Crime Thriller

(GENRE WRITER SERIES)

CRIME THRILLER

HOW TO WRITE DETECTIVE, NOIR, CAPER & HEIST, GANGSTER, & POLICE PROCEDURAL THRILLERS

PAUL TOMLINSON

Copyright © 2019 by Paul Tomlinson

All rights reserved. This book may not be reproduced or transmitted, in whole or in part, or used in any manner whatsoever, without the express permission of the copyright owner, except for the use of brief quotations in the context of a book review.

The content of this book is provided for educational purposes. Every effort has been made to ensure the accuracy of the information presented. However, the information is sold without warranty, either express or implied, and the author shall not be liable for any loss or damage caused – directly or indirectly – by its use.

For country of manufacture, please see final page.

To find out more about the *Genre Writer* series and to receive additional free writing advice and resources, sign up to the mailing list: **www.paultomlinson.org/signup**

ISBN: 978-1092-47296-8

First published April 2019
Publisher: Paul Tomlinson

www.paultomlinson.org/how-to

Cover image and design © 2019 by Paul Tomlinson

Contents

	Introduction	7
1	Hardboiled Private Detectives	10
2	Gangsters	56
3	Crime Sprees & Gun Molls	77
4	Police Procedural	83
5	Forensic Investigation	139
6	Serial Killers & Forensic Psychology	158
7	Undercover Cops	198
8	The Heist	210
9	Burglars & Thieves	242
10	Confidence Tricks	261
11	Prison Thrillers	289
12	Noir Romance	303
13	Vigilantes & Enforcers	319
14	The Buddy Movie	335
15	Informants	348
16	Interviewing & Interrogating	364
17	Surveillance & Stake-Outs	383
18	Missing Person Investigation	394
19	Murder Investigation	403
20	Car Chases	411
	Bibliography	422
	Index	428

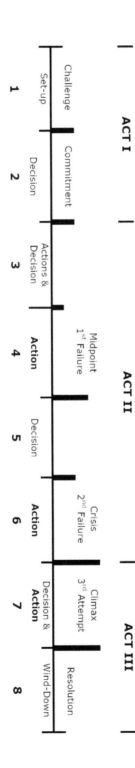

From: *Plot Basics: Plot Your Novel or Screenplay in Eight Sequences* © Paul Tomlinson 2017

Introduction

The crime thriller came into existence between the First World War and World War II. It grew out of the 'inverted' mystery story, in which the criminal was the hero instead of the detective, and documentary-style stories of investigators working for the police, FBI, and private detective agencies. It also drew on elements of the suspense thriller in order to place its hero much closer to the centre of the action and to put him in much greater jeopardy. The eccentric amateur detective who solved a carefully constructed whodunit mystery in the drawing room of an English country house was replaced by a more realistic form of hero and a more realistic form of plot. Though in fiction *realism* is a relative term. In the decade between the first appearance of Agatha Christie's Hercule Poirot and that of Dashiell Hammett's Sam Spade, the conventions of the mystery story changed forever.

Crime Thriller is the third volume in the Genre Writer series following *Mystery* (2017) in which I wrote about the conventions and plot structure of the traditional whodunit, cozy, or classic murder mystery and *Suspense Thriller* (2018) in which I covered the following sub-genres:

- Amateur on the run or 'Hitchcock' thriller
- Spies & espionage
- Political thriller
- Medical thriller
- Legal thriller
- Techno-thriller
- Psychological thriller
- Manhunts & chases

In this book, I will be looking at the conventions and plot structures for:

- Hardboiled/private detectives
- Gangsters
- Crime sprees & gun molls
- Police procedurals
- Forensic investigation
- Psychological profiling & serial killers
- Undercover cops
- Heists & robberies
- Burglars & thieves
- Confidence tricks
- Prison thrillers
- Noir romance
- Enforcers & vigilantes
- Buddies, bodyguards & bounty hunters

In addition, there are chapters on informants, surveillance and stake-outs, interviewing and interrogation, car chases, and the typical sequences of events in a missing person investigation and a murder investigation.

Genre Conventions

Readers of a particular genre of novel or viewers of genre movies are seeking a story that is the 'same only different.' They want to see familiar genre elements presented in a fresh way. As writers, our challenge is to identify those things that need to remain constant and those places where originality is required. The *Genre Writer* series is an attempt to set down the required conventions and highlight ways that you can use them to create something new. The series uses a standard set of genre conventions:

- *Setting:* Where and when the story is set – including physical place, historical period, and 'social milieu.'
- *Iconography:* What objects or props, clothing, or other items appear, and what is their symbolic meaning?
- *Themes:* What human values are defended or opposed? What issues or concepts are explored?
- *Tone:* What is the emotional mood or style of the story?
- *Characters:* What roles are required and what types of people fill them?
- *Plots:* What is the typical sequence of events and what scenes regularly occur?

Some of the sub-genres I cover in this book share the same conventions, especially in terms of things like iconography and settings, so I have tried to avoid duplication as far as possible and have not used the above headings in every chapter.

Deciding on which sub-genres of the crime thriller I should include wasn't easy as there is no standard list or set of definitions. Some sub-genres are distinctly different when it comes to characters and plot – a story about a cat burglar is different to one about a gang of bank robbers or confidence tricksters, but in many places these are all lumped together as 'capers.' *Film noir* is another tricky subject – many films in that category are hardboiled detective stories or police procedurals – and in the end I opted to focus on one sub-genre that wasn't about private or police investigators, the 'noir romance'. I have tried to come up with helpful sub-genres based, for the most part, on differences in plot structure – but be aware that may definitions and divisions may not match exactly those you will find elsewhere. As far as possible, I have tried to choose 'pure' examples of each type of plot I describe, but there is a great deal of overlap between crime thriller sub-genres and you may not always agree with the box I have put a particular film into. I also cheat occasionally and refer to the same film in more than one sub-genre.

Plot Conventions

Genre fiction tends to be plot-centred rather than character-centred with the story people treated as a function of the plot. For this reason, this series is focused mainly on plot structure and the roles played by characters within the plot. The 'buddy movie' which has a chapter towards the end of the book is a rare example where character development has a significant role to play. I will show how changes the main character undergoes can be plotted alongside the action of the thriller.

In the *Genre Writer* series, I use a model for analysing and creating plots that is based on the 'three-act structure' and the 'eight- sequence' model that is often taught to screenwriters. The eight-sequence model was originally devised by Frank Daniel at UCLA and has been widely used by writers since then. If you have never come across it before, you can read about it online or in Paul Gulino's book *Screenwriting: The Sequence Approach*. I also wrote about using it for novels and screenplays in my *Plot Basics* book.

I will deconstruct typical examples of each of the sub-genres, to reveal the fundamental requirements of crime thriller plots. The information presented here also draws extensively on what academics and critics have written about the genre.

Most of the chapters are self-contained, but some do build on or reference ideas in earlier ones. The best approach might be to read the whole book through once to get an overview, skimming the detail occasionally, and then go back and dip into the relevant sections as you develop your own thriller. The chapters towards the end cover subjects that could be applicable to many of the different sub-genres – investigations, interviewing witnesses, surveillance, and car chases – and the section on *victimology* in Chapter Six will be relevant to any story which features the victim of a crime.

1 | Hardboiled Private Detectives

I am using the term 'hardboiled detective' here to refer to private eye stories of the type written by Dashiell Hammett and Raymond Chandler. Their novels provide the model for most detective fiction written today. I'm also using it because terms like private eye, private investigator, or private detective could be said to include some of the detectives of the traditional murder mystery and I want to distinguish between the two. And 'hardboiled dick' just sounds wrong.

A private investigator, private eye, private detective, or inquiry agent is someone who can be hired to perform investigations. They are used by private individuals, companies and organisations, and by attorneys. There is some overlap between private eyes and the amateur detectives found in many traditional whodunit stories, but the PI generally conducts investigations as his primary type of *business* and may be licensed to conduct this business.

Hardboiled versus Whodunit
The hardboiled detective story is often defined in terms of its differences from the traditional whodunit – the 'classical' or 'golden age' murder mystery typified by Agatha Christie's Hercule Poirot and Miss Marple stories. I wrote about the traditional whodunit in some detail in an earlier book in this series, *Mystery* (2017).

The 'classical' murder mysteries of Agatha Christie and co. are often referred to as belonging to the 'Golden Age' of the detective story implying that hardboiled detective stories came later, but in fact, in chronological terms they belong to the same period, the 1920s and 1930s. The first hardboiled story appeared in *Black Mask* magazine in 1922, only a year after the first appearance of Hercule Poirot.

Ian Ousby has said that the traditional whodunit "...never looked more British than when the Americans were attempting it, or the hardboiled novel more American than when the British were attempting it." He's probably referring to British writers like James Hadley Chase who wrote stories about American detectives in American locations in imitation of those who had experienced both first-hand. The style and locations of the hardboiled detective story are distinctly American – this is an American sub-genre. But the changes it brought to the mystery story plot and its cast of characters have influenced private eye stories around the world.

Raymond Chandler was critical of the classic detective story in the English tradition, saying the stories were "… too contrived, and too little aware of what goes on in the world." In his essay 'The Simple Art of Murder,' originally published in 1944, Chandler wrote: "Hammett gave murder back to the kind of people that commit it for reasons, not just to provide a corpse; and with the means at hand, not with handwrought duelling pistols, curare, and tropical fish. He put these people down on paper as they are, and he made them talk and think in the language they customarily used for these purposes."

Chandler highlights two of the significant qualities of the type of fiction Hammett was writing – that it is more *realistic* than the traditional whodunit and that it is written in a more modern *style*. This was the style of Ernest Hemingway, Theodore Dreiser, Ring Lardner, Carl Sandburg, and

Sherwood Anderson – and is sometimes referred to as American Naturalism. Chandler also says that the style is easy to fake, with lesser writers presenting brutality in place of strength, flipness rather than wit, and edge-of-the-seat writing and 'dalliances with promiscuous blondes' just for the sake of it. Raymond Chandler developed his own style filled with what have come to be known as Chandlerisms – more on these later.

The realism Chandler refers to includes the corrupt urban environment in which the stories are set – the world of bootlegging and gangsterism and a constitutional amendment that criminalised anyone who liked to take a drink. Into this environment came a particular kind of hero. In Chandler's words, "... down these mean streets a man must go who is not himself mean, who is neither tarnished nor afraid." That is the hardboiled detective, a 'man of honour', and his story is a "... search for hidden truth."

In the sections on genre conventions in this chapter, I will highlight some of the major differences – and some of the similarities – between hardboiled and whodunit mysteries.

Hardboiled & Film Noir

There is some argument among critics as to whether film noir is a *genre* or a *style* of film-making. The term originated in France in the mid-1940s and may have been inspired by the series of books published by Gallimard from 1945 which were marketed as *Série Noire*. One argument against it being a genre is that it encompasses too many different types of story making it difficult to identify a distinctive set of genre conventions. I'm going to sidestep this debate by covering hardboiled detective stories in this chapter and including a separate chapter for the Noir Romance later in the book. Together these two chapters don't cover all noir plots, but they do cover most of those that fall under the crime thriller heading.

Historical Development of the Private Detective

The first private detective agency was probably that founded in France by Eugène François Vidocq in 1833. Vidocq inspired the creation of Edgar Allan Poe's fictional detective C. Auguste Dupin, who first appeared in 1841, and his memoirs were also drawn on by many other writers.

In the United States, Scottish-born Allan Pinkerton and Chicago attorney Edward Rucker formed the North-Western Police Agency in 1850. It later became the Pinkerton National Detective Agency and still exists today as Pinkerton Consulting and Investigations using the same open eye symbol and slogan 'We never sleep.' Pinkerton famously foiled a plot to assassinate President Abraham Lincoln in 1861 and his agents were hired to track down western outlaws including Jesse James and the Wild Bunch. In 1856 Kate Warne persuaded Pinkerton to hire her and she became America's first female private investigator and she was instrumental in uncovering details of the plot against Lincoln.

The Pinkerton agency's infiltration of the Irish-American secret society the 'Molly Maguires' was one of the inspirations for Arthur Conan Doyle's Sherlock Holmes novel *The Valley of Fear* (1915) and also for the 1970 film *The Molly Maguires*.

In Britain, Charles Frederick Field set up a private 'inquiry office' in 1852, having retired from London's Metropolitan Police. Field was a friend of Charles Dickens, who wrote magazine articles about him and based the character of Inspector Bucket in *Bleak House* upon him. One of Field's employees, Hungarian-born Ignatius 'Paddington' Pollaky left to set up his own agency and advertised his services in 'election, divorce and libel cases' and making 'discreet enquiries in England or abroad'. Pollaky became Britain's best-known inquiry agent and was even mentioned in Gilbert and Sullivan's comic opera *Patience*.

Biographies of Private Detectives
Most private detectives keep a low profile, but there are a few who become 'celebrities' and pen their memoirs or have books written about them. These are fun to read because they tend to include strange anecdotes and observations on the life of a private detective that you won't find anywhere else. Some of their stories are too bizarre to be used in fiction, but others can be used as inspiration for things that happen to your detective.

- Armes, Jay J. as told to Frederick Nolan – *Jay J. Armes, Investigator*. Macmillan, 1976
- Irwin Blye – *Secrets of a Private Eye*
- Gene Caeser – *Incredible Detective: The Biography of William J. Burns*. Prentice-Hall, 1968
- Marilyn Greene (with Gary Provost) – *Finder*
- William R. Hunt – *Front Page Detective: William J. Burns and the Detective Profession, 1880-1930*. Popular Press, 1990
- Josiah Thompson – *Gumshoe: Reflections in a Private Eye*, 1988

Allan Pinkerton also wrote a series of 'Great Detective Stories' detailing work in the field of private detection in late nineteenth-century America.

The Hardboiled Detective in Novels & Films
The first hardboiled detective story is believed to be Carroll John Daly's short story 'Three-Gun Terry' published in the May 1923 issue of *Black Mask* magazine (a prototype hardboiled hero had appeared in Daly's 'The False Burton Combs' in the December 1922 issue). In June 1923, the first of Daly's stories about Race Williams appeared in the same magazine and these proved incredibly popular. But it was Dashiell Hammett – whose unnamed hero the 'Continental Op' (an operative of the Continental detective agency) in the October 1923 issue of *Black Mask* in 'Arson Plus' – who really defined the style of the hardboiled story. When Joseph T. 'Cap' Shaw took over as editor of the magazine in 1926, he wanted writers to emulate Hammett.

Hammett worked for the Pinkerton National Detective Agency from 1915 until the beginning of 1922, though served in the Army during the First World War. Hammett wrote about his time as a private detective in an article for the March 1923 issue of *Smart Set* magazine. It included such recollections as – "The chief of police of a Southern city once gave me a description of a man, complete even to a mole on his neck, but neglected to mention that he had only one arm."

Hammett's first novel *Red Harvest* (1928) also featured the Continental Op, though it is his *The Maltese Falcon* (1929) that virtually defined the hardboiled detective genre, particularly in the wake of the 1941 movie adaptation directed by John Houston. Sam Spade is the archetypal private eye.

The hardboiled detective story combines elements of the classic murder mystery and of the traditional thriller, but also owes something to the lone gunman hero of the Western, and earlier American detective story heroes such as Nick Carter, who appeared between 1886 and 1990 in various guises and by various authors. It is also related to the 'gangster' story, covered in a later chapter, which developed during the same period against the backdrop of Prohibition and the Great Depression.

Martin Rubin, in his *Thrillers* (1999), writes that hardboiled detective films drew on elements from thrillers, and also the "thick nocturnal atmosphere and semi-expressionist style from the Gothic-style horror film; tough-guy dialogue, seedy urban demimonde, and stock criminal characters from the gangster film; and from the spy film, the use of lone wolf heroes, the frequent location of villainy among decadent upper-class types, and a sense of large-scale intrigue and conspiracy." He also notes that, like the thriller hero, the hardboiled detective often begins in a neutral position, but "becomes personally committed in the course of the action, working out a private accommodation between self-reliance and social responsibility."

Raymond Chandler published a series of short stories in *Black Mask*, beginning with 'Blackmailers Don't Shoot' in December 1933, featuring a detective called Mallory, an early version of his Philip Marlowe. Chandler said he taught himself to write pulp fiction by studying the Perry Mason stories of Erle Stanley Gardner, but he also recognised Hammett's influence on the genre.

In his essay 'Murder and the Mean streets: The Hardboiled Detective Novel' (1970), George Grella notes that the writers of these stories "took the professional investigator of real life – usually considered a seedy voyeur – and transformed him into a familiar figure of the popular media ... Though superficially an altogether new kind of folk hero, the detective is actually another avatar of that prototypical American hero, Natty Bumppo, also called Leatherstocking, Hawkeye, Deerslayer, and pathfinder." Grella quotes from Henry Bamford Parkes' essay 'The Metamorphoses of Leatherstocking' (1957), in which he noted the qualities common between this hero and the hardboiled detective: "Technical skill, along with physical courage and endurance; simplicity of character, with a distrust of intellectualism; an innate sense of justice; freedom from all social or family ties except those of loyalty to male comrades; and above all a claustrophobic compulsion to escape from civilization, supported by a belief that social organization destroys natural virtue and by a general critical attitude towards all established institutions."

Almost every writer of detective fiction since the Second World War – with the *possible* exception of those sticking to the classic murder mystery tradition – have been influenced by the hardboiled detective genre, from the creation of lone, somewhat rebellious detectives; to the wide-ranging and fast-moving nature of the investigation; the inclusion of conspiracy and betrayal; and the inclusion of such thriller elements as chases and the use of violence by and against the detective.

Notable names in the development of the genre include Mickey Spillane, whose first Mike Hammer novel appeared in 1947; Ross Macdonald, with his Lew Archer stories beginning 1949; Robert B. Parker, whose Spenser stories began in 1973; James Ellroy (first novel 1981) who writes in a modern *noir* style; Sara Paretsky, creator of V.I. Warshawski, a female private investigator who first appeared in 1982; Sue Grafton, author of the 'alphabet series' featuring private investigator Kinsey Millhone which began in 1982, and Walter Mosely, author of the Easy Rawlins novels, the first published in 1990, which are set in the 1940s to 1960s, and feature a black detective and whose stories are in the hardboiled style but also highlight racial inequality and social injustice.

Reality versus Fiction
In planning this chapter, I had to give some thought to how much information I should include about real-life private detective work. Detective novels and screenplays are fiction, but they must have verisimilitude and credibility, so there are some aspects of the trade that writers ought to be aware of.

There is a fundamental difference between what real-life private investigators do and what their counterparts do in fiction. In novels and movies, the hero is determined to deliver *justice* for his client or some other person connected to the current case. In reality, a private investigator obtains and delivers *information* – he must uncover the truth and present it to the client. Including the parts that the client doesn't want to hear or that don't support the client's ultimate objective. The real private detective often has no part to play in what is done with the information that he provides – that is for the client to decide: the detective may offer an opinion or advice on possible next steps, but the client has the final say. Unless the detective finds himself called to present his information in a courtroom.

Becoming a PI – Training & Experience
Most people enter the field of private investigation either having worked previously in an investigative role – rather than a beat cop – in law enforcement or the military, or by gaining on-the-job experience – paid or unpaid – with a reputable private detective agency. See the section on *Licensing* below for more on the requirements for becoming a private detective in different locations.

Types of Agency
In real life, there are three main types of detective agency – the lone operator, the small business, and the organization.

The Lone Operator – These may still have a secretary, an accountant, an attorney. They may also bring in freelancers or part-timers to work on some cases or specialists and consultants for certain types of work. Part-time helpers may include former police officers and they may or may not be licensed private investigators – or a wannabe detective may be called in to help out. Specialists can include photographers, janitors and domestic staff, electronics experts, computer hackers, criminals, cab drivers, actors, or prostitutes.

Small Agencies – employ between two and maybe thirty full- and part-time investigators.

Large Organisations – Agencies who employ hundreds of investigators and often have offices in different parts of the country.

In fiction, you could have your hero work for any of these three sorts of agency, but traditionally lone operators and two-person agencies are the most common. With a large agency, you're moving closer to the sort of set-up you find in a police procedural novel.

Types of Work
Real private investigators very rarely investigate murder – though a client may ask them to look into a 'cold case' that has been shelved by the police. In fiction, the private detective often starts off with a relatively ordinary case that takes a dramatic turn when someone ends up dead. Listed below are some of the ordinary types of work real-life private investigators carry out. Remember that even a lone operator is likely to work on more than one

case at a time, though not all will be major cases – you can choose additional or secondary cases from the list below.

Loners and small agencies are likely to specialise in one or two areas of detective work; larger agencies probably have specialist departments for all or most of the different types of work with a team of agents whose expertise is in that area. In a smaller town, the private detective may have to take on a wider variety of cases while in larger cities they are (a) more likely to specialise and (b) be part of a larger organisation.

Insurance – This can involve investigating thefts and trying to recover property so that the insurer doesn't have to pay out or gathering information on people suspected of making false injury claims, especially against their employers.

Child Custody – This kind of work may be like insurance fraud work in that the detective is hired to provide evidence that one of the parents is doing something that makes them unsuitable guardians of a child with the aim of persuading a court to grant custody of the child to someone else.

Bounty Hunting – If a bail bondsman puts up the money to allow a prisoner to be released pending their court appearance and that prisoner then fails to appear for their court hearing, a 'bounty' is paid by the bail bondsman to a hunter who locates the missing prisoner and returns them to police custody. In the past, bounty hunters also went after escaped convicted prisoners who had a price on their heads. Bounty hunting is no longer legal is some American states and doesn't exist in the UK. Janet Evanovich's heroine Stephanie Plum works as a bounty hunter.

Private Security – including loss prevention – guarding valuable objects, advising on building security; bodyguarding – including celebrities and protecting people from violent former spouses, or concert and nightclub security. This sort of work requires proper training and insurance. In the UK private security is an area that is regulated and licenced. You might want to read *Introduction to Private Security* (2011) by John S. Dempsey or *Introduction to Security* (2012) by Robert J. Fischer et al.

Background Checks – Some employers hire private investigators to perform checks on prospective employees to determine if everything they say on their resume, including their educational history, is true and if anything significant, such as a criminal record, has been omitted. Some people hire detectives to check into the background of someone they – or their child – is planning to marry, to see if there is a history of financial problems, crime, spousal abuse, or a previous marriage that has not yet been annulled. Other detectives may specialise in checking into the background of companies for investors or potential purchasers, or into the background of a home or piece of property someone is considering purchasing.

Divorce – In the past, obtaining evidence of infidelity in order to petition for divorce was more common than it is today. Many places now allow 'no blame' divorces meaning evidence is not required – you would need to research the position for the place where your story is set. But detectives may still be hired to work for a spouse who is seeking release from alimony payments and needs proof that his or her former spouse is now in a new 'supporting' relationship or has even remarried. Or the detective may be asked to provide proof of spousal abuse. The police tend to avoid becoming involved in domestic disputes – and so this type of work, either before or after a break-up, often falls to the private detective. Real-life detectives must avoid getting emotionally involved in such cases – though, in fiction, this may be exactly what you want to happen. They must also be aware of any consequences that may arise when he delivers his evidence – he doesn't want to be responsible for a furious spouse going after his or her partner with a loaded shotgun. There is a certain amount of counselling required in this sort of case.

Debt Collection & Repossession – See Fay Faron's *A Private Eye's Guide to Collecting a Bad Debt*. Creighton-Morgan Pub Co., 1991 (earlier editions are listed with the titles *Take the Money and Strut* or *A Nasty Bit of Business*).

Electronic Surveillance and Counter-Surveillance – or bugging and debugging. See Patricia Holt's *The Bug in the Martini Olive and Other True Cases from the Files of Hal Lipset, Private Eye*, Little Brown & Co., 1991 (published in paperback in 1994 as *The Good Detective*). I've written a little more about this in the chapter on surveillance.

Attorney-Related – Some investigators are either directly employed by lawyers or district attorneys – or are hired by them on a case by case basis. Erle Stanley Gardner's Perry Mason called on the services of Paul Drake.

Political Investigations – Digging up the dirt on client's political rivals.

There are a number of kinds of work where the detective acts as a go-between for the client, rather than conducting an investigation as such:

Process Serving – There may be situations where a detective delivers other papers or items for a client, either to provide proof of delivery or to protect the item until it is handed over. In most places, you don't need to be a licensed private detective to serve subpoenas, though you may need to be authorised by the local sheriff's office or court.

Missing Persons – This covers a range of people including runaway teenagers, abducted children, payment defaulters, rogue tradesmen, high school sweethearts, lost relatives, and heirs to unclaimed fortunes. The skills and resources for this type of work are also used by police detectives and I have included a separate chapter on missing person investigation towards the end of this book.

Exchange of Stolen Property – Thieves may sell stolen property back to an insurance company or the owner and the client will ask the detective to handle their side of the exchange.

Blackmail or Kidnapping – A detective may be hired to drop-off any payments made or to be present for the exchange, either supporting and protecting the client or representing them.

There certain areas of detective work that are common to both private detectives and those working for a police department – I have included separate chapters about these at the end of the book: surveillance and stake-outs; interviewing and interrogation, and informants. There are also chapters on the structure of a missing person investigation and a murder investigation. Plus a chapter on car chases.

If you intend to write a private detective story, you should probably read up on the real-life work of detectives and the equipment and procedures they use – you don't have to make your stories true to life, but you should be aware of how far you are moving away from reality. Two good books on the subject are Steven Kerry Brown's *The Complete Idiot's Guide to Private Investigating* (2013) which is in its third edition as I write this, or *Practical Handbook for Private Investigators* (2013) by Rory J. McMahon. Also worth a look are *Be Your Own Detective* (1998) by Greg Fallis and Ruth Greenberg and *I, Spy: How to Be Your Own Private Investigator* by Daniel Ribacoff (2016).

Gathering Evidence
There are three main types of evidence:

Testimony – statements from witnesses. Many private detectives spend their working days travelling around interviewing people who know things because they are connected to the case or who know things because they are experts in their field.

Documentary – papers containing information, including formal records and signed agreements of various kinds.

Physical/Tangible – weapons, vehicles (possibly damaged), fibres, fingerprints and footprints, blood stains and other fluids, personal possessions

If a private detective goes to a crime scene that has already been professionally examined by an official forensic team, how likely is it that he will discover something they missed? It depends on the nature of the evidence. Edgar Allan Poe's short story 'The Purloined Letter' shows how the amateur detective finds something that has been missed by the police and you could use a similar approach. The police may miss something if it is something that they are not actually looking for – a CSI team is unlikely to miss carpet fibres or human hairs, but they may miss the significance of an automobile that is the wrong type or parked in the wrong way if they don't recognise its significance. Police examiners also tend to use a routine approach and will consider the job done when everything on their usual list has been ticked off. But what if the evidence lies outside the sort of things discovered by that routine? Or requires a mindset that is beyond their routine approach? Or what if the evidence shows the opposite of what they are looking for? What if they have no incentive to perform a certain kind of search or to seek a certain kind of evidence – because they lack a piece of knowledge that makes that approach seem appropriate? There is also the fact that sometimes the *absence* of something is a significant clue, but you must be aware that it should have been there.

This is one reason why it is important for your detective to visit the scene – even if it is some time after the crime took place. He needs to be *in* that environment to be able to understand the context of whatever happened or was found there. Having gained an understanding of the location, he can then look for anything that seems unusual – either as he's standing there or from the photographs the police took of the scene. Is there something there that shouldn't be? Or is something missing that should be there? I wrote in more detail about clues and red herrings in *Mystery*.

In exploring a crime scene, the hero will search in a *spiral* widening out from the point of the crime, or he will use a *grid* search method covering the whole area around and including the point of the crime. And he will make detailed records of what he observes – perhaps speaking into a digital Dictaphone – and take photographs. The photographs will include wide 'establishing shots' taking in the whole of the scene before moving on to close-ups. And any tangible evidence he finds will be photographed *in situ* before being collected for further analysis.

Generally speaking, private detectives don't have access to crime labs in the way that the police do. DNA testing is probably not an option. Though they may use something like a simple test to show whether blood is or is not present at a scene.

If the physical evidence a private detective finds will be presented in court at a later date, the detective must follow the rules relating to the *chain of evidence*, collecting and storing it properly and documenting every stage of the evidence's journey from the moment it was found until it is shown in the courtroom, in order to be able to demonstrate that it has not been tainted or tampered with.

As mentioned before, if a private detective won't be required to present a watertight case in court, he can use more unorthodox methods – such as manufacturing evidence in order to bluff and perhaps trick a suspect into an admission of guilt.

Private Detectives & The Law

Private detectives are not official law enforcement officers and are, for the most part, private citizens with no additional rights or privileges. If anything, they must demonstrate a greater understanding of and adherence to the law than an ordinary person – otherwise, they might find themselves in court.

Your detective is unlikely to be a legal expert – unless he originally trained to be a lawyer and actually practised for some years – and so will probably retain the service of an attorney or lawyer. This may be the character to turns up to help when the hero is arrested or he may be a more mentor-like character who advises the hero on what he can and cannot legally do in various circumstances.

Having said that, real-life detective work may require many small violations of the law – bending rather than breaking it, in most cases – and in fiction, even more liberties are taken.

Particular areas of the law that private investigators need to be aware of include the following – laws and regulations vary from country to country and from state to state, so you will need to check up on the position in the place where you choose to set your story.

Licensing – does your hero need a license to operate as a private detective?

Firearms – what are the regulations relating to carrying handguns and does the private detective need an additional license – on top of his detective's license and his firearm license – to carry a weapon for work purposes? See below.

Recording of Conversations – in some states it is necessary to have the permission of at least one person in a conversation, in others the permission of both people is required, and in other places recording of private conversations is not permitted by a third party. There is state by state information on firearms and audio recording laws as well as other general advice

https://privateinvestigatoredu.org/private-investigations-laws/

Contracts – does the hero ask clients to sign formal contracts drawn up by his attorney?

Searches – what are the rules regarding the searching of private premises or vehicles? Some states require an attorney to file a motion for discovery.

Arrest – A private detective can only carry out a citizen's arrest *after* a crime has been committed and not if he suspects a crime is going to be committed. Getting this wrong can result in a charge for false arrest and a civil suit.

Bounty Hunting – In some states this is no longer permitted.

Evidence – The private investigator must understand the rules regarding the use of evidence in court and the proof of 'chain of custody' for any piece of evidence presented.

Accessing Personal Data & Other Records – laws and guidance on personal data are being tightened as a result of the amount of information being collected and stored digitally – in Europe, the General Data Protection Regulation came into effect in 2018 and similar regulation is being looked at in the USA and elsewhere. Personal data such as medical records have always been subject to confidentiality and other types of data are only available to authorised agencies and personnel.

Use of Force – for personal protection, to defend others, and during a citizen's arrest.

Character Defamation – a private detective needs to know when his words or actions cross the line and constitute a false statement to a third party that harms a person's reputation.

Chain of Evidence – more on this below and in the chapter on the Police Procedural.

Court Appearances & Depositions – if the detective is called as a witness in court or gives a deposition, he needs to be aware of their legal context and the rights of himself and other individuals in the case.

Subpoena – a detective can be legally compelled to produce his own records relating to a case; if he doesn't keep them or destroyed them upon conclusion of the case, he cannot produce them.

Privacy – You must know the law relating to an individual's right to privacy. The Fourth Amendment to the U.S. Constitution protects Americans from unreasonable search and seizure. These rules apply to journalists as well as private detectives and most countries have something similar in place. As a rule of thumb, if a person's activity can be observed from a publicly accessible viewpoint, the person does not have a reasonable expectation of privacy.

Licensing

Each country has its own system for regulating the work of private detectives and you will need to research these for the location used in your story. Here I briefly cover the United Kingdom and the United States.

United Kingdom – Regulation of the private security industry in the United Kingdom is covered by the *Private Security Industry Act 2001*. Licencing is overseen by the Security Industry Authority (www.sia.homeoffice.gov.uk). In December 2014 the Home Office announced that private detectives would be licenced by the SIA, but this was not brought into effect – currently, there is *no* licencing or regulation of private detectives in the UK. However, there are specific forms of private security activity that do require licences from the SIA – manned guarding of premises, property, and individuals including the roles of doormen or 'bouncers'; guarding cash or valuables in transit, and close protection work such as that carried out by a bodyguard. A licence is also required for the manned supervision of public space surveillance by CCTV and for the immobilisation, restriction, and removal of vehicles.

United States – Licensing of private investigators in the United States varies from state to state. Some states require no license. Some require a city or state business licence. And some, such as Virginia and California, require private investigators to undertake training and testing and to have a number of years' experience in the field. In some states, both the individual and the agency that employs them are required to be licensed. There are some agreements that allow a detective licensed in one state to work temporarily in another, but not all states participate in such reciprocal agreements. There may also be different licensing requirements for armed versus unarmed private detectives. *PI Magazine* maintains a list of the state associations for private investigators with links to their individual websites – from there you should be able to find information on state licensing requirements and other local information: http://pimagazine.com/pi-associations-usa/

Wherever your fictional private investigator is working, make sure you give them the appropriate level of license or make it clear that they are working 'unofficially' without a license.

Recording Telephone Conversations

In the USA it is illegal to record a telephone conversation if the participants in the conversation are unaware that it is being recorded. Law enforcers must obtain a warrant to tap someone's phone. In some states ('single party') it is legal to record a telephone call if *one* of the participants has given permission – so you can record your own calls. In many states ('all party') *all* participants in the call must give permission. If a telephone call involves people in different states, whichever state has the stricter laws is the one whose restrictions should be adhered to.

Firearms

When it comes to writing about weapons there are two things you should research thoroughly – the weapons and laws relating to their use. What types of gun might a private detective carry? Are hammerless handguns the better option? Which types of gun can have a silencer fitted to them and to what extent do they really 'silence' the sound of a shot? After firing six shots in rapid succession, is a gun barrel hot enough to burn you? If you drop a handgun, can it go off?

In the United Kingdom, private detectives are ordinary citizens and are not permitted to carry firearms. There are also strict rules on what sort of knife a person can carry in public.

In the USA, your detective may be permitted to carry a gun – in some states an additional license is required. In those states he then makes a *choice* whether to carry a gun or not. Some people are not 'gun people' and that says something about the kind of person your detective is – and the kind of clients and cases he takes on.

Genre Conventions

Settings

The Urban Milieu – The detective thriller is set against a modern urban backdrop. Beneath the bright façade lies a world of corruption and exploitation. This world is controlled by a secret alliance between glamourous wealthy citizens and powerful criminal bosses. As John G. Cawelti writes in *Adventure, Mystery and Romance*, this world is "profoundly decadent and ... the key to its decadence is a link between crime and respectability..." The world of the hardboiled detective story is a world where corruption has infected every strata of society.

The first hardboiled stories were written during the same era as the gangster story – the Roaring Twenties and Prohibition, followed by the Great Depression of the 1930s. "Grinding poverty, unemployment, homelessness, bank and small business failures in alarming numbers, ongoing police and political corruption and rampant gangsterism, violent clashes between union organisers and management scabs in both industry and agriculture," this was the social milieu, as described by Bill Pronzini and

Jack Adrian in their introduction to *Hardboiled: An Anthology of American Crime Stories*.

'Urban milieu' is a phrase I've taken from *The Oxford Companion to Crime and Mystery Writing*. In it, Frankie Y. Bailey says that the "...anonymity and peril of the city are attractive to writers who concentrate on the reality of crime." Bailey also notes that while 'cozy' settings such as a country house serve as *closed* worlds in which suspects and clues are planted, the city provides an *open* environment. In the same book, Bonnie C. Plummer writes about the 'mean streets milieu,' referring to Raymond Chandler's essay on the sub-genre. "The city itself might be San Francisco or Los Angeles or New York," Plummer writes, "but ... the description was the same: a dangerous place, frequently viewed at night, filled with strangers capable of violence, motivated by greed, lust, and hatred; even the people one knows in the mean streets may not be what they seem." Plummer also says that the size of the city and the diversity of lifestyles within it provide the writer "...a wide range of possible suspects and victims and threats to the detective and his or her clients." Another aspect of the crowded city streets is that the hunter or the hunted can quickly disappear.

The city is often described as a pressure cooker, bringing together many different – rich and poor – in a small space, a microcosm of society. The hardboiled detective can pursue his investigation through all levels of this world – from the mansions of the wealthy and powerful, to the night clubs and back alleys of the seedier side of town. He usually works out of a shabby office somewhere on the margins of town – the kind of place favoured by unsuccessful dentists and ambulance-chasing lawyers. This office is the detective's sign that he has not succumbed to the glamour of easy money – he remains incorruptible, paying his own way as best he can. It's marginal location also an indication of his status as a loner – he doesn't *belong* in the world in which he works and regards himself as separate from it.

As the years have gone on, private detectives have 'hung out their shingle' in all manner of cities. And the world around him (or her) has changed – but the setting of these stories is still one of glamour – or perhaps ordinariness – hiding a corrupt underbelly. The upper echelons are still involved in criminal conspiracies, and the forces of law and order are not always able – or willing – to see that innocent people receive the justice they deserve.

The Detective's Office – In real-life many lone private eye's operate out of their own homes rather than an office. Many clients may not want to be seen walking into a private investigator's office and would prefer to meet somewhere else – though this can be alleviated to some extent if a PI rents an office in a building where many businesses share a street entrance and lobby.

You can personalise the detective's workspace so that it reveals something about his or her personality – or about the type of client they work for. Robert Crais describes Elvis Cole's office as having several items of Disney memorabilia and that helps to create a visual impression of the place and tell us something about the detective. The décor of the office needs to reflect the detective's financial situation – or indicate what he wishes people to believe his financial situation to be. Its location will also reflect this. And the location will determine what sort of people walk in as clients.

If your detective doesn't have an office in town, you need to consider how he or she gets new clients. Word of mouth recommendations? Referrals from lawyers or the police? Do they advertise – if so, where? The days are gone where someone picked a name out of the Yellow Pages. Today a detective needs to be listed in online directories, have a social media presence, and have a website. If your detective does none of these things, that also says something about his character and about the sort of clients he works for. If your detective pins flyers to the noticeboards in local coffee shops or laundromats or hands out business cards, you need to tailor these towards the sort of client he makes money from – does he want to give the impression of being a Sherlock Holmes-like thinker? Or a more traditional Sam Spade sort of hardboiled detective? Does his advertising indicate that he is discreet or does it emphasise the fact that he carries a gun?

The type of client a private detective receives will, to some extent, be determined by his social milieu. What sort of people does he encounter on a daily basis? This includes the places he visits in his off-duty hours and his hobbies and interests. Every businessman tries to network with people who can help him improve his income.

Iconography

The detective's shabby office with the name painted on the frosted glass of the door is such an iconic image that it has become a cliché. So too the battered fedora that the detective wears, and the revolver in the shoulder-holster slung over the back of his chair. Then there's the bottle of whiskey in the bottom drawer of the desk, the filing cabinet he never files anything in, the fan that serves for air-conditioning, and the dusty Venetian blinds that hang at the window.

In the hardboiled story, the detective typically moves through locations that contrast sharply: from the bright sunlight to midnight shadows; from elegant mansions to seedy bars and gyms frequented by down-at-heel boxers. There is often an irony in this contrast – good people are found in dirty places, and corrupt criminals beside the gleaming water of their vast swimming pools.

Other locations the detective may visit include police headquarters or a lawyer's office – both of which places symbolising law and order, but possibly harbouring corruption.

Violence too is a part of this world. As well as the revolvers we may see knives, blackjacks, and brass knuckles. The hero may be shot at, and he'll probably be beaten up at least once by henchmen who warn him to stop 'poking his nose' into things that shouldn't concern him. And when he refuses to give up the case, he'll be clubbed unconscious and kidnapped, dragged off to some out of the way place where he'll either be drugged or tortured (or both) to find out what he knows about the conspiracy at hand. There may also be a woman who is threatened with torture – or worse – but only in the most sadomasochistic of tales is she ever really harmed.

Not all women in these stories are victims – some of them are as deadly as the men. Or deadlier. The hardboiled detective story is one where we often find the female betrayer or *femme fatale*.

As well as visual imagery, the hardboiled detective story is defined by the style in which it is written, particularly in terms of the dialogue of the characters. We'll look at that in more detail below.

Themes

Barbara Norville in *Writing the Modern Mystery* says: "The primary attribute of the private eye is his unique sense of justice, and this is the *theme* of all private eye novels." What is important here is that the detective's sense of justice – his moral code – is *his alone*. It is not something he necessarily shares with the rest of society. The detective chooses to be an outsider – but he's not an intellectual bohemian like the classical detective, rather he is a freelance professional, answerable to no one but himself, and his isolation "represents his outright rejection of a society whose values and attitudes he cannot accept or even understand. A self-styled existentialist, he has refined his own personal, pragmatic code based on traditional, outmoded values like rugged individualism and fair play." (Thomas Schatz, *Hollywood Genres*)

Schatz highlights two things worth exploring in more detail: that the hardboiled detective may be an existentialist, and that he defends traditional, outmoded values. We will cover both in the section below on the hardboiled detective himself. Here I'll just say that the detective's outdated moral code is often compared to the chivalric code of medieval knights, and that the hardboiled detective is an existentialist in that he recognises that human existence is essentially meaningless, except in that every individual is solely responsible for giving meaning to their own lives. He believes that we should live 'authentically' – that is, passionately and sincerely, in accordance with our own values.

Existentialism

Dennis Porter writes that if "... there is any literary realism in *The Maltese Falcon* ... it is to be found in a kind of witty, laconic, hard-bitten philosophy of life that insists on the absurdity and randomness of events, and the individual's existential loneliness..." In Dashiell Hammett's novel, there is a much-discussed anecdote that Sam Spade relates to Brigid O'Shaughnessy – an ordinary man named Flitcraft went out to lunch one day and never returned. Spade tracked the missing man down and learns that he had walked out on his old life following a near-miss that had almost claimed his life – a falling metal beam almost killed him. This caused him to walk out on his old life, but he soon readjusted and started a new life that turned out to be exactly the same as his old one.

Life is disorientating and confusing: things happen randomly and are essentially meaningless. This is the starting point for the philosophy of existentialism. Gary Cox, in *How to be an Existentialist* writes: "Existentialists are nihilists because they recognize that life is ultimately absurd and full of terrible, inescapable truths. They are anti-nihilists because they recognize that life does, in fact, have a meaning: the meaning each person chooses to give his or her own existence. They recognize that each person is free to create themselves and make something worthwhile of themselves by striving against life's difficulties. Life, or rather death, will win in the end, but what matters is the striving, the overcoming, the journey." Existentialism, he argues, is a positive, optimistic philosophy because it says that we can live an honest and worthwhile life in spite of the fact that the universe is indifferent to our fate – "... each person exists first, without meaning or purpose, and strives thereafter to give himself meaning and purpose."

Kierkegaard said that each individual – not society or religion – is responsible for giving meaning to their own life, and for living that life authentically. That is, to be true to themselves. What existentialists take from this is that everyone is responsible for his or her own life and for their own actions. We have total freedom to choose what meaning our lives will have, and we have absolute responsibility for the actions we take. This can lead people to suffer from an overwhelming feeling of dread or 'existential angst.'

Existentialists also understand that human beings are not purely rational – we cannot be completely objective, and so we make decisions based on subjective meaning. If the world outside of us is random and irrational, the only meaning available to us is that we provide ourselves. Therefore decisions must be subjective. If we do not live according to our own values – if we ignore them in order to make some sort of material gain, or if we try to be something we are not in order to please or impress others – then we are being inauthentic. We should always act in accordance with our own values. We should act with integrity and be *authentic*. This ties in with the hardboiled detective remaining true to his own values, despite the corruption and temptation he finds all around him.

But what *are* his values?

The Hardboiled Chivalric Code

"*Chivalry! – why, maiden, she is the nurse of pure and high affection – the stay of the oppressed, the redresser of grievances, the curb of the power of the tyrant – Nobility were but an empty name without her, and liberty finds the best protection in her lance and her sword.*" – Walter Scott, *Ivanhoe* (1820)

Chivalry, or the chivalric code, was a system of approved behaviours associated with medieval knights, developed in the period 1170 to 1220 ad. It featured in medieval and in later romantic literature. There is no single document which can be identified as *the* code, and various attempts have been made to identify what the code might have been.

Chivalrous behaviour has been broadly categorised in three areas:

Duties of a Warrior – including serving one's lord (carrying out one's feudal duties) and loving one's country; being willing to sacrifice one's life for another; protecting the weak and the poor (including widows and orphans); and such knightly virtues as honour, courage or valour (not recoiling before the enemy), fairness, justice, honesty and integrity, self-control or forbearance, largesse or generosity (while having nothing but contempt for bribery), and mercy.

Duties to God – including being faithful to God, observing the teachings of the Church, and defending the Church (this tended to include making war on 'infidels'); being a champion for good over evil, and protecting the innocent.

Duties to Women – this includes the idea of 'courtly love,' which requires that a knight serve his own lady, and after her to demonstrate gentleness and graciousness to all other women.

This code of conduct has been associated with the hardboiled detective by a number of writers. As we have already seen, the hardboiled detective tends towards an existentialist viewpoint rather than espousing religious beliefs, and so 'duties to God' would need to be replaced with a more suitable secular heading, what Dennis Porter refers to as "... an updated secular humanist ethic ... that embodies an idea of duty and of a professional code of conduct," but other than that the code might serve our purposes.

John G. Cawelti: "Despite his involvement in the contemporary urban metropolis, the hardboiled detective's ethical attitudes and modes of judgment usually evoke some earlier era, most commonly the chivalric code of the feudal past ... Like the Western hero, the tough-guy detective's action-oriented code of honour enables him to act in a violent world without losing his moral purity and force."

The most quoted extract from Raymond Chandler's 'The Simple Art of Murder' is this one:

... down these mean streets a man must go who is not himself mean, who is neither tarnished nor afraid. The detective in this kind of story must be such a man ... He must be, to use a rather weathered phrase, a man of honour... if he is a man of honour in one thing, he is that in all things.

Chandler makes a number of references to knights – to the age of chivalry – in his stories. In *The High Window,* Philip Marlowe refers to himself as the 'shop-soiled Galahad.' *The Big Sleep* opens with Marlowe describing his client's mansion: "there was a broad stained-glass panel showing a knight in dark armor rescuing a lady who was tied to a tree..." And later in the same story says: "Knights had no meaning in this game. It wasn't a game for knights."

H.R.F. Keating in *Writing Crime Fiction* says of Hardboiled detectives: "They are, in fact, none other than the knight-errant of the fairy tales (as witness Chandler calling his hero originally Malory, after the author of *Morte d'Arthur*, and Robert Parker calling his Spenser after the poet of *The Fairy Queen*). They are the lone crusader righting wrongs, rescuing damsels, killing dragons."

In *The Long Goodbye,* Philip Marlowe makes a number of references to the values that he lives by. He says that he doesn't do all kinds of detection, "only the fairly honest kinds." And: "I've got a five-thousand dollar bill in my safe but I'll never spend a nickel of it. Because there was something wrong with the way I got it." And later: "I'm a romantic, Bernie. I hear voices crying in the night and I go see what's the matter."

While Raymond Chandler overtly compares his detective to a knight, Dashiell Hammett makes the reader draw his own conclusions from the actions Sam Spade takes. At the end of *The Maltese Falcon,* he admits that he has feelings for Brigid O'Shaughnessy, but he hands her over to the police anyway because that is the 'moral' thing to do.

The hardboiled detective often continues to investigate after his client has been killed, or after he has been fired by the client. He feels a moral compunction to go after *the truth* – the crusade has become his now.

The detective is often warned off through the threat or use of violence, or he is offered a bribe to drop his investigation. The villain cannot understand why the detective continues to investigate – especially if he's no longer receiving payment from the client. What's in it for him? The villain doesn't see that, for the hero, discovering the truth in and of itself has a value.

In his introduction to the 1934 edition of *The Maltese Falcon* Dashiell Hammett said of Sam Spade: "He is a dream man in the sense that he is what most of the private detectives I worked with would like to have been and in their cockier moments thought they approached. For your private detective does not – or did not ten years ago when he was my colleague – want to be an erudite solver of riddles in the Sherlock Holmes manner; he wants to be a hard and shifty fellow, able to take care of himself in any situation, able to get the best of anybody he comes in contact with, whether criminal, innocent bystander or client."

The hardboiled detective's marginal position in society, his mistrust of the wealthy elite, his anti-authoritarian rebelliousness, and his frustration at being unable to fix a broken and unjust world, are all qualities that American readers could identify with when the stories first appeared.

As John Patterson wrote in 'A Cosmic View of the Private Eye,' in *The Saturday Review* (22nd August 1953): "He is everyman's romantic conception of himself: the glorification of toughness, irreverence, and a sense of decency too confused and almost half-ashamed to show itself."

Other Themes
In her article 'Naturalism in American Literature,' Donna M. Campbell lists the themes of this literary movement – all of which are found in the hardboiled detective novel:

[Charles Child Walcutt, in *American Literary Naturalism: A Divided Stream*, 1956] identifies survival, determinism, violence, and taboo as key themes.

The 'brute within' each individual, composed of strong and often warring emotions: passions, such as lust, greed, or the desire for dominance or pleasure; and the fight for survival in an amoral, indifferent universe. The conflict in naturalistic novels is often 'man against nature' or 'man against himself' as characters struggle to retain a 'veneer of civilization' despite external pressures that threaten to release the 'brute within.'

Nature as an indifferent force acting on the lives of human beings. [In contrast to the] romantic vision of Wordsworth...

The forces of heredity and environment as they affect – and afflict – individual lives.

An indifferent, deterministic universe. Naturalistic texts often describe the futile attempts of human beings to exercise free will, often ironically presented, in this universe that reveals free will as an illusion.

Tone & Style
Raymond Chandler: "My whole career is based on the idea that the formula doesn't matter, the thing that counts is what you do with the formula; that is to say, it is a matter of style."

The detective thrillers of the 1920s and 1930s that are still known today are celebrated for their 'hardboiled' style. It combines quickfire dialogue with its own slang terms, sarcastic wisecracks, and cynical first-person storytelling riddled with ironic similes.

Carroll John Daly, credited with writing the first hardboiled stories, was popular with *Black Mask* magazine readers, but he lacked the style that later writers would bring. Pronzini and Adrian have written that he was "a crude and badly flawed writer. He was cursed with a tin ear where speech was concerned and possessed no talent at all for characterisation. His action sequences (on which all his tales relied heavily) were invariably implausible, his plotting was weak and obvious, all his characters seem hewn from the same block of wood, and the East Coast environs in which Race Williams operated were no more authentically portrayed than those in the dime-novel detective stories."

Dashiell Hammett was a much more accomplished writer: his novels are in print today, where Daly's name is known only to fans of the early hardboiled stories. *Black Mask* editor Joseph T. Shaw thought highly of Hammett, holding him up as a model for the type of stories he wanted to publish. Later Shaw would write that the *Black Mask* style was 'hard, brittle,' fast-moving with 'economy of expression' and 'authenticity in characterisation and action.' Shaw also believed that dialogue was a key element. In June 1939 he wrote an article on dialogue for *Writer's Digest* magazine: "A cardinal rule in practically all writing is that the author should keep out of it entirely and allow his characters to tell the story," he said. "Nothing weakens or spoils even good dialogue so much as to have the author act as interpreter between the quoted lines." Shaw didn't want to see a line of dialogue followed by something like this: *Bill was not smiling when he said this. He was angry. Moreover, he wanted to make Ed angry, force him to make the first move, to reach for his gun.* This was something Dashiell Hammett knew: in a review of *The Glass Key*, *The New Yorker* said "He does his readers the infinite courtesy of allowing them to supply descriptions and analyses for themselves. He sets down what his characters say, and what they do."

Joseph T. Shaw's article on dialogue included advice that is still relevant and worth extracting here:

- *you must know your respective characters thoroughly, just what sort and type of men and women they are, how they will act and react in any given situation.*
- *you know your plot and just in what manner you want to develop it.*
- *let the characters you have portrayed tell the story you have setup, themselves; not in your language and with your own expression, but their own.*
- *it must always be in character, not only with respect to the personalities to whom you give speech, but also with regard to the actual situation and its natural requirements.*
- *written dialogue should be edited ... As a rule, it should be terse, with only significant expressions remaining.*
- *cast yourself into the character that is to speak and express the thought, the feeling and the meaning that particular character would naturally express under the circumstances and in his language and in his way of speaking.*
- *Dialect dialogue is not a short cut to characterisation. It may denote personality, whether a person is black or white, foreign or domestic, ignorant or educated. It should never be difficult to read and understand...*

Raymond Chandler, in 'The Simple Art of Murder', approved of the way Hammett wrote, describing it as "...spare, frugal, hardboiled..." An example that has often been quoted is the opening of Dashiell Hammett's first novel, *Red Harvest* (1929): *I first heard Personville called Poisonville by a redhaired mucker named Hickey Dewey in the Big Ship in Butte. He also called his shirt a shoit...*

Dennis Porter in his chapter on 'The Private Eye' in *The Cambridge Companion to Crime Fiction* quotes this opening paragraph and says "Hammett showed how the apparently ordinary, spoken American language could be made to transcend itself in the direction of a new urban poetry. With its staccato rhythm, its echoing vowels, its alliterative energy, its no-nonsense American names, its use of period slang (mucker), and its laconic wit, the evocation of Personville is a sophisticated verbal exercise in the anti-picturesque. At the same time, the voice establishes itself as a distinctly male voice, the voice of a man who has knocked about a bit, and knows how to handle himself on a tough urban street or in an unfashionable neighbourhood dive."

Chandler knew that this style didn't belong only to Hammett, or to anyone else, it is "the American language (and not even exclusively that any more)..."

Pronzini and Adrian say that the style's "... emphasis on dialogue, its use of the vernacular, and its basic colloquial rhythm were offshoots of the styles employed by Sherwood Anderson and Ring Lardner and polished and simplified by Ernest Hemingway." If we look even further back, we see that this colloquial and dialogue-rich style owes much to Mark Twain.

Raymond Chandler recognised that this style of writing was capable of more than Hammett was using it for and, according to Porter, his Philip Marlowe speaks in the American vernacular, but "...it is the vernacular with a difference, the vernacular heightened and burnished to the level of street-wise poetry..." Chandler combined "... the epigrammatic flourish of Oscar Wilde with the moral environment of Hemingway's *The Killers*."

What does he mean by that? Porter is referring to what has become known as the 'Chandlerism':

I left her with her virtue intact, but it was quite a struggle. She nearly won.

She threw her arms around my neck, and nicked my ear with the gunsight.

If you don't leave, I'll get someone who will.

These are all taken from *The Notebooks of Raymond Chandler*. Sometimes he strains a little too hard for the ironic simile, and the last quoted above has more than a hint of Groucho Marx about it.

Among the most famous Chandlerisms are probably:

He looked about as inconspicuous as a tarantula on a slice of angel food. (Farewell My Lovely)

She gave me a smile I could feel in my hip pocket. (Farewell My Lovely)

The subject was as easy to spot as a kangaroo in a dinner jacket. (Playback)

Chandler acknowledged that the hardboiled, or 'realistic,' style was "...easy to fake; brutality is not strength, flipness is not wit, edge-of-the-chair writing can be as boring as flat writing; dalliance with promiscuous blondes can be very dull stuff..." The only comment to add to this is that writing in the hardboiled style is fine – but trying to write like Raymond Chandler is pointless. He is unique. Many bad writers have tried to copy him, and they just sound like bad parodies. The thing about writing in a colloquial or vernacular style is to use one that you are personally familiar – and comfortable – with. If it is an exaggeration of your personal style, it will flow more naturally. Be authentic – in an existential sense.

If it isn't already obvious, we should observe that the hardboiled detective's cynical, flippant attitude is a defence mechanism. He is not, as we will discover later, a nihilist – he doesn't believe that life is pointless – he has *hope*. But he thinks hope makes him vulnerable, so he seeks to hide it with wisecracks and self-directed putdowns. There is irony in his irony.

Dennis Porter has written that the classical murder mystery owes something to the comedy of manners, but that hardboiled detective stories have more in common with 'American literary realism.' He also draws a comparison with the 'literary naturalist' writers Stephen Crane and Theodore Dreiser. Realism was a literary movement that strove to depict ordinary life as it really was, rather than presenting it in a stylised or romanticised manner. Naturalism grew out of this, attempting to demonstrate that such 'natural forces' as heredity, socialisation, and physical environment influenced human character and behaviour. Naturalistic writing tended to focus on the darker aspects of life, including poverty, violence, bigotry, corruption and human vice.

Although Raymond Chandler has argued that hardboiled detective fiction is more realistic than the classic murder mystery, others have argued that while it may portray violence and corruption in a more realistic way, the plots and characters of these stories are themselves highly stylised and – if we accept the detective as a chivalrous knight – tending to romanticism rather than realism. Carolyn Wheat says it best in *How to Write Killer Fiction*: "... the private eye novel isn't any more real than the country-house cozy. It's an 'existential romance,' a pseudo-realistic vision that is considerably more stylized than truly authentic."

William Denton compiled *Twists, Slugs and Roscoes: A Glossary of Hardboiled Slang*, originally published by Miskatonic University Press in 1993, it is now available online: www.miskatonic.org/slang.html

Characters

The hardboiled detective thriller features a cast similar to that of the classic murder mystery, but there are some important differences in how they are presented and used. The main difference has as much to do with setting as character: in the hardboiled detective story there is no closed circle of suspects. Part of the detective's investigation will be to discover who is connected with the crime – they are not all present when he arrives at the scene of the crime.

The detective thriller does not focus on uncovering the identity of *the murderer*, it is not a whodunit – therefore the role of the murderer is somewhat different. In all probability, the main villain will not be acting alone – he is part of a criminal conspiracy, a gang or network – and the actual act of murder may be carried out by one of his henchmen or associates. The person who *commits* the crime may be different from the person who is *responsible* for it.

The victim may not be known personally to the murderer (or even to the person who ordered him or her killed) – they were probably killed because they were part of, or had become aware of, the criminal conspiracy.

The detective is usually a private eye – a professional, licensed investigator, but not part of an official criminal investigation authority. He may have another job – a journalist, photographer, or a bail bondsman's bounty hunter, for example – but he is less likely to be an amateur in this type of story.

The Watson is not typically found in the hardboiled detective story. The detective either tells his own story in the first-person, or we follow him closely in a restricted third-person viewpoint in which we do not hear the thoughts of other characters or see things from their point of view: the point of the story is to follow the detective's investigation and learn things as he learns them. Some detectives have partners who they work with on occasion – sometimes the partner provides specialist assistance or provides the 'muscle' – but the hero effectively works alone even then.

Suspects and witnesses play somewhat different roles in the hardboiled detective story. As mentioned above, there is no closed circle of suspects, so we do not have a story where the 'finger of suspicion' points at each suspect in turn, until the actual murderer is unmasked. First, the hardboiled detective must discover *who* the suspects are – who is connected to with the crime – and only then can he begin to uncover the nature of their relationship to the victim and to the other characters. And – once the nature of the criminal conspiracy has been discovered, about midway through the story – what their connection to the conspiracy might be.

The investigation involves piecing together a web of relationships which is woven around an (initially) unknown conspiracy, with the villain setting at the centre of the web. The detective will need to discover previously unknown links between individuals, and between circumstances or events. Typically, he will find that seemingly honest individuals with wealth and power are an integral part of this web.

Some of these characters will try to prevent the detective from completing his investigation – either because they are part of the main criminal conspiracy, or because they have guilty secrets of their own which they are afraid he will uncover. These characters will either use threats and violence to try and get the detective to give up his case, or they will try to buy him off with a bribe – 'What's your price?' – not realising that the hero cannot be bought. Or blackmailed, or otherwise coerced.

And then there is the *femme fatale* who might try to distract him long enough for the conspiracy to be completed; or she may lead him into a trap; or she may seek to trick him into doing her dirty work for her. Or she will lead him into a situation where the detective himself seems guilty of murder so that the police hunt him – distracting him from his investigation.

There is one final character that is found in most detective thrillers, but who is an optional character in the classic murder mystery – *the client*. This is the person who first comes to the detective and offers him money to investigate a case. This person may be the *femme fatale* or it may be another character – but whoever it is, they are not usually being one hundred per cent honest with the detective. Their motive for hiring him is not always clear, and the client may turn out not to be who he or she claims to be. Sometimes the client is the first murder victim, and the detective carries on investigating to discover why they were killed. This happens especially if the detective was hired to protect the client – he feels a sense of duty, not to mention guilt, for having failed to prevent their death. In many cases, at some later point in the story, the client will ask – or order – the detective to stop investigating. Which, of course, he doesn't, as he now wants to know the client's motive for ending the investigation.

Let's look at the major characters in more detail, saving the detective himself until last.

Villain & His Henchman

In keeping with the fact that, in the hardboiled detective story, people are not what they seem, the main villain may turn out not to be the murderer. In *The Maltese Falcon,* the main villain is the 'fat man,' Caspar Gutman – played by Sidney Greenstreet in the 1941 movie. He is a greedy, obsessive, and ruthless man who will do whatever he has to in order to get his hands on the jewelled statue of the falcon. Like many of the best movie villains, he has a henchman, the young 'gunsel' Wilmer Cook (Elisha Cook, Jr.)

Gunsel is American underworld or hobo slang and means 'catamite,' referring to a young male kept as a sexual companion, usually by an older man. It is thought to come from the Yiddish word *genzel*, possibly a corruption of the German *Gänslein* meaning 'gosling.' The word 'goose' is connected to a range of sexual slang terms. Dashiell Hammett seems to have sneaked it into *The Maltese Falcon* – had his editor known its true meaning it would have been given the blue pencil. The word also found its way into the 1941 movie, and Hammett's success at avoiding the censor means that gunsel is now widely believed to mean a young gunman.

Some writers have suggested that Hammett's use of the word means that there was a sexual relationship between Wilmer and Gutman; others have said that Joel Cairo is the only 'pansy' in the gang and that Sam Spade is taunting Wilmer about his possible homosexuality. Cairo is obviously attracted to Wilmer, though Wilmer seems repelled by the idea. Gutman says "I feel towards Wilmer just exactly as if he were my own son." Whatever Gutman's true feelings, he is quite happy to allow Wilmer to be the fall-guy if that is the price that must be paid for his own escape: only Cairo seeks to protect Wilmer.

Making some or all of the males in the criminal gang homosexual makes for interesting relationships between them and the *femme fatale*, Brigid O'Shaughnessy. They would be immune to her dangerous sexual allure – and even if he is straight, Gutman is more interested in the falcon than in sex – and would simply regard her as an equal, a fellow rival for the black bird. There is even a suggestion that she and Joel Cairo were rivals for the love of the same boy in Istanbul. An interesting thing about the male members of the gang in *The Maltese Falcon* is that they are all openly criminal and open about their desire for the falcon. Only Brigid pretends to be something that she is not.

It is a feature of *The Maltese Falcon* that there are no genuine friendships or romances – except for Sam Spade's platonic relationship with his seemingly virginal secretary Effie.

A quick aside here about villains. There is an argument which runs along the lines of 'if you make your villain female, it's because you're a misogynist who hates women; and if you make your villain homosexual, it's because you are a homophobe who hates gays...' This is nonsense. Hollywood doesn't cast classically-trained British actors as villains because of a hatred of Brits – they cast them because these actors make *great* villains and have the chops to chew the scenery. And actors accept the roles because villains are great characters to play. And because Hollywood movies pay better than British theatre. There's only ever an issue of bigotry if you believe that *all* women are betrayers, and all gays (or blacks or Jews or Hispanics or whatever) are criminals.

And this doesn't mean you need to balance out every female villain with a female heroine – but it does mean you should create *individual* characters rather than adopting stereotypes.

In *The Maltese Falcon*, Gutman is the 'Mr. Big,' but turns out not to be the murderer Sam Spade seeks. In other stories, the main criminal may be *responsible* for one or more murders – though he may have had someone else pull the trigger. The villains in hardboiled detective stories are more like the villains in a James Bond movie, or like Don Corleone in *The Godfather,* or Sherlock Holmes' nemesis Professor Moriarty – directing criminal activity remotely. These characters often appear to be innocent until very late in the story, usually appearing to be successful businessmen or occupying positions of power in society.

With tough-guy thrillers – including gangster stories and spy thrillers – the inclusion of homosexual men and *femmes fatales* allow for queries to be raised about what it means to be 'hardboiled' – being tough obviously isn't an all-male, or even an all-straight-male, preserve. And being an optimistic romantic doesn't make you feminine or less of a tough-guy. It is a key feature of the hardboiled story that nothing can be taken at face value – ambiguity goes with the territory. In the hardboiled detective story, almost nobody is what they seem, and most of the characters cannot be trusted – they're either part of the criminal conspiracy, or have a guilty secret of their own to hide. Or both.

In the classical murder mystery, sympathetic or romantic characters are frequently suspected along with everyone else. They may even – for a while – be made to seem to be the 'most likely' suspect. But they are usually cleared at the end when the final solution is revealed. In the hardboiled story, the *opposite* is often true – a character the detective is romantically involved with, or someone he regards as a good person, or even a friend, will turn out to be guilty; they will be shown to be part of the criminal conspiracy. They will have betrayed the detective's trust – providing him with further proof of just how widely corruption runs in society.

Criminal characters – whether overtly or covertly criminal – will seek to put an end to the detective's investigation by either persuasion, coercion, bribery, or temptation. In part they will be acting out of fear – however small their part in the conspiracy, they will be afraid that he will uncover their corruption or seek to bring them to account for it. The *femme fatale* is among the most interesting of the criminal characters found in this type of story, as we shall see later.

The Femme Fatale

The romantic co-protagonist doesn't really exist in hardboiled fiction – instead, we have the *femme fatale*. She is a central character in the Noir Romance, so we will explore her in more detail in Chapter 12.

In hardboiled detective fiction, the *femme fatale* employs deceit as well as sexual allure: she is a trickster character who pretends to be what a man desires in order to be able to manipulate him. Often, she will pretend that she is a helpless victim, trapped in an unendurable situation, playing on a man's compulsion to 'rescue' her. *The Maltese Falcon* and *The Lady from Shanghai* are just two examples of this behaviour.

John G. Cawelti notes that the hardboiled detective is typically much more sexually attractive than the hero of the classic murder mystery and that in most stories he plays either seducer or seduced. "But sex tends to be represented in a double-edged way in the hardboiled story. It is an object of pleasure, yet it also has a disturbing tendency to become a temptation, a trap, and a betrayal." Cawelti also notes that in nineteenth-century novels there was a tradition for blondes to be presented as chaste, while brunettes were more sexually active, but in hardboiled stories, the blonde woman is more likely to be threatening and aggressively sexual. He says the presentation of women demonstrates a "fear of feminine aggression and domination ... which often manifests itself in the plot in the form of the terrifying female murderess..." Women represent "certain basic challenges to the detective's physical and psychological security." This fear of women may show itself in the detective's emotional reserve and reluctance to enter into relationships – because he knows he will be disappointed, and possibly harmed by them: he has been hurt in the past.

Allies & Friends

John G. Cawelti writes that the function of friends and allies is to "...help the detective to solve the crime and certify his worth by judging him a good man despite his façade of brutality and amorality." They also provide the detective with someone to talk to – someone who understands the world in which he operates. Cawelti again: "The cynical but honest reporter is a favourite figure for the role of friend and confidant, because he can be presented as a man who has seen the sordid side of life and is frustrated by his inability to do anything about it. The honest ex-policeman who has been fired for trying to do his job, and even the noble racketeer, a male version of the respectable prostitute, also turn up on occasion as allies. Whatever the type, the essential characteristic of the detective's allies is their disgust with society's corruption and their recognition of the inherent virtue under the detective's cynical exterior."

Being a friend to the hardboiled detective is a tough role because he has very high standards himself and expects similar of his friends. In *The Long Goodbye,* Philip Marlowe finds himself disappointed in his friend Terry Lennox when he finds they do not share the same moral values.

Of course, as someone who is essentially a loner, the hardboiled detective cannot have too many friends. He is also unlikely to have a work partner or 'buddy' – Sam Spade's partner Miles Archer gets bumped off early in the novel and Spade doesn't waste much time getting Archer's name taken off the office door. It also seems that Spade was friendlier with Archer's wife than a friend ought to be.

If the detective previously worked for the police or district attorney, his relationship with former colleagues tends to range from the guarded to the outright confrontational – and we get a feeling that the hero wasn't an easy man to work with.

Other Characters

The Victim(s)

Raymond Chandler noted that the murder in a hardboiled detective novel does more than provide a body and a puzzle. In the classical murder mystery, the victim is usually unknown to the detective and – especially in the 'First Act Murder' plot variation – unknown to the reader. In the hardboiled detective story, the victim is often someone the detective has a relationship with or an emotional attachment to. The first victim might be the client who just hired him. In *The Maltese Falcon,* it is Sam Spade's business partner. In *I, the Jury* it is Mike Hammer's best friend. Almost from the very start, the case becomes personal for the hardboiled detective: he has a stake in the outcome. The relationship he has with the victim may also imply that the detective himself is at risk, increasing the stakes. Making the first victim a sympathetic character – someone whose death is regrettable – increases reader involvement in the story. And the villain is made to seem more powerful and despicable.

The nature of the murderer's relationship to the victim, as we have said, also differs from that in the classic murder mystery. In the classical story, the murderer has a *personal* reason for wanting the victim out of the way. In the hardboiled detective story, the motive is more akin to a business decision. The victim is killed because of his or her connection – either accidental or planned – with the criminal conspiracy that lies at the heart of the story. In the classical story, the murder is at the centre of the detective's investigation; in the hardboiled story, the murder is almost peripheral, and while it may instigate the investigation, the detective will go on to uncover the greater criminal conspiracy that (indirectly) motivated the murder.

The Informer

Not all private detectives cultivate informers, they are more common with police detectives who are not as close to the criminal underworld as the private detective. I have included a chapter on informers towards the end of the book.

The Police

As with the classic murder mystery, in the hardboiled story you need to get the official detectives out of the way so that your private eye can investigate. And you need to make sure they can't come in and take over the case before the investigation is finished.

Typically a client will come to a private detective because either (a) they don't think they will get true justice through official channels (or they have already failed to do so); (b) their case isn't the sort of thing the police can give time to; or (c) there is something about the case that means they don't want to go to the police with it – they have their own guilty secret of some kind; they may be being blackmailed, for example. Sometimes private eyes are asked to look into 'cold cases' where the police have given up; or they're asked to locate someone who the police don't regard as being missing, or they're asked to investigate a death that the police consider to be accidental or a suicide, but which the client is convinced is murder.

In the hardboiled detective stories of the 1920s and 1930s, the private detective gave his reason for acting as judge, jury and executioner as the fact that the police and/or district attorney's offices were corrupt themselves, or that lawyers in court could twist the legal process such that the guilty got away with their crimes, effectively proved innocent. And some cases are such that the client or victim cannot wait for the tortuously slow movement of standard police procedure and/or the court system.

The relationship between the private detective and the police/district attorney's office is typically antagonistic: he regards them as bureaucratic, incompetent, or corrupt, and they regard him, at best, as interfering and disrespectful of legal process, and at worst a muckraker stirring up trouble, or a vigilante taking the law into his own hands.

Some officials have reason to fear him, if they are corrupt themselves: they may know he is incorruptible, and that he will expose their wrongdoing if he gets sufficient evidence. These officials – whether they are a beat policeman or a police chief – may actively try to prevent the private eye from succeeding with his investigation. They may harass him, arrest him, employ violence, frame him for murder, discredit him in some other way, try to revoke his licence, or arrest or threaten someone the detective cares about.

The detective may have decided that the behaviour of the police is at odds with his personal values. In Raymond Chandler's *The Long Goodbye*, Marlowe describes the working methods of Captain Gregorius, who "solves crimes with the bright light, the soft sap, the kick to the kidneys, the knee to the groin, the fist to the solar plexus, the night stick to the base of the spine..."

Even if they are not involved in the main criminal conspiracy – or are not being bribed to turn a blind eye to it – policemen and official detectives may still regard the private eye as a sort of pariah. Often this is because he was previously employed by the police or the D.A.'s office – but left because he couldn't stomach the hypocrisy and corruption. His ex-colleagues dislike him because he thinks he's better than them – and because he makes them feel guilty for taking their regular back-handers. Or the detective may have been injured in the line of duty and quit because he didn't want to risk his life for a force that fails to bring justice to those they allegedly serve. Or, worst of all, he may have exposed corruption within his own organisation, effectively betraying 'one of our own.'

Philip Marlowe doesn't trust the police. In *The High Window,* he says: "Until you guys own your own souls you don't own mine. Until you guys can be trusted every time and always, in all times and conditions, to seek the truth out and find it and let the chips fall where they may – until that time comes, I have a right to listen to my conscience, and protect my client the best way I can."

Occasionally the detective may have one or more friends or allies in the force or the D.A.'s office. And in modern-day stories, the antagonism between police and private eye is more likely to be in the form of professional rivalry.

The Private Investigator – How to Hard-boil Your Detective

The hardboiled detective, like the classical 'great detective,' is an outsider. Being an outsider allows him to view people and situations objectively. The traditional Sherlock Holmes-like detective remains aloof and sees things from a purely intellectual viewpoint – an example of the 'Thinker' archetype. But the hardboiled detective is more active: he doesn't just want to solve problems for intellectual stimulation, he wants to do something to try and make situations better. He combines elements of the 'Warrior' with the 'Thinker,' which makes him an example of the *Crusader* archetype. He doesn't just observe and make judgments on what is right or wrong, he wades into the middle of things and tries to fix them. A Crusader is someone who fights for a *cause*, a moral purpose. The character type is also sometimes referred to as the 'Advocate,' because he or she will speak out for those who have no voice. Human rights activists and environmentalists also belong to this group – they fight for political, social, environmental change. They are idealists and reformers.

The hardboiled detective is typically a *private* detective – he works for himself. He may have been employed by the police or the district attorney's office in the past but left because he became disillusioned – either because of the corruption he saw within the organisation, or because abiding by the written rules meant that the organisation was not always able to bring the guilty to justice or protect the innocent.

The private eye has a strong moral code – there are lines he simply will not cross. But this code is his own – it is not the religious doctrine of a priest, nor is it fully in accordance with the moral beliefs of the society in which he lives. He can be both more pragmatic and more stringent in his actions in pursuit of justice. At the positive end of the scale, the hardboiled detective is *more* moral than society – he has 'old fashioned' moral values, which – as we have said – are often likened to the chivalric code of medieval knights in shining armour. The hardboiled detective has witnessed the corruption all around him in all levels of society, and so regards his own moral code as being superior. He is not corrupt or corruptible. At the same time, he is prepared to take action – even to risk his own life – to defend this less than perfect society from those who seek to exploit it for personal gain.

At the darker end of the scale, the detective may believe that his cause is just, so that the ends justify the means. Here he is in danger of becoming a vigilante or 'punisher' – judge, jury, and executioner, and answerable to no one. These two sides of his character mean that the hardboiled detective's motives are usually morally acceptable, but that he is able to engage in behaviours – such as the use of violence – that some would find unacceptable. The dark and light sides of his nature also mean that he can move between the sunny everyday world and the darker, seedier underworld. And his moral code means that however deeply he travels into the shadows, he is not at risk of being corrupted by this world. But the fact that he has witnessed the corruption that exists even in the ordinary world means that he has become 'world-weary' and cynical. He knows that appearances cannot be trusted – that something unhealthy can lie beneath. And he knows that people – including himself – are not perfect or perfectible. We have weaknesses, we make mistakes, and sometimes we are untrue to ourselves.

His position as an outsider means that the hardboiled detective has elements of the *rebel* in his character. He not only challenges criminals but those in authority whose actions – or inaction – he believes to be insufficiently moral, according to his own beliefs. In his view, people with wealth, power or a position of authority should not be deferred to without question.

But while the hardboiled detective is a cynic, he has not lost hope. He believes that things can be made better – and he is prepared to try and make this happen. He directs his attention toward what is wrong, what needs fixing, and seeks to help those who are suffering injustice. He knows that his efforts will not change the world – he is a realist – but he strongly believes that his energies are not being wasted. He wants to make a difference.

In part, the hardboiled detective's cynicism is a defence for his vulnerability. Showing commitment to, and enthusiasm for, a cause is not currently fashionable. Selflessness is not trending. We prefer to belittle or ridicule the enthusiasms of others, rather than have any of our own. People who start out with enthusiasm often have it knocked out of them as they are ground down by the world around them. We have moved from looking after the greater good of our community, and instead just look out for ourselves. The hardboiled detective stands against this tide: he does what he believes is right, and damn the consequences.

He is dedicated to living his life according to his own moral code, and this requires him to make sacrifices and to act selflessly. Anyone who does this and who feels that their sacrifices are not being appreciated or even recognised, risks becoming disillusioned. He becomes frustrated because other people do not see the necessity of what he does, or refuse to acknowledge it, or are in denial of its importance. He cannot force other people to his way of thinking – the best he can do is lead by example.

Worse still, while people do not, cannot, or will not see what he has achieved, they may recognise and draw attention to what he has *failed* to achieve. He is not perfect or omnipotent, he can only do his best. But he may find that only his failure is noted, and there is a danger that he will dwell on his own failures or perceived failures. He needs a sense of reality, of cynicism even, to help him deal with the fact that he cannot achieve everything that he might wish to. Circumstances and his own human fallibility don't allow for perfection – and he must not beat himself up about this.

Where the 'great detective' of the classic murder mystery is fallible as a human being – sometimes humorously so – he is generally infallible when it comes to the solution of the mystery itself. He sees all, knows all, and understands all. The hardboiled detective does not – he is more like a man blundering around in the dark hoping to come across some clue that will take him a little further in his quest for truth. And when he does discover it, the solution may not turn out to be grand or miraculous. It may not even be complete. And often it is not fulfilling – serving only to confirm that there is corruption in the world and he has merely uncovered another dollop of it.

The Crusader Character Archetype

The hardboiled detective conforms fairly closely to the *Crusader* archetype, demonstrating most of the positive qualities and some of the negative ones. I wrote about this character archetype in depth in *Character Creation* – here I will recap the main features of the Crusader archetype. Most systems of personality or character archetypes include a 'crusader' – sometimes called an idealist, reformer, moralist, or advocate – and it is one of the six archetypes I prefer to use.

Motivation: To bring about change by taking action; to act morally and with integrity. He feels he *must* act to bring justice to those who need it – cannot leave the responsibility to others.

Behaviours: responds to life with a combination of the head and the gut; he instinctively *feels* what is right, and then seeks to rationalise it. He has strong moral values and aims to live up to them at all times. He has difficulty trusting or forgiving others. He can sometimes feel guilty – judging that what he is doing is not good enough.

Values: The Crusader has a strong sense of *justice*, not simply as a theoretical concept, but as a practical outcome we should strive to achieve. He values logic and reason only insofar as he can use them to justify what he feels to be right. He also believes that however bleak the situation, there is always *hope*.

Weaknesses: The Crusader risks seeing everything as black or white, right or wrong. He may apply his strict personal values to others and judge them to be unworthy and may have difficulty forgiving their imperfections. He risks becoming disillusioned by the world around him, and he may become frustrated and angry because other people do not accept the importance of his 'crusade' to bring about a more just world.

Fears: The Crusader fears not living up to his own standard of behaviour – he is afraid of being judged not good enough. As a result, he may fear making mistakes – or owning to them when he does. And he fears being proved wrong – that is, learning that his value system, the justice he is fighting for, is in some way misguided – because it is all he has to give meaning to his life. He is afraid of failure because he knows he only has himself to blame.

Needs: The Crusader needs to stop trying to be perfect – he needs to be able to forgive himself his own human failings, and then he will be able to do the same for others. He needs to be able to relax and have fun, get away for a while from his compulsive need to fix things. And he needs to be able to accept people for what they are – all that they are – without trying to change the parts he doesn't 'approve of.' The Crusader would like to be seen as a rational Thinker, valuing intellect over instinct or gut feeling. Others may see him as self-controlled and cool, but he may be troubled by doubts and passions inside. He represses his anger, afraid that he would be unable to control any outburst once it started.

Backstory: The Crusader developed a strong set of personal values, perhaps as the result of a significant event in his life, a turning point:
- he may have witnessed someone acting as a Crusader and been inspired
- he may have witnessed injustice or corruption and made a decision to do something about it – sticking up for the underdog

- he may have been the victim of injustice – an underdog – himself and vowed that he would not allow anyone to suffer as he did

A person who has very high expectations for himself may have been subject to severe and constant criticism as a child or may have experienced a profound sense of failure in something that he wanted to achieve. He may have been made to feel that he needed to justify his own existence and so had to achieve things and do things perfectly. His father may have been absent or weak, leaving him with a need to fulfil the role of his own father-figure or protector. He may have become responsible for his own wellbeing – and perhaps that of others – at an early age before he was really ready to accept this responsibility. He may have had to suppress his own needs and help others, leading to feelings of frustration and anger.

Relationships: The Crusader is often disappointed in his relationships with other people. He has high expectations of his friends and lovers and feels that fidelity and integrity are hugely important. Other people may feel that he expects them to prove themselves worthy of his love or friendship and may feel repulsed by what they take to be his superior attitude: he thinks he is better – more moral – than they are, and may come across as patronising. He needs people to share his values and ideals, and as a result may become uncompromising and controlling as he tries to make friends or lovers meet his ideal. He may be over-critical, believing he is doing it for the other person's own good, but can end up undermining their confidence so that they give up, knowing that they can never achieve his standards. When people fail to meet his standards, he may feel that he should be punishing them for their transgressions. The worst thing anyone can do to the Crusader is to make him feel that he has been *betrayed*. This is an action that he cannot accept or understand. He is unforgiving. Because the Crusader is dedicated to his cause, he may regard romantic feelings as selfish and a distraction from his important work. And his own insecurities – his belief that he must be perfect and that he may not have been good enough to have 'earned' love – can also hamper his relationships. He may be afraid of making a mistake, of being 'wrong,' and he may be afraid of being rebuffed or ridiculed if he attempts to initiate a relationship. He can be extremely sensitive to criticism, and his insecurity can mean that he is afraid to admit that he has made an error: he may feel compelled to try and defend his action, rather than learn from the experience and move on.

Shadow: The shadow or dark side of the Crusader is the punisher or vigilante. This is someone who believes that his way is the only way and that he is justified in taking whatever measures are necessary to achieve his goals. He believes that it is his job to 'fix' people and make them fit his idea of perfection. He risks seeing a person as a problem to fix, rather than as another human being. He seems emotionless when he makes decisions, claiming to be objective, but really he is acting on gut instinct. He is uncompromising, stubborn, unyielding and punishes harshly. He cannot afford to allow doubt to creep in, because it might undermine his resolve.

The Crusader's beliefs are based on what he feels is right and moral, and as such he has difficulty defending them intellectually. Rather than explaining *why* he believes certain moral values are important, he is more likely to say *what* he believes in, his ideals, and then he comes across as opinionated, self-righteous, dogmatic, and moralising. You should behave in this way, he says, because I feel that this is the right way to behave.

Even if other people do think that what he says is correct, they may still be turned off by his attitude – the Crusader can be tactless and abrasive, even when speaking to people he likes. And rather than being able to see the good in people, he is more likely to see only their faults. People may want to join him in his crusade but will be made to feel that they are not up to the task. Only the Crusader himself is able to fix the problem, and it must be done *his* way.

A consequence of embarking on a one-man crusade can be that the Crusader resents having to take on the burden of 'doing everything.' He may become frustrated and angry, particularly when it appears that his efforts are actually achieving very little by way of change.

Character development is not usually a significant element in the detective thriller: the hardboiled private eye *is* he does not *become*. This being the case, we will not spend time here exploring the character arc of the Crusader character type. But I will mention the characteristics of the type of person – whether a friend or a lover – who is best suited to be with the Crusader.

To have a successful relationship with a Crusader, a person would need to be able to:
- share responsibility and do their fair share of the work
- acknowledge both the sacrifices the Crusader is making, and what he has achieved to date
- reassure the Crusader when he is being too self-critical
- show that they value the Crusader's advice
- try to be fair and considerate – 'moral' – in accordance with the Crusader's values
- help the Crusader to be able to forgive by apologising for any mistakes or transgressions
- listen to the Crusader's concerns and frustrations
- gently encourage him to relax and even to laugh at themselves when the Crusader is being too uptight.

'Twenty-five dollars a day and expenses'

Derek Porter describes private eyes like Philip Marlowe as "the small businessman as hero." Unlike the 'upper-class swells' of the classical detective story, "Marlowe works in a service industry where he does what it takes to make an honest living." There is no private inherited income for the hardboiled detective, he must make his own way in the world. Bear in mind too that the early novels in this genre were written in the shadow of the Great Depression.

As a freelance, the hardboiled detective usually has an employer, a client, but as Cawelti writes, "... in the long run he refuses to let the client shape either the goals or the methods of his investigation. Telling the boss off is as important to the private eye as exposing the corruption of the rich and respectable, and many hardboiled novels have central scenes in which the confrontation of employer and hero results in the putting down of the client. In such actions, the hero indicates his rejection of the drive for success by refusing to conform to the employer's authority. In effect, the hardboiled detective refuses to become a successful but conformist executive. Instead, he demonstrates that those who have achieved wealth and status are weak, dishonourable, and corrupt."

The hardboiled detective is not a small businessman who dreams of being in big business – he is, in a real sense, a self-made man, and he wants nothing more than to remain true to the self he has created. His shabby office is not a symbol of failure, but a demonstration of his integrity.

The Hardboiled Tough Guy

John G. Cawelti writes that the hardboiled detective is "first and foremost a tough guy. He can dish it out and he can take it," and he is "accustomed to a world of physical violence, corruption, and treachery..." When he is hit over the head, the injury is not a demonstration of weakness, or of the closeness of death, rather it "symbolises his toughness and ability to survive." And it shows that he is willing to suffer in pursuit of his goal.

Pronzini and Adrian: "The history of the United States abounds with larger-than-life loners whose accomplishments, whose very survival, depended on an uncompromising toughness and a willingness to enter into struggles against seemingly insurmountable odds: Daniel Boone, Kit Carson, Davy Crockett, Jim Bridger, Mike Fink, Jim Bowie. Such rugged individualists inspired the creation of mythical heroes – Paul Bunyan, for instance – and fictional men of action. Both James Fenimore Cooper's Natty Bumppo and Herman Melville's Captain Ahab are hunters driven by forces outside themselves, and in that sense are perfect paradigms of the modern private eye. Even Mark Twain's Huck Finn, and certainly Jack London's Wolf Larsen, have elements of the hardboiled knight in their makeup."

This tough guy element of his character comes from the fact that the Crusader character archetype combines elements of both the Thinker and the Warrior. As a Warrior, he takes action – he pushes back at those who seek to bully him into submission. But his Thinker aspect means that he considers his actions – he thinks about the consequences of what he's done, and he questions whether such actions are consistent with his convictions. But once he has made up his mind, he acts decisively. He is principled, strong-willed, self-controlled, and purposeful – when he has started something, he doesn't quit.

His opponents in the story will test him, both physically and mentally. They will attack him to warn him off; they will try to persuade him to give up his cause, arguing that it is in no one's best interest, least of all his own; and they will seek to tempt him – offering him money or sexual favours. But the hardboiled detective has the courage of his convictions and will not give up responsibility for his crusade once he has taken it on.

The Hardboiled Tough Gal

Carolyn G. Heilbrun has written that "...the first genuine woman hero ... may be found incarnated as the contemporary female detective in fiction. Starting in the 1970s, women detectives who were neither conventional nor committed to the safe and sure began to emerge in mystery narratives." And "...the contemporary female detective scorns the dictates of custom, history, and the earlier restrictions of womanhood..." These characters entered a field previously regarded as 'men's work' and achieved the same autonomy as men where they "...willingly engage, though differently, with the same kinds of risks and dangers as men."

As examples, Heilbrun gives Sara Paretsky's V.I. Warshawski, Margaret Maron's Deborah Knott, Laurie R. King's Kate Martinelli, P.D. James's Kate Miskin, Janet Neel's Francesca Wilson, and Marissa Piesman's Nina Fischman. Other notable female detectives include Marcia Muller's Sharon McCone and Sue Grafton's Kinsey Millhone.

Like their male counterparts, these women often shun romantic relationships – valuing their independence. In part, this is because, as Heilbrun writes, "...they are not prepared to sacrifice their own need for moral action to others' principles. They do not put men first in their lives, but they are rich in friends, sometimes men, and in lovers, sometimes women. Marriage cannot lure them, at least, not more than once, and then briefly. Childless, they often mentor girls and young women."

See also: *Hardboiled Dames: Stories Featuring Women Detectives, Reporters, Adventurers, and Criminals from the Pulp Fiction Magazine of the 1930s* (1986), edited by Bernard A. Drew and published by St. Martin's Press.

Appearance

Appearance is one way we can characterise our detective – though it's important to remember that the hero will wear different clothing to the first meeting with a client, where he wants to make a good first impression by seeming professional, than he will on the job where he wants to blend in and go unnoticed. In that initial meeting, he probably wants to look the way people expect a private eye to look – unless not looking like a detective is a significant part of his character. When he is working in the field he probably wants to look as little like a detective as he can.

Clothing, grooming, and personal hygiene may vary in each of these situations. And the hero may wear glasses in one and contact lenses in another, depending on what impression he wants to make. Out in the field, he'll probably need to wear comfortable shoes that he can walk long distances in – and run in if necessary. He's unlikely to wear a trench coat and fedora unless he's going to a fancy-dress party.

Personal Life

There are a number of things you might want to consider exploring when it comes to your detective's personal life:

Paranoia & Suspicion. Because a private detective is often suspicious of people's motives and is an expert at spotting deceit, his personal relationships can be affected. He is also occasionally a little paranoid – usually with good cause – and this can put additional strain on a friendship or romance.

Stress. Long hours, running a business alone, and dealing with intense emotional reactions or disturbing evidence can have an impact on a detective's mental health. It can also affect his life outside of work.

Social Life. Becoming deeply involved in an investigation can mean that the detective neglects his social life. True friends will probably understand this – but others may not.

Alcohol. Private detectives stereotypically deal with the stress and lack of social life by having a bottle of whiskey in the bottom drawer of their desk. To function properly, a detective needs to keep a clear head when he's on the job – but the job often means meeting people after dark and the meeting place is often a bar. Even if the detective is on the wagon, it is difficult to avoid temptation. Your detective may avoid cliché and not touch a drop and whether or not he or she feels the need to explain this may say something about their character.

Temptation. Another cliché in the hardboiled detective novel is that women throw themselves at the hero – and they're often naked in his bed when he gets home from the office. Typically, the hero tells them to put their clothes on and get out, he's not interested. This is another way of showing that the hero is a chivalrous type who doesn't take advantage of people. It's up to you whether your detective occasionally succumbs to temptation.

Rotten Apples

There are some real-life 'private investigators' who are not in the slightest bit heroic – they are in the business in order to exploit the innocent and vulnerable and are motivated by the usual forces – money, ego, and sex. The may falsely claim that someone may be heir to an unclaimed fortune and offer to provide the necessary proof for the client to claim this inheritance – for an up-front fee plus ongoing expenses. Or they may create cases for themselves in other ways – preying on the bereaved or people who believe their spouse could be cheating on them.

Plot Structures

The plot of the detective thriller is much less constrained by convention than the classical murder mystery. It does have a fundamental structure, but there is more scope for variation within it. It centres on a 'criminal conspiracy' rather than a single murderer-victim relationship. A murder may be part of the conspiracy, or it may be a by-product, perhaps accidental, that draws the detective's attention to the conspiracy.

As we will see when we examine the structure of the detective thriller in detail, it usually involves two separate cases which at first appear not to be connected, but which later prove to be linked by the secret criminal conspiracy. Thomas Chastain has observed that in both *The Big Sleep* and *The Maltese Falcon* "...the authors deliberately misdirect the eye (the private eye of the story and the eye of the reader) while working toward the solution of the mystery. Interestingly enough, in both books the mystery posed in the story was contained in the subplot while the main plot line was given over to what was essentially the misdirection of the eye."

The plot also combines elements from both the classic murder mystery and the traditional thriller – and it has some things in common with the gangster story and espionage thriller, which we will look at in chapter two.

The plot of the private detective story broadly follows the stages of the investigation of the main case in the story. Those stages will look something like this:

    (a) First contact with the client
    (b) Meeting the client (may be combined with first contact)
    (c) Taking the Case – Commitment
    (d) Beginning the Investigation
    (e) Interviewing – There are multiple instances of this
    (f) Contact with the Opposition
    (g) Investigating Another Person Related to the Case
    (h) Interviewing an Expert/Specialist
    (i) Investigating Vehicles, Property & Other Documentary Evidence
    (j) Investigation of the Circumstances of the Crime
    (k) Interviewing Other Witnesses
    (l) Impasse – The investigation stalls
    (m) The Catalyst – Making Things Happen

These stages don't necessarily occur in this order, some stages may occur more than once, and not all will feature in every investigation. In the plot template below, I have indicated where these elements might typically occur. Not that although I have labelled this a 'hardboiled detective' plot, this structure is used for the vast majority of contemporary detective stories, including many cozies – it is the basic investigation story structure and can also be used in other genres.

There will generally be between six and twelve major clues. Clues might include:
- something physical discovered at one of the locations
- a similarity between this case or murderer and another one in the recent (or distant) past
- something documentary, e.g. a newspaper article or the ownership of a piece of land or company
- a relationship between two characters; including, perhaps, a stormy or antagonistic one
- a tip-off to check out a new location
- a motive for the first victim's murder, pointing to the conspiracy
- something strange that happened recently that doesn't seem to be connected
- something else related to this strange occurrence or situation that provides a link to the present case(s)

The detective himself will be narrating the story in the first-person or we will be closely following his action in 'over the shoulder' third-person, which means that we will see whatever he sees as soon as he sees it. In the traditional whodunit, the investigation was filtered through the Watson character, who didn't always understand what the detective had found and didn't know what the detective was thinking. You can still fudge things a little bit by having your hero say something like 'I didn't know what this proved, but I knew it couldn't be good.'

Erle Stanley Gardner noted that "...that many of the clues these days are clues of action. In other words, the detective doesn't find a broken cuff link or a fragment of curved glass at the scene of the crime. Instead, one of the characters does something that turns out to be the significant clue."

There will also be four or five attempts to get the detective to end the investigation, such as:
- threat by a henchman
- physical attack or attempt on detective's life
- warning from the villain of how powerful he is
- seduction by a 'betraying female' or femme fatale
- bribery or an attempt to hire the detective by the villain
- police warning the detective to drop the case
- detective is fired by his client, or his client is killed or disappears

Often the detective is abducted and drugged, beaten-up or tortured and interrogated. Erle Stanley Gardner wrote that this is "...an inherent improbability in most of the hardboiled stories. The hero is usually captured by the big, bad villains, given a shot of morphine, awakens in an isolated house with a huge gorilla sitting in the room, methodically chewing gum. The hero asks questions, makes wisecracks, and from time to time the gorilla calmly gets up, walks over to the bed and beats up on the hero. After that, three or four other villains come in and start exercising. The hero is beaten into unconsciousness two or three times, but eventually manages to slug his way into the clear. Thereafter the only evidence of his beatings is shown by the increased tempo with which he dashes around making love to complaisant women and killing villains." Gardner is exaggerating slightly, but we should bear his comments in mind and not make our hardboiled hero impervious to concussion.

Three Acts – Four Quarters Plus Midpoint

The basic structure of the private detective story looks like this:

Act I: Set-up
Act II.1: Acting in ignorance of the conspiracy
Midpoint: Identifying the Villain and the nature of the conspiracy.
Act II.2: Following up the lead – proving the case
Act III: Climax and Resolution

The template below breaks this down into eight sequences, two for each of the quarters identified above.

The Hardboiled Detective Plot Template

Sequence 1

This typically consists of (a) *first contact with the client* and (b) *meeting the client*. These may be combined or the first contact, perhaps a telephone call to arrange a meeting, may have occurred before the first scene we actually see. The first contact may be made directly by the client or the client may be referred to the detective, perhaps by the police or an attorney or a mutual acquaintance. First contact with a client will typically take place by phone or perhaps e-mail. But a detective isn't likely to take on a new case without having a face-to-face meeting first. A great deal is revealed by body language and people behave differently when dealing in person than they do in the relative anonymity of a call or message. The private detective's job is based on meeting people, interviewing them, and forming an opinion about their reliability – why would he not use these skills when choosing new clients?

The opening scene might be:
- the client walking into the detective's office
- the detective going to the client's home or place of work
- or the story begins with the investigation underway and then the details of the detective being hired by the client are filled in as backstory.

This opening scene serves to introduce the hero and his ordinary world. One of the reasons we often meet the detective in his office is that it serves to characterise him – in the same way that Sherlock Holmes's Baker Street rooms revealed much about him. H.R.F. Keating writes that the 'shabbiness' of the private detective's office indicates that he is a 'person of integrity'. He's not getting rich off his clients, rather he is an honest man doing an honest job. The office also indicates that he is in *business* – this is his profession, he's not some sort of effete amateur dabbling in investigative work. If we don't see the hero in his office, the same characterisation is achieved by a description of his car and/or his appearance. We also learn something about him from his attitude to the work and the way he talks to his client.

When we first meet the detective, he may be dealing with a personal problem of his own – this may affect why he takes a case that he wouldn't normally touch, perhaps motivated by the fact that he's almost bankrupt.

Or this personal issue may play out in a subplot in the novel – or across a story arc spanning several novels in a series.

Meeting a client is a business meeting and it is important for the detective to make the right first impression. At the same time, the detective will be sizing up the client to decide whether he wants to work for this person. In assessing the client, the detective will consider a number of things:

Objective – What does the client, ultimately, want to achieve and is the goal they are currently proposing the right way to reach that objective? Are there any legal issues relating to what the client wants done and/or how they want it to be done?

Character/Personality – Does the client have character flaws that make working for them a risky proposition? Does the detective like them and trust them enough to be their champion? Or is this the sort of person that the hero is going to clash heads with?

Mental State – Is the client's current state of mind and/or emotional state affecting their ability to make reasonable decisions? Are they acting in anger or out of revenge? Are they upset? Are they afraid? Paranoid? Does the story they are telling seem rational and credible? Is their proposed action a sensible choice? Sometimes the best course of action for a detective is to talk the client out of doing what they say they want to do.

Consequences – If the client gets what they're asking for, what will the consequences be – both for the client and any third party they want investigating? Will the client go after his cheating spouse with a shotgun? Will finding out the truth be worse than not knowing?

Money – Can the client afford to pay what the work will cost? Sue Grafton's Kinsey Malone gives this serious thought for some of her potential clients. As a sole trader, the detective is free to set his own rates for the job. And some jobs he will price differently to others. If you are going to mention the rates your detective charges, I would avoid quoting actual dollar (or other currency) amounts, unless your story is set in a specific historical period. Saying your detective charges $50 an hour plus expenses might quickly date your novel if the economy changes and fifty dollars no longer buys what it used to. Rates will also depend on the location of your story – urban versus rural, say – and on the type of clientele your detective serves. They will also take into account the sort of experience required to do the job and any perceived level of risk in carrying it out.

Does the detective ask for a retainer? A flat fee? A day's payment in advance? And what does he say to the client so that they understand nonpayment of the bill will have consequences? He may make it clear that nonpayment amounts to a breach of contract and if that happens the client confidentiality agreement no longer applies. The detective may also run some checks on the client before the meeting to make sure they don't have a criminal record or a history of unpaid debts. Sometimes a detective may mention something he's learned about the client – as proof of what a good detective he is.

With some clients, a detective may decide he wants to have a formal written contract in place so that there is no misunderstanding later. He may have his own boilerplate contract template for this or he may have his attorney draw it up for him. If you want an idea of what a contract should look like, Google 'sample private investigator contract' – but I wouldn't quote one in full in a story, summarise the most important bit(s) and say (or hint) why this is important to the hero for this particular client.

There are other questions the detective may ask himself during this first meeting:

Is the client telling the whole truth? And if they seem to be hiding something, why are they doing that? Every private detective says something like 'Expect everyone to lie to you – especially your client.'
Why me? Why has the client come to a private detective rather than doing the work him or herself or going to the police?
Am I the right person for the job? What the client requires may fall outside the detective's area of expertise or may involve a type of work that he doesn't like doing. In such cases, he may refer the client to a more appropriate private investigator. In a novel, this often results in the other investigator ending up dead and then the hero feels obliged to investigate himself.
Caseload – Is the detective's current list of ongoing investigations so large that he cannot take on another client? Or is he so desperate for paid work that he'll take anything?

Typically, we would say that being asked to take the case is the *challenge* or 'call to adventure' given to the hero at the end of Sequence 1. He would then spend some time being *reluctant* to take it and would finally accept the challenge at the end of Sequence 2 and make his *commitment*. In the hardboiled detective story, we want to get things moving quickly and the commitment is made in Sequence 1 – or has already been made as the sequence opens with the hero at work on the case.

Given all of the above, private detectives still sometimes take cases that logic and their gut feelings tell them they shouldn't. Sometimes it's because they feel they ought to play the good Samaritan and sometimes it's because they need cash for grocery shopping. Reluctance may be expressed, but the hero *takes the case* (c) – this may be an explicit statement or implied by the fact that the hero begins working. Often the detective knows, or suspects, that the client hasn't told him the whole truth – or he feels that something isn't quite right. The case itself, as he initially accepts it, is something fairly mundane – to find a missing person, to follow a cheating spouse, to offer security advice, or any of the other types of task mentioned earlier.

Before the end of Sequence 1, or perhaps not until Sequence 2, we may see (d) *beginning the investigation*. The detective will review the available information and plan his first moves. We see the detective at work – perhaps interviewing the client or some other source of information; perhaps visiting the scene of a crime or disappearance. We also see his abilities as an investigator, and his attitude – and usually an early demonstration of his moral code.

Sequence 2

Here we begin the investigation work with (e) *interviewing*. Meeting with the first witness, expert, contact, or informant – this person may be reluctant to provide what the detective wants. Assessment of the reliability of the interviewee. What this person says – or doesn't say – gives the detective a clue to the next location he needs to visit, and/or the next person he needs to speak to. There will be a number of these interviews throughout the investigation. I have included a chapter on interviewing and interrogation later in the book. This first interviewee may become the detective's second client, or a murder victim, a murderer, or someone who is suspected of murder but is innocent.

The detective's early actions in the investigation will have consequences. He will attract the attention of the villain, who may regard him as a threat and have him followed. He may also attract the attention of the police – either honest or corrupt cops, or both. He may cause problems for other important individuals – perhaps causing them embarrassment. Or he may lead the bad guys to the location of someone who is in hiding or living incognito.

Often we see more of the detective's home life – he lives simply and honestly – further demonstration of his integrity and moral code. His home and/or office are typically in stark contrast to the wealth of the places occupied by his client and/or the criminal types he encounters during his investigation.

To the second location, where he questions one or more people who are unhelpful, evasive, or threatening. Having learned nothing from them, the detective may stake out the location and follow one of the people he has spoken to.

The detective may be spoken to or harassed by the police – why are they interested in such a mundane case?

Before the first murder, we are often introduced to a second 'client' – this may be someone who actually employs the detective formally, or it may be someone he ends up working on behalf of. They could be the person the detective has been hired to locate and may have a seemingly separate problem of their own that they want help with. This second client may appear to be a villain – they may appear to be powerful and in control, and they may threaten or bully the detective. They are a contrast to the victim-like first client. This second client does not appear to be connected to the first client in any way – though a link between the two will come to light later.

The order of the appearance of these two clients can be switched, and either of them could be the first murder victim. Or the first murder victim could be someone else entirely.

The first client may reiterate their need for the detective's help – perhaps they have been threatened or have some other reason for feeling afraid. He may confront them about not telling him everything, and he may learn more of the truth, or a different lie – but still not *all* of the truth. The client will typically make themselves out to be a victim, telling the detective that they are afraid. But still not giving him all the details of what they are afraid of.

The detective may learn something about the police's interest in his case – something related to the first or second clients, a suspect, or perhaps even a victim. We may learn something of the first client's backstory – but rather than clarifying things, it will raise more questions. We may also learn something about the victim – either before or after he is murdered. And/or we could learn something about the relationship between the victim and the first client.

End of Act I – *The first murder*. The victim may have been killed as a result of the client's or the detective's actions. The victim may be his client, or someone the client asked him to locate, or a person who is in some other way connected to the client. Initially, there may be no apparent link between the victim and the client – it may seem to be a coincidence that the victim died in the vicinity of the detective – but a link with the case he is investigating will be discovered later.

We are now at the end of Act I and roughly one-quarter of the way through the story. The rest of the story will involve the detective exploring three possible solutions to the case – two wrong ones and a right one – and one in each of the remaining three quarters. The division of the action won't be that obvious, but that is the underlying approach we're looking for. The first attempt at a solution the hero tries (during Sequences 3 and 4) will lead him to a midpoint revelation – where he discovers that not only is his solution wrong, but he's involved in something much bigger – a conspiracy – than he ever suspected.

Sequence 3

This will begin with the aftermath of the discovery of the murder. The police are now definitely interested and question the detective about the murder. They have discovered some link between the detective and the victim. They will probably warn him that this is now a 'police matter' and he should leave it to the professions, abandoning his own investigation. There is antagonism between the hero and the police detectives and suspicion on both sides. The murder may mean that the detective feels he has failed in some way – or feel that he was in some way responsible for the death. Did he lead the killer to the victim? Did his asking questions draw attention to the victim?

If the murder victim is not the client, the murder may result in the client being threatened, harmed, or humiliated. As a result, he or she may fire the detective. The detective may confront the client about not having told him the truth. He may pretend that he knows more than he really does, in order to get the client to reveal something. This puts the detective at risk – the bad guys may think he knows too much and this makes him a threat to their plans.

The detective may be suspicious of the client's motives for firing him – and he decides to carry on the investigation for his own curiosity or peace of mind. One or other of the clients – or both? – reveal that there is a third major player, and they hint that this is the *real* villain. This villain is the one who is responsible for the victim's death.

The detective may be threatened, or an attempt made on his life. This is another attempt to get him to drop his investigation or to stay away from someone – perhaps one of the clients or the villain. The detective's next step will normally be to investigate the background of the murder victim or to try to interview or find out more about the person he has been warned to stay away from.

There may be an initial indication or clue that the second client's small-scale case is in some way linked to the murder.

Note that if the client doesn't fire the hero in this sequence, there is probably another attempt by someone else to get him to abandon his investigation. The hero may be fired by his client at the midpoint instead.

We may also see the hero at home again and a further development in his personal problem subplot.

The detective may tell one or both of his clients that he thinks their case is connected in some way to the murder – and/or that the two cases are linked in some way. The client doesn't believe this – or doesn't want to. The detective and his client may disagree over this – with the detective saying he'll investigate the case in his own way. The client may warn him to stay away from someone, saying 'they're not involved in this.'

Remember that there is often something at the end of Sequence 3 that pays off or comes back to haunt the hero at the end of Sequence 5. This could be a person who is reluctant to speak to the hero or who is afraid to speak or who says something cryptic that the hero doesn't understand the significance of.

Sequence 4

The detective may play the two clients off against each other – he trusts neither and does not pledge his allegiance to either. If one of them is the *femme fatale* she will attempt to seduce him, either to try and get him to give up his investigation or to find out how much he knows, or to try to manipulate him to do her dirty work for her.

Investigating the victim – a clue that leads the detective to the next location/source of information. The detective goes to this location/source and learns something new about one of the clients or about the victim.

First sight of the villain. Villain or his henchmen may threaten the detective, or he may be beaten up, or an attempt may be made on his life. This is a clue that he is getting close to something important.

Midpoint

The detective makes a significant discovery – something that proves his 'first solution' or suspicions wrong. The detective may seek to speak with the client's 'opponent' or this person may seek out the detective. Often he meets and talks to the villain – (f) *contact with the opposition* – who tells him he is way out of his depth. The villain may demonstrate the extent of his power. He will not tell the detective anything. Again the detective may pretend to know more than he does to try and draw the villain out. He doesn't trust anything the villain tells him – especially when the villain offers to do the detective a 'favour' by telling him the truth about what is going on – and about why he cannot trust either of his clients or the police. The villain may try to hire or bribe the detective. The detective's moral code will not allow him to accept. The detective may also learn something about the nature of the conspiracy, and/or about a significant secret relationship between two of the characters.

If the midpoint involves the hero being fired by one of his clients or being physically threatened or attacked, then he knows he's on to something important. He may have learned something important, but he doesn't have the evidence he needs to identify the murderer. What is he missing?

The midpoint may involve a romantic encounter – perhaps with the *femme fatale*.

Something unconnected with the case may give the detective a clue or point him towards something important. The clue may not register immediately, so may only be mentioned in passing. It could be an observation about something he sees happening, or it could be an anecdote he hears, or it may be the detective musing over an earlier case or other event from the past that has something in common with the current investigation.

Sequence 5

The detective may stake out the home or headquarters of the villain – or of the villain's henchman, or someone else connected with the villain – (g) *investigating another person related to the case*. Following up on a lead, the hero talks to or investigates the background of another person whose name has been linked to the case. He follows them or discovers a clue which leads him to a new location.

The detective asks questions at the new location – learns something about the activities that the villain is involved in, and possibly something about the relationships between the characters. The detective also learns something significant about the conspiracy and the people involved in it. As a result, the detective may be drugged or kidnapped, beaten or tortured so the villain can see how much he really knows.

We may gain the villain's point of view on what is happening and his backstory. He may feel that he is the injured party seeking justice and feel that he has a legitimate claim to whatever wealth or power lies at the heart of the conspiracy.

The detective is released or escapes. He may be stopped by the police detectives and warned off the case again – or they may tell him that they have been ordered to drop their investigation by the 'higher-ups'; they aren't happy about this and may hint that they want him to continue his investigation. Or they may warn him that powerful individuals or organisations are involved so he should drop his case. Or perhaps the hero's second client asks him to give up on that investigation – and he suspects that this client may also have been threatened.

The detective, refusing to give up on his investigation, may go in search of another source of information – but this person has disappeared, refuses to answer questions, runs away, or attacks the hero. The hero may go and seek information from a more friendly source – an old newspaper editor friend or someone like that.

The detective discovers a clue – to a new location. He goes there and learns something new. This may be a false clue, a setback, or a twist. It may turn the detective's investigation upside down, upsetting his favoured theory – but it is ultimately the final piece of the puzzle that he needs to understand the conspiracy and everyone's roles in it. Or so he thinks.

The hero may gain a clue or be given some information that appears to solve one or both of his cases – but this convenient 'solution' has been manufactured in order to get the private detective and possibly the police to give up on their investigations. This evidence seems to resolve the whole mystery or to 'prove' that the private detective's two cases are not connected. The police may be satisfied with this and back off – but the hero may remain suspicious. This solution may be that the first murder was an accident or suicide, or that the 'vagrant' (or some such) who was recently arrested was responsible or that someone has conveniently confessed to it. Doubting this explanation, the hero may feel that he is the only one now who can investigate properly and get justice for the victim.

Remember that there was something at the end of Sequence 3 that pays off or comes back to haunt the hero at the end of Sequence 5. This may be a clue that didn't make sense back then but means something significant now.

Sequence 6

The detective begins to put his plan into action. He makes arrangements or sets up meetings. He may locate or obtain the thing that everyone is looking for. Now he has this thing and/or knows the truth about the conspiracy, he must decide what to do. His decision will be in accordance with his moral code. The detective formulates a plan. He may share what he has learned with his client(s) and/or the police.

But the clients or the villain (or perhaps the police) have other ideas – they take action of their own, usually pre-emptive. An attack, a raid, a kidnap. Typically the *femme fatale* or one of the clients deceives the detective – possibly even setting him up. She may try to distract him by attempting to seduce him or continue their romance. She may try to persuade him to abandon his plan, warning him how dangerous the villain can be.

At this point, or at any other point during the investigation, the hero may need (h) *interview an expert or specialist*. This may involve gaining specific information relevant to the case or a general understanding of a subject associated with it. The expert or specialist isn't necessarily an academic or a scientist, they are just someone with knowledge in a particular area. Their area of expertise might be people trafficking, drug smuggling, counterfeiting or something as mundane as cheese-making. The detective may need this information in order to understand a clue he has found or perhaps to test a theory.

The detective may also investigate (i) *vehicles, property, or other documentary evidence*. Again, this is something he might do at any point in a story, often with the hope of proving a connection between a person and a place or object, or to discover something about the history of a place or person, or to uncover previously unsuspected relationships between characters.

As a result of something he learns, the detective may decide to revisit one of the people he has already interviewed – but instead of finding them, he finds a body. This body could be the person he wanted to re-interview, it could be the person he suspected previously, or it could be one of his clients. Or, less commonly, it could be the villain, the henchman, or one of the detectives investigating the first murder.

As a result of information the hero has shared with the police or a client, someone may have decided to take the law into his or her own hands. Perhaps someone is killed or hurt as a result. Or perhaps it is the hero's own direct actions that cause someone to be harmed. At the end of the sequence, the detective's plan has unravelled – and he feels responsible/guilty. It is his fault that people are hurt, kidnapped, or dead.

Sequence 7

The end of Sequence 6 is effectively the failure of the hero's second attempt at a solution and he is left in a situation which makes him feel that not only has he failed to solve his client's problem but his actions have actually made their situation worse. The end of Sequence 6 is a 'darkest hour' for the hero and it seems that a solution to the problem is further away than ever.

Having seen his second attempt to solve the case fail, the hero may pause and reflect on everything that has gone before – trying to see where he went wrong or what he missed. This often involves (j) *investigation – or reinvestigation – of the circumstances of the crime*. There may be something that the hero and everyone else have taken for granted and which, on further investigation, proves to be false or a red herring. This then leads to (k) *interviewing – or re-interviewing – other witnesses*. Given his new perspective on the case, the detective may have new questions to ask. But despite these renewed efforts, the hero doesn't seem to be getting any closer to an actual solution.

The detective may search the second victim's home and discover a clue that links the victim to the first murder victim or to one of the other characters or to the conspiracy. The detective may consult a friendly source to find out more about the second victim. Building on what he has learned, the detective is able to demonstrate a relationship between the second victim and one of the other characters. The detective may confront this character and be told to back off – warned that this character has powerful friends. Does this mean the police, the villain, or someone else? Although this encounter is antagonistic, the other person may let something slip that is helpful to the detective.

The detective may return to an earlier reluctant source and pressure them into revealing what they know.

The police or someone else may contact the detective and warn him that his life is in danger.

The detective reviews all that has gone before –

What he knows and can prove, including links between some of the characters and lesser crimes committed by some of them.

What he knows or suspects but cannot prove, such as links between the villain and various people probably involved in the conspiracy; the thing that links all of the important players, e.g. drug smuggling; the link between the first murder and the second, and the identity of one or both of the murderers.

What he still doesn't know, such as why the first victim was killed; why the second suspect was framed, and why the first suspect was murdered.

Having failed to prove his second solution is the correct one, the hero is at an (l) *impasse* – the investigation has stalled and he needs to do something to get it moving again. Sometimes in an investigation – and in writing a story – things just stall and nothing seems to be happening. At this point, the hero may need to do something to stir things up. It is time for (m) *the catalyst* to make things happen.

If the hero can figure out what will motivate someone to take action, he can give them the appropriate 'encouragement' – either directly or indirectly. Placing people under stress reduces their ability to think rationally – they just want to act to escape from the unpleasant feeling and so may act rashly. Part of the job of a storyteller is to place characters into high-pressure situations so that they reveal their true selves by their reactions. Private eyes do a similar thing. When someone is under strain they reveal their true emotions and their real character. 'Prodding' often involves preying on someone's weakness – which is usually some form of greed, lust, jealousy, or fear.

Alternatively, the detective might use a 'honey pot' to draw someone out and ensnare them – this might include offering prizes or free gifts to bring someone out of hiding. If a private detective is not expecting to have to put together a case that will stand up in court, he is more leeway than the police to 'make things happen' – the rules concerning entrapment don't apply to him in the same way. In the case of an insurance fraudster, for example, the catalyst will be something that causes him to do something that proves he is faking his injury. 'Winning' a free day's surfing or a bungee jump may do the trick. Or maybe just having him chase down the street after a $100 bill. Private detectives can't usually set up complex or expensive scams – ingenuity is usually called for. And again, it is important to target the person's weakness – usually in the form of something that they *desire* and will take action to get without considering the risk or the consequences.

Sometimes the catalyst is a bluff. The hero pretends to have some evidence or to know something in order to see how someone reacts. If a suspect tries to disprove or destroy a piece of non-existent evidence, there is a good chance he's got something to hide. Sometimes the hint is enough to have a character say, 'You know, don't you?' and the detective doesn't have to say or do anything except allow them to confess. Obviously, you don't want to trick the *real* villain into a full confession – that would be unconvincing and an anti-climax. But the detective can use this approach on one of the villain's associates.

These techniques don't just apply to criminals and suspects – the detective may have to use them against reluctant witnesses or experts too.

Having identified his final suspect, the hero goes after them or goes to someone who knows where this suspect is and persuades them to give up the location.

Sequence 8
Climax and Resolution – the conspiracy revealed and thwarted, and the detective explains who killed the victim and why. Perhaps a final twist/revelation. The guilty handed over to the appropriate authorities, or justice is served in some other way according to the detective's moral code.

Denouement – In a real-life investigation, the private detective's last contact with the client is often the presentation of a report – either written or verbal. I wouldn't advise ending your novel with the hero's full written report, but you might tie up any loose ends by having him summarise it, perhaps just for the benefit of the reader, or to have a scene where he makes his verbal report to the client, filling in any missing details and consequences that haven't yet been explained in the story.

It may be helpful in planning this final scene or chapter to think in terms of the structure of the written report the detective would make. The beginning, middle, and end of the report would be an introduction, the main body of the content, and the conclusion, followed by an appendix of supporting data if necessary. The report should be concise, including only that information which is necessary. The format used for the report may depend on the nature of the client – for a spouse, an envelope of photographs showing their partner cheating, along with details of where and when they were taken, will probably be enough; for a businessman, a formal written report in a presentation folder may be necessary. In both cases, straightforward language should be used to ensure clarity of communication.

The *introduction* will contain a summary of what the detective was asked to achieve by the client, the purpose of the investigation, along with the circumstances under which the investigation was undertaken, a summary the main stages of the investigation, and an outline of the evidence that will be presented.

The *body* of the report is effectively a chronological summary of the investigation. It will seek to demonstrate that the investigation was thorough and that no avenue was left unexplored. It will also include any details that are unfavourable to the client's case as well as those that are favourable – this should demonstrate that the detective did not allow bias to influence the course of the investigation. The details provided should be precise, including exact quotations from the persons interviewed. And the information provided should be objective and factual, avoiding assumptions or opinions. These details should include the *who, what, when, where, how,* and *why*.

The *conclusion* of the report should summarise the information gathered and what was or wasn't proved. It may also include the detective's opinions and/or recommendations on next steps.

Plot Functions of Characters
I want to talk about characters here purely in terms of their functions or roles within the plot. In the traditional whodunit, the detective is presented with a *closed* situation – a body and six suspects, and one of the suspects must be the murderer. The six people all serve as *suspects* – any one of them could be the murderer – and as *witnesses*, since all of them were present at the time of the murder.

The six suspects are each typically interviewed *twice* by the detective – once as he gathers their initial stories and a second time after he has compared their accounts for discrepancies and also pieced together information about their backgrounds based on what other suspects have said about them. The detective's investigation involves proving who had the means, motive, and opportunity to commit the murder. There is no *client* as such – the detective is effectively working for the good of the innocent suspects and restoring equilibrium to their world.

The hardboiled detective story differs in that the hero is faced with an *open* situation – he doesn't know who the suspects or the witnesses are – they could be anyone in the city and there are millions of people in the city. He has to *locate* these people before he can interview them. And in the hardboiled detective story, there are usually *two* clients – and two apparently unrelated investigations which eventually prove to be related to a larger conspiracy. There is also a villain or antagonist who is responsible for the criminal conspiracy but who may or may not be responsible for the murder(s). There may be two or more murders, committed by the same person or by different people for different reasons – but both connected in some way to the conspiracy.

What characters are needed for a hardboiled detective story?

As well as the hardboiled detective, there are a number of roles that need to be filled – and a single character can fill more than one of these roles. I will list the roles first:

- Client 1
- Client 2
- Victim 1
- Victim 2
- Murderer 1
- Murderer 2 (optional)
- Suspect 1 (innocent)
- Suspect 2 (innocent)
- Villain
- Femme Fatale
- Henchman (optional)

Now let's look at which roles could be occupied by the same character – this is where it starts to look complicated, but it isn't as bad as it looks.

The *femme fatale* could also be a client, a murderer, or the villain behind the criminal conspiracy. She will almost certainly *not* be a victim.

A *client* could also be a victim, a suspect, or responsible for one or more murders.

The *villain* could be the *femme fatale* as we've said and will almost certainly be a suspect. The villain may or may not be a murderer. They will almost certainly *not* be a victim and probably not a client – the hero wouldn't agree to work for them, unless he is unaware of their villainous status at the time they become his client (this would be the case if the *femme fatale* was both client and villain).

The *henchman* might be a suspect, a murderer, or a victim.

The *victim* of the second murder could be the murderer of the first victim.

Virtually any of the roles could be filled by someone who is also a policeman.

There may be a number of witnesses, informants, experts, or contacts who are interviewed by the detective but who fill *none* of the roles listed above. But any of the above roles could also be a witness or source of information and most of them will probably be interviewed by the detective.

Reading all of that may have made your head spin, but it will make more sense when you come to create your own cast of characters. I should probably have said that the *femme fatale* is actually optional, but why would you not include one? If you are familiar with *The Maltese Falcon,* and you should be if you want to write one of these things, try figuring out which of the characters fills which of the above roles.

I said above that there are two innocent suspects plus one guilty one – and possibly (optionally) a second murderer. Roughly speaking, the hero – and the reader – will suspect one of them in the second quarter of the story (Sequences 3 and 4), one in the third (5 and 6), and the real murderer will be revealed in the last quarter (7 and 8). In some stories, one of the suspects is apparently cleared in an earlier sequence, only to be proved guilty at the end – this often happens in the case of the *femme fatale* or one of the clients.

How you handle these three suspects is up to you, but options you might consider include:
- someone we 'want' to be guilty of murder (usually the villain) turns out not to be
- someone we *don't* want to be guilty has so much evidence pointing in their direction that they must be considered a suspect
- the real murderer turns out to be someone close to the hero and possibly someone he is attracted to (usually the *femme fatale*)
- someone cleared of the first murder might be responsible for the second, and vice versa
- the person who commits the second murder might try to make it look like the work of the murderer who committed the first one
- the first suspect becomes the second murder victim
- the hero is suspected of one (or both) of the murders by the police and has to find the guilty person to prove his innocence. Perhaps someone (the *femme fatale* or the villain?) has set him up and planted evidence to frame him
- the *femme fatale* may appear to have been framed and have the hero prove her innocent, only for him to discover that she was guilty all along
- one of his clients or the *femme fatale* may deliberately cause the hero to suspect an innocent person – either in order to deflect attention from themselves, to distract him for their own purposes, or to protect a third party

2 | Gangsters

The gangster thriller is very much a *crime* thriller rather than a detective thriller. Investigation plays little or no part in the story and attention is focused on the activities of the criminal. In this chapter we will look in detail at the 'classic' gangster story – that is, the stories of a small number of gangster movies that defined the genre in the 1930s.

These stories are set in an urban environment – usually Chicago – and follow the rise of a criminal character to a position of power and his rapid and dramatic – and usually violent – fall. His story is essentially a tragedy and, on the surface at least, demonstrates that crime doesn't pay. Rather than investigating the gangster's crimes, the story explores the psychology of his character and shows how his 'tragic flaw' leads to his own destruction. W.R. Burnett, author of the gangster novel *Little Caesar*, said that his aim was to present the story from the point of view of the criminal, a novel idea in 1929: "You had crime stories but always seen through the eyes of society. The criminal was just some son-of-a-bitch who's killed somebody and then you go get 'em. I treated them as human beings."

Writing in his book *Bloody Murder,* Julian Symons said that the crime novel, in comparison to the detective novel's conservative social attitude, was "...often radical in the sense of questioning some aspect of law, justice, or the way society is run." The gangster story explores the darker side of the American Dream – the idea that America is a land of equal opportunity and that anyone who works hard can succeed and have a good life. Lee Horsley says that the gangster story has a "... double appeal, allowing readers and filmgoers to experience a sense of vicarious participation in gangster violence but also giving them the retributive pleasure of seeing violence turned against the gangster himself." And that they could "...identify with criminal rebellion against a corrupt, hypocritical society, but at the same time could indulge in fantasies of revenge against criminals ... identified as the 'public enemy' responsible for the decline of all standards of decency and order."

The classic' gangster story takes place before the 'Castellammarese War' that took place between February 1930 and April 1931 – a violent power struggle for control of the Italian-American Mafia that ended with the establishment of a governing body called The Commission. Mario Puzo's novel *The Godfather* (1969) is set in the decade from 1945 to 1955 and was inspired by the real-life histories and more formal structure of the 'Five Families' in New York. Later in this chapter, we'll look at how the plot structure of *The Godfather* differs from that of the classic gangster thriller.

Historical Development of the Gangster Story
There were gangs in New York in the 1780s after the American War of Independence and there was a peak in gang activity just before the Civil War. *The Gangs of New York: An Informal History of the Underworld* (1927) by Herbert Ashbury is an account of these criminal gangs and it was the inspiration for the 2002 Martin Scorsese film *Gangs of New York*. 'Gangsters' as we know them emerged in New York and Chicago after the

end of the First World War and grew in influence as a result of three significant events: the expansion of the urban environment and a growth in urban population, the Depression, and Prohibition.

Urbanisation. Rapid industrialization in the United States radically altered the way in which people lived and worked. In 1790 around one in twenty people lived in cities, by 1870 it was one in four and by 1920 half of the population lived in urban areas.

The Depression. The worldwide economic downturn that became known as the Great Depression began in the United States with the 'Wall Street crash' in October 1929 and lasted for the best part of ten years. Many wealthy people lost their fortunes and huge numbers that weren't wealthy were plunged into absolute poverty.

Prohibition was a constitutional ban on the production, importation, transportation, and sale of alcoholic beverages applied across the whole of the United States from 1920 to 1933. Supporters of it regarded it as a victory for public health and morals. It effectively criminalised anyone who enjoyed consuming alcohol and gave rise to an underground industry of illicit alcohol production and distribution that criminal gangs capitalised on. It is estimated that by 1925 there were between 30,000 to 100,000 speakeasies in New York City. It also cost the government tax revenues during the years of the Depression.

Al Capone and his seven-year reign as the head of the Chicago Outfit inspired much of what we regard as being typical of the gangster story. The early films and novels were created while Capone was still active and incorporated events almost as they occurred. There was the murder of North Side Gang leader Dean O'Banion in his flower shop; the assassination of Hymie Weiss across the road from the Holy Name Cathedral, and the St. Valentine's Day Massacre – these and more have found their way into the movies in various forms.

Gangsters Around the World

The is no formal definition of a 'gangster' beyond the fact that it denotes someone who is a member of a criminal gang. Originally, gangs would have been small local groups or street gangs engaged in relatively low-level crime, but the term has become associated with organised crime and with the Italian-American Mafia. The Italian Mafia is believed to have come into existence in the early to mid-1800s in Sicily and the first mafiosi – the terms Mafia and mafiosi were not used by the organisation itself – are thought to have arrived in America during the late 1800s.

But criminal gangs have existed throughout history and across the world. In China, the Triads date back to the mid-1600s and the Japanese Yakuza came into existence early in the same century. The Russian mafia or Bratva can be traced back to the 1720s. India has its history of organised crime too and a number of high-profile and 'celebrity' mobsters. Gangsters have also featured in Indian cinema with films about the Mumbai (formerly Bombay) underworld and the dacoits or 'bandits.' In England, gangs of outlaws have existed for centuries and following the Industrial Revolution were found in many major cities. In the 1890s, Birmingham had the 'Sloggers' and their rivals the 'Peaky Blinders,' whose exploits formed the basis of the BBC drama series first broadcast in 2013. In the 1840s the Northern Mob was formed as groups from Liverpool, Manchester, Derby, and Nottingham banded together and in the 1860s Sheffield had its own gangs including the Guttapercha Gang. In the 1920s conflict between the Sheffield gangs was such that it was dubbed 'Little Chicago.'

Graham Greene's 1938 novel *Brighton Rock* is the story of psychopathic young gangster Pinkie Brown. It was filmed in 1948 with Richard Attenborough in the title role and released in the USA as *Young Scarface*. A 2010 film based on the novel is set in the 1960s, the era of the Mods and Rockers. In the 1950s and 60s, the Kray twins, Ronnie and Reggie, led a gang referred to as 'The Firm' in the East End of London, responsible for murder, armed robbery, arson, and protection rackets. Like Al Capone, the Krays capitalised on their notoriety, making friends of politicians and rubbing shoulders with people like George Raft, Judy Garland and Frank Sinatra, who hired minders from one of their companies. Several films have been based on the Krays, including *Legend* (2015) in which Tom Hardy plays both Ronnie and Reggie.

Gangster Movies

The earliest surviving gangster film is believed to be *The Black Hand*, released in 1906. Subtitled 'True Story of a Recent Occurrence in the Italian Quarter of New York' it was directed by Wallace McCutcheon and had a running time of 11 minutes. Another early example is *Musketeers of Pig Alley* (1912) directed by D.W. Griffith and starring Lillian Gish, which ran for 17 minutes.

Underworld (1927) was a feature-length silent movie directed by Josef von Sternberg. The screenplay was based on a story by former Chicago crime reporter Ben Hecht, inspired by the Irish-American gangster 'Terrible' Tommy O'Connor who escaped from a Chicago courthouse in 1923, four days before he was due to be hanged for the murder of a policeman. Hecht received the first Academy Award for Best Story for *Underworld* and was also one of the screenwriters of *Scarface* (see below).

The Racket (1928) was a full-length silent movie directed by Lewis Milestone and based on a 1927 play by Bartlett Cormack, who co-wrote the screenplay. Edward G. Robinson played the racketeer in the original Broadway production. The story's portrayal of corrupt police officers and city officials led to the film and the play being banned in Chicago. It was remade in 1951 with Robert Mitchum playing the honest cop and Robert Ryan as the mobster.

The Warner Bros. Gangster Movies

Lights of New York (1928), a tale of New York bootleggers, was Warner Bros. first 'all-talking' picture. The film opens with a title card that reads: *This is a story of Main Street and Broadway – a story that might have been torn from last night's newspaper*. Critics labelled the film a melodrama and hokum, but it proved popular with audiences. Warner Bros. followed it with *The Doorway to Hell* (1930) directed by Archie Mayo and starring Lew Ayres as a Chicago gangster and James Cagney as his right-hand man. The screenplay was based on a story by Rowland Brown, who was nominated for 'Best Original Story' at the Academy Awards in 1931. The title card at the beginning of the film says 'based on the story 'A Handful of Clouds' by Rowland Brown' but George Peary, writing in the journal *The Velvet Light Trap* (Fall 1976) says that 'A Handful of Clouds' was a play. Screenplay and dialogue are credited to George Rosener.

The Doorway to Hell has been overshadowed by later Warner Bros. gangster films, and is a little slow and stagey in places, but it does contain some classic moments that became part of the genre's iconography. Dwight Frye – Renfield in 1931's *Dracula* – has a small role as a hoodlum. He exits a pool hall carrying a violin case and says, "I'm going out to teach a guy a lesson." This may be the first time that a violin case was used to carry a gun in a gangster movie. James Cagney as Mileaway, the hero's right-hand man, has some of the best scenes including those where he's having an affair with the boss's wife. There is also a great scene depicting the 'all-out war' between rival gangs featuring a lot of guys fighting and shooting machine guns and a car being set on fire and exploding.

But it was three later films that came to define the 'classic' gangster movie: *Little Caesar* (January 1931), *The Public Enemy* (April 1931), and *Scarface* (April 1932). 1931 also saw the release of *Smart Money*, a story about illegal gambling, in which James Cagney and Edward G. Robinson appear on screen together for the first and only time. The film was shot while Cagney was still working on *The Public Enemy*.

Little Caesar & W.R. Burnett

W.R. Burnett's novel *Little Caesar* published in 1929 more or less created the gangster genre in novels and the adaptation of it is one of three movies that defined the genre in cinema. William Riley Burnett was born in Springfield, Ohio and as a young man worked in Columbus as a statistician for the State of Ohio. He hated the office routine and decided to quit and move to Chicago. At that point, he had been writing in his spare time but in six years had sold nothing. In an introduction to a 1958 edition of *Little Caesar*, Burnett wrote about arriving in the city: "On me, an outsider, an alien from Ohio, the impact of Chicago was terrific. It seemed overwhelmingly big, teeming, dirty, brawling, frantically alive. The pace was so much faster than anything I'd been used to; rudeness was the rule; people seemed to have no time to be friendly, no time to desist for one moment from whatever it was they were pursuing. Broke, jobless, a nobody, I fought hard to keep my balance in one of the most blankly indifferent, one of the toughest cities in the world." And at that moment in Chicago's history, "Capone was King," and "Gangsters were shooting each other all over town..."

In a story embellished by the skills of a storyteller, Burnett recalls his 'first night' in the city where he was staying in a fleabag hotel on the North Side: "Just as I was falling asleep there was a terrific explosion directly across the street. Windows rattled; curtains blew wildly, and my bed gave a leap that nearly threw me to the floor. Almost at once there were two more explosions, blocks away this time, but close enough. I got up, dressed, and went down to the lobby, where a sleepy-eyed night clerk explained that there was a price war going on among garage owners, things had got rough, and apparently the 'boys' had decided to toss a few 'pineapples.' The clerk did not appear to be disturbed or even very interested. The whole thing seemed natural enough to him."

The people of Chicago took such things in their stride or pretended they weren't going on, but Burnett was fascinated by it all. He talked to a police reporter, began to make notes and gradually these developed into an idea for a novel about the darker side of the city. Unhappy with his early chapters, he threw them out. Burnett began reading books about crime and one of them was a 'coldly factual' text about gangsterism published by the Chicago University Press – this was probably *The Gang: A Study of 1,313 Gangs in Chicago* by Frederic M. Thrasher, published in 1927. In it was an account of the rise and fall of the Sam Cardinelli gang that Burnett used as the basis for the novel that was originally titled *The Furies* and was published as *Little Caesar*.

Burnett struggled to write the novel until he found the right angle from which to tackle it – he referred to this using the Hollywood terms 'wienie' or 'gimmick' – which was to tell the story entirely from the point of view of the gangster: "Further, the book should be written in a style that suited the subject matter — that is, in the illiterate jargon of the Chicago gangster. I threw overboard what had been known up to then as 'literature.' I declared war on adjectives. I jettisoned 'description.' I tried to tell the story entirely through narration and dialogue, letting the action speak for itself. I also jettisoned 'psychology' — and I tried hard to suppress myself and all of my opinions."

The gangster's point of view involved treating criminal activity in a business-like way. Burnett said he learned this from a young barbershop owner who worked for a North Side gang, referring to the man as 'John'. John explained to him how gangsters handled 'business' rivals: "You give him a chance, see? A good chance. You reason with him. You say, 'Look, fellow, there's room for all of us, so don't be so greedy.' If he won't listen, if he stays greedy, lousing you up – then – *pow!* He asked for it." Burnett also discovered that the gangsters didn't share his old-fashioned notions about murder. Did they not suffer pangs of conscience or remorse? "John stared at me in consternation, then almost choked laughing. Was I kidding? Do soldiers in a war suffer stuff like that? What was the difference if a guy rubbed out Germans or 'impractical' business rivals? I must be nuts."

In a foreword to the 1958 edition, writer and critic Gilbert Seldes said that we have all seen and read so many crime stories that it is difficult to read *Little Caesar* and see it as its first readers must have read it. "You read ... *Rico rushed him, pumping lead* — and you smile. You think not only of Mickey Spillane, but of S.J. Perelman's 'Somewhere a Roscoe...' [a *New Yorker* article celebrating the excesses of *Spicy Detective* magazine]. But this book was published in 1929! I don't know if anyone ever pumped lead before, but I do know that something authentic about Chicago and its gangsters was being said in this book."

It is often taken for granted that the central character of Rico Bandello (Edward G. Robinson in the movie) was *based* on Al Capone – perhaps because he became best-known of all the Chicago gangsters, but while Burnett was aware of the activities of Capone's Chicago Outfit, because they were going on around him, Capone's story didn't come to an end until after *Little Caesar* was published. The St. Valentine's Day Massacre occurred *after* the book was finished.

Rico isn't based on any specific gangster, rather he is an example of a 'type,' as Burnett told Ken Mate and Pat McGilligan in an interview published in 1983: "I was reaching for a gutter Macbeth – a composite figure that would indicate how men could rise to prominence or money under the most hazardous conditions, but not much more hazardous than the men of the Renaissance." Burnett explained the quotation from Machiavelli that is the novel's epigraph – *The first law of every being is to preserve itself and live. You sow hemlock and you expect corn to ripen.* – saying that it meant "...if you have this type of society, it will produce such men. That's what I was looking for, a type. Rico was doomed from the first. If he had a tragic flaw, it was over-impulsive action. But he is the picture of overriding ambition." Rico was an ambitious man with no legitimate outlet for his energy and so he turned to crime so that he could 'be somebody.'

W.R. Burnett didn't know at the time, but the style he adopted for *Little Caesar* – light on adjectives and heavy on dialogue and action – made his story ideal Hollywood movie material. It was also published at a time when

Warner Bros. producers had already recognised the filmic possibilities of gangster stories. Burnett would go on to write almost forty novels, a number of which were adapted into movies including *High Sierra* (1941) and *The Asphalt Jungle* (1949). Burnett moved to California where he also wrote screenplays, beginning with a co-writing credit on the Warner Bros. movie *The Finger Points* (1931) about a newspaper reporter who takes bribes from gangsters in exchange for not publishing details of their crimes. Other credits include *Scarface* (1932), *High Sierra* (1941), and *This Gun for Hire* (1942). W.R. Burnett created not only the 'ideal' gangster story plot, but also managed to have the ideal life of which many writers dream.

The 'Classic' Hollywood Gangster Movies

In his book *Hollywood Genres,* Thomas Schatz writes that the gangster movie "...enjoyed possibly the briefest classical period of any Hollywood genre." The first examples appeared in 1931 and the formula was effectively abandoned in the mid-1930s as a result of public and federal pressure. Despite the title card at the beginning of *The Public Enemy* stating *'The purpose of this film is to depict an environment, rather than glorify the criminal'* – these films, though popular, were regarded as dangerous because they both celebrated the life of the criminal *and* portrayed law enforcement officials and politicians who were corrupt.

The most successful gangster films of this 'classic' period were *Little Caesar* (1930) directed by Mervyn LeRoy, *The Public Enemy* (1931) directed by William A. Wellman in 1931), and *Scarface* (1932) directed by Howard Hawks. These three films established the 'formula' for this type of film – and we will look at their plot structure later in this chapter.

The Public Enemy (1931) was based on an unpublished story (some sources say novel) 'Beer and Blood' by John Bright and Kubec Glasmon. Bright had been a newspaper journalist in Chicago and had worked with Ben Hecht there and Glasmon had been a pharmacist. Both went on to be successful screenwriters. Harvey Thew, who had been writing for films since 1916, is credited as adapting the story.

Scarface (1932) was based on the novel by Armitage Trail (a pseudonym of Maurice R. Coons) which was inspired by the life of Al Capone. Four screenwriters are credited, including W.R. Burnett, author of *Little Caesar,* and Ben Hecht, who had co-written the silent gangster movie *Underworld.*

Based on a True Story?

Warner Bros. liked to proclaim that their stories were ripped from the newspaper headlines, but similarities between the onscreen characters and their real-life counterparts were minimal – though it has been suggested that some real-life hoodlums learned how to dress, talk and behave by watching the movies. Edward G. Robinson's portrayal of Rico Bandello in *Little Caesar* has been compared to Al Capone, but all that was really borrowed from him were his taste in clothes and cigars and the violent actions of his hoodlums; we know that W.R. Burnett broadly based the biographical structure of his novel on an account of the career of Sam Cardinelli. James Cagney's character, Tom Powers, is said to have been inspired by Hymie Weiss – largely because the character's demise occurs on the steps of a cathedral and Weiss was killed opposite one. Paul Muni's character of Tony 'Scarface' Camonte is said to have been modelled directly on Al Capone.

Sudden Demise of the Gangster Movie

In his survey of the genre, Thomas Schatz writes that the 'classic' gangster movie went into decline after 1933 and was replaced by two 'watered-down' versions, the 'gangster-as-cop' movie such as *G Men* (1935) in which James Cagney's character joins the FBI and helps track down a violent gang of criminals. And the 'Cain-and-Abel' variation, which featured both criminal characters and law enforcement or other pro-social characters in equal opposition – *Angels with Dirty Faces* (1938) has James Cagney's gangster facing off against Pat O'Brien's Catholic priest. Deliberately lacking the moral ambiguity of the classic gangster story, these films aren't nearly as interesting.

A third variation identified by Schatz is what he calls the 'middle-man' story, featuring a character who is not aligned with the gangsters or the law enforcers. This story effectively takes the Ally character from the classic gangster movie (see *Characters* below) and makes him the hero. He is usually a man with some criminal connections or perhaps someone about to join a criminal gang, who is motivated to turn his life around when he falls in love with a good woman and sees the error of his ways. Perhaps the best-known example of this type is *The Roaring Twenties* (1939) in which gangster Eddie Bartlett, played by James Cagney, tries to redeem himself and win the love of the good woman, played by Priscilla Lane. This variation is more interesting in the fact that the central character is faced with a dilemma – a life of crime versus redemption and pro-social values that may reward him with a relationship he desires. These stories tend to be stronger as they centre on a strong central character in which the character can be both good guy and bag guy – Cain *and* Abel – and so tend to be more focused.

By the late 1930s and into the early 1940s, the gangster film was pretty much gone, replaced by what Schatz describes as 'rural gangster' or 'bandit' films, taking the criminal character out of the city and placing him into a rural setting. Examples include *The Petrified Forest* (1936) based on Robert E. Sherwood's play which was inspired by the crimes of John Dillinger; *You Only Live Once* (1937); *High Sierra* (1941) starring Humphrey Bogart, based on a novel by W.R. Burnett, and directed by John Huston; and *They Drive By Night* (1940) based on the novel *Long Haul* by A.I. Bezzerides.

Later examples include *Bonnie and Clyde* (1967) starring Warren Beatty and Faye Dunaway; Robert Altman's 1974 film *Thieves Like Us,* based on the novel by Edward Anderson which was also the basis of the 1948 film *They Live By Night,* and the Quentin Tarantino-scripted movie *True Romance* (1993). These stories are sometimes referred to as belonging to the 'couple on the run' sub-genre, an early example of which was the film *Persons in Hiding* (1939) based in part on one of the accounts in J. Edgar Hoover's book *Persons in Hiding* (1938). There is also some crossover here with the noir romance and neo-noir sub-genres.

Two films from the post-war period of the late 1940s marked the end of the original gangster movie era – *Key Largo* (1948) and *White Heat* (1949). *Key Largo,* based on the 1939 play by Maxwell Anderson, stars Edward G. Robinson as ageing gangster Johnny Rocco hiding out in a Florida hotel out of season. Rocco used to be a big-time criminal but is now almost forgotten – he is hoping to pull off a major crime that will re-establish his reputation. Second World War veteran Frank McCloud (Humphrey Bogart) is initially reluctant to take action when the gangster and his men take over the hotel and bully the owner and the gangster's moll, but as the situation escalates he is forced to take a stand. The film is the last of four in which Bogart and Lauren Bacall play onscreen lovers. The ending of *Key Largo* marks the death of Edward G. Robinson's on-screen gangster persona.

The demise of James Cagney's gangster in *White Heat* is even more dramatic. Cody Jarrett is a ruthless gangster of the old school who will kill members of his own gang as easily as he will kill the cops who oppose him. He is emotionally unstable and has a relationship with his mother that Freud would have described as Oedipal. Jarrett's father, we learn, was a mentally unstable outlaw and his mother trained him to be a criminal and gang leader, making him a product of genetic inheritance and off-kilter nurturing – meaning this time that society isn't to blame. Edmund O'Brien plays an undercover detective who infiltrates Jarrett's gang – he is intended to portray the pro-social viewpoint to balance the narrative, but Cagney's gets the most screen time and the best lines. Rather than being an example of the cops versus gangsters story, O'Brien's character serves more in the role of the ally who betrays the hero and brings about his tragic downfall. The final scene – 'Made it, Ma! Top of the world!' – is a Hollywood classic.

The 'classic' Hollywood gangster movie appeared during a specific moment in cinema history. *The Jazz Singer,* which effectively marked the end of the silent movie era, appeared in 1927 and *Lights of New York,* the 'first all talking' gangster film was released in 1928. The limitations of the technology meant that films were restricted to studio sets and the streets in the backlot, making gangster stories ideal material. But by the end of the 1940s, filming and sound recording had advanced to a point where films could be made on location again and the claustrophobic crime movie was no longer necessary.

The other reason for the swift demise of the gangster movie was the introduction of the Production Code.

Censorship & The Motion Picture Production Code

The Motion Picture Production Code was a set of moral guidelines established by the Motion Picture Producers and Distributors of America (which became the Motion Picture Association of America in 1945) in 1930 and which remained in force until 1968. The code replaced a list known as 'Don'ts and Be-Carefuls' drafted in 1927. The code is also sometimes referred to as the 'Hays Code' after Will H. Hays who was president of the organisation from 1922 to 1945. Until 1934, the code was largely ineffectual, but in 1934 Hays appointed Joseph Breen to oversee its enforcement. The Code was replaced by the MPAA rating system in 1968.

In the 1920s, Hollywood produced a number of risqué films and there were off-screen scandals such as the murder of William Desmond Taylor and the alleged rape of Virginia Rappe by Roscoe 'Fatty' Arbuckle. Religious, civic, and political groups questioned the morality of the industry and individual states were adopting censorship bills. The Code was developed as a form of self-regulation.

In 1933 the Legion of Decency was founded by the American Catholic Church. Catholics were told that viewing any film that had been condemned by the Legion was a mortal sin, though it has been suggested that any film condemned came to be regarded as a 'must see' in some Catholic neighbourhoods. Nevertheless, it increased pressure on the industry to enforce its Code.

The 'classic' gangster movies were produced before the Code was properly enforced. And they were one of the reasons it was decided that enforcement was necessary. Enforcement of the voluntary code within the industry was seen as preferable to large-scale public boycotting of cinemas or federal intervention and censorship.

Of particular impact on the gangster movies was the section on the depiction of crime which stipulated that films must not show crimes in such a way as to teach people how to commit them; inspire potential criminals to imitate what was shown on screen, or make criminals seem heroic or justified in their actions.

The *Wikipedia* entry for *Scarface* shows the sort of issues that makers of gangster films faced and there is little wonder that film studios sought to change the moral tone of their films – if not the action actually portrayed on screen – effectively replacing the violent gangster with the violent law enforcer.

The *General Principles* state that:

- No picture shall be produced that will lower the moral standards of those who see it. Hence the sympathy of the audience should never be thrown to the side of crime, wrongdoing, evil or sin.
- Correct standards of life, subject only to the requirements of drama and entertainment, shall be presented.
- Law, natural or human, shall not be ridiculed, nor shall sympathy be created for its violation.

The text of the Code can be found online in several places and makes interesting reading as a social document reflecting the values of the time in which it was written.

Characters in the Classic Gangster Story

Hero

The classic gangster film is essentially biographical, showing the rise and eventual fall of the main character. This character's goal is to rise from poverty and achieve success – to 'be somebody.' Success is usually seen in terms of material wealth and power in the form of being a leader in the criminal community.

The protagonist of the gangster movie is an *anti-hero* rather than a hero in the traditional sense. He is motivated by personal greed and desire and uses violence to get what he wants. How do you make a protagonist – a 'hero' – out of such a character? I wrote a chapter on creating 'Tricksters, Rebels & Anti-Heroes' in *Character Creation* which explored why readers find them engaging story people. With the gangster, the qualities that most attract us are probably his self-reliance, ambition and determination, and the fact that he is a rebel who flaunts social convention. He knows who he is, he knows what he wants, and he takes action to get it – these are qualities, at least in the abstract, that we can all aspire to. Horsley describes the gangster hero as "...strutting, snarling, and posturing, possessing a blatant, anarchic appeal." In terms of a character archetype, he is the Warrior-Businessman – ambitious and ruthless.

The hero's individuality and rebelliousness are what ultimately dooms him. He refuses to conform to standards of acceptable behaviour approved by society *and* he refuses to abide by the 'rules' which govern behaviour within and between criminal organisations. The gangster-hero's tragic flaw, according to Schatz, is the fact that his overwhelming need to express his individuality and his inability to channel his energies into lawful activities mean that he is at odds with society, its legal system, and also the other criminal leaders who regard him as a threat. With all of these forces ranged against him, it is inevitable that he can remain on top of the world for only a brief period.

The prototype for this character was Rico Bandello, played by Edward G. Robinson, in *Little Caesar*. Thomas Schatz refers to Rico's irrational brutality, disdain for law and order, and enterprising business mentality as being inherent elements of his character. He stands out from the dull-witted hoodlums around him and the inept, and possibly corrupt, policemen who represent law and order. Rico's character appears on screen fully-formed and we never really find out where he came from and how he became the man he is – the story concentrates on his rapid rise to power.

Rico expresses his beliefs in a few memorable lines. "Money's all right, but it ain't everything," he tells his ally, Joe Massaro. "Be somebody, have a bunch of guys who will do anything you tell 'em, have your own way, or nothin'!" And the way to achieve this ambition is to be ruthless. "Shoot first, argue afterwards – if you don't, the other fellow gets you," he says. "This game ain't for guys that's soft!"

The Public Enemy, starring James Cagney as Tom Powers, made some attempt to show how someone might become such a gangster. The film opens with images of the inner-city tenements that house those who have been most severely affected by the Great Depression. We see Tom as a boy receiving a severe beating with a strap by his father – a scene that generates sympathy for the character and also shows how power through violence was a part of his upbringing. We see a similar thing in *GoodFellas*. Tom's older brother is a war hero who gets a job as a streetcar conductor leaving Tom as the archetypal over-shadowed second son who can never quite be as successful in his family's eyes – and his own – as his older brother. That Tom drifts into petty crime doesn't come as a surprise to us – nor does the fact that he wants to be the one handing out violence rather than being the victim of it.

Tony 'Scarface' Camonte, played by Paul Muni in *Scarface,* achieves power in the criminal world less as a result of his dominant personality and more because he is one of the first gangsters to get hold of a machine gun. In this story, the technology that had proved so devastating during the First World War is brought to the city streets. Schatz writes that the character of Camonte is not the self-made man we see in Rico Bandello or Tom Powers and that his "...primitive brutality, simple-minded naïveté, and sexual confusion made him a figure with little charisma and with virtually no redeeming qualities."

The 1920s American gangster was usually from an immigrant community – and in the movies that usually meant Italian or Irish. In different decades and different geographical locations, other national or ethnic groups live in poverty and turn to organised crime as a way to escape. In most cases, there is a strong sense of *belonging* to a community and the criminal gang, while strictly hierarchical, is more like a family business than a faceless corporation. It is debatable how much honour there really is among thieves – the ruthless gangster often sacrifices his own soldiers – but loyalty is expected and betrayal is punished harshly.

John G. Cawelti (1976) in *Adventure, Mystery, and Romance* writes that an important aspect of the gangster protagonist was his lower-class social origin. "Surely one of his most endearing traits was that he never became assimilated into an upper-class lifestyle but remained an unregenerate barbarian. Suspicious of culture, art, and manners, he was always ready for a fight, and tough on women..."

Cawelti also writes about the difference between the gangster and the hardboiled detective, saying the gangster was "...supremely egotistical. His actions were solely motivated by the desire to achieve enough wealth and power to impose his own will on the world; because his ambitions were limitless and boundless they could lead only to destruction. He resembled in this way the figure of the overreaching tycoon." Cawelti also notes that the similarity between the gangster and the tycoon was one of the themes explored in F. Scott Fitzgerald's *The Great Gatsby*. Lee Horsley also compared the gangster to the hardboiled detective, saying that "...unlike the private eye, he is awed by those who are socially above him, and motivated not by the urge to set things right but by the spirit of emulation." And, in contrast to the private eye, the gangster's "...dissociation from the past leads not to the condition of living in the present but to an obsessive preoccupation with future goals."

Tragic Flaw
The gangster is a tragic figure and he has to die because the conventions of social order and morality require it – but at the same time, the audience regrets the demise of this self-reliant rebel who refused to give up who he was even in the face of death. The gangster protagonist may be given an opportunity to reform and seek redemption – and is often encouraged to do so by a mentor-like investigator or priest – but his need to rebel and express his individuality, to prove himself, is overwhelming.

Although the gangster seems supremely self-confident, under his bravado and his determination to 'be somebody' lies a sense of isolation and despair – a fear that he is, in fact, nobody and that no matter what actions he takes, he will never be able to fill the void, the lack he feels inside himself. At the end of the story, his fears are fulfilled – he lies dead in the gutter back where he began, a nobody.

Ally
The hero's ally is a significant character in gangster stories. He is typically a lifelong childhood friend and functions as a 'reflection' of the hero – they are two men from the same background but with different personalities, whose lives eventually diverge and take different paths. The ally is usually less Warrior-like and more introspective and caring – and as a result, suffers pangs of conscience of a type that never trouble the hero. In the early parts of the story, the ally is swept along by circumstances and the hero's dominant personality. But as the hero's ambitions and use of violence grow, the ally becomes increasingly uncomfortable and distances himself from his old friend.

In *Little Caesar,* the ally character is Joe Massara, played by Douglas Fairbanks Jr. When he meets a nice girl and falls in love, his own personal ambitions are rekindled – he wants to sing and dance professionally – and the only way he can ever have the life he wants is to betray his friend Rico and turn state's evidence. Rico's discovery of this betrayal and his attempt to seek vengeance lead to the ultimately tragic ending of the story.

In *The Public Enemy,* the ally is Matt Doyle, played by Edward Woods. He too falls for the love of a good woman but is killed in an ambush intended for Tom. Tom vows to avenge his friend's death and by attacking the gang responsible effectively seals his own fate.

George Raft played the ally character in *Scarface*. Guino 'Little Boy' Rinaldo established him in his trademark role of a coin-flipping hoodlum. He makes the mistake of falling in love with his best friend's sister, ultimately resulting in a tragic ending for himself, the sister, and 'Scarface' Camonte.

Villain

If the hero of a story is a 'bad guy', who is the villain? The main character in a gangster story faces opposition in two forms – from the law enforcers who want to put an end to his criminal activities and from other gangsters who regard the main character as a threat. Both sides are more or less content to let the hero go about his (criminal) business until the hero's ambitions draw their attention because they represent a threat – and there comes a point when they can no longer turn a blind eye. Often this occurs when the hero kills a rival gang leader in order to take over their territory. Other gang leaders may band together against the protagonist, afraid he'll come after their territory next, and the police will feel the need to take action because they fear that the gangs will start a war that will harm the city and its people.

Occasionally, opposition will come from the protagonist's ally who feels he must betray the protagonist, his friend and boss, either to protect his own interests – he usually wants to escape gangsterism and settle down and marry a nice girl – or because the protagonist's actions have become so outrageous that they are a threat to everyone.

Robert Schatz has suggested that what ultimately opposes the gangster protagonist is American society as represented by the city: "His urban environment, with its institutionalized alienation and class distinction, has denied him a legitimate route to power and success, so he uses the depersonalizing milieu and its technology — guns, cars, phones, etc. — to plunder its wealth. But somehow the massive, unthinking city, that concrete embodiment of civilization and urban order, is more powerful than either the self-reliant criminal or the generally inept police who pursue him."

Romantic Co-Protagonist

Women are typically used as objects to indicate social status in the gangster movie and they are often treated badly. The only 'nice girl' is usually the ally's girlfriend and the closest we come to a strong female character is the gangster's mother – there is no *femme fatale* in the classic gangster movie.

There has been some speculation in academic literature about the fact that the gangster protagonist may not like girls and that there is a homoerotic subtext to his story. While there have been gay and bisexual gangsters – Ronnie Kray being a notable example – I think it is a misreading of the classic gangster story to suggest there is a homoerotic subtext. The misreading, I think, arises as a result of three things. Firstly, gangsters are vain and take an interest in the way their hair and clothes look. This is a demonstration of their self-centeredness and desire to *appear* successful rather than a suggestion of effeminacy.

Secondly, the stories place a great deal of emphasis on male friendship and loyalty to one's friends. This was found in many immigrant communities where single young men arrived in the USA in the hope of making money to send back home to their families – having no family in America led them to value friendships with men from their home countries. There is also the fact that ordinary expressions of friendship in Italian culture –

including hugging and kissing on the cheek – seemed alien to many Americans who had never been exposed to such behaviour. In the movies, the friendship between the protagonist and ally reflects this kind of Italian immigrant experience – and Rico sacrificing himself for his friend at the end of *Little Caesar* is only an extension of this.

And thirdly, there is the way that gangsters treat their women in these stories. In *Little Caesar*, Rico seems to have no interest in women and is contemptuous of the ally's relationship with a nice girl. But this is probably more of an indication of Rico's dedication to achieving his own ambitions than of the fact that he wants the ally for himself. Rico sees romance as a distraction and possibly a weakness – he's a classic Warrior-Businessman. Also, when you love yourself as much as Rico does, you don't need anyone else to love you and you don't need anyone else to love.

James Cagney's character Tom in *The Public Enemy* demonstrates the sort of relationship a gangster might have if he *does* have a relationship. During the movie he has two girlfriends, the first being Kitty, played by Mae Clarke, who gets a grapefruit in the face in the famous breakfast scene. She represents the nice girl, the sort of woman you could settle down with and marry – but Tom doesn't want to settle down. His need to express his own individuality means that he has to rebel against any attempt to 'domesticate' him or to get him to obey the 'rules' of a marital relationship. He wants a girlfriend, but he wants one on his terms. Tom leaves Kitty and takes up with Gwen Allen, played by Jean Harlow, a blonde who confesses she loves bad boys – this means she accepts Tom as he is, not wanting to change him, and she allows him to treat her badly without complaining. Her overt physical attractiveness also allows Tom to show her off like a possession – she is another demonstration of his success – and he has 'traded up' from Kitty to Gwen.

The so-called 'gangster's moll' as we traditionally think of her – cigarette in one hand and a gun in the other – doesn't belong in the classic gangster story – we'll meet her in the next chapter.

The Gangster's Mother

The mother in a gangster movie tends to represent traditional Catholic values and also the idea that a mother will love her son no matter what he does. She is also a working-class mother who has struggled to provide for her children during the difficulties of the Depression – often having to survive without the support of a husband due to the fact that he was killed in the war or is travelling the country in search of paid work. James Cagney's Tom in *The Public Enemy* is devoted to his mother and the actor's character Cody Jarrett in *White Heat* (1949) is even more attached to his mother. Tony 'Scarface' Camonte is also very close to his mother and, as originally scripted, she loved him unconditionally, having no issues with his lifestyle and accepting the money he gave her.

Settings

Originally, the setting of the story was 1920s Chicago during the time of the Depression and Prohibition. Other locations have been used since, but there is usually a similarity between them in that there is a dual aspect to the place, with parts of the city featuring bright lights, wealth, and gaiety and other areas in the gloom and dirt of grinding poverty. The hero's aim is to drag himself out of the gutter and into the bright lights.

Buildings we see in gangster films include casinos and speakeasies, pool halls, and bars. We often see a home in a tenement – usually belonging to the hero's hardworking mother. This is often seen in contrast to the hero's glamorous 'nouveau riche' apartment. And somewhere in between the parties and the poverty sits the gangster's hideout, often somewhere in a warehouse district or close to the docks, convenient for shady business activity.

Locations are often claustrophobic and dimly lit – and even when they are filmed in colour, gangster movies often have extended sequences that are almost monochrome with blues dominating to give an impression of night time. Colour is saved to give emphasis to the brightly lit world of the wealthy and powerful. You can also reflect this sort of contrast in the descriptions you create in a novel.

In his essay 'The Gangster as Tragic Hero,' Robert Warshow writes that the gangster is "...the man of the city, with the city's language and knowledge, with its queer and dishonest skills and its terrible daring ... For everyone else, there is at least the theoretical possibility of another world – ... [the] brightly lit country – but for the gangster there is only the city; he must inhabit it in order to personify it..."

Thomas Schatz writes that the dark, rain-soaked streets of the city represent "...a complex, alienating, and overwhelming community that initially creates the gangster and eventually destroys him." The city is the arena in which the violent action takes place, but also "...represents the forces of progress and social destiny which the gangster cannot hope to conquer. The intangible forces of social order and civilization which have created the modern city certainly will crush a single anarchic malcontent."

Iconography

The iconography of the gangster film can be divided into two: that relating to *materialism* and that relating to *violent crime*. Relating to the theme of the 'American dream' and a desire to live the high life, gangster movies contain images of expensive suits, gleaming black shoes, fedoras, big cigars, jewellery, cars, alcohol, bundles or roles of cash, big shiny cars with running boards, good food and alcohol. Cost is typically more important than taste and we will often see the gangster demonstrate this with a garishly decorated apartment, or a hideous pin-striped suit, two-tone shoes, and a huge patterned tie. The dark shirt and white tie is a combination that came out of the gangster movies. Set against this are images of knives, handguns, Tommy guns, 'pineapples' (hand grenades), and dead bodies. Depending on the era in which the story is set, criminality will be represented by illegal alcohol or illegal drugs or whatever illegal commodity criminals are currently making large profits from.

Typically, the victims of this crime and its consequences are *not* shown – you rarely see images of drug addicts, but if you do they're presented as 'losers' or in some way 'un-American.' And prostitutes tend to be the classy 'hooker with a heart of gold' rather than exploited sex slaves. The worst you tend to see is some unfortunate shop owner given a beating for not paying protection money to the right people or for buying his black-market goods from the wrong gang – and he quickly learns his lesson. The crime most often seen in the classic gangster movie is bootlegging, which was regarded as a lesser crime because many ordinary people were opposed to Prohibition. Interestingly, the wealthy upper-class, politicians and law enforcement officials were often seen to enjoy a drink of illegal whiskey – it was a crime that united all classes. The films often featured images of the police smashing open barrels of illicit whiskey and letting it drain away or of gangsters smashing up bottles of booze that came from a rival gang – if you were a drinker in the Prohibition era, this in itself might have looked like a crime.

Themes

There are two main themes that appear in the classic gangster story. First, it is a morality play warning of the dangers of selfish ambition – W.R. Burnett refers to *Little Caesar*'s Rico Bandello as a 'gutter Macbeth.' Julius Caesar too was betrayed by Brutus who was concerned by Caesar's ambition. The theme is not so much that good conquers evil, but that evil destroys itself. The second theme in the gangster story is a criticism of the 'American Dream' – or rather, of the fact that some people have more opportunity to achieve this dream than others. These two themes are connected by the main character's desire to achieve success – to 'be somebody.'

John G. Cawelti in *Mystery, Violence and Popular Culture,* writes that "...'Crime does not pay' was an official motto, a bit of publicly acceptable moralism. The actual sympathies of the audience were probably as much with the gangster who initiated the violence as with the lawman who retaliated against it." Cawelti also writes that the gangster story has something in common with the monster movies that were also successful in the 1930s. Both are about "...social outsiders whose monstrosity seems as much a result of accident and circumstances as of evil intentions. One can even sympathise with their attempts to gain acceptance or success in respectable society. But the desire to move from the margins to the centre of society leads them to overreach themselves and to threaten society itself, thus necessitating their destruction."

Ambition

A central theme of the gangster movie is the conflict between individuality and the need for social order. Society approves of men who work hard and try to improve their situation but can quickly turn on anyone who achieves success – out of a combination of jealousy and fear. Robert Warshow wrote that "...the gangster is doomed because he is under the obligation to succeed, not because the means he employs are unlawful. In the deeper layers of the modern consciousness ... every attempt to succeed is an act of aggression, leaving one alone and guilty and defenceless among enemies: one is *punished* for success. This is our intolerable dilemma: that failure is a kind of death and success is evil and dangerous, is – ultimately – impossible. The effect of the gangster film is to embody this dilemma in the person of the gangster and resolve it by his death."

The gangster protagonist *does* achieve success, but it is short-lived and things begin to fall apart before he's really had an opportunity to enjoy his new status.

The gangster's ambition means that he is trying to stand out from the crowd, to be a leader – a 'Little Caesar' – and anyone who seeks to set himself above others is ultimately a lonely figure. But as Warshow writes, "No convention of the gangster film is more strongly established than this: it is dangerous to be alone. And yet the very conditions of success make it impossible not to be alone, for success is always the establishment of an *individual* pre-eminence that must be imposed on others, in whom it automatically arouses hatred ... The gangster's whole life is an effort to assert himself as an individual, to draw himself out of the crowd, and he always dies *because* he is an individual; the final bullet thrusts him back, makes him, after all, a failure."

The danger of being alone, of being unable to trust even those closest to him, can result in the gangster becoming paranoid to the point of being afraid to go out in public for fear of assassination. But even when he reaches this point, he is unable to give up his ambitions.

Rags-to-Riches & The American Dream

John G. Cawelti (2004) writes about the 'myth of equality through violence' in "...stories of how lower- or middle-class individuals use their skills in violence to achieve a level of equality with persons of established wealth and power." This myth arises from the idea of "...America as a frontier society in which violent confrontations are part of the ordinary course of life. This is a pervasive vision in our popular literature and films, whether set in the Wild West or the jungle of the modern city." But where the use of violence is an acceptable part of life to defend against attacks by Indians or outlaws, its use for "...the mere achieving of equality or status is rarely treated as sufficient justification for the hero's violence."

Cawelti refers to the genre's portrayal of "...the gangster's rapid rise from obscure poverty to power and affluence as a variation on the Alger story, the protagonist's technique of success being not pluck and luck but his free and easy way with a .45 or submachine gun." Other writers have also noted the way in which gangster stories are almost a dark parody of a Horatio Alger story.

Horatio Alger Jr. wrote *Ragged Dick, or Street Life in New York with the Boot Blacks* in 1867. Aimed at boys, it is the story of a poor bootblack who rises to middle-class respectability. Ragged Dick is a young teenager with a determination to succeed and a strong moral conscience. His good deeds draw the attention of wealthy benefactors and mentors and after rescuing a drowning child he is rewarded with a new suit and good job and leaves his vagabond life forever. Alger wrote dozens of such stories and his name became synonymous with the rags-to-riches story.

Manuel Peña has said that "Tenacity ... along with faith in God, industry, sobriety, honesty and the notion of limitless individual power over one's destiny form the basic rags-to-riches narrative..." and it has been argued that anyone in America can succeed on these terms: Benjamin Franklin's 'The Way to Wealth' said it in 1758 and Andrew Carnegie said it in his 1885 'The Road to Business Success: An Address to Young Men,' and many still believe it today. Built into this argument is the implication that if you fail to achieve success then you must look to your own failings. And it also comforted those that *did* achieve success, or have it thrust upon them, by allowing them to think that they *must* have deserved it.

The fact that some of those who prosper in business are clearly *not* good men might lead you to suspect that faith in God, sobriety, and honesty might not actually be *necessary* for success and that perhaps tenacity, industry, and belief in your own power to shape your destiny are all that is required. That certainly seems to be what Rico Bandello believes and he proceeds on that basis and the story shows his rise to power.

Al Capone regarded himself as a businessman and at the height of his power in 1929 managed an empire of hundreds of brothels, speakeasies and roadhouses and his annual revenue from gambling, prostitution and illegal alcohol was estimated to be almost $100 million. In abstract terms, he appears to prove that you can live the American Dream and Tom Nicholas and David Chen even wrote a case study of Capone as entrepreneur published by Harvard Business School in 2009. David Bell (1953) in his essay 'Crime as an American Way of Life,' wrote that crime "...has a 'functional' role in the society, and the urban rackets — the illicit activity organized for continuing profit rather than individual illegal acts — is one of the queer ladders of social mobility in American life."

Tone
As we have already seen, the tone of the gangster story is tragic. The protagonist is doomed and it is his own ambitions which ultimately and inevitably lead to his downfall. But within the tragic structure, there is often ironic or gallows humour and the gangster protagonist himself – especially if he is played by James Cagney – is often a boyish, optimistic and joyful figure, at least during the first half of the story.

Gangster Thriller Plot
The gangster story offers plenty of scope for conflict. The gangsters are opposed by the forces of law and order *and* by rival gangs who want to take over new territory or defend their own. Within the protagonist's gang, there are power struggles – the hero comes to power by staging some sort of coup and later finds himself opposed by people in his own gang – and often by the ally who think the protagonist is going 'too far' in order to achieve his ambitions. And there may also be a conflict within the hero himself – his desire to be a success vying with his fear that he is a nobody.

The plot template below is drawn from the structure of a number of the classic gangster movies including *Little Caesar* (1931), *The Public Enemy* (1931) and *Scarface* (1932). More contemporary gangster movies such as *GoodFellas* (1990) often consciously reflect this same structure.

The gangster genre came back into vogue following the release of the 1972 movie *The Godfather,* and we'll look at the plot of that film later.

Sequence 1
The hero and his childhood friend, the ally, involved in some small-scale criminal activity. They're poor and they come from a working-class immigrant neighbourhood. They complain that they are nobodies. They both have ambitions – the hero wants to 'be somebody,' a big shot in the big city; the ally usually has more modest ambitions. They head for the city, usually Chicago, or if they're already in the city, they seek to become associated with one of the criminal gangs.

Introduction to the gang. The boss tells them that he's in charge and that things are done the way he says they're to be done. As they enter the gang, there's usually some hint that this is a one-way journey: once you're in the gang, you don't get to leave it and go back to a normal life. Often it's the ally's more mundane ambition that highlights this point – he gives up his own dream when he goes with the hero and pledges his allegiance to the gang. Sometimes there is a warning, perhaps from a girl the ally has met, that they shouldn't take up this way of life, but the warning is ignored.

Sequence 2
The hero, still a novice, accompanies the gang boss and learns from him. Often the hero is chastised for being too quick to reach for his gun: being trigger-happy is unwise, you have to know when the use of violence is appropriate. Killing people attracts attention and that can cause problems. The corrupt police and politicians can be bribed to look the other way most of the time, but too many murders may bring a crackdown on the gangs. In

this sequence, the hero and the ally may be given guns for the first time, as a sort of 'graduation to the big time' present.

The hero and the ally now become involved in planning a crime with the gang. This their first chance to prove themselves as true gang members rather than gophers. The hero may try to show his leadership skills, but he's put in his place by the boss: 'I'm in charge.'

There may be a scene with the hero and his mother – she may not want his 'tainted' money and threatens to disown him because of his criminal lifestyle. Or she may take the opposite view, proud of the fact that her son is living the American Dream that she came to America in search of.

Sequence 3

The crime is carried out. Typically it is a raid on a nightclub owned by the boss of another gang. They may have been ordered not to use their guns unless they have to, but the hero shoots someone anyway. Back at their hideout, the leader is angry and nervous about the hero's actions. Seeing this as a weakness, the hero challenges the boss for dominance, telling him he's getting old and weak, too comfortable and too complacent. The hero is tired of taking orders from him – and he's not happy about taking a lower cut of the money. The hero's appearance often changes at this point, his clothing and lifestyle reflecting the success he has achieved. The hero has become popular with the other gang members and has their backing, and so is able to depose the old boss and take his place. This may be a bloodless coup, with the old man retiring quietly, or there may be a fistfight or a shootout between rival factions within the gang.

Sequence 4

One of the weaker gang members may be troubled by the killing that has occurred. His mother may remind him of the values of his Catholic upbringing. Fearing that he is going to betray the gang, the hero may end up killing this person. Or this mother-figure may be the hero's mother or the ally's. Meanwhile, the ally is also having second thoughts – and he would leave the gang if he thought it was possible.

Midpoint: The hero is referred to as the 'Boss' for the first time. He begins dressing and acting like a boss and also enjoys the publicity he's achieving as a successful 'businessman' and supporter of the poor and local charities, etc. He feels that he has earned the success that he set out to achieve.

Sequence 5

A rival gang boss says that the hero has gone too far and needs to be stopped. He's nervous because the hero has begun encroaching on his gang's territory and also because his violent methods risk bringing the authorities down on all the gangs. A plot is hatched to assassinate the hero.

An attempt is made on the hero's life – he is injured, but he survives. The hero is shaken by this experience, having felt that he was invulnerable. And this makes him angry. He confronts the rival gang boss and says he's taking over the rival's territory. The rival is killed or steps away quietly and the hero's empire has expanded again. This draws more attention to him – from the authorities and the other big bosses, who must now take him seriously as one of their number.

Rising tensions in the gang world threaten all-out war and this prompts the authorities to begin making plans to crack down on the gangs. At the same time, politicians and law enforcers become annoyed because the gangsters are being romanticised by the media – and the gangsters may capitalise on this by charitable work among the poor.

Sequence 6
The hero moves among the wealthy and successful, but he is not accepted by them and doesn't fit in. He feels uncomfortable and embarrassed when he reveals his ignorance. There are visible material signs of the hero's success – he now dresses like a boss and has an expensively decorated apartment, showy rather than tasteful. But he's still a working-class guy with no idea about the finer things in life. He is offered more territory and takes it. But his ambitions continue to grow – he wants to take over the territory of one of the big bosses.

Needing to protect his own territory – and his own neck – means the hero has become increasingly paranoid. He may come to suspect that his ally is about to betray him – especially if the ally has tried to persuade him to tone down his excessive behaviours. The hero can't understand why he and the ally don't hang around together like they used to in the old days, but at the same time, he expects to be able to give the orders and have the ally jump to obey them. And the hero may become jealous of a romance that has developed between the ally and his girlfriend – he blames the girl for having changed the ally and for taking the ally away from his childhood friend.

Another attempt may be made on the ally's life by a rival gang – he survives but is injured or badly shaken. This makes him more angry and determined to get his revenge for the attack.

Sequence 7
The ally wants to leave with his girlfriend but can't see how they will manage to escape and live somewhere that they can't be tracked down. They know they will never be able to live in peace until the hero's rule as boss is ended. Will the ally betray his friend to the authorities or to one of the other bosses?

Things rapidly unravel for the hero. The ally may betray him – or the ally's girlfriend might. The ally may then be killed. The hero's gang is raided by the authorities and most of his men are arrested. The hero escapes and goes on the run from the police. He is alone again and has no money and nobody to help him.

Or the hero may kill the boss of the rival gang that tried to assassinate him – this risks starting a gang war and means that both the rival gang and the police are intent on bringing down the hero. He may even be opposed by facts in his own gang or by the ally.

Sequence 8
The final showdown. Often the hero's ego forces him out of hiding to face the police or rival gang who are hunting him. He is shot down and dies in the gutter.

In the gangster movies of the 1930s, the gangster-hero had to come to a sticky end as proof that crime doesn't pay. Since the end of the Production Code, that limitation is no longer placed on gangster stories.

The Godfather
Mario Puzo's novel *The Godfather* (1969), adapted into a movie directed by Francis Ford Coppola in 1972, took the traditional gangster story and reshaped it. *The Godfather* also depicted the workings of the Mafia within

the format of a historical family saga, exploring the Sicilian heritage of the Italian immigrants who became America's gangsters.

John G. Cawelti, in *Adventure, Mystery, and Romance* has said that the single most significant impact of *The Godfather* was in the "use of the central symbol of 'the family' ... Puzo extends the symbolism of the family beyond the actual progeny of Don Vito Corleone to the criminal organisation of which he is the leader."

Marlon Brando's performance of Vito Corleone in the movie version of *The Godfather* was deemed worthy of a Best Actor Oscar, though he turned down the award. But while his performance dominated the movie, the lead character – in both book and film – is actually his son Michael (played by Al Pacino). In telling Michael Corleone's story, Mario Puzo spun the gangster story in a new direction. Instead of having a character who was seduced by the gangster lifestyle and who is ultimately destroyed by it, Puzo made Michael a *reluctant* gangster. Both father and son wanted Michael to stay *out* of the family business. Vito wanted his son – and ultimately his whole family business – to be legitimate. It is the circumstances of the story that draw Michael into becoming a 'gangster.' As Cawelti writes: "The novel is a tale of family succession, showing the rise of the true son and heir and reaching a climax with his acceptance of the power and responsibilities of Godfather." But at the same time, *The Godfather* is also a tragedy – or is at the very least deeply ironic – in that Michael's 'success' in becoming the head of the family, is also a failure: he didn't escape to the legitimate life his father dreamed of him having.

While *The Godfather* does show some of the violence of the world of the gangster – images in the movie come close to the crime scene pictures of the murders of real criminals – it has been noted that it shies away from depicting any of the criminal activities from which the family made its money: loan sharking, protection rackets, illegal gambling, or prostitution. Both film and book have also been criticised for presenting a stereotypical image of Italian-Americans, and the novel has been described as being misogynistic in its portrayal of women as victims of spousal abuse, submissive wives, or obsessed with the size of men's penises.

Rather than telling the story of the rise and fall of an over-ambitious gangster leader, *The Godfather* shows us a man who wants to avoid becoming part of his father's successful criminal empire but finds himself reluctantly drawn into it. He is unable to escape his fate.

Here's a rough breakdown of *The Godfather* plot – film and novel have pretty much the same structure, though the novel spends more time on the singer Johnny Fontane.

Sequence 1 – We meet the old Don and the son who does not want to be like him.
Sequence 2 – Introduces the situation that will snowball out of control and change Michael's life.
Sequence 3 – Michael is drawn into the situation and demonstrates his abilities.
Sequence 4 – Michael gives up his old, civilian, life and becomes a gangster. (Midpoint)
Sequence 5 – Downfall of the hot-headed son who is not fit to lead the family.
Sequence 6 – Romantic interlude for Michael – brought to a dramatic end that forces him back into the main action.

Sequence 7 – Michael in charge of the family – the new 'Don' in all but name. His father acting as mentor as he hands over power. Death of the old Don.
Sequence 8 – Michael proves himself the new leader, accepts the mantle of Don.

The Godfather's plot structure is very simple – but very effective. As a novel it was a bestseller, and it still reads well today 50 years after it was written. The Hollywood adaptation is one of the finest motion pictures ever made, regularly appearing on 'best of' lists.

Where the original 1930s gangster movies put the spotlight on a single, tragic figure – showing his rise, his 'over-reaching' in his quest for power, and his inevitable demise; *The Godfather* presents a similar character arc from a different perspective. We see Michael's rise, but the story ends with his ultimate success – he has become the boss. But he is still a tragic figure, as his success is – ironically – a failure: he has not achieved what he and his father both wanted his success to be. We also witness his story not as outsiders slowing down as we drive by the car wreck of his life, but rather as insiders who have empathy with his character and with his family. We don't approve of the *actions* of these people, but we understand their emotions and their motivations. The story allows us to *belong*, vicariously, to this family. One of the things that makes *The Godfather* more than the sum of its parts is the paradox of Michael's character – we want to see him succeed, to get revenge on the bad guys and defeat them, and yet – at the same time – we don't want to see him fail and become the same as his father. If you can make a reader have contradictory feelings in this way, you've given your story that extra something that raises it to the next level.

3 | Crime Sprees & Gun Molls

If you look at the 'List of Depression-Era Outlaws' on *Wikipedia,* you'll see that many criminals in the 1920s and 30s weren't city-based gangsters. Some of the best-known criminals of the period operated in gangs that were more like the Dalton Gang or Wild Bunch of the Old West. These gangs travelled around and engaged in bank robberies and other 'stick-ups'. And a key part of many of these gangs was a female member who played an active role in the crimes as either driver or 'gun moll.'

The word *moll* in 'gun moll' or 'gangster's moll' comes from the English term 'molly' meaning a whore, which was in use in the 1600s and possibly before. The *gun* in gun moll has come to be associated with the weapon carried by female criminals, but is thought to have originally come from the Yiddish word *gonif* – from the Hebrew *ganev* – meaning a thief or crook. Gonif's moll became gun moll. The *Wikipedia* entry for 'Gun Moll' lists a number of female associates of gangsters and other criminals. The gun moll was more than just the gangster's girlfriend and, unlike the *femme fatale*, was in love with her man and loyal to him. Theirs is typically a doomed romance, as together they suffer the same fate as the city-based gangster. This is a character that has probably been underused in fiction.

In movies, these are the films that Thomas Schatz referred to as 'rural' gangster movies. A classic example of the gun moll who manipulates her man like Lady Macbeth is the character of Annie Laurie Starr played by Peggy Cummins in *Gun Crazy* (1950) which was also released under the title *Deadly is the Female*. It was based on a short story by MacKinlay Kantor published in *The Saturday Evening Post* in 1940. The screenplay was by the blacklisted writer Dalton Trumbo. The Production Code was still in force at this time, so there was a limit to how much sexuality could be portrayed and to what extent the two main characters could be 'turned on' by guns. The 1992 film *Guncrazy* starring Drew Barrymore was inspired by the 1950 film but was not a direct remake. W.R. Burnett's novel *High Sierra*, filmed in 1941 with Humphrey Bogart and Ida Lupino, also belongs to this sub-genre. The novel was filmed again in 1955 as *I Died a Thousand Times* with Jack Palance and Shelley Winters.

Where the 'classic' gangster story was defined by three movies, the crime spree story is best known by the names of some of the real-life criminals and the fictional accounts of their activities. The best-known of all are probably Bonnie Parker and Clyde Barrow, whose story was told in the 1967 film *Bonnie and Clyde*. Their story, as can be seen from the examples below, is typical of the short-lived careers of many of these crime spree criminals.

George 'Machine Gun' Kelly was active in bootlegging and minor crimes during the late 1920s and with his wife Kathryn was responsible for the kidnapping of oil tycoon Charles F. Urschel, a crime which would lead to the arrest of the couple in 1933. Kathryn is said to have purchased the Thompson submachine gun and encouraged Kelly to use it. She is also believed to have built up his reputation as a dangerous criminal. Kathryn tried to secure a lenient sentence for herself and her mother by offering to betray Kelly to the FBI, but all three were captured before a deal was completed – they all received life sentences. The 1958 film *Machine-Gun Kelly* was directed by Roger Corman and starred Charles Bronson in his first lead role – it was originally released as a double feature with *The Bonnie Parker Story*. In the film, Kelly's partner is the tough-talking Flo Becker who dominates him and cajoles him into 'proving' himself by committing crimes.

John Dillinger was leader of the Dillinger Gang who operated in the American Midwest from September 1933 to July 1934. Baby Face Nelson's gang are thought to have helped Dillinger escape from prison and they then joined his new gang. This gang's robberies were more carefully planned than the usual 'stick-up' with military-style tactics learned from the crimes of 'Baron' Herman Lamm. The gang were also referred to as The Terror Gang and are believed to have been responsible for the robberies of twenty-four banks and four police stations. They were accused of killing ten men and wounding seven. Dillinger himself escaped from prison twice – including the 'wooden pistol' escape from Crown Point, Indiana. From October 1933 until her arrest in April 1934, Evelyn 'Billie' Frechette was Dillinger's companion – hiding him in her apartment and on one occasion driving the getaway car after Dillinger had been shot. She was not an accomplice in the gang's crimes and served two years for harbouring a criminal. Frechette's side of the story was published in a series of articles published in *The Chicago Herald and Examiner* beginning 27th August 1934. Dillinger was betrayed to the FBI by the madam of a brothel – Dillinger was shot by special agents as he tried to escape from the Biograph Theatre on 28th July 1934. Films about Dillinger's life include *Dillinger* (1945) starring Lawrence Tierney; *Young Dillinger* (1965); and *Dillinger* (1973) starring Warren Oates. Johnny Depp plays Dillinger in the 2009 film *Public Enemies*.

Baby Face Nelson had been involved in petty crime from an early age and began his gang-affiliation while in his mid-teens. By 1929 he was involved in armed robbery – he was arrested in 1931 but escaped during a prison transfer. Towards the end of 1933, he formed his own gang of bank robbers. In early 1934, Nelson's gang teamed up with John Dillinger. In April of 1934, Nelson, Dillinger and other gang members and their girlfriends arrived at the Little Bohemia Lodge in Wisconsin. The FBI was tipped off and a raid was mounted – innocent customers were shot by the FBI and a federal agent was killed by Nelson, who then escaped in an FBI car. None of the gang was captured and the FBI was severely criticised for the handling of the raid. The FBI captured or killed a number of gang members, and Dillinger was killed in July 1934. Baby Face Nelson was the only member of the gang to remain at large and, having killed a federal agent, was named Public Enemy No. 1. The FBI staked out one of Nelson's former hideouts. A gun battle – the 'Battle of Barrington' – took place at the end of November 1934 and Nelson and two FBI agents were mortally wounded. The film *Baby Face Nelson* (1957) directed by Don Siegel starred Mickey Rooney in the title role. The screenplay was based on an unpublished novel by Irving Shulman.

Kate 'Ma' Barker is (wrongly) believed to have been the leader of the Barker-Karpis Gang which was active from 1931 to 1935. The gang included her sons Fred and Arthur along with Alvin 'Creepy' Karpis. At its height, the gang had twenty-five members, who were engaged in robberies and kidnapping. After the death of Baby Face Nelson, Alvin Karpis – the real head of the gang – was declared by the FBI to be Public Enemy No. 1. The myth about Ma Barker being the ruthless mastermind leading the gang is believed by some to have been deliberately created by J. Edgar Hoover. Films about the gang include *Queen of the Mob* (1940) based on an account in J. Edgar Hoover's book *Persons in Hiding; Ma Barker's Killer Brood* (1960); *Bloody Mama* starring Shelley Winters and a young Robert De Niro (1970), and *Public Enemies* (1996).

Edna 'Rabbit' Murray was a waitress with two failed marriages before she met Volney Davis and became his lover. Davis was a robber who was an early associate of the Karpis-Barker Gang and was sentenced to life after a night watchman was killed during a burglary at a hospital. Davis escaped from prison on a number of occasions and was ultimately sent to Alcatraz. Edna married a jewel thief who was executed for murder in 1924 and then married another criminal, Jack Murray, in 1925. Husband and wife were sentenced to 25 years for their parts in a holdup, during which Edna earned the nickname 'the Kissing Bandit' after she allegedly kissed one of the victims. Edna made several prison escapes, earning herself the name 'Rabbit', and teamed up with Volner again in 1932 and the two joined the Barker-Karpis gang. The pair were also associated with John Dillinger. Murray was arrested in 1935 and co-operated with the authorities, giving evidence against other gang members. She also wrote articles including 'I Was a Karpis-Barker Gang Moll,' published in *Startling Detective Adventures* in October 1936. Volney and 'Rabbit' appear as characters in Stephen King's short story 'The Death of Jack Hamilton' (2001) which is told from the point of view of one of the members of Dillinger's gang. The story was turned into a short film (45 mins.) by director Jamie Anderson in 2012.

Pretty Boy Floyd was a bank robber whose exploits received considerable coverage in the early 1930s and he was viewed as a sort of hero outlaw by locals in Oklahoma, sometimes referred to as the 'Robin Hood of the Cookson Hills.' Floyd's criminal career began when he was eighteen and by 1929 he was wanted in connection with a number of cases. He was convicted of bank robbery in 1930 but escaped from prison. In June 1933, four law enforcement officers were killed in the 'Kansas City massacre' and the FBI named Nelson and his associate as the prime suspects, though it is not clear whether they were actually responsible. Having narrowly escaped the FBI on a couple of occasions, Floyd was located and shot in October 1934 – there are three different versions, told by the FBI, local law enforcers, and others present, about what actually occurred. Larry McMurtry and Diana Ossana wrote a fictionalised account of Floyd's life, *Pretty Boy Floyd*, published in 1995. Floyd is also referred to in John Steinbeck's *The Grapes of Wrath*, where Ma Joad says she knew his mother. The movie *Pretty Boy Floyd* (1960) features John Ericson as the title character. Floyd is a character in a number of other films, notably *Dillinger* (1973) and *Young Dillinger* (1965), and he was played by Channing Tatum in the 2009 film *Public Enemies*.

Clyde Barrow engaged in car theft, safecracking, and robbery from the age of seventeen and was sent to brutal Eastham Prison Farm in 1930. His experiences there changed him from a 'schoolboy to a rattlesnake' according to one fellow prisoner. Barrow committed his first murder in prison, killing a man who had beaten and raped him repeatedly. Released from prison in 1932, Clyde Barrow was reunited with Bonnie Parker – the two having first met in 1930. Barrow and another former inmate originally began their robberies in order to finance a 'liberation' of others held at the Eastham Prison Farm. As well as Barrow's brother Buck and his wife, the gang included several other members at various points – these were all merged into the character of C.W. Moss the 1967 movie.

Newspaper stories about the gang were initially favourable and photographs that they had taken of themselves have become part of the legend. In 1934, the gang did help some prisoners escape during the 'Eastham Breakout' and an embarrassed Texas Department of Corrections brought in ex-Texas Ranger Frank A. Hamer to hunt down the gang – it was the authorities that were humiliated by the gang, not Hamer personally as the film depicts. Officer Thomas Persell was captured by the gang at one point, and it is his gun that can be seen in the photographs taken by the gang. In the ambush that killed them, Bonnie Parker and Clyde Barrow suffered around twenty bullet-wounds each – what the film does not show is the gruesome frenzy of souvenir hunters after the couple's death.

Retellings of the couple's lives include the films *The Bonnie Parker Story* (1958) and *Bonnie and Clyde* (1967), directed by Arthur Penn and starring Warren Beatty and Faye Dunaway. Non-fiction sources include Blanche Barrow's autobiographical account *My Life with Bonnie and Clyde*, written between 1933 and 1939 and published in 2004; John Neal Philips' *Running with Bonnie and Clyde: The Ten Fast Years of Ralph Fults* (1996), an account from the point of view of one of the gang members, and a more recent and detailed account is *Go Down Together: The True, Untold Story of Bonnie and Clyde* (2009) by Jeff Guinn.

Plot Structure of the Crime Spree Story

The plot template below is based mainly on the 1967 film *Bonnie and Clyde*. It is typical of the basic structures of many of the films mentioned above and also of films such as *Badlands* (1973), *Dirty Mary, Crazy Larry* (1974), *True Romance* (1993), *Kalifornia* (1993), and *Natural Born Killers* (1994). The plots of the 1969 Western *Butch Cassidy and the Sundance Kid* and the 1991 film *Thelma & Louise* also have a similar structure.

Sequence 1

Our criminal couple meet – I'll refer to them as the hero and romantic co-protagonist, though they're equally important in this type of story – and there is typically banter and flirting. They are immediately attracted to each other. He tries to impress her by telling her he's a crook. She obviously likes the fact that he's a bad boy – but she doesn't take his boasting at face value and goads him into proving it. He takes her along when he commits a crime – probably asking her to keep an eye open for trouble. No one is hurt during this crime. She is thrilled by the adventure of it.

They steal a car and flee. There is more romance bonding – over a hamburger or a coke in a late night diner. He plays along to her fantasy, telling her that they're not like other people – they need freedom and adventure. Something of her backstory is revealed – she usually has a dull life, working as a waitress. Part of the attraction of this bad boy is that he will take her away from that. He indicates he will and says that together they could really be something. In some stories, they make love that first night – other stories are more chaste and spending time together in some other way takes the place of sex. Before the end of the sequence, he will probably show her how to shoot a good. The implication is that they will be partners the next time they rob somewhere.

Sequence 2
Their first crime as a team. It doesn't go well and he ends up shooting someone, injuring but not killing them. He is angry because the victim's actions 'forced' him to shoot. We see law enforcement officers investigating the robbery. The couple meet a young man – we'll call him the ally – and he joins their 'gang' and acts as the driver for their next robbery. A mistake by this young man leads to a situation where the hero has to shoot and kill someone. This raises the stakes and marks a point of no return.

Sequence 3
The hero is angry with the ally because he 'made' him kill someone. After the hero has stormed out to cool down, the romantic co-protagonist teases the ally, embarrassing him and making him forget the hero's anger.

Later, the hero and romantic co-protagonist may make love, but it will be awkward and unsatisfactory as they're worried about the situation they now find themselves in – they're wanted fugitives from the law. Two more people may join the gang, though this optional. They are usually known to the hero but not the romantic co-protagonist, being old prison buddies, life-long friends, or relatives of the hero. One or more of them may also have a girlfriend or wife. The romantic co-protagonist didn't know they were going to arrive and she isn't pleased to see them. There are awkward introductions and she finds herself left out of the friendly banter and reminiscences about adventures she wasn't part of. She just wants to be alone with the hero.

The gang may end up goofing around and taking photographs of each other. The guys are all happy but she is just playing along to humour them. There is a moment of suspense when there is a knock at the door – but it is just food being delivered. But then... the law enforcers have found the gang's hideout. There is a shoot-out and the gang escapes – but in doing so they kill at least one law enforcer and injure others. Again, the stakes have again been raised.

Sequence 4
The hero and the romantic co-protagonist have an argument about the new gang members – she blames them for the poor way they handled the shoot-out and escape, and she wants to be rid of them. One of the new gang members and/or his female companion may actually *want* to leave, but they can't because they have been seen by the police and identified as members of the gang – they all have to stick together now.

During their escape or afterwards, the gang may encounter a lone policeman or investigator and make him their captive, humiliating and disarming him before they let him go. The gang carries out another bank robbery or other crime – and this one is much more professional than their previous efforts. They make a clean getaway and no one is hurt. This positive moment marks the *midpoint* of the story – things will go downhill from here.

Sequence 5
This sequence concentrates on the relationships between the gang members – especially between the hero and the romantic co-protagonist. The haul from the bank is disappointing and there are arguments among the gang members over who deserves what, who took the greatest risks, etc. The romantic co-protagonist is feeling homesick – she is surrounded by the hero's 'family' and is missing her own. She may decide that she wants to

take her share of the money to her mother – but the hero will veto this, telling her it is too dangerous. The romantic co-protagonist disappears – she's heading back home without telling the others. They search for her and the hero eventually catches up with her and tells her they'll all go together.

Sequence 6
The romantic co-protagonist visiting with her family. Perhaps they have a scrapbook filled with newspaper clippings about the gang's exploits. The hero tries to reassure the mother that the romantic co-protagonist is safe – but the mother sees through this and tells them to keep running. The romantic co-protagonist doesn't want to leave, but knows she has to.

The romantic co-protagonist and the hero have a quiet moment together – she says that when she first ran away with him, she thought they were going somewhere. She now realises that the 'going' is all there is and they have to keep going. He says that he loves her. She asks if he loves her enough to die with her because she thinks that is where they are heading. He says yes. The police spot one of the gang members getting food. A raid on the motel where the gang are staying. Shoot-out. One of the gang is shot and seriously wounded as they escape. Their situation is so dire that even the gang members who don't like each other bond and comfort each other.

Sequence 7
The gang have been surrounded while they sleep – there are dozens of armed men out there. They are advised to surrender. The gang don't open fire, they just try and sneak away. But they are spotted and are fired upon. The hero and/or the romantic co-protagonist are shot and injured or are hurt when their getaway car hits a tree. The gang member who was seriously wounded before has to be left behind – his girlfriend or closest friend stays with him, even though they know it means being captured.

The other members of the gang manage to get away – but only just. They may be helped by some local people who regard the gang as folk heroes. The ally drives them to a place of safety – a farm belonging to his father, uncle, or cousin. The law enforcers are still on the gang's trail and are not far behind them. Newspaper reports may paint the gang in a bad light or publish untruths about them that make them look bad. This angers the hero, who wants to set the record straight.

At the hospital, the severely injured gang member has died. Investigators speak to his friend or girlfriend who accompanied him, perhaps offering a deal in exchange for information. Whether they intended to or not, the girlfriend/friend reveals some clue that will help the investigators find the gang's latest hideout.

Sequence 8
There is a nice romantic moment as the hero and romantic co-protagonist recover from their wounds. But it is bittersweet as this is the calm before the storm and their romance is doomed.

A more positive story about the gang may be published in a newspaper or magazine. This improves the hero's mood – he finally feels as though he has made it, he is a someone important – a legend.

The ally, the ally's lover, or a member of the ally's family – or someone else close to the gang – may betray the hero and the romantic co-protagonist to the investigators, perhaps in exchange for a deal to get the ally a lighter sentence. An ambush is set up. The hero and romantic co-protagonist are gunned down.

4 | Police Procedural

The police procedural – occasionally referred to as a police crime drama or police routine novel – is a sub-genre of the detective mystery. Hillary Waugh, who wrote one of the earliest examples, has said that police procedural novels are "...stories in which professional policemen, using police resources and police methods, are the ones who solve the crimes."

George N. Dove's *The Police Procedural* was the first in-depth academic study of the sub-genre and in it he set down two requirements: "First, to be called a police procedural, a novel must be a mystery story; and second, it must be one in which the mystery is solved by policemen using normal police routines."

The detective is officially employed by a police department and it is his job to investigate crimes. This distinguishes him from the amateur or consulting detective of the traditional whodunit – Sherlock Holmes or Hercule Poirot – and from the self-employed or privately employed hardboiled private detective in the Phillip Marlowe and Sam Spade tradition. But there is more to the creation of a police procedural than just making your hero a police detective.

While the police procedural has things in common with both the classic murder mystery and the private eye novel, it is also a type of 'expert thriller' of the type that I wrote about in *Suspense Thriller*. And it has links with the Legal Thriller – which I covered in the same book – in that both operate within the limits of the legal system. Having explored the law and the legal system at some length in *Suspense Fiction* I don't want to repeat that information here and will concentrate only on those aspects of the law that relate to the investigation of crimes.

Police Detective Novels versus Police Procedurals

Hillary Waugh wrote that "...the procedural thrusts the detective into the middle of a working police force, full of rules and regulations. Instead of bypassing the police, as did its predecessors, the procedural takes the reader inside the department and shows how it operates. These stories are not just about policemen, but about the world of the policeman." By this definition, the Charlie Chan novels are not police procedurals, because even though he is a police detective, his investigations do not really involve the workings of the police department. Even in the Maigret novels, where other policemen do appear, the detective operates pretty much on his own in the manner of the consulting detective and the private eye. The Charlie Chan and Maigret stories are examples of the 'Police Detective' sub-genre.

In the Police *Detective* novel, we have a lone detective – often with a Watson-like partner – who investigates a single crime, usually murder. He is employed by a police department, but the workings of that department do not feature much in the story – they are deep in the background. In the Police *Procedural*, the detective is a member of a team and the workings of the police department play a much more significant part in the story. As George N. Dove says, the term 'procedural' refers to the "...methods of detection employed, the procedures followed by policemen in real life."

Dove notes that police detectives have been around since the early days of the mystery genre, including Emile Gaboriau's Monsieur Lecoq, Wilkie

Collins' Sergeant Cuff and Georges Simenon's Maigret – but these stories are not police procedurals for two reasons:

1) While these detectives belong to a police organisation and are assisted by other policemen, they always solve the mystery single-handed. In the police procedural, as we will see, the investigation is conducted by a team of policemen, some of them specialists in particular fields, who work in collaboration.
2) The methods used by Lecoq, Maigret et al. are the same powers of observation and deduction used by the 'Great Detectives' of the classic whodunit rather than being the investigative methods – the 'procedures' – used by real-life police detectives.

Other examples of the Police Detective story include Colin Dexter's Inspector Morse series, Reginald Hill's Dalziel and Pascoe stories. P.D. James's Adam Dalgliesh and Ruth Rendell's Wexford are also police detectives. And it's probably fair to say that any series that is identified by a single detective's name is going to be in the Police Detective sub-genre rather than the Police Procedural. There are significantly more police detective novels written by British authors than by American ones – perhaps because the private eye novel has been more popular in the USA. The British police detective grew out of the country house whodunit tradition, with Michael Innes's Sir John Appleby being one of the earliest examples in *Death in the President's Lodging* (1936, published as *Seven Suspects* in the US).

George N. Dove also points out that not every story that centres on the work of policemen is part of the police procedural sub-genre. To qualify, a story must include an element of *mystery*. By this definition, the police novels by Joseph Wambaugh are not procedurals because the policemen in them are not detectives who solve a mystery.

This may seem like splitting hairs, but for our purposes – for examining the *plot* and *genre conventions* of a police procedural – this is an important distinction. The story in a Police Detective novel can be structured in the same way as a traditional whodunit murder mystery or in the same way as a hardboiled private eye novel. The Police Procedural novel cannot – it has a different sort of hero and a different sort of plot structure. In theory. I am going to emphasise the *differences* between the police procedural and other types of detective novel, but in practice, you will find that many police procedurals – particularly those in long-running series – are very similar to police detective novels.

I am not going to treat the *Police Detective* novel separately. As I've said already, the plot can follow the traditional murder mystery or private eye novel structure. The hero in such a story will be a combination of elements from the traditional 'Great Detective' (or the Private Eye) *and* the police procedural detective that we explore in this chapter. And the milieu in which the police detective operates – the police department in which he works – will be a toned-down version of the background described here.

Before we go on to explore the 'pure' police procedural, it is important to recognise the one thing that the police procedural has in common with the whodunit and the private eye novel – all of them feature an element of *mystery*. Because, as Hillary Waugh pointed out, if there's no mystery there's no suspense and no story. George N. Dove states that the police procedural "...belongs in the mystery genre, and people read them at least in part for the satisfaction of watching detectives detect, of participating in the solution of a problem."

The Myth of Realism

Ranking the three main types of detective story we would say that the classical murder mystery (or whodunit) is the least realistic, the hardboiled detective novel is more realistic, and the police procedural is the most realistic of all. But just how realistic is the police procedural novel? The answer, if we're brutally honest, is 'not very.' But there are good reasons why this is the case.

In his essay, Hillary Waugh pointed out that most real-life murders are committed in a state of high emotion and for personal reasons, such that the police know the identity of the murderer in five minutes and the motive for murder very shortly after that. This sort of situation cannot be used for a novel because there is no mystery and no suspense. A police procedural novel has to feature one of the less common types of murder in which the identity of the murderer is a mystery or where obtaining the necessary evidence to secure the conviction of a suspected murderer offers some other sort of challenge.

George N. Dove highlights another aspect of the police procedural that is at odds with the reality of police work – the unsolved case. A significant proportion of real-life crimes that require investigation ultimately remain unsolved. Police procedurals almost always end with a solution – to leave the case unresolved risks leaving the reader feeling dissatisfied with the story. But while the main case in a story may not remain unsolved, detectives often refer to the large number of other unsolved or 'cold cases' on their files.

Ultimately what really matters is *plausibility*. Writers must know enough about the world of the real police to make their stories plausible, including procedures and routines, a policeman's way of thinking, and the sub-culture of which he is a member. We will look at all of these in this chapter.

An Element of Chance

Related to the need for realism is the idea that chance plays a much bigger part in real-life police work than it does in fictional investigations. In the classical murder mystery or whodunit, one of the 'Rules of the Game' – as laid down by S.S. Van Dine in his 'Twenty Rules' – is that "The culprit must be determined by logical deductions – not by accident or coincidence or unmotivated confession." And in his 'Decalogue,' Ronald Knox stated that 'No accident must ever help the detective.'

If we expect the private eye novel and the police procedural to be more realistic than the whodunit, chance or coincidence should play a larger part. But this presents us with a problem as storytellers where unmotivated events and unearned good fortune are regarded as being 'a rabbit pulled out of a hat' or as *deus ex machina* and therefore 'cheating.'

This relates to something I have written about in *Plot Basics* and elsewhere – stories make sense while real life often does not. Part of the appeal of a story is that there is a clear pattern of cause and effect – we get to understand *why* things happen. Real life isn't always this simple. Another reason we enjoy stories is because we like to see the protagonist take responsibility for his or her own destiny – they become the cause of the good things that happen to them. Or the bad things.

If we accept the idea that the police procedural is more realistic than the traditional whodunit or the private eye story, then we have to accept that chance will play more of a role in events and that the protagonist may not be in control of his own destiny. But this is another one of those cases where *plausibility* is more important than strict adherence to reality. We need to make it *seem* that our procedural detective is subject to the whim of Fate.

The one unbreakable rule is that a major investigation in a novel should never be solved as a result of luck or coincidence. If you want to show chance at work, save it for a minor investigation that is occurring at the same time as your main one. And highlight the irony of Fate's intervention. But it is okay if bad luck makes things more difficult for your protagonist or impedes his discovery of the solution.

This is in line with general storytelling 'rules' which say that when it comes to significant plot points, you can use chance to make the hero's situation worse but it is 'cheating' if you use luck or coincidence to get your hero out of difficult situation.

Bad breaks can occur in the form of an important clue that isn't spotted straight away because it is buried in a mass of reports that have been gathered by those working on the case. Or in the form of a vital piece of information that one detective in the team has but that isn't shared with the other detectives because its significance isn't realised. Obviously, criminals get bad breaks too and a mistake they make may turn out to be beneficial to the protagonist. In theory, all clues discovered by the police are the result of a mistake or bad break for the criminal, so this is less like cheating than having a clue drop into the detective's lap purely by chance.

Use of Multiple Points of View

In his essay on the British police procedural, Michael Gilbert noted the important difference in point of view between the major types of mystery novel. In the traditional whodunit, the reader views the murder investigation from the outside, watching the detective piece together the clues and then eventually announce the solution. We never get to share the thoughts of the Great Detective, because that would give the game away too early. In the 'inverted' mystery or crime story, we experience the story from the point of view of the murderer, watching him make his plans, carry out the crime, and then try to avoid detection. In the police procedural, as in the private eye novel, we *do* get to share the thoughts of the detective (or detectives) investigating the crime. We, the readers, share in the day-to-day experience of what Gilbert describes as "...the fascinating, infuriating, vital job of the professionals whose job it is to catch the murderer." We also get a glimpse of the home life of our hero and get to share in his personal hopes and fears, as well as his professional ones. It is the motives and actions of the police detectives that concern us more than those of the suspects and the murderer.

Whodunits are typically told from a single point of view – either the reader stands at the detective's shoulder watching, or he experiences the story from the viewpoint of a 'Watson' who is standing at the detective's shoulder. The private eye story is usually told from the viewpoint of the detective – and often in the first-person. But a procedural novel often features more than one viewpoint character. One detective may be the main viewpoint character, but – as Keating says – "You will probably have to see events through the eyes of one or more detectives, of a scene-of-the-crime officer, of various laboratory experts and of the man who sits in his office at headquarters and directs the operation."

Even if the story follows a single detective throughout, other members of the team will also be working on the case – gathering statements or carrying out ballistics tests or DNA analysis. This means that some suspense can be added to the story as the main detective waits to hear the results from other people and it means that reader and detective can be surprised by unexpected developments.

Historical Development of the Police Procedural

The Police Detective novel predates the Police Procedural by some margin. A number of early mysteries had detective heroes who were operating in an official capacity, including Emile Gaboriau's Monsieur Lecoq novels published between 1865 and 1868, referred to by *The Oxford Companion to Crime & Mystery Writing* as the first police detective.

The first Police Procedural novel has not been formally identified, partly as a result of the overlap with the Police Detective sub-genre. Several early examples are usually cited in histories of the police procedural. The earliest is Henry Wade's *Lonely Magdalen* (1940) which tells the story of a murder investigation from the point of view of two police detectives who investigate it. Aside from the middle section that serves as a flashback exploring the life of the victim, it is a straightforward example of a police procedural. Maurice Procter's *The Chief Inspector's Statement* (1951, published as *The Pennycross Murders* in the US) is another British example, telling of the investigation of a murder in a village from the point of view of the main investigator. Lawrence Treat's *V as in Victim* (1945) is probably the first American police procedural and Hillary Waugh's *Last Seen Wearing...* (1952), which is having established the format for the procedural. Waugh said that the novel was inspired by an account in a book of true crime cases, and it has been suggested that the crime in question was the unsolved disappearance of Paula Jean Welden in Bennington, Vermont in 1946. Both Treat and Waugh wrote series of novels featuring police detectives. Waugh himself acknowledges *Dragnet* – on radio from 1949 and on television from 1952 – as an important influence on the sub-genre. Note that the 1987 film *Dragnet* starring Dan Aykroyd and Tom Hanks is a 'parody and homage' and shouldn't be taken as representing the style of the earlier stories.

The popularity of the procedural grew after the Second World War, partly as a result of the success of a number of 'semi-documentary' films that claimed to authentically depict police work, with some of them being based on actual cases. Titles included *The Naked City* (1948), *The Street with No Name* (1948), *He Walked by Night* (1948), and *Border Incident* (1949). *He Walked By Night* is notable in that it served to inspire the creation of *Dragnet*. The 1951 film *Detective Story*, featuring Kirk Douglas, is an account of one day in the life of a police precinct and is based on a successful 1949 play by Sidney Kingsley.

Similar films were produced in France and Britain, and Japanese director Akira Kurosawa's 1949 film *Stray Dog* has been described as a police procedural, a film noir, and the precursor of the 'buddy cop' film sub-genre.

Elizabeth Linington wrote eighty or so novels, most of them police procedurals, under her own name and as Anne Blaisdell, Lesley Egan, Egan O'Neill, and Dell Shannon. As Shannon she wrote thirty-eight novels featuring Luis Mendoza of the LAPD, beginning with *Case Pending* in 1960. Under her own name, she wrote thirteen books about Ivor Maddox and the Hollywood Police Department, the first being *Greenmask!* (1964).

John Creasey, writing as J.J. Marric is said to have written his George Gideon of Scotland Yard series in response to a challenge from a police inspector who said 'Why don't you show us as we are? You don't have to put in the dull part.' *Gideon's Day* was published in 1955 and a film adaptation (titled *Gideon of Scotland Yard* in the US) was released in 1958 and twenty more followed, plus another five ghost-written after Creasey's death. Creasey wrote more than 600 novels during his lifetime and had twenty-eight pseudonyms. Under his own name, he wrote over forty books featuring Detective Inspector Roger West beginning in 1942 with *Inspector West Takes Charge*.

John Wainwright, an ex-policeman, published 78 novels, many of them police procedurals. His novel *All On a Summer's Day* (1981) is an account of a twenty-four-hour period in a police station in the north of England. Wainwright joined the West Riding Constabulary in 1947 and claimed to have been involved in six full-scale murder enquiries and to have spoken to the murderer in each case. He wrote an autobiographical account of his time as a policeman, *Wainwright's Beat*, and another detailing his experiences as a rear-gunner in a Lancaster bomber during the Second World War, *Tail-End Charlie*.

Maurice Procter wrote fifteen novels featuring Detective Chief Inspector Harry Martineau of the Granchester City Police. The first, *Hell is a City* (*Somewhere in This City* in the US) was published in 1954 and a film adaptation starring Stanley Baker was released in 1960.

The author most closely associated with the police procedural is Ed McBain (a pseudonym of Evan Hunter, author of *Blackboard Jungle*). His 87th Precinct series began in 1956 with *Cop Hater* and features as its 'hero' the detective squad in the imaginary city of Isola, based on New York. Although a single detective, Steve Carella, appears in many of the novels, others in the series have other detectives from the squad as their protagonist.

John Harvey wrote eleven novels featuring Detective Inspector Charlie Resnick based in the City of Nottingham, beginning with *Lonely Hearts* in 1989 and ending in 2014.

While not a writer of police procedurals by our definition, I want to mention the work of novelist Joseph Wambaugh here. His 1971 novel *The New Centurions* was one of the first to explore the reality of the lives of working policemen. Wambaugh was the son of a police officer and himself served in the LAPD for fourteen years. *The Choirboys* (1975) marked a change in the tone of Wambaugh's writing, featuring more dark humour and outrageous situations. His novels influenced the television series *Hill Street Blues* (1981-1987), which every writer of police procedurals should watch, and he also helped create the NBC series *Police Story* (1973-1978). These two shows are said to have influenced the development of later series such as *Law & Order* (1990-2010), *NYPD Blue* (1993-2005), *Homicide: Life on the Street* (1993-1999), *The Wire* (2002-2008) and *The Shield* (2002-2008).

Although a number of police procedural novels have been adapted into films, it is notable that in recent years, the police procedural has proved more successful on television. An ongoing television series provides more space to develop an ensemble cast and to portray the overlapping storylines typical of the sub-genre.

Many of those who have written police procedural novels, including some of those mentioned above, had experience working in a police department – is that a necessary qualification for writing in this sub-genre? H.R.F. Keating, in his *Writing Crime Fiction*, says not. It is better to be a good fiction writer researching how a policeman works than to be a good policeman trying to figure out what an author does. What you really need, Keating says, is empathy – the ability to see life through the eyes of a policeman.

Genre Conventions

George N. Dove in his book *The Police Procedural* notes that the main conventions of the sub-genre can be viewed as handicaps that the writer has to overcome. But while these added restrictions can be frustrating for the author, the reader arrives expecting to see 'proper' police procedure and the writer is under an obligation to supply it.

Michael Gilbert says that the reason most early mystery stories featured an amateur detective – and why many still do – is that the writers are amateurs who know very little about real-life detective work. Ruth Rendell once admitted that she avoided errors in describing police procedure by leaving it out. You don't have that luxury with the procedural.

George N. Dove credits Lawrence Treat with having established many of the conventions of the American police procedural novel in his *V as in Victim*. Treat had his characters use the routines and procedures of real policemen. He also "introduced the reader to the police mind, a constellation of attitudes and prejudices that characterise the main detective in the story..." and he established "a tension between the old-fashioned, largely disorganised approach to police work and the emerging development of police technology." Two developments were added by John Creasey (writing as J.J. Marric) in his *Gideon's Day* (*Gideon of Scotland Yard* in the US): the multi-storyline plot, which we will look at later, and the inclusion of elements of the main detective's private life. Gideon was shown as "husband and father, a policeman often torn between commitment to his profession and the demands of family life."

Early writers in this sub-genre had to establish the parameters of this world. But aspects of it have become so familiar as a result of novels and television, that modern writers can safely assume that the reader or audience is familiar with the way this world – or the fictional representation of it at least – works. That being said, it is probably still worth exploring some of the key features of the police 'milieu' and its relationship with the wider world.

Police procedures are an important element in this sub-genre, so much so that I have included a separate section on them later in the chapter. Before that, we'll look at some of the more familiar genre convention headings.

Settings

If a police procedural takes place in a small town, then a murder investigation will be a major event. In real-life, as Hillary Waugh points out, there is probably one such murder in a century; in a police procedural series there may be two (or more) a year. Readers are prepared to suspend their disbelief to allow this. In a major U.S. city there are hundreds of homicides a year, but only a small percentage of those will be the sort of case that requires the sort of investigative work that we require to create the plot for a novel. Again, the reader will forgive us for concentrating on these exceptional cases.

If you plan on publishing a series of two or more novels a year, a city location probably gives you more scope of murder investigations.

The location of a story and the size of the local population can also affect how easy it is to locate witnesses – suspense can be added to a story by making a witness difficult to locate. Or by having them try to escape from the police. And once caught, they may be reluctant to answer questions – not necessarily because they have something to hide, but because they are suspicious of, or simply dislike, the police in general. People may harbour, assist, or provide alibis for criminals for the same reason.

Dell Shannon says that the advantage of having a police station as a setting is that there is always something interesting going on. Other cases are under investigation alongside the main one in the story and eccentric, amusing or tragic characters may or incidents may appear on stage briefly to help break-up the routine nature of day-to-day police work.

In terms of geographical location, you have the choice of setting your fictional detectives in a real location or a made-up one. If you use a real one, you will need to become familiar with the real-life structure, procedures and customs of the police force there. If you create a fictional setting that is based on a real one, as Ed McBain did, you allow yourself a little more freedom and can avoid some of the research.

The physical settings we see in the police procedural – the crime scenes and police stations and courthouses etc. – are pretty much those we have seen in every cop show on television – to the extent that it is difficult to avoid cliché here.

The Hero

Under *Plot Structure* below I discuss two main types of police procedural novel – those that centre on the investigation of a single crime and those that feature multiple investigations. Broadly speaking, in a single investigation you *can* have a single protagonist who is the point of view character throughout the whole novel, while in a multiple investigation novel you *will* have more than one protagonist/viewpoint character. There are exceptions to this, but as genre writers we need to understand the usual approach before we tackle the unusual.

Even in a story with a single main protagonist, that detective will almost always have a partner. This is because (a) most real detectives work that way, with two heads being better – and safer – than one, and (b) it avoids your character having to talk to himself. In a detective partnership, you may want to have one being the hero and the other being the sidekick – effectively playing the 'buddy' or 'ally' role in the plot – or you may treat them as equal co-protagonists, having them share the work and the credit. Either way, you can use one or both of them as your viewpoint characters. If you're comfortable writing a multi-viewpoint story, I would go with that option as it gives you more flexibility – especially if you're planning to write a series and/or want to explore the lives of your characters away from the day job.

In a multiple storyline novel you will have two or more *pairs* of detectives who are protagonist-ally or co-protagonists of their particular investigation.

However many duos you have to create, you need to make it so that your reader knows which one is which. On television they have the blond one and the dark-haired one. In movies it is usually old cop and rookie cop. In novels you can use some combination of male/female, married/unmarried, idealistic/cynical, caring/combative, old-school/new-school, maverick/straight-laced, humorous/serious, healthy/hypochondriac... You can add more ideas to this list, but ideally you want something that characterises each of your story cops and makes them instantly recognisable each time they appear on the page.

With those general thoughts in mind, let's look at creating a procedural detective protagonist in more detail.

The Ordinary Mortal

I've said already that one of the conventions of the police procedural is that the detective is an 'ordinary mortal' rather than a superhero. He is not an intellectual genius like Sherlock Holmes and he is not a tough guy private eye who can withstand torture and multiple whacks on the head and still fight off the villain's henchmen and fulfil his role of knight-errant. The procedural detective is an ordinary person without exceptional abilities, just like you or me. Except he isn't really. But he has to *seem* that way.

We can make our hero seem ordinary by giving him a home life like ours; by having him complain about his job and his boss like we do; and by giving him the same values and prejudices that we have. We also make him a member of a team rather than a loner or outsider. We have to give the impression that he's like the guy next door getting up and going to his day job. Or nightshift.

But if you are going to write about ordinary men investigating everyday crimes, how do you avoid writing dull stories? Ironically, Keating and other writers have suggested that one of the key appeals of the procedural is the detective with his ordinary abilities and his ordinary life. Concentrate on the humanity of your policemen, Keating advises, "Think with them. Feel with them. Make them real people." Relationships between different members of the police department can be explored, as can those detective's homelife. And, he says, one advantage of these 'human interest' aspects is that they do not require research as they can be found by "looking into your own heart."

The public image of this type of detective – held by the common people and the media in both fact and fiction – suffers in comparison to Sherlock Holmes because he does not perform the same feats of deduction and seems uneducated, unimaginative and uncultured. This conforms to the opinion that Holmes held of Inspector Lestrade. He also suffers in comparison to James Bond and Philip Marlowe due to his lack of heroics. The world of the police procedural detective is seen as dull and shabby. The general opinion seems to be that these detectives are either inept or lazy and that this accounts for the rise in crime in society and the poor clear-up rate for reported crimes. And if the police are seen to take action, they are branded as heavy-handed and provocative. As a result, the police tend not to be held in high esteem, and even law-abiding citizens treat them with indifference, contempt, or hostility.

When it comes to self-image, the detective tends to see himself as flawed. He is anxious about the extent of his own abilities and decision-making skills. If he is young, he worries about his lack of experience. If he is older, he worries that age may be slowing him down and that he may be getting out of touch with both society and modern police techniques. If he has managed to reach a position of authority, he may worry about his own leadership skills and decision-making processes. He is plagued by self-doubt, afraid that he's failing as a detective, husband, father, son, brother, friend, and in any other role he sees himself occupying. At the same time, he wants to be able to see himself as competent and hard-working, taking pride in the professional standards he applies to his work in terms of dignity and respect, confidentiality, vigilance, pragmatism, and objectivity.

Lillian O'Donnell, who wrote a series of police procedurals featuring Nora Mulcahaney, was probably joking when she wrote that 'Procedurals are dull and their heroes are even duller.' But there is a question about how you are supposed to write an interesting story if your detective is an ordinary man who investigates an ordinary crime. The answer is, of course, that both detective and crime only *appear* to be ordinary. This allows us to satisfy the convention of apparent realism – or rather plausibility – while still being able to write a gripping story.

The trick is to establish that police work in general is a case of uninteresting people doing uninteresting tasks, but the specific case you are writing about is one of those rare exceptions that has an untypical protagonist investigating an unusual case. And you do that for all twenty books in your series and – if you do it well enough – the reader is prepared to go along with this. This allows us – as readers and writers – to have our cake and eat it. As well as having all of the characteristics of the 'ordinary mortal,' our detective is also allowed to demonstrate occasional flashes of deductive brilliance and, while generally shunning heroics, he is capable of occasional acts of heroism. When he does these things, George N. Dove says, the detective will surprise himself, reinforcing his own image of his ordinariness.

The Day Job
The procedural detective is doing his day job and as such his attitude towards it will have much in common to anyone else who has to go out to work every day. Our detective tends to regard his job as thankless and to dream of doing something more rewarding or of retiring to somewhere warm and peaceful. Most detectives in procedurals regard theirs as a 'dirty' job and say you have to be crazy to do it.

This attitude is generally expressed as a result of the frustrations that the detective feels – which arise as a result of his current case and of the nature of his job in general. These frustrations include a lack of clues or leads; an ever-increasing workload caused in part by lack of resources; being 'hamstrung' by laws, regulations, and bureaucratic red tape; lack of respect and assistance from the general public, and a court system that imposes short sentences or non-custodial sentences because the prisons are already over-crowded. Added to that is the fact that his job is not particularly well-paid and the hours are long. The detective will never express these frustrations to outsiders – they are only ever aired in front of colleagues and close family members.

Given this attitude towards their occupation, some thought has to be given to why your fictional detective doesn't just quit. He will probably talk about leaving and doing something more rewarding, but you need a reason for him to stay – especially if you want to write a series of books about him! He may stay because of job security and the promise of a pension at the end of it. The older he gets, the more significant that pension becomes to him. He may like the people he works with – that's a reason many people give for staying in a job they complain about. Simple inertia and dislike of change is another reason. Most detectives would probably say that they couldn't see themselves doing anything else or that they're not qualified to do anything else. And most would actually miss the lifestyle.

Some police detectives do quit and become private eyes – these are usually those with a stronger streak of the maverick in them. And some who retire early going into private security work – working for private companies as guards or night watchmen. We know this because in many police procedurals and private eye stories, the protagonist often runs into an old colleague in one of these positions and gets the information he needs because even ex-cops are still part of the fraternity and ready to provide favour.

To some extent, complaining about the job is something almost everyone does as a way to let off steam. Threatening to quit has a therapeutic function because it allows us to convince ourselves that we *could* quit at any time – if we wanted to. It helps us to believe that we are in control of our own destiny. It is one of those little lies we tell ourselves.

In the earliest police procedurals, the protagonists mostly seem to have become policemen because their father or favourite uncle was a policeman and they themselves never really had any ambitions to become anything else. And in those early stories detectives joined the force as a uniformed policeman, walked a beat, and gained experience on the job. This was the tradition and gut instinct was valued above a college education or technology. There is still an element of this in more recent police procedurals, especially among the older generation of detectives, but a college education and use of technology are much more common than they were. But while the desktop computer has replaced the old typewriter, detectives still hate keeping records and writing reports.

Personality Archetype
If we want to consider our detective in terms of the personality archetypes I wrote about in *Character Creation*, which of the six does he most resemble? The protagonist in a police procedural is most likely to be a Warrior. We have said that he lacks the deductive/reasoning skills of Sherlock Holmes and that means the Thinker archetype is not a significant element in his personality. This also rules out his being a Crusader who is a Warrior-Thinker hybrid.

There is a question as to what extent the Carer influences the personality of this character. He is a public servant whose job is helping others – to 'protect and serve' – and so we would expect the Carer to be present. The relative importance of *belonging* to the police fraternity and the fact that he is typically a married man also suggest the influence of the Carer.

Although he is a Warrior, which brings to mind an image of a soldier and so fits with the idea of the police being a military-like organisation, the detective is typically a soldier rather than a military officer. Uniformed policemen serve in the trenches while detectives have achieved the status of specialists but not leaders. In most police *detective* novels, the protagonist tends to be serious and professional; but in the police *procedural* he is more likely to be a bit of a maverick – getting his job done by subverting the rules to some extent. Such detectives often find themselves being warned by their captains to reign in their rebellious nature. The rebel in this case, I would suggest, comes from the Adventurer archetype, a Warrior-Carer hybrid. The rebel isn't a major part of our detective's character – unless you're writing something like a *Beverly Hills Cop*-style comedy – but there is a hint of the maverick in him.

Alienation
Detectives have to deal with abnormal people – with the worst aspects of human nature – and so they sometimes feel ashamed of their profession when they are not with other cops. This can also lead them to withdraw from any form of social life that doesn't include other policemen and this can lead to a sense of social isolation.

Coupled with this is the problem that since they deal with criminals on a daily basis, they are more likely to recognise the everyday 'crimes' committed by people around them. Cops tend to suspect *everyone* because in their work it can be fatal if they don't. And they may end up carrying the work-related fear, distrust, and contempt into their home lives. And at its worst, this can lead to paranoia.

Police detectives work long hours and even when they are at home or out grocery shopping, they may feel that they are never really off-duty. Being a policeman isn't a nine-to-five job, it defines who the detective is – and this can ultimately lead to a loss of identity: he is no longer a person, he is a cop.

Personal Values

George N. Dove's book *The Police Procedural* was published in 1982 and covers novels published between the 1940s and end of the 1970s. These novels tended to reflect the public values of the decades in which they were published. Based on these novels, Dove summarised the sorts of values held by police detectives.

These men were middle-middle or lower-middle class and held conservative middle-class values, especially in terms of social behaviour, morality, and the importance of family life. Most detectives had worked on the street at uniformed police officers and 'worked their way up.' They valued practical experience – 'street smarts' over book learning – and had a tendency to be anti-intellectual. They distrusted 'experts,' especially sociologists, psychiatrists, and criminologists and were suspicious of abstract theories and statistics, preferring to trust their own gut instincts and first-hand experience on the 'front line.' They also tended to complain about liberal 'bleeding hearts' and 'do-gooders' who seemed to value the rights of criminals above those of victims. And they tended to demonstrate prejudice against minority groups.

During that period, police detectives tended to be white and male so that the detective squad was not representative of the racial and gender mix of the geographical area in which it operated.

It is almost forty years since Dove's book was published and things have changed somewhat in the real and fictional worlds of the police detective. In large cities in America and Britain, the racial mix within the detective squad will more closely match that of the city it serves and there will be more female detectives than was the case in the 1970s. In some smaller communities, it may be the case that most detectives are still male and white. This is something you would need to check for the location you choose for your novel.

Today it is much more common for detectives to be university graduates and fewer detectives come from the uniformed ranks, though again this is something that you would need to research for a particular area. Detectives are also much more open to using technology and science and rely less on 'old school' methods. Whether or not detectives are less conservative in terms of their personal values is something else which may be dependent on location.

Teamwork

Most of the heroes we explore in the *Genre Writer* series are individuals who take charge of their own situation and seek to solve their own problems. The reason why this sort of character appeals to readers and audiences for all genres is that we all like to feel that we are responsible for our own lives – we can choose who and what we want to be. Our fiction heroes serve as models of our own autonomy. The romance genre is an exception in that it shows how two people – joint protagonists – resolve their individual differences in order to make their relationship work.

But while we are all seeking autonomy, we are also social beings and seek some form of *belonging*. We want to feel that we are part of a larger community or family and that our individual qualities and abilities are respected by and contribute to the group. Some stories emphasise group membership and the specialisms and character differences of different group members. The heist movie, as we'll see later, is one example where criminals with different skills work together for a common goal. And the police procedural story is another example. The detective in a police procedural story will demonstrate both heroic individualism but also the ability to work with others and to respect the fact that they have skills and experience that he lacks. He may also need to demonstrate the ability to serve as a 'warrior' who is able to contribute to the strategic plans of his leader.

The Villain & The Crime

Hillary Waugh has said that the traditional whodunit and the private eye novel both pit an exceptional hero against a murderer who is some sort of 'evil genius.' In the police procedural, the detective is a man of ordinary abilities and the villain is not a criminal mastermind – he (or she) is also an ordinary person. H.R.F. Keating describes the traditional whodunit as being a duel between a brilliantly clever murderer and a genius detective. The villain has to be brilliant in order to provide an adequate challenge to the Great Detective. In the procedural, the murderer's opponent doesn't need to provide a challenge at that level. It is more a matter of being able to bluff in a card game rather than play chess at grandmaster level.

In many stories, the identity of the murderer – or at least the chief suspect – is established relatively early. The work of the detective then becomes obtaining sufficient evidence to secure a prosecution. Michael Gilbert has suggested that in a real-life murder investigation a quarter of the difficulty is identifying and charging the murderer and three-quarters of it is being able to prove the case against them such that it 'stand up' in court. He quotes a retired CID officer as saying "If you want to know what a murder story really is, I'll tell you. It's a few hundred statements, a few hours interrogating the man you're going to charge, with a cup of cold coffee in one hand and Judges' Rules in the other, a day in court having your character torn to pieces by defending counsel, and a fifty-fifty chance of success."

If you write a procedural where the identity of the murderer is not revealed until the end, H.R.F. Keating advises that you follow the tradition of the whodunit – "your reader will be disappointed if the murderer has not been 'seen' at an early stage in the book, however unlike real life that may be."

The crimes typically investigated by real detectives are physical assaults, rapes, and domestic murders. Most police procedural novels involve these same crimes along with kidnappings or child abduction, gang-related murders, and – very rarely – serial killings.

Romantic Co-Protagonist

The detective hero of the police procedural is, unlike the consulting detective or private eye, usually married and often happily so. Dove writes that this is the 'rule rather than the exception' and that it is also part of the convention that the detective suffers the same sorts of worries as any other husband and father including financial concerns and conflicts with rebellious teenage children. Family problems can affect a detective's performance on the job.

In the traditional whodunit, the 'ordinary world' that the detective seeks to protect and return to equilibrium is typically represented by a young couple who are in love. In the police procedural, this world is more often seen in terms of the detective's home life. Protecting his wife and children – and other ordinary folks like them – are the reason he chooses to do the job that he does. The hero in the procedural novel is not an outsider, he has a vested interest in protecting his community. Some detectives, almost inevitably, are separated or divorced.

Writing about clichés to avoid, Dell Shannon said that the "detective's wife-who-wants-him-to-quit-because-it's-dangerous has been met a bit too often..."

Considering romantic relationships more generally in the police procedural, and particularly in the multi-storyline structure, we often see quite a few minor romantic subplots. Cops may date cops or people from other agencies – paramedics, lawyers, firemen, FBI agents, or whatever. Or cops may date witnesses or victims of crimes. They might even date suspects or criminals. These relationships may occur between characters within a single criminal investigation or between characters from different investigations – so a detective from one storyline may become romantically involved with a suspect from another detective's case, for example.

There may also be relationships that do not include a detective – criminals date criminals, criminals date lawyers, paramedics, victims or witnesses. A character from one novel – whatever their role in that story – may reappear in a later novel as someone's romantic partner. A relationship may begin, perhaps shakily, in one book and develop in subsequent books in the series. And a book might show a relationship from an earlier story ending.

Obviously, the more continuing characters you have in a series, the more possible permutations you have for relationships. Some of these relationships are inadvisable and some are obviously doomed from the start – but these are often the ones that are more interesting to explore in a story.

Other Characters & Character Development

With a detective or pair of detectives as your protagonists, there is usually little or no opportunity for character development – particularly if you are writing a series. Even across the span of a series, character personalities rarely develop very much beyond the fact that a young, idealistic detective may become more cynical as he grows older and wiser. There may be some *situational* development in a character's home life or relationships – detectives get married or divorced, they have children, children become rebellious teenagers etc. – but there is no appreciable character arc. This is pretty much the nature of all series characters and many genre characters in one-off stories.

But you *can* have a character development arc for a minor character – a victim or witness to a crime, for example, who finds themselves changed as a result of their experience. Or you may have a character who gradually come to feel – perhaps during the course of several books – that police work isn't for them, climaxing in their decision to leave the force.

Victims, Suspects & Witnesses. These are the ordinary people or street criminals that appear in stories but are not major or continuing characters.

They function in much the same way as their counterparts in the private eye novel and the whodunit. Victims here aren't restricted solely to murder victims, as police detectives may be involved in investigating many different types of crime, including domestic abuse, sexual and physical assault, robbery and burglary, and any other crime found in a modern city. I have written more about suspects and witnesses in the chapter on interviewing and interrogating.

The Mentor. Either an older *relative* or close family friend who was a cop and who influenced the detective's choice of career. Ed McBain also refers to the 'rabbi' –a well-placed friend or relative, who is in a position to advance a policeman's career.

The Informant. In the police procedural, Hillary Waugh has said that "...a detective is only as good as his informants..." The information provided by an informant is often more important to the progress of an investigation than a physical clue. Because the informant is also found in other types of crime thriller, I have covered this type of character in a separate chapter.

Tone

Early examples of the police procedural aimed for documentary-style realism – imagine a crime-scene photograph brought to life. As a result, the sub-genre gained a reputation for being grim and occasionally sordid. 'Gritty realism' is still the tone some writers aim for – particularly in showing the reality of the aftermath of violence and other forms of crime. But it is now more common to find an element of ironic and/or macabre humour in these stories.

People who deal on a regular basis with injury and death often develop a sort of gallows humour as a way of dealing with it. You see this in emergency room doctors, the autopsy room, and among mortuary workers. Policemen develop it too.

Humour is also a way of dealing with our own disappointments and disillusionment in life. Idealism and enthusiasm are often replaced, in various walks of life, with world-weariness and cynicism. And we tend to reflect this in a sort of cynical or sarcastic humour.

The fact that life – real life – isn't fair and often doesn't make sense is another reason why we turn to humour. How else can you deal with a world filled with corrupt politicians and businessmen, starving babies, and people with mental health issues thrown out onto the streets? Innocent people are often found guilty and guilty people are freed by the courts. The wealthy seem to have a better chance of seeing 'justice' than do the poor. And one bad choice can ruin an entire life. How do you cope with this unless you can resort to a sort of ironic humour?

The randomness of life and the bizarre and absurd situations it occasionally throws up – especially if you're a policeman operating in the community – can sometimes only be dealt with if you have a sense of humour: it isn't a matter of callousness or bad taste, it is a matter of protecting your own mental wellbeing.

The humour in police procedurals isn't quite at the level of the wisecracks of the private detective. It is more wry and has an element of resignation – a shoulder shrug – 'This is what life is like – what can you do about it except deal with it?' Imagine yourself in the position of the people who have to deal with our garbage day in day out or sort out problems with our sewage system – the daily life of a policeman is often more like that than it is the life of a detective in a whodunit. You really have *got* to laugh.

Themes

Moral Values

Dell Shannon believed that the detective novel was "the morality play of the twentieth century" and that while it was no longer crude black versus white, it still dealt "primarily with basics: with truth versus lie, law and order versus anarchy, a moral code versus amorality." The good guys were the law officers and they always came out on top. "I try to involve the reader *from the police viewpoint*. For I believe that this is no more than the duty of those of us who have taken sides, as it were, in the never-ending struggle between good and evil."

Elizabeth Linington, the woman behind the Dell Shannon pen name, was also a right-wing political activist and member of the John Birch Society, and she had strong views on the 'amorality' of the century in which she lived. Her views on the purpose of the police procedural novel have to be viewed in this light. "The police-routine novel ... makes an emotional connection between the reader and the police," she wrote. "When the evil forces of conspiracy, encouragement of lawlessness, are today making the police officer's job a thousand per cent more difficult, it is salutary that somewhere, in some fashion, the upright forces of law and order should be shown as 'the good guys' – which they largely are. I do not mean to say that we writers in this field should show police officers as winged and haloed, but as they really are..."

George N. Dove refers to this viewpoint as "...the myth of the Moral Absolutes..." and says that while the policeman is employed to defend society, he may privately wonder whether it is worth defending. The detective in the police procedural also knows that he is fighting a never-ending battle in which good does not ultimately triumph.

The College of Policing in the UK produces ethical guidance: www.college.police.uk/What-we-do/Ethics/Documents/Code_of_Ethics.pdf

The Police & Society

It is the policeman's job to 'protect and serve' the community that employs him. He is an officer of the law, upholding the rules that society has put in place so that people can live together in harmony – or as close to harmony as possible.

As mentioned above, the police detective is not an outsider with an objective viewpoint and a mission to restore equilibrium to a community, the police detective and his family are members of the community.

Society as a whole, and smaller communities within it, are hierarchical. The policeman often has to deal with a complex web of official and unofficial hierarchies. It is rarely a good idea for him to upset the wealthy or the powerful – but sometimes that is what the job requires.

Attitudes of Society to the Police

Criminals may regard the police as 'the enemy' or as an occupational hazard, but the policeman usually knows where he stands with them. Attitudes of ordinary people towards the police are more difficult to assess – as, indeed, is the attitude of the policeman towards ordinary people.

To a doctor, a lawyer, or even a private eye, the person they work for – who pays their fee – is a *client*. But the policeman does not have this sort of relationship with the public he serves and whose taxes pay his wages. And at the same time, he is a member of the same community who also pays taxes. He is, paradoxically, too close to and yet distanced from the people he serves. Which, as Dove notes, leads to feelings of ambivalence and alienation. "His responsibility is to his lieutenant or chief, and his loyalty is to his fellow cops."

Public attitudes towards the police are equally ambivalent. Even ordinary, law-abiding citizens can be suspicious or afraid of policemen. Just the sight of a policeman is enough to make many of us feel anxious and guilty, afraid that we will be punished for some minor infraction. Someone who's recently received a parking ticket or a speeding fine will feel they have a grievance against all policemen everywhere. And someone whose property has suffered vandalism and theft is going to feel aggrieved because the police have 'done nothing' to prevent such crime or solve this particular instance.

Other people may see the police as representatives of an 'Establishment' that that does not treat all citizens fairly – defending the rights of only the wealthy and the powerful. They may even regard criminals as modern-day Robin Hoods, champions of the underdog or the oppressed. While others look down on policemen, regarding them as 'jumped up civil servants,' and if challenged by them will point a finger and say, 'I'm a taxpayer, I pay your wages.'

Many people regard the police as a 'necessary evil' and even those who are opposed to them or feel aggrieved by them will probably call the police if they find themselves the victim of a crime.

Any of these feelings can mean that ordinary people don't want to get involved in 'police business,' to the extent that witnesses don't want to share what they have seen and victims don't want to report crimes. There is also a fear that the bureaucracy of the police and the court system can take up a lot of your time, even if you're only a witness, and cross-examination in court is going to leave you feeling as though you're being regarded as a criminal rather than someone participating in a process intended to secure justice for a victim.

These attitudes are part of the reason why policemen feel alienated from the ordinary public. Another reason is that they spend so little time with ordinary people since most of their working day is spent dealing with suspects, criminals, or others involved in law enforcement and the legal system. In some cases, the police detective may feel that he has more in common with criminals than he does with the public he serves.

Attitudes of the Police to Society

Like the private eye, the police detective operates in a world that the average person doesn't see and doesn't understand. And part of their role is to protect people from it – to the extent that they would prefer that ordinary, law-abiding citizens never came into contact with it. The police detective rarely shares the full reality of his working life with his wife and children. This is part of the reason why police officers only talk about their work with their fellow-officers – because they understand what the 'real world' is like. This can mean that police detectives regard ordinary members of society as naïve and/or over-protected or unrealistic in their belief that justice will prevail and expectation that all crimes will be solved.

The Law versus Justice

In the case of the police detective, the obligation to uphold the law is much stronger than it is for the Great Detective or the private eye, who have more freedom to see that justice, according to their own moral code, is served.

But while the police do not generally question the validity of the laws they are employed to enforce, they may express concerns in the way in which people from different backgrounds are treated within the legal system and – as a public servant paid for by taxpayers – may feel it is wrong that people with wealth and power can 'buy' justice or escape prosecution.

There are occasions when the application of formal legal procedures is not the most effective way of dealing with a situation – either because the situation isn't sufficiently serious to warrant it or because the legal system would not deliver genuine justice. In the first category is the drunken street brawl where both parties are equally at fault. Is it the public interest to arrest and prosecute the men? Or would it be better for the beat officer to give them both a stern talking to and send them on their way? Given that hundreds of such situations occur every week, the justice system would not be able to cope if each one was dealt with formally. In more serious situations, the degree to which policemen or detectives should be allowed to exercise their discretion is less clear-cut.

One reason why the police detective has less freedom to apply his own brand of moral justice is the fact that, unlike the amateur sleuth, he works in a system alongside colleagues and overseen by superiors and the system is designed to ensure, as far as possible, that the law is applied objectively and fairly, with no one person taking the role of judge, jury, and executioner.

Sub-Rosa Justice

The legal system is not perfect and there are occasions when criminals cannot be brought to justice and when, due to a variety of circumstances, the courts allow guilty persons to go free. The sheer volume of cases and the fact that finite resources mean that not everyone who should be imprisoned can be locked up. The police are more aware of these weaknesses in the system than anyone. For this reason, the police in real life, and more so in fiction, have unofficial methods for trying to maintain order and, on occasion, dispense justice. These methods tend to be based on what the police community mutually regard as morally appropriate and just.

George N. Dove refers to this as a 'sub-rosa' system of justice. The police effectively circumvent formal legal procedures and police regulations and take matters into their own hands. Illegal searches, which seem to occur almost routinely in stories, are one example of the law being broken because it is considered to be 'in the public good.' How far can this unofficial system of justice go? Dove suggests that the police may make judgments about guilt or innocence and even provide an appropriate punishment. If it proves impossible to obtain the evidence to prove a criminal guilty of one crime, they may seek to frame him for another.

The ultimate punishment in this system is death. Executions are rarely carried out, even if it is clear that a murderer will escape justice – but the police may pass word on to someone who will do it for them – a rival gang or someone with a grievance against the offender. But this lies at the extreme of the sub-rosa system. How far you allow the system to go in your own stories is up to you.

While sub-rosa justice might be considered to exist in a moral grey area, there are other types of police behaviour that definitely fall into the criminal area. I include mention of them below because they exist in the real world – you must decide to what extent they should be a part of your fictional world. Remember that a corrupt police officer doesn't have to be a hero or anti-hero, they can serve as villain or antagonist.

Police Wrongdoing – Corruption, Brutality & Prejudice

Corruption

The Knapp Commission was an investigation into corruption in the New York City Police Department in the early 1970s. Its report said that there are two types of corrupt police officer – the *meat-eaters*, who "aggressively misuse their police powers for personal gain", and *grass-eaters*, who "simply accept the payoffs that the happenstances of police work throw their way."

A number of types of police corruption have been identified:

Gratuities – complimentary drinks, meals, and other free stuff received solely because someone is a police officer.

Extortion / Bribery – demanding or receiving payment in order to overlook a past or future criminal offence. Services provided by policemen for such payment may include protection from arrest, ticket fixing, altering testimony in court, destruction or loss of evidence, and provision of privileged information or tip-offs. Includes 'shakedowns' where payment is demanded for not arresting an offender.

Theft – Unlawful removal of property from a crime scene, victim, or criminal. Includes 'confiscation' of drugs. May also include theft from the police department's evidence room.

'Fixing' – Undermining criminal prosecutions by destroying or 'losing' evidence, by watering down or ineptly providing testimony in court, or by-passing information to the defence. Fixing may be done for payment or as a favour.

Perjury – lying in court to protect him or herself or a fellow officer or a known offender.

'Frame-ups' – Planting or manipulating evidence to increase the likelihood of a person being charged and/or convicted.

Ticket Fixing – Cancelling traffic tickets as a favour to family or friends.

Brutality

Use of excessive force by law enforcement officers when dealing with criminals, suspects, or members of the public – including use by police of batons, tasers, tear gas, pepper spray, and firearms. Includes public protests, arrest-related deaths and death whilst in police custody. Complaints made against police officers in England and Wales are investigated by the Independent Office for Police Conduct (IOPC). In the USA such complaints are typically handled by internal police commissions and/or district attorneys. Amnesty International investigates and highlights police brutality around the world and civilian organisations such as 'Cop Watch' also monitor police activity. Increased use of smartphones for video recording of police activity and use of body cameras by police officers mean that better evidence can now be provided by both sides.

Racial Prejudice

In both the USA and the UK, official statistics show that a disproportionate percentage of non-white persons are subject to arrest, stop and search/frisk, police brutality, death in custody, and – in the USA – shooting by police officers. The shooting of unarmed black men and incidents such as the beating of Rodney King in 1991 have led to public protests, including the 'Black Lives Matter' campaign and even riots. The 1981 riot in Brixton area of South London was also caused by tensions between African-Caribbean community and the Metropolitan Police Force – a report commissioned by the British government concluded that there had been disproportionate and indiscriminate use of 'stop and search' powers by the police against black people in the period before the riot. And a report into the police investigation into the murder of black teenager Stephen Lawrence in 1999 concluded that the Metropolitan Police Service was 'institutionally racist.' An independent Police Complaints Authority was set up to investigate incidents involving police officers and this has become the Independent Office for Police Conduct (IOPC).

Internal Affairs
In the United States police misconduct by individual officers is handled by internal affairs departments within a police force. Internal commissions and/or district attorneys may investigate allegations involving multiple officers and on occasion, a city mayor may instigate an independent commission to investigate. In the most extreme circumstances, where federal crimes may have been committed, the FBI will investigate.

In England and Wales, alleged misconduct by individual officers is investigated by a police force's own professional standards department, overseen by the Independent Office for Police Conduct (IOPC). The IOPC was set up as a result of the *Policing and Crime Act 2017*. It conducts independent investigations of serious allegations of misconduct or criminal offences by law enforcement officers and complaints against police forces. It also conducts investigations if a person dies during or following police contact. See www.policeconduct.gov.uk

The Never-Ending Tide of Crime
We've already noted that in the whodunit, a murder investigation is a one-off unique event that impacts on a self-contained community, but that in the police procedural the crime is just one in an ongoing series that makes up the detective's day job. It's a tide that may ebb and flow, but it never actually stops. We've also acknowledged that multiple cases can occur at the same time and that some cases inevitably remain unsolved. This results in two important conventions in the police procedural sub-genre. First, the police are overworked – there are always too many cases and not enough detectives to work on them. And second, shortage of manpower means that detectives are under pressure to solve a case as quickly as possible and move on to the next one. George N. Dove refers to this as the 'tyranny of time'. This pressure means that if a case cannot be solved quickly, it may have to be set aside and as a result, it may never be solved at all.

I mentioned above that in real life, murders are often committed in the heat of the moment by someone closely related to the victim so that the identity of the murderer and the motive for the killing can be discovered quite quickly. There is no mystery to investigate. This leads to something that is often said in police procedurals – If the murder isn't solved within forty-eight hours, it probably won't be solved at all. This, in turn, acts as a sort of assumed deadline that puts the detectives under pressure to achieve results quickly.

Time-pressure – a deadline or a countdown or a rising tide – is a way of heightening the suspense in any story. It can be applied in the procedural in a number of ways. Superior officers often put pressure on their detectives simply because of the sheer volume of cases that need to be dealt with. Where the amateur detective or private eye takes on only one or two cases at a time, a police department receives new cases every day and that means only a finite amount of time can be allocated to each one. A detective also probably has several open cases at any one time. Political pressure can also be applied – particularly if, say, a governor or district attorney is campaigning for re-election or if the victim of the crime has wealthy and powerful friends or relatives.

Circumstances may also dictate rapid action – the uniformed officers making door to door enquiries may be available for only a short period before they are assigned to another task such as policing a sporting event, presidential visit, or political rally. The investigation of a child abduction or a kidnapping has time-pressure built into it.

Public pressure may also be applied in some cases with newspaper headlines asking, 'Why haven't the police caught this maniac?' There may be accusations of incompetence, collusion, or wasting public money.

It is actually very rare for the major crime in a police procedural to be solved within a forty-eight-hour timeframe. J.J. Marric's *Gideon's Day* takes place during the course of a single day as does Ed McBain's *Hail, Hail, the Gang's All Here!* But most stories unfold over a period of a month or more. Minor cases that make up subplots may be cleared up more quickly – or may even go unsolved.

The Police Force

The policeman is a public servant whose job is to maintain law and order. The nature of this occupation makes it a combination of military organisation and civil service department – and a combination of the best and worst qualities of both of these.

The Hierarchy

If you are going to write about a professional police department or force, you will need to have an understanding of its hierarchical structure. While the civil service is also obsessively stratified and hierarchical, the hierarchy in the police – including its use of different 'ranks' and uniforms – is closer to the military model, especially in the USA. The structure of a police department varies from country to country and within different areas within individual countries, so I am not going to attempt to describe the possible permutations here. You can find details online of the hierarchy for the force or department you are using in your story – or for the one you are using as a basis for your fictional one. If you want to have a look at an example, try the *Wikipedia* entry for 'New York City Police Department.'

If you have ever worked in a hierarchical organisation of any type, you can bring this experience to writing about the police. Certain things are common to all hierarchies.

A hierarchy is a power structure – the higher up you are, the more power you wield. People lower than you in the 'pecking order' have to obey instructions that you give to them and they must (or should) treat you with the respect as a result of the status you have achieved. Within a hierarchy, there are *official* channels along which communications – information and requests for information – are meant to pass. And in every hierarchy, ways are found to subvert these official channels.

Hierarchies also present opportunities for promotion to higher positions and – usually – increased pay. The higher up in the structure you look, the fewer positions are available, and so competition for these positions becomes more intense. And the more likely 'internal politics' are to be a part of who gets the vacant slot. Personal ambitions can develop into feuds and can have a detrimental effect on the teamwork necessary to get the job done effectively. Threats of blocking a promotion – or of demotion – can be used to keep employees in line or to intimidate them. And those who do not 'toe the line' can be punished by being assigned to undesirable duties – in police stories detectives are frequently being threatened with 'traffic duty' or being busted back to walking the beat.

The larger an organisation becomes, the more regulations are put in place to govern the behaviours of the people working there. For policemen, there are the regulations and codes of conduct within their own force or department and the wider regulations of the legal system in which they operate. These rules are intended to ensure consistency and fairness, to protect the policeman as well as the rights of the suspect or criminal, but in practice, police detectives often feel that the rules hamper their investigations and ways of getting around or bending the rules without breaking them are sought. Every individual's need for autonomy also means they have a hint of the rebel or maverick in them with a desire to avoid being controlled or restricted by another person or 'the system.'

A hierarchical system governed by restrictive rules coupled with work that is often repetitive and boring provides a need for employees to vent their frustration. This is true for the military and it is true for the police. Banter and horseplay are a part of this, as are friendly rivalries, insults, pranks, and petty acts of revenge. These things also help to foster camaraderie and may be used as a way of dealing with the tensions and horrors that policemen sometimes face. Related to this may be initiation rites for new recruits.

In any large organisation, a grapevine develops and rumours circulate. A police force is no exception. This informal communication channel can sometimes conflict with the official need for confidentiality or secrecy and jeopardise the work of the department.

Cliques and strategic friendships are also formed in large organisations. Knowing the 'right person' often means that you can avoid the usual bureaucracy or 'red tape' to get the information or resource that you need. A system of favours owed and repaid is also an important part of the unofficial network within the department.

Specialisation within large organisations – especially unionised ones – means care must be taken to respect another person or team's 'territory.' Within a single team, geographical territory – 'our patch' – may be jealously guarded and people talk about 'owning' a particular case or investigation.

Status & Internal Rivalry

As well as affecting the relationships between people in the same organisation, status – a person's position in the hierarchy – affects relationships between people from different organisations. The higher rank of someone from another organisation has to be respected, and that person is also in the position of being able to 'pull rank' if they want to. As in any hierarchical organisation, some people enjoy dominating and humiliating those who are lower down the pecking order. Also, someone who has just been denigrated by their superior may turn around and take it out on someone subordinate to them.

People of the same or similar rank typically have to work more closely and participate in the exchange of favours, so their relationships tend to be more along the lines of friendly rivalry. Lieutenants, medical examiners, and lab personnel interact at more or less the same level.

A Brotherhood or Close-Knit Community

Police detectives and uniformed officers are often portrayed as belonging to a sort of fraternity in which they not only work together but also mix socially. They band together for protection not only against the criminal world but also against the ordinary public who are often suspicious of or hostile towards the police.

This attitude of belonging to a special group whose experiences cannot possibly be understood by outsiders is something policemen share with soldiers. There is a sort of siege mentality, a feeling of being under attack on all sides, and of having to 'look after your own.' This feeling of 'specialness' means policemen have a sort of superior attitude, looking down on ordinary people who do not understand what it is 'really like out there.' In this sense, they are similar to the characters I wrote about in *Suspense Thriller* who are aware of a conspiracy – of another world that ordinary people know nothing about.

The police fraternity has typically been shown as overtly masculine and includes the same sort of hazing, pranks, and heavy drinking as its military or college counterparts.

A clear rule of the police community is that it is closed and civilians – other than family members – do not *belong* in it and must be kept out. Officers do not discuss their fears, weaknesses, or mistakes in front of civilians. Civilians cannot be trusted. The lowest-ranking policeman is welcome where the highest-ranking civilian is not. One upshot of this is that the only places that a policeman feels safe to relax are at home and at headquarters.

Members of this police fraternity or band of brothers are fiercely loyal to one another – to the extent that loyalty to the group takes precedence over adherence to police regulations (membership of the department) and to the community they serve (membership of the wider society). A consequence of this is that policemen will protect one of their own even if he has made a mistake or done something wrong – even if the something is illegal. Superior officers may also cover for their subordinates. In the USA this is sometimes referred to as the blue wall of silence, blue code or blue shield.

If an officer is guilty or suspected of committing a crime, his colleagues will still seek to cover for him or defend him. The nature of the crime will determine the level of inner conflict – duty to the law versus duty to a brother – that other officers feel. Like the hero of a Legal Thriller, the protagonist in a police procedural has a somewhat ambivalent attitude to the law. Detectives, especially on television shows, seem to regularly engage in illegal searches of suspects' homes. Some help themselves to stolen goods or expect 'favours' from criminals and honest businessmen. There are apparently acceptable degrees of police corruption – with 'graft' being regarded as 'clean' money, at least in the police world of some stories, in comparison to 'dirty money' which comes from other activities. One cop's attitude toward the criminal activities of another – whether he informs on or accuses him – will depend on whether the offender is regarded as having 'betrayed' the fraternity. If other cops have been harmed as a result of an individual's actions, he may earn the label 'dirty cop' and find himself an outcast.

A problem with this loyalty to fellow officers arises when the public becomes aware that the police band together to protect their own resulting in feelings of distrust or a suspicion that policemen regard themselves as above the law. Sometimes this public suspicion is justified. The 1973 movie *Serpico*, based on Peter Maas's biography of Frank Serpico, a policeman who went undercover to investigate police corruption, explores this aspect of the police community.

The attitudes of policemen also vary in terms of what level of violence or intimidation they regard as being acceptable in their treatment of criminals and suspects. One man's 'reasonable force' is another man's police brutality. The level of violence in a story is one of the things that determines its tone (see below).

Defence of a fellow officer also occurs in the more literal sense and at a more official level. If a policeman finds himself in danger or under threat, his comrades will come to his assistance, dispatched as a matter of urgency. He can always rely on the fact that someone has 'got his back.'

We can think of the policeman's world in terms of concentrate circles – the outer ring is society as a whole; within that is what Dove calls the Police Establishment, and within that is the fellowship of police officers who will, if necessary, subvert the authority of the Department to protect each other. And the fellowship is such that they will do this even for colleagues who they personally dislike – loyalty to one's fellows transcends personal animosity.

Death in the Line of Duty

Another situation that brings the loyalty within the police community to the fore is the killing of a policeman. No matter what his fellow officers thought of him when he was alive, his death galvanises them into action. There is an element of revenge in the actions that go into the investigation and there is a risk that objectivity and professionalism may be sacrificed as a result.

The Detective's Role

The consulting detective in the whodunit and the hardboiled private eye both work alone and have no superior to report to. They are also self-contained in that they know everything they need to do their job and undertake all of the tasks needed to complete the investigation. The role of the detective in the police procedural – and in real life – is very different from this. He is a member of a team and has all the resources of a police department behind him. This means that he doesn't search the crime scene for clues, a specialist team does this, and whatever they find is taken away for analysis in the police laboratory. The police detective doesn't have to knock on every door in a street or an apartment block to interview witnesses – a team of uniformed officers will make the initial enquiries and the detectives will then sift through their reports and decide which witnesses to question further. And if a kidnap victim or a criminal gang is located, he doesn't have to break down the door to make an arrest, a SWAT team (or the equivalent) has the equipment for that.

One disadvantage of teamwork is that it can discourage detectives from taking risks for fear of making a fool of themselves. They might not speak up when they have an idea no one else has thought of, perhaps because it is a little off the wall, or it might prevent them from making intuitive leaps or proposing new theories.

Compared to the consulting detective and the private eye, the procedural detective suffers a number of disadvantages. Unlike them, he cannot refuse to accept cases that do not appeal to him – investigating crime is his *job* and he has to take every case that drops on his desk. He also doesn't have the same flexibility as them to disregard the law – or to act as judge, jury, and (perhaps) executioner. Police detectives have to obey the law and follow the rules regarding evidence and the questioning of suspects, otherwise he risks having his evidence discounted when the case comes to trial. He will also work long hours and may be called up at any time of day or night – he is never really off-duty. Police departments also have incredible workloads and not enough staff to keep on top of it – and this pressure can affect a detective's health and home life, and it can also have an impact on how well he can do his job.

But there are also advantages to being a police detective – they have job security which the private eye doesn't have and they also get insurance and a pension. And if he gets into trouble, the police detective can call for back-up and know that it will be sent immediately. And even if the worst happens and he is killed, the police detective will get a proper funeral and his colleagues will do everything they can to bring his killer to justice.

The procedural detective has access to official databases that are not accessible to outsiders. And the authority that comes with his job has other benefits – as an *official* investigator, he can obtain permission to enter premises and conduct searches and he can gain warrants that allow him to bring in suspects for questioning. Their authority also means that people may be more likely to offer information so as to avoid any official unpleasantness. Uncooperative members of the criminal world know that a policeman can make life difficult for them.

With all of the procedures and resources available to the professional police detective, the odds seem to be stacked against the criminal. But the one thing that a police department lacks is the time necessary to deal with all of the crimes that occur in their territory. And each new procedure or resource brings with it an increase in the amount of available information that needs to be sifted through and evaluated.

The fact that the procedural detective works as a member of a team has one other disadvantage for the writer – you can't just throw in a surprise attack on the detective by the murderer to liven things up. The fact that the consulting detective and the private eye work alone means that they individually pose a threat to the villain – such that the villain may decide to try and bump them off. But the procedural detective shares his information with his co-workers and his superior rather than keeping it all in his head – if he is killed, someone else can pick up where he left off.

Much of the day-to-day work carried out by police detectives is repetitious and boring. Dull administrative routines – keeping accurate records – take up a lot of time. A lot of time is also spent waiting around – whether that is sitting around in a car on a stakeout or hanging around the courthouse waiting to be called to give evidence in a trial.

Rivalry Between Departments & Agencies

There are rivalries between different teams or squads within a department and between the police and other agencies. These rivalries can be used to add conflict, obstacles, and/or humour to your story.

Any publicly-funded organisation is in competition for tax-payers' money and has to prove itself both worthy of and in need of increased funding – this is true whether funding is provided locally or nationally. Proving your worth is a matter of public and political recognition, credit, and reputation. Fighting to obtain or to keep these can put agencies into conflict.

The flip-side of this is the battle to avoid blame for failure and to avoid having your agency's workload increased or made more difficult by rival agencies. The police can find themselves at odds with the court system, the prison and probation systems, healthcare – especially in terms of mental health – and social welfare.

Antagonism in the police procedural is usually based on one of three things – status, territory, or trust/friendship.

Negative Effects of Rivalry
Some of the negative consequences of inter-agency conflict have already been covered above. Another result of it is that those who supervise teams – and this is true of any organisation – find themselves engaged in a form of diplomacy in order to keep the peace and encourage rivals to work together to achieve a common law enforcement goal. Obviously, this requires a leader to set aside his own feelings about the rival agency, which is more difficult for some than others. The greater one's status in the hierarchy, the more one has to deal with the politics of situations.

Positive Effects of Rivalry
Rivalry also has some positive consequences for law enforcement. If an individual or team feel that they are in competition with a rival, they tend to work more efficiently and put in the extra effort necessary to 'win.' This can serve to build morale and promote teamwork. Friendly rivalry also acts as a safety valve for frustration and other negative emotion that people may feel if they feel threatened.

Trust/Friendship
Personal friendships also have an impact on the relationships between different departments or agencies. Policemen who have worked together before or trained together at 'the academy' are likely to have a level of trust that does not exist between strangers.

Territoriality
Some departments in law enforcement have distinct geographical territories and the borders of these are jealously guarded. But some agencies operate on the same 'patch' – the police and the fire service, for example. Then there are teams whose 'territory' is a particular type of crime within the same geographical area – narcotics and homicide, perhaps. And finally, there are organisations whose territory may encompass the smaller territories of other groups – in the USA, for example, you may have district, state, and federal law enforcement agencies. In Britain, there is local policing and national policing, with more serious crimes investigated by the National Crime Agency. Criminal activities that potentially impact national security, such as terrorism, are likely to involve yet another organisation. Incidents involving biological or chemical weapons require the input of specialist teams, as do bomb threats and hostage situations.

As mentioned above, status influences the nature of these professional rivalries – and in general, in a serious law enforcement situation a temporary truce is called and different agencies co-operate with those of similar rank engaging in friendly banter and insults.

Issues of territoriality or jurisdiction are related to questions of who takes *responsibility* for the investigation if things go bad and who gets the *credit* if things turn out well. As mentioned previously, detectives try to avoid increasing their workload by seeking to avoid taking responsibility for a case – this is related to the old military attitude of 'never volunteer for anything.' But once a case has been assigned, detectives tend to regard it as part of their 'territory' and refuse to give it up. To have a case taken from you and given to someone else is seen as a sign of failure and as damaging to your status and reputation. This is especially serious if you have ambitions to progress in your career. To have someone else put in a position where they can potentially claim credit for the work you have already done is especially galling.

The flip-side of this is trying to avoid taking on the responsibility for someone else's case either because doing so won't bring any personal benefit or because the detective wants to avoid the associated paperwork and subsequent court appearance.

Surrendering jurisdiction or allowing someone to 'invade' your territory is also connected to the issue of status. In movies and television, it is almost a cliché to have the FBI enter a local territory and pull rank, upstaging and offending the local law enforcement officers. A perfect example of this is the character of Special Agent Albert Rosenfield played by Miguel Ferrer in *Twin Peaks*. Scotland Yard occupies a similar place in British detective fiction. On occasion, a local sheriff or police chief takes great pains to try and keep the FBI out of a case so that he can remain in charge of the investigation – the events in David Morrell's thriller *First Blood* (and the Sylvester Stallone film adaptation) are based on this sort of situation.

When considering issues of rivalry, it is also important to remember the tightly-knit fraternity to which a policeman belongs. If one member of their team is offended as a result of a territorial dispute or someone pulling rank, then the whole team will rally to support their colleague. Outsiders who come in to work with a team sometimes forget how close the members of the team are and are caught off-guard when a slight towards one person causes everyone else to close ranks.

Part of the issue between local and national agencies is that the investigators on the national team are outsiders and people are always suspicious of, and feel threatened by, strangers.

Police Procedures

The reader of the police procedural chooses this sub-genre because they want to see police procedures from the inside. There are basically two broad types of procedures – those based on modern science, including forensic analysis of things like flakes of paint, voice-print identification, and DNA. And those often referred to as 'old school' that have been gained on the street or passed down from earlier generations of police detective. While a successful police detective uses both kinds of procedure depending on circumstances, stories often reflect a rivalry between proponents of the two types.

On the job experience over a period of time can provide knowledge that cannot be taught in a classroom. Building up an understanding of, and a rapport with, local people can be invaluable to a policeman. As can being able to spot when something has changed in a location or situation. It also allows a local policeman to be involved in the give and take of favours that is often vital to a successful investigation.

There isn't space here to explore all of these procedures in detail, but I will include a few notes about the sort of things you should know and where you can find further information. Some of these procedures are standard but many will vary according to local practices and laws. I will refer only to the United Kingdom (and more specifically England and Wales, since Scotland as a separate legal system) and the USA here, but you should be able to find similar sources of information for other countries. Many of the examples I include here are from the UK, mainly because there is much more standardisation of laws and procedures nationally than in the USA, where each state and many smaller jurisdictions within states have their own regulations and procedures. The examples I give here should give you some idea of the sorts of things to look for when researching (or creating) those for the area where you set your story.

There are some procedures that are also relevant to other types of crime thriller, so I have included separate sections on these in later chapters: forensic science and pathology, forensic psychology, informants, interviewing witnesses interrogating suspects, surveillance and tailing including stakeouts. There is also a separate chapter on the car chase.

A more extensive list of police procedures can be found on *Wikipedia* under the Category 'Law Enforcement Techniques'.

In an introduction to the *MWA Mystery Writer's Handbook,* Lawrence Treat suggested that the writer's reference shelf should contain up-to-date texts on criminal investigation, forensic medicine, and police science. Dell Shannon provided a list of such texts in her 1972 article, but these books are only of historical interest now. In the late 1990s, Writer's Digest Books published the 'Howdunit Series' that provided a lot of factual information for crime and mystery writers – the original versions are a little dated now, but some have been made available in updated ebook editions and are worth having.

In terms of up-to-date texts in the areas that Treat mentioned, what you really need are the sort of textbooks that appear on a college or university reading list for those studying to work in criminal investigation. These will vary from country to country and in the USA – to some extent – from state to state. You must select texts that reflect the laws and practices that are used in the location where you intend to base your novel. Even if you decide to use a fictional location, it is a good idea to base it, at least in part, on a real location so that if you need to refer to a local law or practice, you have something to look at to find the right sort of detail and wording.

Routine work solves cases. Ninety per cent of the job is repetitive information gathering and analysis, following one clue to the next and putting together the pattern. Every lead has to be followed and nothing left to chance. Theories must be made to fit the facts – all of the facts – rather than trying to fit facts to theories; otherwise you risk missing something significant by only seeing what you expect or want to see. Objectivity should be paramount – personal feelings or prejudices shouldn't be allowed to affect your judgement. Don't just rely on the technology – trust your own understanding of people; this is sometimes referred to as a hunch or instinct, but it can be key in understanding *why* someone did what they did. When it comes to understanding motivation, remember Occam's Razor: the simplest explanation – the one requiring the least speculation or the least number of assumptions – is usually the best one.

Training & Experience

If you are going to write about real-life detectives, you need to have an understanding of what sort of training they receive to become police officers and what experience is required for them to become detectives – and what additional experience is required for them to become detectives who specialise in particular areas of investigation. Again, police training is something that varies from one jurisdiction to another so you will need to research current practices for the place that you set your story – or for a place similar to your fictional location.

In the USA it takes around six months to train to gain a law enforcement certification and become a police officer. Some states require additional certification to become a detective but in many, police officers become detectives as a result of promotion and may then receive additional investigator training. Four or five years' experience as a police officer is normally required before someone can take a promotional exam to become a detective.

The situation in the UK used to be similar to that in the US, but more recently pathways have been created to allow people to become a trainee detective constable immediately, beginning with 20 weeks of training as part of a two-year program that includes completion of the National Investigators Exam.

Each of the 43 police forces in England and Wales (see www.police.uk/forces) has its own application and training process. Beginning in 2020 there will be three entry routes: a degree apprenticeship, degree-holder entry, and a three-year undergraduate policing degree followed by on-the-job training. Details of the National Policing Curriculum can be found at the UK's College of Policing: www.college.police.uk

Weapons

If you are writing about the use of weapons by police officers, it is vital that you research the types of weapons used by a particular police force and the way in which officers are trained to use those weapons. Many readers will know more about these things than you do, so double-check everything and talk to experts if you can.

In the United States, police officers usually carry a handgun while on duty and many are required to do so. They may also be required to carry a concealable off-duty handgun. Some police departments also permit qualified officers to carry shotguns or semiautomatic rifles in their vehicles. Police officers may also use non-lethal weapons such as mace, pepper spray, electroshock guns (Tasers), and beanbag shotgun rounds. The side-handle baton or nightstick often seen in television series and movies has been replaced in many police forces by a telescoping baton.

Two useful texts on the use of handguns by the police are *Police Pistolcraft: The Reality-Based New Paradigm of Police Firearms Training* (2007) and its sequel *The Officer's Guide to Police Pistolcraft: The New Paradigm of Police Firearms Training* (2009) both written by Michael E. Conti and published by Saber Press.

The majority of police officers in England and Wales do *not* carry firearms. Use of firearms by the police is covered by the *Police and Criminal Evidence Act 1984* and by the Home Office *Code of Practice on Police use of Firearms and Less Lethal Weapons* and the Association of Chief Police Officers (ACPO) *Manual of Guidance on Police Use of Firearms*. In the UK firearms are only carried by specially trained officers who are only deployed in certain places and under certain circumstances.

Vehicles – Marked & Unmarked

In this subject area, you need to be aware of what type of vehicles are (or were) used by a particular police force and what modifications and equipment were added to the vehicle to make them suitable for police use. As well as standard patrol cars and unmarked vehicles used by detectives, there are also specialist vehicles used for 'fast response' or high-speed pursuit. And SWAT teams also have armoured vehicles. Remember that 'vehicles' also includes boats and aircraft as well as cars and motorcycles. There is also the vehicle for transporting suspects – known as a paddy wagon, patrol wagon, police carrier, Black Maria, or – in the UK – police van. The origin of the term 'Black Maria' is uncertain but it was used in the French detective novel *Monsieur Lecoq* (1868) by Émile Gaboriau.

Things to note about police cars in the USA. Patrol cars can run without the keys in the ignition – 'runlock' keeps the engine running to ensure that onboard systems have enough electricity to function – which means that your characters can't jump into an unlocked police car and drive off with it. The doors of police cars can be reinforced with Kevlar or other materials to make them bullet-proof, so a car door isn't as unlikely a shield to hide behind as it may first appear – just don't try it with an ordinary station wagon. The different siren sounds are typically used in different circumstances - the 'wail' is used when travelling at speed on open roads and approaching intersections at it is easily heard by people in other vehicles; the 'yelp' is used in crowded traffic situations to goose other drivers and get them to move out of the way, and if that doesn't work there is a louder airhorn. Modern patrol cars contain licence plate recognition systems and automatic cameras that take images stamped with the date/time and location.

Beyond the actual vehicle, you need to know what sort of training police officers receive – especially those involved in high-speed pursuits – and what guidance governs what they are, and are not, permitted to do whilst driving a police vehicle. You should also know what equipment is carried by a police car. In the UK, for example, many cars used by traffic police now carry automatic number plate recognition systems and are linked directly to police databases.

You should probably also be aware of the colours and livery of police vehicles in the area where you set your story.

Wikipedia has an excellent article on 'Police Vehicles in the United States and Canada' covering the makes and models used in different jurisdictions. Another useful source is www.policecararchives.org which also has a section on the various lightbars used on top of vehicles.

Wikipedia also has an article on 'Police Vehicles in the United Kingdom.' The site www.ukemergency.co.uk contains many images of British police and other emergency vehicles. And www.emergency-vehicles.co.uk includes images from the UK and many other countries. For vehicles from previous decades check out the Blue Light Vehicle Preservation Group (www.blvpg.co.uk). A useful document relating to the use of police vehicles is *The Law, Guidance and Training Governing Police Pursuits: Current Position and Proposals for Change* (2018) which contains links to other sources. There is also information on police driving at www.college.police.uk

Good practice for UK police drivers is set down in two books, *Roadcraft: The Police Driver's Handbook* and *Motorcycle Roadcraft: The Police Rider's Handbook* published by The Stationery Office. These texts are used as the basis for a number of advanced driving tests in the UK including the Class 1 Police Driving Test.

Communication & Other Technology

Most US police departments have a centralised communications centre used for dispatch and patrol cars use VHF, UHF and more recently digital radio transceivers. Officers also carry handsets attached to their uniforms or headsets or earpieces. Most patrol cars are also equipped with portable computer systems that have access to their state's department of motor vehicles, criminal records, and other databases.

In the USA there is also the National Law Enforcement Telecommunications System (NLETS) - a secure private network that states have access to and that enables access to state databases for criminal history, driver's license, and vehicle registration as well as federal systems including Homeland Security, Immigration and Customs Enforcement, the Drug Enforcement Administration, and the Federal Aviation Administration Aircraft Registry. The network also allows access to non-US sources such as Interpol.

In the UK, the mobile communications network used by the emergency services, including the police, is provided by Airwave Solutions Ltd (www.airwavesolutions.co.uk) with a much-delayed replacement, Emergency Services Network (ESN), now due in 2022.

Identifying Criminals – Line-Ups, The Police Artist & Mugshots

Line-ups or Identity Parades

In real-life, line-ups – referred to as 'identity parades' in the UK – involving people physically present behind a one-way mirror are relatively rare and witnesses are more likely to be asked to pick out a suspect from a 'line-up' of photographs or video images. This is quicker and cheaper to organise – a physical line-up in the UK used to take anything up to ten weeks to organise. The video system used in England is called Viper – Video Identification Parade Electronic Recording which has a database of thousands of images classified according to various physical attributes that may occur in an eyewitness description.

Psychological research suggests that witnesses tend to concentrate on unique features, so if they witnessed a crime where the perpetrator had a facial scar or a squint, they will pick a person from a line-up based on this feature, even if the person with the scar or the squint isn't the actual perpetrator. The number of false identifications from line-ups increases if the witness is made to feel that that *must* select a subject – accuracy is greater if they are told that the perpetrator may or may not be present in the line-up.

Physical line-ups have the advantage that persons in the parade can be asked to speak a specific line heard during the incident, though voice recordings can also be used for a separate 'voice identification parade'. Physical line-ups may not be an appropriate method of identification for victims or even witnesses of particularly violent crimes or sexual assaults as seeing the perpetrator again may prove incredibly traumatic.

There are a number of potential problems with line-ups where law enforcement officers can intentionally or inadvertently influence the selection made by an eyewitness. The other people in the line-up may not sufficiently resemble the description given by the witness before the line-up. Or there may be significant differences in appearance, as in the example of the scar or the squint mentioned above. And witnesses may end up comparing the people in the line-up against each other to see who looks most likely to be a criminal, rather than relying on their own memory of the incident. And, as mentioned above, a witness may feel pressured into identifying *somebody* from the line-up, even when they cannot make an identification based on their own memory.

For these reasons, a suspect in the USA has the right to have an attorney present during a physical line-up (but not if photos are used instead). If a line-up is used without the suspect's attorney present, the lawyer may seek to have this evidence suppressed at trial. There is also research that suggests that once a person has made an identification - either right or wrong - they are likely to make the same identification again in future, meaning that there are no second chances when it comes to line-ups.

The US Department of Justice has published *Eyewitness Evidence: A Guide for Law Enforcement* (1999)

Facial Composites

These were traditionally drawn by a police sketch artist based on descriptions given by an eyewitness or suspect. 'Identikit,' a mechanical system using drawings of facial features on transparent acetate sheets, was introduced in the US in 1959. In 1970 the 'Photofit' system using photographs of different facial features was introduced in the UK, and more recently computer-based systems have been developed and are continuing to be developed. These include Identikit 2000, PortraitPad, SketchCop FACETTE, and FACES in the USA and E-FIT and PRO-fit in the UK. The websites for these products include examples and other information about their use.

The accuracy - judged by the correct naming of a suspect based on an image - ranges from 20% to 60% depending on the system used and the nature of the interviewing process used to draw information from the eyewitness.

Reviewing research on forensic art, Caroline M. Wilkinson listed the following observations:

- Eyewitnesses have better facial recall when the cognitive interview is utilized.
- Where more than one eyewitness produces a composite of the same person, then an average of these composites will be more effective than any single composite for recognition.
- High detail facial images may not be any more effective than low detail facial images.
- Configural relationships in a face can be altered and the face will still be recognizable.
- Pigmentation cues are as important as shape to face recognition.
- Facial features presented on their own may be enough for recognition, especially eyebrows and eyes.
- Caricatured faces are better recognized than accurate faces.
- Facial features are processed holistically and one feature can affect the recognition of another feature in a single facial image.
- Faces are better recognized when lit from above to simulate daylight.
- Faces are better recognized in three-quarter view or a moving view.
- The correct hairstyle can be an extremely powerful cue for recognition.
- Cropped images of faces are more effective than whole head images.

CRC Press publishes books on forensic art, including *Forensic Art and Illustration* (2000) by Karen T. Taylor and *Digital Forensic Art Techniques: A Professional's Guide to Corel Painter* (2018) by Natalie Murray.

Caught on Camera

Many UK police forces publish 'Caught on Camera' images – from CCTV cameras, dashboard cameras, or smartphones – of people they would like help from the public to identify. These include people seen in the vicinity of a crime as well as alleged perpetrators. Similar approaches are used by police departments in other parts of the world.

Mugshots

The police photograph or booking photograph to provide a record of an arrested individual and for use in identifying suspects by victims, witnesses, and investigators was formalised by French police officer Alphonse Bertillon in 1888, though photographing of criminals began soon after the invention of photography. They were later used on 'wanted' posters and displays of a 'rogues' gallery' of persons wanted by a police department. A typical mugshot consists of a front view and a side view of the person's face and upper body using a standard lighting set-up and a plain background. The image sometimes has the subject holding a placard with their name, date of birth, booking reference number, arrest date, or other information. 'Mug books' were collections of photographs of local criminals shown to witnesses or victims so that they might identify a criminal - these have been replaced by photographic databases.

The front and side view images of mugshots are so familiar to the public that the format may be regarded as prejudicial – photographs of someone presented in this format tends to make people believe that they must be a convicted criminal – and so care must be taken when using them to identify suspects.

Forensic Art & Digital Imaging

This includes composite sketches of suspects based on eyewitness descriptions, facial reconstruction of victims from human remains, age progression of a suspect or victim based on a photograph taken earlier in their life, and image enhancement including sharpening of CCTV pictures and other sources.

News Media

There is usually media interest in most crimes, especially the more dramatic sort of incident that appears in police procedural thrillers. News agencies seek to report as much information as possible about a crime, both because it is a matter of legitimate public interest and also because a 'juicy' crime story sells newspapers or draws readers to online news sites. The police, as a publicly-funded body, has to balance public interest (and also issues of public safety) against laws and regulations regarding confidentiality and the right to privacy of suspects and victims, and also the issue of not prejudicing a criminal trial. A person 'tried in the court of public opinion' might claim that they are unable to obtain a fair trial in court due to the publicity surrounding their case, and this can lead to cases being dismissed or collapsing in court.

Most police forces produce guidelines for law enforcement officers on dealing with the media – you should consult those for the location in which you set your story – or those for an area similar to your fictional location.

The College of Policing in the UK produces guidance on media relations.

Confidentiality

Personal information on individuals collected and used by law enforcement agencies is protected by different regulations in different jurisdictions. In England and Wales there is the *Data Protection Act (1988)* and the *Human Rights Act (1998)*. The European General Data Protection Regulations (GDPR) and the *Law Enforcement Directive* (LED) came into effect in May 2018. Guidance is published by the Information Commissioner's Office (www.ico.org.uk) and the College of Policing.

Confidentiality may also be an issue when law enforcement officers are seeking to *obtain* information from other agencies or institutions. There are strict regulations concerning the release of medical records including those relating to mental health. There is also a lawyer-client privilege and in the Catholic Church priests may not disclose anything they learn as a result of an individual's confession, to the extent that they should not even confirm that the confession took place. A priest breaking the 'Seal of Confession' faces excommunication.

Writing Reports & Record Keeping

Police work is sometimes referred to as 'death by paperwork' and many detectives – real and fictional – complain about the amount of time they have to spend completing paperwork. Unfortunately for him, it is not the detective's job to simply conduct an investigation – he must also carry out all of the administrative duties that will enable the evidence he gathers to be properly presented as a case file so that a decision can be made to prosecute (or not) and then taken to trial.

Recording Incidents

Incidents, including crimes, are recorded for the purposes of investigation by the police and also to provide statistics to the public and governing agencies that provide the funding to police departments. In both cases, it is important for crimes to be properly identified and consistently recorded. To that end, most legal systems have adopted standard naming and descriptions for crimes. In the USA, for example, the FBI produced the *Crime Classification Manual: A Standard System for Investigating and Classifying Violent Crimes*. The National Standard for Incident Recording (NSIR) published in 2011 by the National Policing Improvement Agency includes the National Incident Category List and is designed to ensure consistency in recording and handling of incidents by the police in England and Wales.

Preparing Case Files

In England and Wales, there is a National File Standard (NFS) that sets out how case files should be maintained as an investigation progresses. *The Prosecution Team Manual of Guidance For the Preparation, Processing and Submission of Prosecution Files* uses a system of around twenty different 'MG' forms for different stages of the process. The guidance including samples of the forms can be found online by searching under the title.

In the USA, individual police departments have their own guidance for record-keeping and report writing. An example that I found online that includes samples of reports is the *Baltimore City Police Department Academy Report Writing Manual*. And the Cincinnati Police Department also includes guidance in their detailed procedure manual which is accessible online.

See also rules of evidence below.

Searching Records

In the United States, law enforcement agencies in different states traditionally kept their own systems of records and there was little exchange between different states and different agencies. A number of national databases have been created to improve this situation. The Interstate Identification Index (III - or triple-eye) is a national index of criminal history records (rap sheets) maintained by the FBI's National Crime Information Center (NCIC). It lists which states have a record for an individual but the investigator has to contact the individual states for the specific details of that person's criminal history in that state. NCIC databases also include missing persons, identity theft, immigration violation, sex offenders, gang members, wanted persons, and stolen property records. The FBI also maintains the National Instant Criminal Background Check System (NICS) used to determine whether or not an individual is eligible to purchase firearms or explosives.

In England and Wales, police forces and other agencies have access to the Police National Computer (PNC) and the Police National Database (PND) – these are scheduled to be decommissioned and combined into a new system as a result of the National Law Enforcement Data Programme. The PNC consists of a number of databases including information on individuals who have been convicted, cautioned, or recently arrested, with links to fingerprints and DNA; vehicle registration records, stolen and found property records, and driving licence records. The PND contains records created by individual police forces and other law enforcement agencies. Various agencies other than the police have access to these records – the *Wikipedia* article on the 'Police National Computer' lists them – and access and record keeping is subject to the terms of the *Data Protection Act 1998*. Records relating to crimes involving firearms are co-ordinated by the National Ballistics Intelligence Service (www.nabis.police.uk) in a similar way to the US Integrated Ballistics Identification System.

Rules of Evidence

A fundamental rule in the police procedural – as in real-life police work – is that the case that is built against a suspect must be sufficiently strong to 'stand up in court.' There must be sufficient *evidence* to ensure that a prosecution can be made. In this respect, the police detective doesn't have any of the freedoms enjoyed by the amateur detective in the whodunit. If the detective has a theory about what happened at a crime scene, he must be able to demonstrate that his theory is correct based on the available evidence – there can be no intuitive leaps or comparisons based on experience gained in other cases.

There are legal guidelines on how, where and under what circumstances suspects can be interviewed and how the answers must be recorded. If the police detective doesn't follow the rules and obtain evidence lawfully, it can be ruled as inadmissible in court. And the police detective cannot engage in entrapment or trick the suspect into revealing or confessing his own guilt.

In the USA, federal courts adopted the Federal Rules of Evidence in 1975 (see www.rulesofevidence.org) and many states have adopted these or similar rules. In England and Wales, guidance for police forces on admissible evidence was originally set down in the *Judges' Rules* in 1912 and these were subsumed into the *Police and Criminal Evidence Act 1984*.

The Right to Silence

In the USA a suspect has the right to remain silent – sometimes referred to as 'pleading the Fifth' as the Fifth and Sixth Amendments to the US Constitution lay down this and other rights of suspects. In order not to beach a suspect's rights, the police are required to provide anyone taken into custody with a Miranda warning. The requirements of this were set down by the judge in the 1966 case of *Miranda v. Arizona,* where it was decided that the police had violated the Fifth and Sixth Amendment rights of Ernesto Arturo Miranda.

In England and Wales, the right to silence – or the privilege against self-incrimination – is more limited than in the United States. Prior to 1994, a policeman would say something along the lines of 'You do not have to say anything but anything you do say will be taken down and may be given in evidence.' But this was amended by a 1994 Act of Parliament to: 'You do not have to say anything. But it may harm your defence if you do not mention when questioned something which you later rely on in court. Anything you do say may be given in evidence.'

The Right to Counsel

In the USA, the Sixth Amendment of the US Constitution guarantees criminal suspects the right to counsel during police interrogations – that is, they have the right to have their lawyer present and the police must not try to question a suspect without counsel unless the suspect formally waives that right. This right was formally tested in court by Escobedo v. Illinois in 1964.

In England and Wales, a person arrested is entitled to free legal advice before being questioned (see www.gov.uk/arrested-your-rights/legal-advice-at-the-police-station). The rights of suspects in terms of detention, treatment and questioning are set out in Code C of the *Police and Criminal Evidence Act 1984*. If you are writing a historical police procedural you would need to refer to earlier Acts, all of which should be available online.

Court Appearances

Having passed the first test and reached the courtroom, the detective's evidence must then be sufficient to withstand cross-examination by a defence lawyer *and* convince a jury of laymen and women of the suspect's guilt. I have explored the workings of the court in terms of the Legal Thriller in *Suspense Thriller* – the work of the police detective effectively covers what happens before a case gets to court, but must be carried out with one eye on what will happen in the courtroom. This aspect of police work often affects the outlook of the police detective and his relationship with the society in which he works.

Detectives often have to appear in court in relation to cases they have investigated – with the trial often occurring many months after the detective's work was done. Police detectives are typically resentful of the time that is 'wasted' hanging around the courthouse waiting to be called as a witness and at the way in which lawyers conduct cross-examinations as they attempt to discredit the detective's testimony by making him appear incompetent, dishonest, or even corrupt.

Other Types of Procedure

Although we are discussing the *police* procedural, it isn't only police methods that are included in these stories – criminals' methods are a part of many stories too. If the crimes in a story revolve around a particular occupation or hobby, 'inside' details of that might be included too. Ed McBain's *Mischief,* which I'll talk about more later, includes information about a criminal putting together a team for a heist, how a homeless shelter operates, what it's like to work in a lap-dancing club, the activities and folklore of graffiti artists, and behind the scenes of an open-air music concert. None of these things are explained in exhaustive detail because we see them from the point of view characters who consider these things part of their normal routine lives, but they give a feeling of having access to areas that ordinary people don't usually see.

As well as planning for a heist, you could include a criminal's point of view as he prepares to carry out an assassination – which I explored in some detail in *Suspense Thriller* – or a professional hit. You might find it helpful to read Frederick Forsyth's *The Day of the Jackal,* which shows a single crime – an attempt to assassinate General de Gaulle – from the point of view of the assassin planning to carry it out and of the police who seek to prevent the killing. You might also find ideas for your police procedural in later chapters in this book which explore other types of crimes.

The 'King of Procedures' was bestselling novelist Arthur Hailey – he spent a couple of years researching the background workings of the settings for each of his books, the best-known of which are *Hotel* (1965) and *Airport* (1968), the film adaptation of the latter kicking off the 'disaster movie' craze of the 1970s. Of more interest to us is Hailey's 1997 novel *Detective* in which a Miami Police detective's latest case demonstrates the investigative methods of a homicide department. A 2005 television adaptation didn't do the story justice – seek out the original novel which, while dated now, offers an interesting glimpse into the world of the detective.

Plot Structure

There are two basic structures for the plot of a police procedural novel which I will refer to as the 'single case' and the 'multiple storyline.' First, we'll look at the single case plot in some detail and then see how it can be adapted for the multiple storyline novel.

The Single Case Plot

The police procedural grew out of the traditional murder mystery or whodunit, with the police detective novel as a sort of intermediary stage. Like the whodunit, the plot is fundamentally a chronological account of the different stages of the investigation of a mystery, from the discovery of the crime to the point where the guilty party is identified and arrested, with sufficient evidence to 'stand up in court' having been gathered between these two points. The investigation usually centres on a murder.

Discussing Lawrence Treat's novel *V as in Victim* as having established the format, George N. Dove says that as well as using the same structure as a traditional murder mystery, the police procedural also observes the convention of 'fair play' in that when the detective discovers a clue it is shared with the reader. I covered the structure of the classic whodunit story in some detail in my book *Mystery,* but a summary of the eight-sequence structure looks something like this:

Where the police procedural differs from the whodunit is in *who* does the gathering of the evidence and *how* that evidence is analysed and interpreted. In other words, the detective himself is different and the *procedures* he uses are different. As we have already seen, these two things lie at the heart of the conventions that define this sub-genre.

Where the private eye moves from location to location and engages in a series of situations of increasing danger, suspense and excitement, the police detective's investigation contains much more repetitive work and waiting around.

The mystery in a traditional whodunit centres on exploring whether each of the suspects had the Means, Motive and Opportunity to carry out the murder. If they didn't, they are eliminated and the pool of suspects gradually decreases until the murderer is revealed. Investigations in the police procedural do not follow this pattern. A body is found in the middle of nowhere, there is no 'hermetically sealed' location and no discrete set of suspects to be questioned. Even the identity of the victim may be unknown initially. The investigation does not take the form of a puzzle where all of the pieces are placed on the board from the outset.

Single Case Plot Structure

Sequence 1

There are three things to achieve in the first sequence: introduce your detective(s), introduce the crime they will investigate, and establish the pattern for point of view – Will we see events from just one character's viewpoint, from a couple of different viewpoints, or from multiple viewpoints?

There are a number of different ways that you can handle the opening of your story – whether it is the first scene or a short 'prologue' that sets things up. If you are writing a series of police procedurals, it is useful to have different options for beginning your stories – here are half-a-dozen or so ideas for first scenes.

- Open with the victim, showing events leading up to the crime.
- The discovery of the crime. Typically this means that a body is found, but it could be a missing person or an abduction/kidnap or some form of assault.
- Begin with a setting – the police department at work or the place where the victim is working or spending their time before the crime.
- The main character(s) – the detective or a pair of detectives, either at work or off-duty. You might want to introduce your detectives investigating some smaller crime which may or may not be related to one of the main crimes that will make up the bulk of the story.
- The discovery or commission of a smaller crime that will result in the main detectives being called in. Again, this may or may not turn out to be related to the main storyline.
- An intriguing incident related to the planning of the main criminal plot – something related to setting up the heist or a crime that involves obtaining a resource or a person who will be involved in the main crime. This could be shown from the criminal's point of view or that of a beat detective who discovers it in progress or having been completed.

Whatever type of opening you choose, it needs to captivate the attention of the reader – to intrigue them so that they want to keep reading and find out more. Introduce either an interesting character or an interesting incident that implies that more interesting things are to come.

I would say that it is probably best to create something that is *not* a self-contained incident – leave it hanging open or with a cliff-hanger or with some significant question unanswered so that the reader *has* to keep turning the pages.

Typically you will introduce your detectives as they are notified about the crime or as they arrive at the crime scene. You will characterise the two partners by their interaction with one another – usually with banter and insults – and the way they treat other people at the scene – uniformed officers, the medical examiner or paramedics, witnesses, a victim, etc. As mentioned before, you need to quickly establish them *in character* so that readers can recognise them and tell them apart – the grumpy one versus the cheerful one or the sensitive one and the foul-mouthed brute, or however you want to create them. You probably want to establish them such that one can play 'good cop' and one can be 'bad cop' when they come to interrogate suspects later in the story. Though you may also want to have some fun and have the more caring of the two *play* bad cop in the interrogation room. You can also characterise your detectives further by showing their home lives and/or off-duty relationships.

At whatever point in Sequence 1 the crime is discovered, the procedures described for dealing with it must be those that the police would use in real life.

It is helpful to know the main stages involved in dealing with a crime scene from the moment the body is discovered to the time when the area is released by the police and is no longer a crime scene. I included a broad outline of these stages earlier in the chapter, but you may need to fill this out with specific details about how things are handled by the police in the specific location where your story is set. Who discovered the body (or other crime)? Who did they call? Who was the first 'official' on the scene – a beat cop, a paramedic, or someone else who was close enough to make the first response? What actions did they take first? Who did they 'call it in' to? How did they 'secure the crime scene'? How were the people at the scene managed? After the crime scene had been secured, what are the various stages of a crime scene investigation? If there is a body, who examines it? Who removes the body and where is it taken to? What records have to be made by the people attending the scene? Who has overall authority/responsibility? What happens if news photographers or reporters arrive on the scene? Or if people have taken 'selfies' with the body? How is a forensic examination of a crime scene carried out? Is there a difference between a crime scene outside and one inside? What happens if it's raining or very hot?

There may be representatives from different official agencies at the scene and there will almost certainly be people of different ranks – you will need to show how these people interact with one another. How are rivalries handled? Who shows deference or respect to who? Who pulls rank and seeks to humiliate those of lesser status? How does this affect the atmosphere at the scene?

You have to decide how much detail you want to include about the police and other agency procedures at the crime scene. You can manage this by your choice of point of view character. An experienced detective is going to take proceedings for granted and not make many detailed observations about what is occurring – it is all *routine* to him. Someone relatively new to this sort of situation will notice a lot more – and some of it will seem strange or confusing. They may also see other professionals treating it as routine and may be surprised or upset by their apparent callousness or inappropriate humour – even though this is just a coping mechanism for those who have to deal with such grim scenes week after week. If a rookie is partnered with an experienced officer, there is scope for one to ask questions and the other to explain things – which allows the writer to sneak in some of that fascinating research he has done into police procedures.

Detectives may identify and question witnesses at the scene to get an initial broad idea about what happened. Or they may leave this to uniformed officers who will report what they find. Who discovered the body? Who saw or heard something? Witnesses may make remarks that only become significant later. They may have seen or heard something that seems unrelated. Or they may say something that is initially dismissed or not believed. The police may believe that they are unreliable or mistaken. In *V as in Victim* a witness heard a woman screen ten seconds *before* a crime was committed – Why would she do that? And, of course, some witnesses may be genuinely unreliable, either from incompetence or because they themselves have something to hide.

During this scene, detectives may muse on the work involved in this type of case – paperwork, court appearances, meetings with lawyers, explaining to superiors – and the writer can use this to give the reader more of a flavour of the true nature of police work. And of his characters' attitudes towards it.

You also need to consider how other people are *affected* by the crime. There will be witnesses, perhaps including someone who has just discovered the body. There may be relatives, friends or colleagues of the victim. If the crime is something other than murder, there may be a living victim. These people have their own lives and personalities. Some people don't like to talk to the police. Some people just like to talk, period – even if they have nothing useful to say. Though there may be important nuggets hidden in their dialogue or monologue. To show the *impact* of the crime – on people to whom crime is not commonplace – you might want to have a short section from their point of view if you're writing a multi-viewpoint story.

Crime scenes have been seen so often in movies and on television that you need to spice up the cliché somehow. You might want to include something unusual or even bizarre. In *V as in Victim* there is a dead cat which may or may not be significant and in *Mischief* murdered graffiti artists are 'decorated' with coloured spray paint. Unusual visual elements like this can help the reader to 'see' your crime scene. Or you may find that effective use of point of view or an unusual character in the scene is enough to generate interest without the need for a visual 'gimmick.'

Don't include too much investigating in Sequence 1 – have just the minimum that must be done at the scene of the crime. You will probably want to say that uniformed officers have gone out knocking on doors in the neighbourhood and collecting statements or that they are checking with local businesses to see what CCTV footage may be available – but save analysis of this material for later chapters.

Even in a single case novel, you may want to introduce mention of another case being received. This case may be mentioned several times in the background as you concentrate on the single case your protagonist is investigating, or it may just sit there, ready for your detectives to tackle after they've finished the current one. Either way, it reinforces the impression that there is a never-ending stream of crimes for them to tackle.

Sequence 2

The second sequence is where we establish that this isn't a run-of-the-mill, solution in forty-eight hours type of murder committed in the heat of the moment by an angry husband (or wife). This crime is a *mystery* that will need more extensive investigation – and a pair of detectives will have to commit their time to the investigation. The mystery may be established by the fact that this crime is similar to one or more previous unsolved crimes. Or there may be something else about it that indicates that this isn't just another domestic or gang-related killing.

Sequence 2 is where we also deal with the *immediate* aftermath of the crime. Who is affected by it and how do they respond? The nature of their response may be significant – especially with close family, friends, or work colleagues. Does someone have a guilty secret? Was there some sort of family feud – either recent or long-standing? Who benefits from the victim's death? Some people may be devastated by the loss of the victim. Others may be ambivalent. And others may be glad they're gone. Those most upset – assuming their grief is genuine – will need to be reassured by the police that the murderer will be brought to justice as swiftly as possible.

Once the crime becomes public knowledge, it may attract the attention of reporters – either local or national depending on the nature of the crime. The police will need to handle this – as may the relatives of the victim.

And we will see initial police routines for this type of case. They may be a search for the murder weapon, with a team of officers looking in dumpsters, trash cans, sewers, etc. The *scale* of this kind of search is very different from any similar search in the traditional whodunit.

Detectives will put together a list of the people they want to talk to – and this will not be the tidy half-dozen suspects who are interviewed in the whodunit. There may be forty or fifty people on the list, some of whom are only partially identified, e.g. a taxi driver who picked up the victim around 7pm on the night of the murder.

There may also be some discussion among the detectives about similar cases, including speculation on possible motives – from the commonplace to the jokey or outlandish – and how previous cases turned out. There may be an indication here that all cases are not solved and that some just end up in the 'cold case' file.

Reports will come in from the uniformed officers who conducted door-to-door interviews. Some of these will confirm – or perhaps contradict – statements given by witnesses at the scene. Some names may be added to the list of people the detectives want to talk to – either for follow-up interviews with someone the uniformed officers spoke to or because a name was mentioned by one of the witnesses – 'I saw a homeless guy with a shopping cart hanging around after it got dark.' These early reports may also include some local knowledge or gossip – 'That's Angelique's corner, you should talk to her' or 'Everyone knows that guy was going to end up dead in a gutter, the way he treated his people.'

There may be some initial report from the crime lab on samples gathered at the scene – 'The gun used was a .38' or 'The victim had red nylon fibres under the fingernails of the left hand.' This evidence shouldn't be of the sort you find in whodunits – 'You're looking for a man with dark hair, approximately six foot two inches tall, with a slight limp on the left side and wearing a type of Nikes manufactured in 1996.' The detectives might piece something like this together from separate clues over a period of days or weeks, but we don't want to make it this easy for them early on. Early clues should be so general as to be virtually useless.

At this stage, you want to be adding to the amount of work it seems the detectives and their colleagues will need to do. And making it seem more and more unlikely that the murderer will ever be identified.

Before the end of Sequence 2, there will also be some indication from a commanding officer that this case has been assigned to or continues to 'belong' to our protagonists. This is the equivalent of the end of Act I 'commitment' or 'acceptance of the challenge' in story structures like the hero's journey. It marks a change from 'a problem we're aware of (and was hoping would be given to someone else)' to 'this is my case to solve (I'm stuck with it).'

Initial 'legwork' on the case carried out by the detectives may include visiting the home of the victim and talking to his or her friends, neighbours, relatives, and/or colleagues. They begin to build up a picture of the victim

– and may discover that different people have a different idea about what sort of person the victim really was. There may also be an early suggestion – genuine or malicious – that the victim had a secret life that his or her family didn't know about.

If another case wasn't introduced during Sequence 1, it will be introduced here. Again, the aim is to highlight the workload pressure of the team of detectives. If you have a second investigation going on in parallel to the main one – either in the background or the foreground – don't repeat procedures etc. already covered in the first case. Police work may be dull and repetitive, but you don't want your story to be.

Time pressure may be placed on the investigating officers here – because of the victim's wealthy family, the D.A., politicians, or circumstances. This pressure will also be such that there isn't an option for this case to go onto the 'unsolved' pile. Relatives may put pressure on the police because they don't feel that enough is being done quickly enough – they are frustrated and just want to see *something* being done. The detectives may have to do something conspicuous just to appease them. Or perhaps the family offer a reward for information that leads to an arrest, which brings various amateurs and sleazy private eyes out after the money – who only serve to make things more difficult for the detectives by muddying the waters. Offering a reward may be done in Sequence 2 or later in the story.

There may also be some sort of personal connection for one of the detectives such that he wants to see the case solved – maybe it's similar to something that happened to someone he knew or a case his father worked on or a case he failed to resolve earlier in his career. Or maybe it is just the sort of crime he doesn't want to see go unpunished. Or it may be that he just needs to solve a case – any case – successfully to restore a tarnished reputation or to restore his own faith in his ability to 'make a difference.' Alternatively, one of the detectives may be reluctant to work on the case for the same sorts of reasons, but they have no choice because this is their job.

Sequence 3

This is where the investigation moves from initial routine teamwork to a more in-depth approach by the main detectives assigned to the case. The detectives will work through the mass of reports they have received from uniformed policemen, the medical examiner or forensic medicine team, from database searches, and from scientific analysis of samples from the scene. The volume of information dwarfs anything that the investigator in a whodunit amasses – and finding anything relevant is like searching for a needle in a haystack. Or several haystacks.

The detectives begin to try and put the pieces together into a 'story' that accounts for all of the facts that they have. Initially, this will be a generic story – one that they have seen in other crimes of this type and that the reader probably recognises from cop shows and other novels. But there will be unique features and clues that mean this case can't be explained by the generic story. What is the significance of 'X' discovered at the scene? Or of 'Y' seen or heard by one or more witnesses? Or why was 'Z' *not* found at the scene?

Again, we are demonstrating why this is not a run-of-the-mill case – and we're assessing and discounting the usual and most obvious possibilities that a reader would expect the detectives to consider. We are also – as in this sequence in all stories – removing the obvious or easy solutions and making the heroes' lives more difficult. There can be no quick fixes. All possible hiding places for the murder weapon may come up empty. Obvious suspects with strong motives will have concrete alibies. More work is required to identify a suspect.

One or two people from the list of 'persons of interest' may be placed under surveillance. This may be carried out by the detectives themselves or, more likely, by other people in their team. Others on the list may be tracked down and interviewed – and either eliminated as being of interest or shown to have nothing to offer as a witness. Dead ends.

Part of this is a narrowing down of options. The procedural doesn't have the enclosed setting and select group of suspects we see in the whodunit, so we need to reduce the area of the search and possible list of suspects down from 'everywhere and everyone.' But we disguise this to some extent, making it seem that the detectives' job is getting harder not easier as options are eliminated. The focus of the investigation will become sharper in later sequences, but in Sequence 3 we are mainly eliminating the obvious.

Media reports about the murder and the investigation may bring out people who want to 'help.' Witnesses, amateur investigators, psychics and the like. The police will have to handle them – Are they genuine, self-serving, or just crazy people? There may also be anonymous notes or 'phone calls – either from people alleging to have information or perhaps claiming to be the killer. Is this really the killer writing/speaking? They may even get confessions from people who are not guilty and who simply want notoriety – but still, the police have to deal with them, just in case. Though they may recognise the culprit as a known 'serial confessor.' The investigation may also be hampered by people trying to benefit from the situation in other ways – a man may kill his wife and make it look like the work of a serial killer. Or someone may commit a similar crime just because they are a copycat killer. Often the police withhold some significant fact about the original crime to help them weed out these copycats and time wasters.

There will usually be at least one significant clue discovered in Sequence 3 – though its meaning or significance may not be recognised immediately. There may also be a false alarm resulting in a wild goose chase. Perhaps a copycat or an amateur investigator is caught doing something suspicious.

The detectives talk to more people who knew the victim and continue to build up their picture of him or her. Perhaps this picture contrasts in some significant aspect with that provided by the victim's immediate family. Did the victim have a secret life? Were they part of some small hidden community – defined by a hobby, a secret vice, a health issue, a sexual peccadillo, recent or past life event, or something else that family and colleagues didn't know about? There may also be more information about family or other close relationships that wasn't revealed initially – especially with respect to family feuds and those who had a reason to hate the victim. The alibis of people connected to the victim will also be compared and verified. Ex-husbands or former lovers may also enter the picture or be added to the list.

It is still relatively early days and our detectives will still be waiting for some reports to come in. Remember that real police work involves a lot of waiting. They may be waiting for reports from other police officers who are conducting enquiries about or interviews with people on the list. They could be waiting for laboratory analysis of items recovered from the crime scene. Perhaps they're still waiting for news about an elusive cab driver or homeless person, or a search for a particular vehicle or some other item. Technicians may be analysing CCTV footage – perhaps the victim has been glimpsed in one or two frames somewhere and now they are trying to plot the victim's possible movements forwards and backwards from this point with footage from other cameras. And then they will look to see if anyone seems to be following the victim, either on foot or in a vehicle.

Police work often relies on informants – but they are usually only useful if a crime is committed by someone in the criminal community. But the informant may prove useful if it is suspected that a criminal was at or near the scene at the time of the murder and is now avoiding contact with the police. Or an informant may be able to provide information about an unusual weapon.

Later in the sequence, other reports may come in. Perhaps a lab report on a piece of physical evidence suggests a link with another crime or another location. There may be something interesting in the autopsy report. Note that if an autopsy is carried out, you will need to check what the law/procedure is regarding permission for this – Can the family of the victim refuse to give permission? This may vary depending on where you set your story.

If you want to include a funeral scene or an inquest, you will also need to check local procedures. In some jurisdictions the police may not release the body to the family for some considerable time, depending on the circumstances of the murder.

Perhaps a person on the list who the police have been trying to track down is found – and turns out to be no help or to be nothing like the person seen near the scene or captured on CCTV footage.

The detectives may have a 'preferred suspect' in mind – and may have identified them as early as Sequence 1. But this person may have a strong alibi and/or there may be no evidence pointing towards them. But they seem to be the one person who actually benefits from the victim's death – or to have had a strong motive for wanting them dead. With nothing else to go on, the detectives may assign someone to follow this suspect.

A theory may be put forward suggesting what happened on the night of the murder – but it is an unlikely or perhaps outlandish story, like something from an old-fashioned locked room mystery, and it is treated as a bit of a joke. Sometimes you have to get these ideas out of your head to make space for something more

If we haven't seen this already, we will see one or both of our detectives at home with his family or engaged in a romantic relationship. We need to see them as ordinary people and members of the community – even if they are never truly off-duty.

Sequence 4

Sequence 4 builds to a midpoint revelation or discovery – or to some other significant turning point in the story. The midpoint could be another murder, an arrest, or a confession. Or it may be the discovery of some evidence that seems to prove, beyond doubt, that someone is guilty of the murder.

One way to structure the investigation of a mystery is to have two wrong 'solutions' followed by a final correct one. In this case, Sequence 4 can be devoted to putting together the first wrong solution. The midpoint will then either *appear* to prove this solution correct – this often happens if the 'guilty' person is a sympathetic character who the reader will not want to be guilty. Or the midpoint proves the theory wrong and sends our detectives back to the drawing board. The midpoint may 'prove' someone innocent even when the reader and/or the police are convinced – or may know for a fact – that this person is guilty. If the police can find proof and come up with a successful second attempt at a solution, a murderer will walk free.

As part of its focus on the 'wrong theory', Sequence 4 will examine in more detail the backstory and relationships of the suspect in question. It may even be told, in whole or in part, from this person's point of view. We may see the activities of the detectives through this person's eyes. And we will also experience first-hand the effect that the crime and its investigation is having on them (the suspect) personally. Whether or not the guilt of this person is revealed to the reader at this point depends upon the author and the needs of the story.

In the procedural, the *identity* of the murderer is often less of a mystery – at least to the reader – than it is in the whodunit. The reader, and perhaps the police, may know the identity of the killer from the beginning or may discover it at any of the key turning points (at the end of any of the first seven sequences) in the story. The mystery then becomes whether or not the detectives can put together enough evidence to enable them to prosecute – and then achieve a conviction in court.

The midpoint of a story might also seem to prove a guilty person guilty. This can be particularly effective if the reader has known the guilt of this person and has been following events, to a significant extent, from the point of view of the murderer, such that he or she is almost a joint protagonist with the detectives. Being proved guilty at the midpoint is a significant setback for this character and may be portrayed as such from his or her p.o.v. rather than being seen as a positive development for the detectives. Or we may get to see it from both viewpoints.

Alternatively, we may see a suspect – guilty or innocent – making a mistake and wondering whether the detectives will discover it and use it as 'proof' of their guilt. This can provide suspense if the reader is allowed to see things from the suspect's viewpoint – as the police seem to get closer and closer to discovering the mistake.

If the case the detectives have been investigating was a missing person or an abduction/kidnapping, the midpoint may involve the body of the missing person being discovered. At this point, the story then becomes a murder investigation. This may cause you some issues if it causes a change in jurisdiction with a homicide squad or other agency coming in and taking over the case.

There are other things that can be included in Sequence 4. A wealthy relative of the victim may be dissatisfied with the progress the police have made and decide to hire a private eye. Reports in the media may criticise the police for their apparent lack of progress. Both of these things increase the pressure on our detective heroes. Or the detectives may decide to use the media and have a relative make a television appeal for information that might help identify the killer.

If a body is discovered at the midpoint or earlier in the sequence, it may prove to be a false alarm or a red-herring. It may be the work of a copycat or an opportunist, as mentioned previously. Or it may be a random murder that is unconnected to the present case. But reporters may insist that there *is* a connection and blame the police – saying that this person may still be alive if the police had solved the original case. The police may know that there is no connection because of some unique feature about the original killing that they are not releasing to the public – but they cannot reveal it to the press, and so just have to accept their criticism.

In Sequence 4 another clue – significant or minor – is often discovered which will either prove something the police knew or suspected – or disprove something.

Whatever occurs at the midpoint of the story, the press may pounce on it and report it – against the wishes of the police. And whether the 'proof' discovered at this point is correct or not, it raises the stakes and revitalises the investigation.

Sequence 5

This sequence – as in virtually all stories in all genres – concentrates on (a) the response of characters to the midpoint discovery, and (b) relationships between characters.

The detectives may quickly suspect that the midpoint 'proof' may not be what it first appeared and set out to test it.

When it looks as though their preferred suspect may be innocent, the detectives have to go back to the drawing board – or back to their original list of suspects – and try to figure out who really did it. Whatever was revealed at the midpoint, Sequence 5 is the unravelling of their first theory. Where did we go wrong? This is a major setback for them.

But perhaps the midpoint does provide them with something that causes them to look at all of their existing information in a new light. If 'X' wasn't true – or was – what implication does this have for 'Y' and 'Z'? Does it indicate that another suspect or witness lied? Does it suggest that something thought wrong or insignificant is, in fact, true and important?

The midpoint may also cause the detectives to reconsider relationships between different characters. Or events at the midpoint may impact on a relationship of one of the detectives – especially if he had feelings for a suspect who now appears to be guilty of murder! Or whatever he discovers about other people's relationships may make the detective appreciate his own – and he will spend more time with his wife or lover.

One of the detectives may interview a 'femme fatale' character – someone who is flirty or make overt sexual advances. He may be tempted but backs away – not wanting to jeopardise his relationship at home which is too important to him.

The detectives may learn something new and significant about a relationship between the victim and a family member, friend, or colleague. Or they may discover that a relationship existed that wasn't revealed before. There may be questions about an inheritance and who benefits. Or who benefited from an earlier inheritance.

A character may fear that someone they care about is guilty – or think the police believe them to be guilty – and so seek to protect this person. They may lie to the police to give the person a false alibi, or they may make a direct or indirect confession of their own guilt. This action in itself may provide a clue to the detectives. Why would someone make a false confession? Who are they protecting? Or the person may seek to direct blame towards someone else by strategic revelation of facts. Or they may fabricate a 'frame-up.'

Even if the police still have a prime suspect and feel they merely need to prove their guilt, they cannot completely ignore the possibility that someone else may be guilty.

New forensic evidence may be discovered – or something, a car perhaps, or someone the police have been searching for for some time may be found. This may cast new light on the investigation. They are ready to formulate and test a new theory – and perhaps even arrest a new suspect. This sets up Sequence 6 of the story.

Sequence 6
Sequence 6 builds to a major turning point in the story. In many plots in various genres this is a crisis point and typically marks the hero's darkest hour. He seems further from success in his 'quest' – whatever form that takes – than he has ever been so far in the story. He loses old things that he has valued for some time and he loses everything new that he has gained in his quest to date. How do we apply this to a police procedural plot?

Ideally, we want to end Sequence 6 with a situation that makes it seem that the detectives are further from a solution than at any point in the investigation. If we want this to be their darkest hour, we want to see them disheartened and possibly humiliated by what has just happened to them. What has just happened is their second attempt to put together and demonstrate a solution to the mystery. The end of Sequence 6, their crisis, is when this second theory is proved wrong – and dramatically so.

But we don't want the reader to see this crisis or disaster coming. During the course of Sequence 6, they will see what seems to be good progress being made in the investigation, such that a solution seems imminent. New clues are discovered – often buried in reports or information that they have held for some time.

A mystery person who has been on the list of people to be questioned since Sequence 1 may finally be identified and located. They may be regarded as a suspect or potential witness. What they have to say may prove to be relevant or they may turn out to be another red-herring.

The narrowing down of the list of suspects or persons of interest will continue so that the list of 40 or 50 is reduced to about a dozen and then towards the end of this sequence to just two.

The two detectives working on the case may each favour one of the suspects as the murderer. And one of them may be biased as a result of being attracted to one of the suspects.

Evidence of a motive for one of the suspects may be identified, leading to the detectives confront them and try to make an arrest. The victim may escape and go on the run, making it seem that they must be guilty. But are they?

This person's escape – or some other reason – will cause the press, the D.A., the victim's family, their own commanding officer, and the general public to put pressure on the detectives to redouble their efforts and solve the case. This may cause them to cut corners or to do something that breaks their usual code of conduct – as an act of desperation. Or they may decide to ignore a piece of evidence that doesn't fit their present theory. And it may look as if this will pay off as it appears to bring them close to a solution and to the proof they will need to secure an arrest and a conviction.

Sequence 6 mirrors Sequence 4 to some extent in that it presents a possible solution and then ends with it being proved wrong. In Sequence 6, the stakes are higher and the failure more dramatic – to the extent that the detectives are threatened with demotion or dismissal if they don't turn things around quickly and bring the killer to justice. This threat may come because not only have the detectives embarrassed themselves with their failure but the image of their captain or the D.A., mayor, or some other politician has also been tarnished and this never goes down well.

Sequence 7

Sequence 7 builds to another turning point – either a final significant clue that appears to prove someone's guilt or an arrest. Possibly both. It begins as a reaction to the failure of the second solution at the end of the previous sequence.

The detectives discuss the case, one of them pushing his theory about the guilt of one of the major suspects.

The meaning of one of the odd clues, bits of evidence, or witness statements from Sequence 1 is finally uncovered.

At this stage in the story, the list of suspects has been reduced to two characters that the detectives have met and interviewed. There may also be a third 'mystery' suspect that the detectives have known about since Act I but have not been able to locate.

Often in this sequence, one of the suspects does something that makes them appear to be guilty of the murder. Or some significant piece of evidence is found that seems to prove their guilt. They may be caught in a lie regarding their relationship with the victim and/or a lie that shows that their alibi for the night of the murder isn't true.

There may be another murder and one of the two main suspects is caught red-handed – effectively standing over the body with a smoking gun in their hand. They are arrested. It seems that one of the detectives was right about this person being the murderer and the other wrong. But they still have to put together enough evidence to prove that this person is guilty of the original murder.

If there isn't another murder at this point, the suspect may instead be caught engaged in some other suspicious activity that suggests a connection with the original murder. This may be discovered as a result of the police having the two main suspects under surveillance.

Or perhaps something occurs that leads the detective to believe that there is about to be another murder. One of the witnesses or an innocent person unconnected with the case may be the potential victim. Or the intended victim may be one of the two remaining suspects. This may relate to an actual planned murder or it may be a false alarm triggered by circumstances that have been misread. Either way, the police can't take any chances and have to respond to the threat. In mysteries, it is not uncommon for a murderer to make it appear as if they have been targeted by the killer and had a narrow escape – they believe this will deflect the detectives' interest away from them.

As a result of their suspicions about another murder, the police may 'rescue' the intended victim – only to discover that they didn't need rescuing. This can lead to a hugely embarrassing situation for them. The 'rescued' person will be angry and confused and will seek to defend the suspect that they were 'rescued' from. But are they unknowingly defending a murderer? The detectives have to question the rescued person to try and discover if they know anything that could help advance the investigation. Perhaps they do inadvertently reveal something useful – something that indicates the guilt or innocence of the suspect in custody.

Sequence 7 typically sees the detectives having one of the suspects in custody and this suspect is either guilty but appears to be innocent or is innocent and appears to be guilty. Either way, the detectives need more information in order to be able to prove who the murderer really is. They have some circumstantial evidence against the suspect they have in custody, but 'nothing that will stand up in court.'

Media reporters may have an idea that 'something' is going on and come sniffing around. Not wanting to reveal their hand early and tip off the murderer, the police may tell reporters that the case is stalled and that they have no new leads. Reporters may accept this, or one may go off and start digging around and potentially put the investigation in jeopardy.

There could be one piece of crucial evidence that the detectives need but have been unable to find. This may be a vehicle that they need to locate – but it is a common make of vehicle meaning that finding the right one is almost impossible – even assuming that it hasn't been crushed in a scrapyard. Or they may need something that proves a connection between the first victim and the suspect at the time of the murder – a hotel reservation, for example. To locate this evidence, the police may have a team of uniformed officers out doing routine *legwork* – laboriously checking every registered car of that make and colour or checking registrations at every hotel in the area. Again, this serves to show how police routine differs from the work of the detective in a whodunit.

The 'mystery' suspect that the police have been trying to find is eventually located. He or she is eliminated as a suspect, usually because they have an alibi that can easily be proved as genuine. Or you may want to have it that this mystery person isn't a real person at all – it was the killer in disguise and so has to be one of the two remaining suspects.

If the suspect they have in custody appears to be innocent, the detectives will have to release them. But they may arrange to have them followed. If the suspect in custody appears to be guilty, they can hold them for a while as they try and put together enough evidence to make a formal arrest. Failing that, they may have to let this 'guilty' person go.

The police may interrogate the 'guilty' suspect, playing good cop/bad cop, in the hope of getting them to confess their guilt. Or you may want to save the interrogation scene and use it as part of the climax of your story in Sequence 8.

Sequence 8

Sequence 8 is the third and final attempt to come up with a solution and prove that it is the right one.

At this point, the detectives may have a suspect in custody – and this suspect may be guilty or innocent. Or they may have had to release the suspect – and the person they released was guilty or innocent. As the detectives begin formulating their final solution, they may begin Sequence 8 in a position where they are trying to prove an innocent person guilty or a guilty person guilty. The reader may know which, but the police won't be 100% sure either way until they have all of the evidence in the right sequence.

If the reader doesn't know which of the suspects is guilty, it may be that they want one of them to be innocent because the story has been such that they have grown to like this person. It's up to the writer to decide whether this person will be exonerated or not – but either way, the situation should be milked for as much suspense as possible!

Sequence 8 will contain, at some point, an explanation of what happened – how and why the crime was committed, who did it and what the sequence of events was both before and after the murder. This is the equivalent of the 'drawing room scene' in a whodunit where the detective gathers all of the suspects together and exonerates the innocent before finally pointing the finger at the murderer. In the police procedural, the suspects aren't gathered together in this way, but there still needs to be a final 'story' that puts all the pieces of evidence in their proper order and explains their meaning. Typically, in the police procedural, this explanation occurs either near the beginning of Sequence 8 or at the end. If you want to get it out of the way early – because explanations aren't particularly dramatic – then you can have the detectives formulate their theory, telling each other (and the reader) the story, and then they go off and prove it and the rest of the story is them in action. Or, if you need the solution to contain an element of surprise, you can have the murderer admit what happened at the end when they are finally captured. You could also split the explanation between these two points so that the detailed explanations about evidence are done away with early and their final significance is revealed at the end.

A statement by a witness may be shown to be a lie. They lied either in a misguided attempt to protect someone else or because they were afraid to tell the truth – perhaps because of some guilty secret of their own or because of some hold the murderer had over them.

False 'evidence' planted by the murderer to prove their innocence is demonstrated to be fake.

New evidence may be found – but it doesn't support their theory and cannot be made to fit it. Does this mean the theory is wrong?

The detectives may need to review the whole murder file – everything they have discovered to date – trying to view it objectively rather than trying to make it fit a theory. Is there something that they missed the first time through? A vital piece of evidence overlooked? Perhaps the clue is not something that they found but something that was missing at the crime scene. Something taken from the victim? If they find this object, it may be the last piece of evidence they need.

Other evidence may come from distant parts of the investigation – the missing vehicle may be located or details of the hotel registration that show the victim and one of the suspects *were* together on the night of the murder. Or some evidence may be found that shows a statement by a witness or suspect isn't true – which may have a knock-on effect for other parts of the story of what happened on the night of the murder. If one or more alibis depend on the statement being true, the innocence or guilt of suspects may need to be re-evaluated.

During these final crucial stages of the investigation, the police need to keep media reporters at bay so that they don't accidentally tip-off a suspect that the detectives are closing in.

The murderer doesn't know how close the detectives are to proving his or her guilt. They may feel confident that the alibi and false evidence they have planted is enough to prevent the police from ever identifying him (or her). Or the murderer may be afraid of being captured at any moment and be worried, paranoid, and on the alert. In a multi-viewpoint story, we may even see this from the murderer's point of view.

If the detectives are concentrating their efforts on the *wrong* suspect, they may interrogate the suspect and try to get them to 'crack' under the pressure. It may be that the reader – and perhaps one of the detectives – wants this person to be innocent, but the case against them seems incredibly strong. The detectives are able to prove part of their theory that shows this person guilty – but not all of it. They can demonstrate the proximity of the suspect to the victim – the can prove *opportunity* and perhaps even a *motive* – but they cannot (yet) prove conclusively that the suspect did actually murder the victim. They need just one more vital bit of evidence to seal their case against the suspect.

Interrogation of this suspect may become pretty intense. The detectives may suggest that an accomplice has already confessed all and implicated the suspect. Or that a witness who had been bullied into keeping quiet has finally revealed what they know. Under pressure from the good cop/bad cop routine, the suspect may become angry and/or upset and finally say something that seems to indicate his or her guilt. Not an admission, but a final missing bit of evidence – or an indication of where that evidence may be found. This evidence will either demonstrate the suspect's guilt – or prove that the other suspect is the murderer.

The police can finally piece together the real meaning of all of the clues/evidence and tell the real story of what happened on the night of the murder.

If you don't want to make an interrogation the centrepiece of your final sequence, you could have one of the two suspects – either the innocent one or the guilty one – attempt to flee, apparently demonstrating their guilt and inadvertently leading the detectives to a clue that demonstrates their guilt or innocence.

Or you could have the murderer become so worried about the police closing in that he or she attempts to trap the innocent suspect in a situation that will make them look guilty – perhaps even involving an apparent suicide and a letter of confession. Or by having the innocent suspect found by police standing over a body with a smoking gun in their hand.

At some point in the writing process – either in the early planning stages or perhaps not until you have reached the midpoint of your first draft – you need to decide how you want to end your story. What sort of scene do you want it to be and where do you want it to be set? Ideally you want the ending to reflect something that occurred in Sequence 1 to make the whole novel seem more of a piece – but obviously, you can tweak Sequence 1 in rewrites to make this happen. When you know what your ending is, you can work backwards towards the midpoint – or even right back to the opening of the story. This technique is common in writing mystery fiction and is referred to as 'back plotting.' There will almost always be an element of this – because once you've worked out the explanation for your mystery, you will need to go back and plant clues to support it. And you'll also need to plant a few things to support your detectives' wrong theories. Some writers do all of this during a detailed planning stage before they begin writing – which has advantages in that you always know what you're going to write next. For other writers, the planning stage is less detailed and they use their first draft to work out the details and then go back and fix the structure. There is no one right method for this – every writer discovers ways of doing things that work for them and these may change as their writing career and experience develop.

Limitations of the Single Case Plot

Before we go on to look at the multiple storyline structure, I want to make a few observations about the single case plot outlined above. Firstly, I think the 'pure' single case structure is only suitable for a short novel – say 60,000 words or less – or a screenplay of around 90 minutes. Even if you add a romantic subplot for one or both of your detectives, you will probably struggle to write a longer novel or screenplay – and the second half of Act II is at particular risk of seeming a bit 'thin.' If you want to write a story at the longer length, you will almost certainly need to add a second – and maybe even a third – case to be investigated, either by your main detectives or by another pair from their team. Your main plot will still be the same as above, but your additional subplot will increase the scope for incidents, suspense, and character relationships. Whether the two cases eventually turn out to be related or not is up to you. If you do this, your story will have some things in common with the private eye plot.

Secondly, for the first novel in a series, the single storyline plot – or single storyline with a subplot – is preferable to a full-on multiple storyline story in most cases. The more detailed investigation where two of your detectives get the most 'screen time' means you can introduce them properly to readers and give them a chance to bond. The introductions and backstories of the characters mean you have less space for multiple in-depth investigations. I think this is true even if you're planning to write a series of multi-storyline novels with multiple detectives. In the first book, introduce one pair as the main characters and have a second – and possibly even third – duo working on the subplot(s). Then in your next novel switch the focus and have one of the other partnerships take centre stage. This gives readers a better chance to know your people and gives you more scope for creating them in detail across several stories. One criticism that readers often make about books is that too many characters are introduced and it is difficult to keep track of who is who.

Thirdly, as I've already said, the single case plot structure risks having a weak section during the second half of Act II – the third quarter of the story. A feature of all thrillers is that they are plot driven and contain only limited character development – especially if you're writing a series. This gives you less opportunity for a full character-based subplot – and for the most part, readers don't want this sort of subplot in their police procedurals. So you need more plot to make up for this. But having the police come up with two wrong theories before hitting on the right one can risk your story feeling repetitive and making your detectives look a bit inept. You could probably write a much stronger structure with one wrong theory and then a correct theory – but you'd probably end up with a long novella rather than a short novel. Novellas are often structured more like the two acts of a television episode rather than the three acts of a movie.

You can probably see where I'm heading with this. The multiple storyline procedural novel effectively weaves together two or three (or more) of these novella-like stories, creating a cohesive whole by the addition of other material that acts like buttercream between the different layers. Did I mention that writers like to have their cake and eat it? Let's look at how multi-storyline procedurals can work.

Multiple Storyline Plot

The multiple storyline novel features several investigations going on at the same time and is intended to show how a 'real' team of detectives doesn't have the luxury of concentrating on one case at a time. The separate investigations may have nothing in common except that they are being handled by detectives from the same team – though often a couple of the cases do turn out to be linked in some way.

H.R.F. Keating indicated that this sort of story wasn't his cup of tea, saying he preferred a procedural that tells only one story and has one main protagonist with whom readers can identify. I think he's right in that ensemble stories with multiple plotlines are more difficult to write well and perhaps have a more limited audience. In a standalone novel or movie, it is much easier to 'get into' a story with a single hero whose subjective viewpoint you experience directly. When you're watching a group of protagonists you can't help feeling like an outsider with a more distant viewpoint. But when it comes to a series – either a series of novels or a television series – being able to follow the stories of a larger cast gives you more scope for variety and contrast and helps you avoid falling into an obvious formula.

Elizabeth Linington wrote police procedurals under her real name and the pseudonyms Dell Shannon and Lesley Egan. In an essay on the procedural, she said that she personally objected to procedurals set in large cities that "...imply that sleuths are happily handed only one case at a time to solve ... This is scarcely plausible, if we are trying to give a reasonably accurate picture of real-life police routine." If you want to write a single-case story, she suggested setting it in a small town where a big murder case is very rare.

Real detectives may each have half-a-dozen or more 'live' cases at any one time and a new one will come in before the old one is finished. In a multiple storyline novel, it would be too much to try and give one detective that much to do – the reader would quickly become confused about which case he's working on and the routine 'legwork' involved for each of the cases would make for dull reading. And it would be unrealistic to have the detective tie-up six cases during the course of a single novel – and to leave cases incomplete or unsolved might annoy the reader. More typical is to have a team of detectives investigating a handful of cases at the same time, each pair of detectives concentrating on one of them, and with other cases being referred to or arriving during the course of the story but not being actively worked on. The detectives that get the most 'screen-time' in the novel may investigate two cases at the same time to give more of an indication of the extensive workload 'real' detectives face. A rare exception is *Gideon's Day* which includes six storylines that unfold during the course of a lead detective's single working day.

How Many is 'Multiple'?

How many separate storylines should you have in your multiple storyline novel? More than one but no more than six is as close as I can come to an answer. And not all of them will be equal. In part, the number of storylines will depend on the length of your novel which will range from a minimum of 60,000 words up to a maximum of 100,000. I would say that 75 to 80,000 feels about the right length for a thriller of any kind, with only bestselling authors feeling obliged to push toward the upper limit. Ideally, the length of your novel is determined by the needs of your story, but you do have to bear in mind what you have been contracted to deliver (if applicable) or the typical length for a book in this genre, which counts as one of its conventions. While page-count isn't an issue with ebooks, you do still need to think about the cost of producing physical books for a paperback edition (either now or in the future) and about the cost per finished hour for audiobook versions.

Ed McBain's *Mischief*, which I have analysed in some detail, runs between 96 and 97,000 words. It has three main storylines that occupy 20 to 25,000 words each and another that runs for a bit under 8,500. The rest of the novel is made up of random crimes that are not connected to the main storylines and around 10,000 words following the lives of non-police characters who become victims of the crime that forms the climax of the story.

Multiple Storyline Plot Structure

Between 1956 and 2005, Ed McBain published more than fifty novels and novellas set in his fictional 87th Precinct. I have looked at early examples from the series and some of the later ones to get a feel for how he structured his novels. The first one was *Cop Hater,* which was made into a film in 1958 – it introduces Detective Steve Carella and has a single case plot which centres on the murder of a police detective. McBain deliberately avoided making Carella the hero of all of the books in the series, having other detectives from the same team take the lead in later novels. The later books also used a multi-storyline structure.

I said earlier that I took McBain's 1993 novel *Mischief* as an example to dissect and examine in detail. I chose this one because it comes relatively late in the series – number 45 out of about 55 – and also because one of the storylines features McBain's series villain the Deaf Man. Steve Carella and his wife also feature in the novel. Other characters who have featured in earlier books in the series, along with brief reminders of their stories, are also included.

As I mentioned above, *Mischief* weaves together four separate investigations, three written at novella length and the fourth more like an extended short story at around 8,000 words. There are also there are also four romantic subplots in the novel – one between a detective and the mother of the first victim, a major one between two of those affected by one of the crimes in the story, one between the villain and a woman he hires as a 'wheelman', and one between a detective and a superior officer. We also learn how Steve Carella and his wife met and became involved – events which actually occurred before the first novel in the series.

I could list the sequence in which the four storylines are presented – A,B,B,C,A,B,C etc. but I don't think that would be particularly helpful as the pattern varies from novel to novel. But what is useful is to note that three of the cases – and the pair of detectives investigating each one – are introduced in Sequence 1 and that two of these are resolved in Sequence 7, with the solution to the final one forming the climax of the novel in Sequence 8. The fourth, and shortest, of the cases begins in Section 4 and ends, except for its romantic subplot, ends in Sequence 5 – so effectively this fourth cases exists to provide interesting and dramatic events to lift the centre of the novel on either side of the midpoint. It is probably worth noting that all of the main cases should be introduced before the midpoint and – with rare exceptions – all of the main characters too. And you do not have to introduce all of your main crimes and investigations in Sequence 1, but they should begin before the end of Sequence 2 – i.e. they should all begin in Act I. And the major ones will end in Act III, that is Sequence 7 or Sequence 8.

This middle section storyline is told exclusively from the point of view of the detectives who are involved in it. A case involving the abandonment of old people who are 'dumped' by relatives who can no longer manage to care for them is told mainly from the point of view of detectives handling the case. The two more significant cases are told from the points of view of both the detectives and the criminals involved in them. If we consider the plot that climaxes at the end of the novel to be the main one – and this is one that involves the reappearance of a series 'villain' – there are an additional 10,000 words or so told from the points of view of two ordinary people whose lives will be impacted by the Deaf Man's plot – and theirs is the most significant relationship explored in this novel.

The first crime in *Mischief* is the murder of a graffiti artist – and this is the first of a series of such killings. The second crime introduced is that involving the Deaf Man, and is presented as him preparing for some kind of heist – though his target remains a relative mystery – and also sees him taunting Steve Carella, providing him with obscure 'clues' that are supposed to allow the detective to figure out what the Deaf Man is up to. The third crime is the abandonment of old people in public places. And the fourth crime is a hostage situation that quickly goes bad. Mixed in with these are unconnected shootings and other crimes – vignettes – usually told from the point of view of the criminal or a witness. Together, all of this is designed to show the never-ending tide of crime that is found in a major American city.

If all of this seems complicated, that's because multi-storyline stories *are* complicated – until you break them down and deal with each of the storylines as a separate single case story. One of the pleasures of reading a multi-storyline story is in seeing how the author brings separate strands together and shows how they are related. In *Mischief,* for example, we see the relationship between two citizens develop during the planning of an open-air music concert and we later learn that this is connected to one of the crimes – but we don't learn until very late on, as we approach the climax, just how the crime and the concert are connected – and what impact this will have on the relationship we have seen develop. Other storylines may not be connected, except for the fact that detectives from the same team are involved in investigating them – but we see the interaction of the detectives when they come together in the 'squad room' or HQ and compare notes, swap stories about experiences, and tell each other bad jokes.

The other crimes which occur and which are not seen to be investigated by the police in the novel can be used to add a sense of realism, contrast, or humour to the story. Some incidents are too bizarre to be part of a main plot but you can include them as little sideshows. Some may seem to be connected to one of the investigations but turn out to be red herrings. But occasionally, something that seems random and unconnected may actually be significant in one of the cases. The more random crimes can be inserted at points where you want to cut away from an investigation to show a passage of time or to create suspense if you cut away from the main action at a cliff-hanger moment. Or they can be used to slow down or speed up the pace of the story.

The multi-storyline procedural novel is the story of multiple crimes and so, obviously, needs to be set in a place where multiple crimes occur. This means that it is better suited to a big city location rather than a small town. It is more difficult – but not impossible – to write a multiple storyline police procedural set in a small town or rural community. If you want to try a small-town procedural, I would suggest having a look at the first season of the television series *Twin Peaks*. It is not a procedural as such, and you have to ignore the more supernatural elements, but if you want to see how the discovery of a young woman's body impacts on a small community – and sends ripples out across that community – then you can see it there. The first couple of episodes are still incredibly powerful – especially the performance by the actress playing the victim's mother. You also see the jurisdictional issue as the local police have to contend with the arrival of the FBI – Miguel Ferrer and David Duchovny's roles as FBI officers later in the series are also pretty impressive. And then there is the gradual uncovering of the secret relationships and criminal activities of other members of the community – it's like a cross between a crime show and a dark and twisted soap opera.

Another writer who handles the intrigues that bubble under the surface of small-town life is Stephen King. Again, ignore the supernatural or science fictional elements and look at how he creates characters and their relationships and backstories. Often, especially in the early stories, we see things from the point of view of younger characters. Many of his novels show what happens when something unexpected disrupts the equilibrium of a community. The film adaptations rarely manage to capture the sense of community that King creates, so I'd advise going to the original novels.

You can also find the 'twisted soap opera' setting in shows like *Desperate Housewives* or Grace Metalious's 1956 novel *Peyton Place*.

I've said before that a single murder can have a large impact in a small community. In a big city, murder is more commonplace and ordinary people are not impacted by it in the same way – because in the city everyone doesn't know everyone else. But if the murder happens close to home – literally and/or figuratively – or if there is a series of murders across the city, people pay more attention. But in either location, the crime 'belongs' to the community – ordinary people are affected by it, gossip about it, or have theories about who is behind it and how it should be punished. A key element of the police procedural is creating the community in which it takes place, which is why I have suggested looking outside the genre for examples of 'community creation.'

Even as late as #45 in his series, Ed McBain is revealing new things about the (fictional) city he uses as the location. There are bits of history, folklore, old news stories, and colourful local characters – these all contribute to making Isola seem like a real place that has been in existence for a long time. It's also worth bearing in mind that different people will view the same location in different ways. In a multi-viewpoint story, you can show the same place from the point of view of a criminal, a victim, and a policeman. The policeman will have knowledge of things that occur in the city that ordinary folks aren't aware of, and so his attitude is more world-weary and perhaps cynical. The policeman is also more likely to have an understanding of the consequences of certain actions – which even criminals may not understand or care about. Someone who has lived in a location for a lifetime will have seen it change, so they will see it differently – they may refer to features that no longer exist or refer to the 'Jackson house' even though no-one named Jackson has lived there for twenty years.

5 | Forensic Investigation

What is a Forensic Thriller? The definition on *WritersDigest.com* is: "A thriller featuring the work of forensic experts, whose involvement often puts their own lives at risk." This captures the two essential elements of this type of thriller – the importance of forensic expertise and the fact that an expert protagonist is caught up in a thriller plot.

There is a tendency to think that 'forensic expert' means only a pathologist who examines the body of a victim of crime or a specialist from the crime lab who collects samples from a crime scene and analyses them, but in reality – and in fiction – there is a much broader range of expertise under the forensic heading. We might also think that 'forensic' means detailed scientific analysis, but the term 'forensic' is more specific than that – it comes from the Latin *forensis* which means pertaining to a 'forum' which could be a court, tribunal, or public debate. Today we use forensic to mean pertaining to a court of law, especially in relation to the detection of crime.

While many thrillers *do* centre on forensic medicine and forensic science, some are based on forensic psychiatry or psychology, forensic accountancy, forensic anthropology and forensic reconstruction. Digital forensics – the examination of personal computers, cell phones, cameras and other devices – has also become an important part of investigative work. I'll touch on these and other areas of expertise later in the chapter, but for the most part, I will focus on pathology and forensic science as examples of how such expertise can be used in a thriller plot.

In her book *Forensics: The Anatomy of Crime* (2014), crime novelist and journalist Val McDermid says that forensic investigation focuses on two things, the crime scene and the body of the victim and that ideally the body is discovered at the scene so that the relationship between the two can be used to help the investigator reconstruct the events that led to the death.

The forensic thriller is a type of *expert thriller,* one of several sub-genres that feature a person with expertise in a particular field, like the legal thriller and the medical thriller. The forensic thriller combines elements of the murder mystery, the police procedural, and the medical thriller and – in some cases – the legal thriller as well.

Cases, Cold Cases, and Old Cases

A *cold case* is an unsolved crime that a previous investigation failed to solve and which is later re-opened and investigated again. Some mysteries and thrillers feature an investigation into a crime that was committed in the past – sometimes many years ago – but which was not investigated, and perhaps was not even discovered, at the time – these are historical cases but since there was no earlier attempt to solve them, they are not cold cases.

The re-investigation of old cases is nothing new – the Hercule Poirot mystery *Five Little Pigs* (1942, *Murder in Retrospect* in the US) has the Belgian detective solve a crime that was committed sixteen years previously, based solely on recorded testimony and present-day recollections. Technically, he's investigating a miscarriage of justice rather than a cold case, but the plot structure is the same.

Historical Development of the Forensic Thriller

The history of the forensic thriller is closely tied to developments in the fields of forensic science and forensic medicine. There are a number of excellent books on the history of these fields, as well as texts about developments in specific areas, and I'm not going to attempt to summarise them here. Val McDermid's *Forensics: The Anatomy of Crime* provides an excellent introduction to the subject.

In the early days of the mystery genre, the pathologist, coroner, or police surgeon was usually a peripheral character who came on stage to confirm that a death was, indeed, suspicious and to provide a time and cause of death. The detective-protagonist would then go off and discover who had means, motive, and opportunity and thus unmask the murderer.

The 'forensic scientist,' on the other hand, has been part of the mystery genre since the beginning. If we accept Edgar Allan Poe's 'The Murders in the Rue Morgue' (1841) as the first detective story, the Chevalier C. Auguste Dupin's careful examination of the crime scene and the clues he obtains from it is the first example of a crime scene investigation. His methods were expanded upon by Arthur Conan Doyle when he created Sherlock Holmes, whose scientific study into the identification of cigarette ashes has become almost an in-joke in the genre. The concept of a 'scientific detective' was taken even further by R. Austin Freeman in his stories about Dr. John Thorndyke.

Thorndyke, an expert in medical jurisprudence, first appeared in print in *The Red Thumb Mark* (1907), where his scientific methods were used to prove whether a thumbprint found at a crime scene was genuine or not. Thorndyke featured in a further 20 novels and around 40 short stories. Freeman also pioneered the 'inverted' detective story in which the identity of the criminal is known by the reader from the beginning and the story shows how the investigator discovers and proves this person's guilt.

Another scientific sleuth was Professor Craig Kennedy, created by Arthur B. Reeve and first appearing in the short story collection *The Poisoned Pen* in 1911. The stories feature the latest scientific discoveries of the time including lie detectors, ballistics, and wiretapping.

Reggie Fortune was a medical consultant working for Scotland Yard in over fifty short stories written by H.C. Bailey, gathered into a number of collections, the first being *Call Mr. Fortune* (1920) and the last being published in 1948.

An early writer to use a medical examiner as a protagonist was psychiatrist Ernest Marsh Proate who wrote a series of stories beginning in 1926 for *Detective Story Magazine* featuring Dr. Aloysius Moran, Chief Medical Examiner of New York City. The stories are melodramatic with a hint of the Gothic and the protagonist with his 'Watson' in tow performs the function of a classical detective.

Another pathologist hero was Dr. Daniel Webster Coffee, created by Lawrence G. Blochman, who featured in two volumes of short stories, *Diagnosis: Homicide* (1950) and *Clues for Dr. Coffee* (1964).

The first story featuring the reconstruction of the facial features of a victim based on a skull seems to be *About the Murder of a Startled Lady* (1935) by Anthony Abbot (real name Fulton Oursler). The protagonist, Police Commissioner Thatcher Colt, asks a sculptor who creates waxworks for a Chamber of Horrors to model the image of a young woman whose skeleton was found in a box. The first such attempts in real life are credited to Russian palaeontologist Mikhail Gerasimov who in the late 1930s used a combination of anthropology, archaeology, and forensic science to create the likenesses of primitive men and then later more contemporary figures.

Gerasimov, whose autobiography is titled *The Face Finder*, was the inspiration for the character of Professor Andreev in Martin Cruz Smith's *Gorky Park*.

Forensic dentistry or odontology has an even longer history – Sheridan le Fanu used it in his story 'The Room in the Dragon Volant' published in 1872 and Rodrigues Ottolengui used it in 'The Phoenix of Crime' (1898). The first recorded account of dentistry being used to identify victims in real life is believed to be the fire at the Bazar de la Charité in Paris in 1897.

There were few stories written *by* pathologists until relatively recently. Bernard Knight was a Home Office pathologist who was technical advisor on the BBC television series *The Expert* about a Home Office Pathologist, Dr. John Hardy, broadcast between 1968 and 1976 and wrote a tie-in novel *The Expert* (1976) under the pseudonym Bernard Picton. Under his own name, Knight wrote a series of twelve historical mysteries, published between 1998 and 2012, about 'Crowner John,' a former knight in the 12th century who acts as an early form of coroner.

Modern Forensic Thriller Writers

Patricia Cornwell – Her novel *Postmortem* (1990) about medical examiner Dr. Kay Scarpetta is widely regarded as the first modern forensic thriller. It was loosely based on the case of serial killer Timothy Wilson Spencer, the 'Southside Strangler.' The author was working for the Office of the Chief Medical Examiner of Virginia at the time of the case. The character of Scarpetta was inspired by real-life medical examiner Dr. Marcella Farinelli Fierro. Twenty-four novels were published in the series between 1990 and 2016.

Jefferson Bass – Pseudonym of television documentary maker Jon Jefferson and forensic anthropologist William M. Bass. The two met when Jefferson wrote and directed a two-part documentary for the National Geographic Channel, *Biography of a Corpse* and *Anatomy of a Corpse*, which showcased the work of the University of Tennessee Anthropological Research Facility, popularly referred to as the 'Body Farm.' William Bass established the facility in 1971 as the first research centre to systematically study the decomposition of human remains. Jefferson and Bass collaborated on a book *Death's Acre: Inside the Legendary Forensic Lab, the Body Farm, Where the Dead Do Tell Tales* (2004) and then went on to write a novel as 'Jefferson Bass' – *Carved in Bone* (2006) is the first in the 'Body Farm' series featuring anthropologist Dr. Bill Brockton. In 2007 Bass and Jefferson published *Beyond the Body Farm* a non-fiction book detailing more of the cases Bass worked on.

Jeffery Deaver – Deaver's website describes him as a 'former journalist, folksinger and attorney' as well as a best-selling author. He has written 14 novels about Lincoln Rhyme as of 2018, beginning with *The Bone Collector* (1997). Rhyme was a 'forensic criminalist' working in the field until an accident at a crime scene crushed his spine and left him a quadriplegic able to move little more than his head. In the first in the series, Rhyme's former partner consults with him about a serial killer, the 'bone collector' of the title. Deaver also wrote four novels about Kathryn Dance, beginning with *The Sleeping Doll* (2007), an FBI interrogator specialising in reading body language – she had previously appeared in the Lincoln Rhyme novel *The Cold Moon* (2006).

Val McDermid – Dr. Tony Hill is a clinical psychologist who works as a profiler for the Home Office and the police, specialising in investigations involving in violent offenders and serial killers. He first appeared in the novel *The Mermaids Singing* (1995). A television series *Wire in the Blood* was made in the UK with twenty-four episodes broadcast between 2002 and 2008 – Robson Green played the title character.

Kathy Reichs – A forensic anthropologist and academic who has consulted for the Office of the Chief Medical Examiner in North Carolina. To date, she has written nineteen novels and a collection of short stories/novellas featuring forensic anthropologist Temperance Brennan, whose background and work are based on Reichs'. The first in the series was *Déjà Dead* published in 1997. The television series *Bones* is loosely based on her novels.

Simon Beckett – A British journalist and author who has written six novels about forensic anthropologist David Hunter, the first being *The Chemistry of Death* (2006). The stories were inspired by a visit made to the 'Body Farm' while researching an article for the *Daily Telegraph*. The newspaper article is available on the author's website (www.simonbeckett.com). Of his protagonist, Beckett has said: "There are enough heavy-drinking, maverick tough-guys in crime fiction already, without me adding to them. I wanted a character who was more flawed, who was introspective and even vulnerable in some respects. Hunter's very human - he doubts himself all the time. But there's still a stubborn streak in him. He's got a strong sense of right and wrong, and he'll stick his neck out for something he believes in."

Tess Gerritsen is the *author* of several bestselling medical thrillers. Her 2001 novel *The Surgeon* introduced Boston police detective Jane Rizzoli and *The Apprentice* (2002) introduced medical examiner Maura Isles. As of 2017, there are twelve novels in the series. The TNT television series *Rizzoli & Isles,* based on the novels, ran for seven seasons between 2010 and 2016.

Lisa Black has *worked* as a forensic scientist in Cleveland and a 'latent print examiner' in Florida. She wrote five novels about forensic investigator Theresa MacLean up to 2014, the first being *Takeover* (2008). More recently she has written four novels about forensic investigator Maggie Gardiner and Jack Renner, a killer with a conscience. The first in the series is *That Darkness* (2016).

Meg Gardiner – The 'Jo Beckett' series is about a forensic psychiatrist based in San Francisco. Interviewed by Sandra Parshall for the *Poe's Deadly Daughters blog,* Gardiner said of her character: "Jo calls herself a deadshrinker. She analyses the dead for the police. She's the last resort in baffling cases. When the cops and the medical examiner can't determine the manner of a victim's death, they turn to Jo to perform a psychological autopsy and figure out whether it was accident, suicide, or murder. Jo looks at victims' emotional, moral, and psychological lives to figure out why they died." And she told *Killer Reads* that "Jo doesn't pick up gory bits of trace evidence with tweezers. She digs into people's passions, obsessions and secrets to find out what killed them. Her territory is the psyche and the human heart." The first in the series is *The Dirty Secrets Club* (2008).

Iris Johansen – Twenty-six novels have appeared to date in the 'Eve Duncan' series, the first was *The Face of Deception* (1998). The protagonist is a forensic sculptor. A television adaptation of the second novel *The Killing Game* for the Lifetime channel starred Laura Prepon.

Caleb Carr's 1994 novel *The Alienist* is set in 1896 and features the investigation of a series of gruesome murders by a team who use new techniques including fingerprinting and psychology. A ten-part television adaptation was broadcast by TNT/Netflix in 2018. Dr. Lazlo Kreizler, a psychologist and early criminal profiler, appeared in a sequel *The Angel of*

Darkness (1997) and two further novels were announced but have not yet published.

The Forensic Thriller on Television

Quincy, M.E. – Eight seasons totalling 148 episodes were broadcast between 1976 and 1983 with Jack Klugman starring as Los Angeles County medical examiner Dr. R. Quincy. The series was inspired by the book *Where Death Delights* by former FBI agent Marshall Houts. The character of Quincy is also thought to have been partly modelled on Thomas Noguchi, the former Chief Medical Examiner-Coroner for the County of Los Angeles who became famous as a result performing the autopsies of a number of well-known film stars and politicians including Marilyn Monroe. In most episodes, Quincy sets out to discover the cause of a possibly suspicious death and his investigations bring him into conflict with his boss or the homicide detective on the case. He is assisted by lab assistant Sam Fujiyama. Earlier episodes were often whodunit-style mysteries but later seasons included investigations related to various social issues.

Wojeck was broadcast on CBC Television from 1966 to 1968 – twenty episodes plus a 1992 TV movie. John Vernon played coroner Steve Wojeck who "regularly fights moral injustices raised by the deaths he investigated" according to Wikipedia. The show was inspired by the work of Ontario Chief Coroner Dr. Morton Shulman.

The BBC television series *The Expert* broadcast 1968-1976 (62 episodes) was a police procedural series featuring Marius Goring as Home Office pathologist Dr. John Hardy.

Bones – about the work of a forensic anthropologist, Temperance Brennan, loosely based on the character from Kathy Reichs' novels. Reichs served as a producer on the show – to 'keep the science honest' – and has written three episodes and appeared in one. In the show the lead character also writes novels about a fictional forensic anthropologist 'Kathy Reichs.'

The Wire in the Blood – based on the 'Tony Hill' series by Scottish author Val McDermid.

Silent Witness – A BBC television drama featuring a team of forensic pathology experts originally led by Dr. Sam Ryan (Amanda Burton). The show first aired in 1996 with the 21st series, and has continued into 2019. Between 1996 and 2003 series creator Nigel McCrery published five original novels featuring characters from the series.

CSI: Crime Scene Investigation – A police procedural series focusing on forensics work. Fifteen seasons were broadcast by CBS between 2000 and 2015 with a total of 337 episodes. In the first nine seasons, William Petersen played Gil Grissom, a forensic entomologist. *CSI: Miami, CSI: NY,* and *CSI: Cyber* are all spin-offs from the original series and all are said to exist in the same fictional world as the CBS series *Without a Trace* and *Cold Case*. There was some criticism that the show distorted the nature of crime scene investigators' work and exaggerated its speed and effectiveness, such that the term 'CSI effect' was coined to describe the unrealistic expectations that members of the public and particularly jury members might have of forensic evidence as a result of what was seen on television.

Waking the Dead – a BBC television series with 92 episodes broadcast between 2000 and 2011, with a five-part prequel broadcast on BBC radio in 2018. The show features a fiction London-based cold case unit made up of detectives, a psychological profiler and a forensic scientist. A spin-off, *The Body Farm*, was broadcast in 2011.

Body of Proof – broadcast 2011 to 2013 by ABC with three seasons making a total of 42 episodes. Dana Delany played medical examiner Dr. Megan Hunt.

Crossing Jordan – an NBC series that ran for six seasons from 2001 to 2007. Jill Hennessy played forensic pathologist Dr. Jordan Cavanaugh employed by the Massachusetts Office of the Chief Medical Examiner. The show has been described as more character-driven and less graphic than the CSI series. The show was set in the same fictional world as NBC's *Las Vegas* and there was some cross-over of characters.

Modern Forensics

I will cover forensic psychology in the next chapter which details the psychological profiling of serial killers. Below are brief descriptions of some of the areas of forensic investigation that might be used in writing fiction – this list is provided for information/inspiration only and is not intended to be complete. There are many textbooks covering these specialised areas in detail and I would suggest picking up one of these if any of these areas of forensics strike you as having the potential for a story or series of stories. As with any scientific or technical discipline, seek books that have been published in the last year or two as these are more likely to provide details of the current 'state of the art.' Obviously, if you are writing a story set in an earlier period, you should select reference sources from that time.

Serology & DNA Typing

Serology is the analysis of blood and body fluids. DNA typing has mostly replaced traditional serology, and so the term is being replaced by the broader term 'forensic biology'. DNA typing, sometimes referred to as DNA analysis, has largely replaced traditional blood typing in forensic labs. As well as blood and other body fluids, it can be applied to hair and skin samples. The science has developed rapidly since the late 1980s and it is important to refer to up-to-date texts when referring to this type of analysis.

Forensic Pathology

The primary job of a forensic pathologist is to perform autopsies in cases of suspicious or questioned deaths and to determine the cause, manner, and mechanism/circumstances of death. The pathologist may also be required to establish the identity of the body and estimate a time of death – the PMI or post-mortem interval.

Forensic Toxicology

Toxicology is the analysis of drugs and poisons in blood, body fluids and – in the case of gaseous poisons – lung tissue. Fiction deals mainly with post-mortem toxicology, but the field also includes drug testing, including the use of illegal drugs, drug overdose, performance-enhancing drugs in sport, and blood alcohol levels. In post-mortem forensic analysis, detection of poisons is the responsibility of the medical examiner. Both the substance and the amount of it ingested have to be determined, measured by the LD_{50} or 'lethal dose 50.' Poisons can be organic (e.g. hemlock, strychnine or snake venom) or inorganic (e.g. cyanide, arsenic or mercury) and some exist in gaseous form, such as carbon monoxide. The substance has to be extracted from body samples and isolated before it can be tested and identified.

Forensic Chemistry

Toxicology and drug analysis are subsections of forensic chemistry and in smaller organisations, toxicology and forensic chemistry may be carried out by the same team. Forensic chemistry involves the application of the principles and procedures of chemistry – especially analytical chemistry.

Other areas of analysis where these procedures may be applied include evidence of suspected arson, explosives, paint, fibres, gunshot residue, and other forms of trace evidence. Modern apparatus used includes gas chromatography, mass spectrometry, high-performance liquid chromatography, infrared, visible, and ultraviolet spectrometry, scanning electron microscopes and x-ray diffraction. But as well as this, traditional 'wet chemical' techniques are also still used. Wet chemical techniques are often used in preliminary 'presumptive tests.' Also known as colour, spot, or screening tests, these involve adding a chemical reagent to a sample which results in some form of colour change that indicates the likely presence of a particular substance such as blood, gunshot residue, or explosives. These tests are not definitive but suggest that the presence of a substance is more likely than not and indicate what further analysis might need to be carried out.

Forensic Odontology

According to the *Encyclopedia of Forensic Science,* this involves the application of "dentistry to legal matters in the areas of personal identification, age determination, bite marks, evaluation of wounds and trauma to the jaws and teeth (particularly in potential child abuse cases), and evaluation of alleged dental malpractice or negligence." The fact that teeth have five exposed surfaces – four sides and the top – and that teeth in the jaw have different spacings, including orientations and gaps, and that a person's teeth will acquire unique patterns of wear, extractions, and fillings, the overall pattern is considered to be unique to a specific individual. The principal organisation in this field in the USA is the American Board of Forensic Odontologists, which publishes guidelines.

Identification based on dentition can be made by comparing the teeth of a victim against existing medical records – this can be used for individuals and in identifying people in 'mass casualty' events such as aeroplane crashes. Where there are no records to compare a victim's teeth against, the odontologist can provide only an estimation of the victim's age – unless there are distinctive types of dental work that might indicate where the work was carried out.

Forensic Anthropology

Forensic anthropology is the analysis of skeletal remains as they relate to legal procedures. It is a form of physical anthropology which includes osteology. Work involves determining whether material is actually bone or teeth and if so, whether they are human remains. The age of the remains may also be estimated as can age at death, gender, race, time since death (the post-mortem interval), and possibly the manner and circumstances of death. The American Board of Forensic Anthropology regulates practice and certifies practitioners.

Wilton M. Krogman (1903-1987) was an American anthropologist who wrote an article for the FBI newsletter in 1939 titled 'A Guide to the Identification of Human Skeletal Material' and this was said to have marked the beginning of forensic anthropology in the United States. Krogman was popularly referred to as 'the bone doctor' and his *The Human Skeleton in Forensic Medicine,* the first edition of which was published in 1962, was regarded as the definitive work on the subject.

Forensic Taphonomy

The study of the process of death and its aftermath including decomposition. This includes analysis of bone weathering, the scattering of remains by carnivores and scavengers, and the post-mortem movement of remains, especially by water. Marks found on bones are analysed to try and determine their possible causes. Forensic entomology - especially the effect of insects on the decomposition of remains - can be a significant element of this type of study. Taphonomy can also help determine whether a body was dismembered deliberately or whether scattering of remains was caused by carnivores after the body was originally deposited. It also studies whether the site where the remains were found is the location of the victim's death or if the remains have been removed and reburied.

Fingerprint Analysis

Fingerprints are now taken either with the traditional ink-based process or using digital scanners. Searching of fingerprint databases is carried out using an automated fingerprint identification system and standardised file formats mean that searches can be constructed across multiple databases. While the computer locates the closest matches, a human fingerprint examiner determines the final identification. Footprints and palm prints may also be taken for analysis.

'Elimination prints' are fingerprints of any innocent persons who might have been at the crime scene - including the police - who might have inadvertently left a fingerprint at the scene and need to be eliminated from searches.

Fingerprints have patterns of 'friction ridges' in the form of loops, arches, tents, and whorls the combination of which is estimated to be unique to the point that the chances of two people having the same pattern are one in sixty billion. Fingerprints found at a crime scene can be latent (almost invisible) or visible prints left on a surface. 'Plastic' prints are those left in a pliable material such as chewing gum or modelling clay. Various methods are used for making latent prints visible and for preserving fingerprints – 'dusting' for fingerprints is just one of these and there are different types of 'dust' used. In order for a fingerprint to be classified as a 'match' there must be 6 to 12 points of commonality (the number varies in different jurisdictions). The process of identification is called dactyloscopy. It is one of the disciplines recognised by the International Association of Identification. Others include biometrics, bloodstain pattern identification, facial identification, digital evidence, footwear and tyre track analysis, and forensic art and photography. See www.theiai.org

Ballistics & Firearms

The term 'forensic analysis of firearms' is more accurate than 'forensic ballistics' since ballistics is the study of projectiles and their movement through the air. But most television shows will have someone say 'send this to ballistics.' Forensic analysis of firearms is broader and includes examination of gunshot residue, the chemical analysis of bullets, determination of the distance between a shooter and a victim, and the restoration of serial numbers on weapons.

Often only a bullet or casing is found at the scene of a shooting and analysis will begin by determining the *type* of weapon it came from. Then comes the process of trying to identify the *specific* gun that fired it. When a bullet is fired, marks are made into it as it travels down the barrel of the gun and these striations will be unique to the weapon. This enables a bullet or casing discovered at a crime scene to be matched to any weapon recovered during the subsequent investigation. 'Ballistic fingerprinting' is the process of linking firearms evidence such as a bullet or cartridge casing to a specific weapon. Databases of patterns and marks can now be searched for a match against any weapon used in a previous crime.

In the United States, the National Integrated Ballistics Information Network is co-ordinated by the federal Bureau of Alcohol, Tobacco, Firearms and Explosives.

Bloodstain Stain Pattern Analysis

Bloodstain pattern or 'splatter' is used by investigators to try and reconstruct what happened at a crime scene. The correct interpretation of patterns of blood splatter has been a subject of much debate, with experts sometimes differing in their conclusions. *Flight Characteristic and Stain Patterns of Human Blood* (1971) by Herbert L. MacDonell, published by the US Government, is considered an important report on this type of analysis. See also the International Association of Bloodstain Pattern Analysis at www.iabpa.org and the Scientific Working Group on Bloodstain Pattern Analysis at www.swgstain.org

Bloodstain pattern evidence was used in the 1954 trial of Dr. Sam Sheppard and he was convicted of killing his wife. The case inspired the television series *The Fugitive* which in turn was the basis for the Harrison Ford movie in 1993.

Forensic Art & Sculpture

Reconstruction of the facial features of a victim to aid in analysis can be created two-dimensionally in a drawing or digital painting or in three-dimensions using physical or digital sculpture. In the past, there was a limit to the extent that fragile or damaged skulls could be used for three-dimensional reconstruction and since the skull was itself a piece of evidence, it had to be handled without causing permanent changes to it. In these days of digital scanning techniques, there is more scope to make a 'copy' of a skull to form the basis of a reconstruction. Tissue depths in reconstructions are estimated using data tables and the muscle structure of the face is recreated before creating the skin surface.

Facial Recognition & Biometrics

Biometrics originally referred to the measurement of living organisms but is now used to refer to physical characteristics that are unique to an individual. Fingerprints are the most common form of biometric analysis. Other forms include retinal scans which use the unique pattern of blood vessels in the eye; the pattern of the iris of an eye; speech patterns, and the geometry of the face or hand. Automated facial recognition and tracking systems are being developed and 'gait analysis' - looking at the unique way in which a person walks - is also being studied.

Digital Forensics

Also referred to as 'computer forensics' or 'cyber forensics.' Includes analysis of e-mail, video, sound recordings, digital photographs, online chat or messaging, social media use, and hacking. Recent interest in this area has centred on attempts by law enforcement agencies to gain access to password-protected devices such as cell phones and tablets. Investigation of illegal online activity may also involve the use of forensic psychology to try and profile hackers and discover unique patterns in their activities.

Suspicious, Forged, or Altered Documents

These are often referred to as questioned documents after the 1910 book of that title by Albert S. Osborn. Forged banknotes or wills are obvious forms of documents that might be questioned, but any form of handwritten or printed document might be called into question as part of an investigation. This may include analysis of handwriting (not to be confused with graphology) and determining whether signatures are genuine. Testing of paper and ink and also determining the age of a document may be required. Typewritten or printed documents may also be analysed. Typewriters, copiers, fax machines, and computer printers all have features that mean individual machines can be tied directly the documents produced on them – especially if the machine has been used for some time and developed unique patterns of wear or damage. See the American Society of Questioned Document Examiners and the Questioned Document section of the American Academy of Forensic Sciences.

Forensic Accountancy & Fraud Investigation

A forensic accountant is an expert in accountancy and the law as it relates to finance who also has experience in investigating crimes such as fraud and embezzlement. They may also be involved in the investigation of money laundering, bankruptcy, economic damage calculations, or personal injury and insurance claims. They typically work closely with law enforcement officers and lawyers during the course of an investigation or may be called to appear as an expert witness at a trial. As a form of 'expert thriller,' the forensic accountancy thriller has much in common with legal thrillers, such as John Grisham's *The Firm,* business thrillers, and also the police procedural.

The 2016 film *The Accountant* starring Ben Affleck is an action-thriller in which the protagonist is an accountant who investigates suspected embezzlement within criminal organisations. The Treasury Department is closing in on him while at the same time his present investigation makes him some very dangerous enemies.

Canadian author Ian Hamilton has written a series of a dozen novels about Chinese-Canadian forensic accountant Ava Lee, the first of them being *The Water Rat of Wanchai* (2011).

Forensic linguistics

Involves the analysis of the use of language either in written documents or in voice analysis. Linguists may work on threatening letters or phone calls, ransom notes, disputed wills, and other key documents. Statistical analysis of texts is now carried out by computer software, which has also been used to test documents such as the works of Shakespeare to determine whether parts of the plays had been written by other authors. It can also be used to analyse of court transcriptions or other legal statements.

Other Forms of Forensic Investigation

There are other specialised areas of forensic investigation that you might want to consider as possible subjects for a thriller. *Forgery* of documents and works of art are two areas where there have been a number of high-profile real-life cases.

The investigation of *criminal enterprises* (organised crime) is an area where several forms of forensic activity may be involved, including accountancy.

Environmental crimes, such as industrial pollution of land or water, is also investigated using forensic science – from the identification of the toxic substance to the tracing of its source.

Crimes against *wildlife*, such as poaching of endangered species, are increasingly being investigated using forensic techniques, which are used to identify the poachers but also to test skins and furs, bones and horns, and products made from animal remains. Related to this are crimes against domestic animals and livestock, where 'victims' may be examined in much the same way as humans.

The investigation of fires and explosions – along with the identification of human remains found at the scene – are areas that require particular skills and experience and which might form the basis of an effective thriller.

Genre Conventions

The forensic thriller is effectively a police procedural seen from the point of view of a different member of the investigating team – someone other than the detective.

Hero

The hero of a forensic thriller is an expert in one of the fields of forensic science mentioned above. But while they are an expert in their field, they are not an expert action-adventure hero in the manner of, say, James Bond. The hero here is more along the lines of the ordinary innocent person – an amateur – who gets caught up in a criminal investigation and/or conspiracy. This means they have a lot in common with the hero of the Medical Thriller and the 'amateur on the run' that I wrote about in *Suspense Thriller*.

In terms of character archetype, a forensic expert is a scientist and so the Thinker archetype will be a significant part of their personality. If their area of specialism includes medicine, psychiatry, or psychology then there is also likely to be an element of the Carer in their character. If the character is mostly lab-based, the Thinker will be predominant, but if their work involves going out into the field and working with other people, the Carer will still be a secondary element – at least in professional encounters – but will help make the character more empathetic and more of a team player.

Because the hero of the forensic thriller is not a typical action-hero, we find female characters in this role quite often. And she is often contrasted with more macho detective types with whom she works on cases.

Villain or Antagonist

The villain in a forensic thriller functions in the same way as that in a private eye novel or a police procedural. The villain's identity may or may not be known – to the hero and/or the reader – and it is the hero's job to use his or her expertise to provide evidence that will enable charges to be brought against them and the case proved in court. Often the villain remains off-stage and unidentified until the later stages of the story when the hero is targeted by them, meaning that for the first half or more of the story, the villain is only known through his actions as revealed by the evidence. The serial killer is perhaps the most extreme example of the villain faced by the forensic thriller hero and we will spend time with him in the next chapter.

If there is a conspiracy element to your plot, then the villain will function more in the way of the conspiracy thriller antagonist – and the hero will stumble upon evidence of his conspiracy when applying her expert knowledge and experience to the case.

Romantic Co-Protagonist

The home life of the forensic thriller hero serves a similar purpose as that of the police procedural hero's – it grounds the hero within the community that they serve. It also helps demonstrate the everyday world of average citizens that the hero seeks to protect – it helps show what is at stake from the forces of disorder.

It is something of a cliché to have the female forensic expert in a romantic relationship with a detective, but there are sound reasons for doing this. The forensic expert is only one of many specialists contributing to an investigation – and this means that they are privy only to a very small part of the whole case. In our thriller, we want the hero to be more deeply involved in the investigation, so to provide wider access to the case we put them in a relationship with a detective who is leading the investigation. This gives them an excuse to have dinner and talk about the details of the case, giving the hero more opportunity to participate.

This relationship, especially in the first of a series of novels, often begins in a similar way to a typical romance – the two meet and are attracted to one another but their differences in personality mean that their interaction is quite antagonistic. The detective is too much of an alpha male type and the hero thinks he's a jerk; while he is probably intimidated by her because she is much smarter than him. This is the cliché and you have to find some way to put an original spin on it. Making the hero and detective ex-husband and wife might be interesting. Or you could come up with a more platonic but equally antagonistic relationship – maybe brother and sister or people who have been rivals in another sphere. Have fun with it and make it fresh. And leave yourself scope to expand the relationship if you plan to write a series.

Other Characters

The hero of a forensic thriller may have children from a current or previous relationship, or she may not. She may be living with or caring for an older relative. Don't make your hero a loner with no living relatives – leave yourself options for expanding the cast of characters as your series progresses.

I've already said that characters contributing to an investigation do not work alone, and that means that there can be any number of other characters encountered by the hero during her work. There will be colleagues in the department where she works – experts in other areas and assistants who work in her own area. And as with the hero of the police procedural story, the hero here will probably work for an organisation with a hierarchical structure that may also fit within a larger social hierarchy, overseen by a district attorney or mayor's office perhaps.

Specialists, while experts, often have an older and more experienced mentor character to call upon – often the person who trained them. This person can be used as a sounding board – and gives the writer an opportunity to have two experts discuss subject matter that the reader needs to learn to understand the importance of a particular forensic technique.

Crime & Conspiracy

In a forensic thriller, the crime in question is almost always murder – and not just because a pathologist needs a body to examine. No matter what area of forensic expertise features in your story, the hero and her colleagues are going to be examining evidence – typically physical evidence, but in the case of areas such as psychiatry and psychology, less tangible forms. If the victim of a crime is still alive, detectives can question them about what occurred and the work of forensic experts takes more of a backseat. To bring forensic investigation into the foreground we need a situation where the victim cannot tell their own story and what occurred has to be pieced together from the available evidence.

A conspiracy may feature if a victim's death is part of a larger plot that a group of conspirators are trying to conceal. This may involve a single death or multiple victims over a period of time. The connection between the victim(s) and the conspirators is something that the hero would need to figure out. Often, the hero will come to suspect that there *is* a conspiracy because someone has deliberately manipulated the evidence to make it *appear* that events transpired in a particular way, while concealing what really happened. This is a variation on the technique used by the murderer in a whodunit and helps ad a mystery element to the forensic thriller – Who manipulated the evidence and why?

Settings

Locations used in the forensic thriller include almost everything that appears in a police procedural plus some from the medical thriller and, perhaps, some from the legal thriller if the hero is called on to work with the prosecution or defence team as an expert witness. In addition, there may be one or more settings specifically related to the area of forensic expertise – a pathology lab or some other scientific laboratory, an academic setting where a mentor character may be consulted, or perhaps a specialist research facility such as the now legendary 'body farm'.

Iconography

Again, the things we 'see' in a forensic thriller tend to mirror those of the police procedural and medical thriller. There may also be specific equipment or techniques unique to the particular area of forensic science featured in the story – the body on the stainless-steel autopsy table in a pathology thriller is an obvious example. Fingerprint experts have their own tools, technology and activities and other experts will as well. This is where you need to do your research and watch experts in action – either in person or via documentary-style videos. You need to try and get an understanding of sights, sounds and smells as well as textures so that you can share these with the reader.

Themes

Any criminal investigation will feature some variation on the theme of justice and bringing the guilty to account, but in the forensic thriller this often becomes more personal. The forensic expert pieces together the evidence and feels that they have come to 'know' the victim – they tend to think of the victim as a person rather than just a body in a drawer. This may be emphasised if the hero makes some connection between her own life and that of the victim. And there is a sense that a dead person cannot tell their own story and so the forensic expert has a responsibility to tell this story for them – becoming their advocate. This is where the Carer element of the hero's personality comes into play – her ability to put herself in the victim's position and see things from their viewpoint. This can make the hero a valuable ally to the detective who cannot – or cannot allow himself – to empathise so closely with the victim.

Tone

This sub-genre usually aims for gritty realism – dealing with crime scenes is not romantic or funny and there needs to be a certain clinical professionalism and respect for human dignity when dealing with dead bodies.

Dealing with such unpleasant situations can lead forensic pathologists and detectives to engage in a certain amount of gallows humour when they are away from the general public – it is an insider's way of dealing with the stress associated with work of this kind.

Getting it Wrong – Misuse of Forensic Science in Fiction

There are two areas where forensic pathology is often misrepresented in fiction – in predicting a time of death and in establishing how long a victim might have lived after sustaining an injury. Neither is easy to establish with any degree of accuracy, despite what fiction tells us.

An accurate time of death was often important in whodunits as part of a puzzle that relied on obtaining and testing alibis – Where were you at the time of the murder? Body temperature, the onset of rigor mortis, the amount of potassium in the vitreous humour of the eyeball, and the extent to which food in the stomach has been digested have all be used to determine the exact time at which the murder took place. In reality, the margin of error in using such methods can be several hours either side.

Forensic Thriller Plot Structure

You could take the plot structure of a traditional whodunit, a medical thriller, a police procedural, or a private eye story and – with a few tweaks – use it for a novel or screenplay featuring a protagonist who is an expert in any of the forensic specialisms mentioned in this chapter. In this section, I'm going to examine the plot of the modern forensic thriller that is descended from Patricia Cornwell's 1990 novel *Postmortem*.

Sequence 1

Concentrates on the hero and her job – and the primary case to be investigated. Personal life and relationships – other than a bit of professional backstory – not introduced until Sequence 2.

Characterise hero by her professionalism and her respect for the victim's dignity, treating the victim as a person rather than an object or part of a puzzle.

Begin with the murder being committed – point of view of victim or killer or omniscient.

Or begin with the body being discovered – p.o.v. of a witness or omniscient.

Begin with medical examiner being called out to the scene – first person p.o.v or third limited.

Introduce medical examiner hero. Introduce main homicide detective. Introduce some background to the crime if this is the second or latest in a series of similar killings.

Crime scene – wider perimeter as it has been sealed off; local people and reporters. Inside the cordon – crime scene photographers etc. at work.

Hero's examination of the body in situ – contrasting professional detachment as she does her job with a more empathetic response as she thinks of the victim as a person rather than an object. Reassuring to the reader to know that the dignity of victim respected.

Perhaps introduce a political or other opponent for the hero. Perhaps the result of some former conflict – romantic, professional, etc. Or jurisdictional conflict.

If the hero's romantic interest is a professional one, may be introduced in Sequence 1; if not, it will appear in Sequence 2.

Part 2 of the first sequence – body now in the morgue, being examined by a team of experts. Forensic medicine including autopsy plus physical samples takes and searching for fingerprints on the body, etc. Indication that this is one of several cases morgue is working on – this is their *job*.

Sequence 2
Hero returns home after a long day at the 'office.' Introduce homelife, family, and perhaps a romantic partner.

Introduce the secondary case – this may be something that affects the hero more directly. In *Postmortem* it is the leaking of confidential information to the press. The secondary case may or may not prove to be related to the primary one.

First Suspect identified – someone closely related to the latest victim, e.g. a spouse. They are almost always the first suspect and have to be eliminated first.

First clues related to the primary case – something unusual, unexplained, unique, or unexpected.

Sequence 3
Hero looks at evidence to date and tries to put together a profile of the killer – perhaps with the help of a psychologist or profiler. Also working with other members of her team – e.g. serologist – on samples taken from scene and/or during autopsy. Perhaps some additional circumstantial evidence that points towards the First Suspect being guilty.

Probably a further reference to the impact that the murder is having on the local community – and people's responses to it. Maybe demands for police to make the streets safer. Perhaps wannabe witnesses, investigators, or psychics coming forward but doing little more than wasting police time.

Indication of the legwork police are involved in related to the case and some of the waiting around involved in processing information to sift out useful leads.

A new development in the secondary case.

Further characterisation of the hero in terms of her background and home life. Perhaps some self-doubt – comparing herself unfavourably to a predecessor or mentor.

Additional pressure put on the hero by her superiors and/or politicians. Perhaps she is blamed for a mistake made in the investigation – or for the lack of progress to date. This may relate to the primary case or the secondary one. This is undeserved misfortune that helps the reader feel sympathy for her.

Sequence 4
If the hero has an opponent or rival – perhaps someone from another agency or a politician – the background to this ongoing conflict should be revealed at or before the midpoint since all 'setting up' of the story should be complete by the end of Sequence 4.

To increase pressure on the hero, you could also introduce the first hint of some problem in a significant relationship – romantic or familial. This can be made more overt and developed later.

Uneasy relationship between the hero and the homicide detective and/or between the medical examiner's office and the police. Despite this, they have come – or will come – to respect each other's areas of professional expertise. They discuss the case, trying to find some connection between the victims in a series of murders or some aspect of the victim's life that would make them a target if the case is a single murder.

The detective is probably aware of the hero's undeserved misfortune and his sympathy – or lack of it – makes her feel even more isolated.

Someone may be identified as a potential suspect in the secondary case – though this may be based on gossip or speculation with no real evidence to back it up. This case is currently more of an irritation than a pressing matter – but this may change in the second half of the story.

Developments in the primary case may be such that the first suspect – the spouse or other close relationship – now seems less likely to be guilty. Their alibi checks out, they pass a polygraph, or some other evidence indicates that they are not the killer. This is not conclusive, they're not completely exonerated, but they seem less guilty than previously – probably much to the detective's disappointment, as he would have been hoping for a rapid resolution to the case.

Midpoint: An important clue or some other discovery or observation about the primary case – perhaps something that is missing from the scene or something about one of the victims or killings that doesn't fit the pattern of the others. How might this anomaly be a clue to the killer's methods and/or identity? Or the midpoint could be the discovery of another body or an attempted murder that the victim survived/escaped from. Or it may be the build-up to another murder – the killer usually strikes on the same day/time – but the hours tick away as police and hero wait for the phone call... but it doesn't come. A mixture of relief and disappointment. This 'waiting for a murder' could occur at the end of sequence five instead of here.

Sequence 5

Sequence five is often the reaction to whatever happened at the midpoint. If a body was discovered, we go to the crime scene. If it was expected to but didn't, we deal with the consequences of it not happening. If the midpoint was a twist or revelation relating to the secondary case, we deal with the aftermath of that. Whatever the hero and other characters have to 'deal with' here allows us an opportunity to spend some time in character-related scenes.

Typically, this sequence in stories focuses on relationships of and between the primary characters – or, occasionally, a victim or someone affected by the crimes. We will probably learn more about the hero's family and background – especially if this is the first book in a series. If it is later in a series, the fifth sequence may see more of their current romantic relationship or conflicts within a close family relationship.

If a romantic relationship is going through a rough patch – or if the hero's romantic interest is in some way involved in one of the cases – or just suspected of being possibly involved – then this is the point in the story where the cracks start to show. If either of them wasn't aware that there was a problem with the relationship, this is where it becomes obvious to them. Alternatively, this may be where a new relationship becomes more significant to the couple involved in it – or perhaps where a rocky relationship finds a new balance and seems to be moving in a positive direction. To some extent, the way you handle this relationship moment will depend on how you want to use the hero's romantic partner later in the story – will he or she betray the hero? Have they done so already but the betrayal hasn't yet been discovered? Is the romantic partner guilty of the primary or secondary crime? Or some other, unconnected crime? If you're planning a surprising or shocking development in the relationship, you don't want to 'telegraph' it ahead of time, but you do need to set it up so that it doesn't seem too random or a 'cheat' when it does occur. Obviously, how much you can reveal will depend on your choice of point of view. And just because the hero suspects her partner of something doesn't mean he or she is actually guilty of it – though it may suggest trust issues on her part. How will the partner react when they discover that they have been under suspicion?

Things are often 'planted' in sequence five that will prove significant later in the story. If the hero has a gun, a samurai sword, or a baseball bat hidden under her bed – just in case – we will learn about it here – especially if she's going to use it to fight off an attacker in Act III. Or if an intruder threatens her with it. There may also be some other weird incident or clue that makes no sense here – and which may not even seem related to the case, until its significance is understood later.

We will probably see the hero involved in an autopsy that is not related to any of the story's cases – a reminder that this is her day job.

Suspect 2 is probably identified here. Having been disappointed at Suspect 1's apparent innocence, the detective suggests a new suspect. Or evidence discovered at the midpoint may have pointed the finger at this person. This second suspect seems much more likely than the first one – looks as if he or she *should* be guilty. This is not someone the reader feels sympathy for. The detective actively pursues his investigation of this person – almost to the point of harassment – and wants to hero to assist him in proving Suspect 2's guilt. The hero may initially be pulled along by the detective's enthusiasm, despite any reservations she might have about Suspect 2's guilt. Perhaps she doesn't want this person to be guilty for personal reasons. Or perhaps she feels sympathy for them, despite their apparent unpleasantness or violence. Or maybe she just isn't happy with the evidence against them.

If the midpoint didn't include the discovery of another body, there will probably be one at the end of this sequence – perhaps the killer did strike on schedule but the body wasn't discovered until some later date.

Another incident near the end of this sequence may be to do with the secondary case or the hero's ongoing conflict with a rival or opponent – and the case and opponent may or may not be related. This incident will typically be an apparent solution to the problem that turns out to be short-lived or to have significant negative consequences. Beating or humiliating an opponent can often have consequences such as the opponent seeking to get revenge.

Sequence 6

If sequence five ended with another body, the new sequence will begin with the crime scene or with the autopsy in the lab.

There may be another significant development – positive or negative – in the hero's romantic relationship. Something suspected may be confirmed or proved wrong. Or suspicions may increase if there is no proof either way. The relationship may seem to be heading for an ending – or alternatively, it may seem to be developing in intensity and becoming more important to the hero. The hero may discover something that proves the romantic partner is innocent or guilty of something – but this 'proof' may later be shown to be fake or mistaken. This is the usual on-again off-again stuff of any story relationship – but given an extra thriller/conspiracy dimension.

Pressure on the hero and/or the police about the mishandling the investigation, or lack of progress in it, increases pressure on the hero. This pressure may come from an angry relative of one of the victims or from a politician who is friends with the family of a victim. This may be further intensified by media reports or threats to bring someone 'more competent' in to take over the investigation, replacing either the hero or the homicide detective, or both. This may drive a wedge between hero and detective – or increase their efforts to work together to solve the case in the face of a storm of criticism and blame.

It may feel that the case has stalled and that no progress is being made. The hero's self-doubt may mean that she thinks that it might be better if someone else did take over the case. But support, perhaps from an unexpected quarter, urges her not to give up.

The detective still believes there is a strong case against Suspect 2 and that they should concentrate their efforts on him or her. He may have gathered additional circumstantial evidence and hearsay that support his suspicions. But the hero isn't convinced by his arguments or by the evidence they have – perhaps because there is one bit of evidence that cannot be made to fit or cannot be explained by the detective's theory.

There is probably some significant development in the secondary case and/or the conflict with the hero's opponent or rival. Or just some minor incident that will prove very significant later. This may involve a parallel investigation being carried out by someone in the hero's team – or perhaps by the hero's rookie partner.

The hero may talk to a mentor or friend unrelated to the investigation in order to get a fresh perspective on the investigation. If she hasn't already spent time with a psychological profiler to discuss the murderer, she may do this now. These discussions may bring her to feel that the detective's theory about Suspect 2 is correct – or they may convince her that his theory is wrong and the killer is someone else. If she doesn't support his theory, this may put her into conflict with the detective. Either way, the hero is motivated to move forward and be pro-active, rather than wait for the killer's next move.

Sequence 7

The hero comes up with her own plan to draw the killer out. She may work alone or with members of her term. Or she may work with her mentor, the profiler, or a reporter. The nature of the plan may be such that she has to keep it secret from her superiors and perhaps from the homicide detective. The plan is probably something that puts the hero's career in jeopardy – and perhaps her personal safety. She may not fully understand the risks she is taking – but she is committed to catching the murderer.

There will be some significant discovery in the secondary case – an important clue that will ultimately point to a solution, if it can be properly interpreted. Or there may be a development in the conflict with the hero's opponent or rival – this may be such that it generates suspense by the fact that it will impact the hero's plan to catch the killer. Or it may put the hero's romantic partner in danger. Or the detective. Or the hero's family. Or the hero may be removed from the investigation – suspended or replaced – so that she cannot implement her plan. And the clock is ticking down to the time when the next murder is expected.

The secondary case may be resolved towards the end of this sequence – or a plan put into effect that will resolve it in sequence eight.

A final clue may be discovered – often the anomaly or missing piece identified at the midpoint (or earlier) is explained or understood.

The hero finds a way, with the support of her friends or colleagues, to put her plan into operation. This involves drawing out the killer – upsetting him in some way that makes him react angrily. The hope is that this will cause him to make a mistake that will lead to him being caught. But the plan goes wrong or backfires – or is too successful – with dramatic consequences. This is probably the hero's lowest point – damage has been caused and she is directly responsible.

Sequence 8

The hero has to accept the consequences of her actions. Her superiors are angry and her career is probably over. The detective is angry because she acted without involving him – putting herself and others in danger.

They investigate the clue discovered in sequence seven. This may involve a lot of checking of leads – uniformed policemen knocking on doors or making phone calls. Trying to pinpoint the source of the clue.

Suspect 3 is identified – perhaps a specific person or just a broad category of person – a delivery person, taxi driver, or some other sort of profession.

The hero may have her own suspicions about who the murderer is – which she may not share with the detective because she wants to check them out first. Or perhaps she suspects he is in on the conspiracy.

Suspect 1 is more or less completely exonerated. Suspect 2 may still be a possibility, or they too may be eliminated.

A link between all of the victims is discovered. Or the reason why the lone victim was targeted. This probably comes from the hero checking out her suspicions. She shares what she has learned with the detective. Or perhaps she doesn't. Either way, she is now a target for the killer – either because she is the only person who can expose him/her or because the hero has humiliated the killer in some way as a result of her plot, exposing his darkest secret or his weakness.

The primary and secondary cases will be resolved and explained at some point in this sequence – though the secondary case could be resolved in Sequence 7. The conflict with the opponent or rival will also come to a head. The order in which these things are resolved isn't important – but the biggest climax in this sequence should belong to the ending of the primary case. This typically has the hero at the mercy of the killer.

I would say that you should avoid having your female hero having to be rescued by your detective or some other a male character – she deserves better than that. And avoid having her do something stupid to get into jeopardy in the first place. Set up the ending so that the hero is responsible for her own survival and for capturing the killer – don't have her become another female victim. She doesn't have to do it alone – a quality of most great female heroes is that they are able to work as part of a team, supporting – and with support from – other people.

Equilibrium is typically shown to have been restored by having the hero engaged in some sort of family or relationship moment. This reinforces that people are at the centre of the work she does and that she is a member of the community that she works to protect.

6 | Serial Killers & Forensic Psychology

Forensic psychology is the application of psychological principles to legal issues. It may be used to help a court decide which parent should have custody of a child or to evaluate a defendant's competence to stand trial. It can also be used as part of criminal investigations and in research to understand the behaviour of criminals, witnesses, victims, and trial juries. In this chapter we are looking at two areas of forensic psychology – the profiling of victims of crime (victimology), sometimes referred to as a 'psychological autopsy' when murder victims are profiled, and the profiling of criminals, with particular emphasis on serial killers. I am going to use the term *criminal profiling* for this work as this is a term that became popular in the 1990s in fiction and non-fiction works, though it has gone out of fashion with the FBI and professional forensic psychologists as a result of criticisms of early practices in the field.

Although this chapter focuses on the serial killer, the techniques described can also be applied to profiling other types of criminal including thieves, computer hackers, terrorists, and others who commit more than a single crime. The section of *victimology* contains information that may be used for profiling any murder victim or victims of other types of crime.

Psychology vs. Psychiatry. It is probably worth reminding ourselves of the difference between psychiatrists and psychologists, since both may deal with offenders. Psychiatrists are medically trained and treat those suffering from mental illness – they may examine patients and prescribe medications. Psychologists are not usually medically trained and instead specialise in social and behavioural sciences.

History of Criminal Profiling

Bloom (2013) and others have suggested that 'profiling' of a sort was used in the past during religious inquisitions and witch hunts. The methods used to identify suspects were not based on rational processes and they were applied in order to give a veneer of legal authority to what was effectively the scapegoating of a group within the population.

In the wake of Darwin's theory of evolution, nineteenth-century attempts at categorising and identifying criminals tended to assume that people who committed crimes were in some way 'less evolved' – that criminals were born rather than made, and that the 'criminal class' was in some way more primitive. These ideas even went as far as suggesting that criminals *looked* more primitive than ordinary folk. The most famous proponent of this approach is probably Cesare Lombroso, who published several works containing illustrations of what various criminals looked like, including *L'Homme Criminel: Atlas* which you can find online.

Treating criminals as a sub-species of human beings that has distinctive physical traits was an error that continued into the early twentieth century. And there is still a risk of committing a similar sort of error when we consider human psychology rather than physiology to establish criminal types. It seems laughable now to think that an 'ugly' face means that someone is a criminal, but an 'ugly mind' denoting criminality seems much more plausible. We have to be cautious not to fall into this trap.

Jack the Ripper
In October 1888, Sir Robert Anderson, Assistant Commissioner of the London Metropolitan Police, asked Dr. Thomas Bond for his assistance in the investigation of the Whitechapel Murders. Bond's response was one of the earliest examples of a profile of a serial murderer and was based on Bond's observations of one of the victims. Jack the Ripper was never identified so it is impossible to know how accurate the profile was.

Hans Gross
Hans Gross (1847-1915) was an Austrian criminologist who wrote two of the first books in the field, *Criminal Investigation: A Practical Handbook* (1906) was adapted from his *Handbuch für Untersuchungsrichter als System der Kriminalistik* originally published in 1893, and *Criminal Psychology: A Manual for Judges, Practitioners, and Students* (1911) the first English translation of *Kriminal-Psychologie* published in 1898. Having worked as an Examining Jurist – a combination of investigator, prosecutor and judge – Gross applied his practical experience to devise methods that would be of use to investigators and the courts and he is regarded as a founder of modern criminology and criminal profiling. He also warned of the dangers of using inferences rather than verifiable observations.

The Vampire of Düsseldorf
Peter Kürten was a German serial killer active between 1913 and 1929 – he was found guilty of nine murders and seven attempted murders. Psychologist Karl Berg interviewed Kürten following his arrest and wrote the book *Der Sadist* which was published in 1932 and first published in English as *The Sadist* in 1938. Kürten admitted to being sexually excited by the sight of the blood of his victims. While Berg did not profile the murderer before his arrest, his book is one of the earliest studies of a modern serial killer. The 1931 film *M* by director Fritz Lang is thought to have been inspired by this case.

James Brussel
Between 1940 and 1956, almost thirty homemade bombs were left in public places throughout New York. The bomber sent letters to newspapers saying he was seeking revenge because he was the victim of 'dastardly acts' committed by the Consolidated Edison Company. Unable to identify the bomber, the police sought the help of psychiatrist Dr. James Brussel who had performed counterintelligence profiling work during the Second World War.

Brussel examined crime-scene photographs, the bombs (half of them didn't explode), and letters sent by the bomber and produced a 'portrait' of him. In December 1956, the New York Times published a summary of Brussel's description of a man the police had been seeking for sixteen years: *Single man, between 40 and 50 years old, introvert. Unsocial but not antisocial. Skilled mechanic. Cunning. Neat with tools. Egotistical of mechanical skill. Contemptuous of other people. Resentful of criticism of his work but probably conceals resentment. Moral. Honest. Not interested in women. High school graduate. Expert in civil or military ordnance. Religious. Might flare up violently at work when criticized. Possible motive: discharge or reprimand. Feels superior to critics. Resentment keeps growing.*

Present or former Consolidated Edison worker. Probably case of progressive paranoia.

When the Mad Bomber, George Metesky, was eventually arrested, much of Brussel's description was discovered to be accurate. This was much publicised and he set the level at which criminal profilers were expected to perform. He was a modern-day Sherlock Holmes. Except, he wasn't really. Objective analysis shows that his profile contributed almost nothing to the investigation. Brussel's only real help was to suggest that details of the bombings and the bomber's letters be made public – the police had been keeping them secret. As a result, a clerk at Con Edison looked through their files for any employees who had made threats as part of their compensation claims. Metesky was identified because his file contained letters with similar wording to those of the bomber. As to the fastened double-breasted suit – most men wore them in those days and it would not have helped the police single him out from the crowd. Brussel was also consulted in the case of the Boston Strangler.

The FBI's Behavioral Science Unit

Rising murder rates during the 1950s and 1960s led to the FBI being given responsibility for the investigation of serial crimes. The newly-expanded FBI Academy opened in 1972 and one of the units formed was the Behavioral Science Unit. Those teaching there were looking at ways in which theories from psychology and sociology could be applied to their work – and one of those teachers was Special Agent Howard Teten.

"I developed the FBI's original approach to profiling as a lecture course in 1970," Teten said in an interview (see Webb). "This course was based on a concept which I had originally developed while working as a police crime scene specialist. The idea was conceived in about 1961-62. However, it was necessary to test the approach using solved cases for about seven years and to check with several psychiatrists to ensure I was on firm ground in terms of the characteristics of the different mental problem areas before I felt it was ready for presentation ... I expanded the course by asking that unsolved cases be brought in for use as examples."

The first case to be solved using Teten's profiling techniques was that of seven-year-old Susan Jaeger who was abducted in 1973. Teten and his colleague Patrick Mullany created a profile describing a young, white, male loner who lived locally. Police identified David Meierhofer as a suspect but had insufficient evidence to charge him. Following the disappearance of a woman known to Meierhofer, Teten and Mullany refined their profile and were also able to offer advice on a strategy that eventually led to Meierhofer's arrest.

Another aspect of the Behavioral Science Unit's work was to conduct interviews with convicted serial killers, gathering information about how and why certain characteristics were found at crime scenes. Robert Ressler began conducting the interviews in 1976 and was joined in this project by John Douglas who joined the BSU that year. Taylor writes that the "...information from these interviews was stored on a computer database and cross-referenced with evidence from the crime scene, forensics and victim reports, as well as recorded personal offender details. The combination of information enabled Ressler to examine the underlying gratification served by the crimes committed, and the motivations behind them."

Robert Ressler & John E. Douglas

Ressler and Douglas collected data on thirty-six incarcerated offenders. In his book *Mindhunter: Inside the FBI's Elite Serial Crime Unit* (1995), Douglas said: "By the time Ressler and I had done ten or twelve prison interviews, it was clear to any reasonably intelligent observer that we were on to something. For the first time, we were able to correlate what was going on in an offender's mind with the evidence he left at a crime scene." Ressler and Douglas's interviews had led them to classify sexually-motivated serial murderers and similar offenders as either 'organized' or 'disorganized' – we will consider these in more detail under *Types of Profiling* below.

Concentrating their efforts on sexual offenders, Ressler and Douglas, along with Ann W. Burgess, conducted a study which led to the publication of *Sexual Homicide: Patterns and Motives* (1988) which outlined the characteristics of sexual killers. The three also collaborated on the *Crime Classification Manual*, published in 1992.

John E. Douglas provided a profile of the killer responsible for a series of murders in Atlanta between 1979 and 1981, correctly identifying the murderer as a young black male. The case was the basis for the 1985 film *The Atlanta Child Murders* and the 2000 television movie *Who Killed Atlanta's Children?*

Ressler also profiled the 'Nebraska Boy Snatcher' and the FBI were able to link the crimes to an earlier murder and two other assaults. John Joubert was identified as a suspect, tried, and found guilty. Ressler co-authored (with Tom Shachtman) three non-fiction books – *Whoever Fights Monsters* (1992), *Justice is Served* (1994), and *I Have Lived in the Monster* (1998) – which contain accounts of his work and interviews with convicted serial killers. Ressler claimed to have coined the phrase 'serial killer' in 1974 in relation to the Son of Sam case, but the German equivalent *serienmörder* appears to have been used as early as 1931.

Ressler and Douglas were both consulted by Thomas Harris when he was doing research for *The Silence of the Lambs* and Douglas was also a consultant on the film version. The character of Jack Crawford is modelled on Douglas. The characters of Jason Gideon (Mandy Patinkin) and David Rossi (Joe Mantegna) in the television series *Criminal Minds* were also based on Douglas as was Holden Ford (Jonathan Groff) in the series *Mindhunter*, which was based on the book written by John Douglas & Mark Olshaker

Douglas eventually became head of the BSU and retired in 1995. The BSU became the Behavioral Analysis Unit in 1997 and is now the Behavioral Research and Instruction Unit. Ressler helped Pierce Brooks to establish the Violent Criminal Apprehension Program (ViCAP) which was set up by the FBI in 1985. At the heart of ViCAP is a database of details about violent crimes including sexual assaults, kidnappings, missing persons, and homicides. State and local law enforcement agencies can search the database for similarities with crimes they are investigating.

The work of the FBI's Behavioral Science Unit was pioneering and generated a great deal of interest in law enforcement circles and among the general public. But the early dramatic successes were not matched by later investigations and critics began to feel that the accuracy and usefulness of profiling had been overstated. Academic research also cast doubts on the methods used. Since then, the FBI has moved away from profiling and have developed a broader method known as Criminal Investigative Analysis (see

Types of Profiling below) which built on the original work of BSU staff, combining it with other investigative methods.

Serial Killers in the Media

Hickey (2010) notes that while only a few films about serial killers were made in each of the decades from the 1920s to the 1970s, there was a sudden explosion during the 1990s which continued into the 2000s. There was also a rise in non-fiction titles published including: *Hunting Humans* (1986) by Elliot Leyton; *Mass Murder: America's Growing Menace* (1985) and *Overkill: Mass Murder and Serial Killing Exposed* (1994) by Jack Levin and James Alan Fox; *Serial Murder* (1988) by Ronald Holmes and James DeBurger; *Profiling Violent Crimes* (1990) by Ronald Holmes, and *Serial Murder: An Elusive Phenomenon* (1990) and *The Killers Among Us* (2001) by Steve Egger.

Hickey also writes about the way in which serial murders are covered in the media, with each one being assigned a colourful alias based on some aspect of their crimes – 'The Boston Strangler,' 'The Torture Doctor,' 'The Atlanta Child Killer,' 'The BTK [Bind Torture Kill] Strangler' – names that are "...designed to evoke our disgust, horror, and fascination." These men are sexual sadists who enjoy killing and "...have engaged in necrophilia, cannibalism, and the drinking of victims' blood. Some like to bite their victims; others enjoy trophy collecting..." their trophies including human body parts. The popular image of them also has them as a sort of Jekyll and Hyde character – a monster who looks like an ordinary man and could be your next-door neighbour. It is perhaps little wonder that such murderers caught the imagination of thriller writers. Among the best-known writers in this sub-genre is Thomas Harris, whose *Red Dragon* (1981) and *The Silence of the Lambs* (1988) were adapted into successful movies. An early example of the investigation of a serial killer is Agatha Christie's *The ABC Murders* (1936) in which the killer taunts Hercule Poirot in a series of letters.

Bloom writes of the appeal of such stories, saying that "...depictions of profiling from popular culture communicate that the world is controllable, can be influenced, is predictable, and can be understood."

A number of novels have also been written from the serial killer's point of view, including Jim Thompson's *The Killer Inside Me* (1952) which has been adapted for the screen twice, in 1976 and 2010; Ramsey Campbell's *The Face That Must Die* originally published in 1979, but seek out a later version with the restored text; and Brett Easton Ellis's *American Psycho* (1991) which was adapted into a movie starring Christian Bale in 2000 – the original novel has more to offer writer's than the screen version. The film *Henry: Portrait of a Serial Killer* directed and co-written by John McNaughton and starring Michael Rooker was inspired by the crimes of Henry Lee Lucas, a serial killer who claimed responsibility for over 600 murders and was convicted on eleven.

Reality versus Fiction

David Canter (2010) is one of those critical of the way in which forensic psychology has been portrayed in modern fiction. The popularity of the 'profiler,' he says, is due to an "apparent need for a modern-day Sherlock Holmes" in crime fiction and that "...these clever, but usually flawed, fictional characters are portrayed as seeing into the criminal's mind ... the 'profiler' seems to have the uncanny ability of knowing what the murderer thinks and feels. These insights appear to be based on little more than the crime scene and other odds and ends of clues." This popular image of the profiler was created during the early days when the work of profilers was "...written about in a heroic light (not unusually by the 'profilers' themselves)..." The profiles produced during the period, viewed in retrospect, were rarely of any direct practical help in an investigation.

In his 2012 book, Canter says that television crime dramas do not provide a true picture of the real-life work of the forensic psychologist. They do not interrogate suspects in dark alleys or go "...charging into dangerous locations in front of armed police..." Although many people regard psychologists as having the necessary skills for criminal investigation, the codes of conduct for professionals emphasise the importance of not operating outside of their areas of competence.

In real life, the forensic psychologist usually serves as an advisor to someone in another profession – a police detective investigating a crime, a lawyer preparing a case for court, parole or probation officers concerned with the future risk posed by offenders, or politicians and civil servants responsible for policies relating to offenders and victims. Canter (2010) suggests that the forensic psychologist is always the bridesmaid and never the bride and in his 2012 book says that despite what we see in crime novels, "...psychologists very rarely get actively involved in investigations. They may pop in and give a few hints, but they contribute far less than the Crime Scene Investigation (CSI) experts who deal with fibres and fingerprints, blood splatters and all those forensic science matters." Ramsland too says "...the intent of a profile is not to solve a case. Profilers are consultants to investigations, not the primary detective."

Although we may talk of criminal profiles, studies have demonstrated significant diversity among criminals such that it is not possible to develop a standard or generic profile of a burglar, a murderer, a rapist, a computer hacker, or a terrorist. And individual criminals may change over time as a result of their crimes and other life experiences. The 'profile' that typically appears in fiction includes a variety of details concerning the personality, lifestyle, motivations, family relationships, and other characteristics of the criminal that real-life profilers are rarely able to provide with any accuracy. According to Canter, the areas in which psychology can most usefully be applied to criminal investigations are in terms of suggesting where an offender may be based – geographical profiling – and how to narrow down searches of existing police records to identify an offender.

Canter is also critical of the way in which 'psychopaths' are portrayed in fiction and film, saying that such stories "...never really provide any psychological insights into the actions of the monsters who are the anti-heroes of their dramas. They are presented as pure evil. The rather more psychologically interesting films such as *Psycho* or *The Boston Strangler* provide pseudo-Freudian explanations for the nastiness of their villains, but still present them as rather alien individuals who can appear unthreatening but deep down are malevolent."

How Do You Become a Forensic Psychologist?

In the UK there is a formal professional pathway for becoming a 'chartered forensic psychologist' and this is overseen by the British Psychological Society. Study may include a degree in psychology and then Master's programme or specialised training leading to a Diploma in Forensic Psychology, and finally they must complete two years in practice, supervised by someone who has already achieved chartered status. In the USA certification is awarded by the American Board of Professional Psychology (ABPP) and ethical standards are set down in the American Psychological Association's code.

Profiler vs. Serial Killer

The fact that criminal profiling and other investigative procedures have featured in television dramas and documentaries means that serial killers, as well as the general public, have a greater understanding of how investigations are carried out. American serial killer John Joubert read true crime magazines because he was excited by the images in them, but he also said that he learned things in them that helped him avoid getting caught. Joubert's crimes were the inspiration for Alex Kava's first novel *A Perfect Evil* (2000). Other killers such as Colin Ireland, Dennis Rader and Israel Keyes all researched earlier serial killers – perhaps seeing them as heroes or role models, but perhaps also learning from the reported mistakes of these killers. Keyes in particular made conspicuous efforts to avoid engaging in predictable behaviours and to vary the locations of his killings.

Any effort by a serial killer to avoid 'signature' behaviours or acts, to avoid having a typical victim type, and to avoid operating in a small geographical area will make it more difficult for investigators to link crimes or to create a 'profile' of the killer. But at the same time, many serial killers seem to enjoy seeing their crimes reported – at least until they are identified as a suspect – and so may deliberately or subconsciously leave clues that allow the police to link crimes.

Profiling Criminals – The Serial Killer

The purpose of a profile is to provide information on the characteristics and traits of an unidentified criminal such that investigators can differentiate him from the general population – it is meant to reduce the pool of viable suspects and help focus the investigation by prioritising the remaining suspects.

Profiling is based on the assumption that behaviour during a crime, like all other behaviour, is determined by the personality of the individual. It also assumes that these behaviours remain fairly constant over time for individual offenders. Human behaviour is also influenced by the situation in which an individual finds him or herself – behaviours are triggered by circumstances. The behaviours at a crime scene and the circumstances in which the crime took place have to be considered together to try and determine characteristics and traits of the personality of the person who committed the crime. In his book *Mindhunter* (1995), FBI profiler John E. Douglas said that *how* plus *why* equals *who*.

Serial Killers

The FBI (2008) defines serial murder as "...the unlawful killing of two or more victims by the same offenders in separate events." In the past, there has been some discussion about what actually constitutes a serial killer. In an attempt to distinguish serial killers from other mass murderers such as spree killers it was suggested that a serial killer had a 'cooling-off period' between killings and that this period should be 30 days or more. The FBI definition now states only that a serial killer kills his or her victims in separate events. Homant & Kennedy (2014) note that "The main point is that the first killing has temporarily satisfied whatever motives are driving the killer, and the subsequent killings are part of a separate sequence of behaviours."

Also discussed was the number of killings required for someone to 'qualify' as a serial killer, with various numbers being suggested. The FBI now says two or more. There is an argument that says a minimum of three is required to establish a pattern – two similar killings might be a coincidence but three makes it seem more likely to be part of a series – but we have to remember that every serial killer begins with a single murder. In fiction, we tend to make our serial killer's crimes so distinctive that it is pretty obvious that the second murder was committed by the same guy as the first one. But establishing that there *is* actually a link between different killings may be part of the plot of a serial killer story.

Hickey (2010) notes that serial killers have a number of common traits, regardless of their ethnicity or nationality. Most suffer some form of mental disorder or have experienced severe psychological stress as a result of rejection, abandonment, loss, humiliation, and hatred. Their alienation is combined with a capacity for violence and eventually manifests in violent acts that are part of some fantasy that the serial killer believes is real. They are rarely judged to be insane and are regarded as being responsible and culpable for their own deliberate actions. Hickey also writes that with serial killers there is usually a "...pattern in their killing that can be associated with the types of victims selected or the method or motives for the killing. This includes murderers who, on a repeated basis, kill within the confines of their own home, such as a woman who poisons several husbands, children, or elderly people in order to collect insurance."

Serial Killers – Motivations

Various attempts have been made to classify serial killers into types – one way uses the dominant motive of the killer – *why* they kill their victims. We will look at another form of classification under 'Four Types of Serial Killer' below.

Killers with the same motive are believed to have other traits in common that mean they can be distinguished from other types of serial killer. Motivation is something that can – possibly – be inferred from evidence at a scene, but there is an element of educated guesswork about it. David Canter believes it should not play a part in the profiling process and questions the extent to which it is helpful to investigators.

Canter (2012) says that courts do not need to know what a criminal's motive was, they only need to know that the crime was committed by the defendant and that he knew what he was doing when he did it. He also believes that the term 'motive' is too vague – "It can mean an explanation, a purpose, a reason, an unconscious urge, the set of actions it was part of (such as 'we were all drunk and having a laugh') and some form of narrative (as in 'I don't let people push me around')." This ambiguity means it is difficult to establish and even more difficult to prove. In fiction, murderers are typically motivated by revenge, jealousy, greed, or fear but in real life the actions of a serial killer may be the result of a complicated mix of emotions, psychological trauma in childhood, life experiences, and biological inheritance – and the killer may not even be consciously aware of these things.

Not all psychologists share David Canter's views on the usefulness of motive in profiling serial killers. A 2006 symposium organised by the FBI's Behavioral Analysis Unit listed the following as the primary motivations of serial killers:

Anger: offenders are motivated by rage or hate toward society as a whole or specific subgroups within it

Criminal enterprise: offenders commit serial murder to gain status or other tangible or intangible rewards with an organized crime environment. Contract killers would probably be included here

Financial gain: the primary focus of the offender is monetary gain from the killings. This includes 'black widow' killings and some healthcare killings, serial robbery homicides, and multiple homicides linked to insurance and welfare fraud or inheritance. Also included may be those killings that are committed for non-tangible gains such as public notoriety

Ideology: serial murders are related to the goals of an extreme ideology and may target members of specific religious or ethnic groups or those with a particular lifestyle. These killers often believe they have a 'mission' to complete which may (or may not) be seen as fulfilling the will of their god – they regard themselves as 'reformists' and are often determined to rid society of people of a certain type – but this belief is not the same as the 'vision from God' that psychotic killers may claim to have received (see below). Included here are terrorists who carry out multiple murders with the intention of evoking terror in a civilian population

Power thrill: persons who commit serial murder for excitement and empowerment including a desire for dominance or revenge. Also included here are those who kill simply for the joy of killing

Sexual: people who kill to gain physical sexual gratification and/or fulfil sexual fantasies – often involving sexual sadism, torture, and/or mutilation. Some psychologists differentiate between sex murderers and lust murderers. Sex murderers kill out of fear and a desire to eliminate the only witness to their crime. Lust murderers kill because causing pain – and perhaps death – is part of their sexual fantasy

Psychosis: persons with serious mental illness that may include visual or auditory hallucinations, delusions, and/or paranoia. These are sometimes referred to as 'visionary' killers who believe they are being instructed to kill by a god or some other entity

In thrillers, the serial killers usually engage in murders in the lust, thrill, and power/control categories – and usually involving an element of sexual assault or sexual sadism, though some also have a mission element as part of their motivation. Occasionally we find a 'visionary' killer with a severe mental illness, but more typically we see the 'sane' serial killer in the form of some kind of psychopath.

Where sexual assault is an element of serial killings, the act itself may not be motivated simply by a desire for sexual gratification. Sexual assault is often related to frustration and anger which is demonstrated in a desire to control the victim. The display of dominance, of power, may be more important to the attacker than sexual pleasure. Studies of rapists have identified four main types of sexual assault: anger retaliatory, anger excitation, power reassurance, and power assertive.

Anger retaliation – the victim is seen as responsible, in reality or symbolically, for some transgression against the offender. The attacker is trying to get revenge on a person or group he is angry with and the sexual assault is intended to punish and demean the victim and so is typically violently aggressive. One study of sexual murderers showed that around a third of attacks fell into this category.

Anger excitation – a planned sexual assault, usually against a stranger, where inflicting pain on the victim is required for the satisfaction of the sexual and ego needs of the offender. The offender may also gain gratification from the planning stage, fantasising about the attack. One study showed that less than ten per cent of attacks fell into this category.

Power reassurance – the offender is effectively acting out a conquest fantasy, demonstrating the offender's power over the victim. The victim's lack of compliance will anger or panic the offender who then kills the victim. The offender will be frustrated that the sexual assault wasn't completed and the anger resulting from this sexual failure may cause him to engage in a sexual act with the dead victim and/or mutilate the body. In one study this form of assault accounted for around twenty per cent of cases.

Power assertive – the offender commits a sexual assault to reassure himself of his own masculinity. Severe harm or traumatisation of the victim are not a primary intent, though violence will result if the offender's power and control are challenged. If the victim is killed, there is typically no mutilation of the body. This type of assault, which shows the least amount of sadism, accounted for a little under forty per cent of the assaults in one study.

Approaches to Profiling – Inductive vs. Deductive

I wrote in some detail about inductive and deductive reasoning in *Mystery*. Deductive reasoning is based on gathering evidence, exploring possible theories for the meaning of the evidence, testing the theories against the evidence and refining them. It is evidence-based. Inductive reasoning is case-based or uses analogy to come up with *probable* explanations based on previous experience and/or statistics. Both inductive and deductive methods involve making *inferences* based on available evidence – that is, coming up with possible theories – but in the deductive method, there is more emphasis on testing the theory against the evidence.

Canter (2012) writes that the inferences psychologists make are 'informed assumptions' rather than definite conclusions and that they may be based on previous research or derived from general principles.

Methods of Profiling

There are three main profiling methods in use and written about in academic literature – *Criminal Investigative Analysis* and *Investigative Psychology* are predominantly inductive, while *Behavioural Evidence Analysis* is a more deductive method. It is important to remember that these are only tools and that it is not necessary to restrict your investigators to one particular method – most investigations, fictional or real life, will use a combination of these three and along with other forensic specialisms. It is also worth noting that there is overlap between the three models – victimology (the profiling of victims), identifying 'signature' behaviours, and some form of geographic profiling are common to all and I discuss these separately later in the chapter to avoid duplication.

1. Criminal Investigative Analysis – The FBI Method

This method is the most well-known and developed out of the early work of the Behavioral Sciences Unit at the FBI. It has been taught to investigators from a number of countries and so is used around the world. A number of writers have produced lists of the various stages of the 'FBI Method' – mixing and matching them we get this:

- Information gathering
- Evaluation of the information

- Classification of the offender
- Determining the offender's *modus operandi*
- Determining the offender's 'signature' behaviours
- Criminal profile
- Investigative suggestions

Information Gathering

Information gathering involves bringing together all of the 'inputs' that will be used to produce the profile of the offender who is being sought by investigators. Sources of information will include crime scene photographs or video, the autopsy report, police reports, victim profiles, witness statements, maps and aerial photographs. The victim profile will include all the details covered under *Victimology* below.

Evaluation

Evaluation of the data involves looking for individual items and patterns that may help determine the nature of the crime, intent of the offender, victim and offender risk, escalation, and time and location factors. The *nature of a crime* is typically evaluated according to the criteria set out in the *Crime Classification Manual*. *Time Factors* are taken into account, including the length of time between the offender making contact with the victim and the time of the murder; the time it took to commit the crime, including any acts performed before, during, and after the killing; and the passage of time between death of the victim and disposal of the body. Time of day, week, month, or year may also be a factor. In serial crimes, the length of time between each incident is also significant.

Classification

In the FBI method, this involves looking at the information available about the crime and deciding whether the actions of the criminal most closely match those of the 'organized' or 'disorganized' type of offender.

Organized and Disorganized Serial Killers

Hickey lists the characteristics of the *Organized killer*:

- Highly intelligent
- High birth-order status
- Masculine image
- Charismatic
- Socially capable
- Sexually capable
- Occupationally mobile
- Lives with partner
- Geographically mobile
- Experienced harsh discipline
- Controlled emotions during crime
- High interest in media response to crime
- Model inmate

The organised killer may return to the crime scene and even seek to assist investigators, volunteering genuine or false information and being friendly with police officers.

The characteristics of the *Disorganized killer* are given by Hickey as:

- Below-average intelligence
- Low birth-order status
- Socially immature
- Seldom dates
- High school dropout
- Father often under- or unemployed
- Lives alone
- Has secret hiding places
- Nocturnal
- Lives/works near crime scene

- Engages in unskilled work
- Significant behavioural changes
- Low interest in media attention
- Limited alcohol consumption
- High anxiety during crime

The disorganised murderer may return to the crime scene, attend to the funeral of his victim, keep a diary or scrapbook relating to his crimes, and may change jobs relatively frequently.

It should be noted that this organized/disorganized classification was originally developed in the 1980s and has been criticised by some psychologists and practitioners. Many real-life offenders are classified as being 'mixed' – that is, their crimes display some 'organized' and some 'disorganized' behaviours.

Modus Operandi
The crime scene and the behaviour of the offender are assessed to try and reconstruct the sequence of actions undertaken in order to determine the offender's method of committing the crime. This assessment is usually carried out by comparing the crime currently under investigation with previous similar crimes looking for common patterns of activity.

Signature
Where *modus operandi* looks at actions and behaviours necessary for the offender to commit the crime, a 'signature' is a more idiosyncratic act or pattern of behaviour that is not necessary for the completion of the crime but which satisfies some psychological or other need of the offender. See *Signature Behaviours* below.

Profile
Putting together everything learned in the previous stages, the profiler now identifies a number of characteristics that the offender is believed to possess. These will range from things that the evidence suggests are almost certain characteristics down to things which are based on probability, previous experience, and 'educated guesses.' Characteristics provided can include any of the following – this list for a 'basic profile' is taken from Ramsland: Approximate age; Sex; Race; Typical MO; Geographic comfort zone; Probable living situation, including approximate location; Education level; Likelihood of full-time work; Work hours; Evidence of military experience; Travel patterns; Likelihood of a criminal or psychiatric record; Psychological traits or disorders; Fantasy scenario that compels

Investigative Suggestions
The profile will also provide advice to help the investigators target their resources. Usually, these suggestions will be related to characteristics of the offender that help to narrow the pool of suspects and will focus on those things in the profile most strongly supported by specific evidence. In some circumstances, the FBI also provide advice to investigators on how to handle media interest in a crime – particularly if the public or a section of the public are regarded as being at risk from future attacks.

Criticisms of Criminal Investigative Analysis & FBI Profiling
Every profiling method has strengths and weaknesses, and the FBI method has the advantage of being refined since it was first used in the 1980s. The classification of offenders into 'organized' and 'disorganized' types has been criticised by some academics and practitioners because it was based on just

one interview-based study of only thirty-six convicted criminals. A more recent study of a hundred serial killers showed that their crime scenes all featured both organised and disorganised elements, suggesting that the organized/disorganized typology offers little of use to investigators. There has also been little research into whether disorganised behaviour at a crime scene is matched by disorganised behaviours in other, non-crime related, aspects of a criminal's life.

There are also risks inherent in basing the classification solely on inferences drawn from the crime scene. If the same offender leaves behind two very different crime scenes with no linking 'signature' behaviour, there is a danger that the crimes would be classified as having been carried out by two different types of offender which could impede the investigation. A single offender's behaviour at a crime scene could be affected by a number of factors – drug or alcohol use, being interrupted during the commission of the crime, or a sudden change in mood provoked by the victim or other factors. It is also possible that an offender will become more proficient and more cautious over time and therefore appear less 'disorganized'.

2. Investigative Psychology – David Canter

Investigative Psychology is an inductive, research-based approach to understanding offender behaviour that was developed by British psychologist David Canter. Canter (1998), like most modern practitioners, seeks to distance himself from the term 'profiling'. "Investigative psychology is a much more prosaic activity. It consists of the painstaking examination of patterns of criminal behaviour and the testing out of those patterns of trends that may be of value to police investigators ... Investigative psychologists also accept that there are areas of criminal behaviour that may be fundamentally enigmatic."

This method is based around five factors relating to the offender's past and present life: interpersonal coherence, significance of time and place, criminal characteristics, criminal career, and forensic awareness.

Interpersonal coherence refers to the way an offender interacts with other people. Canter believes that the way an offender treats his victims will be consistent with the way he treats people in his everyday life. So, for example, a criminal who exhibits selfish behaviour towards family, friends, and colleagues will also exhibit selfishness in the way he attacks his victims. This belief in the consistency of behaviour is common to all types of offender profiling.

Significance of time and place refers to the fact that an offender chooses a time and place for his attack and this choice – along with the offender's behaviour within and around that location – reflects something about the offender himself. This relates to the concepts of geographical profiling mentioned previously. Canter was a pioneer of geo-profiling in Britain and wrote a book on the subject (2003).

Criminal characteristics uses data about the nature of similar crimes – based on interviews with criminals and empirical studies – to provide investigators with characteristics which may help them to identify a specific offender. This aspect is inductive and is similar to the FBI model that uses an organized/disorganized split to differentiate types of offenders. Also included here is an analysis of any developments in criminal behaviour demonstrated across a series of crimes – i.e. any refinements in the criminal's methods based on experience gained from earlier attacks. And any precautionary behaviours the offender uses are also of interest because they might provide clues about any previous contact the offender may have had with law enforcement or the legal system.

Forensic awareness refers to whether the offender demonstrates any experience of law enforcement and the criminal justice system. This may include wearing a mask to prevent visual identification, gloves to avoid leaving fingerprints, or use of a condom during a sexual assault to avoid leaving DNA evidence.

Criticisms of Investigative Psychology are those common to any inductive analysis. In addition, there are concerns about those areas which are dependent on statistical analysis because these rely on both the quality and quantity (sample size) of data available and also the interpretation of this data. There is also a danger in any statistical approach that any generalisation may or may not apply in a particular case.

Petherick writes that different offenders may perform the same act for different reasons and that interpreting the significance of the action is impossible without understanding its context. He gives the example of offenders biting a victim during a sexual assault. For one offender this might be foreplay, for another the inflicting of pain may provide gratification or stimulation, and in a third case the offender might bite the victim in order to gain their compliance. "The same behaviours are borne of different motivations, mean different things to the offenders, and are intended to serve different functions or fantasy behaviour. Simply reducing the variable to 'biting' tells us little, if anything."

3. Behavioural Evidence Analysis – Brent Turvey

Forensic scientist Brent Turvey interviewed convicted serial killer Jerry Brudos and discovered some significant discrepancies in what Brudos told him and what was recorded in police case files. Given that most criminal profiles were based on inferential analysis of serial killer interviews and/or police case file data, Turvey became concerned about the validity and accuracy of generalisations resulting from inductive profiling. This led him to develop a more *deductive* method, Behavioural Evidence Analysis.

Behavioural Evidence Analysis is based on forensic science, specifically the collection and interpretation of physical evidence to understand what it reveals about the offender. It relies on the evidence from a specific case rather than being based on generalisations based on previous cases. Profilers conduct a detailed examination of the scene to understand the behaviours of the offender at the scene – inferences about characteristics of the offender are then made from these specific observations. Petherick notes that the strength of this approach lies in the fact that the profiler uses only what is *known* – nothing is assumed or surmised – making for a more objective profile.

There are four main stages in Behavioural Evidence Analysis: *Forensic Analysis*, *Victimology*, *Crime Analysis*, and *Criminal Profile*.

Forensic Analysis refers to the collection, examination, testing, and interpretation of physical evidence. The handling of forensic evidence must be done by professionals trained and experienced in this area. As well as training in forensic science, it requires people with an understanding of legal requirements for collection, documentation, handling, testing, and storage of physical evidence who can ensure that the evidence is fit for acceptance in a court of law. And those examining a crime scene must be aware of 'evidence dynamics' – that is, anything that alters, relocates, obscures, or destroys physical evidence, whether such actions were the result of a victim or a criminal or paramedics, firefighters or policemen attending the scene. Weather and other environmental effects must also be noted.

The evidence retrieved is then used to try and piece together the 'story' of what occurred at the crime scene – to effectively *reconstruct* the crime. The evidence is analysed to separate that which is relevant from that which is not. Inductive and deductive logic are applied in this reconstruction. Crime scene reconstruction based on physical evidence lies at the heart of this method of profiling.

Victimology involves an investigation into all aspects of the life of the victim. Since in most crimes the victim is known while the offender is not, as much time is spent examining the victim's life, personality, and behaviour as is spent on the offender. In part, this stage tries to determine the possibility and extent of any relationship between the victim and the criminal. Also explored is 'victim exposure' – see below under *Victimology*.

Crime Analysis considers factors such as the way an offender approaches and attacks a victim; the location chosen; any methods used to control the victim; the weapon or any other materials used, and the nature and sequence of any sexual acts. Precautionary measures used to avoid identification or detection are also considered here. Locations involved in the crime might include the place where the attacker initially made contact with the victim; the place (or places) where the assault and/or murder took place, and the place (or places) where the body was left or buried. Evidence at the crime scene will usually show whether or not the victim was attacked at the location where the body was found or whether it was brought to the location after death.

Criminal Profile – or 'offender characteristics' – is the final stage. Information gathered during the first three stages is brought together and assessed using scientific method and deductive reasoning to determine characteristics of the offender. Turvey says that a profile produced via this method *cannot* determine age, gender, race, or level of intelligence as these require inductive reasoning and are not based on physical evidence.

Although Behavioural Evidence Analysis is based on deductive reasoning, it is not purely deductive. Inductive processes are used to produce theories – particularly when it comes to reconstructing the crime – which are then tested against the evidence. Evidence is then said to be 'consistent with' the theory – or not. There is also some reliance on information gathered from previous crimes in terms of, for example, wound patterns and assessing risks associated with certain lifestyles during the victimology stage. Forensic science also relies on an existing knowledge base including the way characteristics of a knife blade are determined from the wounds in a body or the way patterns of blood splatter are interpreted. But in all cases, these things are explored in relation to the physical evidence found.

Given that Behavioural Evidence Analysis is based on physical evidence, profiles produced will only ever be as good as the evidence that is available to the profiler. If there is any sort of problem which casts doubt on a piece of evidence, any deduction based on that evidence must also be suspect. And if some kinds of evidence are absent from a scene, it will be impossible to make any deductions that are normally based on that type of evidence. A further weakness of this method relates to the inductive elements where theories are produced for testing – if the profiler does not properly test the theory against the available evidence to establish its veracity, elements of the resulting profile will be compromised.

There are some aspects of criminal profiling that are relevant to all three methods of profiling - I will cover them here under the headings *geographical profiling, signature behaviours, serial killer methods*, and *serial killer victims*.

Geographical Profiling

Rather than trying to define characteristics of a criminal, a geographical profile seeks only to determine the offender's likely location. It will not pinpoint a home location precisely but does suggest areas where investigators should prioritise their search, significantly narrowing down the search area.

Geographical offender profiling is based on two assumptions. First, that the further an offender is from home, the less likely he is to commit a crime. And second, that if the *opportunities* for crime are evenly distributed around his home location, his crimes are also likely to be distributed around that location. People in general tend to be consistent in their habits. We typically shop in the same stores, for example, and when we travel we have preferred routes. Criminals are believed to behave in a similar way, committing their crimes in a preferred locality. While this is not true for all criminals in all circumstances, there is evidence that suggests it is sufficiently common that it can be of use to investigators.

If a criminal's crimes are plotted on a map, it should be possible to draw a circle which will enclose his crimes and which will have his home location somewhere within it, probably close to the centre of the circle. Five or more crimes are required for this kind of profiling which means that other methods may be used earlier in the profiling process to determine whether two or more crimes are actually linked.

Geographical profiling may be concerned with more than one location. It may include where a victim was selected or abducted, where the murder was committed, where the body was found, and what routes were travelled by the offender and the victim. It is also concerned with where the victim and the offender's homes are or may be in relation to these locations. Distance and travel time between locations have to be born in mind. If an offender selected the victim at a location other than the crime scene, locating the place where the victim was first seen or stalked by the attacker may allow investigators to identify additional witnesses – and possibly even people who the killer had previously targeted and approached but who avoided becoming victims.

Another thing to consider is the nature of a location – is it wasteland, former industrial, modern office blocks, gang turf, farmland, woodland, or suburbia? What sort of cover and/or hiding places are available? Are there places where an attacker could wait and watch a victim? The nature of the local terrain is also important as are local weather conditions.

The profiler will also try and determine how an offender might have come to know a particular location? What else might they have done in this place? Do they live locally? Work or attend meetings? Engage in a hobby such as hunting or fishing? Or take part in some kind of sport or other activity?

When thinking about geography it is important not only to think in terms of external physical maps – people also have 'mental maps' and we each tend to perceive locations and distances differently. A criminal will typically commit his crimes in a place where he or she feels comfortable or confident. The extent of the area of comfort varies from individual to individual. Someone who normally travels very little in their life may choose a small area that is local to them; a truck driver who travels long distances regularly may have a much larger 'patch' in which to commit his crimes. Also of interest are any boundaries – physical or psychological – that define a criminal's territory. A state line or a river may mark one edge such a territory. Or an offender may only feel safe within a particular community. Or his targets may belong in a particular community. Familiar routes or forms of transport, especially escape routes, may also be a consideration.

When an investigation gets close to an offender's usual area of activity, this may cause the criminal to commit a crime in a different area. A change in life circumstances may also cause a change in location.

Signature Behaviours

There are some characteristics that are common to many serial killers including anger, low self-esteem, fantasy, and objectification of victims. But there are other behaviours or patterns of behaviour that are less common and more distinctive.

The signature is sometimes referred to as a 'calling card' or 'trademark' or a 'paraphilic footprint' and is a feature of the attacks by some serial killers and serial rapists and also in other types of crimes. Signatures may include things said by the killer or acts he performs and they may part of a 'ritual' that relates to his own particular fantasy or 'narrative' or an underlying psychological need. A signature behaviour may be 'active' – that is conscious and deliberate – or 'passive' – unintentional or subconscious. These things are not *necessary* for the successful completion of the crime and are separate from the criminal's *modus operandi* (method of operating or MO). The way that a killer carries out his crime may evolve as he becomes more experienced and confident, but his signature will often stay constant.

Signatures are often identified as a result of what Hickey refers to as 'paraphilia profiling.' Referred to as sexual deviation or perversion in the past, paraphilia refers to sexual arousal caused by atypical non-sexual objects, fantasies, or individuals. It may include fetishism and/or extreme or dangerous situations. In cases of serial murder with a sexual element, associated paraphilias may include recording or photographing victims, posing victims after death, use of specific forms of binding, acts performed on the victim's body before or after death, or use of a particular type of weapon.

It is also worth noting that just because a behaviour is repeated by the killer at different crime scenes this does not make it a signature behaviour. A signature behaviour has some psychological or emotional significance for the killer.

Amy L. Bronswick in her dissertation *Using Sexually Related Crime Scene Characteristics to Profile Male Serial Killers* provides a list of signature behaviours:

- Aberrant sex
- Attacks at the face
- Body disposal
- Cannibalism
- Decapitation
- Dismemberment
- Mutilation
- Necrophilia
- Penile/object penetration
- Picquerism (sexual arousal from repeated stabbing of a victim)
- Restraints
- Souvenirs (photographs, clothing, jewellery, newspaper clippings)
- Torture
- Trophies (victim body parts)
- Weapons

Signatures may be one of the ways investigators can use to link crimes as being the work of a single offender or team of offenders. Even if the killer changes or varies other aspects of his crimes, the signature may remain the same as it is an important part of his fantasy. The term 'signature' suggests that these behaviours can be used to uniquely identify an individual offender, but the fact that we can have a list of frequently found signatures shows that this is not the case. A 'signature' of this kind is *not* sufficient to identify a specific individual – at best it can be said that evidence at a crime scene indicates a pattern of behaviour that matches that found at another scene and that this is consistent with them having been committed by the same killer(s).

If a serial killer does have a signature, there may be crime scenes where it is not found – perhaps because he was interrupted before he could complete his 'ritual'.

Ritualistic behaviour that is not *necessary* for the commission of the crime is evidence that increases the risk of the offender being caught. But this behaviour usually meets some need in the offender and they are unable or reluctant to give it up – it is part of *why* they do what they do. The longer the offender spends on these behaviours, the greater the chance that physical or behavioural evidence will be left behind for investigators to see. It is easier to create a profile for a serial killer that has particular ritual habits – and these sorts of behaviour also make for more dramatic fictional crimes.

An important factor in forensic evidence of all kinds is that of *individuation*. A piece of evidence may be shown to be *consistent* with a theory or to be a *match* with a particular type of thing – fibres from a carpet, say – but this is not the same as saying that the evidence identifies a source to the exclusion of all others allowing for *individuation* of an item. It's the difference between having fibres that identify a type of carpet that may be in use in thousands of homes or vehicles and having a sample that identifies a specific piece of that carpet in a particular location such that the sample could not have come from anywhere else. Behaviours, even apparently unique 'signatures', are – according to Petherick – best regarded as identifying a type of offender rather than pointing to a specific individual. Behavioural evidence cannot be regarded as definitive proof in the same way as a fingerprint or DNA.

Serial Killer Methods

Here we consider choice of location, type of attack and use of violence. From the *location* of the crime it is possible to identify four types of serial killer according to Rossmo (1997): the *hunter* (or marauder) who goes out from his home location in search of victims and who may lure them back to his home to kill them; the *poacher* (or commuter) who uses another place as the base for his attacks and may travel some distance to find victims; the *troller*, whose seizes any opportunity that presents itself, and the *trapper* who carefully plans his attacks. Other aspects relating to location were covered under *Geographic Profiling* earlier in this chapter.

Three different types of *attacking behaviour* have also been identified – blitz, con, and surprise. A blitz attack is sudden and unexpected and has also been referred to as a 'raptor' attack – such attacks tend to be opportunistic and the victim is chosen almost at random. A con is a trick or some other method of luring the victim – it involves deliberate targeting and is also referred to as an 'ambush.' Surprise attacks involve stealth and again involve deliberate targeting, with the attacker perhaps stalking the victim and then sneaking into her home to carry out an attack.

The use of *violence* is another way in which we can think about differentiating serial offenders. Two main forms have been suggested. *Expressive violence* is an outburst of aggression caused by emotions that arise when the person is challenged or frustrated. The individual feels a need to hit out or to 'explode.' This demonstrates an inability to control impulses and this will also be evident in other behaviours such as substance abuse and volatile personal relationships. As it is triggered by emotions, this type of violence is sometimes referred to as *affective*. *Instrumental violence* is physical aggression used to achieve a particular purpose. Violence or the threat of it is used in a calculated way to control another person and make them do what the offender wants. Use of violence in this way is considered – it has thought behind it – and so is sometimes referred to as *cognitive*.

Four Types of Serial Killer

We can take the classifications of victim as *object* or *vehicle* and combine them with the two forms of violence – *cognitive* (or instrumental) and *affective* (or expressive) and combine them to create four types of serial killer: *affective-object, affective-vehicle, cognitive-object,* and *cognitive-vehicle.* 'Healthcare killers' are slightly different in this respect and we'll look at them separately below.

In broad terms, the two *affective* types of killer correspond to the FBI's 'disorganized' killer, in that they are more impulsive and emotion-driven; while the two *cognitive* types are 'organized' as their attacks demonstrate more pre-planning.

Godwin summarises the key characteristics of these four types of serial killer, based on studies of convicted serial killers in the USA.

The Affective-Object Serial Killer
Model Characteristics: Disorganized, Low self-awareness, Impersonal attachment, Rage
Signature Behaviours: Blitz attack, Use of bindings, Bludgeoning victim, Biting, Objects inserted into victim. Possible use of a gun as a weapon.
Background: Typically white and aged around thirty; sex-related crimes, use of pornography, sexual fetishes; possibly paedophilia; employment status and education level vary.

The Affective-Vehicle Serial Killer
Model Characteristics: disorganized, Low self-awareness, Impersonal attachment, Rage.
Signature Behaviours: Forced entry into victim's home, typically at night; ransacked property and often theft of victim's vehicle or property; victim fully dressed; restraints used, possibly made from victim's clothing; weapon often something found at the scene and left at the scene – though punching and kicking may be used instead of a weapon; often sexual assault or attempted sexual assault with semen found at the scene.
Background: White or black and typically aged around thirty. Juvenile convictions – crimes including burglary, robbery, and violent offences including kidnap, rape, and murder. Sex crimes including voyeurism and possibly paedophilia; use of pornography; sexual fetishes. Employment status and education level vary.

The Cognitive-Object Serial Killer
Model Characteristics: Organized, High self-awareness, Personal attachment, Sadistic
Signature Behaviours: Sexual acts on victim post mortem; dismemberment and scattering of body parts – though body may be buried and forensic evidence destroyed; cannibalism. Uses a ploy or con to approach victims. Holds victim captive. Carries a 'kit' of tools/materials for crimes or may stash them at strategic locations often some time in advance of use.
Background: Typically white and thirty years of age. Use of pornography; sexual fetishes. Convictions for sex-related crimes other than rape. Possibly paedophilia. Typically in employment; educational level varies.

The Cognitive-Vehicle Serial Killer
Model Characteristics: Organized, High self-awareness, Impersonal attachment, Sadistic
Signature Behaviours: Ritualistic activity with the victim being tortured and the body left posed. Piquerism. Offender retains trophies. Victim is often drugged, gagged and blindfolded, bound with electrical cord. Sexual assault
Background: Typically white and aged around 28. Juvenile convictions for violent crimes including kidnap, rape, and murder. Use of pornography; sexual fetishes; voyeurism. Typically employed; educational level varies.

Serial Killer Victims

I will cover the profiling of victims in more detail later, but there is one significant aspect that I want to cover here – the serial killer's treatment of the victim. Canter et al. (2004) used the Radex model to classify the victim in the crime in terms of what they represented for the offender. The killer may regard the victim as an *object,* a *vehicle,* or a *person* – and this is revealed in the way in which the offender treats the victim.

Victim as object sees the killer regard the victim as simply a thing that allows them to achieve their goal – and this means the offender may inflict horrific injuries on the victim without any concern for them.

Victim as vehicle sees the offender target the victim in the belief that they represent something or someone. If the offender has strong emotions towards, for example, his own mother, then he may express his aggression and desires on a victim he sees as representing her. The things the killer does to the victim are things that he wants, on some level, to do to his mother. Often a specific type of person is targeted – they fit a 'type' the killer wishes to direct his actions against or demonstrate his control of or power over.

Victim as person involves the offender seeing the victim as a person who has feelings. The victim typically has something that the offender wants and manipulation and violence are used to try and obtain it. The victim may be the offender's usual sexual partner or someone the offender has been stalking. If there is a sexual assault, the rapist may not fully accept or understand the nature of his actions – he may believe that the victim wants to engage in the sexual act. Serial murderers rarely see their victims in this way and are more likely to treat that as an object or a vehicle.

Creating the Profile

I'm not going to advocate using any one of the three types of profiling here – you should choose whatever methods best suit the needs, characters, and circumstances of your story. In real life, I think the evidence-based deductive approach is probably the better method, but when it comes to fiction I would probably want to add some of the more inductive content as this gives a much better feeling for the inner workings of the serial killer. I doubt that it is actually necessary to include a full profile within the text of a novel – you probably want only three or four short paragraphs spread across a scene or a couple of scenes plus a few references in dialogue – but I think creating a profile for your own use might have benefits – particularly if you like to spend time creating biographies for your other characters. Here we'll look at how a profiler might go about creating a profile including what information they may need (inputs) and what the finished profile might include (output).

Profiling Inputs

The quality of a criminal profile is dependent on the information used to produce it and, generally speaking, the more information the better. Sources of information include:

- Photographs of the crime scene including the body in the position in which it was found.
- Photographs of the victim including close-ups of any wounds or other marks on the body.
- Details of the neighbourhood in which the body was found, including details of the types of people who live and/or work there.
- Map of the area and a record of the victim's movements in the hours before their death, plus details of a last siting of the victim alive.
- Pathology/autopsy report, including photographs, detailing any damage to the body, estimated time of death, toxicology findings, presence of bodily fluids from the attacker, and whether wounds were inflicted before or after death.
- Investigator's report with date, time, and location of the body's discovery; details of the weapon, if known; witness statements, and the investigator's reconstruction of the sequence of events based on the scene and other evidence.
- Background information on the victim including age, gender, ethnicity; physical description including clothing; marital status; education and intelligence; lifestyle including any recent changes; occupation; present and former home addresses and their distance from the crime scene; relatives, friends, and colleagues; physical and mental medical history; social and sexual habits; personality and attitudes; involvement with law enforcement or the legal system, and any other details that might indicate why they might have been chosen as a victim.

Ramsland lists the following crime scene factors used in profiling:

- Approximate time the incident occurred
- How long it went on
- Why it stopped
- Whether the offender arrived prepared
- Whether something or someone at the scene facilitated offender behaviour
- Whether the incident was inside or outside
- How many victims at each scene
- How many other potentially connected scenes

- Whether there is one primary scene per incident or several associated scenes
- Weather conditions at the time
- The time of day
- Details about if and how a body was moved
- The environment around the crime scene
- Whether similar incidents have been reported nearby
- Neighbourhood demographics
- Geophysical features

In evaluating the evidence to discover characteristics about the offender, Ramsland says, profilers will consider the modus operandi, any ritualistic or signature behaviours that occurred before, during, or after the attack, and the way in which the victim was approached. These will be used in conjunction with the victimology – including victim risk exposure levels, and crime scene evidence, including where the body was found and how it had been treated – buried, hidden, left exposed, or posed.

Geographical profiling will also be carried out for the crime scene and any other locations related to the crime. Crime scene elements can give clues about whether the offender has a set routine, preferred hours or times of the week/month/year for committing offences, full- or part-time employment, access to a vehicle, and experience with weapons, perhaps gained in the military.

Profilers often look at the crime scene to try and envision how the offender experienced it. What significance did a particular action or object have for the offender? Does it symbolise something? Did the killer surprise the victim? Or did they use cunning to lure them to the scene of the attack? Or did the killer just take advantage of a chance opportunity that presented itself? How did the killer control the victim during the course of the attack? Was the victim a captive for any length of time before the murder? Do the places where the bodies were found suggest that the murderer has an occupation that involves travel? Or does it seem that local knowledge was required? Do the attacks take place in the killer's home, the victim's home, or at some other location? These things all offer clues about the type of person who committed the crime.

Output – Profile Contents

Claire Ferguson writes that studies into what can reliably be obtained from available information include only five characteristics: Motive; Special Skills or Knowledge of Methods and Materials; Knowledge of or Relationship to the Victim; Knowledge of the Crime Scene or Location, and Criminal Skill/Forensic Awareness.

Motive: The physical, psychological, or emotional needs that drove the criminal to carry out the attack.

Special Skills or Knowledge of Methods and Materials: Any specific experience or expertise that was required to carry out the crime in the manner in which it was committed.

Knowledge or Relationship to the Victim: Did the victim know the attacker? Evidence that they did include absence of signs of forced entry or struggle and lack of defensive wounds. Evidence at the scene may also indicate that the attacker knew the victim's daily or weekly schedule, route, or other habits.

Knowledge of Crime Scene or Location: Did the offender demonstrate specific knowledge of the location where the crime took place? Evidence that they did may include knowing where objects were located, knowing access routes or exits, or knowing where the victim's vehicle or home was located.

Criminal Skill and Forensic Awareness: Did the attacker demonstrate knowledge of police procedures or of the ways in which forensic evidence is gathered? Did the criminal engage in planning, precautions, or deliberate acts designed to deceive investigators and hamper attempts to identify him/her? Attempts to avoid leaving evidence at a scene or to destroy evidence may indicate that the criminal is experienced – which may mean he has committed similar attacks before. Or it may be an indication of his/her level of intelligence.

Inferences
Once the data has been gathered, the profiler assesses and interprets it and begins to compile a profile of the attacker's characteristics. Different approaches to this produce profiles with differing levels of detail. This stage involves drawing inferences from the information available. David Canter (2012) writes that creating a 'profile' of an offender involves collating details of the crime and then making some 'if–then' assumptions. As an example, he says that if a man has been violent to women in the crimes then it is highly likely that he is someone who has been violent to women on other occasions and may be someone known to the police because of this.

Inferences are often in the form of 'Given what we now know, where should we look next to find further information?' The danger here is that an investigator applies too much imagination and makes a huge leap between evidence and inference, such that the inference isn't really based on what is *known*. Many fictional profiles contain inferences that aren't supported by the evidence, with the profiler drawing on either gut instinct or experience of similar cases – neither of which can be entirely relied upon in the present case. But, there is evidence from studies of solved cases of what Canter (2010) refers to as the 'consistency principle' – "The actions in a crime will be generally consistent with how the offender acts in non-criminal situations, even though they may be more extreme when part of a crime."

Canter suggests five questions that should be asked:

- What does the crime indicate about the intelligence and knowledge of the offender?
- What does it suggest about his degree of planning or impulsivity?
- How does the criminal interact with the explicit or implicit victim?
- What do his actions indicate about the degree of familiarity with the situation or circumstances of the crime?
- What particular skills does the offender have?

As Canter notes, these questions relate to the crime itself rather than to the perceived personality of the criminal and their coverage is not quite as broad as the five characteristics suggested by Ferguson.

Criticisms of Profiling – Accuracy, Utility & Investigative Relevance
Accuracy or validity refers to whether correct linkages have been made between events – i.e. did the profile prove to be factually correct. *Utility* is concerned with the extent to which valid information provided by the profile was actually useful in understanding or solving the crime. The degree to which information included in a profile can actually be utilized by

investigators to solve the crime is also known as 'investigative relevance.' The profile needs to provide something that the investigators can act upon.

David Canter is critical of the content of some profiles, noting that it is unlikely that a detailed account of an as yet unidentified criminal's personality will contribute much that is of use in solving the crime. An understanding of a criminal's psychology can be of use after they have been identified and detained – in terms of how they are questioned by investigators and, later, in trying to help the jury understand how and why the criminal did what he did.

There is also a danger in assigning a characteristic or indicator to an unknown criminal. If a profiler advises investigators to search for a man with military training, for example, then the police may allow a killer to escape simply because he doesn't have military training.

Ramsland writes that our natural desire to place things in a logical narrative order is a risk that profilers must be aware of in themselves and in others. He says that our familiarity with the pattern of stories means that we "...form expectations of how the narrative will develop and how it will (or should) end. A narrative with holes is vulnerable. Listeners will add details that make the story make better sense." Profilers and other investigators have to make themselves consider alternative scenarios rather than just accept the most obvious 'story' that appears to fit the evidence. The classic mystery or whodunit explores how different theories of what might have happened fit with the clues that have been discovered and there is still an element of this in the forensic thriller.

Linking Crimes

With the case of a serial murderer, one of the first things that has to be done is to establish that there is a link between two or more murders. Physical evidence such as fingerprints, fibres or DNA may show that two or more crimes are connected and probably the work of a single offender. Where there is no such evidence, it may be possible to show that the behaviour of the offender – their modus operandi or a 'signature' – in two or more crimes suggests a link, especially if that behaviour is unusual. Obviously, the fact that something is 'unusual' would need to be supported by statistical evidence.

Hickey notes that some serial killers are highly mobile and – in the USA – may commit crimes in several law enforcement jurisdictions while still operating in a relatively small geographic area. Some killers choose strangers as victims, meaning that there is no former relationship that may link victim to murderer. And, thanks in part of media reports, documentaries, and movies, offenders may possess sufficient knowledge of forensic and other investigative procedures that they are able to avoid leaving behind obvious incriminating evidence. All of these and other factors can mean that it may be some time before a link is made between the crimes of a single serial murderer. Also, if a body is not found, there may be no way to link a missing person report with the actions of a serial killer.

Linking a Cold Case

Some serial killers operate over an extended period of time and there are also instances where it appears that a serial killer ceased killing for some time – perhaps as a result of being imprisoned for another crime or due to some other change in life circumstances – but then begins killing again at a later date. For these reasons, investigators need to be aware of earlier unsolved cases that may be linked to a current investigation. Databases exist in most countries listing the various characteristics of unsolved crimes which can be searched and cross-matched against new reports of similar crimes.

Advances in techniques such as DNA analysis mean that older unsolved cases – 'cold cases' – can also be reinvestigated. This often occurs when an offender is convicted and is then linked to earlier crimes. Even without DNA evidence, behavioural analysis may link an offender to unsolved crimes, providing new directions for further investigation.

Victimology – Victim Profiling

Turvey (2014) says that victimology is one of the most important aspects of an investigation, second only to the gathering of physical evidence at a crime scene. Knowledge of the victim may offer insights about the person who murdered them.

Profiling the victim of a serial murderer has much in common with the way in which a 'psychological autopsy' (see above) is conducted.

Specific areas in which victimology can assist in an investigation include:

Assisting in understanding elements of the crime. Examining the victim, their lifestyle and their environment allows the victimologist to understand the relationships and interactions between victim and crime scene, offender and crime scene, and victim and offender.

Assisting in developing a timeline. Retracing a victim's last known movements and actions is critical in understanding the victim as a person, their relationship to the environment and events, and in discovering how and when the offender first came into contact with the victim.

Defining the suspect pool. In any case, where the identity of the offender is unknown, victimology can help to define the suspect pool. The victim's lifestyle and activities offer clues as to who had access to the victim both in general terms and at the specific time and/or location of the crime. An understanding of how the offender came to select the victim can establish a link between offender and victim. Links may be related to geographical area, occupation, school or college, hobbies, or related to a regular schedule of movements or activities for the victim.

Providing investigative suggestions. A victimology can offer a list of suspects to interview, locations to visit to seek witnesses or suspects, and the timeline might highlight discrepancies in statements made by witnesses or suspects. An understanding of the victim's activities may also help establish the relevance of actions, objects, or other pieces of evidence. It may also indicate that items are missing or that certain behaviours were out of character for the victim and need further investigation. Ramsland offers the example of a missing woman's care found backed into a parking spot, which would not appear unusual, but "...if her husband insists that she hated to back up her car, this would raise the likelihood that someone else manoeuvred the car or forced her to."

Assisting with crime scene reconstruction. An understanding of the victim's patterns of behaviour can be helpful in accurately reconstructing what happened at a crime scene. Knowing why a victim was at a particular location and what they planned to do there provides context for what happened both previously and subsequently.

Assisting with development of the offender's modus operandi. Knowing why a victim was at a particular location and what their actions were can help establish how the offender selects his victims. A location with multiple potential victims may suggest that the offender goes to that place looking for an opportunity to acquire a victim. A location with no one but the victim in it may suggest the offender has targeted the victim previously and followed them. If the victim was ambushed in an isolated location, this may suggest that the offender was aware of the victim's usual schedule of movements.

Assisting with development of offender motive. The more information that is gathered about a victim, the better the chance that investigators will be able to work out *why* an offender targeted them.

Assisting with case linkage. In the absence of physical evidence to demonstrate a link between crimes, investigators may seek similarities in offender behaviour as a link. Selection of victims is an important element in behavioural analysis. Examination of the victims in a series of crimes may also identify factors that the victims have in common. A comparison of victim exposure levels may also confirm (or refute) that there is a link between crimes.

Assisting with public protection advice. If investigators understand how and why an offender is selecting his victims, then they can try and predict what sort of person he might target in future. Knowing this, advice can be provided to those groups who are most at risk so that they can reduce their own exposure to danger.

A victim profile is a list of the characteristics possessed by a specific victim. According to Turvey (2014) the profile will include "...physical, biological, mental, social, educational, occupational, and personality descriptors..." and he suggests the profile be open-ended rather than confined to a checklist. He also says that "...the victimologist must be willing to sift through each victim's history carefully, with no preconceived theories..."

Sources of Information About a Victim

In profiling a criminal whose identity is unknown, the sources of information are relatively few – there is the crime scene and some clues about behaviour may be deduced from what appears to have taken place there. The victim, however, is typically present – either as a survivor of the crime or as a body. The identity of the victim is also often known – either immediately or following a relatively short period of investigation, though some victims do remain unidentified. The physical presence of a victim and knowing their identity means that there is a much greater range of information about the victim for investigators and profilers to analyse. Based on the list given by Ramsland and Turvey (2014), we can group these sources under a number of headings.

Personal Details. These include some or all of the details that we typically find on a character creation checklist – gender, ethnicity, height, weight, hair colour and style, tattoos and other distinguishing marks such as scars, and eye colour. Clothing, jewellery and personal items – including a wallet, purse, handbag, backpack or briefcase – may also be included here. Interests such as sports or hobbies, gym or club memberships, and routine social activities are also of interest, as are any recently attended or forthcoming events or commitments.

Digital or Online Life. Cell phones are an important element in many people's lives today and they can provide a lot of details about a person. There will be a list of contacts for phone calls, chat and messaging, and e-mails – along with the person's recent exchanges. There may also be photographs, video, and perhaps GPS data with stored locations. Much of this digital evidence will be date and time-stamped. Internet browser history on a phone or computer is another source of recent information. Website 'favourites' and social media accounts – including dating apps – also help fill out the picture of a person's interests and activities.

Home Details. A person's home offers clues about their personality and their community. The type of residence – house, apartment, rented room – and its location reveals something about the social status of the individual. The physical condition of the building and the interior decoration and furnishings also add to this picture, as does the type and physical condition of any vehicle owned or used. Possessions give clues about interests, hobbies, and taste in things like movies, books, foods, and music. Files of paperwork and correspondence can offer information about friends, business, financial, or medical matters. Personal items may also reveal something about a person's sex life. Items that appear to be missing may also be relevant to the investigation along with any signs of intrusion or violence. If the living space is shared with others or there is evidence that one or other person has been in the home recently, this may give investigators new names to add to the list of those to be interviewed. Records of telephone calls made to a landline in the home and of any 911 or other calls made from it may also offer clues. CCTV video footage from the victim's home may also be available. The building's trash will also be searched.

Relationship Details. Investigators will want to identify and locate and present or former spouses, lovers, or sexual partners; relatives – by blood and by marriage; roommates or lodgers; friends, classmates, co-workers, and acquaintances.

Employment & Education Details. Schools, colleges and/or universities attended and educational achievements will be noted as will current and former occupations including job titles and work schedules. Employment history will also include the person's relationships – good or confrontational – with bosses, colleagues, and customers. A work computer, phone or GPS device might offer similar clues to those in personal devices. Odometer readings or other logs for a work vehicle may also be significant.

Financial Details. Online banking and other financial records can also be accessed by investigators. Bank and credit card statements can offer clues about payments made to individuals or organisations, items purchased, and places visited. Investments, insurance policies, and property ownership details will also be checked.

Physical & Mental Health Details. This will include any toxicology report on the victim, with details of any alcohol, recreational drugs, or other substances found. There will also be information about any recent prescriptions or medical treatments for short- or long-term medical conditions, including addictions. Investigators will also be interested in recent medical appointments and contact with medical and other healthcare professionals including doctors, dentists, or counsellors.

Legal or Criminal Details. This would include an instance of the victim having previously been a victim, suspect, or witness in any legal proceedings along with any criminal history including warrants, arrests, convictions, protection orders, or other interactions with the courts, social services, or law enforcement.

Having been identified and gathered, these sources can then be used to compile a timeline (see below) and lists of the victim's routines and habits; family members, friends, co-workers, and other associates, and movements and activities during the period prior to the attack

Creating a Timeline: The Last 24 Hours
Turvey (2014) says that an effective approach to creating this chronological account of locations and events includes at least the following steps:
- Compile all witness data.
- Compile all available forensic evidence and findings.
- Compile all the police/media crime scene photographs and video.
- Compile all security stills and video covering the crime scene and any paths taken by the victim or offender to or from it.
- Create a linear timeline of events and locations.
- Create a map of the victim's route for the 24 hours before the attack, as detailed as possible.
- Physically walk through the victim's last 24 hours using the map and forensic evidence as a guide.
- Document expected background elements of the route in terms of vehicles, people, activities, professionals, and so on for the time leading up to, during, and after the victim was acquired. It is possible that the offender is, or was, masquerading as one of those expected elements.

Then attempt to determine the following:
- The point at which the offender acquired the victim
- The place where the offender attacked the victim
- How well the attack location can be seen from any surrounding locations
- Whether the offender would need to be familiar with the area to know of this specific location or get to it
- Whether knowledge of the route would require or indicate prior surveillance
- Whether this route placed the victim at higher or lower exposure to an attack
- Whether the acquisition of the victim on that route placed the offender at higher or lower exposure to identification or apprehension

The Victim's Exposure to Risk
Victim exposure to risk is the amount of contact the person has to harmful elements and/or their vulnerability to these elements. Profilers consider two aspects of this: *lifestyle exposure* and *situational exposure*.

In exploring how a victim's lifestyle or actions might have contributed to their becoming a victim of crime, it is important to note that we are not in any way blaming the victim for their own suffering. Victimologists must avoid making personal or moral judgements about the victim – and they should not make assessments about what the victim should or should not have done in any situation.

Generally speaking, lone individuals are more at risk than pairs or groups, but there are offenders who will target pairs so that they can use threats towards one of them to control the other – a mother, for example, will do what the offender asks if she believes her child is at risk.

Lifestyle Exposure to Risk
Lifestyle exposure refers to the victim's experience of potentially harmful elements as a result of their usual environment and personality traits. It also takes into account past life choices. Lifestyle factors can affect the possibility of harm in three ways: by increasing a person's contact and

interactions with criminals; by creating conditions that bring them into conflict – real or perceived – with an offender, and by increasing an offender's perception of the person's vulnerability.

The victim's lifestyle can offer clues about how and where they might have met their murderer. Ordinary people do not typically encounter or engage in relationships with dangerous criminals – and when they do become victims it is often because the attacker enters the victim's home or targets them in some other way. For ordinary people, situational risk (see below) is more of a factor than lifestyle risk.

Lifestyle factors that can affect a person's level of risk include physical and mental health and their personal, professional, and social environments. Some groups of people have lifestyles that put them at higher risk of encountering dangerous individuals. High-risk victims, according to Ramsland, "...include those engaged in marginal behaviour, such as substance abuse, prostitution, sexual role-playing, memberships in risky clubs, and exotic dancing." Anyone whose occupation, social habits, or behaviours bring them into contact with groups that contain a disproportionate number of criminals or violent individuals is more likely to become a victim of one of those criminals.

Prostitutes are vulnerable because their work involves being alone with men that they do not know. They may also be targeted by 'mission' killers or by a killer who sees them as representing some female figure that he has intense feelings about or a grudge against.

Homosexual men are also at risk if they seek to be alone with a man that they do not know particularly well. Gay men are typically targeted by homosexual serial killers rather than straight men, and the initial contact between victim and killer may take place in a social situation without any apparent warning signals. Hickey notes that there is "...fallacy in suggesting that homosexual serial murders are more bizarre than heterosexual serial killing. Serial murder is, by its very nature, obscene. The homosexual serial murders by Dahmer, Gacy, Baumeister, and Kraft are equally rivalled by the heterosexual savagery of Bundy, Kemper, Robinson, and DeSalvo."

Traits that Influence Lifestyle Exposure

Aggressiveness: People who are confrontational or who express anger regularly are more likely to evoke aggressive behaviour in others (see *Precipitation of Risk* below).

Impulsivity: Actions taken without planning or consideration of consequences mean that impulsive individuals are at greater risk of encountering situations they are unprepared for.

Self-destructive behaviour: Some behaviours are known to be dangerous but individuals engage in them anyway. As well as the risks inherent in binge drinking, drug use, or thrill-seeking trips to isolated or dangerous locations, there is an added risk of criminals taking advantage of this recklessness.

Passivity: Some people allow themselves to fall or to be led into dangerous situations or behaviours. They are either too trusting of others or unable to take responsibility for their own safety. Again, such people are at increased risk of being targeted by offenders.

Low self-esteem: This brings with it a number of risk factors. People suffering from depression may engage in self-destructive behaviours that increase their risk of victimisation. Or they may allow themselves to be led into dangerous situations in order to win the approval of others. And it can lead to the victim feeling that they *deserve* to be victimised.

Sexual behaviour: Sex with strangers entails a higher-level risk than other forms of relationship – and the risks increase if this is combined with alcohol or drug use. There are also behaviours during sex that increase risk including bondage and erotic asphyxiation.

Precipitation of Risk

Precipitation refers to characteristics or behaviours that a victim has that are perceived as triggering the offender to target them. Precipitation can be passive or active. *Passive precipitation* occurs when a victim has a characteristic or behaviour which, unknown to the victim, is perceived by the offender as threatening or encouraging. The offender's perception may be a misreading of the situation – the result of a misunderstanding or a subconscious influence. It may also arise because the offender sees the victim as *symbolic* of another individual or group and therefore a legitimate target for acts of punishment or vengeance.

Active precipitation occurs in situations where the victim knowingly provokes the offender. Provocation may take the form of criticism, insults, or even physical assault by the victim. The victim then suffers greater harm – perhaps out of all proportion to the original provocation – as a result of the offender's retaliation or 'defence.' The victim makes the first move but suffers the greatest consequences. While provocation is usually the result of words or deeds directed at the offender, there are some behaviours and lifestyle choices that while not being specifically targeted at an individual offender might be seen by that offender as provocative. The extent to which the victim is aware that they are being provocative in these behaviours or choices – i.e. the extent to which they are deliberately seeking to provoke responses to them – determine whether they are active or passive precipitation.

Turvey (2014) writes that "...victim lifestyle exposure must be established to help place the crime in context from the victim's perspective. Specifically, it assists with establishing the victim's physical and mental faculties, as well as disposition, coping mechanisms, and perception of reality." Different people perceive situational threats in different ways and also vary in their responses to them. An understanding of the victim's everyday experiences also provides a baseline against which the 'extraordinariness' of the situation of the crime can be assessed.

Situational Exposure to Risk

Where lifestyle exposure to risk refers to factors that occur within a person's typical life circumstances, *situational exposure to risk* refers to harmful elements experienced by the victim resulting from their environment and personal behaviours and disposition *at the time the crime was committed*.

Situational harm may come from the people, the environment, and the circumstances present at the moment when the crime was committed – all of these things must be investigated.

Time of Incident. Some particular times of day can present a greater risk of harm occurring than others. This factor must also be considered in combination with the location – a particular place at a particular hour might be necessary for the crime to be committed unobserved.

Location of Incident. What are the characteristics of the location that led the offender to choose it as his location for an attack? Did he need to isolate the victim in a place that would leave them undisturbed for a considerable period of time? Is the location a 'lawless zone' where no one is likely to come to the victim's assistance? Other factors to consider include:

Ownership: Who owns the location, if anyone? Was the victim aware of the location's ownership status?

Relationship to the victim: What is the relationship of the victim to the location? Do they live or work there? Is it a place they frequented socially? How familiar were they with the location? Were they familiar with it at that particular time of day? How did they arrive at the location – voluntarily on their own or as a passenger of an acquaintance, or were they taken there against their will? Where was the victim coming from or going to?

Security: What security measures are in place in terms of doors, locks, cameras, or patrols? How easy is it to get into the location unobserved? Are there security cameras on nearby buildings or approach roads? Investigators need to locate and secure any recordings.

Lighting: What lighting is in place at the location and how much of the area does it cover? Is artificial lighting in use after dark? Is it all in working order?

Adjacent locations: What is the nature of nearby homes, businesses, and other locations? Could the harm from one or more of these crossed over to the crime scene location?

Witnesses: Which areas overlook the crime scene and provide possible vantage points for witnesses? Which places provide line of sight to the scene or entrances or routes to it? What places are within hearing distance of the crime scene? Investigators will need to identify any potential witnesses in these places.

Criminal history: Is there a history of crime in this location? Do any of the people within it have a criminal history? Have emergency calls been made from the location in the past? Has the location ever been used as a base for criminal activities? What other forms of activity have been associated with the location? As well as crimes, any 'near misses' or other complaints about activity will need to be investigated.

If a victim was abducted and killed in a separate location, the place where they were taken may also offer clues as to what they were doing at the time and who else might have been present when the abduction took place. This may also allow investigators to decide whether the attacker planned the abduction beforehand or saw an opportunity and acted impulsively.

Victim Selection

Victim selection refers to the process an offender uses to choose a victim – it may be *targeted,* that is selected in advance, or *opportunistic*.

Opportunistic selection means that the victim just happened to be in the wrong place when the offender decided to attack. Either the offender was looking for a victim, any victim, or the situation was such that it suggested to the offender that an attack could be carried out. In such cases, the identity of the individual targeted is not relevant to the crime. The victim is selected because of their availability and accessibility to the offender, their vulnerability, and their location at the time of the attack.

Although opportunistic attacks are more spontaneous, there may still be an element of selection in the offender's choice of victim. Some selection criteria relate to traits necessary satisfy the offender's fantasy – he is attracted to a specific 'type' of woman, for example. Other offenders select according to symbolic criteria – the victim must have characteristics representative of another individual or group that the offender wishes to target.

In fiction, we might want to choose victims that do not obviously belong to an 'at risk' group. In *Red Dragon* Thomas Harris has his serial killer target families – as a method of engaging his reluctant hero and of gaining the sympathy of the reader. In real life, such killings are rare – there is added risk for the serial killer in targeting multiple victims in their own home and more opportunities for something unexpected to happen. And in the USA there is an added risk in that the homeowner may also be a gun owner. Richard Ramirez, 'The Night Stalker', did kill multiple victims during some of his attacks but those attacks seem more like spree killings that typical serial killer attacks. Most serial killers seek to spend time alone with their victim in order to satisfy whatever needs prompted the attack.

It is also rare for a serial killer to abduct more than one victim, again because of the added risk – two against one – and also because it is easier to control and dominate one person. One exception to this is where serial killers operate in pairs or teams.

Vilification & Deification of Victims

In victimology, it is necessary to gain a full picture of the entirety of the victim's life – including their secrets. While family members, friends, and work colleagues can provide details about the victim's home and work lives, and even some aspects of their social life, it is more difficult to obtain details of a person's sex life. This and other aspects of the victim's activities may not be known by even close family members or best friends. And even if details are known or suspected, witnesses may be reluctant to reveal them for fear of 'tarnishing' the victim's reputation or 'speaking ill of the dead.' This means that the things about the victim that may be most relevant to the investigation of the crime may be the ones that are the most difficult to ascertain. A 'secret life' doesn't have to be related to sex, but that is the most obvious example.

Deification refers to the way in which friends, family, teachers and/or employers tend to idealise victims after their death. It is natural to want to remember the victim's better qualities and achievements and also to try and demonstrate that they 'didn't deserve' what happened to them. The press and the public also tend to treat victims in a similar way – especially if the victim is young, attractive, and/or 'one of us.'

Vilification is the opposite and refers to the way in which some victims are regarded as not being worth sympathy or to have 'deserved' their fate. Victims with certain lifestyles, religions, ethnicities, social class, or behaviours are regarded as having contributed in some way to their own victimisation – they were, effectively, 'asking for it.' Prostitutes, drug users, drug dealers, runaways, the mentally ill, the homeless, homosexuals, and other marginalised groups are often among the most vulnerable members of society but are morally judged as being not worthy of the same sympathy as 'normal folk.' While vilification of victims is an issue when it occurs in the media or public opinion, it more directly impacts an investigation when it occurs among potential witnesses and among the police and other investigators. If the victim is a dead hooker or junkie, their murder may not be investigated with the same enthusiasm as the death of a wealthy businessman or an attractive female student or a child. This fact may actually be exploited by serial killers who select victims that are both vulnerable and whose deaths will not receive one hundred per cent of the investigators' attention.

Note that in Chapter 16, I have included information on questioning surviving crime victims and on some of the issues that arise.

The Serial Killer Plot Structure

In this section, I will refer to the serial killer as 'he' and the victim or victims as 'her' – statistics indicate that most serial killers are white males and most of their victims are white females, and most serial killer novels reflect this. The hero in the thriller can be male or female, reflecting the hiring practices of modern-day police forces and the FBI. Mentors tend to be older and more experienced and so are more likely to be male, reflecting hiring practices in these organisations in the past. Having said that, Clarice Starling investigated her first serial killer in 1988, so she'd have thirty years' worth of experience by now, so could well take on the mentor role... In the template below, I will refer to the hero as 'she' and the mentor as 'he.'

Four Quarters

I have based this plot template on a simple investigation based structure that breaks down into four quarters and three acts as follows:

Act I – First Quarter: Introduce the characters and the crime(s)
Act II, Part 1 – Second Quarter: Early investigation and first attempt at a solution with a failure or major setback at the *midpoint*.
Act II, Part 2 – Third Quarter: Further investigation and a second attempt at a solution with a failure or major setback at the 'darkest hour.'
Act III – Fourth Quarter: Third and successful attempt at a solution, final confrontation with the villain, and resolution.

This doesn't look like much, but breaking the plot into quarters like this really helped me make sense of what appeared to be very different and complex plot structures in a number of serial killer thrillers. Breaking each of these quarters into two parts gives us our eight-sequence plot model.

Main Characters

There are five types of main character involved in this plot:

1) *Hero* – often a 'rookie' or a reluctant hero, or both.
2) *Mentor(s)* – this role may be filled by two separate characters, a buttoned-up traditional boss and an unconventional or eccentric expert. In the template below, 'mentor' refers to the eccentric expert only.
3) *Rival* – someone who serves as an obstacle to the investigation at a key moment. Possibly an investigator from a 'rival' investigation team, e.g. the FBI, or a news reporter.
4) *The serial killer*
5) *Victims* – there will be anything from 1 to 5 victims who appear as characters and become victims of the serial killer, plus a number of others who are killed 'offstage' and who may already be dead as the story opens.

The *victims* in your story have a significant part to play and help to define the structure of the story. You need to decide how many *victims* you want to introduce in your story – that is, victims the reader or audience will see as live people rather than just bodies. There may be additional deaths – of law enforcement officers or unfortunate witnesses – but by 'victims' we mean people targeted by the serial killer and subjected to his ritualistic behaviours.

You will also need to decide whether the serial killer enters the victims' homes to kill them, lures them back to his home, or abducts them and takes them back to his hideout.

Suspense can be increased in a story, and a 'ticking clock' urgency added, by having a live victim abducted and imprisoned for the second half of your story – the heroes then have to solve the case before the serial killer kills the victim.

A victim can be abducted at the end of any of the first six sequences in the story. And you can have the killer abduct more than one person at a time – though as mentioned earlier in the chapter, multiple person abductions are rare because of the increased difficulty for the killer to control two people.

Jeffrey Deaver opens *The Bone Collector* with a double abduction and then has victims abducted in sequences 3 and 4 and another double abduction in sequence 5. The nature of his story requires this, but I would say that this is the top end for a victim abduction count.

At the opposite end of the scale are Thomas Harris's two novels, *Red Dragon* and *The Silence of the Lambs* where two or more murders have occurred before the story opens and only one victim is abducted during the story. Though Harris does have other killings that are not part of the 'serial sequence.'

How many victims you have your serial killer abduct depends on what significance the victim plays in the story. In *The Bone Collector,* the victims are more or less pieces in a game and we learn only a little about who each one is. In *The Silence of the Lambs,* the victim Catherine Martin plays a more significant role – she is abducted in sequence 2 and her fate is not decided until sequence 8.

The longer that a victim remains a captive of the killer, the more we will learn about the victim as a person and the more interaction we are likely to see between victim and captor. Also, the more time a reader or audience spends with a victim, the more they will care about that character – and the more they will want her to survive. You can also create scenes of suspense as the victim wonders whether *this* is the moment when they will be killed. And you can include scenes with the victim planning an escape attempt, putting the plan into effect – and failing to escape.

It is also possible to let the audience get to know a victim *after* she is dead. In *The Silence of the Lambs,* we see Clarice visiting the home of one of the murder victims and putting together a victim profile. You can use this to create sympathy for a victim and make the reader *want* to see the killer brought to justice.

Bearing in mind that the plot structure for the investigation requires two failed attempts to find the killer before the successful one *and* the fact that you want rising tension and rising action as the story progresses, you can place your victims accordingly. The placement of the victims in the template below is one way in which this can be done.

Sequence 1

One half of this introduces the main characters who will act as protagonists – usually the hero and his or her mentor. And the other half will introduce the crimes of the serial killer. Crime can come before characters or vice versa. Or you can just mix the whole lot up together or alternate scenes between the two.

You will want to begin your story with either action or intrigue. You could show a victim being murdered in front of our eyes. Or you could show the killer 'posing' the victim straight after the killing. Or you could have an unusual or bizarre murder scene being discovered or investigated. Any of these will draw your reader into the story and make them want to know more.

Victim 1 provides the first 'onscreen' body and crime scene clues for the investigators to examine. This victim isn't someone we got to know when they were alive, so we do not feel any great emotional attachment to them, beyond the fact that they were a human being who suffered a horrible fate. If you *do* want to increase audience sympathy for this victim, you can show the impact her death has had on her relatives and/or have one of your investigators put together a victim profile as Clarice Starling did.

The evidence from the body and the crime scene will usually reveal some sort of 'signature behaviour' that allows this murder to be linked to one or more previous killings that occurred before your story opened – this shows that Victim 1 *was* murdered by a *serial killer*. This signature behaviour should be something usual that will pique the interest of the reader and draw them into the investigation. It may also allow you to give your serial killer a colourful nickname, used by the police or the media.

You almost certainly need to introduce your hero by the end of sequence 1. This character may be a reluctant hero (Will Graham in *Red Dragon*), a rookie (Clarice Starling in *The Silence of the Lambs*) or both (Amelia Sachs in *The Bone Collector*). Will Graham is like a cross between a retired private eye and a war veteran – worldly wise and physically and mentally scarred by the job that he walked away from. His reluctance to return, as with all reluctant heroes, gives some indication of the dangers the job entails. A rookie doesn't have that level of experience, but a rookie character – in any story – gives the writer an easy way of explaining things to the reader as the newbie learns on the job; it provides an excuse for including background material and explanations.

You can include the mentor-expert in sequence 1 – or you could wait until sequence 2, perhaps having introduced them *by reputation* in sequence 1 to build them up before they actually appear on stage. The mentor-expert may be reluctant too. Neither Hannibal Lecter in Thomas Harris's novels nor Lincoln Rhyme in *The Bone Collector* wants to be involved in the investigation. A reluctant mentor also serves as an antagonist during some parts of the story – especially so in the case of Hannibal Lecter. It could be argued that Lincoln Rhyme is the hero of the story, playing the part of a Sherlock Holmes or Nero Wolfe, with Amelia playing his Watson or Archie Goodwin, especially in the movie adaptation, but this doesn't really affect the plot structure we are exploring here.

I would say that you should almost certainly have a crime scene in sequence 1, even if it is introduced at the very end and the investigation of it occurs in sequence 2.

In sequence 1 or 2 you can also introduce your *rival* character or at least some hint about his or her existence. In *Red Dragon* this role is filled by Freddy Lounds, the newspaper reporter, played by Philip Seymour Hoffman in the movie adaptation; in *The Silence of the Lambs* it is the head of the mental hospital, Dr. Chilton, and in *The Bone Collector* it is Fred Dellray, who leads a team of FBI investigators. This character serves as a significant obstacle or causes some other dramatic twist at one of the major turning points of the story, usually the midpoint.

Sequence 2
More on the characters and the crimes. And perhaps the abduction of another victim.

If you had a reluctant hero or reluctant mentor in sequence 1, you will have to show them overcoming their reluctance during sequence 2 and committing themselves to the investigation. This may be a short-term commitment – 'I will work with you until the latest abducted victim is found' or something like that. Here we will also learn more about the backstory and expertise of the mentor-expert. He typically makes some Sherlock Holmes-like deductions based on the crime scene and/or physical evidence. He may also produce the beginnings of a profile of the serial killer. Or perhaps a profile of the victim, created to try and discover what the killer's victims may have in common.

The evidence from the body of Victim 1 and its crime scene, along with evidence from the previous killings, will normally provide enough content to carry the story through to the middle or end of sequence 3. Aside from the signature behaviour, one of the first things learned from the crime scene will be the serial killer's *modus operandi* (M.O.), that is, the way in which he carried out the attacks and the actions he took during the attack. The investigators try to reconstruct the crime as it happened at the crime scene.

In the second half of sequence 2 or in sequence 3, we may begin to see scenes from the serial killer's point of view – though his actual identity may not be revealed.

Also in sequence 2 or 3 the presence of the *rival* character will be reinforced or perhaps introduced for the first time. This is setting up events for later.

If the first sequence focused on a dead body at a crime scene, then sequence 2 might have a live victim – Victim 2 – being abducted by the serial killer – or a report of someone going missing who sounds like they could be the serial killer's 'type'. The abduction of a live victim provides a reason for reluctant characters to commit to the investigation, it increases the stakes, and it adds a deadline – they have to solve the case and find the killer before the victim is killed.

We may also see things from the point of view of Victim 2, though they will probably be bound and blindfolded or in a dark and claustrophobic place. They may hear or smell a few things about their location. And they may or may not realise that they have been kidnapped by a serial killer. As mentioned earlier, we had minimal emotional involvement with Victim 1, and with Victim 2 we will have a small amount of emotional involvement – we will get to know a little bit about who she is and we will get some sense of the fear she feels in her present situation – but we aren't going to grow attached to her as a main character because, harsh as this sounds, she'll probably be found dead at the end of Sequence 4. We may also catch a few glimpses of the serial killer through this victim's eyes.

Sequence 3
First stages of the investigation. Sequence 3 is where the usual methods and easy options are applied to try to solve the case – matching details against the database of known crimes etc. We have to get these things out of the way before our characters can get down to demonstrating their

unique investigative abilities. Part of the way that we demonstrate that our expert *is* an expert is by showing 'mere mortals' failing to achieve what he is brought in to do.

Here we often encounter details of the technical tests that are carried out to identify fibres, hairs, or other samples of physical evidence found at the scene. The aim is to try and find a clue as to where the serial killer may live or where the victim may have been abducted from – or any other fact that might help to narrow down the search for the killer. As well as forensic science being used to examine the physical evidence, forensic psychology will be used to profile the serial killer and/or the victim(s).

As the investigators examine the various bits of evidence, there is usually a discussion about evidence that is of a type – e.g. a carpet fibre that may be found in thousands of homes – and that which is *individuated*, i.e. is unique to s specific object or individual and can have come from only one place, e.g. fingerprints, DNA, or bite marks.

It will seem that the heroes are making good progress in their investigation. The analysis of clues identifies possible leads and teams of uniformed officers or detectives are dispatched to do the 'legwork', checking hundreds of examples of something – vehicles, grocery stores, manufacturers of widgets, or whatever – to try and find a match for the clue they have.

Another body may be found, one from an earlier killing that had lain undiscovered for some time. An autopsy may reveal new clues – or not.

Perhaps more from Victim 2's point of view or from the serial killer's point of view.

Perhaps more about the rival – and the growing possibility of them getting in the way of the investigation or affecting it in some other way.

The hero and the mentor may discuss a plan to try and draw the serial killer out or force him into acting quickly – in the hope that forcing his hand may lead him to make a mistake that will lead to his capture. At the same time, they remain aware that any action they take could mean that the captive victim is killed.

Sequence 4

First attempt at a solution and midpoint failure or setback. The first failure by the investigators at the end of sequence 4 may be the death of Victim 2 – but it doesn't *have* to be. It could be another death connected to the investigation, but not involving the serial killer's ritualistic behaviours.

In this sequence, newspaper reporters may be sniffing around for a story and risk getting in the way of the investigation or publishing something that the investigators do not want to be made public as they don't want the serial killer to know what they have discovered about him.

The mentor may produce a more detailed profile of the serial killer – and it, or a version of it, may be shared with the media. It may include details designed to upset the killer, with the hope of prompting him to make contact and set the record straight. Here we may also see that the relationship between the hero and the mentor is deepening as they grow to like and trust each other. The midpoint failure or setback is often associated with interference by the rival character who in some way disrupts the investigation. In *The Bone Collector,* the hero and mentor are taken off the case and an FBI team take over. In *The Silence of the Lambs,* Dr. Chilton derails the investigation as a result of his own desire for fame. And in *Red Dragon,* the newspaper reporter Freddy Lounds gets an exclusive 'interview' with the serial killer.

If the actions of a rival do disrupt the investigation, this may occur late in Sequence 3 or early in Sequence 4. The hero and mentor could be taken off the case *before* the midpoint. This could mean that the those who take over the case are responsible for the midpoint failure – so that hero and mentor are only indirectly responsible. The rival and his team may misinterpret a clue or become distracted by a red herring or fall for a trick planted by the serial killer. This false or misleading clue may lead the rival and his team to a person they think is the next victim or to the location where they think Victim 2 is being held or to a location where they believe they will find the serial killer himself – his home, his place of work, or his favourite 'pick-up' spot. They are unaware that the killer is deliberately misleading them. When the rival and his team move in to make their raid, it turns out to be a humiliating failure. And worse, it may have deliberately distracted them in order to allow the serial killer to murder Victim 2 and leave her body where it can be found.

Alternatively, the hero and mentor may be taken off the case *at* the midpoint, because the failure *is* the fault. If rivalry does not disrupt the investigation, a first attempt at a solution by the hero and mentor may be tried – and fail. This may involve setting a trap for the serial killer. Or an attempt to find his home or hideout. Clues may lead to the location where Victim 2 is being kept – but when the police go there, the police may find that the serial killer has moved the victim or they may discover everything is gone except the body of Victim 2 – or part of it. If Victim 2 has been moved, it will be assumed that she has been taken to the place where she will be killed. If you do decide to have the hero and mentor taken off the case at a crucial point, it doesn't *have* to be because of a jurisdictional conflict. Their superiors may remove them due to internal or public politics, adverse news coverage, lack of progress, insubordination, or simply because someone had to be blamed for the fact that the most recent killing wasn't prevented and the hero and mentor were nominated as scapegoats.

Sequence 5
Reaction to the midpoint. Character relationships. Reassessment and recommitment. The serial killer selects his next victim. Sequence 5 begins with responses to, and/or consequences of, events at the midpoint. There may be conflict over who has jurisdiction of the case. The midpoint may have brought new evidence and perhaps another body, but the hero and the mentor may be denied access to it because they have been taken off the case. The hero may try and infiltrate the rival investigator's camp – and she may or may not be successful. But she probably manages to gain access to at least some of the new evidence – as a result of persistence, charm, a mistake by the other investigators, or pure luck.

After the midpoint, we will often see the serial killer selecting his next victim. This time we're much closer to him and observe his actions from an earlier stage. We may see where and how he first becomes aware of the potential victim and what it is about her that attracts his attention. We will probably see him following her and spying on her. He may take photographs or video of her – and all the while, she is unaware of his interest.

The serial killer may seek to contact her or even befriend her. Or she may be someone he knows already. The aim here is to have the audience become concerned for her safety – because they know of the danger she's in but she is completely unaware. You might also create a false scare by having it seem as if the serial killer is about to abduct or murder her – but then he backs away. Of course, we assume this is only a temporary reprieve. Unless this apparent victim is a red herring – designed to fool the reader who is then caught by surprise when the killer abducts someone else – perhaps a character we've already met and grown to like...

This red herring victim may be what causes the rival investigators to make their mistake and set-up a raid that goes nowhere. They may become aware of the killer's apparent interest in her and concentrate their efforts on watching her, hoping to catch the killer when he makes his move to abduct her. Or perhaps she is not the red herring. The killer may have planted clues that mean the rival and his team are following a man they *believe* to be the killer, but the man is completely innocent or he's a minor criminal of some kind. When the SWAT team descend on him, the rival and his team end up with egg on their faces.

While all this is going on, time may be running out for a victim – either Victim 2 who is being held by the serial killer or the person the killer has chosen to abduct as his *next* victim. Aware that they are on a deadline, the hero and the mentor may be desperate to continue their investigation – especially if they believe the team that has taken over is not doing the right thing or not moving quickly enough in the right direction. They may offer to help or issue warnings, but their advice is not heeded.

Sequence 5 typically focuses on relationships so we may see further development of the relationship between the hero and mentor, often involving the sharing of secrets and personal ambitions or fears. Or the sequence may concentrate more on the life story of the serial killer and the traumatic incidents and relationships that helped turn him into what he is today. This may include abusive relationships in which he was the victim and examples of behaviours typical of a psychopath such as mutilating animals when he was a child.

Whenever it happens, the embarrassing failure of the rival team results in the hero and the mentor being brought back on the case – either to replace the rival team or to work with them. Their recall may have been a result of the fact that they warned the rival team beforehand that they had made a mistake and were on the wrong track. While the investigators were distracted by all this, the serial killer may have abducted Victim 3, a totally different woman in a different location.

The hero and the mentor, now back on the case, examine clues from the midpoint incident and investigate Victim 3, beginning a detailed victimology. The mentor may also revisit his profile of the serial killer and deduce something significant about him. He begins to understand what it is the killer hopes to achieve by the killings. Based on all of the new information, the mentor is able to formulate a new theory and – perhaps – predict what the serial killer will do next and/or begin to narrow down the search area.

Sometimes another red herring is introduced in this sequence that does not 'pay off' until much later in the story. This may be related to a clue about the identity of the serial killer or of someone inside the team of investigators who is betraying them by passing information to the killer.

We may see the situation that Victim 3 is in through her eyes. She realises who the serial killer is and what is likely to happen to her very soon. Knowing she has little time, Victim 3 makes the first moves in an escape attempt that will depend on surprising the serial killer. We will probably learn a lot more about Victim 3 than we did about the earlier ones – both via her own thoughts and via the hero and/or mentor putting together a victim profile. To increase the emotional stakes, we want the reader to feel much more sympathy for this victim and really care whether she survives.

Sequence 6

Second attempt at a solution and 'darkest hour' failure. The hero and the mentor are back on the case, perhaps instead of or working with the rival team. Based on what he has learned from the latest evidence, the mentor formulates a theory about what the serial killer will do next and where he might do it. Various bits of evidence are cross-matched to try and narrow down the search area – to pinpoint the location where the serial killer lives or where he might be holding the victim.

The 'darkest hour' at the end of Sequence 6 may have several components: Victim 3 makes an attempt to escape – but fails; someone is killed by the serial killer – a 'punishment' killing designed to hurt the investigators because they have upset him or are getting too close to him; a failed rescue attempt; the serial killer has moved on, taking the victim to a new location; the serial killer in this new location making his final plans to kill Victim 3.

Sequence 7

Reaction to the 'darkest hour'. Reassessment of the evidence leading to a third and final attempt at a solution. Probably the introduction of a rapidly approaching deadline to save a victim. The serial killer is making preparations to kill Victim 3. He may have been upset by how close the investigation got to him – he hadn't been expecting this – and has considered postponing the killing or just killing this victim quickly and not carrying out his usual ritual. But he *needs* the full ritual and so has decided to go ahead with it. If anything, he is even more determined and feeling even more violent – as Victim 3 may discover when she refuses to do exactly what he says.

As well as the urgency involved in trying to find the killer before he kills the next victim, the hero and the mentor may also be coming under pressure from their superiors who in turn are under pressure from the media, local politicians and the public. The hero and the mentor may be blamed for whatever went wrong at the 'darkest hour' and told that their careers are on the line. The hero may visit the home of Victim 3 and discover something that connects her to the earlier victims. This clue may mean more 'legwork' is required by the police to locate a specific example of something – a car, a grocery store, or some other object or place that links the victims and the serial killer.

The mentor, meanwhile, is reassessing all of the evidence and realises that they have misinterpreted something or been side-tracked by a red herring. Putting this together with what the hero has discovered, he formulates a third and final theory. The results of the 'legwork' allow them to pinpoint the serial killer's location – which is probably now his home, his hideout having been discovered previously. This sequence ends with Victim 3 being saved – or her body being discovered, if you're feeling really mean. But the serial killer manages to get away.

Sequence 8

Locating the serial killer. Final confrontation and resolution. The final confrontation with the serial killer is usually a personal one with the serial killer targeting the hero and/or the mentor. This confrontation may occur at the killer's home or hideout – or he may have tracked them to their own homes. The serial killer is finally defeated – preferably dead, unless you have an idea of him escaping from his imprisonment and returning in a later story in your series.

7 | Undercover Cops

To go 'undercover' is to assume or disguise one's identity in order to gain the trust of an individual or organisation in order to gather information or evidence. Undercover agents have been used in law enforcement and in political and commercial espionage. I wrote about espionage in *Suspense Thriller,* so in this chapter I will cover only undercover policemen. And I will concentrate on stories where the main character remains undercover for the duration of the story rather than those where a detective assumes a role for part of an investigation. Stories about criminals who pretend to be someone else were also covered in *Suspense Thriller* in the 'Assumed Identity' chapter.

The 'undercover cop' story is a sub-genre of the police procedural story in which a professional investigator uses specific skills to carry out a particular kind of investigation – typically one that involves infiltration of a criminal gang or organisation. The hero is a professional who is carrying out a mission – and this means he has something in common with the professional spy of the James Bond type. The group that the cop seeks to join is usually involved in organised crime of some description – in films and novels, the criminals are often serial bank robbers, drug dealers, or gangsters. But an investigator could potentially go undercover in relation to any form of organised crime, including white-collar crime, so I think there is potential to expand this sub-genre and explore criminal worlds that haven't yet been shown.

A Brief History of Undercover Detectives

Although various agents have gone undercover throughout history, undercover *policemen* have only really existed for as long as there have been official police forces – the first of which appeared in the first half of the nineteenth century in Britain and France. In the less formal law enforcement organisations before this there was much more of a blurring of the lines between law enforcer and criminal – for example, Jonathan Wild (1682-1725), the so-called 'Thief-Taker General' operated on both sides of the law and so didn't need to assume the identity of a crook to gather intelligence. He was hanged as a thief.

Eugène François Vidocq (1775-1857) was also a criminal-turned-policeman, but he dedicated himself to law enforcement and avoided Wild's fate. In 1811 he set up an informal plainclothes unit, the Brigade de la Sûreté (Security Brigade), which was officially recognised a year later. Vidocq trained his agents in the use of disguise and in his memoirs describes how he himself captured various criminals using assumed identities.

In England, the Metropolitan Police force was set up by Robert Peel in 1829 but plainclothes detectives did not operate officially until 1869. They were introduced because they are less obvious than uniformed officers and so, in theory, stand more chance of obtaining intelligence about the activities of criminals. But plainclothes detectives operate under different circumstances to undercover policemen. Plainclothes detectives normally carry police equipment and identification under their own name. Under most circumstances, they must identify themselves as police officers when using their police powers, but they are not required to identify themselves if asked by someone during an investigation. Plainclothes officers also typically have a normal home life to go to outside of working hours.

Infiltration of organised crime and terrorist groups was formally begun in 1883 with the establishment of the first Special Branch of London's Metropolitan Police Service. (Special Branch was merged with the Anti-Terrorist Branch in October 2006 to form the Counter Terrorism Command). The New York City Police Department set up a specialist squad to deal with organised crime in 1906 and several federal agencies had their own undercover teams. The Federal Bureau of Investigation was founded in 1908.

In Britain, undercover operations are referred to as 'covert policing' and the work is carried out by specialist surveillance teams. The nature of the work carried out by undercover policemen means that the extent and nature of their activities are rarely made public – though some former undercover agents do publish memoirs which cover some examples of what has gone on in the recent past. More detailed information often only comes out when an undercover operation goes wrong, or there is some form of scandal reported by the media, which results in a formal investigation or criminal charges.

A high-profile example of what can go wrong with undercover operations is the case of Mark Kennedy, a former London Metropolitan Police officer who worked for the National Public Order Intelligence Unit and went undercover for seven years to infiltrate the environmental protest movement. The activities of such officers prompted the British Government to conduct a public inquiry. It also prompted the setting up of an unofficial 'Undercover Research Project' whose aims are stated to be to create "...an online one-stop resource on political policing and undercover surveillance." Their website at www.undercoverresearch.net includes a number of articles including 'Fifteen Questions' used to assess whether someone is an undercover policeman. The website of the official Undercover Policing Inquiry can be found at www.ucpi.org.uk – resources there include a heavily 'redacted' (censored!) version of the police's undercover 'tradecraft manual' in use before the inquiry. A non-fiction account of the Mark Kennedy case and others like it was written by investigative journalists Rob Evans and Paul Lewis as *Undercover: The True Story of Britain's Secret Police* (2013). A play based on a part of Kennedy's activities, *Any Means Necessary*, was staged at the Nottingham Playhouse in February 2016. A documentary about Mark Kennedy, *Cutting Edge: Confessions of an Undercover Cop*, was broadcast by Channel 4 in the UK in 2011 and is available for viewing on Vimeo as I write this (January 2019).

In the USA, the Bureau of Alcohol, Tobacco, Firearms and Explosives (ATF) were engaged in undercover operations between 2011 and 2014 that apparently sought to entrap criminals by enticing them to engage in unlawful actions. The ATF's activities were described by one judge as outrageous and unconstitutional.

Autobiographical accounts by former undercover agents include *Undercover Cop: How I Brought Down the Real-Life Sopranos* (2013) by Mike Russell with Patrick W. Picciarelli; *The Decoy Man: The Extraordinary Adventures of an Undercover Cop* (1973) by Charles Whited about NYPD undercover officer Dan Chiodo; *Ghost: My Thirty Years as an FBI Undercover Agent* (2018) by Michael R. McGowan and Ralph Pezzullo, and *Under and Alone: The True Story of the Undercover Agent Who Infiltrated America's Most Violent Outlaw Motorcycle Gang* (2005) by William Queen.

Search Amazon for 'Undercover' and click on the 'Law Enforcement' category and you will find many more examples. And if you want something a little lighter, you could try Cameron Crowe's account of going undercover, *Fast Times at Ridgemont High* (1981) which was adapted into a movie released in 1982.

There aren't many textbooks on undercover work and books that do cover it tend to concentrate on the relationship between detectives and their informants. *Undercover* (2nd ed, 2000) by Carmine J. Motto and Dale L. June has chapters on informants and suspects but does include a chapter on undercover agents.

Risks Associated with Working Undercover

The physical risks involved in undercover work are obvious – the hero may be unmasked (or 'made') and then suffer torture/punishment and death. This risk will always be in the back of the hero's mind.

Psychological risks associated with working undercover include anxiety and depression resulting from an agent's separation from family, friends, and his normal work and living environment. By necessity, the role involves higher than normal periods of working in isolation and a lack of work colleagues to share experiences and discuss problems with. These circumstances – along with extended periods of working away from home with little or no communication – can put a great deal of strain on family or romantic relationships. Lack of work-life balance – an undercover agent is always, to some extent, 'on duty' – and not knowing when an assignment might end also increase the risk of stress.

When an assignment *does* come to an end, undercover detectives may experience difficulty in returning to normal life and normal duties. They may have been someone else for so long that they have lost touch with their own identity. Some officers experience lifestyle and personality changes as a result of their work. They also often have issues with discipline and the more direct supervision that comes with normal duties.

The expense, time, and risk involved in such operations mean that undercover agents often feel under pressure to achieve results. Particularly as the case being investigated will be a high-profile one that is important to the agent's employer.

The fact that an undercover officer must work without close supervision and outside the boundaries of normal law enforcement work can mean that there is a risk of the officer being involved in corruption. The more time a person spends with criminals the more likely it is that criminal behaviour will seem normal to them. And as with undercover spies, there is a risk that the undercover agent will come to feel he has more in common with the criminals he spends time with every day than with the men behind the desks who are his superiors in the department.

'Sympathy with the enemy' can be a particular problem if the undercover agent is infiltrating a group with extreme views and/or behaviours, because blending in and being accepted will require an agent to appear to believe and promote those views and engage in those behaviours. Part of the reason an agent is chosen for the assignment in the first place is that he is seen as having some characteristics that are similar to those of members of the group he will infiltrate. It is also possible that undercover agents may experience conditions similar to Stockholm syndrome (a victim's sympathy with his abductors) and/or Lima syndrome (a kidnapper's sympathy with his victims) as a result of the dual nature of the agent's relationship with his targets.

Undercover work by its nature involves deceit and betrayal of trust – behaviours that we are taught from an early age are wrong or immoral. To engage in work which *requires* such behaviour can cause anxiety and stress. This risk may be heightened if the agent is betraying a group with whom he shares characteristics – religion, ethnicity, class, ideology – such that he may feel he is betraying his 'own kind' and suffer guilt as a result. In extreme cases, an agent may even undergo a 'conversion' and betray his employers.

The undercover cop's work means that he must remain suspicious of everyone he meets and on his guard at all times. And this vigilance also applies to his own behaviour – he cannot let his façade slip for even a moment, because to do so risks exposing him as a fake and the consequences of that would be swift, painful, and permanent. This heightened awareness borders on the paranoid and the hero can unknowingly slip over into negative behaviours associated with paranoia. This can also impact other areas of his life such that he feels he cannot trust anyone – not even his employers or his own family. If he reaches this point, his behaviour can become neurotic and self-defeating.

The emotional toll of being undercover is one of the themes explored in the film *Donnie Brasco* (1997), based on the experiences of the real-life undercover agent Joseph D. Pistone which were described in his autobiographical account *Donnie Brasco: My Undercover Life in the Mafia* (1988, with Richard Woodley).

Undercover Cops and the Sociology of 'Passing'

One of the themes in undercover cop stories is the impact on an individual of pretending to be someone else. This impact has been explored in terms of other groups of people who have assumed other identities in real life – that is, people who have sought to 'pass' as members of a different group in society.

The *Wikipedia* entry on 'Passing (Sociology)' notes that people may seek to become accepted in other groups that include "...racial identity, ethnicity, caste, social class, sexual orientation, gender, religion, age and/or disability status. Passing may result in privileges, rewards, or an increase in social acceptance, or be used to cope with stigma." Whenever a particular group is persecuted or oppressed, it can lead to individuals seeking to escape this by 'passing' as a member of a non-oppressed group. Obvious examples include light-skinned black people passing as white prior to the abolition of slavery in the USA and Jews who sought to pass as Aryan to avoid persecution by the Nazis in Germany. In India, people may seek to pass as members of a higher social caste. And other oppressed minorities such as gay men may try to hide their true selves in order to avoid prejudice or violence.

Wikipedia again: "Passing ... may also lead to temporary or permanent leave from another community to which an individual previously belonged. Thus, passing can result in separation from one's original self, family, friends, or previous living experiences. While successful passing may contribute to economic security, safety, and avoidance of stigma, it may take an emotional toll as a result of denial of the authentic self and may lead to depression or self-loathing."

Themes

Themes explored in undercover cop thrillers include:

Loyalty versus Betrayal – In most modern undercover cop thrillers, the undercover hero will, at some point, feel that his loyalties are divided. At the beginning of the story, his loyalty firmly belongs to his employer and to the ordinary people of the world who he is sworn to protect. But somewhere around the midpoint of the story he will discover – perhaps to his own surprise – that he feels loyalty to his closest associate in the criminal gang he has infiltrated. This character will have acted as buddy, mentor, and probably protector and will probably have vouched for the hero and got him accepted by the group. This conflict of loyalty will be further increased if the hero has become romantically involved with a member or associate of the criminal group. And things will probably come to a head when the hero feels that he has been betrayed by his own employers. In some stories, the hero discovers that his employers are prepared to sacrifice him for the sake of the mission. In other stories, he discovers that his employer is corrupt and has betrayed their department and the operation. And in some stories, genuine justice is 'betrayed' for political reasons.

Truth versus Deceit – Early in the story the hero's relationship with his employer is truthful and his relationship with the criminal gang is deceitful. But as the story progresses, the boundaries become less clear. The hero may not tell his employer the *whole* truth – either to protect a criminal 'friend' or to avoid revealing his own activities, particularly if he has fallen in love with someone connected to the criminal gang. And while he may not be able to share the *literal* truth of his life with his criminal 'buddy', he may share some emotional truths. And the buddy will share his own personal secrets and fears, unrelated to their criminal activities, which the hero may respect and not report to his employer.

The hero's romantic relationship is often central to this theme. Dating this person usually begins as a cynical move – he begins the romance because he believes the other person can provide inside information or can get him accepted by the criminal gang or the buddy. But then a genuine romance develops and the hero feels uncomfortable that it is based on deceit – he *wants* to tell this person the truth, but that would put the operation at risk. He typically chooses a sort of unsatisfactory half-way approach where he shares personal memories and dreams and fears but never the whole literal truth. And he knows in his heart that a relationship based on deceit is doomed.

Again, this theme intensifies when the hero learns or suspects that his employers are lying to him – or have deceived him from the start – or he discovers that they do not trust him, despite all that he has sacrificed for them.

Identity – In some undercover cop thrillers, the hero *loses* his identity and 'becomes' the person he is pretending to be. In other stories, the hero *discovers* – or is able to *express* – his true identity for the first time. In the latter case, the hero often quits the department at the end of the story and goes off to do something that is personally more fulfilling and less deceitful. This is related to the theme of truth – but here it relates to inner truth, being true to yourself and expressing who you really are as opposed to who you think you *ought* to be. Obviously, this is also connected to the idea of appearance versus reality – as seen in the hero's dual role in the story. In the screenplay of *Deep Cover,* there is a note about the importance of mirrors and how the hero looks at his reflection at various points in the story, as if he is looking to see who is in the mirror.

The Ends Justify the Means – In many crime thrillers, the methods and beliefs of the criminals are compared to those of the law enforcers and the two are found to be surprisingly (or disappointingly) similar. The law enforcers as a group don't see this similarity (or they disregard it) but the hero and the audience have it brought to their attention.

Law enforcers may make the argument that, yes, they use the same violent methods as the criminals – but they are using them for the *right reasons.* They're the good guys, protecting society from evil, and so their actions are acceptable. The problem is that this argument often gets extended too far and is applied to actions which are not acceptable under any circumstances. Being both an insider and an outsider for both camps, the hero sees this more clearly than anyone – and he begins to question the beliefs and motivations of his employer.

As with the private detective, the undercover cop has his own moral code – there are certain lines he won't cross, either in his role within the criminal gang or for his employer. Having seen – and lived in – the reality of the 'mean streets', the hero also shares the private eye's sense of disillusionment and cynicism. It is really only his own moral values that keep him sane. During the hero's 'darkest hour' – at the end of Act II or in Act III – he may come to doubt his own values and will often cross one of his own lines, because he is forced to by his employer or by the criminal gang – or both. Once he begins to question his own values or abandon them, things will quickly unravel – unless or until he can regain his own moral heading.

Examples

Donnie Brasco (1997), *Point Break* (1991, remade in 2015), *Deep Cover* (1992) and *The Fast and the Furious* (2001) are among the best-known undercover cop movies and they're the ones that I 'took apart' to come up with a generic plot template (see below). I also watched the 1987 movie *No Man's Land* featuring Charlie Sheen and D.B. Sweeney which also has a very similar plot.

The earliest examples I could find in this sub-genre were *The Street with No Name* (1948), a follow-up to the 'FBI-approved' *The House on 92nd Street* (1945), and *The Mob* (1951) starring Broderick Crawford and based on the novel *Waterfront* (1951, published in the UK as *Remember That Face!*) by Ferguson Findley (a pseudonym of Charles Weiser Frey).

Infernal Affairs (2002) is a Hong Kong crime thriller directed by Andrew Lau and Alan Mak, remade as *The Departed* (2006) directed by Martin Scorsese, is interesting because it has an undercover police officer infiltrating a criminal gang *and* a criminal 'mole' working inside the police department meaning that there is a sort of cat-and-mouse game going on between the two. Another Hong Kong undercover cop movie, *City on Fire* (1987), was one of the inspirations for Quentin Tarantino's 1992 film *Reservoir Dogs.*

Al Pacino starred in another undercover cop thriller, William Friedkin's *Cruising* (1980) in which the hero goes undercover in New York 'leather bars' and S&M sub-culture to investigate a serial killer who is targeting gay men. The film, based on the novel by Gerald Walker, was criticised by gay rights activists during filming and at the time of its release.

Another example that I'll mention because it involves going undercover in a different setting – a California prison – is the 1990 Jean-Claude Van Damme movie *Death Warrant*.

The US television series *Tightrope!* ran for a year (37 half-hour episodes) between September 1959 and September 1960 and featured Michael Connors as undercover agent 'Nick'. Nick narrated the episodes, telling viewers he was 'living like a hood to catch hoods' and that 'one slip and you're through because you're always walking that tightrope.'

Undercover Cop Thriller Plot

Sequence 1

Movies in this sub-genre often have an opening image or scene under the titles which introduces the world in which the hero will go undercover. Alternatively, the story may open with a crime committed by the gang that the hero will have to infiltrate.

For the first sequence you will need to decide if you will open your story with your hero as a cop and then show him being recruited for an undercover operation – in such cases we often see the hero demonstrating his skills and training and also some aspect of his character that shows his suitability for undercover work – i.e. he is free-thinking, able to improvise, and probably has issues with authority figures. The hero may initially be reluctant to go undercover – perhaps because it will mean being separated from his family or romantic partner; perhaps because of the danger involved – typically a previous undercover agent is said to have been discovered by the criminals and killed, or perhaps because he had plans to advance rapidly in another area of police work and achieve recognition – undercover cops rarely receive awards or public recognition and often even their own colleagues don't know they are police officers.

Alternatively, a story can open with the hero already undercover – we may see him in his undercover role and *then* learn that he is actually a policeman. Again, this is another opportunity to show that the hero is good at what he does. Reluctance here may be demonstrated in frustration at having to stay undercover much longer than originally planned.

Scenes in this sequence will often emphasise the difference between the ordinary, safe world and the unglamorous and dangerous world that the hero is operating in. There is also often a scene that shows the difference between the world of the department-based police officers – colleagues, a partner, or superior – and that of the hero. The hero's personality is often revealed via some form of antagonism between him and the office-based or uniformed cops – but there may also be an older partner or senior officer of 'handler' who acts as the hero's mentor.

Early in the story, we will also see that broadly speaking, the cops are good and the criminals are bad. But as the story progresses, we see that things are not quite as black and white as they first appeared.

This sequence also usually introduces the 'mission' – What is the hero supposed to achieve when he is undercover? Who is he supposed to get close to and why?

Sequence 2

If the hero is not already undercover, this is where he assumes his new identity. We see him adjusting to his new environment, being accepted by people in this 'new world' and carrying off his assumed role convincingly. We may see him make one or two mistakes here and there will be some hint of the dangers that await him if he makes a more serious error and gets found out.

If the hero *is* already undercover when we first meet him, all of the above will be implied in what we see him doing.

If the mission wasn't fully revealed in the first sequence, we learn about it here – and we see the nature of the hero's relationship with his superiors. We also often learn something about the criminal gang or organisation the hero is seeking to gain entry into. This may be in terms of the crimes they commit and their methods, or – if the identities of key figures in the group are known, we learn about their criminal careers, relationships with other criminals, and their place in the hierarchy of the organisation.

The first part of the hero's mission – after establishing his undercover identity – will be to get close enough to the criminals to learn their identities or, if they are already known, to get close to someone relatively low down in the hierarchy and gain their confidence in order to gain access to more senior figures.

The hero may also meet his 'romantic interest' – we'll call her the Romance for simplicity – during sequence one or two, or they may be introduced later.

The most important character relationship to establish early on is between the hero and the co-protagonist character that I will refer to here as the Ally. This is a member of the criminal gang, or someone closely associated with it, who is targeted as the hero's way of getting accepted into the criminal community. The Ally is part antagonist – he's one of the enemy, especially during his earliest interactions with the hero – but he gradually becomes a mentor, protector, and close friend. The Ally is the character of Dominic (Vin Diesel) in *The Fast and the Furious,* Bodhi (Patrick Swayze) in *Point Break*, Elias (Jeff Goldblum) in *Deep Cover,* and Lefty (Al Pacino) in *Donnie Brasco*. Initially, the Ally is just a target – an opponent the hero has to out-think and ensnare, but the relationship between the two then becomes the heart of the story.

In some stories, the hero may target the Romance as a way of getting close to the Ally. The relationship between Romance and hero often begins with the hero cynically using someone and then gradually falling in love with them. This growing relationship can be exploited by the writer as a way of developing characters, increasing the stakes and the tension, and introducing obstacles. There is also often another member of the criminal gang who is attracted to the Romance – we'll call him the Rival – who becomes jealous of the hero's relationship and this will cause him to take action against the hero later in the story. The Rival is often the one who suspects the hero of being an undercover cop and tries to convince the Boss that the hero cannot be trusted – whether his suspicions are initially based on real evidence or simply the jealous words of someone who wants to be rid of the hero varies from story to story.

In his relationships with both the Ally and the Romance, the hero *lies* – he pretends to be someone else in order to gain their trust. This doesn't bother the hero too much at the beginning of the story – but as his relationships grow, he feels more and more uncomfortable about having to maintain the deceit – he begins to feel that he is being dishonest with people that he now cares about.

In this second sequence, we will also often see more evidence of the 'badness' of the criminals – we need to gain some sense of the reality of the impact of their crimes so that we don't begin to regard them as romantic Robin Hood outlaws. We may see the aftermath of one of their crimes or the consequences of crime of this type – examples include innocent victims such as the children of drug users, bank employees or truck drivers who are injured or killed, or minor figures in the world being punished for not paying their debts or not showing the proper 'respect' for gang members. Scenes like this also establish the dangers of the world in which the hero is operating and the stakes he is playing for.

This sequence also shows more of the world against which the story is set – showing the audience a glimpse of sub-culture that may be new to them – the world of drug dealing and drug use, street racing, or surfing.

Sequence 3

Act II begins with the hero and the Ally bonding – getting to know each other and getting to like each other. The hero is often required to do something that 'proves' he's not a cop – doing something that a cop would never do. The hero may get arrested and/or humiliated or beaten up by the police; he may 'take one for the team'; he may save the Ally from arrest or some other form of harm, or he may just demonstrate that he is good at what he does and impress the Ally. In this sequence we see the hero getting *deeper* into his undercover role.

In *Deep Cover* the hero is betrayed by the Rival and arrested by the police in sequence two – and the fact that the hero doesn't 'rat' on anyone else serves to boost the hero's image as someone who can be trusted. It also further sours the relationship between the hero and the Rival.

All through this development of the hero's reputation the Rival will be seething and plotting in the background. And as the friendship between the Ally and the hero develops, the Rival will feel that he is being replaced as the Ally's right-hand man. The hero may be unaware of the Rival's jealousy or he might ignore it. Or he may taunt the Rival – and this will have consequences later.

The Ally typically defends the hero and/or vouches for him – bringing him into the *outer circle* of the criminal gang. The Ally also confides in the hero – revealing his backstory and possibly his ambitions or dreams. But at the same time, the Ally is still feeling the hero out to see if he can trust him. There may also be veiled threats about what will happen if the Ally discovers he *can't* trust the hero.

This sequence often sees the hero become the victim of a rival gang – which the Ally may have to rescue him from via action or diplomacy. In stories where the identities of the criminals are not yet known to the police, the appearance of this rival gang leads the hero to believe that they might be the ones behind the crimes. He may also *prefer* to believe this rather than suspect the Ally's gang.

Sequence three will also show the hero crossing some kind of line that is important to him personally – he either takes some action or he decides not to intervene and prevent something happening. In *Deep Cover,* the hero has to become a real drug dealer *and* nor prevent the death of someone. Sometimes the hero simply does things that a cop would never do – and this may cause difficulty with uniformed officers who do not know he's an undercover cop – or with colleagues who *do* know.

Sequence 4

Here the hero is invited into the Ally's *inner circle*. In *Point Break,* the hero is invited to a party at the Ally's house where he listens to the surfers' 'war stories' and learns about their adrenaline-fuelled escapades. In *The Fast and the Furious* the Ally takes the hero back to his house where a party is underway – and later the hero is invited to a 'family' barbecue. These scenes also serve to fuel the Rival's jealousy – especially if they demonstrate the attraction between the Romance and the hero.

This may lead to an awkward moment where the Rival accuses the hero of being a cop – perhaps even presenting some incriminating evidence to the Ally. The hero is put on the spot and must think fast and improvise his way out of the situation – and in doing so he probably makes the Rival look bad or stupid in front of the other gang members – again storing up resentment which will lead to problems for the hero later.

The hero also bonds with other members of the gang – being accepted by them as he shows that he has much in common with them. He also finds himself beginning to like them and enjoys the fact that he 'belongs' to a group and is no longer an isolated outsider. These people are starting to become his friends.

At the same time, the hero's relationship with the Romance is deepening. Often, they sleep together for the first time at or near the *midpoint* of the story, signalling a raising of the personal stakes – and the first twinges of guilt that the hero is deceiving this person. There may also be a significant moment in the relationship between the hero and the Ally – a relationship which develops along the lines of a non-sexual romance.

In both *The Fast and the Furious* and *Point Break*, the rival gang that harassed the hero earlier is identified as being behind the crimes and the hero's employers plan a raid which the hero will be part of.

In *Deep Cover,* the hero crosses another personal line at the *midpoint* when he has to kill a rival drug dealer. This also marks a significant point in his relationship with the Ally as they agree to become business partners.

Sequence 5

This sequence comes straight after the midpoint and will include the characters' reactions to whatever has just happened there. Action-wise, there may be another crime by the criminal gang and/or a raid by the police on the other criminal gang who have been (wrongly) identified by the hero as being behind the crimes. Sequence five also sets up the action that will take place in sequence six.

As in virtually all stories in all genres, sequence five focuses on the relationships between characters. In this sub-genre, it is the relationships between the hero and his employers and the hero and the Ally's gang that we concentrate on. The hero has grown closer to the gang and feels loyalty to them and he has grown away from his law enforcement colleagues and they begin to doubt his loyalty to them.

If the identity of the criminals is *not* yet known to the police, there will be a raid on the wrong gang – and when it is discovered that the wrong people have been targeted this is highly embarrassing for the police/FBI who were involved in the raid. The hero's bosses may wonder if he *deliberately* sent them after the wrong gang in order to protect his new friends. Or his boss may wonder if the hero's judgment is impaired because he doesn't want 'his' gang to be guilty. The hero will have to convince his boss of his loyalty, promising to do whatever is necessary to get the real criminals – whoever they may be.

By this stage, the hero is feeling conflicted – his career is on the line and he needs to prove himself to his employers, but at the same time he now feels a kinship with the Ally and his gang and wants to remain loyal to them. He may begin to doubt his own judgment or he may begin to feel he's fighting for the wrong side and that he has more in common with the crooks than the cops.

If the identity of the criminal gang members *is* known, this sequence may involve a raid or sting operation aimed at the Ally's gang which goes wrong because the gang seems to have been forewarned. In this case, the hero's bosses may suspect that the hero tipped them off to protect them.

Point Break and *The Fast and the Furious* both include a raid on a wrong gang. After this, both set up the action ready for sequence six. In *The Fast and the Furious,* the hero receives details of the big race. In *Point Blank,* the hero realises that the Ally and his gang *are* the bank robbers – and he also identifies their next target: he and his police partner then stake out the bank.

In *Deep Cover,* there is no 'wrong gang' and sequence five instead expands the relationship between the hero and the Ally – the police raid does not occur until sequence six. By this stage, the hero is a successful drug dealer and has a new apartment and clothes to reflect this – he is also being urged on to do bigger things by his boss in the department. The hero's boss is more concerned with the operation than with any psychological suffering the hero is experiencing as a result of his increasingly violent activities. It also sets up the circumstances such that the hero can get a meeting with the next higher figure in the local drug scene. This means that he and the Ally will go above the head of their normal drug seller, Barbosa, which causes friction and sees Barbosa becoming more of a Rival. A showdown between hero/Ally and Rival, in which the Rival tries to reassert his authority, ends with him choosing to betray the hero, the Ally, and the Romance.

Sequence 6

Her we have action or a dramatic confrontation – or both. In *Point Break* there is the bank robbery and the chase, culminating in the hero having the masked leader of the robbers in his sights – and being unable to pull the trigger. At this point the hero's cover is blown – the gang know he works for the FBI. There is also a crisis point in the hero's relationship with the Romance – he wants to tell her the truth about who he is, but doesn't; she finds out anyway and their relationship is effectively over.

In *The Fast and the Furious,* the action occurs during the 'Race Wars' – including a confrontation with the 'wrong gang' who were raided by the police and blame the Ally for setting them up – and who also accuse the hero of being a cop. The conflict between the two gangs sets up the action for sequence eight.

In *Deep Cover,* the hero is preparing for his meeting with his third target – one above the Rival. But he is told by his boss that a police raid is planned to arrest the lower level criminals – the Rival and the Ally. The hero objects to this – he has been working undercover to get to a point where they can target the higher-level criminals – but his objection is overruled and he is warned to stay away from the raid. The hero's relationship with the Romance deepens – a hint of a happier life that could come after – but this also raises the personal stakes for the hero as he has more to lose. The police raid takes place and the hero intervenes and warns the Ally.

Sequence 7

This sequence marks the lowest and/or most dangerous point for the hero. It is where the hero's relationships with the Ally and the Romance appear to be over and he may also be betrayed by the criminal gang or by his own boss.

It is also where the hero's loyalty is tested. Ideally, he wants the gang – including the Ally – to be arrested cleanly with nobody getting hurt – but he knows this won't happen. He knows the Ally would rather die in a hail of bullets than let himself be taken alive.

In *The Fast and the Furious,* the Ally and his gang go off to commit another truck hijacking. The hero is aware of a danger that they don't know about – the truck drivers are now armed – and he wants to warn them and avoid bloodshed. In order to find out where the hijack will occur, the hero must tell the Romance who he really is – effectively ending their relationship by admitting that he has lied to her. During the hijack, the only way the hero can save the life of an injured gang member is to reveal to the gang that he is a policeman. The Ally feels completely betrayed by the hero and is angry with him.

In *Point Break,* the hero is taken skydiving by the Ally – who then reveals that he has taken the Romance hostage as his insurance plan. The Ally forces the hero to take part in his gang's final bank robbery. In order to try and save the Romance, the hero boards the plane after the robbery as the gang fly off to Mexico.

In *Deep Cover,* the hero is betrayed by his own boss. He is told that the higher-ups want to end the operation – for political reasons. All the hero's efforts, the suffering and deaths of others, have been for nothing. The hero quits and breaks his own rules regarding drink and drugs – and he seeks solace with the Romance.

Sequence 8

This is the final showdown in which the hero confronts the Ally. There is often escape/pursuit with the Ally seeming to have won – until the hero outsmarts him and turns the tables. The hero can do this because he has much in common with the Ally and knows how he thinks, and because the two have become friends and shared private thoughts and dreams, so the hero knows where the Ally would try to escape to. There is probably also a sense of the two of them needing to have this final meeting to achieve closure in their relationship.

Typically, this sequence sees the hero ignoring normal law enforcement protocols and relying instead on his own moral values to achieve what he regards as *justice.* This will often involve a form of 'poetic justice' or irony which sees both the Ally and the hero's boss receiving the 'punishment' they deserve.

The hero may find himself forced to kill the Ally because of the Ally's actions. Or he may allow the buddy to jump to his own death or take some similar way out that means he won't have to go (back) to jail. Or the hero may allow the buddy to escape. Other possibilities include the hero joining the buddy's gang or – if the buddy has escaped or been killed – the hero may replace the buddy as leader of the gang.

The final scenes will also usually publicly expose the immoral behaviours of the law enforcement agency that sent the hero undercover.

Having discovered and/or expressed his own true self, the hero is usually rewarded by being reconciled with the Romance character.

8 | The Heist

What's the difference between a stick-up, a bank heist, a burglary, and a confidence trick, and aren't they all just 'capers'? Plot-wise they are very similar and I could have created some generic caper plots – the crook-versus-cop, crook-versus-crook, and the big score – but I think there are sufficient differences between the four types of crime to treat them separately. If you plan to write one these caper stories, have a look at the chapters on the other types as there are ideas in each that can be adapted and used in any caper story.

In their National Incident-Based Reporting System, the FBI define *robbery* as "...taking or attempting to take anything of value from the care, custody, or control of a person or persons by force or threat of force or violence or by putting the victim in fear..." while *burglary* is "...unlawful entry of a structure to commit a felony or theft." By this definition, a stick-up is a robbery but a heist may be a robbery or a burglary depending on whether or not violence or threat of violence is a factor. The FBI also publishes annual *Bank Crime Statistics*.

In Chapter 3, I covered the Bonnie and Clyde 'stick-up' type of crime spree which was more or less contemporary with the original gangster thriller. Holding someone up at gunpoint – or at the point of some other weapon – is a centuries-old form of theft and hasn't changed much through the years. The heist, as I use the term in this chapter, is a more sophisticated form of robbery that involves more planning and more people. To take the bank as an example – a *stick-up* takes place when the bank is open and involves pointing a gun at a cashier or manager and taking the cash that is in the drawers and maybe, if there's time, cash from the open vault. But a heist takes place when the bank is closed and involves a team of people who break into the closed vault and take the money.

The bank heist is just one example of this type of crime. Gangs may plan a heist against a casino (*Ocean's 11*), a train carrying gold or cash *(The Great Train Robbery)*, a jewellery store *(Rififi)*, a museum or gallery *(Topkapi)*, or an armoured car *(Heat)*. The heist typically requires inside information about schedules, security measures, and the layout and construction of the vault or strongbox or armoured car. It is carried out by a team where different members are usually specialists in a particular area – electronic security systems, driving getaway cars, hacking computer systems, use of cutting or digging equipment, or whatever. And it is planned with what is usually referred to as 'military precision.' The whole story is structured around a single large theft and shows the various stages of the 'mission' – planning, getting the team together, obtaining equipment, preparation and practice, carrying out the heist, aftermath and consequences. There is often a romantic subplot or some other 'human interest' story and there is also typically an external source of conflict – either with an investigator or with the leader of another gang of criminals, though this is optional.

The Appeal of the Heist Story

Why do we like stories about heists? Heist stories appeal in three different ways. Firstly, we like to see experts at work and we like to gain 'behind the scenes' secrets about things so that we feel we have special knowledge or are being treated as an 'insider.' Secondly, we are social animals and we like to see a group of friends working together and having fun in their off-duty hours – especially if the story allows us to feel that we are part of the in-crowd. And finally, stories about thieves exist in a morally ambiguous space – they allow us to spend time with characters who break the rules that we normally live by. They give us the thrill of spending some time with bad boys.

The expertise of the gang of thieves is revealed early on when we see them planning the heist and preparing for it. As viewers or readers, we are in on the plan. And then later, we get the see the thieves putting the plan into operation – and again, we are right there with them, seeing it happen almost in real time. Often in a heist movie, the sense of being there is enhanced by having the robbery scenes play without a musical score – we hear only the actual sounds made in the location.

The fact that we know what the plan is and what is *supposed* to happen means that we instantly spot when something goes wrong and we understand the implications of the problem – the whole plan could collapse like a house of cards as each part is dependent on what goes before it. This increases our investment in the scene and the tension we feel as a viewer-participant.

If everything went according to plan, the story would be predictable and disappointing. One of the other things we enjoy as viewers or readers is seeing our heroes *improvise* when things go wrong. Our favourite story people are programmed like machines putting together flat-pack furniture, they're talented and creative human beings.

Heist stories also provide a logical and understandable story structure, with a clear goal – get the loot – and clear obstacles. The story fits into a simple structure: planning, the heist, and the aftermath – the latter either involving 'getting away with it' or 'things fall apart.' Or perhaps a combination of the two. And within that the heist itself has its own structure, typically getting in, getting out, and getting away.

Historical Development

Gangs of outlaws working together to carry out criminal acts have existed since ancient times. Ali Baba encountered a gang of forty thieves in an old Syrian tale that was added to the *One Thousand and One Nights* collection in the 18th century and there are folktales about outlaws in many cultures. Another early example is the story of Jason and the Argonauts where the leader, Jason, and his crew are on a mission to steal the golden fleece. This story is referenced in the classic heist movie *The League of Gentlemen* (1960).

Bands of warriors who attack and plunder have also been recorded since early times – the Vikings being one example. And then there are the pirates and privateers who did their plundering on the oceans. It's impossible to decide at which point any of these actions became a planned heist as such – though any story written today set in any of those time periods could be structured like a heist.

One example that seems to fit our definition of a heist is that of Captain Thomas Blood, an Irish rogue whose gang attempted to steal the English crown jewels in 1671. Blood also managed to charm King Charles and get himself not only a pardon but was also awarded a piece of real estate that brought him a decent annual income. A film based on these events, *Colonel Blood*, written and directed by W.P. Lipscomb was released in 1934. See also *The Audacious Crimes of Colonel Blood: The Spy Who Stole the Crown Jewels and Became the King's Secret Agent* (2015) by Robert Hutchinson.

There is also a record of an earlier attempt to steal an English King's treasure. In April 1303, a trader called Richard of Pudlicott apparently had a grudge against King Edward I and decided to avenge himself by making off with some of the King's belongings. Richard had previously helped himself to some silver plate from the monks of the Abbey of Westminster. In order to carry off the King's gold, Pudlicott recruited an inside man so he could gain access to the underground vault. Exact details of how the robbery was committed are scant, in part because many of the records were written by the church who wanted to avoid recording that Richard's other accomplices were probably monks. Unfortunately for them, the thieves were careless in their handling of the stolen items and their guilt was quickly suspected. Two judicial investigations led to Richard and perhaps half-a-dozen of his acquaintances being hanged. Any monks involved claimed clerical privilege – they could only be judged and punished by church authorities – and so were released by order of the King, who didn't wish to challenge the authority of the church. Paul Doherty's novel *The Great Crown Jewels Robbery of 1303* (2005) is based on this crime.

The earliest recorded bank heists in the United States are the 1798 robbery of the Bank of Pennsylvania at Carpenters' Hall, where there were no signs of forced entry and $163,000 were stolen. And the 1831 theft of $245,000 from the City Bank of New York where forged keys were used to enter the bank and its vault. Perhaps the first gang to tunnel into a bank were the five men who targeted the Bank of Australia in George Street, Sydney in 1828 – they used a sewage drain and escaped with £14,000 of cash and promissory notes – worth about $25 million Australian today.

The first Great Train Robbery took place in England in 1855 and involved the theft of £12,000 worth of gold bars – equivalent to about £1 million today. Michael Crichton's novel *The Great Train Robbery* (1975) is based on this incident and he directed the 1978 film adaptation which starred Michael Caine and Sean Connery. David C. Hanrahan's book *The First Great Train Robbery* (2011) is a non-fiction account that draws on contemporary sources and reveals that the crime and criminals were much less glamorous than Crichton portrayed.

In August 1963, 'The Great Train Robbery' was committed in England. £2.6 million (c. £50 million today) was stolen from a Royal Mail train travelling from Glasgow to London. A gang of fifteen robbers including leader Bruce Reynolds, Buster Edwards, Charlie Wilson, and Ronnie Biggs halted and robbed the train. There have been dozens of books and documentaries about the robbery and biographies of some of the criminals. The 1988 film *Buster* starring Phil Collins was inspired by the story of Ronald 'Buster' Edwards. The 1967 film *Robbery* starring Stanley Baker is a heavily fictionalised account of the robbery – it was directed by Peter Yates who went on to direct Steve McQueen in *Bullitt* (1968). Agatha Christie's Miss Marple novel *At Bertram's Hotel* (1965) has references to a train robbery, thought to have been inspired by the 1963 crime. In 2013, the BBC broadcast a two-part miniseries, *The Great Train Robbery*, written by Chris Chibnall – the first part showed the robbery from the point of view of the robbers and the second the subsequent investigation from the viewpoint of the police. The British fascination with The Great Train Robbery is such that a board game of that name was created in the 1970s by Bruce Barrymore Halpenny.

The title 'The Great Train Robbery' was lifted from the 1903 silent Western film that was based on an 1896 stage play by Scott Marble. The twelve-minute long film features a number of ground-breaking film production techniques. If you've never seen it, you should be able to find the film on YouTube and other places online. The film may have been partly inspired by train robberies carried out by Butch Cassidy and the Wild Bunch between 1899 and 1900. The 1941 film *The Great Train Robbery* is a 'crime-Western' that was remade as *The Last Bandit* (1949) and – according to some sources – as *South Pacific Trail* (1952). Westerns lie outside the scope of this book so I'm not going to explore 'crime Westerns' in any detail here.

Genre Conventions

Impossible Mission

The most important factor in a heist movie is the *how*. How do you rob a bank? Or steal from one of the other locations mentioned below. In a heist movie we are watching a group of specialists at work, led by an expert leader. The characters have the added attraction of being rebels and tricksters.

If you read mystery fiction, you're probably familiar with the 'locked room' mystery in which a detective has to discover how an 'impossible' crime was committed – a person was murdered in a locked room and no one else was present. The heist is an inverted version of this in which the leader of a gang of thieves has to come up with a plan for committing an impossible crime – and then bring together the people and resources to pull it off.

Once we know what the hero's goal is – to obtain the valuable item – we then learn what obstacles he must overcome to get it – and when these are explained to us in the planning stage the task really does seem impossible. In the *Mission: Impossible* movies, the explanation we get of the site that Ethan Hunt (Tom Cruise) has got to break into is partly shown as an explanation in voice-over with images of the actual location so that we can really *see* what he and his team are up against. And we don't always learn how each of these obstacles will be overcome until we see the heist occur.

How impossible is the crime? Here's Danny Ocean (and one of his team) describing what they're up against in the 2001 version of *Ocean's Eleven*:

> This place houses a security system rivalling most nuclear silos ... we have to get ... through these doors... each one requiring a different code changed every twelve hours ... the elevator ... won't move without fingerprint I.D. – Which we can't fake. And vocal confirmation from the system ... Which we won't get. The elevator shaft is rigged with sensors ... Once we get down the shaft, it's a piece of cake. Just two more guards with Uzis... and the most elaborate vault door ever conceived by man.

Suspense

The heist story has a number of sources of suspense built-in. First, will the plan to rob the vault succeed or fail? Factors which jeopardise a successful outcome include accidents and mistakes, unforeseen circumstances, something overlooked in the planning, over-confidence, lack of preparation by one or more team members, and betrayal. Second, there is the question of what will happen to the loot if the heist is successful – will the thieves get away with it, will the police recover it, or will another gang of thieves take it from them? Thirdly, at almost every point in the story, the police or other security forces will be close by, ready to pounce if they slip-up. And finally, do the thieves escape – with or without the loot – and how many of them make it?

Hero

The hero of the heist story is normally the leader of the gang of thieves. As a leader he is normally slightly older than some of the other team members – we equate age an experience. He has probably spent some time in prison, so is both worldly-wise and somewhat cynical. He is also a pretty good judge of character – seeing the potential in people that others may overlook.

The ideal leader is someone who has the experience of the Warrior archetype combined with the wisdom and experience of the Thinker. He is both practical and a skilled planner and strategist. He is intelligent, 'street smart', a stickler for detail and doing things the right way, but he is also adaptable and can improvise when something unexpected occurs that wasn't in the plan.

The hero may function as a mentor to younger and more inexperienced members of the team. He has experience of what can go wrong and what the consequences are and tries to help others gain from his mistakes – but he is also aware that you can't 'put an old head on young shoulders' and sometimes have to let people learn their own lessons.

The hero is also a non-conformist who lives outside the accepted rules of society. As such he is drawn to other people of a rebellious nature – even though these people are not always the most reliable co-workers. He knows that you cannot effectively 'rule' creative people by laying down laws and trying to control them by fear or even bribes – a mistake that the villain often makes. Instead, the hero values their individuality and makes allowances for their weaknesses. And if he has to make a decision, he will explain the reasoning behind it to try and ensure that everyone else understands it and buys into it. If you have got to have a boss, he is the sort of boss you want to have. There are many books out there on leadership skills – look closely at the ones that emphasise valuing the skills and personalities of individual team members. There are even a couple of good ones that concentrate on how to manage creative personalities if you want to get a gift for your own boss...

Villain

The main antagonist in a heist story is often a rival gang leader who wants to get his hands on the loot stolen by the thieves. He is the hero's equal in many ways but lacks the hero's value system – this makes the antagonist both stronger (he will not hesitate to kill people) and weaker (he underestimates the hero's resolve to protect his own gang members). This antagonist is pretty standard villain material – and as in any other stories, villains can be an over-the-top eccentric or grotesque individual.

There may be other sources of antagonism in a heist story in the form of a member of a betrayer within the gang of thieves or a detective who is investigating their crimes and wants to arrest them. Neither of these usually plays the main 'villain' role.

Romantic Co-Protagonist

In the heist story, the hero may meet a new lover, he may interact with an ex-lover, or he may become entangled with a *femme fatale* who ends up betraying him.

Other Characters

The most significant 'other' characters are the members of the hero's gang of thieves. The gang is a handful of people with different personalities who have expertise in a particular field related to the heist – safecracker, alarms specialist, tunnelling, computer hacking, getaway car driver, or whatever. They may have nicknames relating to their personality or specialism, though this tends to sound a boy clichéd now after a few decades of crime movies.

The gang often includes someone with a weakness – they have an illness, mental trauma, drug addiction, injury, or are being pursued by the police or debt collectors. This weakness makes them vulnerable to external influence and has the potential for putting the team and/or the heist in jeopardy. It often appears that the hero isn't aware of this weakness, but it transpires that he has had it in mind all along and has built protection from it into his plan.

There may also be a betrayer in the team – it may be the person with the weakness mentioned above, or it may be someone who has a long-standing personal grudge against the hero or his team. This betrayer may be a new recruit to the team or maybe a long-time member. Again, the reader is led to believe that the hero isn't aware of this potential betrayer – but he may have plans for dealing with it.

Sometimes it is necessary to recruit new members to the team who have expertise that existing team members lack. This may be because the usual expert is in prison or has died or been killed. But sometimes the nature of the heist means that new skills are required. There may be some awkwardness and feelings of mistrust when new people are brought in and it takes a while for the team to adjust to their presence. The bringing in of someone knew – 'We need someone with more experience' – can cause resentment from someone who regarded themselves as the expert in this area and this may be what leads to them becoming the betrayer.

In the 2006 heist movie *Inside Man,* the needs of the story dictate that the identities of the gang of thieves are not revealed to the audience.

While the hero often serves as mentor to gang members, the hero may have a *mentor* of his own – either as a member of the gang or as a retired expert he consults away from the gang. The hero may have learned all he knows about the heist and leading a team from this man. And this mentor may turn out to be the person with the weakness and/or the potential betrayer.

Other key characters may include the antagonist's *henchman* – who does the heavy lifting and most of the punching in the face for the antagonist. Again, this character is pretty much standard villainous right-hand man material.

And sometimes you may have a victim of the robbery who is motivated to make his own efforts to locate and eliminate the thieves – though this tends to put the victim character into the role of villain or antagonist. But a more inept or less well-connected victim might just be used to provide an unexpected source of antagonism or an obstacle – and perhaps the hero ends up having to save or rescue this would-be superhero. Or recruit them.

Conspiracy & MacGuffin

Sometimes a specific item is part of the thieves' haul of valuables and it plays an important part in some sort of conspiracy. We will look at this in more detail under the 'Heist and Conspiracy' plot variation later in the chapter.

Settings

The setting for a heist movie is normally urban because that is where wealth tends to be concentrated. And cities look cool after dark. Heist stories share many locations with other crime stories – seedy bars, underground car parks, rooftops and such. Unique locations tend to be places that can be robbed – banks, galleries, museums, jewellery stores, casinos, etc. Thieves sneak around in alleys outside these buildings and also climb up the sides of them. Sewers and tunnels also feature quite often – thieves sneak into high-class buildings in the same way as rats get into expensive restaurants.

Another location we often see is the thieves lair – this has been a staple of the genre since Ali Baba learned that 'Open Sesame' got him into the cave belonging to the forty thieves. The lair or hideout is like a members-only club where the gang get together to plan and prepare the heist and that they come back to to divide up the loot. It is also a safe place where friends engage in mocking banter and share their hopes, dreams, and fears. It is the ultimate safe place – and possibly a bit of a man-cave.

All of these locations are often contrasted with ordinary domestic scenes, where we see the ordinary lives of members of the gang of thieves – and possibly of the detectives investigating their crimes. Domestic settings help establish the characters as real people who have real things at stake – typically a wife and young family. These locations are usually relatively low-rent in comparison with the wealth that is on display elsewhere in the story.

Iconography

Heist stories share much of the iconography of other crime stories. Items specific to the sub-genre include places that hold valuable items and the items themselves – bank vaults, especially the kind with huge round doors that are several feet thick and contain complex locking mechanisms; glass display cases containing jewellery or valuable museum artefacts; folded wax paper envelopes of unmounted diamonds, stacks of banknotes several feet high. The valuables all get stuffed into large canvas sacks or holdalls – the sort that are labelled 'Swag' or 'Loot' in cartoon drawings of thieves.

Complex security mechanisms are built into the places where valuable items are stored, meaning that the thieves have to come up with ingenious ways of beating them. There are vibration alarms for doors and windows; thermal sensors to pick up body heat; pressure sensors in the floor; and those laser beams that criss-cross the room and can only be made visible by spraying hairspray through them.

Other iconic items are associated with the thieves themselves and include their equipment for breaking into the place that holds the valuables – explosives, thermic lances, and complex bits of wiring with alligator clips on that are used for circumventing alarm systems. There are harnesses and ropes and other bits of mountaineering equipment adapted to scale buildings rather than rock faces. And there are grappling hooks and those unlikely looking little crossbow things that fire a spike trailing a length of rope such that the spike embeds itself in concrete and will support the weight of a man.

Themes

Brotherhood and 'the Code' – The importance of teamwork – the ability to work together and trust and respect your teammates – is a key part of the heist story. This is not the tale of a lone gangster or a solitary cat burglar, it is the story of how a teamwork with their leader to achieve an almost impossible mission. There is more on the concept of 'brotherhood' in the chapter on the police procedural and many of the ideas considered there also apply to a gang of thieves.

Linked to the idea of brotherhood and trust is the concept of the thieves' code. Non-thieves would have you believe that there is no honour among thieves, but in stories at least this is not the case. There are two versions of the thieves' code – the more modern version is that 'we look after our own and never leave a man behind.' If one member of the team ends up in prison, the others make sure his family are taken care of. The older version, that is seen in *Rififi* is the code of silence or, from the Italian, *omertà*. This states that if you are talking to outsiders or are questioned by the authorities, you never speak about the illegal activities of others – even your enemies.

Planning and Leadership – In the gangster story, we saw that the central character embarks on a personal – and solo – mission to achieve his own corrupted version of the American Dream. His was a quest for personal success – he wanted to *become* the leader, the 'Little Caesar.' In the heist story, the hero begins as the leader – his experience has helped earn him the top position in the gang or, more likely, has attracted a gang of like-minded teammates. He's such a successful coach that people want to be on his team. And they want to be there because he is not selfish – his group share in the wealth that the heist brings in.

The gang follow the leader because he has proved that he is a great planner. He has knowledge and experience that they lack. And he knows how to utilise the expertise of the different team members, allowing them to work together and with mutual respect, to achieve something they couldn't do individually.

Trust versus betrayal – linked to the idea of brotherhood and looking after your own is the concept of trust and betrayal. We can only be betrayed by someone we have placed trust in – by someone we have regarded as a 'brother'. Conflicts and resentments can cause people close to us to betray us – or us to betray them – and this is one of the things that heist stories can explore. The importance of the team working together makes trust a core value.

Rebellion – Some criminals are sociopaths and while they can make fascinating characters, we don't view them as heroes. Other criminals are seen more as non-conformists and can become folk heroes like Robin Hood. Most of us live our lives by conforming to 'the rules' of behaviour necessary for the smooth-running of our community – but our need to *belong* to a group exists in competition for our need to feel that we have freedom of choice and can decide our own destiny. And with our desire to occasionally do something 'wicked' or 'naughty.' Outlaws and other rebels appeal to that part of our personalities – and stories about them allow us a safe outlet for those feelings.

Money versus Self-Worth – Have you ever looked at something like a gold, diamond-encrusted iPhone and wondered who on earth would want to own anything that hideous? Or looked at images in a 'celebrities and their homes' magazine and realised that just because someone has money doesn't mean that they have good taste? Or read about the drug-induced death of another world-famous musician and realised that money doesn't necessarily bring you inner peace and happiness?

Las Vegas, the world capital of money and bad taste, is like Disneyland for gangsters – a fake world of gaudy conspicuous wealth with no soul. You can see why many crime stories are set there – even without considering the history of its founding.

Money – and almost every form of modern wealth – is an abstract concept. A $100 bill is a piece of paper, a diamond is a bit of rock, a painting is pigment on canvas, and gold is a chunk of metal – their value as an item is not intrinsic, they exist as symbols of wealth. Stocks and shares are even more abstract. The value we assign to them is based, in part at least, on a concept of scarcity. The scarcity myth is based on the idea that there is not enough to go around and that we need to hoard things 'just in case' – and it is basically a rationalisation for selfishness and greed. Alongside that, we have the myth that our worth as a person is determined by how much stuff we have. And what we end up with is 'I am wealthy because I have something that you don't. Because I am wealthy, my life has more value than yours.' I have stuff so I am better than you. Anyone who really believes that has self-worth issues and should seek help.

Thieves tend to challenge the scarcity myth. They say 'Look, money isn't scarce, it is just being hoarded by greedy people.' At which the wealthy cry out, 'That is *my* money – I have it because I *deserve* it and I have *earned* it.' But here's a question: Is it really possible, through your own labours, to *earn* more than, say, $1 million per year? Realistically, who can spend more than a million a year without having to go out and find things like jewel-encrusted smartphones to buy? And here's another one: If you *are* getting more than $1 million a year, aren't you getting that from exploiting other people's labours? Or how about: Just because you can *afford* a $10,000 handbag while a family on the other side of town is living in poverty, does that mean that you are morally justified in doing so? Does it make you better than them? If you take considerably more than you need, aren't you effectively stealing from those people who are in need? Doesn't property become theft at that point?

If a thief steals from a poor man, or even an ordinary person, that thief is a scumbag. But if his victim is *obscenely* wealthy and so much stuff that they have to store it away in special fortified storage spaces – and away from the eyes of the tax man – then you have to wonder whether the 'victim' is really going to suffer as a result of the loss.

You are either nodding in agreement with me here or cursing my pinko commie values – but either way, you're thinking about one of the themes of the heist movie. What does the cash represent? Self-worth? Success? Freedom? Escape from oppression? Escape from childhood poverty and powerlessness?

Thieves express their rebellion by treating money with disrespect rather than reverence. In heist movies we see thieves making love on a bed strewn with banknotes, or opening expensive champagne and swigging from the bottle, or lighting a cigar from a burning banknote. And we often discover that, despite whatever dream-life they talk about retiring to, thieves will often squander the money they steal – gambling heavily, throwing massive parties, or literally losing it through carelessness. The money doesn't always have value to them in itself – it is a by-product of thievery. They don't engage in heists because they're greedy for cash – though there is an element of it. In heist fiction, the thief does it – as Clive Owen's character says in *Inside Man* – 'Because I can.'

Tone
The tone of a heist thriller can be light-hearted, as in Donald E. Westlake's Dortmunder series that began with *The Hot Rock* (1970) or the film *Topkapi* (see below), but the majority are more serious thrillers and some can be quite violent, reflecting the nature of many real-life bank heists.

Examples
In the list below I have tried to include a mix of 'classic' heist movies, interesting variations, and ones based on either novels or true-life crimes.

The Asphalt Jungle (1950) directed by John Huston and based on the 1949 novel by W.R. Burnett. The film stars Sterling Hayden and Marilyn Monroe in one of her earliest roles. It is often said to be the first 'caper' film.

Armored Car Robbery (1950) directed by Richard Fleischer depicts in detail a heist that goes wrong and the police investigation of it. The film was released in the same month as *The Asphalt Jungle*. Fleischer also directed *Violent Saturday* (1955), starring Victor Mature and Lee Marvin, the story of a robbery of a bank in a small town and its effect on various characters, based on the 1955 novel by William L. Heath.

6 Bridges to Cross (1955) starring Tony Curtis and based on the article 'They Stole $25,000,000 - And Got Away with It' by crime reporter Joseph F. Dinneen. Tells of the January 1950 armed robbery of the Brink's Building in Boston, Massachusetts in which $2.8 million (equivalent to £28.9 million today) was stolen. *The Brink's Job* (1978) directed by William Friedkin is based on the same crime.

Rififi (1955). Released in France as *Du Rififi Chez les Hommes* and based on the 1953 novel of that title by Auguste Le Breton, this film is regarded as an archetypal heist movie in which the robbery is shown in a detailed half-hour long sequence virtually devoid of dialogue. The heist was based on a real-life burglary that took place in Marseille in 1899. Le Breton's novel was one of the *serie noir* published by Gallimard.

Bob le Flambeur (1956) written and directed by Jean-Pierre Melville, with Auguste Le Breton also credited as having worked on the screenplay – particularly in relation to the slang dialogue. After losing at the gambling tables, the hero puts together a team to rob the casino. The film was to influence New Wave filmmakers such as Jean Luc Godard and films such as *Ocean's Eleven* (both versions) and the Paul Thomas Anderson's first feature film *Hard Eight* (1996). Neil Jordan wrote and directed a remake, *The Good Thief*, in 2002.

The Killing (1956) directed by Stanley Kubrick who also wrote the screenplay with Jim Thompson based on the novel *Clean Break* (1955) by Lionel White. The hero, played by Sterling Hayden, plans one last heist before settling down - he and his associate will steal $2 million from a race track. Another Lionel White novel *The Big Caper* (1955) about a bank heist was filmed in 1957.

The League of Gentlemen (1960) based on the 1958 novel by John Boland. The hero, played by Jack Hawkins, recruits a group of former army officers with expertise in various areas to be his team to rob a London bank of a £1 million delivery of bank notes. In this case, things are literally planned with military precision. The novel was also adapted for broadcast on BBC Radio 4 in December 2000.

The Breaking Point (also known as *The Great Armored Car Swindle*) is a 1961 film based on a 1957 novel by Laurence Meynell about an attempt to steal a shipment of currency.

Topkapi (1964) based on the 1962 novel *The Light of Day* by Eric Ambler and directed by Jules Dassin who had also directed *Rififi*. A group of thieves plan to rob an Istanbul museum.

The Italian Job (1969). Michael Caine plays the leader of a gang who steal $4 million in gold from an armoured car and make their escape in red, white and blue Mini Coopers. The successful 2003 American remake starring Mark Wahlberg used BMW's modern reincarnation of the Mini.

Kelly's Heroes (1970). A World War II bank heist movie written by Troy Kennedy Martin who also wrote *The Italian Job*.

The Friends of Eddie Coyle (1973). Directed by Peter Yates who directed *Bullitt* and starring Robert Mitchum, the film was based on the novel by George V. Higgins. Concentrates less on the bank robberies and more on the character of Eddie who supplies guns to the crooks and information to federal agents. While the film is interesting, I think the novel is one that every writer should read as it tells the story almost entirely through dialogue.

Thief (1981) written and directed by Michael Mann, this film was originally titled *Violent Streets*. It was based on the book *The Home Invaders: Confessions of a Cat Burglar* by Frank Hohimer (pseudonym of real-life thief John Seybold), some sources say this is a novel but it is actually autobiographical non-fiction. Despite the book's subtitle, the film is concerned with a bank heist rather than burglary of private homes.

Heat (1995) written and directed by Michael Mann. Mann originally filmed this for television as *L.A. Takedown* in 1989. In the film version the two leads, a thief and a detective, are played by Robert De Niro and Al Pacino. The story is based on the true story of the criminal and former Alcatraz inmate Neil McCauley and Detective Chuck Adamson who pursued him in 1964.

Ronin (1998). A group of mercenaries, led by Robert De Niro, are recruited to steal a large metallic briefcase from an armed convoy. The briefcase is sought by various groups during the course of the film, though its contents remain unknown – it serves only as the MacGuffin.

Sexy Beast (2001) Retired safe-cracker Gal Dove, played by Ray Winstone, is 'persuaded' by sociopathic henchman Don Logan (Ben Kingsley) to taking part in a heist. Kingsley steals the show.

Heist (2001) written and directed by David Mamet and starring Gene Hackman and Danny DeVito. Hackman's character retires after a jewellery store robbery goes wrong but is persuaded to target a plane carrying gold. There are various twists and turns as you would expect of a Mamet screenplay.

Inside Man (2006) Spike Lee directs Denzel Washington and Jodie Foster. A gang of robbers take control of a Manhattan bank taking staff and customers hostage and over a twenty-four-hour period carry out what they believe is the perfect robbery. Washington's character is the detective who tries to outwit the criminals but finds the thieves outwit him at every turn.

The Bank Job (2008) – British heist thriller written by Dick Clement and Ian La Frenais in which a gang of second-rate thieves are tricked into tunnelling into a London bank by someone who wants to obtain compromising photographs of a member of the royal family in order to avoid a scandal. A fictionalised account of the real-life robbery of the Baker Street branch of Lloyds Bank in September 1971.

There are a few more films that deserve mentioning here. *Cruel Gun Story* (1964) directed by Takumi Furukawa is a Japanese movie about a thief who is forced into carrying out a heist. Quentin Tarantino's *Reservoir Dogs* (1992) is unique in that it portrays the planning and the aftermath of the heist but not the actual robbery itself. *That Sinking Feeling* (1979) is an ultra-low budget Glasgow-set comedy written and directed by Bill Forsyth about a gang of amateur thieves who set out to heist stainless steel kitchen sinks from a local factory.

Virtually all of the films mentioned above are dominated by male characters with almost no significant roles for women. A number of films have been made which seek to redress this balance. *Set It Off* (1996) features Jada Pinkett, Queen Latifah, Vivica A. Fox and Kimberly Elise as working-class women who decide to carry out a bank robbery to get the cash for a better life for their families. *Ocean's 8* (2018) is an all-female spin-off from *Ocean's Eleven* (2003) and its sequels in which a gang carry out a museum heist. *Widows* (2018) is based on the British television series (1983) written by Lynda La Plante, and is the story of a group of women whose husbands were killed during a botched heist. The women decide that they will carry out one of their husbands' planned robberies in order to pay off their debts and get revenge on those responsible for the husbands' deaths. An American remake of the series was broadcast in 2002.

Point Break could be classed as a heist movie, but I have included that and *The Fast and the Furious* in the chapter on undercover cops. There are also other bank job movies that I include in the car chase chapter.

The Heist Story Plot Structure

There are four main variations on the heist plot:
- The pure heist where the only conflict and suspense arise from the robbery itself and the interaction of the thieves involved in it. There are two subcategories of this type – (a) were the thieves undertake the robbery because it is their plan and they *want* to do it, and (b) where they are *forced* to do it by an external 'Mr. Big' gangster character – most examples fall into the latter group, e.g. *Sexy Beast* and *Heist*. There is some overlap or blurring of this second sub-category and the variation (ii) below, where the Mr. Big doesn't force them to carry out the robbery but tries to take the money afterwards.
- The heist plus external criminal conflict in which one gang of thieves seek to commit the crime and another gang seeks to take the proceeds of the crime from them. *Rififi* falls into this category.
- The heist plus its investigation, where more or less equal time is given to the thieves and the investigators trying to stop them from committing the theft or catch them after the crime (or both). *Heat* is an example of this variation.
- The heist plus conspiracy, where the robbery is part of a larger plot in which the thieves are (relatively) innocent victims. The 2008 film *The Bank Job* has this sort of plot.

These all have a similar cast of characters and share many common scenes or story turning points, but the sequence and relative importance of these varies. For example, the heist itself may begin as early as Sequence 4 or as late as Sequence 8, depending on the story being told. In a heist-investigation story, the heist might take up the first half of the story and the aftermath – the investigation and the thieves' attempts to avoid capture – may make up the second half of the story. To some extent, the structure you choose depends on how much of your story occurs in the aftermath of the heist – and how dramatic those aftermath events are, because you don't want them to be an anti-climax after the thrill of the heist. This is also true of other stories that centre on a crime, such as the confidence trick story we will look at later.

The first type of pure heist story as I describe it in (i) above is quite rare – I couldn't find a single example of a novel or full-length feature film that fits the description. There probably are some – there are hundreds of heist movies and I haven't seen all of them, but their relative scarcity means we shouldn't take that type of story as a baseline for our plot template. Instead, I'm going to start with *Rififi,* which is a near-perfect example of a heist plot, and then look at how the other types of plot are variations on it. Obviously, the heist-investigation is a hybrid of the heist plot and a detective story and the heist-conspiracy combines the heist with conspiracy thriller story elements. The *Rififi* plot more or less covers the second sub-category of the 'pure' heist thriller as well as the variation described in (ii), as these are both heists with conflict created among criminals with little or no police investigation.

The 'Pure' Heist
The purest form of heist story focuses solely on the planning, preparation, and execution of the heist and includes no other action or conflict. This is actually the least common sort of heist story. One of the few examples I have come across is the 1960 film *The League of Gentlemen* and I have based the plot template below on this film.

Sequence 1
Intriguing opening sequence – something incongruous to draw us into the story. In *The League of Gentlemen,* the leader of the gang of thieves emerges from a manhole in the street wearing an immaculate dinner jack and bow tie and then drives away in a Rolls Royce. In the next scene, he cuts five-pound notes in half and puts them into envelopes with typed notes and a copy of a paperback book 'The Golden Fleece.' We then see the various potential team members receiving these mysterious packages and at the same time, we see their home circumstances. This sequence serves to introduce the team members and the leader, but leaves a lot of unanswered questions about why they are being contacted in this unusual way.

Sequence 2
The leader brings the team members together for the first time and puts his proposition to them. In *The League of Gentlemen,* the team members attend a mysterious lunch arranged by the leader – none of the team knows each other and they are all confused as to why they have been invited. The leader reveals each team member's backstory – which also provides their motivation for being part of the heist. They learn who the leader is and that he wants them to be part of a team to rob a bank – but no other details are revealed. They are asked to think about whether they want to sign up for the job – they will meet again.

Sequence 3
The leader recruits his second in command – sharing more details of the plan with him (but not the audience). The second in command is sceptical that the heist can be pulled off – but the leader convinces him that a bank doesn't stand a chance against a trained military unit and the first team member commits to the job. The leader insists that each team member, regardless of rank, will receive an equal share of the loot – that way no one will be disgruntled and cause trouble.

The potential team members all meet for a second time and hear more about the plan – again, the details are not shared with the audience – and they all agree to sign on. They all go off to bid farewell to their home lives for the duration of the mission – they will all be staying together in temporary quarters. The youngest and most rebellious member of the team has a new girlfriend and seems to be the least reliable member of the team – and perhaps his recklessness will put the whole team and the heist in jeopardy.

Sequence 4
The team together in their temporary quarters – assigned (military) job titles and duties and told about the leader's rules for behaviour. Then they attend a planning meeting for 'Phase 1' of the plan – they need weapons for their bank heist and they will steal them from an army training camp.

The scam/theft to obtain the equipment they need is put into effect and carried out successfully. The team work well together. Some of the team members' skills are demonstrated as part of this first, small-scale robbery. There is one near-miss when someone stops to offer assistance to the lookout man who is standing beside his 'broken down' car. The gang make it look as though another group were responsible for the theft to divert attention away from themselves.

At the *midpoint,* the gang get away with the guns and other military equipment they need for the heist. 'Phase 1' has been successfully completed.

Sequence 5
The gang begin their planning and preparation for 'Phase 2' – The Removal Business. They will need vehicles of a certain type and the specialists are sent out to obtain them – including a removal truck. Suspense caused by a couple of near-misses – a policeman warning the driver of a parked car to show some lights and a couple making out in the cab of one of the trucks.

Then comes a montage sequence of planning and preparation – the number plates and signage on the truck are changed and a motorcycle is tested. There are some brief shots of a planning session with the team around a model of the bank. Then slides, film, and a floorplan of the bank are used to explain some parts of the plan – 'Operation: Golden Fleece.' Details are given of the security measures they will have to overcome – they are formidable and it will require all of their specialist skills to complete the job. The methods they will use are described – and then preparations are shown. Their target will be surprised and defenceless.

Sequence 6
Another montage of preparations and practice, including getting the weapons ready.

There is a near-miss when a policeman appears in the doorway of their workshop – curious because he didn't realise the premises were in use. This sets up something that will be used in the final sequence of the story.

Final briefing and burning of the plans and photographs. Team members having difficulty sleeping the night before the heist. The younger team member out with his girlfriend again – against the leader's orders – and arranging to meet her after the job.

Sequence 7
The heist and the getaway. Everything appears to go according to plan – but there is one small and apparently important detail that sets up something that will occur in the final sequence.

Sequence 8
The thieves back at their hideout – celebration and the division of the loot. The first members of the gang leave with their share of the cash and more leave as the evening progresses.

In *The League of Gentlemen,* there is a near-miss when one of the leader's old army friends arrives unexpectedly and wants to join the party. As the remaining team members leave, the leader receives a telephone call – it is the police and they have the hideout surrounded. The leader agrees to surrender himself. He asked who betrayed him, but is told no-one did – the detective says that a bit of evidence from the time of the heist was put together with something the policeman saw at the workshop and this led the police to the leader and the hideout.

This 'Phase 1' and 'Phase 2' approach works nicely for a feature film or a full-length novel, but as it is used in *The League of Gentlemen* I think some of the sequences lack enough conflict and suspense for a modern audience. In 1960, the extended preparation and planning sections worked because they had not been seen before, but a lot of heist movies have been made since then. If you were to use this template today, I think you would need to bolster the levels of drama by having more conflict between the team members and by having their introductions in the first two sequences include more of their solo criminal activities – introducing their skills and their personalities in a much more active way: more showing and less telling. I think I would probably also reduce the planning and preparation phases and extend the second heist – Phase 2 – and the getaway to the equivalent of *two* sequences rather than one, because after all the preparation and build-up, you need a satisfying payoff: I would probably make Sequence 6 show arrival at the bank and the main part of the interior section of the heist, and Sequence 7 the getaway – probably with police in pursuit.

A modern 'pure' heist story would probably be more like *Rififi* (see below) and used the 'Heist & Criminal Conflict' plot but replace the *external* villain with an antagonist who is a member of the gang of thieves – perhaps someone who challenges the leader for the top position in the gang. You could even have a heist and then show one of the gang members making off with all of the loot, so that the rest of the team then have to pursue them to retrieve their shares of the cash.

Another way of increasing the levels of conflict and suspense is to include a subplot such as a police investigation, a conflict with another gang of crooks, or a conspiracy – and we'll look at these variations below.

In *The League of Gentlemen,* there are two occasions when the film cuts away as details of the planned heist are given to the characters, meaning that the audience is kept in the dark. I think a modern audience would resent being left out in this way – we are now used to being included in the planning scenes and excluding us seems like a bit of a cheat. The audience or reader should be allowed to know at least the broad details of the plan – but you can still keep some smaller details secret and also keep a few surprises from them.

The plot template above covers the first sub-type of the 'pure' heist plot (ia). The second sub-type (ib), where the leader of a gang of thieves is forced into carrying out a robbery by a 'Mr. Big' character, is similar to the *heist and criminal conflict plot* below. I will also give a version of this (ib) plot in the chapter on burglars and gentlemen thieves.

The Heist & Criminal Conflict Plot

Sequence 1
We meet the hero who will be the leader of the band of thieves who carry out the heist. He is typically older and more experienced than the other members of the group, probably famous as a thief among local criminals. But his luck recently has not been good and he has either just finished a relatively long prison sentence (five years or more) or has debts that he owes to a local loan shark or gangster. Life has made him cynical. He has probably lost the woman he loves to a more successful and wealthier criminal – perhaps the man he owes his debts to.

The *proposition* is made – a plan to commit a heist. The hero may come up with this himself as a way of paying off his debts and maybe winning back his lover, or it may be brought to the hero by a less experienced member of the gang.

There will be some *reluctance* to take part in this plan. If the proposition is made by the hero, then one or more of the other potential gang members may be reluctant to be involved because of the risk it entails. If the plan originates with one of the other gang members, the hero may be reluctant because of the risk – he doesn't want another stretch in prison.

Personal circumstances give the reluctant participant(s) a *push*. The need for money may provide this push. In the case of the hero, an encounter with his lost love may be the encouragement he needs. There should probably be something other than greed for money motivating the various team members if you want to create audience liking and sympathy for them.

Eventually, a *decision* is made and everyone makes a *commitment* to take part in the heist. If someone else put the plan forward, the hero will make his commitment conditional on him taking charge of the operation and making some changes to the plan. His experience and reputation mean that the other group members accept this – though there may be some resentment from the person who originally put the plan forward, and this may have implications later. Another of the hero's conditions may be that no one carries guns – because doing so automatically means longer prison sentences if they're caught. This may not sit well with younger gang members and one or more may secretly ignore this rule, again this may have consequences later.

Sequence 2

The gang of thieves begin initial discussions about the heist, speaking in general terms about what they intend to achieve and how they will carry it out. The new expert recruits join the team for the first time. There may be some awkwardness as the new crew members and the existing ones size each other up and establish their places in the pecking order. There may be mistrust initially – and the hero, as a good leader, may organise some sort of activity that requires teamwork and helps establish friendship. Usually, mutual respect is established as each team member demonstrates his own particular area of expertise and shows that he deserves a place in the gang.

Broad constraints may also be determined – e.g. we must complete the job before 5am when deliveries begin for the surrounding stores. This may also serve to establish a deadline or ticking clock which can be used to increase suspense during the heist. Some initial steps may also be taken, such as contacting a fence to handle any stolen jewellery or to launder stolen money. They may also identify any specialists that they need to recruit if existing gang members lack this expertise. Usually, only one or two external experts are brought in – perhaps a safecracker or security alarm specialist and a getaway driver.

During the second sequence, we also develop the characters of the main gang members by showing their personal relationships and home lives. Typically, the other gang members have happy relationships or intense short-term sexual relationships and the hero is shown to be without a relationship – he is still holding a torch for his lost love. He may meet up with his ex-lover and receive the cold shoulder from her, even though she is probably still attracted to him. And/or the hero may encounter her current boyfriend who warns the hero to stay away from her and may also gloat about the fact she is now his. This sets up a confrontation that will occur later in the story.

In older examples of this genre, female characters tend to be mothers, stay at home wives, or whores and in some stories, including *Rififi,* the male characters use domestic violence against them. In more modern stories, relationships are treated in a less misogynistic way. Male homosexuality – either overt or implied – has been a part of crime stories since the 1930s, though until relatively recently such characters have tended to be regarded as deviants and perverts. Again, the best modern stories take a more enlightened approach to such relationships.

In a majority of genres, Sequence 5 is where personal relationships and character backstories are explored. In the heist story this tends to occur earlier, probably because the relationship serves as motivation – the characters want to use the money they get from the heist to give their family or partner a comfortable life – and also as part of what is at stake: if the heist goes wrong, the family or partner will be affected too. Relationship issues set up in Sequence 2 or 3 may have consequences in Sequence 5 or later, especially if an antagonist uses a lover or family member as leverage to force one of the gang members to betray the others or give up the loot.

Here we may also see another sort of relationship demonstrated – one of the thieves may have an external antagonistic relationship, perhaps with a gangster he owes money to or with a detective who wants a bribe from him or wants to arrest him. This relationship will be kept secret from the other thieves and it potentially puts them all and the heist in jeopardy. It also means that this person could potentially betray the others later if he is placed under pressure by this antagonist. This antagonistic relationship could be between the hero and his ex-lover's new man, but more often it involves another team member. In some stories this team member represents a threat to the gang because of another weakness – he may be a drug addict, a violent sociopath, or suffer from some physical or mental illness (PTSD for example) that may make him an unreliable team member.

Sequence 3

Sequence 3 marks the point where the thieves 'cross the threshold' and enter the world of the heist. They may separate from their families and partners and move in together in a sort of communal or military barracks type arrangement. They also begin *casing* the target of the heist – they visit the location and check it out and they obtain street plans; building plans; details of electricity, water and other utilities, and blueprints of the building or technical diagrams of an armoured car. They may also drive along the escape route and take timings at various points. They will keep an extended watch on the location, noting the times of regular deliveries and police or other security patrols. They may take photographs, video, or measurements. They may conduct tests on various pieces of specialist equipment. In *Rififi*, the thieves obtain an alarm system identical to the one used by their target building and try various ways of beating it. Duplicate keys or other items may be obtained from inside sources. If a safe or vault is to be opened, they will discover its make and model and research details about it to try and understand its weak points.

After all of this planning and preparation, the gang are ready to undertake the heist. They may visit their families or partners – there may be concern and some tension in this meeting, but it usually goes unvoiced. Again, this serves to emphasise the motivation and the stakes.

Sequence 4

This sequence shows the first practical stages in the commission of the heist leading up to the midpoint. At the *midpoint,* the thieves stand in front of the vault, safe, armoured car, or train and now have to get inside it to obtain the valuables. Sequence 4 is everything leading up to this moment – digging the tunnel, bypassing the alarms, scaling the outside of the building, or ambushing the armoured car or train.

The heist occupies virtually all of sequences 4 *and* 5 in this model plot. This sequence shows in detail how the thieves gain the access they need to the place that contains the valuables. During the days of the Production Code, movies were not permitted to show how crimes were committed for fear that people would copy the methods. Non-Hollywood movies of that period, including *Rififi,* and post-Code films can show as much detail as they want. A big part of the appeal of the heist movie is that audiences get to see how to rob a bank or commit some other crime. Your details here need to be thorough and convincing – though not necessarily 100% accurate.

Initially, in this sequence, there may be someone nervousness and awkwardness, perhaps even clumsiness, but the team quickly settle down into performing their assigned tasks. During this first half of the heist, we often see some of the specialists at work, assisted by those whose expertise isn't required until the second half. After the midpoint, people switch their 'expert' and 'helper' roles. In Sequence 4 we may see the alarms expert bypassing the external alarms to get the gang inside the first ring of security. And then we often see the 'heavy' work being done – digging tunnels or demolishing walls or ceilings, all done quietly so as not to attract attention. Or a team member may be an expert climber and scale the building and put in place the ropes that the others can use to make their climb. Lookouts and getaway drivers will also take up their positions.

The team may have to work in accordance with a pre-planned schedule – perhaps ceasing all noise and turning out the lights when a police patrol or security inspection is due or avoiding some other regular event noted during their preparations.

Suspense is often generated by an unanticipated interruption – perhaps an unscheduled police patrol or the arrival of workers or members of the public.

Sequence 5

The second half of the heist. Typically a new expert takes charge of opening whatever vault, safe, strongbox, or vehicle contains the valuables. This may involve the use of specialist drilling or cutting equipment, such as a thermic lance, or careful use of explosives. It often takes a combination of things to open a vault, perhaps involving two or more different experts. Again, their activities are shown in some detail.

This sequence probably involves another close call with the gang being on the brink of discovery by the police or someone else. Perhaps the getaway driver or car arouses someone's suspicion just as the thieves are ready to make their escape. Or someone or something is not in the place it was supposed to be. Or something goes wrong, potentially trapping them or putting the loot out of reach. Just as success seems to be theirs, there should be the threat of it being taken away in some way that has the audience holdings its breath until the crisis is averted.

This sequence may also include the thieves' getaway, usually by car or delivery truck though you might want to try other less obvious forms of transport. If you want to include a car chase, this might be the place to do it.

In the getaway car or in their hideout later, the thieves sit around and look at their haul. Piles of cash or heaps of sparkly things. They might sit in silent appreciation for a moment and then break out the celebration drinks. They will probably talk about what they want to buy with their share of the proceeds, their various dreams reflecting their individual characters. The hero may watch this silently – because at this point he is the only one of them who doesn't have someone to share a dream life with.

There may also be some discussion about what happens next – gold or diamonds may need to be fenced in order to convert it into cash they can spend. New banknotes in sequential bundles may need to be laundered. Or the cash may need to be hidden until the investigation into the robbery has died down. The gang members may get a small share of any available cash to be going on with – and the hero will probably warn them not to spend it conspicuously as this will arouse suspicion. Of course, at least one of the gang is likely to ignore this advice and buy himself or his girlfriend something flashy and expensive, which is exactly what the police or a rival gang of crooks will be on the lookout for. This sets up and foreshadows what is actually going to happen in Sequence 6.

Sequence 6

One of the more flamboyant or less experienced thieves makes the mistake of giving his girlfriend an expensive gift or perhaps even one of the stolen jewellery items. Or he splashes out on an expensive automobile that effectively shouts to the world that he has just come into some cash. Or he pays off his debts. Or he starts gambling heavily. Or he buys more than his usual amount of drugs – perhaps even organising a party for his friends or people he wants to impress. This character is often a younger member of the crew who is either naïve or hot-headed or a risk-taking rebellious type who thinks the rules don't apply to him and that he's too smart to get caught. The relationship with his girlfriend probably began only recently and he feels the need to prove to her that he's a bigshot and not a bum. This ill-advised action will draw the attention of either the police or the criminals in the rival gang, depending on which of these serves as the major opposition in your story.

The police or insurers may offer a reward for information leading to the arrest of the thieves. This offers an additional source of jeopardy and suspense as it means that a peripheral character may be tempted to turn snitch or a disgruntled member of the gang may betray the others.

The main antagonist, the leader of another gang of criminals, decides that he doesn't want to claim the reward, he wants to take all of the money/jewels/gold stolen by the thieves. When he learns of the sudden spending of the inexperienced/flamboyant thief, he sends his men to pick him up. They beat or torture him to get him to say where the valuables are hidden and/or to give up the names of the other thieves. Unable to hold-out, the tortured thief gives them some clue or piece of information that they can use. He may give up the name of the one member of the gang with whom he had an antagonistic relationship, not realising that giving him up will mean that the antagonist can work out the names of the other thieves this person is usually associated with.

There is often a scene in this sequence involving the hero's ex-lover – usually something that indicates that she still has feelings for the hero. She may warn him that his gang member has been captured and betrayed him. The hero will appreciate the tip-off, but his cynical nature may make him feel that her sudden concern for his wellbeing has something to do with the fact that he's just become very rich. But though he may put up a tough-guy front, it's clear that he still has feelings for her. The muted tenderness between them is often contrasted with another scene in which the ex-lover is treated badly by her current boyfriend, who is usually the main antagonist. He is possessive and domineering and regards her as a possession rather than a human being. These scenes set up her motivation to betray the antagonist and for her and the hero to get back together. But as soon as the antagonist realises what is happening, the ex-lovers life is in danger – and the antagonist can also exploit the hero's feelings for her by threatening to harm her if he doesn't turn over the loot. Again, we're setting up and foreshadowing plot developments to come.

The 'darkest hour' moment at the end of Sequence 6 usually involves the death of one of the thieves. This may be the discovery of the mutilated body of the thief who was captured and tortured, or it may be another of the gang who was betrayed by the tortured thief. There may also be a narrow-escape for the hero, who is now being hunted by the antagonist's henchmen.

The inexperienced thief's mistake at the beginning of this sequence sets off a chain of events that is the unravelling of the thieves' fortunes. At the end of Sequence 5 they had successfully completed their heist and were celebrating. By the end of Sequence 6, things have spiralled out of control such that at least one and possibly two of the gang have been killed.

Sequence 7

Perhaps there is a funeral for the murdered thief. The police and/or the antagonist may watch proceedings to identify the other gang members – but the gang knows this and so has to stay away, leaving the dead man's funeral a small and pathetic affair.

Perhaps the fence hands over a suitcase of clean cash to the hero – the stolen valuables have been turned into something that can actually be spent. This becomes the 'MacGuffin' that everyone now wants to get their hands on. Or perhaps the stolen items are still hidden somewhere and everyone wants to know the location and only the hero has that information.

The antagonist increases the stakes in his attempts to get his hands on the loot. He kidnaps and threatens to kill someone who the hero cares about. In *Rififi* it is the hero's nephew, who is the son of one of the other gang members. It could be the wife, partner, or mother of one of the gang members. Or it could be the hero's ex-lover who is now his lover again. Even if the two are not back together, his feelings will be such that he cannot allow her to die.

Learning of the kidnapping, the hero and his fellow thieves make desperate attempts to discover where the hostage is being held, but without success. They may argue over whether to hand over the money in exchange for this person. And they will know that even if they *do* hand over the money, there is every chance that the hostage will be killed – and so will the person who delivers the money. The ideal outcome is that they rescue the hostage, deal with the antagonist so that he can never be a problem again, *and* keep the loot. It is up to you to decide whether the hero achieves all, some, one, or none of these. If you plan to have a tragic ending (the hero doesn't get the cash or the girl and he probably dies), then Sequence 7 will normally end on a positive note – you make the reader or audience believe that the hero could win. But if you want to have a happy ending (the hero gets the cash and the girl and he doesn't die), you will end this sequence with the audience feeling that the odds are so heavily stacked against the hero that he can't possibly win. You will probably have the hero walking into a trap that the audience knows about but that the hero is unaware of.

Sequence 8

This is the final confrontation between hero and antagonist. Here is where we discover who, if anybody, gets the loot; who gets the girl, and who lives and who dies. How this plays out depends on whether you want a happy or a tragic ending. You also have the option of having an *ironic* ending. Here the hero either gets the girl but not the money (he gets what he *needs* but not what he *wants*), or he gets the money but not the girl (he gets what he *wants* but not what he *needs*). Or maybe he saves her by giving up the money and then she betrays him. Again. He gets neither what he wants nor what he needs, but ends up sadder but wiser and lives to fight (or rob) another day. Or you may have set up another sort of ironic-happy ending where the hero gets neither the money nor the girl, but where this is actually the best thing that could have happened to him – he gets something that he *really needs* instead – perhaps a life with an estranged son or daughter or with a new romance who is a soulmate rather than a *femme fatale*. Obviously, you would need to set up the potential for this sort of ending earlier in the story, probably in Sequence 3, with a couple of subtle 'reminders' of this possibility after the midpoint.

In terms of action, Sequence 8 may involve a race against time to save the hostage by delivering the loot. Or it may involve a suspenseful shadowy hunt as the hero sneaks into the antagonist's hideout to rescue the hostage. Or it may include a car chase after the hero has snatched the hostage. Or the hero may be ambushed and involved in a shoot-out. Or any combination of these things.

Ideally, you will want the end sequence to involve the specialist skills of the thieves again – otherwise, it becomes a generic action sequence that isn't properly integrated into the story. If you have a chase sequence, you want it to feature either the getaway driver from the robbery or someone who is obviously *not* a getaway driver, showing why they hired an expert instead of this person for the robbery. If explosives were involved in the robbery, they can be used in the climax. If an alarm system had to be circumvented so they could get in without setting off an alarm, you want a similar situation in the antagonist's hideout. You don't need to show the same level of detailed planning here, but you should imply that something similar has occurred.

The attack on the antagonist's lair can be an ironic variation on the robbery we saw earlier – similar application of skills but to a different purpose. Where before they wanted small, contained explosions, here they may want the opposite. Where the original getaway car was a non-descript sedan that didn't draw attention, here we may have a souped-up hot-rod or a Hummer. In the original robbery there may have been a line of dialogue along the lines of 'If we get this wrong, this terrible consequence will occur (e.g. the roof will collapse in on us).' In the end sequence, this may be exactly what they *want* to happen.

You can effectively allow your thieves to go wild and use their skills to their fullest effect. They can do the things they're not usually allowed to do.

And in this final 'heist' targeting the antagonist, part of the plan may be to gain the attention of the police – the opposite of the original plan. The heroes may want the police to arrive and capture the antagonist red-handed, perhaps with enough evidence to 'prove' that he carried out the original heist and probably with proof that he committed the murder(s) of the gang member(s).

It's up to you whether this ending sequence involves all of the surviving members of the hero's gang of thieves, just the hero and one accomplice, or the hero on his own. Whoever is involved, their actions should be in character and involve the expertise and equipment of a robber and not just generic action-adventure mayhem.

The Heist & Investigation Plot

Next, we'll look at variation (iii), the *heist plus its investigation*. Many heist movies include this to a greater or lesser extent. In Michael Mann's film *Heat* – and it's earlier incarnation *LA Takedown* – the heist and the investigation get equal time with the thief, played by Robert De Niro, and the detective, played by Al Pacino, effectively being protagonists for each of the two plots. In the two-part BBC TV miniseries *The Great Train Robbery*, the first episode is a standalone movie about the heist and the second is about the investigation.

You will have to decide whether your thief and detective are both the 'hero' of their own plot thread, or if one of them is the antagonist to the other's protagonist. If you create a hero detective and a thief-antagonist, you will concentrate more on the investigation than on the thieves pulling off the heist – and you will be writing a police procedural that is about bringing thieves to justice, rather than a heist thriller. If you create a thief-hero and a detective antagonist you can make your detective a good cop, just someone doing his job, or you can make him a Dirty Harry-like cop who isn't afraid of using violence against criminals. Or you could make him a crooked cop, in which case he plays the role of criminal antagonist as in the previous plot template while still carrying on the investigation as in this template.

I said earlier that the heist movie exists in a morally ambiguous zone that explores how our need for order, stability and obeying the rules conflicts with our need to be autonomous and free-thinking rebels. In a story like *Heat*, both of those sides are represented – the law-abiding part of us has the detective as its champion and the trickster side has the thief – and from moment to moment the story teases with the fact that we want one side to triumph and the other side not to lose. Stories that appeal to paradoxes in our own nature are often very popular.

In the plot below, many of the incidents are the same as those mentioned in the previous template, so I won't repeat the details and will concentrate instead on the unique elements.

Sequence 1

With this variation of the heist plot, we need to get the police involved at a much earlier stage – probably by the end of Sequence 1 or in Sequence 2 at the latest – and this is usually done by beginning the story with a heist. This means that this plot variation typically involves *two* heists rather than one. The first one begins *in medias res* – it is already underway as the story opens and we don't see any of the planning or preparation. When we see the planning for the second robbery later, it effectively also serves as a 'flashback' to how this first robbery was planned.

This first heist will probably take up half or three-quarters of the first sequence – it needs to provide an exciting opening to draw the reader or viewer into the story, but at the same time it has to be smaller in length and emotional intensity than the second robbery later in the story. You don't want to blow all your cool stuff in the opening sequence and have nothing left for later. Bad action-adventure movies often have a great opening and then nothing in reserve for Act II, so they resort to generic shoot-outs and car chases, ultimately leaving the audience unsatisfied.

Towards the end of the heist, something goes wrong or a mistake is made – this leaves some sort of clue that the investigator can use to begin his detection process. In *Heat*, one of the thieves disobeys orders and shoots someone and a nickname is spoken that is overheard by a witness. Both of these things have consequences later in the story.

The heist introduces the leader of the thieves – I'll refer to him as Leader – and his crew.

The latter part of Sequence 1 has the investigators at the scene of the heist doing scene of crime stuff and interviewing witnesses. I cover both of these processes in more detail elsewhere in this book. We are introduced to the main investigator – I'll call him Detective. We may see first see him as he arrives on the scene, or we may see him at home getting the call to come out to the scene. The contrast between home life and professional life is often used to characterise the detective hero. In this type of story, the home lives of the thieves are also contrasted with the lives of the detectives, with particular emphasis on the contrast between Leader and Detective – we get to see how they are different but also what characteristics they have in common, even though they are on opposing sides.

The investigation that the Detective carries out will follow the basic sequence of a typical investigation – this is common to private eye stories and police procedurals, so I have written about it as a separate topic later in the book. Initially, we see him doing the basic tasks we would expect any detective to carry out – examining the crime scene, gathering evidence, questioning witnesses, talking to informants, etc. In later scenes, we will see him make more determined attempts to locate and arrest the criminals. In a typical investigation that means two failed attempts, the second of which is a near-miss, and then a final successful one. Whether or not the Detective's final attempt to arrest them is successful depends on whether you want to have your thieves caught at the end. If you want them to go free, you may want to give your detective a partial victory – maybe he catches a crook but not all of the gang, or maybe he recovers the loot but the gang escapes.

Sequence 2

The first part of this sequence concentrates on the thieves – their relationships with one another and their romantic or family relationships. This may include a division of loot scene and a warning from Leader to spend it carefully and without drawing attention. And again we see there is an unreliable member of the team whose actions are likely to jeopardise the others. The thieves may also talk about what they want to do with their money – their ambitions or dream lives helping to characterise them.

Leader may have a romantic partner, an ex-lover, or no partner at all. He is probably cynical, perhaps hurt in a previous relationship. He probably argues that it is a bad idea for a thief to have romantic attachments because you have to be ready to walk away from everything and start over if the police get too close. But he only half believes this and is slightly jealous of the members of his crew who do have long-term relationships. And he may happen to encounter some in this sequence who could potentially be the ideal life partner for him, making him have to rethink his stance on relationships. Again these scenes about relationships serve similar functions as those in the previous template – establishing stakes and motivation.

The thieves also begin discussions about their next heist. This one will be bigger – their biggest ever. Maybe the Leader intends for it to be his last heist so that he can retire – and meeting a new romantic partner finally convinces him he needs to give up his life of crime.

The relationships and dreams of the thieves are typically contrasted with those of the Detective and perhaps one or more of the people he works with in his team. They are scraping by on a public servant's salary and the nature of their work means that personal relationships become strained and may come to an end. I write in more detail about the nature of the professional relationships between policemen in the chapter on the Police Procedural. The police, like the thieves, are usually a close-knit 'band of brothers.'

We will probably also see the Detective working on the heist investigation – perhaps talking to an informer or a local fence. Or perhaps making a first attempt at following up on whatever clue was left at the scene of the heist.

While the police investigation is the main source of antagonism for the thieves, you can also include a secondary antagonist, perhaps a criminal one. In *Heat* the owner of some of the loot stolen by the thieves decides he will locate the thieves and kill them to demonstrate that it is not okay to steal from him. Or you could have a rival gang behave in much the same way as those in the earlier template – but with their story played out as a lesser subplot rather than one of the two major plots.

Sequence 3
The detective follows up on the information he received from his informer or getting information back about another clue found at the scene. This is more standard police work. As a result, he may learn the identity of one of the thieves or someone closely associated with them. He may follow this person himself or send a pair of detectives to conduct surveillance. This person then unwitting leads the police to one or more of the other gang members.

Here we may see the thieves socialising, demonstrating the close bond between the team members and their families. This may be contrasted with a similar scene of the policemen socialising – perhaps in a 'cop bar' without their families. By this stage, two or more of the thieves are being watched by the police.

Sequence 4
In this plot template, you have a cat and mouse game between the thieves who want to carry out another robbery and escape with the loot, and the police who want to arrest them for the previous robbery and prevent them carrying out the second one. To plot this out, it may be helpful to think of it in terms of the police making three attempts to catch the crooks – two unsuccessful ones and a successful (or not) final one. And the thieves making three attempts to avoid capture by the police – two successful one and an unsuccessful (or not) final one.

In Sequence 4 we see the Detective's first full-scale attempt to locate and arrest the thieves. It ends at the midpoint with the thieves getting away or outwitting him. The *midpoint* is the moment when both the Detective and the Leader know that the game is on – each is now aware of the other and the contest has taken on a personal element. And each becomes aware of how good a player their opponent is and realises that they are going to have to be very careful from this moment on. Before, the thieves' story thread and the investigators' story thread were running parallel but separately, each team aware of the existence of the other but not really having any knowledge of the people involved and no direct interaction – at the midpoint they merge and become a single thread and the people involved become known individuals.

Sequence 5
As well as doing the usual planning for the new heist, the Leader now has to include information gathering on their new opponent, the Detective. He will obtain details of the detective's career to date and his personal life. He will be looking for any weaknesses. Perhaps his initial reaction is to try and pay-off the Detective, but he discovers that this cop never takes bribes and comes down hard on those who do. The Detective is a man of principle, and the Leader respects this, even though it makes his task harder. The Leader is going to have to come up with a really good plan to outwit the Detective – and he relishes the challenge.

Now that he knows the identity of the Leader, the Detective gathers information on him and makes a similar analysis of his career and personal life. He will be looking for weaknesses – use of drugs or family attachments that might lead the police to him. But there is nothing obvious that can be used – the Leader is good at what he does, and the times he has been caught before were down to bad luck – something he couldn't have planned for – or betrayal. The Detective has to admire the Leader's professionalism, and he too relishes facing off against a talented opponent.

In *Heat,* Michael Mann has his thief (Robert De Niro) and detective (Al Pacino) sit down together and have a coffee and a chat. They conduct their mutual appreciation face to face, like boxers sizing each other up before a fight, and part saying something along the lines of 'may the best man win.' Each will bring his A-game and try to beat the other. A face to face meeting probably isn't the sort of thing you could pull off in most stories – you probably haven't got a De Niro and a Pacino to bring together. But they might come together at the end of the Detective's first attempt to catch the thieves and perhaps exchange a few words to express their mutual respect – or perhaps this is even done wordlessly with an expression or a mock salute. And both will know that next time things won't end so cordially.

The fact that these two men are the best at what they do helps establish the stakes and the suspense – which one of them will win against their formidable opponent? At the end of Sequence 5 we see the balance tip first in favour of one player and then the other. With the major heist about to begin, the various members of the gang manage to trick and elude the policemen that have been tailing them. Score one for the thieves. But then someone approaches the Detective and offers to betray the Leader and his gang, tipping the balance in favour of the investigators.

Sequence 6

This is the heist sequence. The heist and escape with the loot can occupy just this sequence or carry on and form all or part of the next sequence. In *Heat* the bank heist is Sequence 6 only and is not a detailed heist of the sort we saw in the previous template.

The thieves don't realise that they have been betrayed and that the police know exactly where they will be and when. When the police move in – as the thieves are coming out with the loot, caught red-handed – there may be a gunfight or a car chase (or both!) that results in one or more of the thieves being injured or killed and a similar number of policemen.

As all of this is going on, the betrayer has a Plan B in case the thieves escape with the loot – he kidnaps someone the thieves care about, perhaps the wife or girlfriend of one of them, perhaps the Leader's girlfriend – and holds them hostage so he can negotiate to get some of the loot if the thieves do manage to escape. Either that or the betrayer has his eyes on the loot from the *first* heist and kidnaps one of the thieves or someone associated with them and tortures them to try and find out the location of the hidden loot.

Sequence 7

The aftermath of the second heist. This sequence sets up the climax in Sequence 8.

This sequence may tie up the romantic subplots – we may see that the Leader's romance succeeds or fails and contrast this with the opposite situation (or the same situation) for the Detective.

The Detective will make one final attempt to locate and arrest the surviving thieves – or he may just concentrate on the Leader at this point. He will realise that the Leader will try and rescue the hostage or kill betrayer – so the Detective sets a trap for the Leader.

The Leader and his crew will realise who it was that betrayed them – this person is responsible for the death and injury of two crew members. They are torn between going after this person or making their escape. With the police having gotten so close this time, they decide that the wisest move is to leave the betrayer alone. Perhaps they will just pass word to a contact by phone and leave other underworld figures to deal with the snitch.

Arrangements are in place for the surviving crew members to make their escapes and start new lives in the Caribbean or somewhere equally paradisiacal. Everyone is ready to leave, including the Leader – with or without his romantic partner, when news reaches them that either the hostage is still alive or of the location of the betrayer. Everyone knows that the wise thing to do would be to walk away – and everyone knows that the Leader cannot do this. They take care of their own – and that means either rescue or vengeance depending on the target identified here – hostage or betrayer (though 'both' is also an option).

Sequence 8
The Leader goes to rescue the hostage or to 'deal with' the person who betrayed him and his crew. This is not a smart move – he should just escape with the loot, but there is a principle at stake here. And the Detective is aware of this and has made plans accordingly.

When the Leader reaches the location, he sees that there are disguised policemen waiting – this is an ambush. Again, the wise thing would be to walk away – but he can't. He must use his thief's equipment and expertise to get past the police and reach his target. He may do this alone or with the help of surviving members of his team.

It is up to you to decide how the Leader's final actions play out. Does he rescue the hostage? Kill the betrayer? Or is the Detective waiting for him? Or does the hostage turn out to be a betrayer? Or does the hostage warn the Leader about the set-up? Does the hero get away with the girl and the loot? Just the girl? Just the loot? Neither? How many of his crew survive, if any? Do they live to heist another day?

There should probably be one final face-to-face confrontation between the Leader and Detective – either close-up and nose to nose or across a distance such that only their eyes meet. Perhaps this time the Detective gives the salute instead of the Leader, acknowledging a stalemate or that the thief won this one.

The Heist & The Conspiracy
This variation on the heist plot weaves in elements of the conspiracy thriller which I wrote about in some detail in the *Suspense Thriller* book in this series. In the example below, based on *The Bank Job* (2008), I will assume that the conspiracy in question is a political one, though in theory any of the types of conspiracy referred to in the earlier book could be adapted for use here. Again, I will just focus on those areas that are different from those in the first template above.

The gang of thieves are usually unaware that they are being manipulated as part of a larger plan, though one member of their team – perhaps the Leader – is a 'mole' and is influencing their actions without telling them what they are really involved in.

Sequence 1
There may be a prologue that establishes the nature of the 'MacGuffin' – the politically sensitive material that the security services want to obtain but which they cannot be seen to take themselves. This may be confidential material in the possession of an agent from a country which the security

service's own government is technically not in conflict with. Or it may be something stolen from the government which cannot officially be regarded as missing for fear of a scandal. In the case of *The Bank Job,* it is incriminating photographs of a member of the British royal family. As with any McGuffin, the exact nature of the item isn't that important – it exists only to provide something that the security services want.

The MacGuffin, we learn, is being held in a safety deposit box in the vault of a bank in the city. The security service decides that the best way to obtain it, without tipping off anyone that they are the ones obtaining it, is to have someone rob the bank and empty *all* of the safety deposit boxes. The target for the heist doesn't have to be a safety deposit box in a bank – it could be microfilm hidden in a statue on display in a museum or a painting hanging in an art gallery. It just needs to be something that is hidden in such a way that it could be stolen as one of several valuable items to avoid drawing attention to it being the prime target.

Having established that the security services want to get their hands on the McGuffin by unofficial means, one of their agents sets about blackmailing someone to do the job for them. This person is usually guilty of some crime – smuggling drugs or something of that nature – and is promised immunity if they co-operate and a long prison sentence if they don't. This person has been targeted by the agent because they are known to have criminal contacts who can carry out the sort of heist needed to obtain the MacGuffin.

The person blackmailed by the security service could be the Leader of the gang of thieves. But it is more likely to be someone that the Leader trusts – a lover or former lover, an older thief that served as a mentor, someone the Leader shared a prison cell with. It could be anyone that could reasonably come to the Leader with a proposition – a plan to rob a bank – without arousing the Leader's suspicions. I will refer to the person blackmailed by the security service as the Mole.

If the Mole is an old thief, he may initially and deliberately *not* ask the Leader to be a part of the heist. The Mole may come to the Leader and ask about some other old thieves he used to work with – hinting that he wants to put the 'old gang' together for a 'sure thing.' Of course, the Leader will be intrigued and want to know more. 'Reluctantly' the Mole will tell him about the bank job that he just happens to have detailed blueprints, vault plans, and security system specifications for. The Leader will probably tell him that the 'old gang' really are too old for this sort of job – but that he and his crew would be willing to help out. Of course, this is what the Mole planned all along.

It is up to you how much detail you give about the Mole's dealings with the security service agent, and at what point you reveal this information to the reader. The Leader won't be aware of the larger conspiracy until the midpoint of the story, but the audience will probably learn about it before then. I discuss this idea of putting the reader in a 'superior' position – knowing things that the hero doesn't – and how this can be used to generate suspense, in *Suspense Thriller.*

In Sequence 1 or possibly in Sequence 2, we meet the rest of the Leader's gang of thieves and learn something about their characters and their personal lives and relationships. We also get an idea of what their area of specialisation is as a thief – and what specialisms are lacking in the gang and will have to be filled by outside recruits.

We may also see another criminal who will serve as the main source of antagonism, since the security service will be a largely unseen opponent that operates in the background. The police, as investigators, have a relatively small part to play in this variation. This criminal may be someone who the Leader or another member of the gang owes money to, or they may be someone who has something valuable or incriminating in the bank vault that will be stolen along with everything else, or they may just be someone, as in the first plot template here, who decides they want the loot stolen by the thieves. Or the criminal may be a crooked policeman who fits any of these criteria. Or this antagonist may be a foreign agent who placed the MacGuffin in the bank vault for safekeeping. I will refer to this character as the Antagonist.

The Leader's gang will discuss the proposition – one or more of them being reluctant because of the inherent risks. Others will put forward the benefits and even suggest ways in which they would spend their share of the loot. At the end of the sequence, the gang all agree that they want to be involved in the heist.

Sequence 2

Two or more of the thieves, perhaps including the Mole, case the bank that is the target of the heist. Other members of the team may take photographs or video of the streets around the bank. They may also spend some time watching the location and making records of police patrols at various hours and regular deliveries to nearby stores.

We may also learn something about other people – innocent and criminal – who keep items in safety deposit boxes in the bank. The criminals in particular may take an interest in the thieves later once it is known that the vault has been robbed.

The plan typically involves entering the bank via a tunnel dug from nearby premises or through a wall shared with the bank or through a roof accessed via an adjacent building. An early part of the plan will be to obtain access to this building – perhaps by renting it.

Other early stages may include recruiting specialists – perhaps a getaway driver or someone to handle the tunnelling. Or it may be necessary to hire someone who can wear a disguise and impersonate a particular person or type of person.

As in the earlier example, there may be a scene where the Leader or another of the team bids farewell to his wife and family before going off to carry out the heist. This helps establish the stakes – he's saying goodbye because if something goes wrong he might not see them again for a long time or he may even be killed.

Sequence 3

The whole gang, including the outside specialists that have been recruited, all meet for the first time. As well as looking over the plans of the target and discussing the plan, there may be a demonstration of some of the specialist equipment that will be used.

The Mole reports to his or her contact that the heist is going ahead. The thieves continue their preparations, unaware that they are being followed by agents of the security service who are behind the conspiracy.

The thieves take up their positions and the first stages of the heist begin. The first half of the heist, including any breaking through of walls or ceilings or digging of tunnels, may be shown in the form of a montage or a few brief written mini scenes. As in the first example template, work may be suspended when scheduled deliveries or security patrols take place. And there may be a moment of suspense when an unscheduled visit is made by a policeman who is there by coincidence or because of a report of noises associated with the robbery.

The Mole may seek an opportunity to contact his or her contact – and this behaviour makes the Leader suspicious, even though he doesn't know the reason for the Mole's furtiveness.

A witness may spot something related to the robbery and become suspicious. Or someone with a grudge and who knows something about the robbery may decide to betray the thieves to the police.

Sequence 4

The witness or betrayer contacts the police and tells them they have information that may be useful to the police. Not realising the importance of the information, the police may not treat it as an urgent matter. This contact with the police serves to raise the stakes and increase suspense – will the police descend on the vault and catch the robbers before they get away?

The thieves begin emptying the vault – breaking open the safety deposit boxes and pouring cash, jewellery and other items into large sacks. They may pick out a few unusual or expensive items and draw them to the attention of their colleagues, but for the most part, they tip things into the bags to be sorted through later.

At the *midpoint,* as the thieves empty the vault, the Leader of the thieves finally discovers what the Mole wanted to obtain from the vault.

Sequence 5

The police take action based on the information given by the witness or the betrayer. A squad of cars and armed officers is dispatched to the scene. The thieves may still be celebrating their success in the vault, unaware that the police are heading towards them. They may have a lookout who warns them at the last minute. Or the police may be delayed by having to wait for a key holder to arrive and open the doors of the bank. Or they may get into the back and see the vault door locked shut, the thieves having created their own entrance in a wall, ceiling or floor inside the vault. Or the thieves may simply have made their escape already and the police just see the door hanging open and the ransacked vault.

Another option is that the witness or betrayer actually worked for the Leader and sent the police to a bank on the other side of the city, ensuring that the thieves could make their escape undisturbed. Or the information given to a genuine betrayer or the evidence seen by the genuine witness may have been faked to achieve the same purpose – all the police in the wrong place.

While the police have been given the run-around (or not), the secret service agents have been keeping the real bank under surveillance, waiting to capture the thieves as soon as they come out with the MacGuffin. But the truck they stop is empty – a decoy – and the thieves have escaped another way. The Leader's suspicions were such that he had a Plan B for the getaway and didn't tell the Mole what it was. And now he keeps a tight rein on the Mole so he or she cannot contact the secret service agent and reveal the change of plan or the location of their new hideout.

The secret service agents panic at having lost the thieves and the MacGuffin.

In the hideout, the thieves may celebrate some more, divide up the loot that doesn't need to be fenced, and talk about what they are going to do with their share. Again, the Leader will advise them to spend it wisely and unobtrusively and again we know this isn't going to happen in at least one case. The two experts who were recruited to the team receive their payoffs and leave.

When only the core trusted gang members remain, the hero tells them about the Mole's involvement with the secret service agent. The gang are angry and shocked by this – and afraid because the secret service could just make them all 'disappear' if they catch up with them. The Mole explains why he/she had to do it and the others have some sympathy, but that doesn't solve their problem. What do they do now? The Mole says that if they hand over the MacGuffin, the secret service will let them keep the rest of the loot in payment. The Leader says he doesn't trust the secret service to keep their side of the bargain – especially since the thieves now know what the MacGuffin is.

Afraid of what might happen, one of the younger and less experienced thieves says he wants out – he wants to take his share of the cash and escape, before the 'spooks' close in on them and gun them down. He is the one who is likely to spend his money unwisely. The Leader lets him go, warning him to be careful and stay under the radar.

The bank heist is reported in the media – it is now public knowledge. Anyone with a safe deposit box in the bank knows they are potentially a victim of the robbery. This includes the Antagonist.

The Leader comes up with a plan to deal with the secret service – he gets the Mole to make a telephone call and arrange a meeting: it will take place in a public space with lots of witnesses so that the secret service cannot shoot anyone.

The secret service agrees to the meeting. They also take steps to take control of the police investigation into the bank robbery – they don't want the police to arrest the thieves until the MacGuffin has been recovered.

Sequence 6

The Antagonist learns of the robbery and becomes concerned because he had an incriminating item hidden in one of the safety deposit boxes in the vault, or he becomes interested in getting his hands on the loot which was stolen from a bank in his 'territory.'

Instead of allowing the Mole to meet the secret service agent, the Leader attends the rendezvous himself. He dictates terms – they will hand over the MacGuffin in exchange to safe passage to a Caribbean paradise and immunity from prosecution. The secret service agent agrees and the Leader tells him where and when their next meeting will take place – another public space.

The Antagonist learns the identity of one of the thieves – perhaps because the thief spends money unwisely as in the previous template examples. The thief is picked up by the Antagonist's henchmen. This raises the stakes, as it puts the Leader and the other thieves at risk. It also means that a situation is brewing that the Leader will have to handle on top of his dealings with the security service.

Sequence 7

The captured thief is tortured by the Antagonist and gives up the names of one or more of the other thieves or the location of their hideout. The Leader, aware that one of the crew is missing, has moved everyone and everything from the hideout. A message is left or sent, telling the Leader to contact the Antagonist.

The Leader or one of the other thieves contacts his wife or partner to let her know that he is safe. She guesses that he was involved in the heist that is in the news reports – she is angry and upset by this, but he tries to reassure her that things will turn out all right. He may or may not tell her that one of the crew has been kidnapped.

The Leader telephones the Antagonist and arranges to exchange the incriminating item or the loot for the captured gang member. The meeting will take place in broad daylight in a public place.

The Leader may have to choose between handing over the MacGuffin to the Antagonist or handing it over to the security service. To save the life of the kidnapped gang member, he decides to give it to the Antagonist. He needs some way of making sure that both he and the hostage can get away safely once the exchange has been made.

The security services or the Antagonist may murder one or more of the other gang members, probably the outside specialists who were recruited – the Leader may or may not be aware that they are dead.

Sequence 8

As in the earlier example, there are a number of possible outcomes for this plot and you have to choose what sort of ending you want to create. The ideal outcome for the Leader and his crew is to get the hostage back, get the police to arrest the Antagonist, give the security service the MacGuffin, and escape to paradise with the loot and new identities. If you want to create a happy ending, you will need to set things up so that the Leader achieves all of these things. For a tragic ending, he will achieve few or none of them and probably end up dead. Somewhere between these two are several partial victories.

As Sequence 8 opens, the Leader has arranged meetings with the secret service agent and the Antagonist and promised to hand over the same item to both of them. He may even have arranged for the two rendezvous to take place at the same time in the same location.

To deal with the Antagonist, the Leader may have tipped off the police that he is the person responsible for the bank robbery and that they will be able to pick him up as he meets a fence to pick up his cash at the appointed time in the public place. The Leader may even have a briefcase full of cash – perhaps counterfeit – for the 'fence' to hand over in exchange for the hostage.

To hand the MacGuffin to the secret service agent and the Antagonist, the Leader may have had a duplicate made to give to the Antagonist in exchange for the hostage. Perhaps the duplicate item is dropped and broken as it is handed over and the Antagonist quickly snatches up the microfilm without examining it too closely – particularly when he spots the police and/or secret service agents around the place. Of course, the Antagonist has to be punished for what he did to the hostage – perhaps he is hit by a car as he tries to get away and maybe that car is driven by the Leader's getaway driver.

These are all just suggestions – you would need to think up details of your own that would serve similar purposes.

9 | Burglars & Thieves

Cat burglars and jewel thieves usually work alone, or occasionally in pairs, and tend to commit their crimes without violence or explosives.

Historical Development
There is a long tradition of the 'gentleman burglar' going back to Victorian times. Rocambole was created by French author Pierre Alexis Ponson du Terrail, first appearing in *Les Drames de Paris* (1857, *The Dramas of Paris*). The character is a criminal who later in the series redeems himself and becomes a hero. There have been half-a-dozen French film adaptations (1914-1963) and a televisions series (1964-65) and a number of authors have written novels continuing the adventures of the character.

A.J. Raffles, the Amateur Cracksman, is a gentleman thief created by E.W. Hornung who first appeared in the short story 'The Ides of March' published in 1898. Hornung wrote a total of twenty-six short stories, two plays, and a novel about the character. The author acknowledged that Raffles and his fictional chronicler Harry 'Bunny' Manders were inspired by Sherlock Holmes and Dr. Watson. Raffles has appeared in a number of film versions and a British television movie (1975) and thirteen-episode series (1977) starring Anthony Valentine. A 2001 BBC TV movie *The Gentleman Thief* starred Nigel Havers. The adventures of the character have been continued by a number of authors and Graham Greene wrote a play *The Return of A. J. Raffles* (1975).

An early film featuring burglary is the 1903 five-minute short film *A Daring Daylight Burglary* directed by Frank S. Mottershaw. You should be able to find the film on YouTube and other places online.

Arsène Lupin was a gentleman thief and master of disguise created by French author Maurice Leblanc. He appeared in a series of short stories, the first being 'The Arrest of Arsène Lupin' published in 1905, and a number of novels and plays. The character has appeared in a number of film adaptations around the world, notably *Arsène Lupin* (1932) starring John and Lionel Barrymore and *Arsène Lupin* (2004) starring Romain Duris.

Hercule Flambeau is a jewel thief and master of disguise created by G.K. Chesterton and who appears in forty-eight of the Father Brown short stories, beginning with 'The Blue Cross' (originally published as 'Valentin Follows a Curious Trail,' in 1910). Flambeau is eventually reformed and adopts the role of detective.

A character often referred so alongside the above is Fantômas, a criminal genius created by French writers Marcel Allain and Pierre Souvestre. The character appeared in more than forty novels, the first being *Fantômas* (1911). Fantômas is no gentleman burglar and appears to be a sadistic sociopath. Three films – *Fantômas* (1964), *Fantômas se Déchaîne* (1965, *Fantômas Unleashed*), and *Fantômas contre Scotland Yard* (1967, *Fantômas Against Scotland Yard*) – directed by André Hunebelle and starring Jean Marais portray the character as a master of disguise engaged in James Bond villain style criminal conspiracies.

The following list includes popular and less well-known examples of films in the sub-genre.

To Catch a Thief (1925) by David Dodge is a novel about a retired cat burglar who has to catch an imposter in order to avoid being arrested for the crimes himself. It was filmed by Alfred Hitchcock in 1955 with Cary Grant as the thief and Grace Kelly in her last film appearance.

Diabolik is a long-running Italian comic book series created by sisters Angela Giussani and Luciana Giussani about an anti-hero thief who first appeared in 1962. Mario Bava directed a film adaptation *Danger: Diabolik* starring John Phillip Law. An animated TV series was broadcast by Fox Kids in Europe between 2000 and 2001 (40 episodes).

The Pink Panther (1953) directed by Blake Edwards was intended to be a light-hearted story about a gentleman thief, Sir Charles Lytton played by David Niven, until Peter Sellers performance as Inspector Clouseau stole the show. Niven had played the lead character in the film *Raffles* in 1939.

The Thomas Crown Affair (1968) starred Steve McQueen as a millionaire businessman who masterminds robberies as a game. He is investigated by an insurance investigator played by Faye Dunaway and the two become romantically involved during the course of their game of cat and mouse. It was remade in 1999 with Pierce Brosnan and Rene Russo in the lead roles.

The Thief Who Came to Dinner (1973) starring Ryan O'Neal is based on a 1971 novel by Terrence Lore Smith. The hero quits his job to become a jewel thief and blackmails a wealthy businessman into introducing him into the social world of the elite so that he can learn about potential targets. Warren Oates plays an insurance investigator who is pursuing the thief.

Entrapment (1999) was written by Ronald Bass and stars Sean Connery as a master thief and Catherine Zeta-Jones as the insurance investigator sent undercover to trap him.

In Japan, this type of character is referred to as *kaitō* meaning 'phantom thief'. One example is the 2016 Nippon TV series *The Phantom Thief Yamaneko*, based on the 2006 *Kaitō Tantei Yamaneko* (The Mysterious Thief Detective Yamaneko) series of manga novels by Manabu Kaminaga. *Magic Kaito* (1987) was a manga series written and illustrated by Gosho Aoyama that was adapted as anime TV specials and a 24-episode series in 2014. One of the earliest examples is the manga series *Lupin III* created by Monkey Punch (Kazuhiko Katō) which began in 1967 and features Arsène Lupin III, the grandson of Maurice Leblanc's original gentleman thief.

Genre Conventions

Suspense – in *Suspense Thriller* I said that the act of breaking into someone else's room or home is a situation that has suspense built into it by default. Even if the person doing the breaking and entering is a character that we *want* to see caught, we still empathise with their situation and worry whether they will get away with it. Anxiety related to 'getting caught' is something that we've all experienced – even if our transgression is nothing more serious than stealing cookies.

Conspiracy – As with the heist thriller that I wrote about in the last chapter, you can combine the burglary story with conspiracy thriller elements. The 1996 novel *Absolute Power* by David Baldacci is an example – it was filmed in 1997 with Clint Eastwood playing the jewel thief. The plot template that I gave in the previous chapter can be adapted for use with a single thief instead of a team of robbers. The 'Thief & Crime Boss' plot below could also incorporate conspiracy thriller elements.

MacGuffin – Sometimes an object that is stolen functions only as a thing of perceived value that various characters in a story want to get their hands on. The 'black bird' in *The Maltese Falcon* is a MacGuffin. In a burglary story, the thief may deliberately or inadvertently steal something that functions as a MacGuffin. Or maybe hired to steal the MacGuffin and then find himself pursued or targeted by others that want it.

Settings – As with most crime thrillers, burglary stories tend to occur in urban settings. They can also feature any of the settings I included in the heist story chapter. In the burglars and thieves sub-genre, settings tend to serve thematic functions. There are the places that the thief burgles which tend to fall into two categories – they are either the private home of an obscenely wealthy person, where the thief risks discovery by the homeowner; or they are a public place – a bank, museum, jewellery store, office building, or art gallery – that is accessed at a time when no one is supposed to be there. The thief is an intruder in either of these settings and this fact resonates with anyone who has ever sneaked into a place that they are not supposed to be or snooped around another person's house or office.

The hero's own home and any workshop space that he may have are usually significantly devoid of knick-knacks and personal items. It is utilitarian and contains nothing that isn't of practical use. This can be for one of two reasons – or a combination of both. First, the hero may have served time in prison and his home looks rather like a prison cell to reflect this. And second, the thief's life is such that he may have to up-sticks and move at a moment's notice. There cannot be anything to tie the thief to any particular place – no belongings or relationships that he is unable to walk away from without a backward glance. The less 'stuff' he has, the easy it is for him to move on.

The romantic co-protagonist's living space is probably in direct contrast to the thief's. It very much reflects her personality and is designed to be a comfortable 'nest' where she feels comfortable and safe. Its cosiness and many warm human touches are also in direct contrast to the coldness of the wealthy private houses that the thief burgles. The romantic co-protagonist's possessions probably have almost no monetary value but are filled with personal significance and value.

Iconography – First, there is the thief him or herself, dressed from head to foot in a tight-fitting black costume and soft-soled shoes, perhaps wearing a mask to hide their identity or to avoid pale skin being visible in the darkness. Black gloves to avoid leaving fingerprints – or perhaps latex gloves if delicate work is to be carried out. We see this figure climbing up the side of a building – with or without the aid of ropes – walking along high ledges and leaping from roof to roof.

The thief's equipment including lockpicks; glass-cutters and suction cups; a stethoscope to listen to the locking mechanism in a safe; perhaps explosives or a thermic lance to get into a vault; climbing ropes, harnesses and grappling hooks; crossbows that fire bolts carrying ropes and secure themselves in a distant wall; wires with crocodile clips used for overriding alarm systems; spray cans for making invisible laser 'trip-wires' visible, and various other bits of *Mission: Impossible*-style equipment. Plus there is often the thief's calling card.

There are the things designed to keep thieves out – safes and vaults; guard dogs; uniformed security guards; alarm systems with heat, pressure, and vibration sensors; automatic steel shutters, bars, and bullet-proof glass cases.

Finally, there are the things that thieves steal – traditionally cash and jewellery in velvet boxes or unmounted diamonds in wax paper envelopes. But also valuable artefacts such as Fabergé eggs or paintings by one of the masters. Real-life burglaries may target more obscure items such as rare books or stamps, but the value of these is less evident to a reader or viewer and they are probably best avoided – unless you can weave an interesting backstory for them similar to the one used in *The Maltese Falcon*.

Themes – Themes here tend to be very similar to those explored in the heist story. Stories tend to explore the difference between intrinsic and extrinsic value – meaning versus cost. People versus things. There is again the idea of the 'honest thief' – someone who openly admits that he steals from others – versus the 'covert thief' who pretends to be law-abiding but cheats his colleagues, lies on his tax return, inflates his business expenses, and cheats on his wife. And again there is the thrill of rebellion in contrast to dull conformity. Obviously, your hero can only be a sympathetic hero if the people or institutions he burgles in some way 'deserve' to be targeted.

Tone – Stories in this sub-genre tend to be on the humorous side. There is banter between the thief and the romantic co-protagonist like that in a romantic comedy and there is a sort of tongue-in-cheek quality about the dialogue between the thief and the investigator. This is balanced by more serious threats being made by the antagonist, whose propensity for violent outbursts can suddenly change the tone of a scene and help make the audience feel that the hero and/or people he cares about are really in jeopardy.

Characters

There are five or six main types of character in the burglary story: the thief, the investigator, the victim, the antagonist, the romantic co-protagonist, and (optionally) the thief's apprentice.

The Thief – He is generally the cynical and worldly-wise character we have already met in the private detective story and the leader of the gang of robbers who commit a heist. Even when he is a 'gentleman burglar' our thief-hero is a bit of a scoundrel.

The Investigator is either a police detective or an insurance investigator assigned to either the first burglary or a series of thefts which includes the first burglary that we see in the story. This character could also be a private eye hired by one of the victims of the burglar or by the antagonist.

The Victim – This is the person or organisation the thief steals from. Typically this is a faceless corporation or public institution that is covered by insurance or an obscenely wealthy individual who can easily afford the loss. In this type of story, if we want the reader or audience to side with the thief, we have to make the victim either faceless or deserving of the loss. We can also cast the victim in the role of antagonist.

The Antagonist is either a victim of the burglar or someone who has a grievance against, or comes into conflict with, the thief for another reason. He may be a crime boss who wants the thief to work for him or who is angry because the thief is committing burglaries on his 'turf.' Or he may be a corrupt cop or district attorney who expects the hero to give him a percentage of his loot to encourage him to look the other way.

The Romantic Co-Protagonist – This is the person that the thief is in love with before the story opens or some he meets early in the story. They are the person who makes the hero question his lone-wolf life and seriously consider settling down, hanging up the black mask for good. As we will see later, this character role can be combined with that of the investigator, antagonist, and/or victim. Or they may become an accomplice or apprentice.

The Apprentice – in some stories the thief takes on a protégé, usually a young and inexperienced thief who wants to learn how to be a professional burglar. This character may be present *instead* of a romantic co-protagonist, or *as well as*, or the two roles could be *combined*.

Reformed Thieves

Hornung's Raffles declined in popularity after he went 'straight' and tried to redeem himself, but other reformed thief characters have proved popular.

The Lone Wolf, alias Michael Lanyard, is a thief turned private detective in a series of novels by Louis Joseph Vance, the first of which was *The Lone Wolf* (1914). The American Film Institute Catalog notes that at least twenty-four films featuring the character were released between 1917 and 1949.

Jimmie Dale is a wealthy playboy by day and masked thief The Gray Seal by night. He was created by Canadian author Frank L. Packard in 1914 and appeared in five novels – beginning with *The Adventures of Jimmie Dale* – originally serialised in *People's Magazine*. Dale begins his break-ins for the thrill of it, never taking anything from his victims, but then he is 'found out' by a mysterious woman who blackmails him into using his skills to combat various criminals. The stories introduced many of the staples of the masked hero story including the secret identity, the secret hideout, and even a forerunner of Batman's utility belt. A 16-part silent movie serial *Jimmie Dale Alias the Gray Seal* was released in 1917

Simon Templar, alias The Saint, was created by Leslie Charteris who first appeared in the 1928 novel *Meet the Tiger*. The character appeared in fourteen novels, over a hundred short stories and novellas, and a number of film, radio, and television adaptations. Templar is often described as a 'Robin Hood-like criminal,' but in many of the novels, the Saint functions more or less as a private detective who targets powerful criminals and corrupt politicians, and sometimes he is more like a James Bond-style agent, though some of the short stories do feature elements of the confidence trick.

Modesty Blaise created by Peter O'Donnell was a newspaper comic strip that first appeared in 1963. The title character was a thief and freelance secret agent. O'Donnell also wrote a series of novels and short stories about the character who also appeared in films in 1966 and 2003 and a one-hour TV pilot in 1982.

T.H.E. Cat was a series that aired on NBC for one season of 26 episodes in 1966-67. Robert Loggia played the main character Thomas Hewitt Edward Cat, a former circus aerialist and former cat burglar who acts as a professional bodyguard, operating out of a nightclub the Casa del Gato. The show had a theme by Lalo Schifrin and a nice animated title sequence and *T.H.E. Cat* also featured in a number of Dell comic books.

The Thief as Detective

Somewhere between the gentleman thief and the reformed thief lies the thief-turned-investigator. In these stories, the thief-hero often finds himself accused of a crime he didn't commit and has to use a combination of detective skills and thief skills to identify the real culprit and prove his own innocence. *To Catch a Thief* (1925) by David Dodge is an early example.

My favourite example of this type of thief-hero appears in Lawrence Block's series featuring burglar and bookseller Bernie Rhodenbarr. The first in the series, *Burglars Can't Be Choosers* was published in 1977 and established the pattern for the series – Bernie breaks into a building and discovers a fresh corpse and seems set to be convicted as the killer unless he can prove that he didn't do it. The eleventh book in the series was published in 2013 and most of the novels feature a traditional murder mystery or private eyelike plot structure with a recurring cast of characters and a lot of witty dialogue and first-person narrative. A film (very) loosely based on the second novel, *Burglar in the Closet,* with Whoopie Goldberg playing Bernie, was released in 1987 and is best avoided.

David Baldacci's 1996 novel *Absolute Power* takes the burglar accused of murder idea and turns it into a much more thriller-like plot that also has elements of the political thriller. When the president's wife is killed while he is in the next room, the hero has to prove that he wasn't responsible. There was a 1997 film adaptation starring and directed by Clint Eastwood with a script by William Goldman.

In terms of plot structure, novels and films of this type use a typical investigation or thriller plot, and I have covered those in detail elsewhere. What distinguishes them is that it is the thief-hero's role as a burglar that gets him involved with the murder investigation or thriller conspiracy, and he uses some of his expertise as a thief to gain the evidence or to turn the tables on the conspirators.

The Thefts

There may be as many as four major thefts in this type of story and probably shouldn't be any fewer than two since seeing an expert thief at work is part of the appeal of this sub-genre. If a story requires that a thief commits a series of more than four burglaries, the additional ones can be indicated by montages of short scenes or parts of scenes, news reports, and other forms of precis. You don't want to bore your audience by showing too many burglaries. The four burglaries I suggest here are equivalent to the 'first actions' and 'three attempts' that I have outlined for other types of plot.

How these thefts are distributed throughout the story will determine the structure of the plot. You might choose to put them at the beginning, middle, or end of each quarter of the story. Or you might have one as the opening scene, another at the midpoint, and then the remaining two in sequences six and seven, six and eight, or seven and eight. The 'Cat & Mouse' plot template below features a typical arrangement.

The *first theft* is usually shown going off without a hitch – showing that our thief-hero is an expert. There are usually close-up details of him breaking in, disabling burglar alarms, opening the safe, etc. An exception would be if your thief is an amateur or new to the game, in which case his first break-in may be less than elegant and feature a few mishaps – *The Thief Who Came to Dinner* falls into this category. The first theft needs to be interesting in terms of visual elements and details, and must include elements of intrigue – who is this and what are they doing? – and suspense – will they get caught? – so that the reader or audience are drawn into the story.

The *second theft* probably goes reasonably well too – but there may be an unexpected problem when it comes to the getaway and we see the thief have to improvise an escape. This theft will often differ from the first in terms of methods used and/or building that the thief breaks into. This theft serves to establish a number of things. First, that in any burglary, there are circumstances that are beyond the thief's control; no matter how carefully he plans things, something can go wrong. Secondly, this helps to establish the risk involved in committing burglaries and this can be used to add tension to the story. And thirdly, it shows us that the thief-hero is coolheaded in a difficult situation and able to think on his feet to come up with an ingenious solution to a new problem. This theft's issue relating to the getaway foreshadows a similar problem that will occur – though on a larger scale – in the final burglary.

The *third theft* will include an unexpected problem of another sort, probably occurring *during* the theft – the sudden appearance of a security guard, policeman, or the unexpected return of the homeowner or businessman who owns the premises. The hero is almost caught red-handed and again has to keep a cool head and figure out how to get out of the situation – and preferably still get away with the loot. The third theft should be more daring than the second one but less than the fourth – you need to keep something in reserve for the climactic burglary. It will include more suspense and greater risk of being caught than the second theft. This risk of being caught by the appearance of an unexpected individual probably foreshadows a similar problem in the fourth burglary.

The *fourth and final theft* is a major set-piece that forms the climax of the story. It must be the biggest theft and occupy the most screen time or number of pages in a novel. It should involve more unique methods, perhaps including disguises and special equipment. The theft itself should be more daring and involve greater risk and the escape and getaway should be more difficult. There may be setbacks and unforeseen problems at each of the main stages, as seen on a lesser scale in earlier thefts. Here we see the sorts of things we've seen before – but with the dial turned up to the maximum.

The four thefts may each stand alone, or there may be some sort of thematic or plot-related link between them. It could be that items stolen during the first three burglaries are required to complete the fourth one. Or it could be more like a computer game where the thief has to complete each 'level' before he can move on to the next – either because he needs to gain certain forms of experience or because the proceeds from the first theft are needed to buy the equipment and information to commit the second, and so on.

To avoid making your multiple thefts seem too samey, you can have each focus on a different stage of the burglary process. The first one is a straightforward case of showing an expert (or amateur!) at work. Then the second could concentrate more on the planning process, the second on the commission of the burglary, and the third on the escape after the theft. The final theft will then bring all of these together for one last mega-theft. One theft could focus on what happens *inside* – disabling the alarm, opening the safe or other secure storage place, taking the valuable item(s), and getting out of the building. Another could concentrate on what happens *outside* – getting over a wall or fence, past security guards, dealing with patrol dogs, climbing a wall, avoiding external alarms and searchlights, opening a rooflight or door. And another could focus on the escape after the theft, including perhaps a car chase or ways in which the thief uses vehicles to avoid being caught – e.g. changing number plates, changing the appearance of the car, changing to a different car part-way through the escape, destroying the getaway car, etc.

Another way to add variety to the thefts is to have the thief target different sorts of premises – a private residence, an office building, a gallery or museum, a bank, a laboratory, a prison, or whatever.

Non-Fiction Resources

Two autobiographical accounts of the life of a thief that you might find useful are *Gentleman Thief: The Recollections of a Cat Burglar* (1995) by Peter Scott and *Confessions of a Master Jewel Thief* (2004) by Bill Mason with Lee Gruenfeld.

Richard Byrne's *Safecracking: Tales and Techniques of the Master Criminals* (1991) is an anecdotal history of safecracking up to the end of the 1960s, at which point the skilled manipulation of safe mechanisms had been almost totally replaced by brute force.

There are websites and books about most aspects of a burglar's work, including picking locks, circumventing alarm systems, and cracking safes – and you can buy lockpicks and 'learn how to pick a lock' kits on Amazon. While these are all freely obtainable in the USA, please make sure that it is not illegal to access them in your country.

The Thief as Hero

With a thief hero, you generally want the victims of his crimes to be either *deserving* of the loss or a faceless organisation so that no personal loss is incurred. And while thieves use the money they gain to pay their living expenses, thief-heroes are typically motivated by something other than greed. Many thieves in stories enjoy the thrill of breaking and entering – and could probably make more money by putting their skills and experience to more legitimate use.

Many thieves share the same rationalisation of their activities – the first time I came across it was in Harry Harrison's science fiction novel about a thief in the distant future, *The Stainless Steel Rat Saves the World*. The hero, James 'Slippery Jim' diGriz says: "Of all the varied forms of crime, bank robbery is the most satisfactory to both the individual and to society. The individual of course gets a lot of money, that goes without saying, and he benefits society by putting large amounts of cash back into circulation. The economy is stimulated, small businessmen prosper, people read about the crime with great interest, and the police have a chance to exercise their various skills. Good for all. Though I have heard foolish people complain that it hurts the bank. This is arrant nonsense. All banks are insured, so they lose nothing, while the sums involved are minuscule in the overall operation of the insuring firm, where the most that might happen is that a microscopically smaller dividend will be paid at the end of the year. Little enough price to pay for all the good caused."

Or we could use the argument proposed by French anarchist Pierre-Joseph Proudhon in his 1840 book *What is Property? Or, an Inquiry into the Principle of Right and of Government* – "Property is theft."

Theft of Works of Art & Antiquities

The ownership of works of art such as paintings or sculptures or ancient cultural artefacts can sometimes be a cause for argument. Many of the treasures that appear in western museums were recovered – some might say 'pilfered' – from the countries which originally created them. And during the Second World War, artworks were looted by the Nazis – something that has provided the basis for a number of film stories including the 1964 film *The Train*, starring Burt Lancaster, *The Monuments Men* (2014), and *Woman in Gold* (2015). This contested ownership status and the fact that even the majority of works of art that are legitimately purchased by museums are not seen as *personal* property makes them ideal targets for thieves in fiction.

Headhunters (2011) is a Norwegian film based on the 2008 thriller by Jo Nesbø about an art thief who quickly finds himself out of his depth when he targets an ex-mercenary (played by Nikolaj Coster-Waldau from *Game of Thrones*).

Museums and art galleries have proved popular targets for real-life and fictional thieves. Famous artworks such as the Mona Lisa and The Scream have been stolen – sometimes more than once – and there are a number of high-profile real-life thefts that might serve as inspiration for your fiction ones, including the theft of three paintings from the Kunsthalle Schirn in Frankfurt in 1994; the theft of thirteen works of art from Isabella Stewart Gardner Museum in 1990; the theft of nine paintings from the Musée Marmottan Monet in 1985; and the 1972 Montreal Museum of Fine Arts robbery, also known as the 'Skylight Caper', when eighteen paintings were taken along with figurines and jewellery.

Canadian art thief John Tillmann is thought to have been responsible for the theft of more than 10,000 objects from museums and galleries. He was arrested and convicted in 2013 and released from prison in 2016 – since that time has been working on his autobiography *Stealing the Past* which at the beginning of 2019 is listed as 'forthcoming.'

James Twining has written a series of novels about reformed art thief Tom Kirk beginning with *The Double Eagle* (2003).

The Burglar Story Plot Structure

Leaving aside the 'burglar as detective' sub-sub-genre, stories about thieves tend to follow one of two plots – either there is a cat and mouse game between a thief and an investigator or a thief is forced into committing a crime by some form of crime boss and seeks to outwit him. Although the execution of solo burglary sequences can be suspenseful and entertaining, the fact that they do not involve recruiting and training a team or extensive and detailed planning means that a burglary in and of itself probably isn't sufficient to provide the whole of a plot and its climax in the same way as a large scale confidence trick or a bank heist. The solo burglar usually finds himself involved in either a series of crimes that are being investigated by a character who serves as his opponent, or the thefts are part of a larger conspiracy.

The Cat & Mouse Plot

Sequence 1

Many burglary stories begin with a burglary. Someone dressed all in black demonstrates their skills as they break into a building – a private house, a museum, or a gallery – and steal one or more valuable items. The stages of the break-in and the expert techniques the burglar uses are typically shown or described in some detail. This is the first of three of four 'set-piece' thefts in the story – and this burglary typically occupies between a quarter and a half of the first sequence.

Depending on the needs of the story, the thief's face may or may not be shown. If you want to keep the identity of the thief a secret from the audience in a film, you can hide his features with a mask. In a novel you can simply avoid revealing his (or her) name – an may even conceal the burglar's gender – but you have more flexibility in describing all or part of the theft from their point of view, and can even use first-person narration if you are careful.

It is up to you whether you have your thief leave a 'calling card' as a signature at the scene of the theft – playing cards, business cards, chess pieces, and other items have been used so you may want to come up with something a little more original or unusual.

If you decide the reveal the identity of your thief-hero from the beginning, the second part of Sequence 1 will probably show him (or her) at home after the burglary – perhaps the next day. This is where we find out about the hero's personality, how he lives, and what main relationships he has. We may see the thief handing the stolen item(s) over to his fence – and this could provide an opportunity for dialogue about the hero's life. Or we may see him with his romantic co-protagonist. Or we may see a 'cute meet' that will be the beginning of a romance. With a romantic co-protagonist, you have to decide whether this character knows that the hero is a thief. In a new relationship, when the thief is flirting, he may jokingly or seriously tell the romantic co-protagonist that he/she is a thief, leaving them wondering if this is the truth – and the thrill of the idea and the thief's air of rebellious is something the co-protagonist finds attractive.

Alternatively, the later part of Sequence 1 could introduce the investigator – usually a police detective or an insurance investigator – who is investigating the current theft and possibly a series of similar ones that have happened in the recent past. There will be a cat and mouse relationship between thief and investigator throughout the rest of the story. You will need to decide whether your thief and investigator are already known to each other – you may want to show their relationship from their first encounter. The relationship between them may be similar to that in a 'buddy' movie like *48HRS* or the interaction between the thief and the detective in *Heat*.

If the two are *not* known to one another, you will introduce each of them separately – thief going about his normal daily activities and the investigator beginning his detective work on the case. If the two *are* acquainted, you can – if you wish – have the investigator pay the thief a 'friendly' visit. Typically, the relationship between these two is, or becomes, such that the investigator *knows* – or is almost certain that he knows – that the thief is guilty, but the investigator doesn't have enough evidence to arrest or convict. The relationship between Ryan O'Neal's thief and Warren Oates's investigator in *The Thief Who Came To Dinner* is a great example of this relationship. *The Thomas Crown Affair* and *Entrapment* take the relationship in different directions, with the investigator becoming the thief's romantic co-protagonist. Another take on the romantic burglar is the 1984 film *Thief of Hearts*.

If you choose not to reveal the identity of your thief, you can't show him or her at home, so the second part of Sequence 1 will probably focus on the investigator and/or the aftermath of the burglary.

In revealing your thief-hero's characteristics, you might want to show him engaged in other smaller thefts of crimes – a bit of pickpocketing or some form of short con (see the following chapter) – shown in a tongue-in-cheek way to demonstrate that your hero is a rogue but basically a good guy. You might also show him in some Robin Hood-like helping the underdog activity or giving to the poor. You will probably also want to give some hint that the hero's smart mouth occasionally gets him into trouble – this can foreshadow a complication later in the story when he says something that upsets someone who doesn't share his sense of humour.

Not every thief has a romantic co-protagonist – some of them gain a 'buddy' or business partner, often in the form of an apprentice or protégé. Examples include *The Real McCoy, The Score,* and *Breaking In*.

In summary, Sequence 1 can include a burglary, and introduce the thief and his life, the thief's romantic co-protagonist, and the investigator. If these aren't all in Sequence 1, some of them may appear in Sequence 2. The 'challenge' or turning point at the end of Sequence 1 is either that there is a burglary that needs investigating – allowing for the investigator to first appear in Sequence 2 – or that the investigator begins his investigation.

Sequence 2
If you are keeping the identity of your thief secret, you probably need to introduce one or more characters who *could* be the thief. You might want to treat these like the suspects in a whodunit. There will probably be someone who is the most obvious suspect, who serves as a red herring and leads the investigator up a blind alley, and another who is the 'least likely suspect' who does turn out to be the thief. Or they may be another red herring if the investigator decides being the least likely suspect makes them worth investigating – because investigators read whodunits too.

If Sequence 1 introduced the investigator, Sequence 2 will probably introduce a second source of antagonism – I will refer to this character as the antagonist, though the investigator is likely to be the main source of opposition for the thief. The antagonist is someone who was a victim of the thief and probably lost something that they want back, or they are someone who has a grievance against the thief for another reason – perhaps the thief committed a burglary on the antagonist's turf or the antagonist is a crooked cop trying to shake the thief down for a payoff.

There may be something about an item stolen by the thief that makes it especially important to the antagonist. The item may make his susceptible to blackmail or is something he was using to blackmail someone else. Or perhaps the item proves the antagonist or someone connected to him guilty of a serious crime. Or perhaps the antagonist was looking after the item for someone else and fears punishment for having lost it. Or the item may prove that the antagonist isn't who he is pretending to be. The thief may or may not be aware of the importance of the item he has stolen. This item means that there is something at stake for the antagonist – and it gives him a strong motivation for wanting it back and also, perhaps, for wanting to see the thief punished or even killed. The theft of the antagonist's item may have occurred during the burglary at the beginning of Sequence 1 or it may happen during a second theft in Sequence 2. Or it could have taken place during a burglary before the story opened. It may also have been taken by someone other than the thief, a copycat using the thief's *modus operandi* and perhaps his calling card, so that the thief gets blamed for something he didn't take. And may ultimately have to steal back to save his own neck.

The roles of the antagonist and investigator may be combined – the investigator may be someone the thief robbed, or the antagonist may hire the investigator. Or the roles of antagonist and romantic co-protagonist maybe combined – the romantic co-protagonist may be someone the thief robbed – in which case the antagonist-romance character may or may not know the identity of the thief. And we have already seen that the romance and investigator can be combined. It would probably be too much for the investigator, romance *and* antagonist to be combined in a single character.

With a separate investigator and antagonist, the two would both provide opposition to the thief. But since each has their own agenda, they might at different points in the story do things which advance the cause of the other – or act in opposition to it. That is, antagonist and investigator may help or hinder each other at different times. This also means that each may also inadvertently help or hinder the thief in his conflict with the other.

The romantic co-protagonist, as in any story, can assist the hero or provide opposition at different times.

Does a thief-hero need to have a *story objective* – a goal that he wishes to achieve by the end of the story? That is, something other than avoiding getting caught by the investigator and killed by the antagonist? I think it is necessary to establish the reason why the thief continues his life of crime. Things are likely to get dangerous and we need to give him a reason *not* to give up. He may be addicted to the thrill of burglary – to the extent that this is more important to him that the cash he gets from thieving. Or he may be saving up for his retirement – one more big 'score' and he's finished. Or several more to achieve the size of nest-egg he has decided that he needs. Or the thief, or someone he cares about, may have debts that the thief needs to pay off. He may be saving money for the education and future life of his child – he's usually estranged from the child's mother. He may also be *forced* into committing the crimes, but we'll look at that as a separate type of plot (below).

By the end of Sequence 2, we have two sources of opposition set up for the thief-hero – the investigator and the antagonist – or one character representing both these sources. The thief-hero may or may not know that the investigator and antagonist are pursuing him at this point. He probably learns of one source of opposition before the other.

Sequence 3

If your first major theft was shown at the beginning of Sequence 1, the second one will probably occur in the first half of Sequence 3. If the first theft occurred towards the end of Sequence 1 or beginning of Sequence 2, the second one may occur near the end of Sequence 3 or beginning of Sequence 4.

Where the first burglary went off without a hitch, there is usually some problem with the second one, as discussed in the section on *The Thefts* above. With the second theft, we are likely to see more of the planning stages – in contrast to the first one where we only saw its execution. We may also see the getaway if that wasn't part of the opening theft.

If there is a romance between the thief and another character, it will continue here. If the romantic co-protagonist is aware that the hero is a thief, she (or he) may play a small part in a theft as an accomplice – and be thrilled by the adventure of it. Perhaps they are the look-out, the getaway driver or a decoy. This theft is probably quite small and is an extension of their flirting rather than being one of the thief's major burglaries. Their scenes together may also include a discussion about trust and/or commitment – both things that the thief probably has difficulty with.

There will be some reminder of the presence and actions of the antagonist either late in Sequence 3 or early in the next sequence.

Sequence 4

If the investigator and the thief were not previously acquainted, they may encounter each other for the first time here. It is usually a fairly low-key meeting: the investigator is checking up on anyone who may be related to the location of the first or second crime and the thief's name is on the list along with dozens of others. If the romance is aware that the hero is a thief, she (or he) may be nervous about the investigator getting this close – but the thief just shrugs it off, being friendly towards the investigator and offering whatever help he can while making it appear he has nothing to hide – treating it in the casual way that an innocent person would.

The investigator will also speak to people connected with the thief – perhaps the fence, the romantic co-protagonist, the thief's ex-partner, or close friends. Nobody gives anything significant away, but the fact that the investigator has identified these people serves to increase the stakes for the thief as the investigator gets closer and closer.

The hero-thief may also do a little investigating of his own and discover a secret that the romantic co-protagonist is keeping from him – and which cause him to suspect that she could betray him.

Sequence 4 builds to the *midpoint*, which is either the third theft or a close call with the investigator – or both. At the midpoint, the investigator may realise or become convinced that the hero is the thief – but he doesn't yet have the necessary proof. He commits himself to obtain it and may try to trick the thief into confessing or giving himself up – but the thief calls his bluff. This moment confirms their relationship as opponents – the contest is now out in the open. We may also see that there is something at stake for the investigator – perhaps he will lose his job if he fails to catch the thief. Or perhaps the humiliation would be so bad that he would have to quit. Or perhaps he feels the need to prove himself to someone else – a boss, mentor, wife, father, or lover.

Sequence 5

Sequence 5 is typically the 'relationships sequence'. In the relationship between the thief-hero and his romantic co-protagonist, we may see a first argument or some jealousy relating to the hero's ex-wife or former partner. Or there is a growing feeling that things cannot go on as they are – either the romantic co-protagonist wants the hero to make more of a commitment, or the hero himself does. Perhaps he wants to quit his life of crime and begin a new life with this partner. If the thief has a platonic partner or 'buddy', there may some tension in the working relationship – perhaps because of something the apprentice partner wants to do and the hero doesn't. Perhaps the hero resents the younger thief trying to take on the role of alpha male.

If the thief or the romantic co-protagonist have been concealing their true identities or occupations, they may make a confession here. The other partner is likely to say something like 'I know' or 'I have a secret too.' This unburdening strengthens their relationship, demonstrating the early stages of a commitment, but hints of doubt still remain.

There will probably be a stronger reminder of the presence of the antagonist in this sequence – perhaps a direct confrontation – a further example of things stacking up against the hero. This intensifies the relationship between thief-hero and antagonist.

And having made what he considers to be an important discovery at the midpoint, the investigator now becomes obsessed with the hero, convinced that he is the thief. He follows the hero around. The thief may or may not be aware that he is being tailed – and may decide to ditch the investigator or lead him into some humiliating situation. This obsession may also raise the stakes for the investigator – he may be risking his career or his relationship, staking everything on proving that the hero is guilty. Any setback he receives at this stage only makes him more determined to 'get' the hero.

The hero and his partner begin discussions or planning for the fourth theft. They may engage in dialogue along the lines of 'one more big score and we get away to a new life in paradise.' The romantic co-protagonist may or may not believe this. The hero may or may not believe this.

Sequence 6

This sequence sets in motion everything that will occur in Act III (Sequences 7 & 8) – that is, it sets up the final confrontations with the investigator and the antagonist and also the final theft.

There may be a face-to-face confrontation with the antagonist in Sequence 6, where he says something along the lines of 'Give me what I want or I will kill you/your girlfriend/your child.' The hero may have to make some kind of counter-threat – or make a deal. He may promise the antagonist a payoff from the proceeds of the final theft. At the same time, the hero may put in motion plans to set-up the antagonist so that he is exposed as a crook and captured by the police or the investigator during the final theft. The antagonist deserves this because he resorted to threatening someone the hero cares about. This confrontation with the antagonist may be linked to the romantic co-protagonist's apparent betrayal of the hero at the end of Sequence 5 – either because she *is* in league with the antagonist or because she and the hero staged a falling out to protect her from the antagonist.

The investigator, meanwhile, may be increasingly confident of the hero's guilt or increasingly desperate to apprehend him. He may begin to engage in threatening or unlawful tactics – in *The Thief Who Came to Dinner* there is a nice scene where the investigator resorts to desperate measures and ends up humiliated.

In this sequence, there is often a demonstration or reiteration of the theme of the story. In *The Thief Who Came to Dinner,* the hero says that he wanted to be an honest thief, open about what he does, in contrast to those who are crooked but pretend not to be.

The investigator and the antagonist may meet in this sequence – perhaps for the first time. The investigator may propose a deal – they're both after the same man. If they work together, the antagonist can keep the money and the investigator will get the thief. The antagonist may or may not go for this. The antagonist may also inadvertently reveal some clue that is useful to the investigator – perhaps about the target for the final burglary. Or the investigator may reveal something that is useful to the antagonist.

During their discussion in Sequence 5, the thief-hero may have promised the romantic co-protagonist that he will go straight – he'll retire and they will start a new life in paradise. But then in Sequence 6 circumstances, in the form of the antagonist or a 'golden opportunity', mean that the hero wants to do one last big theft. The romantic co-protagonist may resign herself to this and may even agree to help him. Or she may decide to leave him.

At the end of Sequence 6 we see the thief-hero commit to the final theft and perhaps take the first actions to achieve it, providing proof of this commitment.

Sequence 7

You will have to decide whether you want your final big set-piece theft to occur in Sequence 7 or as the climax in the middle of Sequence 8. This will depend on how much story you have to tell *after* the burglar – how much of the aftermath and consequences you want to show. And also on whether this material is dramatic enough to sustain a whole sequence of your story without feeling anticlimactic.

One way to deal with this is to have your theft towards the end of Sequence 7 and then the getaway in Sequence 8. If you do this, you need to make sure Sequence 8 has other story points to reveal so that the getaway doesn't seem like a car chase that was just tacked on to spin out the story.

Another way to deal with it is to have Sequence 7 show the preparations and first moves in the theft, with Sequence 8 showing the rest. The movie *Entrapment* deals with it by having one theft at the end of Sequence 6, where the heroes obtain a valuable artefact, leading into the main theft at the beginning of Sequence 8.

The Thief Who Came to Dinner uses the more common approach. Sequence 7 shows preparations for the theft in a series of short scenes – the exact meanings of which aren't revealed to the audience. These serve to set things up that will be used during the theft and the getaway. Then the story goes straight into the burglary and escape.

With the final theft, you probably need to show all of the stages – initial idea, planning, perhaps some practising, getting specialist equipment, obtaining a getaway vehicle (or more than one), and working out how to escape if anything goes wrong and the police turn up. The early stages of this may begin as early as Sequence 7 – though it may not be made obvious to the audience that they *are* preparations for the final theft. Having said that, don't spend too much time showing things that the audience has already seen – if we've watched how the hero hot-wires a car in an earlier theft, you can get away with a very brief reference to his doing it in the final theft. Duplication of details will actually have the effect of boring your audience and slowing the pace of the story. The final stages of planning the burglary may occur as late as Sequence 8.

This final theft should be the most daring and the most complex. There are bound to be unforeseen circumstances – problems getting into the building; problems obtaining the valuable object(s); problems getting out, or problems with the getaway. Some or all of these can be used to increase jeopardy and create suspense. You should also include a ticking clock element if you can – 'If I'm not there by ten after midnight, leave without me.'

You also have to decide if the romantic co-protagonist is an accomplice, an obstacle, or an antagonist at this point in the story. You also need to consider whether the antagonist is involved in the final theft sequence in some way. Does it tie-up his subplot? And you have to decide whether the investigator is involved in any way. You might end one or two of these character relationship subplots in Sequence 7 and the other(s) in Sequence 8.

Sequence 8

Sequence 8 is either the whole of the theft, getaway, and aftermath or – if the theft occurred in whole or in part in Sequence 7 – it is the end of the getaway and/or the aftermath.

If the thief was injured as he escaped, he may get medical attention here or get fixed up by a friend or the romantic co-protagonist. The thief may hand the stolen item(s) over to his fence or to a pre-arranged buyer. There may also be a final encounter with the antagonist if that subplot wasn't tied-up in Sequence 7.

There will probably be a final encounter with the investigator, unless that was dealt with in Sequence 7. And even if it was, the investigator may make a surprise re-appearance here. As might the antagonist.

The outcome/future of the thief's relationship with the romantic co-protagonist will also be shown or hinted at here.

There may be a surprise twist in Sequence 8. Someone thought to be an enemy may be revealed as an ally – or an ally may prove to be an enemy. Be careful about having the investigator suddenly turn out to have been in on the thief's plan all along – that has been done a few too many times already. Try to come up with an original way of doing this – a twist on the twist – if you want to include it.

The Thief & The Crime Boss

This basic plot structure can also be used for a heist plot where the leader of a gang of thieves is coerced into committing a heist by a 'Mr. Big' type leader of a larger criminal gang.

Sequence 1

As with the first type of burglar story, this one typically opens with a theft – we see that the hero is an expert at what he does.

We then see the hero's ordinary life and learn something about his personality. He may have an ongoing romance or he may meet someone that he would like to have a romantic relationship with. But the nature of the hero's 'work' means that he is not able to be entirely truthful with this person and that is not a good basis for a relationship. As a result, the hero holds back from complete commitment to the relationship, and his partner is aware of this and probably not happy about it. This relationship is one of the things that makes the hero question his current lifestyle and makes him wonder how much longer he wants to be a lone-wolf criminal.

The hero may have another relationship – perhaps with a mentor character or a former partner – that also causes him to consider what he wants out of life. This older character may have been in and out of prison and have a string of broken relationships behind him – and this makes the hero wonder if he will end up just like his friend.

At some point during the first sequence, someone – perhaps the hero's mentor, his fence, or someone else – tells the hero that someone wants to meet him to discuss a business proposition. The hero says that he doesn't want to talk to them – he works for himself and chooses his own 'propositions' and he doesn't want to change that.

Sequence 2

We see more of the hero and his personal life. He may discuss his romance or some other aspects of his lifestyle with a mentor or 'wise woman' character – and the advice he receives is that you have to be honest with someone you love or the relationship will not survive.

Some incident causes the hero to speak with the Mr. Big character – perhaps someone has been following the hero, or Mr. Big's people do something to make life difficult for the hero or someone he cares about. Or Mr. Big may just turn up opposite him in a diner or sitting in the hero's living room. The hero is initially antagonistic towards Mr. Big – but the crime boss knows how to turn on the charm to get what he wants. Eventually, the hero agrees to hear him out.

Mr. Big wants the hero to work for him – but the hero says he prefers being his own boss. Mr. Big makes his pitch – he will provide inside information for each job, including blueprints and details about safes, alarms, etc., and he will bankroll the jobs. The hero will get an agreed fee for each job – and will make $X million within the year. He asks the hero to give it a try – do two or three jobs for him and see how it goes. The hero says he will think about it, though he's still not keen.

Up until this point, the hero has avoided the attention of the police, but his association with Mr. Big brings him to their attention. They wonder who the hero is and what his business with the crime boss entails.

Sequence 3

The situation between the hero and his romantic co-protagonist deteriorates further and they have some form of disagreement or the co-protagonist challenges the hero or issues some sort of ultimatum. Perhaps the co-protagonist thinks the hero is married and has been keeping this a secret – they are aware that the hero has been keeping something important secret. The hero decides to be completely honest and explains that he is a thief. The co-protagonist may react positively or negatively to this – either way, the co-protagonist is probably worried about the hero's safety. The two speak openly about their respective lives – their backstories, their fears, and their dreams for the future. And they discover that they have more in common than they ever expected – they are *meant* to be together. His co-protagonist will probably end up telling the hero that they will accept whatever decision the hero makes about his future. This forces him to face up to his dilemma – he has to decide one way or the other.

Deciding that he wants to have a life with this romantic co-protagonist, the hero decides that he will make some money and retire from thievery – and the quickest way for him to achieve this ambition is to accept Mr. Big's offer. He will work for Mr. Big for a short time to obtain the cash he needs to finance his new life.

Sequence 4

Mr. Big provides the details for the hero's first burglary under the new contract. The hero begins to put together the specialist equipment he needs for the job.

Believing that the hero must be involved in something shady with Mr. Big, a crooked cop shakes him down, saying he wants a cut of whatever the hero makes from his crimes. The hero says he has no idea what they are talking about. The cop says he's making a mistake – he could make life very difficult for the hero.

The fact that the hero has been honest with his romantic co-protagonist means that they can now be much closer to one another than before – this makes the hero happier, and people who know him comment on the positive change they can see in him. The hero may visit his mentor or 'wise woman' friend and thank them for the advice. The hero and the mentor may also talk about the crooked cop – discussing the fact that thieves are open and honest about being crooks, but crooked cops, judges, and lawyers all pretend they're clean and respectable – and this makes them worse. The mentor may be concerned about the deal the hero has made with Mr. Big – warns the hero that he doesn't know what he is getting into. And perhaps warns the hero that being an associate of Mr. Big may change his life in ways that he won't like.

The hero spends some time considering this. *Midpoint:* The hero decides that he will retire after this job – he doesn't need millions of dollars to start his new life – he'll take his fee for the current job and then quit.

Sequence 5
Sequence 5, which I have referred to as the 'relationships sequence,' focuses on the hero's relationship with his romantic co-protagonist and his relationship with Mr. Big. As the hero and his co-protagonist move in together and begin planning their future, they discover that the hero's past has certain consequences which mean that they cannot do things that ordinary couples do. It may be that the hero has a prison record or that he has no employment record and no history of paying taxes, and this may stand in the way of him buying a property or engaging in some other form of transaction. Or perhaps he just experiences some form of prejudice as a result of being an ex-con or known criminal. In the film *Thief*, the hero and his new wife are not able to adopt a child. Being prevented from having some aspect of what he considers to be a normal life makes the hero angry and upset. His co-protagonist tries to reassure him that this isn't important, but it is clear that they are upset too.

The hero discovers that he is being followed and, perhaps, that his home has been bugged. This is due to his acquaintance with Mr. Big and the fact that he refused to pay off the crooked cops. He speaks to Mr. Big, who says he'll deal with it. Mr. Big also knows about the problem the hero and his co-protagonist have been having. The hero is surprised that he knows about things going on in his private life – and for the first time, the hero realises the extent of Mr. Big's influence. Mr. Big says he will make the problem go away – the hero is now 'family' and he wants to help him. The hero realises that he is now part of a very different world – and this makes him nervous. What has he gotten himself into? He realises that his old life is gone forever.

Sequence 6
The hero's fears are allayed somewhat when Mr. Big is true to his word and makes whatever problem the hero and romantic co-protagonist were having go away.

The hero makes more plans and preparations for the burglary – all the pieces are now in place and he is ready to do the break-in.

The crooked cop hassles the hero again, saying whatever crime the thief is planning, he wants his cut. This time he makes threats and may even resort to violence. Or perhaps the cop has a new proposition – he wants the hero to betray Mr. Big. Either way, the hero refuses. He tells the cop he should go and have a criminal career of his own rather than leeching from 'honest' crooks. The cop tells the hero that he will be watching him closely – one wrong move and the hero will be behind bars.

On the eve of the burglary, the hero demonstrates his improvisational skills by eluding the policemen who are tracking him, leaving them in an awkward or embarrassing situation.

Sequence 7
The burglary – taking up two-thirds or three-quarters of the sequence. But when the hero comes to collect his fee, he discovers that Mr. Big will hand over only a fraction of it, maybe 10%, and will 'invest' the rest for the hero or hold it in trust. He doesn't want the hero to take the money and retire,

so he keeps the hero's money as leverage. Mr. Big starts telling the hero about his next job. The hero cuts him off – there will be no next job, the hero wants the money he is owed within twenty-four hours. Perhaps the hero threatens Mr. Big with a gun. Or punches Mr. Big's henchman and knocks him down. Or maybe he threatens to have a word with the police who are interested in Mr. Big's activities.

Later, the hero is ambushed by Mr. Big's men – perhaps beaten or maybe one of the hero's friends tries to intervene and is hurt or killed.

Sequence 8
The hero has made a mistake in threatening Mr. Big. Mr. Big explains to the hero that they are not partners – the hero doesn't get a say in what jobs they will or will not do. Mr. Big *owns* the hero now. If the hero doesn't co-operate, people the hero cares about will be killed. He tells the hero to be ready to carry out the next job.

The hero realises he was naïve and has made a deal with the devil. It will take decisive action on his part to extricate himself from this situation. And he must take steps to ensure the safety of his romantic co-protagonist in the meantime.

The hero uses his planning abilities and skills as a thief to come up with a way of defeating Mr. Big and getting the money he is owed.

10 | Confidence Tricks

A confidence trick aims to defraud an individual or group having first gained their trust. In his 1940 book *The Big Con: The Story of the Confidence Man*, David Maurer writes: "The *grift* has a gentle touch. It takes its toll from the verdant sucker by means of the skilled hand or the sharp wit. In this, it differs from all other forms of crime, and especially from the *heavy-rackets*. It never employs violence to separate the mark from his money. Of all the *grifters*, the confidence man is the aristocrat."

Confidence tricksters almost never use violence – their crimes rely on persuasion and deception, relying on quick wits and a way with words rather than weapons and threats. Cons usually target people who are hoping to get a 'good deal' or something for nothing and often have an element of delayed reaction – the trickster doesn't want the victim to even realise he or she has been conned until the trickster has gotten safely away.

The term 'confidence man' is thought to have been first used in the USA in 1849 in relation to the activities of William H. Thompson who was arrested in July of that year, but as we'll see, people have been conning each other since ancient times – it was just called something other than a confidence trick. A con is sometimes called a con, confidence game, confidence scheme, rip-off, scam, a grift, a hustle, a bunco, a diddle, a swindle, a flimflam, a gaffle or a bamboozle.

'Bunco' was originally a parlour game, called 'eight-dice cloth' in eighteenth-century England where it was popular, and which arrived in the USA in the 1850s. It became a popular gambling game and, inevitably, people cheated and took money from unwitting victims. The term 'bunco' came to be associated with any form of cheating or swindling and in the USA many police departments had 'bunco squads' to crack down on those involved in swindling the unwary. The modern-day equivalents of these squads deal with all forms of fraud – both *actual* fraud, such as selling something you don't own, and *constructive* fraud, such as selling something you do own but misrepresenting it to the seller. Confidence tricks may fall into either of these categories.

Where bank robberies account for the loss of less than $100 million per year in America, fraud of all kinds accounts for the loss of *billions* of dollars by individuals and organisations. There is internet and telephone and direct mail fraud; investment fraud, and insurance fraud; fraudulent business opportunities; fake health and beauty scams – especially for weight-loss and penis enlargement; there are phoney psychics and greedy preachers; imposters pretending to be related to the rich and famous or pretending to *be* the rich and famous; people pretending to have qualifications and experience they don't have or pretending to be employed in jobs that they don't have; paintings and other artworks are faked and sold; there are real estate cons; lonely-hearts are targeted by people wanting to capitalise on their vulnerability; widows and widowers are targeted by those who wish to take advantage of their grief; and then there are the usual gambling cons – cards, horse racing, sports, bar games – aimed at anyone who dreams of getting rich quickly.

Many real-life cons are targeted at vulnerable people such as senior citizens or are carried out via the internet. These are not the sort of things that make for a dramatic story. To draw an audience or reader in, we need a particular type of victim – one *deserving* misfortune – and a particular type of con – the 'long con' – both of which we'll explore in more detail below.

There are confidence tricksters who like to target other criminals and even other confidence tricksters. Conning their own kind is seen as requiring a special sort of skill and has the added appeal of proving the successful con man the best of the best. There have been real-life cases of con men being tricked out of the money they have scammed out of people – there is a certain poetic justice in that.

The Law and Confidence Tricksters

Investigations into the crimes of confidence tricksters often involve using their own techniques – lies, deceptions, and double-crosses – against them, within the confines of the law. Investigators may set up their own con games or may go undercover and play the role of a mark. Confidence tricksters have been caught because they revealed their whereabouts after being told they had won an item as a prize. And some investigations into scams targeted at senior citizens have used retired people as undercover 'victims' – there *has* to be a story in that idea!

In the USA, responsibility for investigating crimes of this type usually falls to a bunco squad or fraud team within a town or district's police department; at city or county level it is overseen by a district attorney, and at a state level by the attorney general. Certain types of crime are within the remit of particular agencies, including the Federal Communications Commission, the Secret Service, the FBI, the Federal Trade Commission, and many states have a Department of Insurance and Department of Real Estate.

There are a number of websites where you can find information on modern confidence tricks and the measures taken to combat con artists. The National Association of Bunco Investigators website (www.nabihq.org) has a section labelled 'Cons and Scams' that lists dozens of different techniques currently used to try and trick money from people. Advice on insurance-related fraud can be found via the National Insurance Crime Bureau (www.nicb.org). Resources relating to occupational fraud and its prevention can be found via the Association of Certified Fraud Examiners (www.acfe.com). You can also find information on the FBI website (www.fbi.gov) by searching for 'confidence tricks', 'scams', or 'fraud.'

The Appeal of the Confidence Trick Story

One reason that these stories appeal to us is that they show an expert at work – and that expert is something like a magician. His job is to trick people. In many stories we also get to see how the con man does it – we learn how the magic trick is performed.

The actual confidence tricks portrayed also often contain an element of poetic justice in that the victim is often shown as deserving to be conned and the trick itself tends to fit the crime this victim has been guilty of – it is specifically designed to target their weakness.

Many stories have unexpected twists to surprise the reader and some have a surprise ending – but the convention with the confidence trick story is to include an element such that the reader or viewer feels that they have been tricked or conned. This will involve a situation or a character not being what they appeared to be – and this is typically either a character who was seen to 'betray' the hero earlier in the story or someone who appears to be a law enforcement officer seeking to trap the hero but who is actually in on the con. Ideally, you want the reader to come away thinking that you, the author, are an expert at misdirection – a confidence trickster in your own right.

Confidence Tricks and Stories – The Author as Con Man

Human beings think and communicate in terms of stories – we seek a cause-and-effect relationship in order to try and make sense of the world around us, even when events are chaotic or random. We think in terms of chronological sequences – this happened and then that happened – but more often we try and find a reason behind events – this happened *because* that happened. This means that if someone presents us with a story that appears to have internal consistency – if it shows a logical cause and effect sequence – we feel comfortable in accepting this. And we are more likely to *believe* it than an apparently random set of events. Conspiracy theories capture the public imagination because they purport to explain events that defy logical explanation.

Fictional authors and confidence tricksters deal in stories – one stage in the confidence scheme, as we'll see later, is typically referred to as 'the tale.' It is a story to draw in the victim and make them believe that the con is true. As writers we create a fictional version of the world, people it with fictional characters, and then depict fictional events – and we try to convince our readers that these things are really happening. Trust me, I'm an author. Confidence tricksters do exactly the same thing.

In *Plot Basics* I said that one reason why stories appeal to us is because they provide us with an emotional experience. They make us *feel* something. Con artists also seek to reach their victims on an emotional level. All confidence tricks target some form of human weakness – greed, loneliness, lack of self-esteem, vanity, lust, grief – and appeal to the victim on an emotional level. The con artist wants to appeal to an emotional need, because this tends to be much stronger than a victim's rational understanding of a situation. Tell me something I *want* to hear, and I'll believe it. Early on in the confidence game, the trickster will appeal to the victim's emotional weakness in a gentle way, allowing the victim to convince themselves that this scheme is something that they want and *choose* to go for. Later in the con, other stronger techniques are used to evoke emotions, usually fear, that short-circuit the victim's rational thinking processes and allow the con artist to get away with the con.

Historical Development

Some writers suggest that the Devil, in the form of the serpent in the Garden of Eden, was the first confidence trickster. Trust me, I'm a snake. In the New Testament he is referred to as the 'Father of Lies'.

Susan Kuhlmann has said that a couple of early variations of the confidence trickster appear in Geoffrey Chaucer's *The Canterbury Tales* (1387-1400) in the Pardoner of the Pardoner's prologue and the Canon in The Canon's Yeoman's Tale.

One of the earliest and most detailed accounts of swindling is *The Book of Swindles*, also known as *A New Book for Foiling Swindlers, Based on Worldly Experience* written by Zhang Yingyu and published in China around 1617. It contains eighty-four short stories, classified by the method, perpetrator, or location of the swindle. An English edition of some of the stories, *The Book of Swindles: Selections from a Late Ming Collection*, translated by Christopher Rea and Bruce Rusk, was published by Columbia University Press in 2017.

The first use of the term 'confidence man' appears to be in the USA in 1849, but swindlers existed in literature and real life for centuries before that – the Trickster character has appeared in mythology and folklore throughout the ages and the picaro was the hero of a style of novels that originated in Spain in 1554 with the anonymously published *Lazarillo de Tormes*. Immediately before 1849, the term 'diddler' was used for scam artists, perhaps originating in the fictional character Jeremy Diddler in James Kenney's 1803 farce *Raising the Wind* – though the character may have been named after a word already in use. In the play, Jeremy Diddler is a fast-talking scoundrel who tricks a traveller out of the price of a breakfast and he does seem to have many of the characteristics of the more light-hearted con man. Herman Melville refers to the character by name in *The Confidence-Man: His Masquerade* (1857) and Edgar Allan Poe wrote a satirical article 'Diddling Considered as One of the Exact Sciences' published in the Philadelphia *Saturday Courier* for 14th October 1843. Poe's article was reproduced in a collection of items about diddlers and diddling compiled by A.E. Senter, *The Diddler* (1868), which also includes the text of Kenney's play.

Although there are some confidence tricksters in American literature, including several in the stories of Mark Twain, it is real-life con men who tend to be better known.

Famous Con Men
Wikipedia maintains a 'List of Con Artists' from the 17th century to the present day – among the best-known are:

William Chaloner (1650–1699) was a counterfeiter, con man, quack doctor, and dildo salesman who was eventually defeated by Sir Isaac Newton. *Newton and the Counterfeiter* by Thomas Levenson is a non-fiction account of the case.

Dr. David Theodosius Hines (1810-1864) was a swindler, bigamist and stealer of slaves who operated in the southern states of America and published two volumes of autobiography, the first being *The Life, Adventures and Opinions of Dr. David Theo. Hines of South Carolina* published in 1840. He appears to be the model for the southern swindler beloved of American writers.

William H. Thompson (1821-1856) was an American con man operating in the 1840s and is thought to have been the first person to be described in print as a 'confidence man.' Johannes Dietrich Bergman, in an article in *American Quarterly,* has suggested that Melville's *The Confidence-Man* was based on Thompson. But according to Braucher and Orbach, contemporary accounts reveal Thompson to have been a 'clumsy burglar' and 'unsophisticated swindler'. A farce titled *The Confidence Man,* designed to capitalise on the publicity surrounding Thompson's arrest was staged in July 1849.

William Miller set up a scheme in 1899 that promised investors 10% interest per week, earning him the nickname '520 Percent'. He defrauded investors of $1 million dollars. His scheme was similar to that of Charles Ponzi and pre-dated it, but it was Ponzi whose name became associated with this sort of con.

William 'Canada Bill' Jones (1837-1877) was a British-born con man, gambler and card sharp active in Canada and the United States. In Canada he perfected his skills at three-card monte and later he became a gambler on Mississippi riverboats, teaming up with George Devol, Holly Chappell and Tom Brown. Allan Pinkerton, founder of the famous detective agency, wrote about Jones in his reminiscences.

George C. Parker (1860–1936) was an American con man best known for his attempts to 'sell' the Brooklyn Bridge, the Statue of Liberty, and other landmarks in New York.

Fred and Charley Gondorf were brothers who operated in New York City and elsewhere during the late 1890s through to their arrests in the mid-1900s. They were poker players who also employed the wire and big store cons and are believed to have made $1 million a year. Their exploits inspired the film *The Sting*, in which Paul Newman's character is named Henry Gondorff.

Joseph 'Yellow Kid' Weil (1875–1976) became one of America's best-known confidence men as a result of his own account of his life of crime, in which he describes many of the cons that appear in the film *The Sting*. *'Yellow Kid' Weil: The Autobiography of America's Master Swindler* by J.R. 'Yellow Kid' Weil as told to W.T. Brannon was originally published in 1948 and reprinted as *Con Man: A Master Swindler's Own Story*.

Charles Ponzi (1882-1949) was an Italian-born con man who operated in Canada and the USA in the early 1920s. He operated a fraudulent investment scheme in which early investors are lured into the scheme by promises of high returns and then paid profits from the money taken from later investments – Peter is robbed to pay Paul – and investors are unaware that the scheme is producing no genuine return on investments. The high returns are such that the investor doesn't withdraw his funds and future profits are reported on paper only. This type of scheme was named after Ponzi due to his association with it, but it had been used before and is referred to by Charles Dickens in two of his novels of the mid-1800s.

Victor Lustig (1890–1947) was an Austro-Hungarian con man who was active in Europe and the United States. He is known as the 'the man who sold the Eiffel Tower twice' and also employed the 'Rumanian Box scam' which involved a 'machine' – a box about the size of a steamer trunk – he claimed could duplicate any currency placed into it. He would demonstrate the box 'copying' a bank note, though the output was a genuine note hidden in the box earlier, and then offer to sell the machine for anything up to a thousand dollars.

Natwarlal, real name Mithilesh Kumar Srivastava (1912-2009), was an Indian con man who 'sold' the Taj Mahal and other Indian landmarks including the Parliament House and its sitting members. He is said to have been a master of disguise and escaped from prison several times, the last time in 1996 at the age of 84 and in a wheelchair.

Ferdinand Waldo Demara Jr. (1921–1982) was an imposter who impersonated a ship's doctor, a sheriff's deputy, an assistant prison warden, a lawyer, and – on two occasions – a monk. Robert Crichton wrote two books about Demara, *The Great Impostor* (1959) and *The Rascal and the Road* (1961). In the 1961 movie *The Great Imposter*, Tony Curtis played Demara.

Frank William Abagnale Jr. (1948-) is a former con man and imposter. Leonardo DiCaprio played him in the Steven Spielberg movie based on Abagnale's book *Catch Me If You Can*.

Steven Jay Russell (1957-) is a confidence trickster who escaped from prison a number of times. Jim Carrey played him in the movie 2009 movie *I Love You Phillip Morris*, based on the book *I Love You Phillip Morris: A True Story of Life, Love, and Prison Breaks* by Steve McVicker.

Amy Reading's book *The Mark Inside: A Perfect Swindle, a Cunning Revenge, and a Small History of the Big Con* (2012) explores how Texas businessman J. Frank Norfleet, who was the victim of a stock market swindle in 1919, turned the tables on the con men and beat them at their own game.

Conmen in Movies

You Can't Cheat an Honest Man (1939). You can't have a chapter on con men without mentioning the legendary W.C. Fields. Fields played a variety of bumbling heroes who were never quite on the level. In *You Can't Cheat an Honest Man* he is circus owner Larsen E. Whipsnade who swindles his customers to try and stay ahead of his creditors. The plot doesn't revolve around a con as such, but you watch it to see Fields at work doing what he does best. The title of Fields' 1941 film *Never Give a Sucker an Even Break* sounds like it ought to be a story about a confidence trickster, but it is actually Fields' swansong and, perhaps, an attack on the Hollywood studio system disguised as a film.

The Lemon Drop Kid (1951) is a comedy based on a short story of the same name by Damon Runyon. Bob Hope plays a swindler, The Lemon Drop Kid, who unwittingly takes the cash of a notorious gangster and tries a variety of schemes to try and get the cash to pay him back. A 1934 film with the same title was closer to Runyon's story.

The Great Impostor (1961) stars Tony Curtis as the famous imposter Ferdinand Waldo Demara, based on the biography by Robert Crichton.

Bedtime Story (1964) starring David Niven and Marlon Brando was remade as *Dirty Rotten Scoundrels* (1988) with Steve Martin and Michael Caine, which has now been remade as *The Hustle* (2019, originally announced with the title *Nasty Women*) starring Rebel Wilson and Anne Hathaway. In the original, two conmen who prey on wealthy women engage in a wager to see who can be first to swindle $25,000 from a mark.

Paper Moon (1973) based on the novel *Addie Pray* by Joe David Brown stars Ryan O'Neal as a con man with Tatum O'Neal playing his eight-year-old daughter, who proves to be her father's match as a swindler.

The Sting (1973) The screenplay by David S. Ward was inspired by real-life cons carried out by brothers Fred and Charley Gondorf and other swindlers of the late 1800s and early 1900s.

House of Games (1987) written and directed by David Mamet tells of a female psychiatrist who is drawn into the world of confidence tricksters and persuades a successful swindler to teach her how cons are worked so that she can write a book on the subject – he sees this as an opportunity to cheat her out of a large sum of money. Mamet returned to the world of con men with the 1997 film *The Spanish Prisoner*. The 'Spanish Prisoner' is a real-life confidence trick that originated in the 19th century in which someone pretends to be a wealthy aristocrat in hiding and obtains money from the mark on the promise of a reward when the aristocrat is returned to the rightful position. In Mamet's film, several of the characters are not who they seem.

The Grifters (1990) is based on the 1963 novel by Jim Thompson and has a screenplay by Donald E. Westlake. It tells the story of con artist Roy Dillon who faces the greatest challenge of his life in the form of another grifter – his own mother.

Catch Me If You Can (2002) directed by Steven Spielberg stars Leonardo DiCaprio as famous imposter Frank W. Abagnale Jr. and Tom Hanks as the FBI agent who pursues him. It is based on the 1980 book by Abagnale and Stan Redding.

Matchstick Men (2003) directed by Ridley Scott, is based on Eric Garcia's 2002 novel. The lives of two conmen are disrupted when one learns that he has a teenage daughter. Her unexpected arrival causes him to question his life choices, but she decides she wants to learn the family business.

Confidence (2003) Written by Doug Jung, the story follows a gang of con men who accidentally take the money of a Los Angeles crime boss The King (played by Dustin Hoffman) and agree to mount a scam to earn the money back for him.

Television Conmen

Hustle ran for eight seasons (forty-eight episodes) from 2004 to 2012 and featured Robert Vaughn as the leader of a group of confidence tricksters specialising in the more elaborate 'long cons.'

Leverage ran for five seasons (seventy-seven episodes) from 2008 to 2012 with Timothy Hutton as the leader of a team consisting of a thief, con artist, hacker and 'retrieval specialist' who specialise in righting wrongs by targeting those who seem to be beyond the law.

White Collar ran for six seasons (eighty-one episodes) from 2009 to 2014 and starred Matt Bomer as con artist, forger and thief Neal Caffrey.

Characters

Because confidence trick stories tend to lack large-scale violence and physical action, what the characters do and *why* they do it are more important than in other types of crime thriller. The reader or viewer is interested in understanding the psychology and personalities of the confidence trickster and the victim. At the simplest level, they will want to see the confidence trickster as representing their own rebellious, non-conformist side and they will want to regard themselves as superior to the victim in terms of moral standards and gullibility or overreaching ambition.

The best book I've seen on the psychology of confidence tricksters and their victims is Maria Konnikova's *The Confidence Game* (2016). It takes the various stages of the con game and uses modern research to explore why people think and behave as they do – and why people fall for cons even when they think they won't.

Hero – The Con Man or Confidence Trickster

Edgar Allan Poe's description of the 'diddler' captures many of the qualities of the hero. He is 'guided by self-interest' and is '...ingenious. He has constructiveness large. He understands plot.' He is also '...audacious. He is a bold man...' and '...nonchalant. He is not at all nervous ... He is never seduced into a flurry ... He is cool – cool as a cucumber.' Poe also said that the 'diddler' '...is original – conscientiously so. His thoughts are his own...' and '...impertinent. He swaggers... He sneers in your face... He eats your dinner, he drinks your wine, he borrows your money, he pulls your nose, he kicks your poodle, and he kisses your wife.' And to cap it all, the '...*true* diddler winds up all with a grin. But nobody sees it but himself...' because a diddle '...would be *no* diddle without a grin.' If there seems a hint of bitterness in Poe's description, it may be because he regarded his own creditors as 'diddlers.'

Maria Konnikova says that the con man looks at other people with the kind of attention to detail that most of us only use on ourselves. When we engage with other people, we mostly judge by surface appearances and rely on generalities and stereotypes to 'understand' the people around us. Our brains like short-cuts. Con artists seek a deeper understanding of the person they are targeting – and then they use that understanding to manipulate that person and to gain their confidence. Most of us don't realise how much information we give away about ourselves in ordinary everyday interactions. Con artists gather up that information and put together a picture of the person they are dealing with. The con artist finds out what their victim is like and then behaves in a way that makes the victim think that they have so much in common with them that they can be trusted. How does the con man do this? He uses pretty much the same techniques Dale Carnegie outlined in his 1936 book *How to Win Friends and Influence People*. "Be a patient listener," said 'Count' Victor Lustig, "it is this, not fast talking, that gets a con man his coups."

Gaining the victim's *confidence*, their trust, is vital to the confidence trickster. When we trust someone, we let down our guard and do not feel the need to analyse what they are doing or saying too closely because we do not perceive them as a threat. Throughout the con, until just before the end, the con man makes the victim feel that they are the one in control, the one making the decisions – that they are *choosing* to participate in the scheme.

Some writers, including Susan Kuhlmann, have noted similarities between the confidence trickster and more legitimate occupations including the preacher, as Chaucer showed, the politician, and the businessman – especially the investment banker and the advertising salesman.

Kuhlmann refers to the con man as being self-assured, self-confident, self-knowing but also, possibly, self-deluded. She also says that he is a 'master of self-dramatisation.'

The Personality & Psychology of the Con Artist

The con man believes that he is part of a criminal elite, that he belongs to a different class of crooks to those who use violence. His crimes rely on intelligence, improvisational skills, and experience so he sees himself as a specialist. This belief arises out of egotism and means that investigators or other opponents may use his pride against him – issuing a challenge to draw him out.

His egotism is also demonstrated by his self-confidence – he believes he is smart enough to pull off the con and his scheme is so good that the victim probably won't even report it to the authorities. And even if he was to be caught, he knows that the legal system often doesn't prioritise prosecution and punishment of those involved in non-violent crimes, so he'll either get away scot-free or with a light prison sentence.

There is an element of the rebel in the con artist's character – he is a non-conformist who doesn't like rules. It has been said that con men don't like hard work and so turn to crime instead, but that's not strictly true – any of the long cons involve a great deal of time, planning, and preparation. What the con man doesn't like is having a nine-to-five job where he is not in command of his own destiny.

The con man's rebellious nature and self-confidence probably account, at least in part, for the fact that he is seen as charming and attractive. A person who knows who he is and isn't afraid to go after what he wants can be very attractive. The con artist often lures in his victim by appearing to be the sort of person the victim would like to be or would like to be seen to be associated with. And the con man's skills allow him to *appear* to be just about anybody.

A paradox that seems to lie at the heart of the confidence trickster is that while he has no empathy and little sympathy for the victim of his con, he also has a deep understanding of human nature and motivation and seems to have a finely tuned ability to read other people's minds. This is achieved by his close observation of others.

The con artist isn't necessarily motivated by greed – he doesn't do it just for the money. He enjoys the challenge of pitting his wits against the victim and the thrill that comes from the risk of getting caught.

One characteristic that does mark the con artist out as special is the way in which they are able to treat their victims. Con men seem to lack conscience and feelings of remorse. They have no empathy with the victim and no concern for the consequences of their actions. They also rationalise their work by saying that anyone stupid enough to fall for a con *deserves* to be conned. Or that it is the nature of the wolf to prey upon sheep. Con artists do not regard the victim as an individual with their own hopes and fears, they are simply a player in the game in the position of 'the mark.'

Fay Faron goes as far as suggesting that confidence tricksters suffer from antisocial personality disorder – formerly described as sociopathic – and became this way because of a lack of bonding with their parents. While this may be true of some con artists – particularly those in real-life who prey on the weakest and most vulnerable members of society – I don't think it can be applied to all con men and almost certainly not to those that are the heroes of a confidence trick story. But it is a feature of the con man's character that he cannot form many long-term relationships and has to be prepared to move on. One 'rule' of the confidence game that is sometimes quoted is that you cannot have anything or anyone in your life that you can't walk away from in a second.

I wrote about psychopaths (the most extreme form of antisocial behaviour) and about anti-heroes in *Character Creation*. There is a chapter in that book about creating the 'rebel hero' that I think applies to the sort of character you need to create for a con man (or woman) story. I also referred to the 'dark triad' of personality traits, and Maria Konnikova writes about these in her book *The Confidence Game*. The dark triad consists of psychopathy, narcissism, and Machiavellianism. Psychopathy relates to a lack of empathy and remorse; narcissism to feelings of grandiosity, entitlement, and manipulation of others to get what you want, and Machiavellianism relates to a person's ability and willingness to deceive others for personal gain. Obviously all of these, to some degree or other, relate to our confidence trickster, but – as Konnikova says – the one that seems of most relevance is Machiavellianism.

Niccolò Machiavelli (1469-1527) was an Italian diplomat and philosopher best known for *The Prince* (1513), a text on politics and statecraft. The pragmatic advice he gives is often regarded as ruthless and immoral, such that his name became synonymous with cunning, scheming and unscrupulousness.

Richard Christie and Florence L. Geis created a twenty-statement personality survey to assess a person's level of Machiavellianism. Published in 1970, it is referred to as the Mach-IV test and scores people on a scale of High Machs to Low Machs. If you fancy taking the test yourself (it takes only a few minutes) you can find it online here:
https://openpsychometrics.org/tests/MACH-IV/

According to Jones & Paulhus, Machiavellianism is a duplicitous interpersonal style arising from cynical beliefs and pragmatic morality or even amorality. High Machs are motivated by cold selfishness and pure instrumentality. They give high priority to money, power, and competition and lower priority to community-building, self-love, and family concerns. They tend to focus on achievement and winning at any cost. There is no data to support the suggestion that High Machs have superior mental abilities and they score low in empathy and emotional intelligence. Jones & Paulhus also note that High Machs "...thrive when they have more decision power, fewer rules, and less managerial supervision." They prefer to have 'latitude for improvisation' and "...remain cool, exploit interpersonal relationships, bend the rules, and improvise." They are also adept in face to face interactions. Tactics used by High Machs to manipulate others include persuasion, especially indirect persuasion, selective self-disclosure, deceit, guilt induction, and ingratiation. They also use friendliness and emotional tactics, while remaining emotionally detached from a situation. High Machs lie by commission and omission and are more likely to break promises or contracts they have made. High Machs are also likely to cheat and betray others, especially if there is little chance of being caught or punished. Their cool demeanour means that High Machs are not prone to violence. High Machs may manipulate others for short-term gain or engage in longer-term manipulative strategies in order to make some gain in the future.

Jones & Paulhus write that Machiavellianism may have evolutionary benefits: "The natural selection of selfishness would naturally foster Machiavellian personalities. In ancestral times, those who exploited opportunities to cheat, steal, and manipulate others to achieve their goals would have out-reproduced those who did not. Indeed, this adaptive advantage has been referred to in the literature as Machiavellian intelligence." This evolutionary advantage only applies if there are a relatively small number of High Mechs in a community – too many, and they would all be preying on each other and the advantage would be lost.

Studies have suggested that higher levels of Machiavellianism may be caused by socialisation mechanisms including parental modelling and reaction to a harsh or unpredictable family environment.

High Machs are more likely to be chosen as leaders but people are less likely to want them as friends, confidants, or business partners. There is also evidence that people are uncomfortable dealing with High Machs over a long period of time.

There is a tendency to regard Machiavellianism as a negative trait and associate it with cheating and misusing other people, but it is worth bearing in mind that *cunning* is often seen as a positive trait in folklore and stories. We enjoy seeing the underdog outwitting a stronger and more powerful opponent, using ingenuity rather than brute strength to win.

Types of Con Man

Duane Swierczynski identifies five types of confidence trickster:

The Grifter – Involved in small cons only. An example is the hero of Jim Thompson's novel *The Grifters* and the 1990 movie adaptation who engages in short-changing or 'twenties', betting on a coin toss using a coin that is smooth on one side ('smack'), and betting on the rolling of rigged dice ('tat').

The Imposter – Pretending to be someone you're not is a part of most cons, but imposters assume the identity of another person or claim to be a member of a particular profession. Frank W. Abagnale (*Catch Me If You Can*) and Ferdinand Waldo Demara Jr. (*The Great Imposter*) are examples.

The Insider – This is someone who works inside a company or organisation with the intention of defrauding it and includes embezzlers. Many long or big cons require an inside man, someone with access to materials or information or technology required to pull it off.

The Ordinary Guy – A next-door neighbour, family member, or potential lover who befriends the victim and becomes a part of their life.

The Businessman – Offers business or investment opportunities designed to defraud individuals or organisations – often involved in the long or big con.

Victim – Marks, Suckers, Stooges, Mugs, Rubes & Gulls

Some cons target individuals and some target institutions or businesses – in the latter case, the corporate entity or group will be represented in the story by one or two identifiable individuals, often the equivalent of a villain and his henchman or a leader and his advisor.

The person or group targeted is referred to as the 'mark'. It is often said that 'you can't cheat an honest man,' but I think this is an argument that originated with swindlers who wanted to believe that their 'marks' deserved to be conned. If you look at the various telephone and internet scams that have surfaced in the last decade or so, many of them target vulnerable groups, especially senior citizens, rather than dishonest ones. Confidence tricks exploit the credulity ('gull' comes from gullibility), naïveté, and compassion of vulnerable groups. At the next level are those marks who *ought* to know better but are caught out by scams that exploit their vanity or irresponsibility. And then, finally, there are the 'victims' whose own greed makes them vulnerable. Obviously, if your hero is a con man, you want his victim to be at least as dishonest as he is and preferably more so. The best con man stories have marks who deserve to be conned because they are all-round bad people and greedy as well.

The term 'mark' is thought to have originated from an actual chalk mark placed on a person's back by a crooked carnival game operator to signal to other operators that the person was gullible and likely to fall for other crooked games.

Con men play on common human vulnerabilities – greed, vanity, loneliness, compassion, and low self-esteem. They also exploit the fact that we are more likely to trust someone who we perceive as being like us – they will wait for us to reveal our political or religious beliefs and will then appear to have the same views themselves. Their attitudes towards the opposite sex and minority groups will also be a reflection of the victim's. They rely on the stereotypes we have for people who are trustworthy and people who are shady. They know we are naturally suspicious of strangers and outsiders, so they will also appear to be from our own socio-economic, religious, and ethnic groups.

Confidence tricksters also exploit the fact that we typically seek instant gratification, which is why the short or small con offers immediate rewards. Confidence tricks also exploit our fear of missing an opportunity and so typically involve scarcity – only a few left at this 'price' or only limited spaces available – and deadlines – 'offer expires this weekend.' And if these tactics seem similar to those used in advertising, that isn't a coincidence – marketing too exploits human psychology. The only way to avoid being caught out by a scam is to be sceptical. We are told this over and over again, and yet we still fall for scams – 'If something sounds too good to be true, then it probably is.'

Types of Victim

Victims with different types of personality traits are vulnerable to different types of confidence trick.

Greedy – This is the person who is a bargain hunter or who wants something for nothing – and this makes them susceptible to many scams. They're people who might buy goods at a low price without asking questions about their provenance and this makes them ideal victims for block hustles. They can also be scammed on 'good deal' for services such as car or home repairs. And they may be targets for investment scams.

Gambler – Someone who feels that one day their luck will change and they'll never need to work again. They will risk all they have – and perhaps more – on a 'sure' bet. They're the ideal target for three-card monte and hustles relating to sports and games of skill or chance.

Desperate or Needy – These people make ideal victims for phoney healers and psychics – they effectively select themselves as potential victims; for health and beauty scams, and for sweetheart scams. They also fall for TV evangelists and cults, and for retirement and pet-related scams. Lonely senior citizens fall into this category and are the targets for around 60% of real-life scams. Also in this group are those who are sick or in pain and who are targeted by 'snake oil' medicines and faith healers. And people who suffer from low self-esteem are targeted by health and beauty scams.

Good Samaritan – These are people who always want to help those who are in need – and who naïvely believe that all charity cases are genuine. This sort of person always plays by the rules and believes that other people do as well. This makes them susceptible to charity scams, short-changing, and scam business opportunities. They are also ripe for a bait-and-switch scam. The fact that this sort of person often has a good credit record means they are an ideal target for identity theft.

Small Businesses – These don't have experienced legal and accounts departments to look out for them and so are at risk from machine or building repair or servicing scams; bogus tax experts or inspectors; fake invoices; short-changing; insurance fraud; delivery of good that haven't been ordered; and 'slamming' – unauthorised changing of telephone, utility, credit card processing or other services.

Naïfs – There is an element of naïveté in all victims of scams in that they haven't been cynical or sceptical enough. But there are some groups who are more unwary than others. Young adults, especially those from relatively well-to-do backgrounds, typically haven't had the sorts of experiences that make them cynical. Immigrants and new arrivals don't understand local customs yet and so are susceptible to scams – 'this is how we do things here' – especially if the scammer appears trustworthy or is an official of some kind. Many people come from cultures where bribes, kickbacks, or 'protection' payments are normal and can be tricked into paying them in their adopted country. Senior citizens also tend to be more trusting and they too are often taken in by people who look trustworthy or have an 'official' status. These unsuspecting types can fall victim to block hustles, sweetheart scams, vehicle or home repair scams, telemarketing scams, fake investment or business opportunities, and the block hustle.

People who fall victim to confidence tricks are not necessarily stupid, naïve, or gullible – sometimes they just overestimate their own abilities. "The surest way to be deceived," said François, Duc de La Rochefoucauld, "is to consider oneself cleverer than others." This is the sort of person we often see in confidence trick stories – the over-confident victim who deserves to be taught a lesson.

Allies – The Shill and the Roper
The hero's allies are people who do not appear to be directly associated with the hero. The roper is someone who goes out and finds the victim and steers him towards the con man, perhaps vouching for the hero's legitimacy or dropping intriguing hints about the hero's 'sure-fire' scheme. The roper may test the victim's gullibility by use of some form of short con before introducing him to the hero – this may help determine what type of victim he or she is – and so what type of con they will be most vulnerable to.

The shill is someone who pretends to be a happy customer of the hero's scheme in order to give it legitimacy in the eyes of the victim. The shill appears to be an independent reviewer, but is really in the hero's team. In short cons, the shill will often be seen to bet money and win to 'prove' to the watching victim that it *is* possible to win – though, of course, the hero allows the shill to win.

Mentor
The confidence trickster hero often learns his trade from a mentor, either as his apprentice on the street or during a term in prison.

Opposition
Like all stories, capers and heists need to show the hero facing some form of opposition. Possible sources include:

- the 'mark' or victim. While unaware that he is being targeted, he may do things that interfere with the hero's plans. There is also an ongoing risk that this character may discover what the hero is up to.
- there may be a Mr. Big who set up the crime or bankrolled it – or simply believes that he deserves a cut. He might also demand that the hero does things his way, even though the hero may have a better plan.
- the police or other law enforcement or security people going about their lawful duties.
- the crooked cop who is only out for personal gain and who needs to be paid off to ensure he turns a blind eye to the criminals' activities. May be untrustworthy and may betray the hero even after being paid off.
- an outsider placed in the team to represent someone else's interests, usually someone working for the Mr. Big character.
- an amateur or rookie who wants to be part of the action or to learn how to carry out a con.
- an undercover cop in the team.
- a betrayer – one of the criminals who sells out his colleagues to the police or to the villain.
- a rival within the team who challenges the leader's authority and wants to be in charge himself.

Some of the above may be combined. For example, the outsider may be an amateur who wants to learn how to be a conman or burglar; or he may be someone who feels that he should be in charge.

Romantic Co-Protagonist

As in any story, a romantic co-protagonist can serve as an ally and a source of opposition. They may be threatened or kidnapped by the opposition. They may be persuaded into betraying the hero – or *appearing* to betray them. They may be someone on the inside who has access or expertise that enables the con to be carried out. Or they may be on hand to distract the victim by flirting outrageously or pretending to be attracted to them.

In the 'sweetheart scam' the whole conspiracy revolves around a deceptive romance in which the hero may be the romantic co-protagonist of the victim, or in which someone has to be recruited by the hero to play the part of a romantic co-protagonist.

Conspiracy & MacGuffin

The conspiracy in this sort of story is the confidence trick itself – a non-violent criminal scheme to obtain money or some other thing of value from an unsuspecting victim. Some cons also involve a MacGuffin – a special piece of apparatus such as a machine that can (apparently) duplicate bank notes.

Suspense

In a confidence trick story, there is built-in suspense related to the risk of being *found out* – and the hero often faces risk from a variety of sources including the victim, law enforcement, and perhaps a 'Mr. Big' who is directing and/or bankrolling the crime.

Stakes

In this type of story, there needs to be more at stake than 'does the hero get the money or not?' And often we see that the money is of limited importance to the con man – he is more concerned with outwitting the victim, of proving that he is better than this person. There is also typically an element of justice or vengeance involved in targeting this particular victim. The victim is guilty of some crime and may appear to have escaped justice – the con is designed to restore the balance by punishing them in a non-violent and usually 'poetic' way.

There also has to be something at stake for the victim beyond the loss of a sum of money. The situation of the con has to be such that at the end, after they have been scammed, the victim cannot go to the authorities for help – either because it would mean admitting their own part in an illegal scheme or because it would damage their reputation by making them appear foolish or incompetent.

Settings & Iconography

The locations typically seen in confidence trick stories reflect the origins of such crime in early twentieth-century America. Locations associated with gambling are often seen – racetracks, boxing rings, casinos, betting parlours and also poolhalls and bars. In the long con, a fake office or betting parlour is often constructed to fool the victim, making them believe they are dealing with a legitimate enterprise.

Cons also have a historical connection with carnivals and these are also shown along with street cons like three-card monte. Imposters and assumed identities play a role in confidence tricks and so changes of costume and the wearing of disguises are often seen.

Confidence Trick Lingo
Like any area of expert knowledge, the confidence trick has its own vocabulary or lingo, a subset of what is sometimes referred to as criminal argot. The words used are often designed to obscure the truth – both to confuse outsiders and to provide emotional distance between the confidence trickster and the people he or she targets. A con man doesn't refer to a 'victim,' instead he has a 'mark' – or a sucker, stooge, mug, rube or gull.

Types of Cons
Short cans can be used in short stories and in scenes within longer stories. The long con works better in a full-length novel or movie. The plot structure provided in this chapter is for a long con.

The Small or Short Con
The short con, sometimes referred to as a 'one-liner', is small-scale and happens rapidly, usually in the space of a first meeting with the victim. Susan Kuhlmann also compared the small con to a practical joke where the 'profit' to be gained is a laugh. This type of con is typically designed to take whatever money the mark has with him or to obtain some other small object of value – e.g. a watch. The victim usually becomes aware fairly quickly that they have been duped.

Stages of the Small Con
Fay Faron lists the six stages of the con as being:

Motivation – What will the victim get out of it? Do they get cash or something else of value? The feeling of having helped someone in distress? Or the satisfaction of having helped prevent a crime?

The Come-On – The story that the con man tells the victim to draw them in – it is usually simple but with enough detail to make it sound plausible.

The Shill – The con man's accomplice who backs up the story and perhaps takes up the offer that the con man is making to the victim or tries out the game and wins.

Stress – Some form of pressure to urge the victim to act now – time is running out or there are only a limited number of items or chances left. Under pressure, people tend to think less rationally and this can be enough to overcome any final doubts they have.

The Swap – The victim hands over something of value and gets something of no value in return.

Block – Something that dissuades the victim from going to the police. Usually, this involves making the victim feel guilty because they had chosen to participate in something they knew was illegal or immoral, or that makes them feel so foolish that they don't want to tell anyone about it. Sometimes escaping unscathed is enough – a shill may shout a warning that the police are coming and the victim runs, leaving behind his cash, and is simply grateful to get away. Or the victim may be threatened with exposure or violence and be happy to give up his cash to avoid this.

Not all small cons include all of the steps above, but all will involve the *motivation* and the *swap*.

Types of Small Con
Small cons are similar to street magic or tabletop sleight of hand – and when described in a story they have an appeal similar to learning how a

magic trick is done. Any of the following small cons can be used early on in stories to demonstrate the skills of a con artist character. There is not space for me to give full details of all of these cons – you can find the details, along with variations of each, online. One good place to look is the website www.crimes-of-persuasion.com

Panhandling – this is a simple deception in which someone approaches the victim and says his wallet has been lost or stolen and asks for $8 so he can get his car out of a car park or for the bus ride home. It plays on our tendency to want to help someone in need.

Short-Changing – This is an old trick in which the con man confuses a cash register operator and gets them to give him change from $20 and the original bill back. This is used at the beginning of Jim Thompson's novel *The Grifters*. Another way that you can be cheated on your change is with a folded banknote being counted as two bills. Another way in which a cashier can be cheated is by use of a marked bill – the con man buys something with $10 and then says he's been given the wrong change he gave the cashier a $20 – and he can prove it because the bill had a particular mark on it. The marked bill was given to the cashier by a previous customer who was the con man's partner. This is used in *Paper Moon*.

The Handkerchief Switch – here someone with a large sum of money is shown how to hide it from potential thieves by wrapping it in a handkerchief and stuffing it inside their pants – but the con man swaps the handkerchief containing the cash for one containing a wad of old newspaper. This was used at the beginning of *The Sting*.

Three-Card Monte – also known as 'find the lady.' It is a variation on the old table top trick using three walnut shells and a pea. Place your money down and find the Queen of Diamonds or the pea. There is also a variation involving a shill who whispers a way for the victim to 'cheat' the con man.

The Pigeon Drop – a wallet or briefcase is found which apparently contains a significant amount of money and possibly some indication that it is drug money; the con man and the victim discuss what to do with it and as proof of 'good faith' the victim is asked to come up with a certain amount of cash – that he then loses to the con man, being left with a wallet or briefcase filled with bundles of newspaper.

The Block Hustle – sometimes referred to as a 'white van scam' – it involves merchandise being sold on the street or out of the back of a van. It may involve fake Rolex watches or hi-fi equipment. Usually, the victim is shown an unboxed item and then hands cash over for a sealed box. When the box is opened later the item is either inferior to the item viewed or may be a brick or some other object used to make the box feel the right weight for the item.

Found Valuables and Latin Lotto – Here the victim as asked to hand over cash for something that is apparently much more valuable than the cash sum involved. It may be a winning lotto ticket that the con man says he cannot claim because he is an immigrant. Or it may be a valuable diamond ring or a wallet – here the owner is sometimes phone an offers a high reward for its return; the con man takes a smaller amount of cash from the victim and lets the victim go and claim the larger reward – but the owner is never found, because the person on the other end of the phone was the con man's accomplice and the 'diamond' ring is actually worthless.

Badge Scammers – are con men who pretend to be detectives or FBI or other agency officials, complete with a plausible-looking ID badge, who stop customers outside a bank and tell them the cash they have just received is counterfeit and must be confiscated – they give the victim a 'receipt' for the cash and tell them to go back into the bank and exchange it for real notes. Inside the bank the customer gets nothing and when he or she goes back outside the agent has disappeared.

Hustling – The term 'hustle' has been used to mean all types of con, but originally it referred to scams involving sports or games of skill. The con man or his accomplice pretends to be an ordinary player and demonstrates his ordinary – or below average skills – and the victim is encouraged to play against him. After a few small wins the bets increase in value and the victim eventually loses all of his cash when the hustler demonstrates his true skills. Pool hall hustling is seen in the novels *The Hustler* and *The Color of Money* by Walter Tevis and in the films based on them.

Badger Game – the victim is 'caught' having sex with another man's wife and hands over cash to have it hushed up or to avoid a beating. The 'wife' and the 'husband' are both in on the con.

Murphy Game – a fake pimp says he will send a girl to the victim's hotel room after he's handed over cash, but she never appears. Or the pimp takes the victim's money and sends him up to the girl's room, but that room number doesn't exist.

Panel Game – during sex, the victim's wallet is cleaned out by an accomplice of the person the victim is having sex with. This gets its name from the fact that the thief was hidden behind a panel in the room.

Carny (or Carnival) Cons – these typically involve games of skill such as shooting, tossing rings, beanbags or balls, or throwing darts to win prizes. The games are typically rigged so that the player stands little chance of winning and the prizes given if someone does win are often of lesser quality and value than those displayed.

Gambling Cons – these involving betting on card games and roulette tables, horse races or sports such as football or boxing. Playing cards may be marked. Roulette tables may be rigged with mechanical or electrical devices that control where the ball falls. Card players may engage in card counting. Dealers may deal pre-chosen cards from pre-prepared decks of cards.

Funeral Scams – a death in the family can bring forth all sorts of scams, from inheritance fraud and avoidance of inheritance tax, to forged wills, and strangers turning up to collect debts 'owed' by the dead person.

Bait-and-switch occurs where you offer something to draw someone in – goods or services are advertised at a low price, for example (the bait) – but once the customer arrives at the store, they discover the advertised item is not available or that it is of poor quality, and the salesman then takes the opportunity to try and sell them a higher-priced item or service (the switch). The retail example is the most obvious example, but similar tactics can be used in other transactions of a similar nature. In a confidence trick, the victim is often drawn in and checked out by the criminals via a small-scale con and if they're deemed a suitable mark, they try to switch the victim's attention to the larger-scale con.

The Big or Long Con

The long con, sometimes referred to as the big con or long game, is a scam that unfolds over days, weeks or even longer. It typically involves a team of swindlers and may include role-playing, fake business premises, and elaborate scenes scripted like those in a movie. The aim of the long con is to obtain a flow of money over a period of time or to increase the mark's confidence in the swindlers over time until the point he is ready to trust them with a large lump sum of money or some other object(s) of value.

The long con involves a much more elaborate deception requiring much more equipment and hours of planning and practice. These cons are much more like the large-scale magic tricks performed by David Copperfield. Their set-up includes a larger team working with the con men and often a fake office or other business front – a 'store' – being set up. The larger cons also meant the need for more senior law enforcement officers, politicians and/or judges to be bribed to look the other way.

David Maurer has written that there were originally three types or variations of the long con – *The Wire, The Pay-Off,* and *The Rag.*

The Wire, dating from around 1898, involved a fake Western Union office and a fake betting parlour – the victim was told that they could bet on horse races that had already been run because an inside man at Western Union would hold up the results – then delivered by telegraph – until after the con man and his victim had placed bets on the winner. Having made some small wins, perhaps using the con man's money, the victim then went away to get together a much larger amount of his own (or someone else's) money to bet on another winner. But something would go wrong this time and the victim would lose their cash.

The Pay-Off was a variation introduced in about 1906 in which the victim is in on the fact that a swindle is to be carried out – usually involving a boxer or sportsman who will 'throw' a match or game or a fixed horse race – and is invited to make money from the swindle. It plays out in much the same way as the Wire. The con portrayed in the film *The Sting* is based on the Pay-Off.

The Rag was introduced soon after the Pay-Off and is a variation on it that involves stocks rather than gambling, with an inside man able to manipulate the value of shares and the 'store' being a fake broker's office.

Again, there isn't space in this chapter to give details about the long cons listed below, but you should be able to find more in-depth descriptions online or in one of the books listed in the bibliography for this chapter.

Adoption Scam – an infertile couple is offered a baby for sale. Often a pregnant teenager can 'sell' her baby to half-a-dozen couples and get each couple to pay towards medical and other expenses. Then, just before the birth of the baby, she 'changes her mind' and doesn't want to give up the baby.

Imposter Cons – Frank W. Abagnale Jr., seen in the film *Catch Me If You Can,* and Ferdinand Waldo Demara Jr., seen in *The Great Imposter,* are two of the best-known imposters. Other imposters have claimed to be related to wealthy families – e.g. Christopher Rocancourt – or to *be* famous people – Robert De Niro and Stanley Kubrick both had conmen pretending to be them.

Sweetheart (or Romance) Scams – these include gigolo-types who prey on wealthy older women and gold-diggers who prey on older men. Online dating has brought new variations – and created a larger pool of victims, with con artists able to view the profiles of potential victims and select their best match. Online sweethearts are often in another state or even another country and may initially receive small gifts from their victims – but quickly work their way up to requests to 'borrow' money for medical treatment, passports, visas, and plane tickets so that they can be with their sweetheart. These scams prey on people's loneliness and desire for companionship.

Business Fraud – this usually involves an 'inside man' who misappropriates funds or assets. Schemes may involve fake invoices or wages paid to non-existent employees; skimming cash and ringing up less than was received from the customer; corruption including bribes, kickbacks or bid-rigging; falsifying company accounts – 'cooking the books' – by overstating revenues and under-reporting expenses and liabilities or the opposite, depending on the intentions of the scammer. Often the inside man is a long-time employee who has never cheated the company before – but they have a sudden need for cash (medical bills, gambling or other debts, alimony), they know the system well enough to see how to exploit it without being found out, and they may feel that the company 'owes' it to them or they may have a grudge against the company because of the way they have been treated recently.

If an inside man is only needed for a brief 'incursion' or to obtain something relatively minor, a delivery man, messenger, or cleaner may be used. Businesses are more vulnerable during or immediately after a change of premises, during a refurbishment, or during peak seasons when extra staff are taken on short-term contracts.

Bankruptcy Scams – the con man creates or takes over a business, gets a good line of credit and then abuses it by declaring bankruptcy and leaving suppliers unpaid.

Real Estate Scams – in the past there was the Florida land boom of the 1950s where victims were offered worthless or non-existent tracts of land and in the 1980s there was the 'timeshare' boom. Homeowners have also been targeted by scams relating to the refinancing of mortgages and 'equity release.'

Insurance Scams – these may include arson, faked automobile accidents, fake personal injuries, and even faked deaths. Some scams also involve crooked doctors who provide exaggerated medical reports of injuries suffered and lawyers who exaggerate the dollar value of the impact on an injured person's life. Insurance companies often use investigators to check out suspect claims.

Investment Swindles – these include pyramid schemes and Ponzi schemes in which early investors are paid 'dividends' from the money paid in by later investors – robbing Peter to pay Paul – until the whole thing collapses under its own weight. Other investments fraud involves manipulating the value of company stock and 'insider' dealing of the kind seen in the films *Wall Street* and *The Wolf of Wall Street*.

Boiler Rooms – these are call centres where salespeople use questionable tactics to sell questionable investments. The 2000 Vin Diesel film *Boiler Room* is based in this environment.

Tax Fraud – this involves tax shelters, offshore havens and phoney 'trusts' designed to allow people evade taxes due. The IRS in the USA has a section on its website titled 'Tax Fraud and Abuse' – look at the bottom of the main page for the link at www.irs.gov

With small or short cons, the amount of money that could be taken from a victim ranged from tens of dollars up to perhaps $500. When the Wire was introduced, the amount taken could reach as much as $50,000 and in the 1920s the 'take' could be $200,000 or perhaps even $350,000 and there were even rumours of $1 million or $2.8 million being taken. During the Depression of the 1930s, takings fell to a $25,000 maximum though there were rumours that $100,000 had been taken by at least one big con.

Themes
An obvious theme in the confidence trick story is that of trust and betrayal – of gaining someone's confidence in order to cheat them. Human weaknesses such as greed, vanity, egotism, and such feature as the motivations for victims being sucked into the con – and also as motivations for the actions of the confidence tricksters.

Tone
There is often a light-hearted or humorous tone to this type of story, but with an underlying suspense from the threat of being found out. Often the consequences of what might happen if the hero's scheme is exposed are portrayed early on in the story by some kind of violent act – the murder or beating of someone who crosses the victim or the Mr. Big character.

Plot of a Confidence Trick Story
In stories of crime detection, the plot typically follows the stages of the investigation; in stories about the commission of a crime, the plot usually follows the various stages in the planning, preparation, carrying out, and aftermath of the criminal activity. We see this in the plot structure of a confidence trick story.

Stages of a Con
In his book *Confessions of a Confidence Man* (1920), Edward H. Smith listed six stages plus an optional seventh. In 1940 David W. Maurer published a ten-step model in *The Big Con: The Story of the Confidence Man* and this has been widely adopted, though different labels are often used for the different stages. I'm going to use the labels from Maria Konnikova's *The Confidence Game* and I'm going to add some of the stages that Smith described to fill out the list to fourteen stages, some of which are optional.

1) *Foundation Work* – Smith: "The preparations which are made before the scheme is put in motion, including the elaboration of the plan, the employment of assistants and so forth."
2) *The Put-Up* – Locating and investigating a mark (the victim). Smith says that the 'approach', the "...manner of getting in touch with the victim [is] often most elaborately and carefully prepared."
3) *The Play* – Gaining the mark's attention and confidence.
4) *The Rope* – Steering him to meet the inside man. The 'roper' is a con man who finds the mark, checks them out, hooks them and then leads them into the next stage of the con. He finds out what the mark wants in life and persuades him that he can have it and that he should have it. And then he hints that he may know a way for the mark to get this thing.
5) *The Tale* – The inside man explains how money can be made dishonestly. Smith calls this the 'build-up': "Rousing and sustaining the interest of the victim, introducing the scheme to him, rousing his greed, showing him the chance of profit and filling him so full of anticipation and cupidity that his judgement is warped and his caution thrown away." Confidence tricks exploit human weaknesses and the 'story' part of a con is designed to appeal to the mark on an emotional or gut-feeling level, and discouraging rational processing. Everyone tends to believe that they are unique and special and that they are more intelligent and more socially desirable than they really are. And

they underestimate their vulnerability to risk. People also typically have a sense of entitlement – they feel that they *deserve* good fortune. And most of us are pretty self-absorbed. There are people who are exceptions to this and situations that alter this, but the con artist avoids that type of person and that type of situation. The con man targets those who are egotistical and self-obsessed and seeks to appeal to their vanity. He tells them what they want to hear. And he tells them they can have whatever it is they think they deserve. He is also very subtle in the way that he does it, so that the mark doesn't even know he's being spun a tale. He knows the power of suggestion and he knows most people deny its influence. Everyone thinks they're too smart to fall for a scam – but few of us really are. Even those who have fallen for a scam and ought to have learned better can still be conned again – partly because their experience makes them feel they know what to look for next time. But scams aren't based on intelligence and learning, they're targeted at what we *feel* not what we know. When we have an emotional stake in an idea, it can completely overshadow our capacity to reason logically. Earlier in the chapter, I wrote about the similarity between the tale told by a confidence trickster and the story told by an author – we use similar tools to evoke similar responses from our target audience.

6) *Corroboration* – Smith includes this as an optional stage which "...is important in games where a banker or other shrewd customer is to be the victim." This involves having some apparently objective outside person verifying the scheme genuinely works or providing character references for the con man or men involved. Sometimes this person is in on the con and sometimes the con man has genuinely earned the person's trust during legitimate business interactions. Corroboration may be required after the Tale or before the Breakdown or Send.

7) *The Convincer* – Allowing the mark to make some money to prove that the scheme works. Smith also refers to this as a 'pay-off' and describes it as an "...actual or apparent paying of money by the conspirators to convince the victim and settle doubts by a cash demonstration. In the old banco game, the initial small bets which the victim was allowed to win were the pay-off. In stock swindles, the fake dividends sent to stockholders to encourage larger investments are the pay-off." The Convincer makes the mark believe that the scheme works as described – everything is going to plan. If something isn't broken you don't need to fix it and you also don't risk 'jinxing' it. The Convincer distracts the mark and also prevents him asking questions or seeking other proofs that he should be asking for.

8) *The Breakdown* – Finding out how much the mark is able and willing to invest. This is about testing the mark to see how far he is willing to go. If all is going according to plan, the Convincer has hooked the mark and no further pay-offs are necessary – the con man gains nothing by giving the mark more 'winnings.' The aim now is to get the mark to make a commitment and buy into the scheme in a serious way. Testing the mark often involves a small loss – something doesn't go according to plan and there is no pay-off this time. Will the mark decide to cut their losses or will they commit to the scheme? Most victims commit. Why? Firstly, having been convinced that profit is possible from the scheme, they are afraid of missing this 'golden' opportunity. Secondly, this small failure helps dispel the idea that this scheme is 'too good to be true.' Viewed in this light, a small loss can actually be regarded as

a *good* thing. Nothing worth having is entirely risk-free. By this stage, the con man is not making these arguments to convince the mark, the mark is making them to himself. That is the sign of a well-planned con. Having been hooked by the Tale, and given the Convincer to 'prove' it, the mark is now selective in how he views new evidence, preferring to see it in a positive light and as supporting the decision he now *wants* to make. Desire and greed – emotional feelings – are now crowding out rational thought. The Breakdown is where the con man discovers whether or not the mark is now in this state – and the commitment proves the mark is ready to be fleeced.

9) *The Send* – Sending the mark to get this money – either in cash or by transferring it to a bank account operated by the con man. This is where the victim is asked to invest in the scheme – and to prove his commitment to it.
10) *The In-and-In* – Smith: "This is the point in a con game where the conspirator puts some of his money into the deal with that of the victim; first to remove the last doubt that may tarry in the gull's mind, and, second, to put the con man in control of the situation after the deal is completed, thus forestalling a squeal. Often the whole game is built up around this feature and just as often it does not figure at all."
11) *Pressure* – Smith calls this the 'Hurrah': "This is like the denouement in a play and no con scheme is complete without it. It is a sudden crisis or unexpected development by which the sucker is pushed over the last doubt or obstacle and forced to act. Once the hurrah is sprung the victim is clay in the schemer's hands or there is no game." This is the point at which a deadline is introduced – we have to complete the scheme by X date or call it off – or some form of scarcity is made known – we only have room for X more investors.
12) *The Touch* – Cheating the mark out of his money.
13) *The Blow-Off* – Getting the mark out of the way as quickly and as quietly as possible – the con men don't want him around kicking up a fuss, they just want him gone so that they can disappear with the money.
14) *The Fix* – Forestalling action by the law. This is done in two ways – either by paying off those responsible for law enforcement or, ideally, setting up the con so that the mark cannot go to the police and make a complaint. This is usually achieved by having the mark guilty of participating in an illegal scheme – he cannot go to the authorities without incriminating himself. In some stories – *The Sting* and *Confidence* for example – this is intensified by having the mark appear to be an accessory to murder. Another aspect to this is the issue of *reputation* – many victims of cons do not report the crime even when they themselves are completely innocent because they are afraid of appearing foolish. What sort of idiot falls for a scam like that? Reputation determines how we are viewed by others – do they regard us as responsible, reliable, likeable, and competent? It determines how they act towards us, whether they trust us, and whether they will do business with us. Reputation is often more valuable than the money lost in a scam.

Once the mark has committed himself and handed over his money, he is personally invested in the scheme and no longer views it in a rational or objective way. If new doubts arise or losses are made, the mark will readily ignore them – in part, this is because we don't like to give up on an idea even if it appears to have been a mistake, we don't like to write things off or even admit that we might have been wrong. And we also accept small losses and increased risk in anticipation of making a greater profit later. Another reason why we don't give up on bad ideas is that we tend to regard something that we've invested in as having greater value than a similar thing that is not 'ours.' Even if someone came along and offered to buy the mark's stake in the scheme, he would almost certainly not sell it, no matter what doubts he held about it. People often prefer to stick with what they have – better the devil you know – than risk any form of change that might bring new uncertainties. If the mark did sell his stake, cognitive dissonance would kick in and he'd wonder whether he made the right decision – Suppose he just missed out on making a fortune? It is much better to stay with it and not risk the possibility of losing the 'sure thing.'

Emotion versus Logic
Emotions affect a person's ability to make decisions and this can be seen in two ways. First, if we are asked to make a decision we ask ourselves 'How do I *feel* about this?' In the absence of hard data – and often even when factual information is available – we rely on an emotional or gut reaction. Does this feel right? Am I happy about this or not? We may have doubts about 'facts' that are presented to us, but we rarely question the way we feel. Do I like this or not? Emotion typically comes before thought and influences the decision we make. Con men know this and rely on it to 'hook' their victims and reel them in. As we've already seen, cons appeal to feelings such as vanity, loneliness, a desire for social acceptance, greed, and a variety of other non-rational impulses. They don't seek to persuade us of the *logic* of getting involved in a scam, they seek to arouse an emotional need – and urge us to try and fulfil this need because we think about it rationally. In the early stages of the con, the scammer concentrates on the positive aspects, focusing on what is attractive about having what you want – phrases such as 'imagine yourself sitting on a beach with a cocktail in your hand' and designed to evoke positive feelings. They also downplay the negative side – Why *wouldn't* you do this? You've got nothing to lose.

The second way in which emotions affect decision-making is where the emotion exists before the choice is presented. If we are upset or anxious, we make decisions differently than we do if we're happy. If we are sad, we are drawn to people who are smiling and friendly, because we want to feel the way they seem to. We are also more prone to impulsive behaviour and risk-taking – presumably, we're thinking that things are already bad so what have I got to lose? We also look at the *content* of what a person is saying – seeking something that will improve our situation.

If we are happy, we rely on our feelings – a positive or negative response to something or someone, rather than the details of what they are telling us. We are more open to persuasion – especially if we feel we can trust the person because of their perceived status or expertise.

But if we are anxious or afraid, our irrational feelings tend to overwhelm rational thought. More specifically, and of more importance to confidence tricksters, anxiety followed by relief makes is very persuadable – create a feeling of fear and then offer a solution that makes me feel better, and I'm more likely to believe whatever you then tell me. Anxiety without relief also makes people persuadable, but less so. And an absence of anxiety makes us least persuadable of all.

In the later part of the con, the confidence trickster uses negative emotions to influence the mark's decision-making. He applies pressure to make them feel anxious – that pressure may be a deadline (invest now or miss your chance) or it may be scarcity (only three places left), or it may be a loss, a threat of exposure, or even physical danger. Under these circumstances, people think less logically and less objectively – they are concerned about their own prospects or their own well-being. Both *The Sting* and *Confidence* use a shooting to upset the mark and make them more concerned about escaping arrest than losing their cash.

Establishing Trust
There are a number of different techniques that confidence tricksters use to get victims to trust them.

Legitimate authority – Most people tend to trust a person who is in a legitimate position of authority. We trust surgeons, judges, airline pilots, professors, and others who have achieved their status in a legitimate way. Con artists can capitalise on this by assuming the identity of such a person.

Expertise – We also tend to trust people who are good at what they do, whatever field they work in. We assume that expertise is gained by long hours of legitimate practice and cannot be faked. The 'wire' scam we looked at earlier was based on the fact that the inside man was a telegraph operator who had the expertise to manipulate the system.

Affiliation – If a person is associated with an individual or group that we trust, they tend to gain our trust because of their affiliation. If someone is a member of a creditable institution, they inherit that institutions creditability. This is related to our natural tendency to like people who are similar to us and to distrust those who are different. The same is true if a person belongs to a group that we aspire to belong to or is someone we would like to be seen to be associated with. This comes back to our public image or reputation.

Social consensus – If we see that other people are engaged in some scheme or activity, we view it as socially acceptable and therefore have fewer qualms about being involved ourselves. If we believe that 'everyone' cheats on their expenses or tax returns, then we feel more comfortable about doing it ourselves – and our worries about being caught and socially ostracised are diminished. Con artists often employ shills to appear to be happy customers in the big store in which the con will occur on the basis that the mark will take comfort from seeing so many other people engaged in the scheme.

Start small – Research has shown that if someone does a small favour – for you or for someone else – this makes it more likely that they will do a second, larger favour. This may come from the positive boost that we get from helping someone else – we like the feeling it gives us and so want to feel it again. We are also more likely to trust someone who seems familiar to us, even if our only previous interaction with them has been a brief conversation in the lift that morning – they are no longer a stranger or outsider.

Confidence tricksters are able to gain the trust of even the most unlikely marks. There are even scams that involve promises to help victims recover money that they have been scammed out of!

Plot Structure of the Confidence Trick Story
There is some variation in the structure of the confidence trick plot that depends on what point in the story you want to place the actual playing out of the trick itself. This positioning is determined by how much of the aftermath – the consequences of the con – that you want to show. If you

want to show in some detail what happens after the con, you could place the con itself at the end of Sequence 6; if you want a relatively short aftermath, you can place the con at the end of Sequence 7, and if you want completion of the con to form the climax of your story you can have it occur as late as Sequence 8. To judge how long your aftermath ought to be, you need to consider how dramatic the events of it are in comparison to the action of the con. If your aftermath is not particularly dramatic or doesn't evoke a strong emotional response in your audience, you risk the ending of your story being anticlimactic if it goes on for too long. Having your con begin somewhere in Sequence 7 – either the beginning, middle or end of the sequence – is probably the safest bet as it still gives you room for a long or short aftermath.

The template below is based primarily on the structure of the films *The Sting* and *Confidence,* but also takes into account the 14-stage structure of the confidence trick.

Sequence 1

We meet our hero and we see that he is good at what he does – usually in the form of a short con or perhaps the ending of a long con. We either see the hero working alone or we see him working with his accomplices. This con may simply exist in the plot to show us the hero at work or it may have consequences later. We learn more about the hero (and possibly his accomplices) by the way he (or they) spend the money that they have just earned. Usually, we will see that the money isn't very important to the hero or his friends – easy come, easy go. Though one of the conmen, possibly even the hero, maybe carefully stashing away his earnings so that he can retire relatively soon.

In the first sequence, we may also see the reason why the hero (and possibly his associates) becomes involved in the main con that will define the structure of the story. In both *The Sting* and *Confidence* the hero has scammed money that belonged to a powerful and dangerous criminal – this is the challenge or inciting incident that triggers the rest of the plot events. Another possibility for this turning is to have the hero being caught by a victim who then blackmails him into committing a con of their choosing or into teaching them how to become a con artist. Or a friend of the hero may have financial troubles – debts owed to a violent criminal – so the hero decides to help him by getting money via a con. Or the hero may be in debt and have to carry out a con that is being planned and bankrolled by a Mr. Big crime boss type.

Ideally, we want to see the hero deciding to engage in a con for a reason other than greed for cash – to be a sympathetic hero, we need his motivation to be altruism or a desire for survival or (as in *The Sting*) the need for justice.

Sequence 1 also typically establishes the stakes by showing us what could happen to the hero if he crosses the villain. Often a friend of the hero is killed (this happens in Sequence 1 of *Confidence* and Sequence 2 of *The Sting*) or beaten up by the villain's thugs – or there is the suggestion that this will happen soon. The villain is often spoken of, establishing his reputation, but not seen in the first sequence. He is also likely to be the main victim or mark in the story – having a mark who *deserves* to be scammed helps increase sympathy for the hero

Sequence 2

The second sequence often introduces a second source of opposition for the hero – usually the police in the form of a straight investigator who is determined to capture the conmen or a crooked investigator who wants a big (or bigger) cut of the conman's takings. We may see the hero escape from, outwit, or pay-off this character – but we now know he's on the hero's trail and that we're likely to see him again later.

We may also see another example of the hero's abilities as a conman. And we often see him in his 'home' situation – perhaps alone or with his associates. If the hero or one of the other characters plans to retire or has some other dream life they want to go to, it will usually be established here.

If the challenge at the end of Sequence 1 was to perform a confidence trick for or with someone else, we may see some reluctance on the part of the hero or members of his team – especially if an outsider is going to be part of this new con. An outsider offers a good excuse for the hero to explain what the long con involves, clueing the audience in at the same time.

Here there is often some discussion about the big or long con and how it differs from the short cons we have seen so far.

At the end of this sequence, there is some sort of commitment by the hero – and perhaps his team – a determination to achieve something. In *Confidence,* the hero agrees to carry out a con to repay the money he owes to the villain. In *The Sting,* the hero takes the advice of his old partner and goes to learn how to do the long con from a new mentor. The commitment will be something that relates, directly or indirectly, to the hero becoming involved in a big con.

Sequence 3

Having introduced the main characters and the idea of the con, we now enter Act II of the story where we begin the actual stages of the con itself.

The first two stages of the con, *Foundation Work* (1), if it is necessary, and *The Put-Up* (2) – locating and investigating the mark – occur in Sequence 3, though the mark may have been identified previously.

Here we often see the coming together of the first part of the team – the hero's usual crew. There may be some discussion about the type of con to use against the mark or about the way to carry off the con. We may see members of the crew getting new appearances – hair and outfits – for their roles in the new con.

If the con requires a fake location – a 'store' – it will probably be acquired in this sequence or early in Sequence 4.

The subplot involving the other source of opposition – the investigator(s) – will also be advanced here, perhaps with the investigator having a reason to redouble his efforts to capture the hero. Or perhaps he learns that the hero is planning a big con and wants to make sure he gets a cut of the proceeds. This helps to establish what is at stake for the hero if he gets caught. Not only has he got to avoid falling foul of the villain/mark, but he's also got to stay out of the clutches of the investigator.

We may also see what is at stake for the villain/mark – something along the lines of his position as boss over this territory being in jeopardy if he falls victim to a conman – someone will take advantage of his damaged reputation and take over from him. He can't afford to let the hero cheat him and will do whatever he can to make sure it doesn't happen.

At the end of Sequence 3, we introduce something that will have consequences later, paying off at the end of Sequence 5. Perhaps a team member or a lover will betray the hero and/or the team. Or perhaps the hero or another member of the team has personal troubles – with the police or another gang of crooks – that could jeopardise the whole con, but he doesn't tell anyone because he doesn't want the con to be called off. A lie may be told that will be uncovered later and have consequences. Or someone may be involved in a relationship with someone that they shouldn't be. In *The Sting* the secret is that Robert Redford's character is being pursued by a hitman – he keeps this from the rest of the gang because he doesn't want the con to be called off.

Sequence 4

In this sequence, we see *The Play* (3), where the con men gain the attention of the mark and *The Rope* (4) where they gain his confidence and draw him in to learn about the confidence trick that will make him rich. In *The Sting*, this is the poker game on the train where Paul Newman's character annoys the villain and Robert Redford's character reveals to the villain that Newman is a terrible boss and he wants to get his own back by swindling him. This pitch to the villain/mark is the *midpoint* of the story.

You probably also need to have a midpoint scene for the subplot involving the investigators who are pursuing the hero. The investigator probably discovers some important clue that makes him believe that he is close to being able to arrest the hero – perhaps he knows who the mark selected for the con is, or has identified someone else involved in the con, and will observe them until they lead him to the hero.

Sequence 5

Here is where the villain/mark hears *The Tale* (5), an explanation of what the money-making scheme is and how it works; this may involve *Corroboration* (6), with the villain/mark meeting the inside man and hearing how the technical side of the scheme works. In *The Sting,* the villain meets the telegraph operator and hears how they can bet on a horse race that has already been run and the winner announced.

After the Tale has been spun, the con men have to wait to see if the villain/mark will commit to it – but they are convinced he will. They may discuss how victims typically talk themselves into committing to the scheme having heard the Tale.

Towards the end of Sequence 5 we also see the pay-off of whatever was set up in Sequence 4 – the uncovering of a lie, a betrayal, or whatever it is that threatens to jeopardise the whole con. This may be related to the subplot in which the investigator pursues the hero. In *The Sting,* the gang discover that Robert Redford's character has concealed the truth about the hitman and has jeopardised the whole con.

Sequence 6

Having heard all about how the scheme works, the villain/mark now receives *The Convincer* (7), a chance to put a small amount of money into the scheme and receive a pay-off that 'proves' he can make money from it. Then comes *The Breakdown* (8), where the con men determine how much cash the villain/mark is prepared to invest in the scheme and *The Send* (9), where they get the villain/mark to go off an obtain the cash or transfer it to a bank account controlled by the conmen. Often the con man will appear reluctant to 'allow' the villain/mark to invest in the scheme – this makes the mark even more determined to put his money into it, and he may even increase the amount of cash he'll put in to try and prove his commitment to the hero. Discussion about the money will often include *The In-and-In* (10), whereby the hero will (allegedly) invest some of his own money alongside the villain/mark's. This is designed to encourage the villain/mark to pool his money with the hero's and give the hero control over all of it for the purposes of the scheme. It may also be necessary to apply *Pressure* (11) to the villain/mark here to get him to move quickly before he has had a chance to have any second thoughts about putting such a large amount of money into the scheme. Pressure might come in the form of a deadline or the mention of another 'investor' keen to be part of the scheme.

Sequence 7

Sequence 7 depicts *The Touch* (12), the running of the con and the taking of the villain/mark's money.

A feature of the confidence trick story is that the writer often 'cons' or misdirects the reader or audience. The misdirection often occurs in the subplot involving the investigators who are trying to trap the hero. The misdirection is set-up near the beginning of Sequence 7 and pays off late in Sequence 8. In Sequence 7 we establish what we want the reader to believe – perhaps someone betrays the hero to the investigators and even tells them when and where the con will take place. This sets up an expectation that the con may go wrong, adding another element of jeopardy – the authorities are closing in on the hero. As the action of the con is drawing to a close, the investigators appear to be closing in on the hero, adding to the suspense.

Sequence 8

This sequence may include the conclusion of The Touch, rapidly followed by *The Blow-Off* (13), designed to get rid of the villain/mark before he can start causing trouble for the conmen and *The Fix* (14), which is to ensure that the conmen are not pursued by the police.

Also in this sequence is the pay-off of the misdirection set-up in Sequence 7. The reader is expecting the authorities to arrive and capture the hero and his crew – but the hero has anticipated this and prepared a way to escape... The usual way out is to have the investigator(s) be in the employ of the hero with their appearance being part of the Blow-Off that encourages the villain/mark to get away from the scene quickly. However, having the investigator in on the con has become a bit of a cliché and it is probably better to have a different twist worked out for your plot. In *Confidence,* the subplot involving the investigators is woven together with the main plot in quite a satisfying way – which I won't reveal here as I don't want to give away the ending. Another twist may be that someone who *appeared* to betray the hero actually didn't – their actions were part of the plan. Or perhaps someone in the villain/mark's camp is actually on the hero's side.

11 | Prison Thrillers

A prison is a location and any number of stories could take place there, but we are concerned here with one particular type of story – a story of someone who is placed in the prison and *must* escape in order to survive. These stories are set almost totally within the (literal) confines of the prison, with only a minimal number of scenes (if any) set outside the prison walls. We are not considering escape and chase stories such as *The Fugitive* here as I have already covered those in *Suspense Thriller*.

There are a couple of types of prison story that I am not going to consider in this chapter – the prisoner of war movie such as *The Great Escape* and 'women in prison' exploitation movies. Here I will cover only stories set in men's prisons, as this is where the majority of examples are set, but in terms of story structure and themes, modern thrillers set in women's prisons would, I think, be very similar.

The hero of our prison thriller is effectively a victim who frees himself and is either (a) an innocent man who has been unjustly imprisoned, or (b) a guilty man who deserves to be imprisoned but the conditions he faces in jail are so inhumane that they out of all proportion to the hero's crime. Another variation is that the hero – guilty or innocent – is a prisoner in order to investigate and expose criminal activity being committed by prisoners, prison staff, or both: this variation combines elements of the prison and the undercover agent thriller.

Historical Development

Peter Roffman and Beverly Simpson write that the earliest Hollywood prison movies were "...simplistic moral commentaries, exposing audiences to the cruel injustices of the American penal system." Examples include *The Fight for Right* (1913) which depicted the exploitation of prison labourers; *The Honor System* (1917) about the brutal treatment of prisoners by sadistic wardens and prison guards, and *Intolerance* (1916) which opposed capital punishment.

Roffman and Simpson regard the 1930s as the 'golden years' of the prison film and that the genre had social significance, with films working on dual levels "...both as liberal exposés of prison conditions, and as subtle metaphors for the quality of Depression life." But they note that most prison movies since then have failed to live up to this promise and have neglected to demonstrate the connection between the failings of the prison system and those of America more generally.

The reason prison movies were popular during the years of the Depression is perhaps due to the fact that those suffering from real-life austerity could readily identify with what Roffman and Simpson describe as the 'frustration and entrapment experienced by prison inmates.' There was also the fact that those who were unemployed and hungry were the victims of circumstances beyond their control, like the innocent victims unjustly convicted and sent to prison.

The Big House (1930) shows with the 'processing' of a new prisoner as his individuality is removed and he becomes just one more figure lost in the prison population. It also establishes that prisoners are not always treated fairly. The film was inspired by a number of real-life prison riots.

I Am a Fugitive from a Chain Gang (1932) starred Paul Muni and was based on Robert Elliott Burns's autobiography *I Am a Fugitive from a Georgia Chain Gang!* which was serialised in *True Detective Mysteries* magazine in 1932. Burn's story also formed the basis of the 1987 television movie *The Man Who Broke 1,000 Chains* starring Val Kilmer. Many at Warner Bros. were against making the film, with the story department noting that the violence in the story meant they could only really make it if there was no censorship, but that "...all the strong and vivid points in the story are certain to be eliminated..." The story was deemed depressing and without relief. There were also concerns that the depiction of the brutal treatment of prisoners on chain gangs in Georgia would result in protests in the Deep South. The release of the film and the attention it generated led to improvements in the way that prisoners were treated.

Virtually all of the conventions and clichés of the prison movie – with the exception of prison rape – were established in these 1930s films.

Almost no prison movies were released during the years of the Second World War, but after that the genre became popular again.

Brute Force (1947) starring Burt Lancaster and inspired in part by the 'Battle of Alcatraz' which took place in May 1946 when inmates staged an unsuccessful attempt to escape from Alcatraz Federal Penitentiary. A stand-off resulted and the Marines were brought in to end it. This event was also the inspiration for a 'factually based' TV drama *Alcatraz — The Whole Shocking Story* (1980) and the film *Six Against the Rock* (1987), starring David Carradine and based on the 1975 book of the same title by Clark Howard. *Brute Force* is also interesting in that the inmates share their stories in a series of vignettes that reveal each of them ended up in trouble with the law as a result of falling for a femme fatale.

Caged (1950) was advertised as 'the story of women's prison today' and starred Eleanor Parker who is found guilty of being an accessory to robbery and whose experiences behind bars turn her from a naive young woman into a hardened convict – 'she was part-good before,' the poster says, 'she's ALL BAD NOW!'

Riot in Cell Block 11 (1954). Prison inmates protest about the brutal guards, terrible food, overcrowding and filthy conditions, but politicians are not prepared to make any concessions. The situation eventually develops into a riot and rival groups within the prison vie for power. As things seem about to reach an explosive climax, with the state police brought in to end the siege, a peaceful settlement is negotiated. But the prisoners' apparent victory is short-lived. On the film's release, the *New York Times* critic said the film was "...explosive enough to satisfy the most rabid of the 'cons versus screws' school of moviegoer..." but that it also "...makes a sincere and adult plea for a captive male society revolting against penal injustices."

The 1960s brought only a few notable prison movies.

The Birdman of Alcatraz (1962) starring Burt Lancaster. A highly fictionalised account of the life of Robert Stroud based on the 1955 book by Thomas E. Gaddis. In the film, Stroud is a rebellious prisoner sentenced to life imprisonment and ordered to be kept in solitary confinement after killing a guard. To help pass the time, he starts keeping birds as pets, nursing injured ones back to health and eventually becoming an expert on bird diseases. He remains a free-thinking rebel throughout his life and plays a part in ending a prison rebellion. Although the film and Gaddis' book portray Stroud as essentially mild-mannered, in real life he was a violent pimp and former inmates have described him as a 'vicious killer' and a 'jerk'. One psychiatrist who examined him said he was a highly intelligent psychopath.

Cool Hand Luke (1967) based on Donn Pearce's 1965 novel of the same title. Luke (Paul Newman) is a decorated war veteran with a history of rebellious behaviour who is arrested for damaging parking meters while drunk. He is sentenced to two years in a Florida prison camp. Luke's refusal to accept the established hierarchy among the prisoners results in him facing the much bigger Dragline (George Kennedy) in a boxing match. Hopelessly outmatched, Luke keeps getting to his feet for more – until Dragline refuses to continue. Luke's doggedness wins him the respect of the other prisoners. His optimism, humour, and independent spirit endear him to the others and he continues to challenge the authority of the guards. This makes him a threat to the authority figures who fear he will encourage the other prisoners to rebel.

Luke receives word that his mother has died. Believing that Luke might try and escape to attend his mother's funeral, the Captain has him locked in the box, releasing him only after the funeral is over. Luke then makes two attempts to escape – the first fails and the second is apparently successful, but he is eventually returned to captivity.

Luke is subjected to merciless punishment, being repeatedly beaten and made to dig and then fill in grave-sized holes. Eventually, it appears that Luke's spirit has been broken – he is warned that if he ever tries to escape again, he will be shot and he promises he won't try. The other prisoners are disappointed when it seems that Luke is now a fawning model prisoner. But then Luke makes another escape attempt – with inevitable consequences.

Luke's positive influence on the other prisoners and the punishment he endures at the hands of his captors has led some critics to compare the character with Jesus and some of the imagery in the film suggests this was deliberate. Roffman and Simpson note that this film – along with *The Birdman of Alcatraz* – "...moved away from the traditional complaints about prison life. Both films instead emphasised the struggle against a repressive, conformist society." A key theme of the film is the conflict between the individual and societal rules of behaviour. The same theme is explored in *One Flew Over the Cuckoo's Nest* (1975) based on the 1962 novel by Ken Kesey.

Other notable 1970s prison movies include *The Longest Yard* (1974) directed by Robert Aldrich which takes the conflict between brutal guards and rebellious prisoners and turns it into a gladiatorial contest that takes place on the (American) football field, and *Papillon* (1973) based on the 1969 memoirs of French convict Henri Charrière, played in the film by Steve McQueen, who makes several attempts to escape from prisons in French Guyana including Devil's Island. *Scum* (1979) directed by Alan Clarke and starring Ray Winstone portrays the brutality of life in a British borstal (youth detention centre). It was originally written as a BBC drama but not broadcast due to the violence depicted and was remade as a film. The 2010 Canadian movie *Dog Pound* is reported to be a remake.

Fortune and Men's Eyes (1971) was based on the 1967 play of the same title by John Herbert. The film is significant for openly acknowledging the reality of sexual violence inside prisons. Inmates run the risk of being gang-raped unless they have someone to act as their protector – and are expected to be sexually subordinate to their protector. It also features a prison guard who is blackmailed into taking instructions from one of the more powerful inmates. The subject matter of the play meant Herbert could not get it staged publicly in his native Canada and it was eventually staged in New York in 1967 after having been workshopped by Dustin Hoffman. Since then it has been staged in over a hundred countries.

Brubaker (1980) starring Robert Redford was based on the 1969 non-fiction book *Accomplices to the Crime: The Arkansas Prison Scandal* by Tom Murton and Joe Hyams. Redford initially appears as a new inmate at the prison, but having seen first-hand the treatment of prisoners he reveals himself to be the new prison warden. He sets out to reform conditions in the prison and also investigates a number of unexplained deaths in the prison, leading to a political scandal.

Lock Up (1989) starring Sylvester Stallone and Donald Sutherland sees the hero transferred to a maximum-security prison where he is victimised by the warden as punishment for having exposed the warden's treatment of prisoners during a previous sentence. The film is notable only for Sutherland's over the top performance as the warden.

The Shawshank Redemption (1994) written and directed by Frank Darabont, based on the 1982 Stephen King novella *Rita Hayworth and Shawshank Redemption*. Tim Robbins plays a man wrongly convicted of murdering his wife and her lover and Morgan Freeman is an older inmate who acts as his mentor. The film is a near-perfect example of a prison movie plot, though it is not strictly speaking a thriller. Like *Cool Hand Luke*, the hero in the film has been described as a Christ-like figure.

Also worth noting is the 2001 German film *Das Experiment*, remade in the USA as *The Experiment* (2010), based on the novel *Black Box* (1999) by Mario Giordano and inspired by the real-life Stanford Prison Experiment of 1971. During that controversial experiment, volunteers were given the roles of prison guards or prisoners in a mock prison, with the behaviour and psychological responses of the two groups monitored. Due to the treatment of prisoners by guards, the experiment had to be abandoned after six days.

Starred Up (2013) was written by Jonathan Asser and is based on his experience working as a therapist in a British prison housing violent criminals. Jack O'Connell stars as a violent young man who is transferred to an adult prison where he is encouraged to engage in rehabilitation therapy by his father who is also held in the same prison. The film explores the father-son relationship and the fact that both are victims of their circumstances.

Thematic Argument
The moral argument in the story is relatively straightforward – either the innocent hero has been unjustly imprisoned or the guilty hero's treatment in prison is unjust. The hero's circumstances amount to an injustice. There is an element of irony in this situation in that the prison authorities – those ostensibly on the side of law and order – behave in a way that is more heinous than anything the criminals ever did. Roffman and Simpson write that the "...evils depicted have changed from bad food and solitary confinement to homosexual rape and drug dealing inside the prison, but the message remains the same as in the earliest films – the prison system needs to be reformed."

Characters
There are generally two main characters involved in the conflict of the story – the hero-prisoner and the antagonist-jailer. Sometimes the antagonist is

a prison governor who has a henchman in the form of a brutal prison officer or perhaps a prisoner who is a gang leader within the prison.

Plot Structure

Act I – First Quarter: Imprisonment. We are introduced to the hero either as he is brought into the prison or as he is in the middle of a normal day of imprisonment having been there for a period of time. We learn what sort of person he is and the circumstances that led to him being imprisoned. We also gain some sense of what the prison environment is like – how unpleasant and dangerous it is inside and what happens if you try to escape. We also discover why the hero *needs* to get out of there and why he must do it *soon*. By the end of Act I we have asked the dramatic question – Will the hero get out of prison before the deadline?

Act II – Part 1, Second Quarter: Prison Life & Brutalisation.
Act II – Part 2, Third Quarter: Escape Plan & Preparation.
Act III – Fourth Quarter: The Escape. Things don't go exactly to plan and some unexpected obstacle arises or something vital to the plan isn't where it should be or doesn't happen when it is supposed to. During this act, the hero also often manages to settle the score with the antagonist and score a moral victory beyond his own escape.

During Acts I and II, the antagonist is in control and the hero is virtually helpless, but in Act III the hero gains control of his own destiny.

Prison Thriller Plot

Many prison movies are not *thrillers* as such and some that are – action thrillers such as *Death Warrant* or *Lock Up* – while fun to watch, probably aren't great examples to use as models for your novel or screenplay. Some prison movies focus almost exclusively on an attempt by an individual or a group to escape and the structure of these is much closer to a 'mission' plot or a heist. Here I want to concentrate on a plot that takes its form from the original prison movies of the 1930s but includes an element of *conspiracy* that makes it closer to the thriller. I explored conspiracies in some detail in *Suspense Thriller* so won't go into detail about creating the conspiracy element here. The conspiracies in prison movies are typically criminal conspiracies or political conspiracies.

Before you begin plotting your prison thriller, you need to decide what thematic argument you are trying to prove. Are you saying that the treatment of prisoners in our prison system is inhumane and as much of a crime as the actions that put the prisoners into it? Are you saying that prison does not rehabilitate prisoners and so fails both prisoner and society as a whole? Are you seeking to expose the corruption that goes on within prisons involving both criminal gangs and prison officers – and perhaps even politicians? Or are you showing how the prison system fails to treat inmates as individual human beings – but that an individual free-spirit can still survive within such an environment? You can include elements of all of these, but you need to decide up front – or discover during the writing of your first draft – which will be the dominant thread.

For my money, *The Shawshank Redemption* is one of the best prison movies ever made. It is more of a character-piece – the pace is fairly gentle and the more violent aspects of prison life are glossed over to some extent – but in terms of *structure,* it has just about everything, including a criminal conspiracy element. The template below is based, more or less, on the structure of *The Shawshank Redemption,* but I have woven into it notes drawn from all of the other films I watched and re-watched in researching this chapter.

Sequence 1

There are three things to establish here – the hero and his personality; the circumstances that cause him to be sent to prison; and the hero's first impressions of the prison (which will also be the reader or audience's introduction to the prison).

Generally speaking, the hero will be the viewpoint character – we will experience prison as he experiences it. Staying close to the hero at all times helps to emphasise the claustrophobic nature of the prison. The needs of your story may be such that you need to have scenes set outside the prison that don't involve the hero – but you should try to avoid 'opening up' your story more than you have to.

The first sequence might begin with the hero committing a crime – and the type of crime and his actions will tell us something about who he is. Or you could show the commission of a crime without identifying the culprit and then have your hero arrested for this crime – this leaves you the option of having your hero be innocent and wrongly convicted. Or you could show the crime committed by someone else and make it obvious that the hero is an innocent man wrongly accused and punished. You could skip the crime and begin with the trial and conviction – here again, you have the option of having an innocent hero sentenced to a prison term. Or you could simply have your hero arriving at the prison in the first scene and then fill in the details of how he came to be there a little later.

If you show the crime and/or courtroom, you probably need to keep these scenes brief – using a montage of scene fragments if necessary. Look at the openings of *The Shawshank Redemption* and *The Fugitive*. If you are writing a *prison* story, you want to get your reader into the prison as soon as possible – ideally, by the end of sequence one or by the end of sequence two at the latest. If you do need to show the courtroom, try and emphasise the *helplessness* of the individual within the court process so that the reader gets a sense of the hero being *trapped* even before he reaches prison – *Midnight Express* is a good example.

If you want to begin your story with the hero already inside – or having been there for some time – you lose the advantage of showing the prison and its regime to the audience as the hero first experiences. In this case, you might need to introduce another new inmate to the system and perhaps have the hero acts as a more experienced explaining the ropes and recalling his own induction.

You need to show what sort of person the hero is as early in the story as possible. Is he naïve, submissive, aggressive, rebellious? Show us who he is so that we can begin to imagine or wonder how he will respond once he's inside the prison walls.

If the first half of sequence one introduces the hero and his circumstances, then the second half typically shows him arriving at the prison as a new inmate. If you begin with the hero's arrival in prison on page one, the second half of the sequence usually fills in the details of his backstory – either told by the hero or another character or in flashback. Either way, you should try and establish the hero's personality in the first half of sequence one. You also need to introduce the 'personality' of the prison itself. Showing the structure and location of the prison is often one of the few 'long shots' or panoramic descriptions in the movie. Where does it sit in relation to other places? Is it in the middle of nowhere? Is the landscape around it bleak and dangerous? What do we see of the security measures? Armed guards in towers? Surveillance cameras and searchlights? Stone walls, fences, barbed wire, dogs? Often there will also be some anecdote about what happened to the last person who tried to escape.

New prisoners usually arrive in an armoured prison vehicle, often a bus. Existing prisoners will be interested to see the 'new meat.' It is a bit of a cliché to have existing prisoners greet the new arrivals with wolf-whistles and shouts of 'Hello, ladies!' – but you probably do want to make it so that the new arrivals feel threatened by the attention they receive.

The next stage is usually for the new prisoners to be greeted by one of the officials who run the prison – typically the warden (or governor) – the man in the suit who runs the prison – or by the warden's henchman, the captain of the uniformed guards. Again, the 'welcoming speech' is a bit of a cliché, but it does serve to establish that the prisoners' lives are now completely controlled by the rules and routines of these officials. There is typically some demonstration of brutality by the prison guards – a warning to everyone of what can happen if they step out of line.

New arrivals are then 'processed' – treated like raw material in a factory rather than as human beings. They lose their hairstyles and their civilian clothing – both outward signs of their individuality. They are given a number to replace their name. And they are stripped of their dignity – naked in front of strangers, humiliated by guards, subjected to an invasive strip-search and/or medical examination. They come out of this process looking just like the other prisoners, but their unfamiliarity with the routines and their obvious nervousness makes them stand out as the new guys.

If the hero is sharing a cell, he will probably meet his cellmate(s) late in sequence one or early in sequence two. There may be some antagonism – disagreement over who gets which bunk, for example. Or threats of sexual violence. The occupants of the cell size each other up and positions of dominance and subservience are established.

As the reality of being in prison sinks in, an air of resignation comes over the hero. He has to accept this as his situation – at least for now – and make the best of it. Whether he is guilty of the crime or has been wrongly convicted, he faces a long period in prison – possibly even a life sentence – so he is going to have to adjust to these circumstances as being his new everyday life. And if he is hoping to be released as a result of appealing his sentence, it is not in his best interests to deliberately cause problems for the officials at this early stage. A quality that we often see in hero characters in any genre is the ability to adapt and improvise – the hero is not an automaton or rule-bound bureaucrat, he is a free-thinker and he is resourceful.

Sequence 1 often ends as the prisoners are 'locked down' for the night – doors slam shut and the lights go out. For the new prisoners, this can be unnerving and they may be overcome by claustrophobia and panic. Sounds made by other prisoners in the darkness may also be unsettling – evocative of a Victorian mental hospital. If we haven't already seen the brutal treatment of prisoners by guards, then it may occur her after lights out. A prisoner who causes a disruption is dragged from his cell and beaten – a warning to the others, who quickly quieten down for the night. Alternatively, lights out may result in some prisoner on prisoner violence in one of the cells that is not noticed by the guards – or is not stopped if it is noticed.

Something else you will need to establish early in your story is how you will handle the violence. A movie such as *Midnight Express* establishes a brutal level of realism in the violence early on. This serves to let the audience know that this sort of violence – meted out on a whim by the head guard – can occur at any time. Having established these stakes, the mere threat of violence and very brief scenes depicting the beginning or aftermath of violence are all that is needed in the rest of the story. Once the audience knows what is possible, the threat of violence is enough to generate suspense on an ongoing basis.

Male rape in prison is something that has become a cliché – to the point that a reference to 'dropping the soap' in a communal shower has become a joke. I don't think you can, or should, laugh off the impact of that kind of assault. You don't have to depict the reality of the attack in detail, but you should be truthful in dealing with the consequences of, and impact on, the victim.

Sequence 2

Often this sequence opens with the second day of the hero's time in prison – his first full day behind bars. Scenes in the dining hall and prison yard are common here. In plot terms, we typically see the hero discovering who his allies might be and who his enemies are. He also needs to learn the *unofficial* rules of behaviour and the various territories and hierarchies. There are cliques or gangs, often defined on racial or ethnic lines – the blacks, the Hispanics, the white racists, or whatever.

Not knowing these rules yet, the hero and/or other new prisoners are likely to make mistakes – and the consequences of their unintentional transgressions may be severe. The hero will often do something that 'isn't done,' thereby drawing attention to himself, but also revealing something about his character. The hero speaks his mind, he is a free-thinker, he has strong moral values, he's a rebel, or he's just plain naïve. The action he takes is often to befriend or defend a weaker or unpopular prisoner – the equivalent of 'saving the cat' – and this allows other prisoners to decide whether they like the hero or not. Someone often warns the hero of the dangers of doing what he did – 'You're not going to last too long here.'

There is often an older prisoner who acts as an ally and mentor for the hero. Initially, the two might not hit it off – they don't appear to have anything in common and this is emphasised by having them come from different social, racial, or national groups. This is the Morgan Freeman character in *The Shawshank Redemption* and in *Midnight Express* it is Max played by John Hurt. As in many stories, the mentor is a more worldly-wise and cynical character. The ally-mentor's attitude towards the hero usually softens when he sees that he is a decent man and/or a rebel.

In some stories, the hero saves the ally-mentor from a dangerous confrontation – in other stories, it is the other way around. And in some stories, the ally-mentor just watches as the hero defends another weaker character. This often begins an awkward relationship in which hero and ally-mentor don't initially like or trust each other. They are civil to one another but guarded in what they say. This confrontation, or something like it, also makes the hero his first potential enemy. The bully who initiated the confrontation is often the leader of a gang or clique – and he typically says something like 'You and me aren't done' or 'You're dead, motherfucker.'

The ally-mentor explains the unofficial rules to the hero – who's who, what territory belongs to what group, and who he needs to keep an eye out for – perhaps including the resident snitch who betrays people to the prison guards. The ally-mentor does this in a way that says, 'I'm telling you this for your own good because you're a new guy – it doesn't mean we're friends.' The hero still has to win this character's trust and friendship.

As the story progresses, the ally-mentor will also be a source of prison lore, anecdotes, and of the wisdom and philosophy of someone who has been behind bars for a long time and has learned how to survive – both physically and mentally.

Due to his acquaintance with the ally-mentor, or his cellmate, or another prisoner, the hero will be accepted into one of the looser cliques of prisoners – but he is a sort of associate member. He will still be something of an outsider, independent and/or aloof. The hero's assimilation into the clique and his growing familiarity with prison life may be shown in the form of a montage that gives the impression of the passage of time. Try and avoid leaves flying from a calendar or days being crossed off or a wall covered in scratch five-bar gates as these have all been done to death – try and come up with more imaginative ways of showing the passage of time. Or just state it simply and unobtrusively.

If the hero is innocent, he may be holding on to the hope of an appeal against his conviction or the severity of his sentence. The ally-mentor might warn him against relying on hope too much – it is better to be realistic. But the hero just dismisses this as the jaded words of a long-timer. If you give up hope – what have you got left? During Sequence 2 there may also be a discussion between the hero and the ally-mentor or another prisoner about a dream of escaping, usually across the border to somewhere warm. This is expressed in the form of a fantasy rather than a real hope.

Other characters may be introduced in this sequence. Usually, there is a man with contacts who can obtain contraband items. There is often someone who is regarded as a snitch or a rat who tells tales to the guards and cannot be trusted. In *Midnight Express*, the rat and the black marketeer are the same character, Rifki.

During the whole of Sequence 2, the presence of the guards – especially the main antagonist, the captain – will loom over everything, watching suspiciously and reminding everyone of the dominant authority of the guards by making an example of some poor unfortunate or, more rarely, someone deserving of brutal punishment.

If your story involves some sort of conspiracy – and a prison *thriller* probably should – then there should be some reference to it, or evidence of it, before the end of Sequence 2. This conspiracy should probably be something that is occurring within the prison – or at least the legal and prison system – and involve prison officials. Again, you don't want to open up a prison thriller too widely or you lose the advantage of the claustrophobia associated with such a location – you want your action to occur in a closed, pressure-cooker environment that could explode at any time. You may also want to plant objects or references to events that you will make use of later in the story – or foreshadow things that are to come or introduce symbolic objects, images, or actions.

Sequence 3

Here you need to lock the hero into his prison life and remove any lingering hope of rescue by an outside agency. If the hero was hoping to appeal against his conviction or his sentence, that hope must be removed – either by a failed appeal or a refusal of the opportunity to appeal. This is the equivalent of the hero in other stories trying the easy options before properly committing himself to a quest. Here, the permanence of the hero's situation becomes real to him.

The long-term nature of the hero's imprisonment is also seen in the fact that he's now into the routine of daily life behind bars and is no longer the new guy. Personal items in his cell also indicate that he now regards this as his home. He may also be making short- or medium-term plans about things he wants to do while inside. If escape is his ultimate aim, he might also begin more long-term planning. There is also more bonding with other inmates – sharing of jokes, anecdotes, and also some details of their own life stories, including how they each came to be in prison. If the hero says that he is innocent, the others will laugh good-naturedly – 'Hey, we all are!'

There will be more evidence of the conspiracy and the hero may even ask questions about it, not realising how dangerous this might be. He may inadvertently attract the attention of the conspirators by his questions. Or it may become obvious – to the reader at least – that the hero may have skills or experience that the conspirators will be interested in using.

The dangerousness of the situation that the hero is unwittingly walking into might be emphasised by an act of violence against someone else – perpetrated by the guards or one of the gangs of prisoners, and perhaps related in some way to the conspiracy.

The hero may find himself confronted or attacked by the bully-prisoner he had an altercation with in Sequence 2. Or perhaps it is just a close call, with the violence put off to a later date. The hero may also learn something of the attitudes of other prisoners outside his own clique. In *Midnight Express* when the hero challenges the actions of the snitch following some small betrayal, Rifki says 'You must fuck other men before they fuck you – and you must fuck last.'

Actions and beliefs and relationships within the prison are much the same as those outside, but the claustrophobic atmosphere is like a pressure cooker so that things are much more intensely felt and there is a greater chance of betrayal or violent reprisal. A desire to survive can make some men very selfish and others paranoid. Some men need to dominate others – perhaps as a result of their own self-esteem issues. Some have been abused in the past and now want to be the abuser rather than the victim – believing that you have to be either one or the other. Others have lost everything, their lives shattered, and they feel they have no future to live for and so exist on a day by day basis. And while these attitudes may be most obvious in the prisoners, they may also apply to individual guards.

Here we will probably also see other aspects of the daily lives of prisoners, including work and/or leisure activities. Sports also play a significant part in some prison stories. The hero may also be introduced by other potential allies – people who can get things or do things or have information that might be of use when the hero comes to carry out his escape plans later. In some stories, the hero recruits these people to form an escape committee. In other stories, where he is planning to escape alone, the hero may have to bribe or pay for information and guard against his plan being betrayed to the guards or being forced to extend it to help others escape with him.

The hero may also become aware of some hidden danger that other prisoners are afraid of – something related to the conspiracy. This usually involves the mysterious deaths of prisoners or unexplained disappearances. The hero may ask questions of other inmates and discover they are too afraid to talk. He will probably be warned to stop asking about this – for his own good. We may also see the hero making the mistake of trusting someone he shouldn't, storing up trouble for the future. This person may approach the hero saying he knows something about the conspiracy – when really he is working for the conspirators and trying to find out how much the hero knows. Or it may be one of the people who has something the hero needs and who seems amenable to providing it but who plans to betray the hero – to the guards or to a gang leader – for personal gain.

The hero will also probably engage in some small act of rebellion – just to prove to himself that his spirit hasn't been broken. This act may be observed by the guards, who take note of it but do not take any action. The hero's rebelliousness is potentially a threat to the guards – it is a challenge to their authority and may have to be dealt with firmly before long. It may also be a challenge in that the captain of the guards may – just for the sport of it – decide to break the hero's spirit. As the hero is coming to accept his fate and feel relatively comfortable in his new life, something will happen to shake things up. Typically it is an act of violence. The hero may be ambushed by someone he had a confrontation with earlier. Or something else occurs that reminds the hero of the brutality – physical or psychological – of the environment. The hero realises that he will never be safe here – he can never allow his guard to slip.

Sequence 4

The midpoint that occurs at the end of Sequence 4 is where escape stops being something casually talked about and becomes something that the hero *must* do. His confidence was shaken by whatever happened at the end of Sequence 3, and during Sequence 4 things happen that intensify his need to *do* something about his situation – to get away from this terrible place. Whatever his feelings about what has just occurred, and whatever his ultimate plans, the hero knows that he has to fit in and not draw attention to himself. He will try to be a model prisoner – but will not betray his values or completely give up his individuality. Seeing this apparent change in the hero, the guards may believe that they have succeeded in crushing his spirit – and he may encourage them in this belief.

As a result of his good behaviour and apparently compliant attitude, the hero may earn new privileges – including being assigned special duties as a trustee. This may bring the hero closer to action relating to the conspiracy – and he may even become involved in these actions. In *The Shawshank Redemption,* the hero gives financial advice to the guards and the warden – and ultimately becomes the bookkeeper for the warden's crooked empire.

The hero may have sight of only a small part of what the conspiracy involves and so may decide to investigate to discover more – especially if it involves harm to or the disappearance of prisoners. He may gain some clues at this stage, but not understand what they mean. By digging deeper into the conspiracy he will also put himself at greater risk, knowing that he may be killed if the conspirators discover that he knows too much. The hero may even receive a warning that his investigations have attracted attention and that he could be the next one to disappear. Or the snitch may have seen the hero sneaking around and reported him to the captain of the guards.

At the *midpoint*, the hero may discover the true nature of the conspiracy – and realise that this knowledge puts him in mortal danger. Or the midpoint may be something else that convinces him that he must escape – and he must do it *now*. The hero may realise that he is becoming too much like one of the other prisoners. In *The Shawshank Redemption,* the hero learns that an old prisoner who was just released has killed himself because he had become so institutionalised that he couldn't live outside prison. The hero doesn't want to become that man. Alternatively, the hero may find that he has become like one of the more violent criminals – perhaps he had to kill the snitch character who was set to betray him to the conspirators.

Or the hero may have badly beaten another prisoner and taken his place as the leader of a gang or clique. Or the hero may just feel himself slipping away – his free-thinking rebellious nature being eroded day by day. In *Midnight Express*, the hero discovers that his sentence in a Turkish prison has been extended by another thirty years: his situation has become so desperate that escape becomes his only option. It depends on your particular story whether you need a hard turning point at the end of Sequence 4 – the death of one of the hero's fellow inmates, perhaps – or a softer, more character-based one. It is also important to keep something dramatic in reserve for the turning point at the end of Sequence 6 which is the end of Act II.

Sequence 5

You have to decide whether your hero is going to escape alone or whether he will work with a partner or perhaps as part of a group. Even if he works with a partner or group, the hero may be the only one ultimately who manages to get out. But for the purposes of Sequence 5, you need to know whether the hero will discuss his plans with anyone and whether more than one person will be involved in the preparations for the escape. It may be that another prisoner has equipment or knowledge – e.g. a map or blueprint – that the hero needs for his plan, so that the hero has to take this person into his confidence. Or someone may find out what the hero is up to and insist on being part of it. Or the hero may agree to help someone who won't survive much longer in prison. Partnerships bring added risks – and group efforts even more so. The more people that know about an escape plan, the more chances that it will be exposed and the less control the hero has over things. The hero will need to consider this carefully.

There may be a failed or aborted escape attempt in Sequence 5 – made by the hero or someone else. This highlights the difficulty of the task and the fate of this escapee demonstrates the risks that an escape attempt brings. The attempt may have failed because of a betrayal, so the hero must try and avoid such a thing. Or because of some unexpected obstacle, meaning the hero must have plans for dealing with unexpected problems or things going wrong. Or the attempt may have failed because one of the escapees wasn't physically or mentally up to the task. This may be an issue for the hero as well if he has a partner or team member with a similar weakness.

The failed attempt may also mean that additional security measures are put in place, making the hero's escape harder. But these new measures may also result in new escape opportunities. In fiction, the solution to the hero's problem is often inherent in the problem itself. As the hero (and his team, if he has one) begin preparations for their escape, gathering equipment etc., there may be a sticky moment when a surprise inspection threatens to uncover their plans and/or work to date. But the hero will have thought of his and have a plan in place for dealing with it. Either that or he has to think quickly and improvise something. He may even have done something to trigger the search at a time when it was most convenient – or least inconvenient – for his plans. Or he may have arranged to have the focus of the search directed in a place that doesn't impact his work.

As I've said before, Sequence 5 typically concentrates on character relationships. In the prison story, you will probably explore the relationship between the hero and his ally-mentor. The hero may challenge the ally-mentor to be part of the escape, accusing him of giving up hope for a future outside the prison. The ally-mentor may accuse the hero of harbouring naïve dreams that will fail and eventually drive him insane. The hero will say that he can't stay – he *has* to get out – and challenge the ally-mentor to come with him.

The relationship between the hero and the main antagonist – the prison warden or the captain of the guard – will also be explored here, with the antagonist seeking to prove that he has dominated the hero and broken his rebellious spirit. And the hero either fighting against this or allowing the antagonist to believe he's won. The hero may be more deeply involved in the antagonist's conspiracy at this point and probably knows all of the details of how it works. The hero may find himself forced into doing something that crosses one of his moral red lines in order to prove to the antagonist that he is fully committed to the conspiracy and can be trusted.

If the hero is planning to escape with a group, relationships between the group members will also be explored in Sequence 5. The ally-mentor may try to talk the hero out of the escape plan – warning him that it will be suicide. The hero says he would rather die with a bullet in his back than slowly fade towards death inside the prison walls. This exchange may sour their relationship – the ally-mentor will not be comfortable with the challenge that the hero has issued him.

Sequence 6

Sequence 6 in a story usually ends with a crisis or disaster that sees the hero suffering his 'darkest hour.' In the context of the prison thriller, this could mean that the escape plot is discovered and all hope of freedom is lost. Or it may be that something terrible happens to someone the hero has come to care about. Or both things may happen simultaneously.

The person the hero loses at this point is probably *not* the ally-mentor – though it *could* be. It may be a younger or weaker prisoner that the hero befriended hero and has sought to protect. The hero had probably intended to remain aloof and not allow him to get close to anyone, knowing that someone might exploit this as a weakness. But loneliness and the friendly charm of this character caused the hero to let his guard down. Perhaps the hero saw this character as a younger version of himself – a bit of a rebel – and became something of a mentor to him.

Another option is that this young friend *betrays* the hero his escape plot. Or perhaps the betrayal comes from the hero's ally-mentor, who believes it is the right thing to do in order to prevent the hero from making a suicidal attempt to escape. A betrayal such as this helps intensify the nature of the hero's 'darkest hour.' You can also make things worse for the hero if you make him feel that he is personally responsible for the harm that befalls his friend(s). If the hero hadn't pushed ahead with the escape plan, they wouldn't now be in this situation. Or perhaps the crisis was brought about by the hero's investigation into the conspiracy.

If the hero didn't attack the snitch at the midpoint, he might do it here instead, blaming him for the exposure of the escape attempt and for the punishment meted out as a result. Attacking the snitch may earn the hero a beating from the guards and some time in the hospital or in solitary confinement. In order to demonstrate his control over the hero, the main antagonist may force the hero to engage in some aspect of the conspiracy that goes against the hero's values. When the hero complies, it will seem as if the antagonist has finally succeeded in breaking the hero's spirit. And this time the audience doesn't see any clue that the hero is faking his defeat. Sequence 6 ends with the hero's friend injured or dead, the escape plan finished, perhaps the hero has been betrayed, perhaps he has been badly injured in a beating, and as a result the hero seems to be physically and mentally broken – this is his lowest point.

Sequence 7
The escape. The *real* escape will have been planned in the manner of a caper or heist and we will see it executed as such. Things will have been put together over a significant period of time – and things the audience saw earlier in the story will finally make sense in the context of the escape. Some of the 'disastrous' events in Sequence 6 may actually have been deliberate 'failures' and part of the escape plan – perhaps including the ally-mentor's or friend's betrayal of the hero. Events will have been set up to make the guards look in the wrong direction – perhaps by having the snitch betray misinformation to the guards – so that the final stages of the plan could be put in place. They may have needed to have someone in the prison infirmary, so that even a 'disastrous' injury or beating was really part of the plan.

Prison alarms will sound as the escape is discovered – but the escape plan will have allowed for that as well. Perhaps other prisoners who are not part of the escape will pitch in to cause a distraction – causing a riot – as payment for earlier favours received from the hero. Or the hero may have set-up a war between rivals gangs so that they start a riot without knowing that they have been set up by the hero. There will be moments of tension during the escape as things go wrong, there are near misses, or things expected to be in place are missing. The imagination and resourcefulness of the hero mean these things are overcome. If the hero is escaping with a team, it may be that not everyone gets out – one or more may be caught or unable to get to a specific point at the necessary time; another may abandon his escape attempt because he realises he is not up to the task and risks preventing the others escaping successfully; or one may sacrifice his own freedom to overcome one of the major unexpected obstacles that arise.

However it unfolds, the escape will have been planned in such a way as to make the guards appear incompetent and foolish. It will probably draw the attention of the media – and the guards' triumphant account of how they quelled a prison riot may suddenly be flipped to reveal that they have been duped and the riot was cover for a successful prison escape. The presence of the media will mean that the guards cannot punish the remaining prisoners as brutally as they would normally.

Sequence 8
Escape isn't the main theme of the story – it is about the indomitability of the human spirit and/or the true nature of justice. The final sequence is where we wrap up this thematic argument. As the main antagonist engages in a damage-limitation exercise in front of the media and the public, worse is to come for him – usually in the form of (a) his illegally gained money goes missing, and (b) his conspiracy is publicly exposed. Poetic justice is served when the antagonist is handcuffed – soon to be a prisoner himself. The final shot usually sees the hero living some sort of life that is in keeping with his free-spirit and rebellious nature – and probably something like the sort of life the audience dreams of for themselves.

12 | Noir Romance

There is disagreement among critics as to whether *film noir* is a fully-fledged genre or simply a *style* of film-making. James Damico argues the case for it being a genre because the films have a common narrative template – "Plots in film noir frequently involve some variation of a man lured into a criminal act, often murder, by an attractive but dangerous woman, ultimately leading to mutual self destruction."

Damico expands on this to give an overview of the plot as he sees it: "Either [because] he is fated to do so or by chance, or because he has been hired for a job specifically associated with her, a man whose experience of life has left him sanguine and often bitter meets a not-innocent woman of similar outlook to whom he is sexually and fatally attracted. Through this attraction, either because the woman induces him to it or because it is the natural result of their relationship, the man comes to cheat, attempt to murder, or actually murder a second man to whom the woman is unhappily or unwillingly attached (generally he is her husband or lover), an act which often leads to the woman's betrayal of the protagonist, but which in any event brings about the sometimes metaphoric, but usually literal destruction of the woman, the man to whom she is attached, and frequently the protagonist himself."

Damico gives examples that match this plot: *Double Indemnity, The Woman in the Window, Scarlet Street, The Killers, The Lady from Shanghai, The Postman Always Rings Twice, Out of the Past, Pitfall,* and *Criss Cross. The Blue Dahlia* and *Murder, My Sweet* are variations on it.

It seems to me that Damico is defining a *subset* of *films noir* in which the character of the 'femme fatale' and her relationship with the hero as part of a 'love triangle' is central. There are other films consistently labelled as film noir that do not feature this sort of triangular relationship – and *The Maltese Falcon* has as its hero a character who *doesn't* fall victim to the treachery of the femme fatale.

But we have already explored the private eye thriller that was defined by *The Maltese Falcon* and the *noir*-like gangster film, so in this chapter we will concentrate on the type of story described by Damico, which I will call a 'noir romance' – and which Charles Derry calls the 'thriller of murderous passions.'

The Film Noir 'Style'

In the first full-length study of the *film noir*, French critics Raymonde Borde and Etienne Chaumeton (1955) describe how a 'new kind of American film' was shown in France during the summer of 1946, "...films which had an unusual and cruel atmosphere in common, one tinted with a very particular eroticism..." The term 'film noir' was first used by another French critic, Nino Frank who described them as 'criminal psychology' stories. Borde and Chaumeton also note that the films are typically set in the criminal milieu, differentiating them from police procedural thrillers.

Borde and Chaumeton also wrote about the role of women in these films – "...the femme fatale is also fatal unto herself. Frustrated and guilty, half maneater, half man-eaten, blasé and cornered, she falls victim to her own wiles."

In writing about the 'noir style,' Borde and Chaumeton speak of the way in which the films tend to "...disorient the spectators, who no longer encounter their customary frames of reference." Where in the past, films had offered conventions of a 'clear distinction between good and evil' and characters with 'clear motives' and chaste feminine heroines, these new films offered something different. Criminals are presented as sympathetic human beings with ordinary lives. The victim is not innocent. Policemen may be crooks. The murderer is attractive and likeable. And "...the heroine is vicious, deadly, venomous or alcoholic." While the hero allows himself to be led astray by her. The 'action is confused' and the 'motives uncertain' and the stories are morally ambivalent. The key element of the noir style is "...the state of tension created in spectators by the disappearance of their psychological bearings..." and the creation of "...a specific sense of malaise."

While Borde and Chaumeton refer to Orson Welles film *The Lady from Shanghai* as reviving "...the Expressionist tradition of *Caligari*..." they do not seek to define the film noir in terms of its visual style and are, instead, much more concerned with the psychological aspects of the 'style.'

Later writers have sought to define film noir according to its visual style, noting that it draws inspiration from the German Expressionists and the use of strong shadows contrasting with brightly lit areas of the onscreen image. The term 'chiaroscuro' is often used, in part because it comes from two Italian words meaning clear-bright and dark-obscure. Shots also make use of distorted or exaggerated shadows from venetian blinds, prison bars, the gates of an elevator, bannisters, and silhouettes of human figures. 'Dutch angles' are also used with the camera rotated so that the horizon line and verticals appear off-kilter so as the disorientate the viewer. But while these things may be recognisable in film noir, they are not vital to it – a film noir story can just as easily take place in brightly lit open countryside as it can in the dark, rain-slick city streets. It is the darkness of the psychology of the characters and their cynical and pessimistic themes that define these films rather than their visual style.

The film noir genre (or style) was popular in the 1940s and 1950s, ending with the widespread adoption of colour film. Joan Mellen says that the form was short-lived because it addressed the despair of a particular moment in American history that was replaced by the optimism of the 1950s. Mellen regards the genre as beginning with John Huston's film of Dashiell Hammett's *The Maltese Falcon* (1941) and its 'last great expression' being Orson Welles' *Touch of Evil* (1958). Roman Polanski's *Chinatown* (1974) resurrected the *noir* style and sensibility, reflecting that decade's political disillusionment – it and other more recent films, including Ridley Scott's 1982 film *Blade Runner,* are sometimes referred to as 'neo-noir.' Examples of the neo-noir *femme fatale* include Kathleen Turner in Lawrence Kasdan's *Body Heat* (1981); Isabella Rossellini in *Blue Velvet* (1986); Rachel Ward in *After Dark, My Sweet* (1990) based on the 1955 Jim Thompson novel; Sharon Stone in *Basic Instinct* (1992); Linda Fiorentino in *The Last Seduction* (1994), and Patricia Arquette in *Lost Highway* (1997).

The Femme Fatale

A feature that most critics agree to be a defining element of the film noir is the presence of the *femme fatale*. The *femme fatale* is a character who manipulates men in order to achieve her own goals. She uses intelligence, cunning, charm and sexual allure to persuade or coerce men into doing what she wants. Her ability to use her 'feminine wiles' to entrap or mesmerise her male victim and lead him astray – usually into compromising or dangerous situations – gives rise to comparisons with the enchantress in folklore and mythology. Her seductive charms are regarded as being almost magical, such that she can hypnotise her victim and bend him to her will. The fact that she is seen as seducing and preying on men has led to this type of character being compared to a female demon, a succubus, or a vampire and referred to as a 'vamp.' She is also a 'spider woman' because she lures men into her web. A murderous female who marries a wealthy man and then kills them in order to inherit his wealth is also referred to as a 'black widow.' Sometimes the *femme fatale* is referred to as a maneater, vamp, enchantress, dragon lady or sometimes a 'bad girl'. And sometimes she is just a bitch.

She is a major character in her own right unlike the gangster's molls or gun molls who are the partners of male criminals. The *femme fatale* is a betrayer and a deceiver. She often pretends to be a victim, trapped in an awful situation from which she cannot escape, and then tricking her male victim into becoming her 'rescuer.' She is usually portrayed as villainous or at least morally ambiguous and as sexually attractive but at the same time mysterious and disconcerting.

The *femme fatale* as we know her appeared in the *films noir* of the 1940s and early 1950s. Among the best-known early examples are Mary Astor as Brigid O'Shaughnessy in *The Maltese Falcon* (1941); Barbara Stanwyck as Phyllis in *Double Indemnity* (1944); Ann Blyth as Veda in *Mildred Pierce* (1945); and Rita Hayworth in *Gilda* (1946); Lana Turner as Cora in *The Postman Always Rings Twice* (1946), and Ava Gardner in *The Killers* (1946) based on a 1927 short story by Ernest Hemingway.

The Great Depression of the 1930s meant that many men in the USA were unable to support their families and an increasing number of married women sought work outside the home, usually in poorly paid low-status jobs in the service industries or light manufacturing. America's entry into the Second World War, saw women take on jobs and assume responsibilities that had previously been for men only. As a result, these women – epitomised by 'Rosie the Riveter' – were proudly self-sufficient and had new expectations. Men returning home from the war were confused and frightened by the fact that women were now doing 'their' jobs and didn't want to go back to their old roles as housewives. This fear was reflected in the female characters in *films noir* – many of whom were 'treacherous betrayers'. The films also depicted the way that strong women were now expressing their own sexuality. Mellen writes that *film noir* heroines "...from Bacall and Crawford to Hayworth and Davis were among the strongest, most independent and self-sufficient women to grace the American screen, despite the distinctly misogynous cast of so many *films noir*."

Mellen writes that in the *film nor*, the 'unabashed sexual desire' of these independent women – and its gratification outside of marriage – was often viewed in the same light as their criminal greed and ruthlessness – and regarded as something that the plot should punish them for.

Historical & Literary Precedents of the Femme Fatale

The 'deadly female' archetype appears in the folklore and mythology of many cultures. In Greek mythology there was the temptress Circe who appears in *The Odyssey;* Medea who features in the story of Jason and the Argonauts, and Clytemnestra, the scheming wife of Agamemnon. There were also the Sirens who lured sailors to their deaths with their enchanting songs. Lilith in Jewish mythology may be descended from a much earlier type of female demon from ancient Mesopotamia. According to some texts, Lilith was one of the four original queens of the demons or succubi. The succubus or female demon in medieval legends is similar to the qarînah in Arabian mythology and there are also accounts of such creatures in African mythology. There are several seductresses in the Bible: Eve, Delilah, Jezebel, and Salome – the subject of the Oscar Wilde's 1891 play for which he invented the 'Dance of the Seven Veils.' In Hindu mythology, there is the goddess and enchantress Mohini, whose name is related to delusion or disillusionment and erotic magic. There are also the *Visha Kanya* or 'poison girls' who were young female assassins and appeared in later folklore and Indian literature as an archetype. In Chinese mythology, the 'fox spirit' Daji was the favourite consort of King Zhou of Shang whose infatuation caused him to neglect state affairs resulting in the fall of the Shang dynasty. In the legends of King Arthur, Morgan le Fay is the ambivalent or malevolent enchantress or sorceress.

The *femme fatale* was a popular figure with Romantic poets – John Keats' 'Lamia' (1819) is a poem about the enchantress and serpent-woman from Greek mythology and his ballad 'La Belle Dame sans Merci' (1819) tells of a knight who is doomed after being seduced by a beautiful woman. She has also appeared in paintings and other artworks across the centuries. And she was taken up by writers in the Gothic tradition, notably in M.G. Lewis' *The Monk* (1796) – his wicked woman Matilda is said to have inspired the Marquis de Sade to make a *femme fatale* the heroine of his novel *Juliette, or Vice Amply Rewarded* (1801), and Sheridan Le Fanu created the female vampire *Carmilla* (1871), predating the 'weird sisters' or 'brides' in Bram Stoker's *Dracula* (1897).

Rudyard Kipling's 1897 poem 'The Vampire' is not about the undead, but rather tells of a man who idolises and objectifies a woman, but she can never live up to his expectations and, disillusioned, he bitterly judges her as having used him and cast him aside. The poem is said to have been inspired by Philip Burne-Jones' painting of the same title. The poem in turn inspired Robert Vignola's short silent movie *The Vampire* (1913) in which a woman called Sybil preys on a young man, but then abandons him when he loses himself in the hedonistic life of the big city. Kipling's verse also inspired the 1915 film *A Fool There Was*, which took its title from the first line of the poem. It starred Theda Bara, who became one of the most popular actresses of the silent movie era, and who was typecast for her portrayal of a 'vamp,' a slang term thought to have its origins in the 1915 film, which used the poem in its publicity. Theda Bara also starred in the 1917 production of *Cleopatra*, one of Hollywood's legendary lost films about one of the legendary *femmes fatales*.

The *femme fatale* came back into Hollywood favour during the 1940s and 1950s, especially in what became known as the *films noir*. *The Maltese Falcon* (1941) gave us Mary Astor as the amoral trickster Brigid O'Shaughnessy; Rita Hayworth played *Gilda* (1946); Ava Gardner in *The Killers* (1946); and Barbara Stanwyck appeared in *Double Indemnity* (1944) and Lana Turner in *The Postman Always Rings Twice* (1946).

In an interview for *The Paris Review* conducted in 1977, James M. Cain said that his novel *The Postman Always Rings Twice* (1934) was "...based on the Snyder-Gray case, which was in the papers about then ... Gray and this woman Snyder killed her husband for the insurance money." Walter Lippmann, Cain's boss at *The New York World* attended Ruth Snyder's trial and spoke to Cain about her afterwards. Snyder and Gray were executed in 1928 and a photograph of Snyder in the electric chair was published on the front page of the *New York Daily News*. Cain's *Double Indemnity* (1936) was also inspired by the Syder-Gray case and follows its events more closely.

Neo-Noir movies of the 1980s and 90s, as we have seen, brought us a new batch of *femmes fatales*. She was even spoofed in *Who Framed Roger Rabbit* (1988) in which the impossibly vampy Jessica Rabbit, voiced by an uncredited Kathleen Turner, says: "I'm not bad. I'm just drawn that way."

Typically, the *femme fatale* is always drawn that way – demonised, regarded as a woman who corrupts men and tricks them into committing criminal acts on her behalf; or as a vengeful man-hater who takes a perverse pleasure in bringing a man to his knees and destroying his reputation. But this archetype can be used as an anti-heroine, or even as a romantic heroine who uses her enchantments against villainous men. Some people argue that the *femme fatale* is misogynistic – arising from men's fear of female power. Others say the femme fatale symbolises female independence and challenges traditional female gender roles. Camille Paglia, in *Sex, Art and American Culture: New Essays* (1992) writes that the femme fatale "...expresses woman's ancient and eternal control of the sexual realm."

In her book *Rethinking the Femme Fatale in Film Noir*, Julie Grossman writes that the femme fatale "...threatens to transgress patriarchy." These women are "...lawless agents of female desire, rebelling against the patriarchal relegation of women to the domestic sphere where they are deemed passive and valued only in relation to their maternal and wifely vocation."

Just what is the attraction of the *femme fatale* character? Jessica Morell writes in *Bullies, Bastards and Bitches:* "She is often empowered by anger, a need to survive, or self-fulfillment. She is typically dangerous to at least one vulnerable character in the story, and she can also be self-destructive or dangerous to herself ... Because the bitch character is atypical, she creates a special fascination and tension in the reader, along with an age-old appeal from reading myths and fairy tales with witches, jealous stepsisters, and wicked stepmothers in the cast ... the contradictions of an angel or mother figure masking a demon or a woman with unusual powers makes for potent storytelling."

Julie Grossman: "Most *femmes fatales* are sexual, but that's not their main appeal ... It is the leading female's commitment to fulfilling her own desires, whatever they may be (sexual, capitalist, maternal), at any cost, that makes her the cynosure, the compelling point of interest for men and women."

Themes

Film noir is regarded as being pessimistic and morally ambiguous. The world is essentially corrupt, and characters find themselves trapped in situations which are for the most part hopeless.

Film noir thrillers may have been a reaction against the prevailing conformist attitude in post-War America, and also against the increasing dominance of powerful corporations who sought to influence behaviour through advertising, promoting the 'ideal' American family and preying on threats to it.

"The protagonist killer, the femme fatale and the stranger or outcast are all used by their creators to probe and subvert what they see as the complacent conformity of the time," writes Lee Horsley.

Love

The hero and the *femme fatale* are usually motivated by what Mellen calls 'erotic obsession' and a desire for sexual gratification. Romantic love rarely plays a part – except perhaps at some point late in the story when one of them realises, too late, that they do have genuine feelings for the other.

Mellen notes that occasionally love does triumph in these stories, including "...*The Big Sleep, To Have and Have Not, Key Largo*, and *Dark Passage*, perhaps because Bogart and Bacall as a couple had become icons in their own right."

Nihilism

Joan Mellen writes that the film noir rarely ended happily. "There would be no redemption, no recompense for the innocent paying for somebody else's crime ... The *film noir* was successful because it made no statements, its style alone enunciating the tone of disarray. With stoicism and bravado, shunning explanation (these were never 'message' films), they showed that things are likely to end badly ... the lingering hope that merit will be rewarded or goodness triumph are best left to the fools and the phonies." The American Dream is best regarded as just that – a dream. The corruption within society – and the dominance of the patriarchy – is so deep-rooted that no individual can hope to oppose it.

Thematic Significance of the Femme Fatale

The nature of the femme fatale has been interpreted in different ways by different writers, academics, and critics – she may be a sexual object, selfish destroyer, or tragic victim – or some combination of the three.

In her analysis of women in film, Laura Mulvey (1975) writes that the female is placed on screen as a passive object for men to take pleasure in looking at – she is an erotic object for the male characters in the film and for the male audience. She quotes Hollywood film director Budd Boetticher as having said: "What counts is what the heroine provokes, or rather what she represents. She is the one, or rather the love or fear she inspires in the hero, or else the concern he feels for her, who makes him act the way he does. In herself the woman has not the slightest importance." She is part of the visual 'spectacle' of the film, Mulvey says, "...yet her visual presence tends to work against the development of a storyline, to freeze the flow of action in moments of erotic contemplation."

If you look solely at the images on the screen when Lana Turner appears in *The Postman Always Rings Twice,* you can see that there is certainly some truth in this argument – part of the appeal of such characters is that men are attracted to 'bad girls'. But there is more to the *femme fatale* in film noir than simply the visual presentation of a sexual object. Boetticher is right in saying that she is the thing that makes the hero act as he does – but she also *represents* more than that.

Women throughout history have tended to be represented as either Madonna or Whore. Janey Place writes that the "...dark lady, the spider woman, the evil seductress who tempts man and brings about his destruction is among the oldest themes of art, literature, mythology and religion in Western culture. She is as old as Eve, and as current as today's movies, comic books and dime novels. She and her sister (or alter ego), the virgin, the mother, the innocent, the redeemer, form the two poles of female archetypes." In film noir, which is almost always told from the hero's point of view, the woman is a *destroyer*. If we want to see her as *redeemer*, we have to look outside the genre to a movie like *Casablanca*.

But to see the *femme fatale* as simply a destructive character whose motives are entirely self-centered and who will use men to get what she wants, caring nothing about what happens to them as a consequence, is to miss an important facet of the archetype – her position as a victim in a male-dominated society.

The femme fatale's husband represents the dominant patriarchal system – he is typically wealthy and older than she is, being a controlling father-figure rather than a lover. She is subordinate to him and her role is to stay at home and keep things nice and, ultimately, to bear him a child - preferably a son who will take his place in the dominant patriarchy.

Janey Place: "Film noir is hardly 'progressive' in these terms – it does not present us with role models who defy their fate and triumph over it. But it does give us one of the few periods of film in which women are active, not static symbols, are intelligent and powerful, if destructively so, and derive power, not weakness, from their sexuality."

The femme fatale is unhappy in her male-dominated role and wants to escape from it. She is a threat to the patriarchal system because (a) she has sexual desires of her own that her husband is not fulfilling, and (b) she has *ambitions* of her own – to be something other than a wife and mother. She wants to escape from the role that men have defined for her – and that makes her dangerous to the men who want to control her and who are represented by her husband.

Since the femme fatale has been placed in a position where she is physically, financially, and socially weaker than her husband, the only way she can achieve her own ambitions is to use the 'weapons' she has – or the only weapons society has led her to believe that she has – her sexuality, her victimhood, and her role as a 'mother'.

Using her sexuality she can attract and ensnare a man, the hero. She chooses him because he is younger and more virile than her husband – but also because he is less powerful. The hero is typically unambitious, perhaps even lazy, and a literal or metaphorical drifter. He is also somewhat passive and perhaps masochistic, and so she is able to control him with a strong almost maternal hand – he is an ego-driven man-child and she tells him what to do to get what he wants – which is usually sex and money.

Although the hero is less of a threat to him than her husband, he is still a man and by definition her oppressor. This, coupled with the weakness that she exploits in him, means that she cannot really respect him as an equal partner. But the fact that he fulfils her sexually and seems to adore her does mean that she may come to feel *something* for him. It can also mean that she underestimates the danger he may pose to her and/or overestimates his abilities as a rescuer.

Not all femmes fatales adopt the controlling mother stance – some play up their role as a victim instead, emphasising their apparent weakness and suffering in order to evoke the hero's wish to be her white knight and rescuer.

Whether she controls the hero via her sexuality, maternalism, or victim-status – or a combination of all of these – the femme fatale is deceiving him by deliberately assuming a role or roles that she believes will allow her to achieve her ambitions. She is all of these things and none of them, and part of her tragedy is that she has never been allowed to discover who and what she really is.

And the femme fatale is a *tragic* character because no matter how hard she tries, she cannot defeat or escape from the patriarchy that dominates her world. This society *requires* that she be punished for even attempting to defy it and escape its clutches. This was particularly true in the 1940s when the independent female was only beginning to assert herself and where the Production Code demanded that criminals be seen to be punished.

In neo-noir stories in contemporary settings, the femme fatale is less constrained by patriarchal society – but often her tragedy still arises from the fact that she unconsciously defines herself and defines 'success' or 'escape' or 'power' in terms of her relation to men rather than in terms of her own true self and her own value system. And if she *does* get away with murder and achieve some sort of victory, it is usually a pyrrhic one.

How you choose to portray your femme fatale will depend on the themes you want to explore in your story.

The Noir Romance Plot

The noir romance is structured in two distinct halves – (1) establishing the relationship between hero and *femme fatale* and planning the murder, and (2) consequences of the murder on their relationship and the investigation into the 'accident.' This structure means that this sub-genre is one of the rare cases where a significant character – *the investigator* – is not introduced until after the midpoint of the story. The investigator is a detective, district attorney, or insurance investigator – and he *may* be introduced in a scene before the midpoint, but he doesn't have to be. The investigator effectively controls the action of the story during sequences five and six.

In the first half of the story there is a relationship triangle between the hero, the *femme fatale* and the husband; during the second half of the story, there is a relationship triangle between the hero, the *femme fatale*, and the investigator.

Sequence 1

The hero and the femme fatale meet and there is an instant attraction between them. She is unhappy in her marriage and is knowingly betraying her husband – and he doesn't care.

Sometime during the first two sequences, he realises that she wants to kill her husband. She may deny this – but her denial is unconvincing. She would never go through with the murder on her own – but he agrees to help her.

Sequence 1 ends either with the couple having sex for the first time or with them agreeing to murder the husband.

Sequence 2

The suggestion of murdering the husband may be made here – after sex. They talk about how they would do it without getting caught. It will need to be the perfect murder. She may express some doubts about going through with it or even ask him to talk her out of it. But he does the opposite. She may just be testing his resolve.

There may be a failed murder attempt here – or an aborted one. This makes them rethink the plan and may even cause them to abandon the murder plot altogether – for now, at least. This functions in the same way as a 'reluctant hero' scene – establishing how difficult the task is and showing that something important is at stake.

If there is no abortive attempt, this sequence will concentrate on the planning of the murder attempt. This may involve making sure that something important is in place ahead of time – an insurance policy; a trip by the husband, or something to serve as part of their alibi. This shows the premeditated nature of their murder plot and also gives the opportunity for obstacles and suspense. 'We can't murder him until X is in place.' The couple will also have to sneak around to continue their illicit relationship – they cannot afford to be seen together. Or they may decide that it is necessary that they do not see each other at all until after the murder – which they will find very frustrating.

Sequence 2 serves to establish the amorality of the couple – they are selfish and cold-blooded – she probably more so than he.

Towards the end of this sequence or early in the next, the hero and the *femme fatale* will discuss other opportunities for escaping together – these alternatives need to be disposed of before they commit themselves to the murder plot. That gets out of the way the audience question 'Why didn't they just run away together?' They need a good reason to choose murder – he'd come after them, they want his money, or whatever.

Sequence 3

If there is an aborted murder attempt, the couple may separate for a while to let things cool off. They may even convince themselves that the relationship is over. But fate or desire brings them back together – and the subject of murder is soon back on the agenda – especially if fate also provides them with an opportunity to kill the husband without very much effort on their part.

The husband is unaware that he is being cuckolded or that his life is in danger. He may regard the hero as a close friend and/or as a good employee.

The couple plots the husband's death and may put the early stages of the plan into action. They may need to 'plant' various bits of evidence or witness testimony that will 'prove' their innocence.

Sequence 4

Sequence four ends with the *midpoint* of the story – and this is the point at which the husband of the *femme fatale* is murdered. The murder is almost always designed to look like an accident so that the *femme fatale* can claim on her husband's insurance.

The scenes here show the building suspense as the couple put their plan into operation – making sure any final necessary bits of alibi are in place and carrying out the preparations for the deed itself.

Just before the midpoint, there will be some sort of problem or obstacle that puts the whole plan in jeopardy and/or risks exposing the two would-be murderers. This may be some unanticipated action by law enforcement officers that is unrelated to the murder or it may be an unexpected move by the husband. This marks the couple's last chance to back out – but they forge ahead, finding some way to overcome the obstacle.

The first half of the story ends with the murder of the husband. The actual killing is usually carried out by the hero with the *femme fatale* as accomplice – or she may just watch it happen. She will probably be much cooler about what is happening than the hero is.

Sequences 5 and 6 contain events that are interchangeable – that is, most of the events I describe under *Sequence 5* below could happen in *Sequence 6* and vice versa. These two sequences effectively show a shift in the

fortunes of the hero and femme fatale from positive to negative or from negative to positive:
  (i) *Positive to negative.* The hero and the *femme fatale* seem to have gotten away with the murder – but then something goes wrong that means they are suddenly the prime suspects.
  (ii) *Negative to positive.* The hero and the *femme fatale* are suspected of the murder, but then something happens that seems to prove them innocent – they are freed and seem to have gotten away with it.

Sequence five can be structure as in (i) or (ii) above and then sequence six will be structured as in the other. *Double Indemnity* has (ii) followed by (i), while *The Postman Always Rings Twice* has (i) followed by (ii).

Either way, a great deal of strain is placed on the relationship between the hero and the *femme fatale* and things between them are not the same as they were before.

Here I will make sequence five equivalent to (i) positive to negative and sequence six (ii) negative to positive.

Sequence 5

This deals with the *immediate* aftermath of the murder and the longer-term consequences. The focus here will be on the *relationship* between the hero and the *femme fatale*.

Immediately following the murder, there may be an adrenaline-fuelled moment of relief and euphoria – We've done it! – and the couple may share a romantic clinch or have sex. This is effectively a last moment of freedom before they must deal with the consequences of what they have done. It is also a brief glimpse of the sort of ideal romantic life they had imagined for themselves.

Alternatively, the immediate aftermath may be less positive for the hero. He may feel overwhelmed by the enormity of what he has just done. The stress of it may cause him to double over and throw up. And the *femme fatale* may watch this without emotion or with a flicker of a smile on her lips – she is less emotional about the situation than he is. Or she may be the one who goes to pieces – or at least *appears* to – leaving him to take charge and move them on to the next stage of the plan, trying to convince her that she is strong enough to go through with it.

The couple often discusses what will happen next – having tried to foresee all eventualities. There will be an inquest, she may be arrested and interrogated, there may be a trial, etc. They may even prepare for the fact that she may be accused and found guilty of manslaughter – that she will have to spend some time in prison. She says she's prepared to do that – as long as he waits for her. This all serves to show the audience what the couple think will happen next – allowing the audience to quickly recognise when something unexpected occurs.

The scenes straight after the midpoint may also show the couple completing some parts of their alibi before they have to face the police.

As mentioned above, the *investigator* effectively controls the action of the story during sequences five and six. In order to discover the truth about the 'accident' he will separate the hero and the *femme fatale* in order to try to get each of them to betray the other.

If money was one of the motives for murder, the *femme fatale* stands to inherit her husband's estate and a significant sum from an insurance policy – in this case, the investigator is often working for the insurance company and will be looking for some evidence to show that the company isn't liable and so doesn't have to pay up. They would much rather that the husband's death proves to be suicide or murder rather than a genuine accident.

If the death can be shown to be a suicide, the hero and the *femme fatale* will get nothing for their efforts. Waiting to see if the investigation results in a suicide verdict adds to the stress that the couple is under and increases the suspense – especially when we all know that an accusation of murder will follow if it *isn't* shown to be suicide.

If an insurance claim is not the motive for murder, the investigator is more likely to be a detective or district attorney who will try to determine whether the husband's death really was an accident.

Having introduced the investigator, we reach the point – as discussed above – where the hero and the femme fatale are (i) *not* suspected of murder or (ii) suspected of murder. We'll assume here that they are not immediately suspected of murder by the investigator.

Either way, the stress of their situation may cause the hero and the *femme fatale* to argue – and this is the first sign of the strain on their relationship and the fact that things are not the same as they were.

The investigation will normally be seen from the point of view of the hero because he is the one who has the most to lose – he actually killed the husband. We will also gain some insight into how the hero now feels about the *femme fatale* – is he still infatuated with her?

The *femme fatale's* cold-heartedness during and after the murder may cause the hero to realise that she isn't the kind of woman he thought she was. She is far less vulnerable than she pretended to be. He may even be a little afraid of her – or he may intensely dislike this new version of her – and he may quickly begin to worry that she will betray him, just like she betrayed her husband.

The reality of the murder may also cause the hero to rethink his own position. The murder was probably a lark or an adventure to begin with, but in the cold light of day, the enormity of it – especially if he has never killed a man before – may weigh heavily on him. His instinct may be to run – but that would just risk making him appear guilty and perhaps increase the risk of the *femme fatale* betraying him as a way of punishing him for leaving. Whatever his current feelings for the *femme fatale* – love, lust, fear, hatred, disgust or some combination of these – he knows he's got to stick with her and see how things pan out. He may even have to pretend that he's still in love with her.

Even though they are not (yet) suspected of murder, there is an investigator at work – the hero and the *femme fatale* cannot relax and must be on their guard. They may have decided that they cannot see each other until the investigation is completed – this puts a further strain on their relationship. If they do occasionally sneak away to see each other, there is a risk of them being discovered together.

The situation usually takes a turn for the worst when the investigator finds evidence that the accident wasn't an accident and suicide is ruled out. He will also have either evidence or a strong suspicion that the hero and the *femme fatale* are in a relationship – and were seeing each other before the husband's death. His first task is to gain an admission from one of them that they *were* having an affair.

The investigator's method is to 'divide and conquer' – he questions the hero and the femme fatale separately in order to compare what they say and spot any inconsistencies. The investigator also probably senses fairly early on that the hero is weaker than the *femme fatale* and so puts more pressure on him. The hero initially denies that he was having an affair with the dead man's wife – but the investigator quickly disproves this or tricks the hero into admitting it.

At the end of sequence five, the hero and the *femme fatale* are the prime suspects in the murder of the husband.

Sequence 6

Questioned by the investigator, the hero may have to admit several misdemeanours in his own past when the investigator reveals he has the hero's criminal history in front of him. The hero may also seek to protect the femme fatale by painting her as purely innocent – saying that he seduced her into having an affair – the hero may even believe this is true. But the investigator has seen the *femme fatale* and he doesn't buy this version of events.

Initially during his questioning, the hero will believe that he is in a strong position – even though the accident is now known to have been caused deliberately, he and the femme fatale are only being questioned as a matter of course – there is no evidence against them. And the hero believes they thought of everything and have committed the perfect murder. The investigator will need to shake this confidence before he can achieve anything in his questioning – and will usually do this using some small piece of evidence or witness testimony that shows the couple *didn't* think of everything and may have made a small mistake. The investigator will want to sow a seed of doubt in the hero's mind – if they made one mistake, they may have made more. The investigator will imply that they're following up other leads and will soon have more evidence and/or witnesses.

The hero or the *femme fatale* are often placed in a position where they have to do something that they would prefer not to do – but not doing it would look suspicious and make them look guilty. In *Double Indemnity,* the insurance claim is rejected and so the *femme fatale* has to sue the insurance company. In *The Postman Always Rings Twice,* the hero has to file a complaint against the *femme fatale* because he was injured in an accident when she was driving.

The investigator will look for other ways to put pressure on the hero. The investigator may *say* that he believes the hero is innocent of murder – whether he believes this or not – and then try to get information out of the hero that might incriminate the *femme fatale*. If the hero refuses to cooperate it will look like he has something to hide – and this means he is faced with a dilemma. The investigator may argue that if the hero is innocent and if the husband was murdered, then there is every chance that the *femme fatale* is guilty. The hero can say he doesn't believe this – but if he wants to maintain his own innocence, there isn't much he can offer to try and prove the *femme fatale* innocent.

The investigator may also use the fact that the *femme fatale* betrayed her husband by having an affair with the hero – 'How do you know she won't betray you as well?'

And in the meantime, the hero doesn't know what the femme fatale might be saying to the investigator when she's alone with him. Should he carry on trying to protect her? Or should he just worry about himself? Weighing against this is the fact that if she is found guilty, she is likely to implicate him and take him down with her. This means that no matter what his feelings are for her at this point, he can't betray her.

At some point, the investigator will explain how he thinks the murder was committed. He may have one or two minor details wrong, but overall his theory is correct. This explanation is designed to shake-up the hero and make him think the investigator is close to proving their guilt. But the explanation is mostly speculation – the investigator has little or no proof and he's just trying to smoke the hero out – trick him into a confession.

The investigator may set things up so the *femme fatale* believes that the hero has betrayed her. He may use some small piece of what the hero has said or done as proof of this – having pushed the hero into a corner to get him to reveal this small piece he can use as leverage. The fact that she believes (or suspects) that the hero has betrayed her is significant to the *femme fatale*. She turns against the hero – partly out of revenge and partly because she now regards him as more of a liability than an asset. Or perhaps she has been using him all along and the present situation is just the trigger she needs to let him take the fall for her.

In some stories, the *femme fatale* started out cynically seducing the hero so that she could use him to achieve her murder plot – but then found herself having genuine feelings for him. What she was pretending to feel became real. When it appears that the hero has betrayed her, she becomes angry at having allowed herself to feel anything for this man.

If she believes that the hero has implicated her, she may decide to confess the whole thing with the aim of revealing his part in it all and taking him down with her. Or she may concoct a story that lays the guilt on the hero and shows her to be an unwilling accomplice who went along with the plan because she was afraid of him or because she thought he wouldn't actually go through with it. She may even have had the foresight to plant various bits of evidence that she could use against the hero if this ever became necessary.

If the *femme fatale* doesn't betray the hero by revealing his part in the murder plot, there are other ways in which she can hurt him. The investigator may reveal that she has another lover – and the hero may then learn that she was seeing this person before she met the hero and 'recruited' him for the murder plot. The hero then realises that she has played him for a fool. He may also suspect that he is being set up so that the *femme fatale* and her lover can get away. Rather than allow this to happen, he will want to see her punished – but how can he do that without damning himself? And if the *femme fatale* does betray the hero and set him up to take sole responsibility for the murder, how can the hero account for the new – and possibly fake – 'evidence' that she planted?

At the end of sequence six, the hero – and possibly the femme fatale – appear to be guilty of murder. This marks the hero's 'darkest hour.'

Sequences five and six as I have described them above – with the hero and *femme fatale* having thought they'd got away with murder but then having one or both of them suspected of murder – is a logical and dramatic way of structuring this type of story. But switching things around so that initially they are believed to be guilty of murder but them having something corroborate their version of events or 'prove' their innocence can be equally dramatic. If they are proved innocent at the end of sequence five, sequence six then shows them as being free – and perhaps even collecting the insurance pay-out. They *seem* to have won and sequence six then becomes about their relationship under these new circumstances.

During the difficult period in sequence five when it seemed that they were going to be found guilty, each of them probably said or did things that amounted to betraying the other in order to save themselves. As a result, their relationship has changed – the trust that used to be there is gone. Technically they are even – each of them is as guilty of betrayal as the other

– and they can start over. But one or both of them no longer really love(s) the other. They might try to carry on as before, they may have wild sex, but the original spark is gone.

They have won a pyrrhic victory – they got what they wanted, but now they no longer want to be together – which is ironic if they did all of this in order to be together.

Sequence seven can take one of two courses, depending on whether the hero is guilty or innocent at the end of sequence six.

Sequence 7

Guilty at the end of Sequence 6 – Having been betrayed by the *femme fatale*, the hero decides to kill her – and if she has another lover, he will make it appear that he is guilty of her murder. The hero goes through the process of setting up an alibi for himself as he did before. He arranges to meet her – but is shot himself, either by the *femme fatale* or by her lover. The fact that he has been shot may make it seem that the hero is innocent and that the *femme fatale* shot him because he knew the truth about her guilt. It is up to the dying hero whether or not he tells the investigator the truth – does he want the *femme fatale* to suffer? Or, seeing that he is dying anyway, does he take sole responsibility for the murder and allow her to go free? Or does he allow her to go free but implicate her lover in the murder of the husband, out of spite?

Innocent at the end of Sequence 7 – The 'innocent' hero and *femme fatale* try to make a life together – but disagreements arise because they want different things. In *The Postman Always Rings Twice,* for example, he is a drifter who wants to move on again but she wants to settle down into her dream life. The hero may betray the *femme fatale* by having an affair with another woman. Someone who helped to 'prove' them innocent – either accidentally or deliberately – may turn up and try to blackmail them.

The *femme fatale* may discover the hero's infidelity and threaten to pass evidence to the police that proves him guilty of her husband's murder. She may also have planted evidence that will frame the hero and his lover – and she may even go as far as staging an attempt on her own life that she can blame on them. Or the *femme fatale* may murder his lover and make it appear that he is guilty. Or the hero may have to spurn his lover, treating her badly so that she will leave him, so that she can be safely out of reach of the *femme fatale*. The hero may end sequence seven in the clutches of the jealous *femme fatale* or of a greedy blackmailer.

Sequence 8

In the 1930s and 40s, the Production Code in Hollywood meant that criminals could not be seen to get away with their crimes and so the films had to end with some form of poetic justice. If the hero and/or *femme fatale* evaded justice for one murder, they had to be found guilty of another – perhaps one that they were actually *not* guilty of. Or there may have been a genuine accident that was so similar to the one they faked that it is treated as murder and they are convicted. Or there may be some ironic twist on the way the hero and femme fatale betrayed each other earlier in the story. Or some small action or evidence from an earlier sequence may 'pay off' unexpectedly, damning them both.

Modern noir thrillers are not subject to the same restrictions, so if you want to allow one or both of your murderers escape, you can.

You need to resolve both the plot strand involving the crime and the plot strand involving the relationship. That gives you a choice of four possible endings: *positive* – the hero and *femme fatale* get away with murder *and* they have a successful relationship together going forward. *Negative* – the hero and/or *femme fatale* are found guilty of the crime *and* their relationship goes down in flames. And then there are two more *ironic* endings – they get away with murder but their relationship is doomed, or they are found guilty of murder but their relationship remains strong and they both go to death row knowing that the other still loves them.

A Plot Variation

Somewhere between the private eye thriller (*The Maltese Falcon*) and the noir romance (*The Postman Always Rings Twice* or *Body Heat*) lies a crime thriller like Jim Thompson's 1955 novel *After Dark, My Sweet* (filmed in 1990). Here, the vulnerable hero is ensnared by an alcoholic *femme fatale*, but there is no patriarchal husband to murder – instead, the third person in the relationship triangle is an untrustworthy criminal 'Uncle' Bud who seeks to use both of them in the commission of a kidnapping for ransom with the aim of swindling them out of their share of the profits. Uncle Bud is similar to the character of the scheming Caspar Gutman in *The Maltese Falcon* and while the *femme fatale* Fay has her own agenda, she seems as much a victim of the situation as the hero is. The role of the investigator is replaced by a local doctor who appears to be a sort of mentor character who is concerned about the hero's mental health – and in the film version, there is a stronger suggestion of physical attraction as well.

The basic structure of this sort of story looks something like this:

Sequence 1 – The hero, a drifter, meets the *femme fatale* in a bar – she takes him back to her place. There he encounters an Old Crook who is planning a crime and who wants the hero to be part of it. Realising what they're up to, the hero leaves – an example of the 'reluctant hero' who thinks it would be best for him to avoid getting involved in this crime.

Sequence 2 – The hero encounters the Doctor-Mentor who expresses concern about the hero's health and the risk that he may be taken advantage of. The hero escapes leaves and goes back to the *femme fatale*'s home. There he allows himself to be talked into participating in the crime – despite his better judgment. The *femme fatale* flirts with the hero. The Old Crook narrowly escapes an encounter with a man he once swindled. The Doctor-Mentor tracks the hero down but agrees to let him be.

Sequence 3 – The three discuss the plan for the crime. The hero suspects that the *femme fatale* and the Old Crook may not be what they seem – and that she may be the one who is running the show. She flirts with the hero – but backs off when the Doctor-Mentor reveals details about the hero's criminal and mental history.

Sequence 4 – As the day of the crime approaches, the hero still fears that the Old Crook will betray him. With almost no support from the Old Crook or the *femme fatale* – and taking all the risk himself – the hero carries out the crime. In *After Dark, My Sweet* the hero kidnaps the son of a wealthy family at the midpoint of the story. Just before the midpoint, there is an obstacle or some other setback that makes it look as if the plan will fail and the hero will be caught – but he manages to pull it off. Having successfully completed the crime, the hero says he wants more of a say in what happens next – because he doesn't trust the other two. They pretend to be shocked and offended by this, but agree to his demands.

Sequence 5 – Having successfully carried out the crime, this sequence concentrates on the consequences of this and on the relationships between the hero, the *femme fatale* and the Old Crook – none of whom trust each other. Not trusting the other two, and thinking that the *femme fatale* will side with the Old Crook, the hero says he has stashed evidence incriminating them both that will be revealed if anything happens to him. There are a number of complications – things that don't go as expected – including the sudden reappearance of the man the Old Crook once swindled (see Sequence 2).

Sequence 6 – The hero saves the Old Crook from the man – and says he thinks someone may have tipped the man off so he could find the Old Crook. The Old Crook doubts this as the only person that knew his location was the *femme fatale*. The hero has another encounter with the Doctor-Mentor who says he wants to help him. In this sequence, we see that the Old Crook and the *femme fatale* are cold-blooded when it comes to the well-being of anyone else and this is in contrast to the hero who is much more compassionate.

Sequence 7 – The hero considers ways in which the Old Crook may try to cheat him and tries to think of some way to prevent this. The hero and the *femme fatale* have sex and the hero thinks this means that she genuinely cares about him. He thinks about discussing his doubts about the Old Crook with her and also considers taking off with the *femme fatale* and forgetting about the proceeds from the crime. But then he discovers that the *femme fatale* has betrayed him – and the sex was a way of distracting him while her own plan was carried out. The Doctor-Mentor appears and he figures out that they have carried out the crime. The hero knocks him out and he and the *femme fatale* escape.

Sequence 8 – The final meeting to obtain and/or share out the proceeds of the crime. The Old Crook tries to get away with it all, but the hero was expecting this and outwits him. The Old Crook has been tracked down again by the man he swindled and during their confrontation, either the Old Crook or the man, or both, are killed. The *femme fatale* may have been in a relationship with the other man. With just the two of them left, the *femme fatale* says she wants to be with the hero – the two of them should go away together. The hero knows this would never work out – and besides, the Doctor-Mentor has identified him to the police and he will be hunted down. He decides to sacrifice himself to allow the *femme fatale* to escape, either by provoking her into killing him or by deliberately making some 'mistake' that allows the police to find him while she gets away.

13 | Vigilantes & Enforcers

Revenge is retaliation by one character against another for some real or imaginary injury. The idea of taking 'an eye for an eye and a tooth for a tooth' – of punishment being equal to the crime – is an ancient and deeply held belief and this is what people, on a gut level, regard as *justice*. But our more even-handed modern justice system is designed to take into account things like context and mitigating circumstances – things that the 'revenger' may dismiss as legal loopholes that allow someone to 'escape' justice. The 'revenger' may claim to be seeking *justice*, but by taking the law into his own hands – by taking on the roles of judge, jury, and executioner – he is dispensing vigilante justice. Vigilantes are individuals or groups of civilians who carry out 'law enforcement' without any legal authority to do so. A law enforcement officer who acts beyond the limits of his legal authority may also be considered a vigilante.

Rationalisation
Vigilantes rationalise their behaviour by claiming that the official forms of law enforcement – investigation, trial, and punishment – are either absent, insufficient, inefficient, or corrupt. They claim that injustices are being committed and they seek to redress the balance in favour of the innocent and the (by their definition) good. They typically claim that they are doing what ordinary people want to see done – and there is often significant and vocal support for the actions of some vigilantes. Vigilantes often target people or perhaps organisations that appear to be 'above' or beyond the reach of the law, or who have somehow managed to 'escape' justice.

Proportionality and Violence
One reading of the idea of 'an eye for an eye' in terms of reciprocal justice is that the punishment should be proportionate to the crime – *one* eye for an eye and not more. This is often spoken of in terms of 'the punishment should fit the crime.' This argument is used on both sides – by those who believe that punishments should not be excessively punitive and by those who argue that a person who takes a life should be put to death.

When we think of vigilante justice we tend to think in terms of violent retribution, but 'getting your own back' on someone doesn't have to include violence. The film *The Sting* is an example of non-violent retribution. In stories, a form of ironic or poetic justice is often more satisfying – and more appropriate to the circumstances – than blowing the villain's head off.

Revenge for What?
There has to be an act that prompts the hero to want or need to take revenge. This act is some kind of inciting incident that sets off a chain reaction that continues throughout the story until the hero gains his or her final revenge – or fails to. This incident could be some form of attack on the hero him/herself. Or the victim may be someone the hero cares about – a family member, lover, mentor, or whoever. Or the 'victim' may be society as a whole, threatened by a type of criminal person. Often a vigilante begins with a personal motivation – retaliating for an attack on himself or his

loved ones, but then his 'crusade' takes on a social aspect. 'Defending' society is generally viewed as more heroic than 'selfish' personal revenge.

The Conspiracy and the MacGuffin

There may be a conspiracy element to a revenge story, usually in the form of someone who is an official in law enforcement or the legal system behaving in a way that means justice is subverted. This may be a crooked cop, lawyer, or judge who is, ultimately, regarded as responsible for the injustice that saw the hero and/or the victim come to harm. But a conspiracy is not necessary. The hero may become a vigilante as a consequence of flaws inherent in the law enforcement or legal systems without there being any deliberate actions by conspirators.

A MacGuffin can also be used – an object that was taken by the villain and that the vigilante wants back. It could be a wedding or engagement ring or some other object of sentimental value. It could be something that the victim was trying to protect. It could be the hero's own weapon which has been used by the villain in crimes since it was taken. There is some crossover here if the villain has kidnapped *someone* rather than taken an object. Some serial killer stories and action thrillers such as *Taken* involve a recovery element.

Amateurs, Professionals & Undercover Agents

Some vigilantes are amateurs – the Jodie Foster character in *The Brave One* and Charles Bronson's character in *Death Wish* are ordinary people forced to take the law into their own hands as a result of extraordinary personal circumstances. This means they have a lot in common with the amateur thriller hero I wrote about in *Suspense Thriller*. An amateur vigilante can become a professional over time as their experience builds and as they train themselves to become better at what they do. In the original *Death Wish* series of films, the hero becomes a full-time avenger and the same path is followed by a 'caped crusader' such as *Batman*. Bruce Wayne was himself the victim of a terrible crime when he was a young boy and this prompts him to become a professional vigilante.

Other vigilantes begin as professionals – often in law enforcement – and then step beyond the legal bounds of their official roles and become vigilantes. In the 1971 film *Dirty Harry,* the title character played by Clint Eastwood, was compared to a vigilante because he ignored the rights of suspects and dispensed his own version of justice. This story reflected public feelings of the time where it was felt that the rights of the criminal were taking precedence over the rights of the victim. The filmmakers stepped back from the cop-as-vigilante idea in the sequel, *Magnum Force* (1973), in which Dirty Harry goes up against a group of vigilante cops. Whether the vigilante is an amateur or a professional, the fact that their activities are illegal means that they must operate in such a way as to hide their identity. This means that they have some things in common with the undercover agent hero described in an earlier chapter.

Iconography

The *iconography* of this type of story consists mainly of a lone hero standing in the dark (usually holding a gun) and facing the criminals who exist in the shadows and prey on the good people in the world. Alternatively, if there is a band of vigilantes, we may see them like peasant farmers, arming themselves with whatever weapons they can find, to take on a band of invaders or occupiers.

Setting
The *setting* of these stories is almost always the ordinary world of the hero which takes on a new and darker aspect following the attack on the hero or victim. The actions of a vigilante are almost always taken in defence of the ordinary world of everyday society. The 'strange new world' which the hero enters at the beginning of Act II is typically the same world he has been in all along, but seen differently due to recent experiences. This difference is usually seen in terms of daytime versus night time. But we also often see the hero entering parts of the city or town that he would not normally visit – especially after dark.

The hero often enters the dark 'underworld' that belongs to criminals in order to take his fight to them. He may deliberately make himself look like a defenceless victim in order to draw the criminals out. Unlike the official law enforcer, the vigilante engages in behaviour intended to provoke criminal activity and to entrap the criminal – and by doing this he feels justified in making a violent response. There is a danger here – and this is another argument against vigilantism – that the hero is provoking criminals into committing crimes that would not otherwise have been committed, simply so that he has an excuse to carry out the retributive punishments he wants to carry out.

Suspense & Stakes
There is danger inherent in the act of a lone hero going up against one or more armed criminals – especially if the hero is an amateur. We have typically seen what the villain or villains did to the victim and we know that this – or worse – could happen to the hero. Because the hero's activities are illegal, he is also opposed by official law enforcement agencies. He risks being arrested or shot by a policeman. He is also operating 'undercover' so there is a risk of his identity being discovered. He may also be hiding his actions from a friend, lover, or family members and fear losing them if his activities are uncovered.

There are also psychological risks. The hero may have been traumatised by the original victimising incident and without proper support, their mental health may deteriorate further. If another person was the main victim, the hero may feel some form of survivor's guilt and feel that they must take whatever risks are necessary to secure 'justice' for the victim. Or the hero may feel that he no longer has anything to live for, apart from revenge, and so will take almost suicidal risks because on some level he would welcome death. Even if the hero isn't suffering from some form of PTSD, the actions he takes as a vigilante are likely to impact on his mental wellbeing. He may become desensitised to acts of violence and begin to regard violence as the only solution to problems, carrying it into other areas of his everyday life. The isolation of his vigilante existence may also affect him negatively.

But I Want My Villains to Suffer...
Stories of revenge and vigilante justice are popular. And they are even popular with liberal-minded audiences who *know* that vigilantism is wrong and ultimately doesn't work. They appeal on the basis of a fantasy – they show black and white situations where someone sees to it that the bad guys are punished. It is a reassuring fantasy. And as long as the argument against vigilantism is included somewhere in the story, we're happy to accept that a proper balance has been struck. *Batman* is probably the best-known example of this kind of approach.

The trick for a writer is to set-up your story so that the situation is black and white enough for the reader to accept the actions of your vigilante. There are a couple of ways to ensure this:
- Make the villain's crimes so awful that it is 'obvious' he deserves nothing more than a painful death. This works best in a story that is heavy on action and violence.
- Make the victim's suffering – psychological and emotional, rather than physical – so intense that all of the reader's sympathy is with them. This works better in a more character-centered story.

Characters

There are typically three or four main characters in a revenge or vigilante story:

The *hero* – the vigilante or revenge-seeker

The *victim* – the hero him or herself may be the original victim, but it is more likely to be someone close to the hero who is hurt or killed, with the hero often being a secondary victim

The *villain* – a single person or gang responsible for the harm to the victim. If there is a gang, their leader or most violent member is usually regarded as being the main target for the vigilante

The *antagonist* – this is a non-villainous character whose moral standpoint on vigilante justice is in opposition to the hero's. This character may be a detective, a romantic co-protagonist, a relative, a friend, news reporter, or mentor. Multiple characters may function in this role at different points in the story.

You need to humanise the *victim* so that the reader or audience feels sympathy for them. You have to demonise the *villain* so that the reader regards him as not human and can, therefore, more easily accept bad things being done to him at the climax of the story by the vigilante. In some stories, the villain is a single character, but in others, it is a gang or even a 'type' of person – in these cases, the hero often begins with lower-level criminals and works his way up to their leader or most violent representative.

You need the audience to approve of the actions of the *hero* – to have sympathy with his cause – by making them appear justified. But you do not necessarily need to make the audience feel empathy *with* the hero. In a violent story especially, the hero does bad things for a good reason – the reader accepts the reason but may not want to put themselves in the position of someone carrying out such violent acts. In such cases, you need to establish a little emotional distance between hero and audience. It is similar to the situation where we would not necessarily want to be a soldier ourselves and could never imagine ourselves shooting another person, but we recognise the need for soldiers in fighting a war.

The fact that revenge is related to anger and that the main character in a revenge story is driven by gut feelings about what constitutes justice, rather than by logic or compassion, means that the *hero* will have a strong Warrior element in his personality. If this is mixed with cool-headed planning for revenge, he will probably be a Crusader – Head plus Gut or Warrior plus Thinker. Or he may be driven by more compassionate feelings – he is more akin to the lioness seeking those who wounded her cub – which brings together Head and Heart or Warrior and Carer, giving us an Adventurer, who is more like our private detective character – his emotions are usually hidden, but they are there.

The Vengeance or Revenge Plot
Georges Polti in his *Thirty-Six Dramatic Situations* defined two types of vengeance plot in classical and subsequent literature – (i) Crime Pursued by Vengeance and (ii) Vengeance Taken for Kindred Upon Kindred.

Crime Pursued by Vengeance
The two characters required for this are an avenger and a criminal. Polti lists several possible situations where vengeance might be pursued:

- Avenging a Slain Parent or Ancestor – including vendettas and avenging a father driven to suicide
- Avenging of a Slain Child or Descendent
- Vengeance for a Child Dishonoured
- Avenging a Slain Wife or Husband
- Vengeance for the Dishonour, or Attempted Dishonouring, of a Wife – which Polti says have been the cause of numerous duels, including those where the wife is only insulted
- Vengeance for a Mistress Slain
- Vengeance for a Slain or Injured Friend
- Vengeance for a Sister Seduced
- Vengeance for Intentional Injury or Spoilation – including 'having despoiled during absence'
- Revenge for an Attempted Slaying
- Revenge for a False Accusation
- Vengeance for Violation – including incest
- Vengeance for Having Been Robbed of One's Own
- Revenge Upon a Whole Sex for a Deception by One – Polti includes serial killer Jack the Ripper here

Polti also notes that the broad heading 'Crime Pursued by Vengeance' also covers the professional pursuit of criminals by detectives such as Sherlock Holmes.

Vengeance Taken for Kindred Upon Kindred
This is effectively a specific subset of the revenge story in which the action is confined to members of the same family – all of the main characters are 'kinsmen.' The required characters are an avenging kinsman, a guilty kinsman, and the 'remembrance of the victim' who was a relative of both of them.

Polti writes that this variation 'augments the horror' of another of his dramatic situations – 'Discovery of the Dishonour of One's Kindred.' He also says that the avenger may be motivated to take action against his guilty kinsman for a number of different reasons – desire on his own part; the wish of a dying victim or the appearance of the spirit of a dead one (as in Shakespeare's *Hamlet*); an imprudent promise; a professional duty, or the necessity of saving other relatives, a loved one, or fellow citizens. He also notes that there are stories where the avenger may exact his revenge without being aware that he is related to the guilty individual and stories where 'vengeance' is carried out against a kinsman who is, in fact, innocent so that the avenger effectively becomes a criminal.

Polti again lists several possible situations where vengeance might be pursued but you effectively have any combination of three relatives, one exacting revenge on another for harm done to a third. The closer the relationship between the kinsmen – father, mother, brother, son, sister, husband – the more intense the drama is likely to be.

Historical Development & Examples

In Shakespeare's *Hamlet*, the title character is asked by the ghost of his dead father to avenge his murder. Unsure of the correct course of action, Hamlet investigates and finds proof of his uncle's guilt and so feels he must take the appropriate action. The crime has occurred before the play opens and the story explores its impact on Hamlet who himself is a victim of his circumstances.

Thomas Kyd is believed to have written a play used by Shakespeare as a source for *Hamlet*, but is better known for the play *The Spanish Tragedy* (c.1587) which is said to have established the genre of the revenge tragedy. Kyd drew inspiration for his play from the Roman poet Seneca, whose revenge tragedy *Thyestes*, written in the first century AD, was based on a play of the same name by the Greek poet Euripides probably written between 438 and 405 BC. The revenge plot is one of the oldest there is.

The Count of Monte Cristo, written by Alexandre Dumas in 1844, was inspired by a true crime essay by Jacques Peuchet about a shoemaker who was falsely accused of spying by three jealous friends and who spent years plotting his revenge against them. Inspired in part by Dumas's novel, Lew Wallace's *Ben-Hur: A Tale of the Christ* (1880) is also a story of a man wrongly accused who seeks vengeance and finally achieves it during a chariot race. Stephen Fry's novel *The Stars' Tennis Balls* (2000, titled *Revenge* in the US) is a modern reinterpretation of the *Monte Cristo* story in which many characters have names that are anagrams of those in the original. The revenge plot in the science fiction novel *The Stars My Destination* (1956, titled *Tiger! Tiger!* in the UK) by Alfred Bester has also been compared to Dumas's novel.

Modern examples include the 2000 movie *Gladiator; The Outlaw Josey Wales* (1976), based on the novel *The Rebel Outlaw: Josey Wales* (1972) by Forrest Carter (a pen name of former Ku Klux Klan leader Asa Earl Carter); and the 1974 film *Death Wish,* based on the 1972 novel by Brian Garfield – though the anti-vigilantism of the book was abandoned for a pro-vigilantism movie. There were four sequels to *Death Wish* and the film was remade in 2018 with Bruce Willis in the lead role. Garfield's sequel to the novel *Death Sentence* (1975) was filmed in 2007 with Kevin Bacon in the lead role and the anti-vigilantism theme intact. The 1977 revenge thriller *Rolling Thunder* has a screenplay by Paul Schrader who wrote *Taxi Driver* and tells of two former Vietnam POWs who seek revenge on the gang who killed the wife and son of one of them. A vigilante movie featuring a gang of vigilantes is the 'grindhouse classic' *Vigilante* (1983, also released as *Street Gang*).

There is a sub-sub-genre of this type of story that has been labelled the 'rape and revenge' story, and which is generally regarded as a type of 'exploitation' thriller. Examples include *I Spit on Your Grave* (1978) and *Ms .45* (1981, also released as *Angel of Vengeance*).

Quentin Tarantino's movie *Kill Bill*, released in two volumes in 2003 and 2004, is an homage to – among other things – martial arts and grindhouse revenge movies. Uma Thurman stars as The Bride, who is shot and left for dead by the Deadly Viper Assassination Squad and sets out to avenge herself against its members and leader.

The Brave One (2007) features Jodie Foster as a character who becomes a vigilante following an attack in which she is beaten and her partner is killed. In *Harry Brown* (2009) Michael Caine plays a pensioner on a London council estate who decides to hunt down the gang who killed his friend. *God Bless America* (2011), a black comedy written and directed by Bobcat Goldthwait, is an odd variation on the vigilante theme in which a middle-aged man and a teenage girl take revenge on the rudest excesses of American culture by killing people who annoy them. *Vengeance: A Love Story* (2017) stars Nicholas Cage as a detective investigating the rape of a single mother and who takes the law into his own hands when her attackers are set free by the court – it is based on the 2003 novella *Rape: A Love Story* by Joyce Carol Oates. *Peppermint* (2018) stars Jennifer Garner as a mother who sets out to avenge the deaths of her husband and daughter who were murdered in a drive-by shooting by members of a powerful drug cartel.

Another variation on the vigilante is the masked hero such as Zorro (1919), the Lone Ranger (1933), and Batman (1939). The origin story of Batman, in particular, follows the pattern of a hero who suffers a terrible personal tragedy – the loss of his parents at the hands of a mugger – becoming an unofficial crimefighter in order to rid the streets of 'criminal scum'.

Vigilante thrillers were at their most popular in the 1970s, partly because of popular fears about rising crime rates and the ineffectualness of law enforcement and the courts coupled with a number of high-profile cases of police corruption. This was also the period when people began to fear that the rights of criminals – protected more strongly in law as a result of prosecutions failing as a result of heavy-handed treatment of suspects by the police – were being put ahead of the rights of victims. Clint Eastwood's portrayal of *Dirty Harry* came out of that period as did the popularity of the *Death Wish* movie – both spawning several sequels. It was also the period when the 'enforcer' novels were at their most popular, stories of professional vigilantes typified by Don Pendleton's creation Mack Bolan aka 'The Executioner.' These films and stories were, by standards of the time, regarded as extremely violent and portrayed a type of character whose moral values made some people uncomfortable. I will cover the professional vigilante thriller in more detail under *The Enforcer Thriller* below.

Thematic Argument

If you are going to write a revenge story, you have to decide where you stand on the issue of revenge – at least in terms of your current story. Approval or disapproval of revenge is essentially a moral issue and has to be considered in terms of personal values and societal values. There are three basic positions you can take:
  – Revenge is *bad* – it is self-destructive and ends in tragedy; this includes the negative ironic or pyrrhic victory where vengeance is achieved but somehow backfires or is shown to be no better than defeat.
  – Revenge is *good* – it is cathartic for both 'revenger' and audience, and rids society of a menace.
  – Revenge solves nothing – it doesn't feel as good as the revenger or audience hoped and it doesn't, ultimately, solve society's problems. Included here is the more positive ironic victory with a more ambiguous ending.

Revenge versus Justice

In his essay 'On Revenge' (1625), Francis Bacon wrote: "Revenge is a kind of wild justice; which the more man's nature runs to, the more ought law to weed it out. For as for the first wrong, it doth but offend the law; but the revenge of that wrong pulleth the law out of office." He was basically saying that vigilantes are bad – as bad as, or even worse than, the criminal they seek vengeance upon.

Generally speaking, revenge stories focus more on the act of revenge than on an exploration of the hero's motivations. To the hero, the situation is black and white – someone he cares about has been harmed and that person deserves justice; if the official system cannot deliver that, the hero must do it himself. There is an almost primitive nobility in this idea, however ill-advised the hero's actions. The hero will feel that he is morally justified in seeking revenge – and the audience will probably side with him on this, if he and the victim are presented sympathetically.

In most revenge or vigilante stories, there is usually a moment in the story where the arguments for and against vigilante justice are presented – usually in the form of a discussion between two characters who represent the two differing viewpoints.

In some stories, the hero questions his or her own motives and moral values. In others, the hero is staunchly on one side of the argument and the opposite view is presented by someone else – often by a detective who regards both the criminal and the vigilante as his opponents.

The argument in favour of vigilante justice is basically that the official law enforcement, legal, and penal systems are flawed, inefficient, or corrupt and fail victims by not catching criminals and by not convicting and punishing those who are caught. It may also be argued that the criminal's rights are protected at the expense of the victim's rights. And it is argued that amoral lawyers exploit legal 'loopholes' so that criminals can go free.

The argument against vigilantism – aside from the obvious fact that it is illegal – is that it is wrong for a single person to act as judge, jury, and executioner because there are no safeguards in place to prevent a miscarriage of justice. This is a particular issue if the vigilante has a personal stake in the judgement and is viewing things emotionally and subjectively rather than coolly and objectively. You can't appeal against your conviction if you've received a fatal bullet to the head. The official legal system has measures in place to try and avoid a miscarriage of justice and procedures for handling situations where it is possible that someone has been wrongly convicted. These systems aren't perfect, but they do protect hundreds of innocent people every year.

The legal system also seeks to be as objective as possible, protecting the rights of all concerned – and it seeks to judge the crime within its context, taking mitigating circumstances into account. Situations are rarely black and white and both sides of an argument – or two different versions of events – have to be carefully weighed. The legal system also draws on a great deal of previous experience – of precedence – to try and ensure that people accused of similar crimes are treated equally under the law. None of these legal safeguards is in place where a vigilante is concerned.

In the formal law enforcement and legal systems, suspects and the accused are protected against violence so that – in effect – torture is not used to obtain a false confession. Vigilantes are not limited in this way and may feel comfortable beating an admission of guilt out of someone or obtaining it at gunpoint.

Populism & Mob Rule

Another feature of the vigilante story is that the vigilante's actions against criminals are approved of and celebrated by the media and members of the community. They may also inspire others to take the law into their own hands. There is an element of the lynch mob about this, or of villagers with flaming torches chasing down the monster, and this almost always ends badly. Just because something is popular doesn't mean that it is right.

Genuine democracy recognises both the *rights* of individuals and the *responsibilities* that the individual has towards others. Populism and mob rule tends to concentrate on '*my* rights' at the expense of respecting the rights of others. The formal legal system is based on an assumption of innocence and demands proof of guilt, on the basis that it is better to let a dozen guilty men go free rather than to punish one innocent person. Mob rule tends to work on the basis that it is okay for a few innocents to suffer if that's what it takes to get the bad guys. The only time this becomes an issue is if you end up being one of the innocents who suffer.

Punishment vs. Rehabilitation

This is a theme that we also see in the Prison Thriller and concerns the question of what justice is intended to achieve. Do we want criminals to *suffer* – physical and psychological punishment – or do we want to try and turn them into law-abiding and productive members of society? Mob rule tends to vote for the punishment option. An eye for an eye. Or preferably a death sentence. And that tends to be the option preferred by the vigilante. Prison doesn't work, it is argued, so we need something tougher and/or more permanent.

Revenge vs. Romance

The anti-revenge or anti-vigilantism argument is often portrayed in stories by a romantic co-protagonist character. This character typically comes to suspect that the hero is behind the vigilante killings or knows that the hero is planning revenge against someone, and seeks to talk him out of it. The romantic co-protagonist may be morally opposed to vigilante justice or she may just be concerned for the hero's physical safety and/or mental health.

The co-protagonist may also have been the victim of crime and presents a different form of response to it. She may be more compassionate and forgiving or simply more pragmatic. She knows from her own experience that the law enforcement and legal systems are not perfect, but she regards them as better than the alternative.

The co-protagonist doesn't have to be a character the hero is involved with romantically – it could be a platonic friendship or the character may be an older and more experienced or worldly-wise mentor.

The Vigilante Thriller Plot

Sequence 1

Typically we see the *crime*. The hero is unable to defend the victim against the crime either because he is not present and is unaware it is occurring, or because he is restrained, or is in some other way helpless, and forced to watch what happens to the victim. Obviously, the latter circumstances can only arise in some stories, but they do make the situation worse for the hero and increase his desire for revenge. Another way to make things worse for the hero is to arrange the situation so that he feels in some way *responsible* for what happened to the victim – through his own decisions and actions or inactions – so that his anger and desire for revenge also has an element of guilt mixed with it.

It is possible that the crime has taken place *before* the story opens. In this case you have lost the direct impact of showing the reader what happens to the victim and will probably have to rely on the *impact* of the crime – on the hero or another character who has a relationship to the victim – in order to generate sympathy and outrage – and a desire for revenge – in the reader.

The crime must be sufficiently awful to justify the actions that you want your hero to take later in the story – in order for the audience to be on the side of the revenger, the punishment he intends to mete out must be proportionate to the original crime. The more violence you want your hero to dish out, the more heinous the crime needs to be. Looking at Georges Polti's list, we're in the realm of crimes like rape, murder, incest, or in some other way ruining or taking the victim's life.

We should also see the impact of the crime – its physical and/or emotional consequences – on the victim, on the hero, on others who have a relationship to the victim, and/or on the community as a whole. We must see that the victim did not deserve what happened to them and that they were in no way responsible for it happening – they weren't 'asking for it.'

The *victim* may be the hero him or herself – that is the case in Quentin Tarantino's *Kill Bill* – but it is more often the case that the direct victim of the crime was the hero's lover, friend, or family member and the hero is an indirect victim of the criminal's actions, having been denied the love or companionship of the victim.

Sequence 2

The crime in and of itself is not normally sufficient to set the hero on the path of vengeance. We must first see official law enforcement processes fail to deliver justice. The audience and the hero must feel that the criminal, the antagonist, is going to escape punishment for his crimes and that the victim will not receive justice. Generally speaking, the hero will be a good, law-abiding citizen who the reader feels sympathy for and who is forced by circumstances to take the law into his own hands. He feels an obligation to the victim to seek justice on their behalf. The end of Act I – that is, the end of Sequence 2 – typically has the hero committing himself to achieving justice for the victim.

Sequence 3

As I've said before, Act II typically begins with the hero doing the things that any ordinary person might do to deal with the situation he faces. This means trying the easy options and answering the audience's question 'Why didn't he just...?' We have to show that the obvious solutions don't work. In this case, that might be having the hero attempt legal processes to try and bring the killer to justice – trying to help official investigators by doing their job for them. He may obtain evidence they have been unable to obtain – perhaps in a way that is not technically legal and so makes the evidence inadmissible in court.

The hero's early attempts may also be somewhat amateurish and may even get him into some kind of trouble – with the law and/or the criminal. Either way, he will be advised to 'leave it to the professionals.' This humiliation may cause the hero to rethink or it may just spur him on to more dangerous tactics. We will also see the hero becoming possessed by his desire for vengeance – the combination of anger, guilt, and helplessness is a strong motivator and he will be consumed by his mission and increasingly neglectful in other areas of his life.

Sequence 4
Seeing that lawful actions have not satisfied his desire for justice, the hero will now consider unlawful methods. Instead of trying to assist the official law enforcers, he will step beyond them and take on the role of an unofficial enforcer – he will become a vigilante. He may not initially see himself in those terms, but that is what he is. He will regard himself as being *morally* justified in his actions and see this as more important than their 'technical' illegality.

As with any 'mission,' the hero may need to spend some time planning and getting the necessary equipment together. Obtaining a gun and ammunition may be a significant step for him if he wasn't a gun-owner previously. He may also need to engage in some form of investigation or tracking to identify and locate the villain.

In some stories, the hero is seeking revenge against a single person but in others, he is targeting several members of a group. In *Death Wish,* the hero targets random criminals who he regards as being of the type of person who murdered his wife. The more people your hero goes after, the sooner the killing of bad guys can begin. With multiple targets, you will probably start with the least dangerous or least guilty and work your way up to the most dangerous or the leader or most vicious of the gang. The hero might 'question' one victim to obtain information about the location of the next one.

If there is only a single villain for the hero to hunt rather than a gang, Act II will contain more of an investigation – with the hero learning the identity and location of the villain – then a failed attempt to kill the villain, perhaps with the villain hurting the hero and warning him to stay away. Or the first attempt may fail purely by chance – but it will warn the villain that he is being targeted and the villain may even see and recognise the hero. This will be followed with a cat and mouse chase with each chasing and trying to eliminate the other, the advantage going first one way and then the other.

The first time the hero kills a victim, the impact on him will be significant as he is likely to be the sort of person who has never killed anyone before. Even if the hero has military experience, the situation in which you face a man one to one and end his life in an execution-like way is going to be very different than firing a gun against an unseen enemy. He is likely to experience a combination of sickness, fear, and probably euphoria and you will need to depict this cocktail of emotions for your reader or audience. The death also marks an important turning point in the story – the revenge plan is no longer theoretical, this is happening for real. This marks the midpoint of the story.

Sequence 5
The feeling of strength and power that comes with taking control and *doing* something may carry the hero along into the second killing. It may also make him over-confident – and this may lead him to make an error. The second killing will not be as clean or as simple as the first. The target may fight back and injure the hero. Or the target might be wounded and not killed, meaning that the hero has to pursue him and try to finish the job. The hero may lose his gun and have to face the target in unarmed combat, where he may be at a physical disadvantage – even against a wounded

target. Or there may be a witness – What does the hero do? Kill the witness? Threaten them?

With the second killing or a later one, the hero may discover he has targeted the wrong person and killed either an innocent person or a criminal who wasn't involved in the crime against the victim. The hero will then have to deal with the guilt associated with this. The guilt may make him reconsider his revenge plan – he will suffer self-doubt. But something will happen that convinces him that revenge is still the right course of action. This 'something' may be a visit to the victim, the victim's grave, or someplace he associates with the victim. Or it may be a report of a crime similar to the one suffered by the victim. Or it may simply be something that reminds the hero that the streets are filled with 'scum' and that somebody needs to clean them up.

The second crime may also draw attention to what the hero is doing. The first crime may have been written off as a random killing – the sort of thing one criminal could be expected to suffer at the hands of another. But the second one suggests a pattern – and the third one is likely to confirm it. Even if one of these killings was a wrong man, it will be connected to the others to suggest the work of a serial killer or vigilante.

Detectives will be assigned to investigate the killings, adding an extra source of danger for the hero. He will need to be more cautious and change his *modus operandi* so as not to be caught. Fear of the police may cause the hero to stop and take stock, but he may find that the increased risk just makes the 'game' all the more exciting.

Sequence 6

The detectives investigating the killings may suspect that the hero is behind them. One of them may approve of what the hero is doing – but the other will support the official line against vigilantes and present the argument against them. Or this argument may be put forward by someone else in the hero's everyday life – his son, his lover, a priest, or even the victim. By this stage, the hero is beyond being talked out of his 'mission.' The hero's actions will also have drawn the attention of the media. Depending on the political stance of the reporters, the hero will be presented as a hero or a dangerous psychopathic criminal.

While killing the first target affected him significantly, subsequent killings impact him considerably less. He becomes more confident and more cold-blooded. This may have an effect in other non-revenge related areas of his life. He may be more confident at work and stand up to his boss – which may be a good thing or bad. It may impact his sex life, making him more aggressive or more intense – which his lover may enjoy or find frightening. The hero may also begin to adopt the vigilante justice mentality when faced with other challenges such as bad service in a store or restaurant or rudeness from someone in the street. He may have to consciously control himself so that he doesn't resort to violence in such situations. He may also begin carrying his loaded gun around at all times.

When the criminals become aware that they are being deliberately targeted, they may decide to take action themselves. If they suspect that the hero is behind the killings, they may follow him or pay him a visit to try and scare him off. The hero may be beaten or injured. Or he may take the opportunity to shoot another of the criminals. Or the criminals may go to ground, meaning that the hero has to resort to something risky to draw them out.

Sequence 7
This is usually the final confrontation between the hero and the main antagonist – the leader of the criminals or the most violent and dangerous member of the gang. This may also coincide with a closing in of the detectives investigating the killings. There may even be an ironic situation where the police have to protect the criminal from the avenging hero. The hero's attempt to kill the villain may go wrong, forcing him to improvise. He may find himself at a disadvantage – or perhaps even at the mercy of the villain. Perhaps he is faced with the same fate as befell the victim originally – a fact that the villain takes great pleasure in gloating about.

Sequence 8
How you choose to end your story will depend on what stance you want to take on vigilantism. Does the hero succeed and live to fight another day? Or does he see the error of his ways and quit? Is he killed by the villain? Or shot by the police when he refuses to surrender? Does he end the story having effectively switched roles with the villain – with the villain now in the position of a victim and the hero as his criminal oppressor?

The Enforcer Thriller

John G. Cawelti wrote about 'The Enforcer' in his book *Adventure, Mystery, and Romance* (1976), describing this type of character as a brilliant and ruthless *professional* whose way of life and code of values centre on the skilful completion of assignments. The Enforcer, as Cawelti defines him, is most commonly an assassin – but while his activities are illegal, he is not necessarily involved in organised crime.

The Enforcer appears in *The Godfather* in the form of Luca Brasi and Michael Corleone also takes on the role of assassin to kill those who have betrayed his family. Don Vito Corleone was also an Enforcer and used his professional skills to establish his criminal organisation. Another example is *Get Carter* (1971) based on the 1969 novel *Jack's Return Home* by Ted Lewis, it stars Michael Caine as a London gangster who returns to his hometown to investigate his brother's supposedly accidental death. Learning he was murdered, Carter sets out to avenge his death. The lead character is portrayed not as a victim or a sympathetic character, but as a remorseless killer in his own right.

Don Pendleton's *War Against the Mafia* (1969) is generally regarded as being the first novel of this type. The sub-genre grew out of the American detective story – and Pendleton acknowledged that Mickey Spillane's Mike Hammer was an influence. They also owe something to the old pulp magazine series such as *The Shadow*, *The Phantom*, *The Spider* and *Doc Savage* (who the creators of The Destroyer acknowledge as an influence).

As examples of the Enforcer, Cawelti refers to three series that were being published at the time his book was written: The Executioner, The Destroyer, and The Butcher.

The Executioner. The character of Mack Bolan – The Executioner – was created by author Don Pendleton and the first in the series, *War Against the Mafia*, was published in 1969 and thirty-seven more were published. In 1980, Pendleton sold the rights to the character to Gold Eagle, a division of Harlequin Enterprises. Ghost-writers were employed to write new novels with Bolan heading a team who fought the KGB as well as the Mafia – Pendleton was still credited as the sole author. Bolan was a Vietnam veteran, an expert sniper with experience in intelligence gathering, who begins a single-handed war against the Mafia whose loan sharks were responsible for his father's death.

The Destroyer. Remo Williams – The Destroyer – was created by Warren Murphy and Richard Sapir and the first novel in the series, *Created, The Destroyer*, was published in 1971. 145 titles were published by Gold Eagle Publishing up until 2006 and then the series was taken on by Tor Books. A film *Remo Williams: The Adventure Begins* (also known as *Remo: Unarmed and Dangerous*) was released in 1985 and a television pilot was produced in 1988. Remo Williams was a policeman who was framed for a crime and sentenced to death, but his death was faked by the government who then train him as an assassin.

The Butcher. Bucher – The Butcher – was created by Lyle Kenyon Engel for Pinnacle Books with three ghost-writers working behind the Stuart Jason pen-name. The first novel, *Kill Quick or Die*, was published in 1971 and the 35th and last appeared in 1982. Bucher was a Syndicate enforcer who switched sides and set out to destroy the Syndicate.

"In all of these series," Cawelti writes, "the hero is an absolutely ruthless killer who uses his skill to assassinate the leaders of organised crime who have come to dominate society."

Bradley Mengel, in his book *Serial Vigilantes of Paperback Fiction*, refers to these characters as 'serial vigilantes' and suggests there have been as many as 120 such series. Many of them shared similar characteristics: "After gaining skills in the Vietnam conflict, some event, usually of a violent nature, happens to the hero, causing him to become aware of a threat to society. A violent crusade against this threat is launched, which is either unsanctioned or partially authorised by various government agencies ... In most cases the serial vigilante works alone but teams of serial vigilantes do exist." Mengel also notes that the character's unofficial status allows him to achieve more than 'conventional agencies' are able to.

Kittredge & Krauzer (1978) have noted that the Enforcer's crusade is typically sparked by some event which alters their perception of society – usually one in which they come to realise the negative impact organised crime is having on ordinary people's lives. As with the amateur vigilante, this event is often a crime which harms someone the Enforcer cares about.

As well as acknowledging their debt to Mickey Spillane, Cawelti compared these Enforcer characters to another professional killer, James Bond, who has been described as a government-sanctioned 'assassin' with his licence to kill. Cawelti writes that "The Enforcer is also clearly in the American tradition of the western and hardboiled detective heroes. Like the western hero, the Enforcer is often involved in vengeance plots. Or, like the ageing gunfighter, he may find himself forced to re-examine the meaning of his life. And like both gunfighter and hardboiled detective the Enforcer lives by a code that is deeply rooted in his profession and the maintenance of his honour as a man of supreme skill and dedication to his role."

Mengel describes the Enforcer as 'a crusader for moral order' whose crusade begins after "...a sudden realisation ... that society is not doing its job and protecting people." He determines which organisations pose the greatest threat to society and then uses his skills to mount an aggressive and violent attack. "The serial vigilante has come to the realisation that society's system of justice is flawed, which is generally sparked by a tragedy, and has decided to level the playing field. Just as the criminals operate outside the law and utilise legal loopholes, the serial vigilante also operates outside the law – acting for justice rather than the law."

Enforcer stories, being primarily action-oriented, easily made the crossover into films and comic books – where vigilante stories like *Batman* had always been popular. *The Black Samurai* (1976) is a movie based on the first book in a series of novels by Marc Olden featuring a black martial arts expert. *The Specialist* (1994) starring Sylvester Stallone is based on a series of books by John Cutter (John Shirley). The Destroyer and The Executioner also appeared in comic books. The Punisher introduced in *Amazing Spider-Man* #129 in 1974 was Marvel's version of a serial vigilante and he has appeared in several films. At the 'exploitation' end of the spectrum, we also have *The Exterminator* (1980), described as a 'rip-off' of *Death Wish* by Roger Ebert and as 'grotesque' and 'distasteful' by *Variety*. The film was censored in the UK and banned in several other countries.

By modern standards, Don Pendleton's novel *War Against the Mafia* seems relatively tame and reads like a low-budget action-adventure movie. The action seems so familiar that it is hard to judge how original (or otherwise) it may have seemed in 1969.

The vigilante and the Enforcer have also appeared in various television series in which alone hero or occasionally a team operate outside the law to combat criminals who regard themselves as being above the law. Examples include *Knight Rider* (1982), *The A-Team* (1983), *Street Hawk* (1985), and *The Equalizer* (1985) – remade as a film in 2014 with Denzel Washington in the lead role.

The Appeal of the Enforcer Hero

In stories about Enforcers, the urban setting is similar to that of the hardboiled detective story – a city where corruption and injustice are common. "Criminal activity is just another form of business enterprise," Cawelti writes, "and the criminal syndicate is indistinguishable from any other large corporation." And the Enforcer "...stands out as a man of principle and honour, with the courage and skill to demand and achieve his personal goals ... Like the hardboiled detective, but in a more extreme form, he is a man of honour and courage in a corrupt and hypocritical society. He knows what he is and what he wants, and he is willing to risk his life for his rights." Cawelti also refers to the Enforcer as a "modern urban version" of the Lone Ranger and compares him to 'romantic outlaws' such as Robin Hood, Raffles, and The Saint.

Another part of the appeal of the Enforcer is his lifestyle. Like James Bond, he has expensive taste when it comes to food and drink and other luxuries. But unlike James Bond, we also see the Enforcer off-duty in his own private hideaway or 'bachelor pad', which Cawelti compares to Sherlock Holmes's rooms in Baker Street.

Plot of the Enforcer Thriller

The plot of an Enforcer thriller is generally a 'mission' story, so is very similar to the James Bond style 'Professional Secret Agent' plot that I wrote about in *Suspense Thriller*. Alternatively, it may be structured like the heist or caper thriller described earlier in this book. If we take Don Pendleton's first novel in The Executioner series, *War Against the Mafia*, we can see how the plot is used:

Sequence 1: In a prologue, we learn about the personal incident that causes hero Mack Bolan to become 'the Executioner' – his family were the victims of organised crime and as a result, Bolan decides he will get his revenge on those directly responsible, the Mafia. He kills a couple of criminals and then tells a Mafia loan shark that he has information that will help them track down the man responsible for killing their men.

Sequence 2: Bolan presents his justification for engaging in vigilante justice. The opposing view is presented by a detective who is investigating the deaths of the criminals and suspects Bolan may have been involved. He also warns Bolan that the Mafia will target him for what he has done. Bolan is seeking a man called Leo Terrin who he regards as being responsible for what happened to his family. Bolan assumes an undercover identity in order to get close to Terrin and talks his way into a job as Terrin's assistant.

Sequence 3: Within the Mafia organisation Bolan makes an enemy, Seymour, who sees Bolan as a potential rival and a threat. Bolan, meanwhile, learns how Terrin runs his part of the Mafia empire, overseeing the prostitution business.

Sequence 4: Warned that the Mafia has a contract out on him, Bolan steps up his actions against them, destroying some of their clubs and visiting individual criminals' homes and leaving threats. Unofficially, some of the police support Bolan's actions, but officially efforts to apprehend him are stepped up when military investigators are called in to assist them. The bounty the Mafia has placed on Bolan's head is also increased significantly. This marks the midpoint of the story.

Sequence 5: Bolan steels the money from one of the Mafia's operations. His actions result in the Mafia calling a war council, headed by a more senior member of the organisation. Bolan fires on their meeting, further enraging them. When Bolan visits the home of Leo Terrin, Terrin's wife shoots and wounds him. A local woman hides Bolan and treats his injuries and they begin a relationship.

Sequence 6: after spending more time with the woman who helped him, Bolan goes back to work. He is now wanted by the police for 11 murders. The Mafia think that Bolan is working for the authorities. Bolan discovers that the police have someone inside the Mafia organisation – and he's been undercover for five years. Bolan doesn't have the patience for such a long-term operation. He breaks into a munitions warehouse to stock up.

Sequence 7: Bolan engages in a couple of 'prelude skirmishes', putting Mafia businesses out of operation. The Mafia have increased the size of their army and think they can deal with Bolan. The police think Armageddon is coming. Bolan goes to the Mafia's HQ.

Sequence 8: Bolan, aware that he may not survive, begins his attack on the Mafia HQ. By the end of it, Bolan is responsible for 23 deaths and 51 injured. For him, the battle is over but the war will continue.

14 | The Buddy Movie

When we think of detective stories, one of the first things that comes to mind is probably the television cop show in which a pair of mismatched detectives fight crime and bicker like an old married couple. When I was a kid, my favourite cop show was *Starsky and Hutch* – it was one of many that played on British television. There was *Cagney and Lacey*, *The Sweeney*, *Simon & Simon*, *The Streets of San Francisco*, *Miami Vice* and later *Dalziel and Pascoe* and *Inspector Morse*. The detective duo was the standard format for detective shows until *Hill Street Blues* came along and broke the mould. TV detective duos were inspired by similar pairings of actors in what are often referred to as 'buddy movies.'

Wikipedia defines a buddy film as "...a film genre in which two (or on occasion, more than two) people – often both men – are put together. The two often contrast in personality, which creates a different dynamic on-screen than a pairing of two people of the opposite gender. The contrast is sometimes accentuated by an ethnic difference between the two." The entry also says that "Buddy films are often hybridized with other film genres, such as road movies, Westerns, comedies, and action films featuring cops." In this chapter, I'm focussing on the thriller-buddy movie hybrid. These are often stories featuring the partnering of two radically different personalities as detectives – in television shows as well as films – but this hybrid approach can also involve a pairing of a bounty hunter and his quarry (*Midnight Run*) or a bodyguard and the person he is protecting (*The Hitman's Bodyguard*).

There are all kinds of buddy movies, ranging from *Dumb and Dumber* to *Rain Man,* but this is a book about writing thrillers so I'll pick a couple of my favourites – *48 HRS* (1982) and *Midnight Run* (1988). These may not be classics in the award-winning sense, but they're both good movies based on good screenplays. And both also have great roles for the two main characters. I will also refer to *Lethal Weapon* as another example of the buddy cop movie. The screenplays of *48 HRS, Midnight Run,* and *Lethal Weapon* are all available online and I used these in creating the plot template in this chapter.

Historical Development

Male companionship has appeared in stories since the beginning of time – *The Epic of Gilgamesh*, written around 2,100 BC tells of the friendship between the cultured, urban warrior-king, Gilgamesh, and the wild, nature-dwelling Enkidu. Laurel and Hardy paired up around 4,000 years later (1927) and became one of the world's most iconic on-screen double-acts. They appeared together for the best part of thirty years with their bickering and co-dependence making them seem like a married couple. Odd couples had been paired before – on stage and in film – but Laurel and Hardy's combination of antagonism and trusting friendship became a model for on-screen partnerships that is still used today.

Dean Martin and Jerry Lewis first appeared together as a nightclub act in 1946 then moved into radio before making their first film in 1949. They worked together until 1956. Martin was a handsome, suave Italian nightclub singer who served as straight-man to Lewis, the crazy Jewish comedian. The pair also appeared in a couple of films with comedy duo Bing Crosby and Bob Hope.

Jack Lemmon was paired with Tony Curtis in the 1959 film *Some Like It Hot*. Now regarded as one of the best films of all time, the comedy features two men dressed as women playing it completely straight. But Lemmon's longest-running on-screen partnership was with Walter Matthau – they appeared in fifteen films together. In 1968 they appeared in *The Odd Couple*, a film based on Neil Simon's successful play in which two divorced men share an apartment – Lemmon playing the neurotic and obsessively tidy Felix Ungar and Matthau the easy-going and slobbish Oscar Madison. The way in which their personalities clash and the fact that each learns something from the other and becomes better for it, has become a common theme in buddy movies.

Akira Kurosawa's *Stray Dog* (1949) features the pairing of veteran and rookie homicide detectives and also features a stolen gun plot that found its way into *48 HRS*.

Director Peter Hyams' feature debut *Busting* (1974) starred Elliott Gould and Robert Blake in an episodic story about two vice squad detectives that could easily have served as the template for buddy cop TV shows like *Starsky and Hutch* which was first broadcast in 1975.

Popular examples of the buddy movie include *Butch Cassidy and the Sundance Kid* (1969), *The Blues Brothers* (1980), *The Defiant Ones* (1958), *Freebie and the Bean* (1974), *Running Scared* (1986), *Midnight Cowboy* (1969), *Sideways* (2004), *Stakeout* (1987), and *Thunderbolt and Lightfoot* (1974).

Female Buddy Movies

An influential example of the female buddy movie is the French film *Céline and Julie Go Boating* (*Céline et Julie vont en bateau*, 1974). Other examples include *Desperately Seeking Susan* (1985), *Thelma & Louise* (1991), *Fried Green Tomatoes* (1991), and *Walking and Talking* (1996). *The Heat* (2013) starring Sandra Bullock and Melissa McCarthy is a buddy cop movie.

Buddy Movie versus Bromance

Although there are female buddy movies, this type of story most frequently centres on male characters. As the earlier quote from *Wikipedia* suggested, on-screen relationships between male partners allow for a different dynamic to those between male and female characters, such as that in *The African Queen* (1951). Attitudes towards male relationships have changed in the thirty-plus years since *48 HRS* was first released, but there is still a tendency to regard men as being less able to express friendship and love than women.

Certain attributes, behaviours, and roles are regarded as 'masculine' – but these can vary from culture to culture and in different historical periods. Mosse writes that the stereotype of manliness that we recognise today was created towards the end of the eighteenth century when the medieval aristocratic ideal of a chivalrous knight – "...compassionate, loyal, and ennobled by the pure love of a woman..." – was gradually replaced by something new. Standards of male beauty were drawn from the statues of young athletes from Ancient Greece while ideals of behaviour were drawn from 'Muscular Christianity' which favoured self-control, willpower and courage. This was a period of war and revolution, so bravery and self-sacrifice became associated with manliness, as was patriotism and dedication to a moral cause. It was also believed that women were inferior to men and should obey them. At the same time, intolerance of the non-masculine increased – particularly in the increased persecution and prosecution of 'sodomites.' Effeminacy was frowned upon and men were supposed to demonstrate their differences from females by avoiding overt displays of emotion and 'hysteria'.

This masculine ideal was reinforced throughout the Victorian era and carried on well into the twentieth century. As women and other minority groups refused to accept their assigned inferiority to the patriarchal male, 'angry white men' felt the need to try and reassert their dominance. In the late 1970s – with American masculinity having also been wounded by failure in Vietnam – there was a crisis of identity that led to a need to appear overtly masculine in attitude, action, and speech. This continued into the 1980s and forms the background against which stories like *48 HRS* – with its racial slurs and objectification of women – were conceived.

Attitudes began to change towards the end of the twentieth century. The term 'new man' first came into use in the 1980s, defined by the *Oxford English Dictionary* as a man who "... rejects sexist attitudes and the traditional male role, especially in the context of domestic responsibilities and childcare, and who is (or is held to be) caring, sensitive, and non-aggressive." 1994 brought us the term 'metrosexual' coined by British journalist Mark Simpson and later defined by him as "...a young man with money to spend, living in or within easy reach of a metropolis – because that's where all the best shops, clubs, gyms and hairdressers are. He might be officially gay, straight or bisexual, but this is utterly immaterial because he has clearly taken himself as his own love object and pleasure as his sexual preference." The metrosexual man was compared to the dandy of the Regency period and David Beckham was his poster boy. But this type of man didn't appeal to everyone. Newspaper columnist Barbara Ellen wrote in *The Observer:* "Could it be that post-feminism has created its own Frankenstein's monster? The man who is so like a woman he's unfanciable?"

There was something of a backlash against the 'new man' with a rise in lad culture or 'laddism' and a return to stereotypical of masculinity. Movies such as *Lock, Stock and Two Smoking Barrels* (1998) and *Snatch* (2000) and appealed to the so-called 'new lad'. The post-feminist world also gave us the 'ladette' who the *OED* helpfully tells us is a young woman who behaves in a 'boisterously assertive or crude manner' and engages in heavy drinking sessions. In the USA, as a post on the OED website noted, the term 'bro' came to be "...particularly associated with a certain type of young man, a conventional guy's guy who spends a lot of time partying with other young men like himself." And from this came the twenty-first-century term 'bromance.'

Wikipedia defines a bromance as "...a close but non-sexual relationship between two or more men. It is an exceptionally tight affectional, homosocial male bonding relationship exceeding that of usual friendship, and is distinguished by a particularly high level of emotional intimacy." The word was probably coined sometime in the 1990s but didn't achieve widespread use until around 2005. This, in turn, led to the *bromantic comedy* sub-genre of films which either satirize the stereotypical 'code' of male behaviour or reinforce it, depending on your point of view.

It is hard to say what impact these changes in attitude have had – or should have – on the buddy movie. If you were to pair a modern bromantic type of character with an old-fashioned lad or macho-man, would the ensuing conflict be very much different to that we see in *48 HRS?* And having written that question, I find myself wondering whether relationships between men – and between women and men – have really progressed very far in the last forty years.

Contrasting Personalities
A feature of the buddy movie is that the personalities of the two characters are very different and this gives rise to conflict. They also typically have skills and abilities which complement each other. Both also have a weakness, lack, or flaw that the other helps them to recognise and begin to deal with. Differences are often highlighted by having characters from different racial or cultural backgrounds (*In the Heat of the Night, The Defiant Ones, 48 HRS.*); by having a significant age difference between the two such that one is a seasoned veteran and the other a rookie (*Stray Dog, Se7en, The Rookie*), or by having characters from very different social backgrounds – in *48 HRS* a cop is teamed with a crook; in *Beverly Hills Cop* an unorthodox Detroit cop is teamed with two by-the-book California detectives.

In his review of the 1998 film, critic Roger Ebert said *Rush Hour* was a 'Wunza Movie' featuring a painting of opposites – "...Wunza legendary detective from Hong Kong, and wunza Los Angeles cop. And wunza Chinese guy, and wunza black guy. And wunza martial arts expert and wunza wisecracking showboat. Neither wunza original casting idea, but together, they make an entertaining team."

Beyond the contrasting characteristics of veteran-rookie or neurotic-slob, we can think of the two lead characters in terms of the archetypes I discussed in *Character Creation*. In buddy cop movies, one character is typically a loner, angry and serious and the other is less serious and more relationship-oriented. This suggests some form of Warrior versus Carer pairing, perhaps a Crusader (similar to our existential private detective) and an Adventurer/Trickster. There may also be a Thinker element in one of the characters, as the intellectual-neurotic tends to be obsessive and narrowly focused. Whichever pairing of archetypes you choose, the aim is to show that each character has something that the other lacks – and that each can benefit by learning something from the other.

Characters in the Buddy Movie
The buddy thriller can either be a 'man on the run' type thriller, which I discussed at length in *Suspense Thriller,* but with two men on the run; or it can be an investigation of the police procedural, police detective, or private eye type with two characters investigating.

Midnight Run, as its title suggests, is a men-on-the-run thriller. It features five main sets of characters:
- The *two protagonists* who are on the run together but who also act as antagonists for each other as well as co-protagonists. In *Midnight Run* the protagonists are the Robert De Niro and Charles Grodin characters.
- A *rival* – someone who is seeking the same objective as them and who creates obstacles, problems, and generally gets in the way. Another bounty hunter, Marvin Dorfler, fills this role.
- The *villain* – this is the real bad guy and someone who often only appears in the background, directing the efforts of...
- *Henchmen* – one or two henchmen who pursue the protagonists and generally do the villain's dirty work.

- *The authorities* – the police or the FBI or whatever. Special Agent Alonzo Mosely, played by Yaphet Kotto, is the main representative of the FBI in *Midnight Run*.

In both the 'on the run' thriller and a private detective thriller, we can have our heroes face greater odds by putting them up against a rival, the villain and his henchmen, *and* the authorities. With a police investigation story, you don't necessarily have the heroes up against the villain and the authorities – though they may face obstacles from within their own department or perhaps from a traitor in the department.

In *48 HRS* the characters are:
- The *protagonists* are Nick Nolte and Eddie Murphy.
- The *rival* is Luther, who also wants the same objective as Eddie Murphy's character.
- The *villain* is Ganz, the murderer who takes Nick Nolte's character's gun.
- The henchman is the 'Indian' Billy Bear.
- *The authorities* are represented by the captain of the department who threatens Nolte's character with disciplinary proceedings and dismissal because of his handling of the case.

Plotting Development of the Relationship

With a buddy movie, you have to plot two things – the development of the action and the stages in the relationship between the two central characters. Technically, a buddy story is very much like a romance but without the kissing or sex, except that the action takes precedence over the relationship. In a buddy movie, the action is the A-story and the relationship is the B-story – in a romance, it is the opposite way around.

I'm going to suggest eight broad stages through which the relationship between the two characters may pass. These do *not* coincide with the eight sequences of the plot. Under each, I have listed some sub-stages that you can explore for your characters. Although the eight broad stages will occur, more or less, in the order in which they are listed, some stages or sub-stages are likely to appear more than once. Where many thrillers feature little character development and often have only one significant 'character moment' in Sequence 5, in the buddy movie the relationship tends to develop across much more of the story, beginning when the characters meet and continuing to the final scene.

Stages in the Buddy Character Relationship

I wrote about the development arc of an individual character at some length in *Character Creation* but here I will present some of the key stages that you can often see in a buddy movie.

(1) Antagonism
      a. Confrontation
      b. Grudging respect but dislike
      c. Lack of empathy/sympathy
(2) Thawing
      a. Attempts to get along – usually one-sided and rejected by the other
      b. Raw nerve – one partner says something that is obviously a touchy personal subject of the other

c. Questions and revelations – usually related to work and life in general as personal revelations don't come until later
   d. Personal revelation – usually in the form of backstory or discussion about romantic relationships
(3) *Commonality* – the two discover they have things in common; shared experiences and/or shared values.
(4) *Trust*
   a. Shared danger – they are in it together
   b. Supportive – there is often a romantic subplot or other personal matter where one partner demonstrates support and sympathy for the other – and often dispenses advice which may or may not be welcomed
   c. Vulnerability – the toughest, most macho of the two reveals personal vulnerability. He has come to trust his partner sufficiently to share something personal and painful – a fear, a dream, an obsession, a mistake, or whatever.
(5) *Set-Back* – leading to *mistrust* again
(6) *Working together*
   a. Circumstances dictate that they must work together because success alone is impossible. This is often done grudgingly.
   b. Mutual understanding and acceptance of differences
(7) *Final challenge* – this can involve apparent or real betrayal
(8) *Friendship* – a genuine bond is demonstrated by some final action that reveals both men have changed in some significant way as a result of their adventure with the other.

In the plot structure template below I will indicate where these stages of relationship development are typically found.

Buddy Thriller Plot Structure

In the template/discussion below I'm going to explore the broad strokes of the action and main character relationship in terms of the eight-sequence model of plot. My main examples are *48 HRS* and *Midnight Run* but I will also refer to *Lethal Weapon* as another example of the buddy genre – the sequences as outlined below are based on the *screenplays* of the films and may not exactly match the on-screen running times. As ever, this is not necessarily *the* way to write this type of story, but it is *a* way.

Sequence 1

In the first sequence of your story, you have the option of introducing one of your main protagonists or both of them. If you introduce both you will show them in contrasting work and/or home situations that reveal their character, including their flaw or lack. The challenge or the MacGuffin may be introduced in this sequence. And perhaps a rival, villain, or henchmen. Here or in Sequence 2 or 3 we will also see that the objectives of the two protagonists and/or their methods of working will put them in conflict with one another.

It is often the case that one of the two protagonists has a stronger character development arc than the other. He has a more significant lack or flaw. He has a greater need to *prove* something to himself or to achieve some kind of redemption. The other protagonist serves as the catalyst to trigger and then encourage – through positive or negative actions – the completion of the other's character development arc. It is possible for both characters to have equally strong development arcs, but this is tricky to achieve in the thriller genre where a great deal of action is also required. Here it is more common for there to be a 'primary protagonist' and a secondary one who undergoes a less intense form of character growth.

In *Midnight Run,* Robert De Niro plays the primary protagonist – a down-at-heel bounty hunter who is a loner and an underdog. It is obvious that he has some flaw or personal demon that is holding him back. This makes him very like our 'wounded' private detective hero. Most buddy thrillers have a character who prefers to work alone – this guarantees that there will be conflict when he has to team up with a partner. It is like a bachelor who suddenly has to share his living space.

In Sequence 1, we are typically introduced to the primary protagonist, the loner, first. We need to establish him as a loner and show the 'ordinary world' – usually his working environment and methods – that are going to be disrupted by the arrival of a partner. We will also get some hints about this protagonist's past – which often involves a traumatic or dramatic situation similar to the one he will face in this story.

The first sequence may also introduce the primary protagonist's *rival* – if the rivalry arises out of their work. In *Midnight Run,* the rival is Dorfler, another bounty hunter who tries to capture the same 'skips' as De Niro's character. In other stories, the rival opposes the secondary protagonist instead. In *48 HRS,* Luther is trying to get the same briefcase of cash as Eddie Murphy's character.

We may also see something of the primary protagonist's romantic relationship – especially if this serves to reveal something of his character and his flaw, as it does with Nick Nolte's character in *48 HRS.* His girlfriend, Elaine, also serves as a stand-in buddy for the first two sequences of the story, with Eddie Murphy's character not appearing until Sequence 3.

Sequence 1 of *48 HRS* actually opens with a prologue that introduces the villain (Ganz) and his henchman (Billy Bear), setting up a disruptive force that will upset the equilibrium of the protagonists' worlds. The action alternates between Cates' life and the actions of the villain and henchman. We know that these two plotlines are going to intersect at some point very soon.

Lethal Weapon takes a different approach, introducing *both* of the protagonists in the first sequence, contrasting their on-duty and off-duty lives and establishing that there is bound to be conflict when these two very different detectives are forced to work together.

In *48 HRS* and *Midnight Run,* we don't meet the second protagonist in Sequence 1 – but they are mentioned. And in *Midnight Run,* Mardukas is introduced in dialogue in a way that establishes some of his backstory and reputation.

The *challenge* or 'call to adventure' may be issued to the primary protagonist before the end of Sequence 1. In *Midnight Run,* De Niro's character, Jack Walsh, is hired by a bail bondsman to bring in Mardukas who has skipped bail and gone into hiding. In other stories, the challenge may not be issued and accepted until Sequence 2 – but in Sequence 1 we may be introduced to the MacGuffin that everyone is after. In *48 HRS,* the MacGuffin is a briefcase full of stolen cash that was hidden by Eddie Murphy's character, Reggie Hammond, before he went to prison. We learn about the cash and that the villain wants it before we meet Reggie Hammond, who doesn't appear until Sequence 3.

In *Midnight Run,* Mardukas – the secondary protagonist – is the MacGuffin. Jack Walsh (De Niro) want to deliver him to collect the bounty, as does his rival Dorfler; the villain wants to kill Mardukas to prevent him testifying against him, and the FBI want Mardukas as their star witness. While in *Lethal Weapon* the MacGuffin is the murder investigation that Riggs (Mel Gibson) and Murtaugh (Danny Glover) are teamed up to investigate.

As we'll see later, the primary protagonist has an ambivalent attitude towards the MacGuffin. Jack Cates (Nolte) is more concerned about his stolen gun and bringing the villain to justice than he is about the stolen cash. Jack Walsh is more concerned with proving that he can achieve the task he has accepted than in collecting the bounty. As with Sam Spade in *The Maltese Falcon,* living up to their personal code of conduct is more important to them than getting rich. *Justice* is one thematic element, but there is also the need of the heroes to prove that they live in accordance with their own standards of behaviour and morality. Both the Nolte and De Niro characters have something to prove to themselves.

In the first sequences of *48 HRS* and *Midnight Run* we see the *rival* introduced and set-up so that they can oppose the protagonists – they have the same goal as the heroes. Luther, the rival in *48 HRS,* is motivated by the fact that his girlfriend has been kidnapped to force him to retrieve the cash hidden by Reggie Hammond. Dorfler, in *Midnight Run,* is humiliated by Walsh and set-up as a potential rival. At the same time, we see the FBI targeting Mardukas and warning Walsh to stay away from him. Both stories set up the *external* plot-based conflict early, *before* they bring together the two protagonists and start the character-based conflict.

Sequence 2

The two partners may meet for the first time in this sequence – or this may occur as late as Sequence 3 (but no later). If they haven't already been introduced, the villain, henchmen and/or rival may be introduced here. If the authorities are also going to oppose the protagonists, we will see them too. This establishes the fact that the odds really are stacked against the protagonists and that conflict is inevitable. We will see more antagonism and/or contrast between the characters of the two protagonists. The external challenge may become personal and will be accepted by one or both of the protagonists.

In *Midnight Run,* the villain's henchmen are introduced at the beginning of Sequence 2 – they try and buy Walsh off with a better offer. He doesn't respond directly and the offer is left on the table – a million dollars if he finds Mardukas and hands him over to the villain. But the main part of Sequence 2 involves Walsh's first encounter with Mardukas as our two protagonists become partners in the adventure. The encounter begins as a confrontation – Walsh has a gun and Mardukas has a guard dog. The antagonism between the two begins immediately because they have opposing goals – Walsh wants to capture Mardukas, but Mardukas doesn't want to be caught. Walsh gains the upper hand and takes Mardukas.

As the two begin to travel together we see the early stages of their interaction. There is grudging respect from Mardukas that Walsh managed to catch him. Mardukas asks questions and Walsh responds aggressively. Mardukas attempts to bribe Walsh and when that doesn't work he tries – and fails – to escape. Walsh tries to be reasonable. But when Mardukas expresses a fear of flying, Walsh has no sympathy for him. At this stage, Mardukas isn't a person to Walsh, he is a package to be delivered. Mardukas is an unwilling puppet. We also see the odds against Walsh increase when we learn that both the FBI and the villain's henchmen are receiving inside information about Walsh's whereabouts and plans. At this stage there is a marked difference in the emotions of the two protagonists – Walsh is happy as things seem to be going to plan. Mardukas is the opposite. Walsh makes an attempt to get along, but Mardukas is having none of it. At the end of Sequence 2, Mardukas turns the tables on Walsh and wins this round of the game.

In *48 HRS,* the focus remains on Cates (Nolte) – we learn more about his reputation as a tough cop and a loner. We also see his story intersect with that of the villain and the henchman. The police attempt to capture Ganz and Billy Bear but in the ensuing fight, Ganz takes Cates' gun and shoots a detective with it. Villain and henchman escape. This case has now become *personal* for Cates. His gun is effectively another MacGuffin, symbolising his personal stakes in the action: he made a mistake and a cop got killed. This acts as the challenge/catalyst and his acceptance of the 'call to adventure.' Towards the end of Sequence 2, Cates makes a link between the villain Ganz and an incarcerated crook, Reggie Hammond (Murphy). We learn something about Hammond's history but don't see him yet.

In the second sequence of *Lethal Weapon,* we see more of the contrast between Riggs and Murtaugh. Murtaugh has a steady, sensitive approach to detective work – Riggs is crazy and dangerous. We also learn more about Riggs' reputation – he may have a death wish, suicidal tendencies, because his wife was killed in an accident. Murtaugh finds clues in the murder investigation – and then discovers that Riggs is to be his new partner.

Sequence 3

We see the early stages of the relationship between the two protagonists. One may make attempts at establishing a friendship – but these are unsuccessful. Perhaps a raw nerve is touched, revealing some deep-seated issue for one of the characters. Character flaws may be further revealed through their bickering and/or contrasts in their behaviour and attitudes. If they have not already been introduced, the villain, henchman, and/or rival may appear for the first time here.

In *Midnight Run,* the attitudes of the two characters have flipped around – Mardukas is now happy and Walsh is not. Mardukas makes an attempt to get along, but Walsh responds without warmth or sympathy. Their change of plan – from plane to train – means that they unwittingly manage to avoid being ambushed by both the FBI and the villain's people at the airport. Mardukas tries to bribe Walsh into letting him go, but Walsh makes it clear that he is not a man who takes bribes – this is an important moral standpoint for him and is related to something significant in his backstory that will be revealed later. When Walsh says that he plans to open a restaurant and settle down, Mardukas offers financial advice. He also asks about Walsh's family and it is clear that this is a painful subject for Walsh. Odds are stacked against the heroes when the rival joins the FBI and the villain's henchmen in pursuit of them. Mardukas emphasises the stakes from his point of view – the villain will kill him so he can't testify. Walsh doesn't want to believe this. Differences in character between the two protagonists are highlighted. The FBI and the villains are still receiving inside information about the protagonists' travel plans and are closing in on them.

In *48 HRS* we see Cates and his girlfriend again and she accuses him of putting his job before her and everything else. Cates then meets Reggie Hammond for the first time – tries to manipulate him into helping him locate the villain, Ganz. Hammond knows that Ganz wants the stolen money that he hid, but doesn't tell Cates this. Instead, he manipulates

Cates into getting him released from prison. Their antagonism begins immediately.

In *Lethal Weapon,* the villain and his henchman are introduced and the fact that their criminal conspiracy involves dealing drugs. Murtaugh makes an attempt to befriend Riggs, drawing on their common Vietnam experience, but this is one-sided. We learn more about Riggs – he's a former assassin and classed as a 'Lethal Weapon.' The two admit that they don't want to work with each other. They begin their investigation into the murder. When Riggs risks his life in dealing with a potential jumper, Murtaugh confronts him and demands to know whether he is suicidal. Riggs demonstrates that he just might be. This makes Murtaugh nervous, as he might end up dead as a result of working with this crazy partner. But there is a slight thawing in their relationship as they move on to the next stage of their investigation.

Sequence 4

The stakes for the villain are established or reiterated – by showing how determined he is to get what he wants, we see how intense his fight with the protagonists is likely to become. We may also see the stakes raised for the henchmen as the villain becomes angry at the lack of progress towards his objective. The two protagonists are working together as reluctant partners – there is still antagonism and one may challenge the other for dominance. At the *midpoint,* we see the full-scale of the odds that the protagonists face and we have an understanding of the objectives of both the villain and the protagonists. The objectives of the two protagonists may be at odds with one another, meaning that conflict is inevitable.

In *Midnight Run,* the antagonism between the two protagonists continues and more backstory is revealed. An ambush for the heroes turns into chaos as the FBI and the villain's men clash – and Walsh and Mardukas escape in the confusion. The midpoint sequence sees Mardukas persuading Walsh to visit his ex-wife. It is an awkward encounter, but Mardukas is supportive. Walsh and his ex are partially reconciled and Walsh is happy to have seen his daughter again – it is the first time we have seen emotion and vulnerability from him. It also serves to establish what is important for him – his family as well as his moral values which dictate that he can never take a bribe. We are also aware that his objective is to deliver Mardukas, collect the bounty, and quit his job as a bounty hunter and settle down. Meanwhile, we are also made aware of the strength of the forces Walsh is up against in terms of the might of the FBI and that of the villain, whose men now have a helicopter pursuing the runaways.

In *48 HRS,* Cates and Hammond are working together as partners but neither trusts the other. They confront Luther and learn about the kidnap of his girlfriend. Cates suspects that something is going on, but Hammond still doesn't tell him about the stolen money that he and the villain are both trying to get. Hammond pretends to be a cop, rousting the patrons of a redneck bar – Cates is impressed and this marks the beginning of a thawing in their relationship, but there are still major issues of trust between them. Hammond gains a clue that will help their search for the villain. This marks the midpoint.

In *Lethal Weapon,* Riggs and Murtaugh are ambushed as they investigate the next clue – Riggs saves Murtaugh's life. Murtaugh takes Riggs home for dinner with his family – this is a significant character moment, with Riggs revealing more of his backstory. The midpoint occurs when Riggs comes up with a significant clue regarding the criminal conspiracy they are investigating.

Sequence 5
The protagonists may begin their fight back or decide to take the fight to the villain. In this sequence, character revelations are typically made. Backstory is revealed. The two partners may establish common ground – realising that they share moral values even if they disagree on how to achieve them. One protagonist may challenge the other to demonstrate his moral beliefs – Pick a side. But there is still some distance between them and feelings of mistrust. There may be a fight or some other confrontation – necessary to clear the air and set boundaries. There may also be a revelation – one partner sharing with the other a secret he has been keeping. Or the two may learn something about the external conspiracy – perhaps discovering that someone they know is involved.

In *Midnight Run,* the heroes think they have outwitted their pursuers but end up being confronted by the villain's henchmen. Ironically, they are saved by Walsh's rival, Dorfler, but this means that they are both now Dorfler's prisoners. The relationship between Walsh and Dorfler becomes closer in this sequence – Sequence 5 is typically the 'relationship sequence' in a movie – and they discuss their common moral values in relation to the villain. Relationship development in *Midnight Run* occurs throughout the story – which is why it is a good example of a buddy movie – and is not limited to a character moment in Sequence 5 – major character moments also occur in Sequence 6.

In *48 HRS,* Cates and Hammond fight in the street. This serves to stabilise their relationship as they are equally matched and each earns the respect of the other. Hammond tells Cates about the hidden money and offers him half, but Cates doesn't agree to this. But they will work together to deal with the villain.

In *Lethal Weapon* the 'character moment' occurs in Sequence 4 during the meal at Murtaugh's. In Sequence 5 they identify someone who is involved in the criminal conspiracy and confront him.

Sequence 6
The two partners may become closer as one saves the other from harm or certain death. They may begin to work together as a team. There may be the first suggestion of a feeling of trust developing. But this moment may then be ruined by having one of them restate their selfish motivation or objective. This may result in a setback or confrontation. There may be a character moment in which one partner reveals some insight into the personality and/or fears of the other – and they may also offer unwanted advice. A reminder that the rival, authorities, and/or villain/henchman are in pursuit may concentrate their thoughts and remind them that they have a common enemy and/or objective. The stakes may be raised by having the two partners become separated – perhaps one is kidnapped or captured. Or this separation may occur in Sequence 7. Instead, an important witness or source of information may be killed here – or someone they care about may be abducted. This is a major set-back and they will have to work together to overcome it – and they will have to trust each other.

In a thriller, both sequences 6 and 7 often end with a 'darkest hour' for the protagonists, with the setback in Sequence 7 being on a larger scale than the one in Sequence 6 – worse followed by worst. In *48 HRS,* the heroes follow the rival Luther expecting him to lead them to the villain – but they end up losing Luther, the money, and the villain. The two protagonists become separated at the end of the sequence. In *Lethal Weapon,* the stakes are raised when Murtaugh's daughter is kidnapped by the bad guys – there is a significant moment of trust when Riggs tells Murtaugh they'll get the girl back – his way. In *Midnight Run,* the two protagonists have a near-death experience with Mardukas saving Walsh's life – this seems to be a major turning point in their relationship, but then Walsh ruins the moment by betraying Mardukas and reverting to his former attitude, so the scene becomes a setback instead.

Sequence 7

There is often a reminder of what is at stake for one or both of the protagonists. One partner may deny the extent of the threat, rationalising his point of view. But at the same time, he is now uncertain – something has changed in his relationship with his fellow protagonist. This person's fate is now important to him. In any decision he makes or actions he takes he now has to accept that it is not just his own life that he is risking. In the case of *Midnight Run,* Walsh realises that Mardukas is no longer just a job to him. His partner may issue a challenge – pick a side – or try to convince the main protagonist that by working together they could bring down the villain. But there will still be some reluctance to overcome. This like Humphrey Bogart in *Casablanca* saying he doesn't stick his neck out for anyone but himself. If there is any backstory left to be revealed, it is shared here.

A chase often occurs in this sequence. The outcome may be that the two partners are separated – if they weren't separated in Sequence 6 – resulting in a low moment for the protagonists. One of them may even be captured by the villain/henchman, raising the stakes for them both. The situation requires that the free partner come up with an ingenious plan – and he may fear that he's not up to it, especially if the other partner is normally the better strategist.

In *Lethal Weapon* the two heroes go deep into the villain's lair – a dark and terrible place where Murtaugh's daughter is held prisoner, Murtaugh is beaten, and Riggs is tortured. Although the good guys survive, the bad guys manage to escape setting the scene for the final sequence. In both *48 HRS* and *Midnight Run,* the two protagonists are separated – and in their own ways miss their partner. In *48 HRS,* Reggie Hammond contacts Cates, re-establishing their partnership and demonstrating an increased level of trust and emphasising they have a common cause – they both want to bring the villain down. Cates reciprocates, trusting Hammond enough to allow him to keep a gun. There is a chase, but villain and henchman get away, setting up the final sequence.

In *Midnight Run,* the situation becomes worse for Walsh when he learns that his rival, Dorfler, intends to hand Mardukas over to the villain. He decides to make a deal with the FBI in order to save Mardukas and bring down the villain – setting up the final sequence.

Sequence 8

Sequence 7 often ends at a low point for the protagonists with whatever terrible fate they have been trying to avoid no seeming certain to occur. The villain has the upper hand and it looks like his plan will be successful. The primary protagonist – or both working together – must come up with an ingenious plan – a last do-or-die attempt. All of the opposing forces converge – villain, henchmen, the authorities and the protagonist(s). The rival may turn up too, presenting an unexpected obstacle or threatening to derail the protagonist's plan. There is typically a bit of cat 'n' mouse and some sort of stand-off – and perhaps a final one-on-one fight between protagonist and villain (or henchman). One partner may save the life of the other.

Objectives are achieved and needs are fulfilled. This is typically where we see that the primary protagonist has successfully achieved growth as a character – or is well on the way towards it. He has recognised and overcome his flaw, lack, or weakness and emerged from his adventure a better person. He may have redeemed himself, either in his own eyes or those of someone important to him. It may *appear* – as it does in the case of *Midnight Run* – that the main protagonist has not achieved character growth and is still determined to stick to his old ways, but then there is a twist that shows he has changed – in his own way. An agreement or understanding is reached between the two protagonists – there is still friendly rivalry, but there is also a deep bond of friendship between them.

15 | Informants

In the police procedural, Hillary Waugh has said that "...a detective is only as good as his informants..." The information provided by an informant is often more important to the progress of an investigation than a physical clue. Obviously, the informant cannot simply hand the detective the solution to the mystery – that wouldn't make for a good story. The informant's input has to appear as a stepping-stone on the journey towards a solution, in the same way as a clue in the whodunit. Or perhaps it will function as a red-herring.

An informant or informer is any person who provides privileged information about a person or organisation to another agency. The term is used in politics, industry, and news gathering but is most commonly associated with law enforcement where they are officially known as confidential informants or sometimes 'co-operative witnesses'. Areas of law enforcement where informants may be used include organised crime; general crime including burglaries and rapes; domestic and international terrorism; white-collar crime; drugs; civil rights; national infrastructure protection and computer intrusion; cybercrime; major theft including robberies, and violent gangs. The FBI also utilise other 'confidential human sources' who provide information on a regular basis as a result of their legitimate employment or routine access to records.

In the USA, the FBI and local law enforcement agencies use informants, as do the Drug Enforcement Administration (DEA), Immigration and Customs Enforcement (ICE), the Bureau of Alcohol, Tobacco, Firearms, and Explosives (BATF), the Internal Revenue Service (IRS), and the U.S. Marshals Service (USMS).

There are two main types of informant – the first provides an ongoing source of information about criminal activity, usually to a single detective; the second is when a criminal admits his own guilt and agrees to testify as a witness against his criminal associates, usually in exchange for a more lenient sentence or immunity from prosecution. In the USA, this second type of informer is said to have turned 'state's evidence' and in the UK to have turned 'Queen's evidence.'

When a criminal – or any other person – becomes a witness for the prosecution in cases involving organised crime, drug trafficking, or terrorism, they may need to be offered protection and perhaps even a new identity. In the USA the Witness Security Program (or Federal Witness Protection Program) is provided by the U.S. Marshals Service under the Organized Crime Control Act of 1970 (see www.usmarshals.gov/witsec). The UK Protected Persons Service is overseen by the National Crime Agency (www.nationalcrimeagency.gov.uk) and delivered by local police forces.

Stories involving state witnesses are likely to focus almost solely on the circumstances of the witness as seen from either the point of view of the witness or the person(s) charged with protecting them and ensuring that they are able to get to court to testify. These will typically be 'man on the run' or 'bodyguard' thrillers. In a typical crime thriller involving a private eye or a police detective, we are more likely to encounter the first type of informant – a low-level criminal who provides an ongoing source of gossip about what is going on in the local underworld.

Informants are found in private eye novels as well as police procedurals, but the type of informer tends to be different. In police novels, the informer is typically on the inside of some criminal enterprise and feeds information about the crimes being committed to the detective. The private eye's informer is more likely to be a low-level criminal type who shares gossip about what is going on in the criminal underworld.

The informant is a professional betrayer, and as George N. Dove writes, his "...position is a little like that of the scout in the Western story, in that he has feet in both camps, though he must conceal his anomalous position from the criminal camp. He is more like the 'contact' of the secret agent in spy fiction, and his position is just as dangerous."

Informants, as criminals working for cash or favours, have to be regarded as unreliable. Burt Rapp writes that the police "...prefer to have a 'twist' on their informers. A 'twist' is a means of coercion. A criminal who is caught often has the choice of 'co-operating' with the police or facing a trial and a heavy sentence. 'Co-operating' can get him a reduction of sentence or even complete immunity." The informer is often in a vulnerable position because of the information the investigator has about him. This helps to limit the risk of the informer double-crossing the police or feeding them false or useless information.

In stories and to some extent in real-life, the informant is not used by the whole squad – he 'belongs' to a single detective who usually keeps his identity secret from other detectives. This detective is referred to as the informant's *handler*. A bond of trust tends to exist between informant and handler, and the informant will often refuse to deal with anyone else. The informant-handler relationship is guarded but generally friendly. The system of favours owed and repaid also works between detectives and their informants. The detective may also tip of 'his' man if a 'clean-up' operation is planned. The rapport between detective and informant is helped by the fact that they both operate in the same part of the world – one that is rarely seen by ordinary citizens. And both, to some extent, regard themselves as victims of the 'System' that is seen as hampering both the criminal and detective.

Not all real-world informants are criminals – some are normal, decent people who have information that they feel should be shared with a law enforcement agency. These people are not part of the criminal underworld and don't use the vocabulary that criminals use. They may feel uncomfortable reporting to the police – especially if the information concerns a friend or family member – but they feel they have a duty to do it. Like all informants, they must be reassured that their identities must be protected and they must also be treated in a way that actions are genuinely appreciated, are useful, and will be acted upon wherever possible. Other forms of citizen sources include victims, witnesses, and concerned citizens such as Neighbourhood Watch members.

Some informants, criminals and citizens, are motivated by the fact that they just enjoy sharing what they know with somebody else. This is similar to the 'unwitting informant' below.

Another source used by law enforcers are people who have access to information as part of their normal work, including the department of motor vehicles, utility companies, banks, credit reporting agencies, and other private organisations who maintain records.

And then there are 'street sources' – people whose occupations, lifestyles, activities or place of residence bring them into contact with a broad range of people including criminals. This category includes barmen, restaurant and hotel employees, prostitutes and pimps, cab drivers, and those working in late-night establishments such as clubs, gas stations, and convenience stores. These are the sorts of sources that private eyes will also contact.

But the type of informant we are most interested in here is the *confidential informant* – and in stories, these are usually of the active criminal type. When informants are criminals, it has to be recognised that they might do anything to get out of trouble with the law. They might inform on their criminal associates or other criminals whose activities they know about – but they could just as easily lie to law enforcement officers, perjure themselves in court, fake evidence, and encourage others to corroborate their fake information. Criminals can also be expert manipulators and may be unreliable, providing reliable information one day and misinformation the next. Their loyalty and conscience cannot be relied upon. Fitzgerald notes that many criminals have personalities with many of the characteristics of antisocial personality disorder, including disregard for the rights of others, failure to conform to social norms of behaviour, irritability and aggressiveness, and irresponsibility. They are also impulsive, deceitful, reckless, and lack remorse. Which means that they are exactly the sort of people we need to create dramatic stories with plenty of conflict.

The following pages are concerned mainly with how federal and local law enforcement agencies *should* handle informants to gain the most benefit from them. In fiction we generally don't want to portray the 'best case scenario' and in the guidelines given here, you will find all sorts of opportunities for things to go wrong where informants are concerned.

Slang Terms
In old gangster and prison movies, informants are often referred to as a *canary* because they are guilty of 'singing' to the police. Other slang terms include collaborator, fink, grass and the more valuable supergrass, nark, pentito (Italian for one who repents), rat, snitch, snout, squealer, stool pigeon or stoolie (one who decoys others into a trap), turncoat (one who changes sides), and weasel.

Informant Recruitment Cycle
In their 'Confidential Human Source Program' the FBI describes a Recruitment Cycle for informants that consists of a number of stages:

Spotting – Seeking individuals who can collect evidence or have access to information.

Filtering – Reviewing the access, suitability, susceptibility, and accessibility of the individual and any security issues associated with them.

Assessing – The ongoing process of analysing both potential informants and those recruited. Includes identifying means to induce the potential informant into becoming an information source.

Developing – The process leading to the recruitment of an informant. Includes establishing and building trust between the informant and the person 'handling' them. This may include befriending and creating a seemingly personal relationship. The FBI 'assessing aid' document gives a number of techniques for building rapport. The first contact between handler and informant is sometimes referred to as 'the bump.'

Recruitment – The point at which the informant actually agrees to provide information - including an acknowledgement of the risks associated with this. A one-to-one working relationship between handler and informant is established. Includes the handler making a 'pitch' that outlines the benefits of becoming an informant.

Handling – The ongoing process of managing the informant and obtaining information from them, without alerting the informer's employer, associates, family, or other persons. May involve training the informant in some form of covert information exchange.

Termination or Turnover – Ending the relationship with the informant or passing them on to another handler or agency when they are no longer of use to the handler.

Let's look at some of the major stages in this cycle in more detail.

Recruiting Informants – Spotting & Filtering

Potential informants may be found in a number of places – a criminal may be arrested and the police may seek to recruit him; a prisoner may contact the authorities and offer to provide information; or investigators may have a need for an informant in a particular place or a particular organisation and seek to find someone to fulfil this need.

Investigators need to be able to recognise which potential informants are worth pursuing. In larger-scale criminal enterprises, the people at the top are typically well-insulated from those at the bottom, so that if a low-level criminal is arrested he cannot inform on those higher up because he does not know anything about them. This means that relatively low-status criminals don't have sufficient information to make effective informants. Ironically, having nothing to 'sell' means that low-level criminals often receive higher sentences than more serious offenders who do have information to give in exchange for a more lenient sentence.

Where investigators do not have an individual under arrest or lack sufficient evidence to threaten them with arrest, other more creative strategies have to be used to recruit them. Usually, this involves appealing to their desires or applying pressure targeting one of their weaknesses. A potential informant may be placed under surveillance in the hope of catching him committing a crime or in possession of a controlled substance or other contraband.

Jailhouse Informants – Some criminals may not consider becoming informants until after they have been convicted. They may have been approached at the time of their arrest and refused, but the reality of prison life can lead them to reconsider – and they will offer information in order to stand a better chance of being paroled or to obtain more comforts or privileges while incarcerated.

Unwitting Informants – There are people who provide information without even being aware of what they are doing – they just like to talk about what they know to anyone who'll listen. Sometimes alcohol is what loosens their tongue, but this isn't always necessary for such people. Often their 'stories' are exaggerated, but an experienced investigator can usually pick out the reliable parts. When someone is bragging about what he does and what he knows, most people don't take him too seriously, so it is up to the investigator to recognise when he says something that might be genuinely useful.

Assessment & Evaluation of Potential Informants
The following assessment criteria are based on those used by the FBI:

- Is the person in a position to provide information on illegal activities that fall within the scope of the law enforcement agency in question?
- Are they willing to provide information voluntarily?
- Do they appear to be directed by others who are seeking to obtain information from or about the law enforcement agency?
- Is there anything in their background that makes them unsuitable to be an informant?
- Does the value of the information they can provide outweigh any past or current criminal activity by the individual?
- Is their motivation for providing information reasonable?
- Can the information they offer be obtained from other sources?
- Are they sufficiently reliable and trustworthy? And can their information be properly verified?
- Are they prepared to operate according to the legal and procedural guidelines laid down for the work of the law enforcement agency?
- Will a handler be able to monitor and control the activities of the informant?
- Will the methods used by the informant to obtain information infringe the legal rights of any other person?
- Could use of the informant compromise an investigation, prosecution, or trial?

A check will be made of a potential informant's background including:

- Biographical details and criminal history
- Outstanding warrants
- Driver's license history
- Local and other addresses
- Previous experience as a confidential informant

Agents working for the FBI and DEA are under pressure to recruit new informants and their annual performance reviews are based in part on the development of new sources. This may lead to less rigorous assessment of the suitability of informants if external measures are not put in place to mitigate this.

Gaining an understanding of an individual's motivation for becoming an informant is a key part of the assessment process.

Motivation

Informants can have a variety of motivations and anyone who uses an informant has to be aware of these in order to assess the nature and reliability of the information they provide. The circumstances under which the information is given must also be taken into account – if the informant is placed under duress or is experiencing fear or stress for other reasons, this can affect whether he provides information and the nature of what he gives.

Bearing these things in mind, an informant's motivation will fall into three broad categories – conscience, self-interest, and self-preservation.

Mono & June suggest there are a couple of specific motivations for some female informers – women who want revenge on a lover, husband, or boyfriend and women who have a thing about law enforcement officers and want to be involved in police matters. I think these motivations could equally apply to men. People who inform on their partner can easily patch up their relationship issues and change their mind about giving information. Other informers may be prostitutes who gain their information from 'pillow talk' or drug addicts who are in contact with criminals as buyers.

Fitzgerald writes that it is "...absolutely essential that the investigator and his supervisor know the motivation for the informant's cooperation to ensure that his activities are monitored and he is properly controlled." He also notes that "...an informant may display more than one of the motivators, or his motivation may change during the course of his dealings with the government."

Another thing to bear in mind is that while the investigator tries to assess an informant's motives and weaknesses, the informant will be doing *exactly the same thing* to the investigator.

Conscience
There a few cases where people genuinely see the error of their ways and want to become useful members of society and assist law enforcement agencies. Some are bothered by a guilty conscience and feel a need to do something about it. And some have become disillusioned by the criminal life and want to 'go straight.' Others may be motivated by some form of patriotism or other ideology and seek to help their country rather than make personal gains. Such people do not want payment for their information, feeling that they are paying back society for crimes they have committed in the past, and they will usually take some pleasure in seeing people arrested and convicted based – at least in part – on information they have provided. Police informant Paul Derry has written that "...being an informant ... helped me deal with my own guilt. When I did not like something I had done, I would take down a bad guy, and I would feel better."

Self-Interest
Money/Greed – Informants in this category are sometimes referred to as mercenaries. A professional informer may make his living from selling information and will try and obtain the best price possible for their wares. And even if such a person asks for a ridiculously high price initially, he is likely to have a real idea what is information is worth or what the 'going rate' for similar information might be. And even a first-time informer will probably have decided on his price. Some police informers who provide a steady stream of information will probably receive regular payments. Other informants may have only one opportunity to provide information on a specific criminal act so will seek to maximise their one-off payment.

Payment is generally made when an arrest is made, rather than waiting for a successful prosecution – informants are aware of how long it can take for a case to come to court and of the deal-making that goes on to persuade criminals to turn state's evidence and the plea-bargaining that goes on behind closed doors to avoid cases ever going to court – and they're not likely to agree to a deferred payment that might never come.

While money-motivated informants are usually willing to abide by their handler's terms, there can be problems when information dries up and the informant falsifies information in order to keep getting paid.

Revenge, Spite or Retaliation – There are some informants who betray others because they want to get even with them. The strength of this motivation depends upon the nature of the wrong done to the informant. Paul Derry: "If I didn't like something another criminal had done, I would make a call and get him or her busted. I did not play the revenge card often, but it was among the motivations I have used at least once." Business associates, partners, or competitors may seek revenge by providing damaging evidence. Disgruntled employees, unpaid creditors, or unhappy neighbours may also seek to get even with someone.

Envy/Jealousy – Sometimes the motivation is professional jealousy -- a criminal informs on a rival who has 'moved in' on his territory or simply because the rival has achieved considerable success, perhaps at the expense of the informant.

Adrenaline Rush & Self-Aggrandisement – Some informants have a love of excitement and risk. In his autobiographical account, Paul Derry writes that excitement is one of the reasons why people like him become police informants. "In my case, I got off on the fact that I could travel back and forth between the criminal world and the normal world using information as a tool." Fitzgerald writes that such informants see becoming an informant as a way to fulfil their fantasies and compares them to a would-be James Bond. Such an informant may have valuable information or criminal connections, but he will be difficult to control. He may exaggerate his involvement in criminal activity or inflate his descriptions of crimes he has witnessed – or make his stories up completely. These individuals often give themselves away by dressing and behaving like characters in a movie. And Fitzgerald reports that he may "...purchase a fake police badge, false or official-appearing identification, and will carry a firearm. He is not beyond telling people that he works for the government. He may impersonate his agent handler by using the agent's business cards."

This motivation may be related to a need to increase their social status or compensate for feelings of low self-esteem or a need to receive recognition and praise.

Wannabe Cop – Similar to the above is the type Fitzgerald calls the 'police buff' – someone will a strong desire to be a police officer but whose physical, mental or educational limitations make this impossible – or perhaps they have a criminal record. These people may have a successful civilian career and be active in their local neighbourhood watch. They often have few if any criminal contacts and have little to offer as an informer.

Jailhouse Informant – This type of informant is motivated by a desire to obtain release from prison or, where that is impossible, to gain additional privileges while in prison. One area where prisoners can help the police is in passing on stories heard about 'cold cases.' Fellow inmates may brag about their past crimes and these details may be passed on by the informant.

A trickier area is the use of prison-based informers to target a specific inmate to obtain information or even overhear their confession. Such operations risk violating the target inmate's rights under the Fifth and Sixth Amendments of the U.S. Constitution or similar legal protections.

Prosecution or Judicial Leniency – Some informants seek to avoid prosecution completely, or to plead to a lesser crime, or to receive a lenient sentence in exchange for providing confidential information. Some informants expect the police to turn a blind eye and allow them to continue their own low-level criminal activities in exchange for providing information on more serious crimes committed by others.

Some informants are motivated to assist law enforcement agencies because they want help in dealing with another criminal matter. They will provide information about one crime in order to try and negotiate a lighter sentence or immunity from prosecution for another. The person in trouble with the law may be the informant himself or one of his friends or relatives. Before agreeing to any deal of this sort, an investigator needs to be aware of the full extent of the crime in question, the circumstances under which it was committed, and of any consequences of the crime.

Double Agent – This is an informant to sets out from the beginning to use his relationship with a handler to further his own criminal ambitions. He seeks to learn about the law enforcement agency the handler works for, to see how it conducts investigations or to try and learn the identities of undercover agents, informants, or individuals the agency intends to target. He may even try to use the agency to eliminate his criminal competitors or seek to divert attention away from his own criminal organisation.

Where an informant is motivated by financial gain, there is a risk that he will try and sell information to both sides. An investigator should give as little information as possible to the informant and may need to feed him misinformation to see if it is passed on. Verifying the informant's information, seeking corroboration from other sources, also becomes a priority. Even if an informant's information seems to be good, an investigator must still remain suspicious – just because an informer has some details about some aspect of a criminal activity doesn't mean that he is necessarily on the inside of the criminal operation and able to provide information of the same quality on an ongoing basis. There is also a danger that he may be providing valid information to gain an investigator's trust simply so he can feed him misinformation at a future point when to do so is in the best interests of the criminals he works with.

Self-Protection
Here *fear* is the key motivator – fear of law enforcement activities, fear of punishment for criminal acts, or fear of attack by current or past criminal associates. The potential informer may fear physical harm to themselves or to their friends and family.

Fear is a strong motivator and may cause an informant to fabricate information or seek to entrap his handler's target by any means necessary – means which would jeopardise a successful prosecution of the target. The more desperate his situation, the greater the risk that the informant will resort to extreme measures.

Ex-lovers or spouses may also be motivated by fear of their former partner – particularly if the partner feels that the ex-lover betrayed them.

Threats often occur if someone is suspected – rightly or wrongly – of being an informer; because of jealousy; unpaid debts; the theft of drugs or other contraband, or disputes over 'turf.'

Potential informants who are motivated by fear or revenge typically need to be assessed quickly and their information evaluated. Quick action is advised because a dispute between two parties – especially lovers – may be resolved, removing the desire for an individual to provide information. And someone who is in fear may go into hiding or become a victim of murder before they can gain protection and share their information.

Handling Informants
Handlers should always treat their informants with respect – a fact that isn't always portrayed in TV cop shows, where detectives use terms like 'rat' and 'squeal' to the informer's face and treat them like scum. If an informant is offended by something a handler says – about him directly or about another informer – there is a risk that the informer will withdraw

his co-operation. It should be recognised that an informer is putting himself at risk by passing information, no matter what he receives in return.

At the same time, informers shouldn't be allowed to take control of an investigation. And the informant must never be allowed to believe that he is immune from prosecution, no matter what crimes he commits. Many police officers turn a blind eye to low-level criminal acts by the informer, but care has to be taken that he doesn't progress to more serious crimes. Limits also have to be set on things like 'fixing' speeding tickets or other 'favours'.

If an informant is more than a one-off supplier of information, the handler must continue to maintain contact with him so that if any new information comes to the informer, the handler is in a position to receive it quickly.

One thing a handler has to learn quickly is the extent to which an informer is willing to co-operate. Is he prepared to introduce an undercover law enforcement officer to his criminal associates? Is he prepared to appear in court if a case goes to trial? If he won't arrange introductions, will the informant undertake 'undercover' tasks on behalf of the handler?

Documentation of Informers

Formal records have to be kept about the work of informers. These may include a formal contract between the law enforcement agency and the informer which sets out the obligations and benefits for each side. Evidence – both physical and in the form of testimony – must be recorded according to the legal guidelines that permit its admission in court. And financial transactions related to purchases of contraband and payments to the informer must be properly documented to avoid the possibility of fraud. Keeping such records about a confidential source poses risks and so precautions must be taken to ensure that records do not directly identify the individual and to ensure that the records can be accessed only by a limited number of approved officers. Informers are typically given an identification number or codename and a master list containing the true identities of informers is kept separately in a secure location.

The International Association of Chiefs of Police recognises that investigators may be reluctant to maintain records on the informants they use – either because they fear that security within the department is not sufficient to protect the identity of the informant or because they fear that another officer or supervisor may damage the trust that the handler has carefully built up – or that another officer may 'steal' the informant for his own use.

Trust

The informant and his handler are in a relationship and any successful relationship has to be founded on trust. But, as ex-informant Paul Derry has said, "...given the work atmosphere in which the police officer and informant usually meet, and given the violence, manipulative nature, and ingrained criminality of most informants, it would seem that trust would be nearly impossible." And he has written that the relationship can end up like "...an abusive marriage. One partner has all the control, exercises it often, and does not care about the pain or hurt that the rest of the family suffers, especially the pain of the abused."

Derry believes that trust begins with the handler, the police officer whose job effectively defines him as being trustworthy. A good handler is one that the informant trusts such that he will often refuse to speak with anyone else. On the face of it, the handler/law-enforcer and informant/criminal seem to have little in common and little chance of developing a bond of trust.

The Handler

The qualities needed by a successful handler are:

Empathy – the ability to put yourself in another person's position and understand their responses. An informant is more likely to trust someone who is making an effort to empathise with him – an effort that is obviously authentic. Empathy can exist on several levels. *Cognitive* or intellectual, involving a conscious and rational understanding of another person's perspective. *Affective* or emotional involves being moved by another person's emotional state such that you feel the same emotional response as that person. There may also be *somatic* empathy where you experience the same physical response as the other person. Different people experience these three types of empathy to differing degrees. Emotional empathy is the one most strongly involved with trust – if I believe that you feel what I feel, we have something in common that can form the basis for a trusting relationship. If you are cold and distant and I am unable to 'read' your emotions, I am unlikely to trust you deeply.

Communication – the ability to speak clearly and concisely and make sure that what you say has been understood. And the ability to understand what the informant is saying – both verbally and non-verbally.

Humility – There is room for only one egotist in the relationship and that role is usually occupied by the informant. Anyone who behaves in a way that indicates he thinks he's better than the informant is not going to build the kind of rapport necessary to be a good handler.

Humour – Paul Derry: "Humour can defuse anger, calm fear, lift depression, relieve tension, build rapport, and create bonds. It is vital when dealing with a dark, sinister world." Both informants and handlers need to be able to laugh at their own mistakes and at the absurdities of life. The humour shared is often very dark – a combination of cop humour and rook humour.

Intuition – A good investigator has to trust his gut feelings – they're usually based on tiny clues that his consciousness hasn't made sense of yet. They must also remain alert and in the moment – mindful of what is going on around them and ready to improvise if a situation takes an unexpected turn.

Honesty – Even if it means saying what the informant doesn't want to hear.

Reliability – being where you say you'll be, doing what you say you'll do – and not promising what you know you can't deliver.

Mike Cabana, Deputy Commissioner of the RCMP, and former handler of Paul Derry: "Informants are people, and many of them bring significant baggage and regularly need assistance navigating through personal issues/events affecting them. A handler needs to be prepared to help to the extent possible. This is very much a two-way relationship."

There are a number of potential pitfalls that handlers need to avoid in their dealings with an informer:

- Allowing the relationship to stray from purely professional one by socialising with informants, their families and/or friends.

- Engaging in romantic relationships with informants, or a family member or friend of the informant.
- Accepting information provided by the informant at face value and failing to question its validity or seek corroboration from other sources.
- Failure to properly follow-up or take action on information provided by the informant.
- Lack of awareness and poor documentation of the activities of the informant.
- Promising things to the informant that the law enforcement agency may not be able or willing to deliver.
- Lack of accountability in dealing with money or contraband such as drugs.
- Purchasing items from informants or selling items to them.
- Borrowing money from informants.
- Receiving gifts or gratuities from informants.
- Engaging in business relationships with informants.
- Involving the informant too closely in the planning of an investigation and sharing too many details with him.
- Failure to properly control the activities of the informant and allowing unnecessary or unsupervised contact with the target of an investigation.
- Jeopardising investigations by meeting informants alone and not properly recording all encounters
- Paying informants without witnesses, accepting kickbacks from informants, or submitting false or exaggerated receipts for payments to informants.

Federal agencies in the USA are subject to legislation that criminalises the practice of taking kickbacks from informers. State and local law enforcement agencies have their own policies. You can better understand the temptation and opportunity for kickbacks if you consider that payments made to some informants may be more than a handler's annual salary.

There have also been instances where 'handlers' have created fake informants – either to claim the money made in payment to them or to obtain search warrants based on information from the non-existent 'reliable informant.'

The Informer

We have already seen some of the typical qualities of a criminal informer in terms of personality, but what qualities are needed to be a good informant? Paul Derry has said that "...if you cannot tell a good story or dazzle people with words, you are not likely to ever get anybody to give you information. Gaining information usually requires an ability to talk but also a willingness to wear your sins on your sleeve, so to speak. If you want others to give you information about their dirty deeds, it usually means you have to share your dirt first."

Informers have to be able to manipulate people and work their way into a person's trust. They also need to be expert deceivers because their lives may depend on this. While these things are good for dealing with other criminals, they are less good when dealing with the handler.

Handlers face a number of potential issues when dealing with informants:

Lying – Informants may exaggerate or even make up the information they present about the target of an investigation. Or they may be telling the truth but not revealing the means by which they obtained the information – means which would render their testimony inadmissible in court.

Double-Dealing – An informant can make deals with both the target of the investigation and the law enforcement agency, taking money from each for information about the other. Informants may pass on details of undercover agents, unmarked police cars, and reports on activities planned or underway. Or informants may sell their information to more than one law enforcement agency.

Rip-Offs — Informants are also in a position to set-up their handlers so that large sums of cash arranged for the purchase of drugs or other contraband can be stolen by criminal associates.

Blackmail — If a handler makes the mistake of engaging in questionable or illegal activities as a result of his relationship with the informant, the informant may seek to use his knowledge of this to force the handler into providing payments or other favours to ensure his silence.

Risks Informants Face

Those who inform on the Italian Mafia risk not only a death sentence for themselves but also for their entire families – so even if the informer goes into a witness protection programme, his extended family are still at risk. And if an informer is caught by his criminal associates, the fact that the informer is seen as a betrayer means that his death is unlikely to be quick and painless. His death has to serve as a warning to anyone else who may consider turning informant.

Even relatively low-level informers face danger. Twenty-three-year-old Rachel Hoffman was acting as a police informant when she was killed in May 2008. Her death led to the Florida State Senate passing 'Rachel's Law' which requires law enforcement agencies to give special training to officers who recruit informants, to instruct informants that reduced sentences cannot necessarily be given in exchange for their co-operation, and to permit informants to request a lawyer if they want one. A similar law was passed in North Dakota following the death of twenty-year-old student Andrew Sadek who had also acted as an informant.

George N. Dove: "A well-placed informant ... is so valuable that there have been cases, we are told, where a good policeman was sold down the river in order to protect a good informant."

Compensation for Informants

A problem that law enforcers always face is that they want to know what a potential informer actually knows *before* they commit themselves to a 'deal.' But the potential informer doesn't want to reveal his cards until he has been promised something in return. If the potential informer is under arrest or facing the possibility of being charged, he has the right to have legal representation during any discussions with law enforcement officers and so the lawyer also has to be persuaded that a 'deal' is in the best interests of his client. Written promises will probably need to be given that anything the potential informant says during the negotiation process will not be used against him. After that, an officer can then talk about a *potential* deal that will be contingent on the credibility and value of the information provided by the informant. Ultimately, there will probably a formal written contract between the agency and the informant.

Payments to informants are made from a law enforcement agency's expense or 'discretionary' fund with payments of different levels typically requiring the authorisation of an officer of a certain rank – a police sergeant, for example, might authorise a payment up to a couple of hundred dollars, a commander up to a few thousand, and a police chief above that amount. Payments have to be properly documented with a receipt being signed by the informant, the handler, and a witness to avoid the possibility of fraud.

Not all informants want financial payments – some are looking for a more lenient sentence for a crime they have committed – a 'negotiated plea agreement' – or, if already imprisoned, are seeking assistance in making parole with the help of a 'good word' from the law enforcement agency.

If all else fails, a non-prosecution agreement – referred to in the movies and on TV as 'immunity from prosecution' – may be offered to a potential informant. Care has to be taken to ensure that the agreement relates to the specific crime(s) related to the current investigation and is not intended to provide blanket immunity for past, current, and future crimes.

Controlling the Informant
Fitzgerald writes that "Failure to control informants has undermined costly long-term investigations, destroyed the careers of prosecutors and law enforcement officers, and caused death and serious injuries to innocent citizens and police. In many cases, the sequence of events leading to disaster began during the selection or recruitment of the informant."

Although an informant will usually deal with only the one handler, it is important that the handler's relationship with the informer be subject to supervision and ongoing review. Without external input, the rapport a handler must by necessity establish with the informer may stray towards a deeper relationship and objectivity may be compromised.

Where a relationship between handler and informant becomes unworkable – either because it has become too close or because it has not been possible to build trust between the two – it may be necessary to change the handler. Though here caution has to be taken so that an informer cannot 'shop around' to find a handler that he feels better able to manipulate. As mentioned before, the ideal relationship is trusting but guarded.

It is important that the informant not become aware of the identities of other undercover investigators as this may put them at risk – the informant should only be provided with information that it is absolutely essential to his work as an informer and it should never be assumed that he is now a trusted member of the team.

Some types of informants require special handling. Juveniles must be protected and while agents may seek information from them, they will not be used for undercover work such as controlled buying except under exceptional circumstances and then only with their parents' or guardian's permission. Where the informant and handler are male and female, care must be taken to ensure that an inappropriate romantic or sexual relationship does not develop – and similar caution must also be exercised where there is the potential for same-sex relationships. Handlers and their employers who do not properly monitor and document meetings with an informant may find themselves subject to a sexual harassment complaint or the handler may find the informant trying to blackmail him. Informants who are currently under arrest must be dealt with the knowledge and approval of the relevant prosecuting authority and similar considerations must be given to prisoner-informants.

Whose Informant?

In formal law enforcement circles, there is sometimes disagreement over who an informant 'belongs' to. The detective who has worked as the informant's handler and has built a rapport with him usually feels a sense of 'ownership.' Coupled with this is a sense of responsibility – an informer's handler will feel duty-bound to protect them and ensure their name does not become common knowledge. The more people within a law enforcement agency that know who an informant is, the greater the risk that the name will be accidentally or deliberately leaked to the informant's criminal associates. Some detectives pay their informants out of their own pocket and professional evaluation and promotion in some departments are contingent on recruiting and cultivating a number of effective informants. Most law enforcement agencies also limit which types of employees are permitted to have and work with informants.

In cases where the informant is paid from departmental funds, then the informant technically 'belongs' to the agency and the handler is given primary (but not sole) responsibility for them.

Protecting an informants identity also means that any records maintained about them should refer to them by a number or alias, with the full details only available to those authorised as having a 'need to know.' Applications for arrest or search warrants will usually refer to a 'reliable confidential source,' and possibly any past history of arrests made based on the informant's information, and this is usually sufficient for the warrant to be issued.

Another circumstance that risks exposing the informant is where only he and one criminal associate know the information the informant is sharing with his handler. If law enforcers act on this information, it will be obvious who the traitor was. It may take some ingenuity on the part of investigators to deal with a situation like this such that the informant feels satisfied that he won't be exposed.

The police have privilege not to reveal the identity of an informant, but the rules of discovery mean that the name of an informant must be disclosed by the prosecution where the informer's identity is necessary for the defendant's case. In such cases, a choice sometimes has to be made about exposing the informant or dropping the prosecution. The correct decision depends on the circumstances of the individual case and the specific informant.

Ethics

An investigator should not compromise himself or the informant in the pursuit of information. He should not make unethical promises or deals and shouldn't undertake commitments he cannot fulfil. He should protect the identity of the informant and meetings should be arranged with this in mind – especially in terms of the location and how the investigator dresses and behaves. In some cases, it is necessary to abandon prosecution in a case where the identity of an informant might be revealed and so put him and his family at risk.

Entrapment and Due Process

If a law enforcement official provides an individual with an opportunity to break the law, this does not necessarily constitute *entrapment* – provided that it can be demonstrated that the individual was *predisposed* to commit such an act. If a person commits a criminal act of a type that they wouldn't have considered without the influence of the law enforcement officer, then this would constitute entrapment. Predisposition can be demonstrated by such things as prior convictions for the same crime, prior arrests, previous documented criminal activity of the same kind, or subsequent occurrence of criminal activity of the same kind while not under the influence of a law enforcement officer.

Due Process violations occur if the legal rights of an individual have not been properly respected by law enforcement officers – and by the informants who are acting on their behalf. Issues here include whether the informant instigated and controlled criminal activity, effectively being the cause of it, or whether they were participants in and witnesses of criminal activities that were already taking place. Also, if the informant provides significant resources or expertise, such that the crime could not take place without them, then a violation may have occurred.

Undercover Purchases by Informants & Probable Cause

Informants may be used to obtain sufficient evidence to enable an application for a search warrant to be approved. For example, an investigator may send an informant into the premises in question to make a 'controlled buy' of an item that will serve as evidence. In such circumstances, the investigator has to ensure – and be able to demonstrate – that the informant really did obtain the evidence and didn't just plant it himself to give his handler what he wanted. This may require that the informant is searched before the buy takes place – perhaps to the extent of having to submit to a strip search and body cavity examination. It may also mean that corroboration may be required from video or audio surveillance. Controlled buys are often used in drug-related investigations but can also be used for stolen property. The cash for such controlled buys often comes from the same 'discretionary fund' used to pay informants. And, as mentioned above, there is a risk that an informant may set-up the theft of the money.

Criticism of the Use of Informants

The use of informants has been criticised for a number of reasons:

- Informers are unreliable and by definition they betray others and so may equally well betray the law enforcers he is dealing with.
- Informers are criminals living outside the acceptable rules of behaviour and avoiding attempts to 'control' them, so they are unlikely to abide by the rules of any 'deal' they make with law enforcers or prosecutors.
- Informers may invent 'information' in order to gain certain benefits.
- Some of their 'information' may be given with an ulterior motive, e.g. they may seek to 'get rid of' a rival or someone with whom they have a vendetta.
- If an informant is given a contract such that he is required to 'deliver the head' of a specific individual to an investigator or prosecutor, this provides a clear incentive for the informant to manufacture evidence and to frame the individual.
- Payment of informants is seen as rewarding or even encouraging criminals instead of punishing them.
- Jurors are suspicious of evidence obtained from paid informants and are typically warned by the judge to treat such evidence with extra caution.

As well as the sources quoted in the bibliography for this chapter, there are a number of resources available online relating to the use of informants by US law enforcement agencies. Search for the titles of any of the following documents to retrieve the full – or sometimes redacted – texts. Many state and local police authorities publish online their guidelines for the use of informants.

- *The Attorney General Guidelines Regarding the Use of Confidential Informants*
- *The Attorney General Guidelines on Federal Bureau of Investigation Undercover Operations*
- FBI – *Manual of Investigative Operations and Guidelines* (Section 137)
- FBI – *Legal Handbook for Special Agents*
- *The Federal Bureau of Investigation's Compliance with the Attorney General's Investigative Guidelines* (Chapter 3)
- *Internal Revenue Service Manual* (Part 9.4.2.5)
- *Drug Enforcement Administration Agent's Manual* (Chapter 66)
- International Association of Chiefs of Police – *Confidential Informants, Concepts and Issues Paper*, June 1, 1990
- House of Representatives Report – *Everything Secret Degenerates: The FBI's Use of Murderers as Informants*

The *Wikipedia* entry for 'Informant' has links to two FBI documents (both originally published on www.theintercept.com) – the *Confidential Human Source (CHS) Assessing Aid* and the *Confidential Human Source Policy Guide* – the latter is redacted, with the whole section on the Witness Security Program blacked out.

See also *The Informant: A True Story* (2000) by Kurt Eichenwald, filmed in 2009 by Steven Soderbergh as *The Informant!* with Matt Damon in the title role of a corporate whistle-blower.

James J. 'Whitey' Bulger was an organised crime boss and FBI informer who was the subject of a 2014 documentary *Whitey: United States of America vs. James J. Bulger* and he was played by Johnny Depp in the 2015 film *Black Mass*, based on the book *Black Mass: The True Story of an Unholy Alliance Between the FBI and the Irish Mob* written by Dick Lehr and Gerard O'Neill. Bulger also served as inspiration for Jack Nicholson's character Frank Costello in Martin Scorsese's *The Departed* (2006). The NBC television series *The Blacklist* starring James Spader as an FBI informant was also inspired by Bulger.

16 | Interviewing & Interrogating

The type of evidence gained by police detectives includes physical evidence found at the scene of the crime plus statements obtained from witnesses and suspects. Crime scene analysis features less in the work of a privates detective who is more likely to use a combination of documentary evidence and interviews with witnesses, suspects, and experts. For both types of investigator, good interviewing skills are essential.

Unlike the police, a private detective cannot compel anyone to answer questions – he has to rely on his skills of persuasion. But he does have the advantage of being able to use a less formal or an unconventional approach. His less onerous caseload may also mean that he can take longer over an interview and build a stronger rapport with the interviewee. Real private detectives rarely use bribes or threats to obtain information.

Police interviews of suspects are often more formal and – if the subject has been arrested or is likely to be arrested – may be conducted using recording equipment and with the suspect's attorney present.

Wherever possible, detectives will avoid conducting interviews over the telephone because being able to read a person's non-verbal communication is vital in determining whether the statements they are making are truthful.

In stories, interviews are typically portrayed verbatim as dialogue. But some interviews reveal nothing of value and are a waste of time – you can summarise these rather than showing them 'live'.

Interview versus Interrogation
The terms *interview* and *interrogation* are often used interchangeably, with interrogation typically being regarded as a stricter or harsher form of questioning. Interviews are conducted in a wide variety of circumstances – by employers seeking to recruit new staff, by doctors seeking to understand a patient's symptoms, or by journalists seeking answers from a politician or a celebrity. Interrogations tend to be conducted by law enforcement officers or military intelligence officers. Interrogation is also often linked in people's minds with coercion and torture.

I wrote about torture in *Suspense Thriller* and have nothing to add here other than to quote from the Council of Europe's *A Brief Introduction to Investigative Interviewing:* "There are no circumstances that can justify subjecting a suspect to intimidation, threats, abuse or violence of any kind, whether physical or psychological, in order to obtain information, implicate another or extract a confession. Not only is this unethical, contrary to the ethical standards of professional policing and a breach of domestic and international law, *it simply does not work* ... There is a considerable body of scientific evidence to show that torture and inhuman treatment do not work. They do not elicit accurate or reliable information, which should be the goal of the police interviewer."

Interview & Interrogation Techniques
There are two main approaches to the questioning of suspects and witnesses that I want to cover here – the traditional interrogation approach

and the more recent investigative interview. With the interrogation approach, the purpose of the questioning is to obtain a confession or some other form of admission; with the investigative interview, the objective is to obtain accurate and reliable information.

This is not a textbook on best interview techniques – my aim here is to provide information about options you can consider. You will need to choose the most appropriate technique for the circumstances and characters of your story. Older police detectives and those with military training are more likely to use – and approve of – the interrogation approach; younger officers are more likely to have been taught about the risk of false confessions arising from the more confrontational forms of questioning.

Because private investigators have no authority to detain and question suspects, they usually employ a less confrontation approach by default – though the personalities of some private detectives may lead them into harder-edged interrogation techniques on occasion.

One of the best-known forms of the interrogation approach is the Reid Technique™ which I will introduce briefly below. A form of investigative interviewing used in the UK and some other countries is the PEACE model, which I will cover in more detail as documentation about it is freely available and it also provides an overall framework for interviewing that can be adapted for any form of investigation.

Kinesic Interrogation - The FBI Method

In 2013 an accidentally leaked copy of the Federal Bureau of Investigation's interrogation manual revealed that the Bureau used the Reid Technique. The FBI is also reported to have made use of the non-confrontational interview techniques taught by Wicklander-Zulawski & Associates (www.w-z.com).

The Reid Technique^{TM}

Originally developed by John E. Reid in 1962, The Reid Technique of Interviewing and Interrogation® has been widely used in the United States by both the police and FBI. It is a proprietary technique owned and taught by John E. Reid and Associates (www.reid.com) consisting of a Fact Analysis, a Behaviour Analysis Interview, and then – if appropriate – the Nine Steps of Interrogation. The standard text on the technique is *Criminal Interrogation & Confessions* (5th ed.) by Fred E. Inbau, John E. Reid, Joseph P. Buckley, and Brian C. Jane, published in 2011.

The interrogation aspect of the technique appears to begin with an assumption of guilt and has been criticised for advocating the use of deception and intimidation to secure a confession. There have been a number of documented cases in which false confessions were obtained using the technique.

Investigative Interviewing & the PEACE Model

One of the advantages of investigative interviewing is that its principles can be adapted for interviewing criminals, suspects, witnesses, and victims – and also for use in a variety of non-law enforcement situations.

The PEACE model was outlined in two documents published in 1992 by the Central Planning & Training Unit of the British government's Home Office – *Investigative Interviewing: The Interviewer's Rule Book* and *Investigative Interviewing: A Guide to Interviewing*. The information can now be found on the website of the College of Policing:

www.app.college.police.uk/app-content/investigations/investigative-interviewing/

The stages of the model as defined by the acronym are:

P – Planning & Preparation
E – Engage & Explain
A – Account, Clarification & Challenge
C – Closure
E – Evaluation

The details below are drawn from the College of Policing website and Black & Yeschke's book *The Art of Investigative Interviewing* (2014)

Planning & Preparation

Steven Kelly Brown writes that if a private detective receives a new case from an attorney or insurance company via fax or e-mail, it is still a good idea to go to their office and review whatever files they have on the case before proceeding with the investigation. The detective himself is in the best position to judge what information may be of use in preparing to interview a witness or suspect. Police detectives will have the case file available as a normal part of their work and have access to other background information that can be reviewed before the interview.

Black & Yeschke write that preparation "....involves attitude, psychology, intuition, flexibility, curiosity, imagination, and research."

Attitude – Adopting an authoritarian attitude will cause resentment, retaliation, and reluctance or refusal to co-operate. To encourage an interviewee to participate you must avoid expressing negative feelings, being judgmental, or behaving in an antagonistic way. Instead, adopt a positive and friendly attitude demonstrating warmth, empathy, acceptance, tolerance for human weakness, caring, and respect. Attitude is expressed through verbal and non-verbal signals and most people can read these things without even thinking about them. If you remain calm and show that you are actively listening to the interviewee while at the same time seeming professional and confident, you stand the best chance of conducting a successful interview.

Psychology – You need to be aware of the emotions of the interviewee and the needs or fears that cause them. Interviewees want to feel safe and valued and tend to fear chaos and the unknown. Different personality types have different fears – I wrote about these at length in *Character Creation* – and a successful interviewer is aware of this and tailors the style of interview accordingly.

Intuition – instinct, gut-feeling, or a 'hunch' – is based on a subconscious combination of imagination, knowledge, and awareness. Concentrating your awareness on the issue at hand – being mindful – allows you to respond spontaneously to whatever course the interviewee takes in their replies to questions. It is important to be able to recognise when something is worth pursuing, even if it means going off the planned course for a while, and when something is an unnecessary distraction that needs to be closed down.

Flexibility – During an interview, it will probably be necessary to adapt to changes in an interviewee's responses, tone, or behaviour and alter the line of questioning accordingly. Whatever attitudes or beliefs an interviewee expresses, it is important not to judge or challenge them during the early stages of an interview. Your aim is to learn about the witness and gain information about them, not to engage them in a debate. If an interviewee says something that catches you off-guard, you need to be able to deal with it quickly and maintain the momentum of the interview. And if an interviewee is uncooperative, you may need to try a number of different approaches to get them to respond to your questions.

Curiosity – An interviewer must have a genuine desire to find things out, to be inquisitive. They should also want to probe beneath the surface and try to uncover the 'why'. Curiosity is a positive interest in obtaining information and is preferable to negative approaches such as cynicism or suspicion or accusation.

Imagination – This is linked to empathy in that you need to be able to put yourself in the place of the interviewee – whether they are a witness, victim, suspect, or criminal – and think about how you would feel or behave in their situation. Given the circumstances that they experienced, how would you have reacted? Given their situation now, faced by an interviewer, how would you respond? People are able to rationalise or justify all kinds of illogical behaviours and you have to be able to imagine what is causing them to do so.

Research – It is always best to obtain as much information as possible *before* the interview. The more you know about the people and places connected with the investigation the better. The earliest questions you ask an interviewee will often be confirmation of fact – by demonstrating to them that you have done your homework, you reinforce the impression that you are a professional. Also, if you demonstrate that you understand what they are saying – are familiar with the work they do or vocabulary they use or milieu which they inhabit – you can make them feel that you are like them and can, therefore, be trusted as one of them.

Preparation also involves deciding the *purpose* of the interview. In an interrogation, the emphasis was always placed on obtaining a confession or an admission of some other sort. With an investigative interview, the purpose is to obtain factual information. A confession might still occur, but if it doesn't, the interview will still be regarded as a success if credible information is gathered. Generally speaking, an interview is conducted to obtain *facts,* not opinions or gossip – but there are other reasons. An interview may be conducted for show – because it is expected that someone, or everyone, will be questioned as part of an investigation. Or an interview may be designed to act as a *catalyst* – with the interviewer seeking to get someone to do something in order to move the investigation forward. In fiction, the detective may reveal or imply that he knows something – which may or may not be true. Or he may sow disinformation in order to provoke some sort of response. An interview can also be used to plant information – e.g. a form of words that the detective wants a witness to use in court or in some other situation.

All of the above will help determine what style of interview should be used and what techniques may need to be applied. Preparation includes deciding what questions to ask and how to ask them.

If the investigator is able to decide where and when an interview will take place, these factors will also be included in the planning phase and can include things down to the level of how to position the chairs and desk in the interview space.

Engage & Explain

Greetings and first impressions – Everyone knows that we tend to form our first impressions of someone within a fraction of a second of meeting them. That first impression then influences how we treat them or respond to them from that point on. This impression is based on a range of characteristics, usually beginning with visual ones such as age, race, physical appearance, and posture followed by vocal ones such as accent, language, and tone of voice. The fact that human beings are generally accurate in their initial assessment of people who present themselves truthfully – an ability that probably developed as a survival trait – probably explains why it is very difficult to replace the first impression with a new one.

Most of us receive advice on 'making a good first impression' before we first go to college or job interviews. We want to make a good impression as an interviewee. But it is also important for an *interviewer* to make an appropriate impression. An interrogator typically wants a subject to be afraid of them and behaves in a manner that gives the impression that he is in a position to do harm to the subject either physically, socially, or psychologically. An investigative interviewer, on the other hand, needs to give the impression that they are professional, can be trusted, and want to help the interviewee give a good account of themselves in the interview. The style of the 'cross-examining counsellor' or trial barrister is probably closer to the interrogator in that the questions tend to be adversarial and the attitude is one of 'I'm here to trick you into saying something that proves you're either a liar or incompetent.' This is an impression that the investigative interviewer should also avoid.

Much has been written about making a good impression via body language, especially posture, and every writer should have a working knowledge of non-verbal communication of this kind. 'Impression management' and self-presentation have been areas of study since the publication of Erving Goffman's *The Presentation of Self in Everyday Life* in 1956. Goffman's book explores the subject in terms of an actor performing a play.

Advice for making a good first impression as an investigative interviewer is pretty much the same as that for a human resources interviewer or a television talk-show interviewer. Be welcoming, invite interviewees in, treat them with respect, understand that they may be feeling nervous, try to make them feel comfortable, and treat the interview as a conversation where they are invited to do most of the talking, rather than a rapid-fire question and answer session. The reason those 'questions from viewers' sessions on TV or *YouTube* feel so awkward is that they lack the flow of a conversation.

With formal police interviews, a video or audio recording may be made and it may be necessary to explain this procedure to the interviewee. You will need to research the procedures for such an interview in the place where your story is set – but the recording often begins with a statement of date and time and the naming of the interviewer and interviewee and any other person's present. This formality and the presence of recording equipment can dramatically affect an interviewee's behaviour and the tone of the interview – people are much more forthcoming in a more casual environment, which typically gives the private detective an advantage.

Engaging the interviewee – You want to get an interviewee talking as soon as possible during the interview and you want to get them nodding and agreeing with you. You also want them to feel confident in being able to answer questions 'correctly' and honestly. You do this by beginning the interview with questions that are easy to answer and that are asked in a friendly and encouraging way. If you can also use these questions to show that you and the interviewee have things in common, so much the better. Factual questions where you already know the answer are a good place to start – they show that you are a professional who has done their homework and they get the interviewee nodding and talking. Don't ask questions that might cause the interviewee to suspect you have an ulterior motive for asking them – if they become suspicious they will be defensive. The first few questions will be like those you ask a stranger when engaging in small talk – you're trying to begin a conversation at this stage rather than trying to find things out.

How you engage an interviewee in conversation will depend to some extent on their background and personal characteristics. You will need to try and read their emotional state and pitch your early questions in a form that will help them feel at ease.

Explaining the purpose of the interview – One step towards winning the interviewee's confidence is to explain to them the purpose of the interview and how you intend to conduct it. This helps to eliminate the 'fear of the unknown' element. Tell them what you want to talk to them about and why. Tell them what you hope to achieve by the end of the interview and why you feel that the information they have is important to you as it will help you achieve your objective. You may need to explain to them why you have chosen to interview them rather than someone else. And you may need to reassure them that you are not intending to try and make them look foolish or guilty. But obviously, you shouldn't lie to them if your objective really is to establish their guilt or innocence – they will know if you're lying.

Building rapport – Rapport is defined as a close and trusting relationship in which people communicate well and understand each other. In the early stages of an interview, the interviewer tries to achieve this sort of relationship with the interviewee. Some interviewees will actively resist this. Establishing rapport helps the interviewee to feel more comfortable answering questions and helps the interviewer feel less inhibited in asking sensitive or personal questions.

Rapport doesn't require that interviewer and interviewee become emotionally involved with each other, only that trust and respect are established. It is important that the interviewer maintains their objectivity throughout.

You can find a lot of information online about building rapport in various social and business situations. There are a few basic approaches that I will mention briefly.

Commonality – If two people discover they have things in common, such as interests, hobbies, football teams or whatever, then this common ground can make communication easier. We always find it easier to trust someone we feel to be like us in some way.

Co-ordination – We sometimes refer to this as being 'in sync' with someone else. One way of achieving this is by mirroring the other person's verbal and non-verbal behaviours, including posture and gestures and ways of speaking. This has to be done sensitively otherwise it risks looking like mockery. As social animals, humans naturally tend to engage in mirroring behaviours to some extent. Have a look at one of the good illustrated texts on body language to see how mirroring and other forms of non-verbal communication can be used.

Mutual Attentiveness – Each person is focused on and interested in what the other person is saying or doing. Ways of demonstrating this include looking at the other person and making eye contact, nodding, and smiling. With eye contact, it is important not to stare as this can be seen as threatening. Active listening skills (see below) also contribute to this. Touching can also be an indicator of attentiveness, but whether or not this is appropriate depends on the circumstances.

Account, Clarification & Challenge

Account refers to the information or description of events as seen from the interviewee's point of view. In the case of a victim or witness or criminal, it is their 'version' of events – what they saw and what they did. This is usually gained by using a few questions as prompts and be engaging in active listening.

Active listening – Active listening requires the listener to concentrate on what is being said, understand, respond, and remember. In interviewing, it enables the interviewer to identify important topics during the course of the interview and manage the conversation by keeping it on topic; communicate interest in what the interviewee is saying and demonstrate that their information is relevant and valuable, and identify facts that are significant as clues or evidence for the investigation. Active listening involves understanding what the interviewer *means* rather than just hearing the words that are said.

If someone senses that you have lost interest in what they are saying or are bored by it, they will stop speaking or will revert to talking about inconsequential matters. Poor interviewers often concentrate on what their next question will be rather than listening attentively to the answer to their previous question.

Also be aware that when an interviewee becomes aware that you are not listening, they may seek to take advantage of this or will test you by saying something outrageous to see how you react. It is impossible for an interviewer to control an interview if they are not fully engaged in what is being said.

Active listening is usually non-judgmental – the listener encourages the interviewee to continue speaking by appearing to accept what is being said without challenging it. You want to encourage them into thinking that anything they want to say is permissible. A good listener will avoid offering their own opinions, value judgments, or criticisms. If an interviewee feels they are being judged, they will become more guarded in what they say or may seek to say what they think the interviewer wants to hear. They will also avoid interrupting the speaker and will wait for a natural pause before speaking. The interviewee may express beliefs which the interviewer finds unacceptable or may describe actions which the interviewer finds repugnant – in such cases, it is important that to remain detached.

Active listening requires patience and calmness. You need to allow the interviewee time to answer questions and not be too eager to move them on to the next one. Impatience tends to ruin rapport. If an interviewee becomes impatient or angry, the interviewer should avoid becoming defensive or angry in response. Expressing emotion may alienate the interviewee or encourage them on to further angry outbursts. It is much better to calmly accept what they say and respond with something along the lines of 'I can understand why you might feel that way.' Sometimes an interviewee will try and provoke you in order to test you – your response may determine whether or not they feel able to trust you. Patience is also related to persistence. If an interviewee avoids or refuses to answer a question, you have to be prepared to come back to it, rephrase it, or find some other way of getting back onto the topic – and this may require several attempts. And patience may sometimes require that you say nothing. Don't use the 'silent treatment' to punish an interviewer, don't stare at them, instead treat it as an opportunity for the interviewee to speak without prompting. Some people – interviewees and interviewers – feel uncomfortable with silence and try to fill it. Some interviewees will just sit patiently and wait for your next question. If an interviewee seems determined to maintain the silence, you could try breaking by casually asking them what they are thinking. And if an interviewee lapses into silence or doesn't respond immediately to a question, it may be that they just need time to think and consider their response, so you have to resist the urge to fill the silence.

Ways of demonstrating active listening include asking relevant questions, paraphrasing what has been heard, and reflecting on what has been understood.

While the interviewee is giving their account, the interviewer should be encouraging and supportive. Questions may be used to *clarify* details and to get the interviewee to *expand* their account.

Questions

To maintain the trust of an interviewee, questions should be objective and not imply that you have already formed an opinion or 'taken sides.' During the initial account gathering and clarification, questions should be regarded as prompts to elicit information – and not delivered in the form of a cross-examination of the type seen in courtroom dramas. The interviewee should feel that you are helping them remember, not trying to catch them in a lie. Avoid seeming belligerent or sarcastic and never scoff at what the interviewee says. Using unexpected or trick questions or backing the interviewee into a corner will only make them defensive which will be counterproductive.

If an interviewee is unwilling to answer questions and only gives monosyllabic responses, you have to try and make it difficult for them to avoid answering. For example, if you ask 'Have you seen Bart recently?' the interviewee can say 'No.' Asking 'When was the last time you saw Bart?' prevents them from being able to answer negatively. They may still answer with a single word, 'Friday,' but that at least gives you an 'in' – you can get them to expand on it by asking another question.

You will probably already be aware that there are different kinds of questions that may or may not be appropriate in certain situations.

Open-ended questions cannot be answered with a yes/no or other single statement response. They require a longer and more considered answer. An example might be 'How did you first meet Harry?' or 'Tell me about your relationship with Sally.' They can be used to gain the initial account and to encourage the interviewee to expand it – 'Why did you do that?' or 'What made you say that to him?' or 'What does he use that for?'

Closed questions require limited replies and are best used for confirming facts – some require a yes or no answer – 'Did he hit you first?' or 'Is your date of birth 1st April 1984?' – and some require a simple factual statement – 'What day was this?' or 'How many shots did you hear?'

Forced-choice questions offer the interviewee a limited number of responses to choose from – 'Was it Monday or Tuesday?' or 'Was it a light blue car or dark blue?' The problem with this type of question is that none of the options might be right – What if the car was turquoise? And they also allow the interviewee to pick an answer, even if they don't know the truth.

Multiple questions – 'How tall was he? What was he wearing? Where did he stand?' – can be confusing for the interviewee and they may feel stressed by trying to remember all of the bits they are supposed to answer and the sequence in which they were asked. Single, specific questions are better.

Leading questions suggest a particular answer or contain the information the interviewer is seeking to have confirmed – 'He was the one holding the gun, wasn't he?' Their use in a courtroom is restricted – opposing counsel may object that counsel is 'leading the witness' and trying to direct or influence the evidence being presented. During an investigation, the use of leading questions risks distorting the interviewee's memory and can lead to testimony that is regarded as less credible. In a story, a leading question might be used to trick an interviewee into revealing information that they have not already mentioned, e.g. 'When the stranger entered, what was *she* wearing?'

Oblique questions do not go directly to the point and can be less stressful for interviewees to answer, e.g. 'Your neighbours say they often heard the Smiths arguing – did you?' The reference to the neighbours suggests that answering the question has already been sanctioned by others and the interviewee would not be revealing secrets by replying.

Self-appraisal questions ask the interviewee to evaluate or judge him or herself. 'Do you think you made the right decision?' or 'Do you think that was a reasonable thing to do?'

Diversionary questions – If an interviewee responds angrily to a question or refuses to answer, it may be necessary to reduce tension and try to restore rapport with them. You can defuse things by saying something like 'Let's set that aside for a moment' and then diverting onto a new topic, introducing it in a few words in such a way that the interviewee has time to calm down.

Loaded questions contain a controversial or unjustified assumption such as a presumption of guilt – the classic example being 'When did you stop beating your wife?'

The questions that you use should encourage the interviewee to speak openly and without fear of reprisal. People are reluctant to reveal anything that makes them feel ashamed or embarrassed or that they fear may bring some form of punishment. They are also hesitant to say anything that could expose another person to the same feelings.

Recording & Note-Taking

It is important that interviews are recorded in some fashion. Formal police interviews with suspects are often recorded – either in audio or video form. Witness statements may be recorded or written up for the witness to sign. These records may be submitted as evidence or during disclosure if a case is to go to trial.

Private detectives investigating cases that aren't likely to go to trial are also advised to make detailed notes after an interview. Recording an interview with the subject's permission or making notes during the interview can have a negative effect on rapport and on the subject's willingness to speak candidly.

Good notes are important because human memory isn't always as good as we believe it is and the detective may want to look back at exactly what a subject did or didn't say. Notes can also be helpful if the detective has to provide a written report for his client. An interviewee may also change his or her story at a later date and the notes provide a record of what was originally said. The change of story may be the result of poor memory or it may have been caused by the person's exposure to the statements of other witnesses. Or the individual may deliberately change their story for their own reasons. Whatever the reason, the notes of the original interview can be used to demonstrate that the change has occurred.

If a case does go to court, the detective's notes can be subpoenaed and submitted in evidence and their accuracy (or otherwise) may then affect the detective's reputation.

Challenging Accounts

Once the interviewee has had an opportunity to give their full account, the interviewee can review what they have heard and seen – in terms of non-verbal communication – and look for inconsistencies or gaps in the account. If the interviewer suspects that the interviewee has not told the truth at certain points in the account, now is the time to test those responses with further probing. While it may be useful to suggest that you have some doubts about what has been said, you should avoid stating your suspicions overtly or directly challenging the interviewee. Rapport is still vital at this stage. If the interviewee is suddenly challenged or if the interviewer raises their voice or uses inflammatory language, the interviewee will become defensive and may refuse to cooperate further. Or they may make greater efforts to bolster their deception. Allowing an interviewee to embroider their lies can sometimes be an effective strategy – they may go so far as to say something that is patently and provably untrue and this may be what you need to begin unravelling their story.

The PEACE model advises approaching each element of deception in the account as a separate objective. Picking them apart separately helps avoid a situation where the interviewee can provide a plausible story that covers all of the deceptions. His attempts to 'prove' one incidence of deception may actually provide evidence of the falsity of another part of his story – or at least highlight an inconsistency.

One way of testing the truthfulness of an interviewee's account is to explore the sequence of events as they have described it. If the story has been fabricated, the interviewee will have made up the events in a logical sequence that is easily remembered. Asking him to go over the sequence again in reverse order or jumping around – 'Did X occur before after Y?' – can reveal that his account is false. If we actually witness events, it is easier to recall what happened even out of sequence and we are less likely to falter or have to work our way through the sequence from the beginning.

At the end of the interview, it may or may not be appropriate for the interviewer to announce their conclusion to the interviewee – 'I don't believe you have told me the whole truth' or 'I think you are holding something back.' Or even, 'I think you did it and I want to get to the bottom of it.' Such a statement may cause the interviewee to become angry and defensive or it may prompt further revelations or even an admission or confession. This will depend upon the nature of the character and the needs of your story at that point.

Confessions

Spontaneous confessions do happen in real life – 'You know all about it, don't you?' – and the criminal may even feel relieved that he doesn't have to keep up the pretence of innocence. In a story, this is probably best reserved for a reluctant witness or a minor criminal, rather than the main antagonist or villain because confessions can seem anticlimactic – especially if the investigator didn't have to struggle to obtain the confession. In real-life, somewhere between forty and fifty-five per cent of criminals confess – though the percentage of people confessing to serious crimes including murder and rape is much smaller. Stories typically feature more serious crimes and so the incidence of confession should probably be low.

One way that investigators use to obtain a confession is used when multiple suspects are involved. They tell suspect one that suspect two has already confessed and is blaming it all on suspect one. To save himself from being unjustly accused of all of the criminal activity, suspect one may then confess his part and reveal what part suspect two played in the crime. This same technique can be used on both suspects simultaneously and may result in two accounts that the police can then compare and contrast.

Factors influencing a person's likelihood of confessing, according to St-Yves and Deslauriers-Varin, include:

Age – those under 21 confess more often than older suspects.

Feelings of Guilt – Criminals may feel a sense of relief at having been 'found out' and unburden themselves.

Personality – Introverts confess more readily than extroverts.

Criminal Background – First time offenders are more likely to confess than those who have previous experience of arrest and questioning, perhaps because they are less familiar with their rights in such circumstances or less aware of the techniques interrogators use to obtain a confession.

Nature of the Crime – People are more likely to confess to non-violent crimes – especially those least associated with feelings of shame, rejection or humiliation.

Seriousness of the Crime – Suspects are less likely to confess to serious crimes, probably because of the heavier penalties for such crimes and possibly because in such cases the suspect is more likely to rely on the advice of an attorney.

Evidence – A suspect's decision to confess may be based on the strength of the evidence he *believes* the police have against him.

Questioning Techniques – Interrogation techniques yield more confessions than investigative interviews - but they also, as mentioned previously, lead to more false confessions.

False Confessions

Why would anyone confess to a crime that they did not commit? Torture can be used to make people confess to anything and interrogation methods that involve coercion some way short of torture can also elicit false confessions. But not all false confessions are extracted from people in this way. People who have a low IQ, lack confidence in their own ability to remember, suffer from psychological disorders and demonstrate susceptibility to suggestion or to unquestioningly following instruction are at greater risk of making a false confession. If they are repeatedly told that they did it, they may come to believe this. If they are told that signing a confession is in their best interests, they may sign it. Others may confess because of the attention they receive as a result.

Determining whether a confession is genuine can be achieved by comparing the details given by the confessor against evidence discovered by the police and not revealed publicly. A fake confession will probably also include some of the 'red flags' listed in the section on False Allegations of Crime below.

Closure

Think of the interview as a scene that requires a beginning, a middle, and an end. It needs a proper ending and should finish abruptly or just fade away. The interviewee should also be made aware that the interview is drawing to a close. If more than one interviewer is involved, the first may ask the second if they have any other questions. After that, the interviewer will often summarise what the interviewee has said – allowing the interviewee to make any additions or clarifications along the way.

Steven Kelly Brown: "Sometimes the interview takes an unexpected turn; the witness reveals some information you were unaware of, and in the heat of following the new lead, you forget to ask everything you need to ask about the facts you had to begin with. That's why you should always make a list of the topics you want to cover. If the interview gets really exciting for some reason, be sure to go over your list before you leave the witness and cover any topics you originally intended."

It is also good practice to ask the interviewee if they have any questions they would like to ask. Sometimes you may deliberately avoid asking an interviewee a question that you know they are expecting and they may say 'Why didn't you ask me about the car?' Or they may ask a question designed to try and discover what you know about something that wasn't mentioned in the interview.

You should also ask the interviewee if there is anything that they would like to tell you that wasn't covered by your questions. They may have something – truthful or deceitful – that they are dying to tell you or an answer that they prepared ahead of the interview and haven't had an opportunity to give.

In a formal recorded interview, the final stage will be a statement of date and time and the recording equipment will be turned off. In some cases, a transcript or a copy of the recording may be required by the interviewee or their attorney.

In most cases, you will want to try and maintain rapport and end the interview in a cordial manner. Thank the interviewee for their time and let them know that their contribution is valuable and appreciated. If necessary, leave the way open for further discussion with them. And if appropriate, let the interviewee know what will happen next. Obviously, if the interviewee will face formal charges as a result of the interview, you then enter a new stage of police procedure.

In less formal interview situations, the interviewer must stay alert – the subject may let their guard down when the formal interview is over. Or they may attack! A private detective will also leave a business card and ask the subject to contact him if they think of anything else that might help his investigation.

Evaluation

The final stages of the interview are to evaluate what has been said by the interviewee and to decide what to do next. Evaluation takes place both towards the end of the interview and after the interview has ended. Drawing together all of the interviewee's verbal and non-verbal responses, the interviewer must decide whether they have answered the questions put to them fully and truthfully and then choose which of the following describes the interviewee:

- Truthful

- Probably truthful
- Possibly truthful
- Possibly deceptive
- Probably deceptive
- Deceptive

A single interview may not be sufficient to come to a definitive conclusion and a follow-up interview may be required, but this is not always possible.

If the interviewer has not been able to decide on the interviewee's truthfulness before the end of the interview, Black & Yeschke suggest a couple of possible ways to deal with this, other than a follow-up interview. First, tell the interviewee that it appears that they might have more information to provide, or second, "...give the impression that you suspect that the interviewee is hiding or holding back important information."

In the case of a suspect where the interviewer has formed a strong suspicion of their being guilty of the crime, or of protecting someone who is guilty, the Reid Model and Black & Yeschke suggest that moving on to interrogation techniques should be considered. This does not form part of the PEACE model. Where any interviewer is strongly suspected of lying, Black & Yeschke write that a 'detection of deception' test could be administered using a polygraph. Polygraph tests are not routinely used in the UK and there are concerns regarding their accuracy and usefulness (see below).

Deception
Deception is an act or statement designed to mislead, hide the truth, or promote something that is not true – and it is usually carried out for personal gain or advantage. In the investigative interview, you need to ask yourself what the interviewee seeks to gain by lying. What are they trying to achieve or what are they trying to avoid? What are the interviewee's desires, needs, and/or fears at that particular moment?

A number of external factors – social pressures, loyalties, obligations, and personal needs or objectives – influence whether a subject will answer questions truthfully. It must also be recognised that some people are less reliable than others. Others are uncooperative simply because they have issues with authority figures and don't want to help 'the man.'

Given that the objective of the investigative interview is to obtain full and accurate information, determining whether an interviewee is lying – by commission or omission – is a vital part of the interviewer's job.

Truthfulness tends to be shown by the ability to recall details, demonstrate an understanding of events, and provide an uninterrupted narrative. These things vary according to the individual concerned - some of us are better storytellers than others - but the basic principles apply. It is easier to recall and describe something than it is to make up or edit an account.

Choosing not to reveal information requires a conscious effort and that effort takes time – it may only cause a brief pause as the subject collects their thoughts and decides what to say, but the pause may be recognisable. Lies tend to be less spontaneous and involve less physical movement and display less emotion – liars believe that by appearing calm and still, they are revealing nothing. Their answers also tend to be more evasive – instead of saying 'No, I didn't,' they say something like 'What would I have to gain by doing that?' Or they may answer a different question to the one asked. Or their answer may be convoluted and confused. Look at the way politicians respond to questions and you will see these techniques of avoidance.

Black and Yeshke write that deceivers may also "...attempt to distract the interviewer with inappropriate friendliness, compliments, or seductive behaviour."

For the non-expert, lying is more stressful than telling the truth, so signs of stress may be signs of deceit in some circumstances – especially in an individual who normally tells the truth. The stress arises from a fear of consequences and feelings of shame associated with breaking a rule. 'Pathological liars' and psychopaths do not suffer from this kind of stress.

Non-Verbal Clues to Deception

Non-verbal behaviours can signal deception – refer to an illustrated text on body language to see what these signals are and consider how you might use them in your scenes. An interviewer also needs to be aware that if a subject is lying, they will be closely observing the interviewer's body language to see whether their lies are being believed.

Be careful about assuming that if a person avoids eye contact then they are lying. Research shows that this is not necessarily true and that you have to be able to read more subtle and short-lived facial expressions to spot if someone is lying.

Paul Ekman's book *Telling Lies: Clues to Deceit in the Marketplace, Politics, and Marriage* (2009) is the best-known text on reading 'micro-expressions.' Ekman's work was used as the basis for the television series *Lie to Me* starring Tim Roth.

Verbal Clues to Deception

Phrases such as 'To be perfectly honest,' 'To tell the truth,' or ones that begin 'Frankly' or 'Honestly' are often at least partly deceptive. The speaker is trying to convince both himself and you that what he is saying is the truth. 'Honest to God' and 'Swear to God' are also suspect phrases as are 'Ask anyone who knows me' and 'Swear on my mother's grave.' In an investigative interview, a subject who knows they're telling the truth doesn't need to use such phrases. But they can occur in an interrogation if an honest subject feels that they are not being believed and so are in danger and can also occur in someone who has been interrogated before or has a criminal history and believes that this will be used to assume they're lying.

Honest interviews make simple denials if asked 'Did you do X?' Dishonest ones are more likely to construct more elaborate denials that often include objections – 'Why would I do something like that? I'm an honest man with a good job – I don't need to do X?' In the second example, the subject doesn't actually say he didn't do it, he only says that he doesn't *need* to.

Rationalisation and Projection

Rationalisation refers to a way in which individuals seek to justify their own impulses, characteristics, or behaviours to others and to themselves. No one wants to feel that their actions are irrational or immoral, and so they seek ways of justifying them. Interviewees can demonstrate empathy by accepting the subject's rationalisations – 'I can understand why you would feel that way.' Kinesic interrogations use rationalisation in a more active way, offering up possible rationalisations for criminal or deviant behaviour and seeing if an interviewee will agree with them or adopt them.

In psychology, *projection* refers to a defence mechanism by which an individual's ego tries to defend itself against 'unacceptable' impulses or qualities by denying them in themselves and attributing them to others. So a person who feels subconscious guilt regarding their own gluttony may accuse others of being greedy. They seek to shift the blame. The same behaviour may be demonstrated by subjects in the investigative interview. It can also be used for comic effect in otherwise innocent characters.

Polygraphs – The Use of 'Lie Detectors'

Polygraph testing is based on the belief that the measurement of physiological changes such as blood pressure, pulse, respiration, and/or skin conductivity, can be used by a trained 'expert' to determine whether someone's responses to questions are truthful. Unfortunately, some innocent people 'fail' polygraph tests and some guilty ones can 'pass' and be freed to commit further crimes.

The National Research Council in the United States found no evidence of the effectiveness of polygraph tests and some scientists consider polygraphy to be pseudoscience. The US Supreme Court has stated that there is "...simply no consensus that polygraph evidence is reliable," and that "Unlike other expert witnesses who testify about factual matters ... such as the analysis of fingerprints, ballistics, or DNA found at a crime scene, a polygraph expert can supply the jury only with another opinion." Despite this, as *Wired* magazine reported in October 2018, an estimated two-and-a-half million polygraph tests are given each year in the USA and the industry is worth $2 billion.

There are two ways in which subjects can 'cheat' a lie detector test, referred to as *general state* and *specific point*. CIA officer turned KGB mole Aldrich Ames used the general state method saying that his Soviet handler told him to get a good night's sleep and go into the test feeling relaxed and confident. "Be nice to the polygraph examiner," he was told, "develop a rapport, and be co-operative and try to maintain your calm." The specific point method involves altering the supposed baseline response during the initial control questions by artificially increasing the heart rate by the subject thinking of something scary or exciting or by secretly pricking themselves with a pin – this then means that responses given to the main questions will not reveal significant deviations from the baseline.

Truth Serum

'Truth serum' is a popular term used for a number of psychoactive drugs, the best-known of which is sodium pentothal, which was commonly used in operating rooms as a general anaesthetic but has been replaced by more modern alternatives. Other drugs tried include 'date rape' drugs such as scopolamine (or hyoscine) and Rohypnol (flunitrazepam), and barbiturates such as sodium amytal (amobarbital). Generally speaking, it seems that the effects of these drugs are little different to alcohol intoxication – and ethyl alcohol has also been injected as a truth drug – so the question to ask here is: Do people lie or talk nonsense when they are drunk? Most of the drugs mentioned here have serious side-effects in some people and can be lethal if overdosed, so these are probably not the sort of thing you should have your hero using.

Hypnosis

The use of hypnosis in investigations probably came about as a result of its use by Sigmund Freud to assist patients in retrieving lost or repressed memories of past events. It is based on the assumption that things are recorded in the memory even though we may not be able, or willing, to consciously recall them. Freud eventually abandoned its use, but the idea of it being able to retrieve memories has continued to attract storytellers.

One theory about hypnosis is that the subject is induced into a trance-like state but this is challenged by theories which argue that no change in state is involved.

One of the issues with hypnosis is its similarity to the use of alcohol or 'truth serum' – it serves to relax the subject and reduce conscious critical thinking, i.e. those thoughts that make us self-edit. Another issue with hypnosis is that it makes subjects more susceptible to suggestion – so that rather than help retrieve memories it can cause them to create false ones and believe that they are true.

These issues mean that evidence obtained under hypnosis is treated differently in different jurisdictions. If you want to use it in a story, you will need to check how it is regarded in the place where your story is set. Even where it is allowed as testimony, strict guidelines will probably be in place regarding who is permitted to carry out the hypnosis and how it is used.

In an article titled 'The Rise and Fall of Forensic Hypnosis in Criminal Investigation,' Newman and Thompson concluded: "Investigatory forensic hypnosis was based on a well-intentioned but scientifically untenable position: that detailed memories could be accurately retrieved and utilized in criminal investigations. Although anecdotally helpful in some cases, courts recognized the risk hypnotically elicited memories could pose to the rights of a defendant in a criminal case..."

Good Cop – Bad Cop

A good cop/bad cop routine or friend and foe negotiation is a technique involving two people who take opposing approaches to the interviewee. Each may interview the subject alternately or at the same time. The 'bad cop' takes an aggressive stance, effectively employing interrogation techniques including accusation, insults, threats, and attempts to intimidate the subject. In contrast, the 'good cop' appears more sympathetic and understanding. By causing the subject to seek to defend themselves against the bad cop, it is believed that they will come to trust and confide in the good cop. Because it involves elements of the interrogation approach, this technique carries the same risks of eliciting false confessions.

'Good cop/bad cop' is a genre convention that has been used on television so many times that it has become a cliché. George N. Dove refers to it as 'roleplaying' used for "...the purpose of harassing a suspect and at the same time tricking him into a confidential relationship."

Interviewing Witnesses & Victims

Most of this chapter has been slanted towards the interviewing of suspects, but a great deal of the work done by a police or private detective will be interviewing witnesses to and victims of crime. In theory, the non-confrontational investigative interview technique can be applied to witnesses and victims in much the same way as it is used for suspects, but there are some additional factors that must be born in mind.

Evaluating Witnesses

The dependability of a witness needs to be determined in much the same way as that of a suspect. What constitutes a reliable witness? We have to establish that they were actually *present* to witness the events in question and that they were in a conscious mental state that allowed them to see and understand what was happening. We also need to know how good their powers of observation are – both in terms of the reliability of their physical senses and their ability to focus them on events that occur. And we need to have a sense of how clear-headed or objective they are – mental or emotional disturbance can affect their ability to accurately recall events.

Studies have shown that eyewitness accounts of events can be extremely unreliable, especially when it comes to identifying criminals – see the National Academy of Sciences report *Identifying the Culprit: Assessing Eyewitness Identification* (2014).

False Witnesses

Not everyone who comes forward as a witness to a crime is genuine and not all of the information provided by genuine witnesses is true. Some people claim to have witnessed a crime – especially a high-profile one – because they either want to interact with the police and feel like an investigator or because they are seeking attention and want to be regarded as important.

People who *were* present during or immediately after a crime may have unreliable memories or poor senses and so provide unreliable information – but others make things up for reasons similar to those of the fake witness. Human memory works in such a way that people are actually able to convince themselves that the unreliable or fake evidence they have provided is genuinely true and accurate.

Victims of Violent Crime

I wrote about *victimology* earlier in the book mainly in the context of someone who dies as a result of violent crime. Here I will briefly cover the survivor in terms of their role as a witness to be interviewed by an investigator. I am concentrating on violent crime because this is where the impact can most obviously be seen – but similar responses will be observable in victims of other crimes but to a lesser extent.

Harvey Wallace defined three broad stages through which a victim may pass after being subjected to a violent crime: the *impact* stage, the *recoil* stage, and the *reorganisation* stage. The impact stage is the victim's initial response and the intensity and length of this will vary according to the individual, the nature of the crime, and any physical injuries suffered. Recoil involves the victim's early attempts to deal with the impact of the crime upon them – it can include feelings of sadness, anger, self-pity, fear, and sometimes guilt. They may become emotionally detached and may even enter a denial phase as they try to deal with the experience. The final stage is reorganisation – feelings of fear and rage diminish and the victim directs their attention towards life's everyday activities. Some people pass through all three stages reasonably quickly, others never complete the process.

The impact of violent crime can result in serious mental health issues such as Acute Stress Disorder, Post-Traumatic Stress Disorder, Battered Woman Syndrome, Stalking Trauma Syndrome, or Rape Trauma Syndrome.

A victim's response to the crime they have suffered can obviously impact their mental well-being and this can affect their ability – or even their desire – to function as a reliable witness.

In gathering information from others about the victim, there are two issues that have to be born in mind by the investigator. The first, 'deification of the victim' was mentioned in an earlier chapter and refers to a tendency people have to describe the 'saintly' qualities of the victim and avoid reference to any of their negative characteristics or behaviours – this can actually impede an investigation as the withheld information might contain important leads.

The second issue is 'blaming the victim.' In his 1971 book *Blaming the Victim* William Ryan used the phrase in reference to the way poor people are blamed for their own poverty rather than the real cause which is inequality and lack of opportunity. The phrase has been used subsequently for other victims who have been blamed for exposing themselves to risk and therefore 'deserve' whatever happens to them. The classic example is rape victims who 'choose to dress provocatively' or who flirt with strangers. A known criminal who becomes the victim of a violent assault may get little sympathy from those who saw it happen – if you lie down with dogs, you shouldn't complain if you get up with fleas. This attitude can also impede an investigation and presents challenges for the investigator trying to interview witnesses.

The issue of 'blaming the victim' is the flipside of the issue of false allegations of crime (see below).

Witnesses as Victims

With a violent crime, there may be secondary or 'collateral' victims in that relatives and friends of the victim may be affected by what has happened as may people who actually witnessed the crime. When interviewing either group, it is important to be aware that they may have been impacted emotionally or psychologically by the crime even though they were not involved directly as a victim.

Peter Weir's 1985 film *Witness* starring Harrison Ford presents another take on the way in which a witness – in this case, an innocent Amish boy – can become a potential victim.

False Allegations of Crime

Individuals may falsely report being the victim of a crime for a number of reasons. They may seek to gain financially; they may have a need for sympathy; they may want to get revenge on the person they have accused; they may be trying to cover up another crime, or they may be trying to provide themselves with an alibi.

Dr. Park Elliot Dietz and former FBI Supervisory Special Agent Roy Hazelwood have proposed twenty 'red flags' that could indicate a false report – here is the list, taken from Turvey (2014):

- The story tends to be bizarre or sensational.
- The pseudo-victim injures himself or herself, sometimes seriously, or simulates injury for the purpose of gaining support.
- The pseudo-victim presents in such a way that people believe no one would do this to himself or herself.
- The pseudo-victim does not initially report the incident to the police.
- A stranger is accused.
- The pseudo-victim claims that overwhelming force was used, or that he or she resisted greatly, or that there were multiple assailants.
- The account is either overly detailed or very vague.
- The pseudo-victim reports having his or her eyes closed during the attack or was unconscious, or passed out, or has no memory of what happened, or was drugged, and so cannot provide details.
- The pseudo-victim is indifferent to his or her injuries.
- The expected laboratory findings are absent.

- The pseudo-victim is vague about the location of the assault, or there is no evidence at the scene to corroborate the complaint.
- Damage to the clothing is inconsistent with the injuries.
- There are escalating personal problems in the life of the pseudo-victim.
- The pseudo-victim has been exposed in the past to accounts of similar things.
- The pseudo-victim's post-assault behaviour is inconsistent with the allegations.
- The pseudo-victim is uncooperative with the investigation.
- When the pseudo-victim talks to the authorities, he or she tends to steer the conversation away from the specific to the unprovable.
- There is writing on the body of the pseudo-victim.
- There is a history of making other false allegations.
- There is a history of extensive medical care.

It should be noted that these are suggested as being suspicious and worth investigating further and do not indicate *proof* of a false claim.

17 | Surveillance & Stake-Outs

Surveillance is the close observation of a person, place, or thing – and in the case of the private eye, it is usually carried out in a secretive manner. If the person being followed spots whoever is shadowing them, it is referred to be being 'burned' or being 'made.' If the target has not actually spotted their tail but becomes suspicious that they might be being followed, they are sometimes referred to as being a 'warm' target. Though there may be occasions when an observer *wants* the target to know that he or she is being followed and so allows themselves to be seen. This can be useful if a detective wants to put pressure on someone and provoke them into doing something.

There are two types of surveillance – that relying on the latest sophisticated (and expensive!) electronic equipment and that relying on traditional tactics. I will touch on electronic surveillance in this chapter, but for the most part will concentrate on practical methodology as that is what appears most commonly in novels and screenplays. Some surveillance methods require a team of watchers and such a team may be available to a police department if you're writing a police procedural, but not to a lone private detective. I will include examples of both team and solo approaches here. In the following sections, I will assume 'you' are the detective engaged in the surveillance operation.

Purpose of Surveillance

Suspects, criminals, and the associates of such people may be observed for a variety of reasons related to information gathering. Someone may also be followed after a drop-off or pick-up related to a blackmail or kidnapping case. A place may be watched to find out what is going on there – e.g. is it being used for gambling, drug sales, illegal fights, or some other criminal activity? Or the place may be a known hideout or hangout of a person of interest. An object may be observed to protect it from theft or damage or the object may have been placed in order to attract the attention of a criminal in order to trap him.

Going undercover is another form of surveillance that can be used for a short one-off or an extended period of time. I covered undercover work in an earlier chapter.

Fact versus Fiction

In his book *Shadowing and Surveillance: A Complete Guidebook,* Burt Rapp writes that surveillance as portrayed in novels, films, and television shows is often inaccurate. One exception he notes is in the film *The French Connection* where Popeye Doyle follows a suspect through the streets of New York. "This sequence would make a good training film, because it showed moving surveillance as it really is," Rapp says. He notes that at one point Popeye "...broke his profile by taking off his hat and coat." This was an attempt to make it less obvious to the target that he was being followed.

Surveillance sequences in films are typically short and end in success. In real life, stake-outs can be long and boring and ultimately produce no results, while shadowing someone can involve being out in the rain and cold or blistering heat. Rapp highlights the film *Contract on Cherry Street* as showing some of the problems that stake-outs bring: "Keeping a large warehouse under observation for many days is not as easy as it seems, even though the subject is large and stationary."

Planning & Preparation

Before beginning a surveillance operation, the watcher should thoroughly research the area where the surveillance is to be conducted and also learn as much as possible about the person, place, or object to be watched. Equipment such as maps, a camera, a phone (and charger or spare battery), binoculars, may be necessary. Binoculars should be of good quality, with a high level of magnification and lenses that provide good low-light performance.

Communications

Where more than one person is involved in a surveillance operation, especially if tailing a moving target, it is important that proper communications are established between those involved. This may involve physical hand or body signals, cell phones, or radios.

Evidence & Law

The police and private detectives are subject to the same laws relating to illegal entry, telephone tapping, invasion of privacy, and such – but if a private detective is not preparing evidence for a trial, he is subject to less formal scrutiny than a police detective. In a court case, the prosecution must reveal all of their evidence to the defense – if it becomes apparent that the evidence was obtained using illegal methods, the defense can ask the judge to rule it inadmissible in court.

Stationary Surveillance – The Stake-Out

Choosing Your Observation Post

This involves watching from a stationary vantage point and usually relies on the watcher remaining unobserved. In movies and TV shows, a stake-out consists of two men in a car parked close to wherever the subject is. This is sometimes referred to as *'fixed mobile' surveillance* since the car doesn't move. Two men sitting in a stationary car for hours is so obvious that it is bound to draw the attention of neighbours or the subject. A man and a woman could pretend to be engaged in a romantic encounter, at least for a while, but they would need to be pretty well acquainted. In theory, two guys could also be making out, but sadly that is still likely to draw attention due to being out of the ordinary.

Another Hollywood cliché is the telephone company truck or the maintenance gang digging a hole in the road. These are so obvious that even kids are going to recognise them as being a stake-out. And a beat-up panel van with blacked out windows may as well have a 'Stake Out' sign stuck on the side. The parked vehicle approach also assumes that local parking regulations allow you, a non-resident, to park on the street for long periods of time – this may not be the case in some locations.

Another problem with using a parked vehicle as an observation post is that it is uncomfortable and impractical. Cars can be freezing in winter or like a greenhouse in summer and running the engine to adjust the internal temperature is just likely to draw attention to you. Then there are issues of food and drink – and the absence of toilet facilities. With all this in mind, it is much better to carry out a stake-out from a nearby building – ideally from a room with all the facilities you need, such as an apartment or a hotel room. Having an entrance in a place where the subject cannot see you enter or leave is also an advantage. If the entrance is visible, you will have to limit your comings and goings.

If you borrow or rent an apartment or hotel room, you will need to avoid arousing the suspicions of the landlord or manager. You don't want them to see you behaving suspiciously as they are likely to conclude that you're going something illegal. And if you're in a hotel room, you may need to conceal your equipment from the housekeeping staff.

Of course, sometimes your detective's fixed surveillance location has got to be up in a tree or hiding in the bushes. In such situations, a military camouflage outfit may not be the best idea – they're difficult to explain away if you're spotted by neighbours or the police – you might have to pretend to be a 'twitcher' waiting to see a very rare bird. If you are conducting surveillance at night, be aware that some types of clothing make noise and even coins rattling in your pocket can draw attention on a quiet evening. And remember to put your phone on vibrate only.

Rooftops are sometimes used as observation posts – this can be uncomfortable, depending on the weather and has the same lack of facilities as a stationary vehicle. If a rooftop is used, the watcher has to be careful not to take up a position that makes their silhouette visible against the sky. Walking around on a rooftop also risks having a witness call the police to report a potential 'jumper.' Another possibility is to watch from a public building such as a library – loitering isn't a problem there, we call it browsing – or from a coffee shop or restaurant.

Rural areas, especially open ones, have additional problems. Local people tend to know everyone else and will be immediately suspicious of a stranger. Open vistas also mean you can be seen approaching from miles away and it can be difficult to get into a hiding place – assuming there is one – without being observed. Whatever observation post a watcher chooses, they should also take some time to learn about the location beforehand. Knowing every building, street, and alley means that if their stationary surveillance suddenly becomes a moving one, they do not lose their target.

Other situations that make crop up while on surveillance include:

Dealing with the Neighbours. Steven Kerry Brown has a couple of suggestions for ways in which private investigators can deal with nosey neighbours. First, he says tell them you are a private detective and say that you aren't watching any of their neighbours, you are waiting for someone to drive past. Second, if the neighbour is female tell her you are working for a female client who thinks her husband is cheating on her, and if the neighbour is male tell him you're conducting surveillance on a cheating wife.

Dealing with the Police. Explain what you are doing and why – and hope the policeman is sympathetic to your cause. If he accuses you of loitering and tells you to move on, it is probably best to do as he says and avoid trouble. You could try and head off any problems by letting the local police station know about your planned surveillance beforehand, but that does draw attention to you and will probably result in them sending a police patrol to check you out. If you're questioned by the police, you do not have to reveal the name of your client or that of the person you are watching – and in some US states, it is against local laws to reveal anything about your case to anyone, including the police. In the UK you'll have to bluff and claim investigator-client privilege.

Confrontation by the Subject. In any form of surveillance, there is the risk of being 'made' by the person you are following and that they will confront you directly – and in all cases, the approach you take will be the same. First, deny that you're following them and do not tell them that you are a private investigator. Never reveal the name of your client – to do so might put them at risk. And give up on the surveillance for the day – once you've been made, there is no point trying to continue. You can start over on another day, but you will need to allow for the fact that the subject has seen you and possibly your vehicle, so you will need to make some changes.

Private investigators and police detectives conducting surveillance as part of a criminal case which may eventually go to court have to be careful not to make contact with the subject as it is unethical to question a suspect without allowing them to have their lawyer present. Even a casual exchange of words may be enough for evidence gathered from the surveillance to be ruled inadmissible.

Photographs & Video
With photographs or video recording, the aim is to be as far away from the subject as possible – to reduce the risk of being spotted – while still obtaining good quality images where the facial features of the subject are still clearly identifiable.

Surveillance photographs are often taken of people doing things, going to a specific place, or meeting with someone else – and these pictures are taken to provide evidence of something. But photographs can also be taken of locations or objects, either to provide a visual record of them or for comparison purposes – a recent photograph may be compared with one from an earlier date.

Photographic surveillance is portrayed in movies and on television as requiring a camera with a huge telephoto lens like the ones used by paparazzi being wielded by a man in a car or hidden in the bushes or up a tree. That may be suitable for some circumstances, but there are other options.

Photographs or video can be taken by cameras that are hidden beforehand and left unattended, and then tripped automatically by a sensor detecting movement or sound. This sort of camera is often used by wildlife filmmakers.

Sometimes the photographer has to do a 'drive-by shooting' – capturing images quickly as they pass and trying not to draw too much attention while doing it.

There is equipment available for taking photographs in dim light and even using infra-red or 'night vision' scopes. If you want to have your character use something like this, it is a good idea to research how they are used and what they are *realistically* capable of.

Legal Issues. It is normally legal to photograph someone who is in a public place or is clearly visible to a photographer who is in a public place. Photographing someone on private property without the property owner's permission isn't legal. Nor is pointing a camera through someone's window – especially if it is necessary to climb a wall or a tree or penetrate some sort of barrier to capture the shot.

Mobile Surveillance – Shadowing
Shadowing or tailing involves following a person, usually without them being aware of the fact. It is carried out to discover where the target goes, who they meet, and/or what activities they engage in. Mobile surveillance can be carried out on foot or using vehicles.

Surveillance on Foot

This is best done with two or three people, perhaps with one of them in a vehicle, as this allows the watchers to switch places to avoid the target becoming suspicious of a single person close behind them all the time. Having someone in a vehicle means the watchers are prepared to follow if the target gets into a vehicle.

Burt Rapp describes three different types of tail:

A *loose tail* is following the target at a distance with priority given to remaining unseen by the target. There is a greater risk of losing the subject, but less chance of the tail being 'made.'

A *close tail* increases the risk of being spotted but is used where the priority is to avoid losing the subject.

A *rough tail* is one where it doesn't matter if the tail is spotted and might be used where a detective is following his partner in order to provide back-up if necessary. In such cases, the target will co-operate with the tail.

A person who is shadowing a target should ideally be of ordinary appearance – there should be nothing about them in terms of physical build or clothing that makes them stand out or cause them to be memorable. During the shadowing, it is important that the tail avoids eye contact with the target – but he should not look away suddenly if the target turns, as this is likely to seem suspicious and draw attention. Following someone on the other side of the street may be one way of avoiding the risk of being 'made' in this way.

Burt Rudd highlights a number of situations which may occur during the course of a shadowing operation:

Public Transport – If the target boards a bus, streetcar, or train a lone tail risks being made if he boards after the subject – a pair of tails or a team have more options in this regard. If a target suspects he is being followed, he may board a train or bus to see if anyone follows and then jump off just as the vehicle moves away. It may be possible to follow a bus by hailing a taxi and with a train, it may be possible to board as part of a crowd or further down the platform, preferably behind the target, without being spotted.

Elevators pose a similar risk to public transport. To avoid getting into the same elevator car, racing up the stairs may be an option, though you have to check every floor to see when or if the target gets out, or if there is more than one elevator you can take another car up. This is one place where knowledge about the target may come in handy – if you are aware that he knows someone in the building, you can guess where he is going.

Multiple Exits – If the target enters a building with multiple ways out, and there is no way for you to observe all of the possible exits, you will probably have to follow them in. If the target has become suspicious and is checking to see if he is being followed, entering a building like this is one way of confirming his suspicions – he can be on the lookout for anyone who enters after him and who also leaves when he does. He may do this by entering through a door and then quickly turning around and exiting the same way – anyone who does the same thing will look suspicious.

Changing Pace – Slowing down and speeding up is one way that a suspicious target might use to check for a tail. Anyone who keeps pace with him becomes suspect. Sudden changes of direction can be used in the same way. The tail has got to try and keep the target within their sight without seeming to mirror their erratic movements.

Confrontation – Sometimes a target will turn and challenge a tail directly. All the tail can do then is play innocent and give up – there is little point continuing once you've been made.

Ambush – The target may turn a corner and stop and then ambush the tail or wait to see what the tail's reaction is on seeing him waiting there. As with a confrontation, the tail must play the innocent – showing no change in expression when he spots the target waiting and moving away as if nothing has occurred, or in the case of a physical ambush, deny everything and back away.

Target's Own Tail – Occasionally, a suspicious target will have one of his own people follow him to see if there is anyone shadowing him. This means that a tail must be on the lookout for anyone who is also following the target and/or also tailing him.

Litter Drop – A target may drop a piece of paper or some other small item to see if anyone following stops to pick it up. Unless it is something the tail *must* retrieve, it is better ignored. In a two-man team, the person furthest back can pick up the item when the target has moved out of range.

Empty Spaces – It is easy to disguise the fact that you are following someone in a crowded place but in an empty street or sparsely populated area there is a much greater risk of being made. In such spaces, the tail can drop further back as there is less danger of the target being lost in the crowd, and it may be possible to continue the tail by taking an indirect route around the perimeter of the space instead of crossing it directly as the target has done. With an empty street, you may have to take a parallel street and hope to pick up the subject at the next cross street. This is another situation where in-depth knowledge of an area can pay off.

Meet-Ups – If the target meets someone and interacts with them briefly, the tail has to decide whether to continue following the original target or to follow the other person instead. This can be a particular issue of the target is carrying something from a pick-up or a drop-off and it is the carrier that is to be tailed rather than the specific individual. What happens if you cannot tell if an exchange has taken place? This is a situation where having two or more people involved in a shadowing operation is an advantage.

If two people are tailing the target, the lead will stay relatively close to the target while the second person will follow some way behind the lead. Alternatively, they could follow the target from opposite sides of the street.

When tailing someone on foot, it can be helpful for the follower to be able to change his appearance to avoid being spotted – sunglasses, a hat, and a reversible jacket can be used to make subtle changes so that the target doesn't notice the same person behind them for an extended period. The tail doesn't need to be a master of disguise, because as Burt Rapp says, it is used "...for the purpose of 'breaking the profile' rather than radically changing appearance." And when tailing someone on foot it is a good idea to have cash in the form of small bills and coins, in case you have to follow the target onto public transport or into some location that charges for entry.

Surveillance Using Vehicles

There are different ways of tailing depending on how many cars are available to follow the target – the police will probably have at least two and possibly three vehicles available but a lone private detective may only have one. Following someone in a car is more difficult than following someone on foot if you are operating alone because the target can move more quickly and there is more opportunity for losing the target because of traffic restrictions and other road users. Again, this is an area where having a detailed knowledge of the area, including alternate routes, can be extremely useful.

With three cars, a typical set-up the lead car follows about 'a block' behind the subject – a block being the distance between two streets or avenues, or between 80 and 300 metres or so. The second car follows about a block behind the lead. And the third car follows parallel to the target on another street. This works for American cities that are laid out in blocks but not so well in UK cities.

Two cars can follow the target in the one block and two blocks behind positions as above, with the two cars swapping lead position occasionally so that the target doesn't become aware of the same car behind them for an extended period. Alternatively, one car may travel parallel to the target on the same or another street, or one car may follow the target the other may take up a position in front of it. A good time to change the lead car is when the target turns a corner – because he may be making the move to see if someone is following him.

A single car can really only follow a block behind and hope not to lose the target. In busy traffic, following a car of a common make and colour, it may be necessary to mark the target's car in some way to make it easier to spot.

The riskiest part of surveillance in an automobile is actually starting up. Pulling into traffic after the target can draw attention to you – especially if you do it like in the movies, tyres squealing as you pull a tight U-turn.

Situations that might be encountered when tailing someone in a vehicle include:

Running a Red Light – If the target crosses a junction just as the light turns red, what should you do? That may depend on circumstances, but generally speaking, you won't risk injury to yourself or others by ignoring a red light on a busy street. If you know the area, you will have an idea of how long you will have to remain stationary at the light. You will also know if light further along the road will stop the target, giving you an opportunity to catch up with him when the lights change.

Parking Lots and Garages – This is similar to the situation where a person on foot enters a building with multiple exits. Do you follow them in? If it's a small parking lot where you can see all of the exits from the street, you may not need to go in. Otherwise, you might enter the parking lot using a different entrance to the one used by the target. If it's a busy lot with lots of cars entering, you could enter through the same entrance behind a few other cars. With an underground or multi-storey parking garage, if you enter you risk being made, confronted, or finding yourself ambushed. But if the target is waiting for you, the chances are you've already been made and the game is up anyway.

Corners – If the target turns a corner and is temporarily out of view, you need to be prepared for the fact that he may have stopped just around the corner – in which case the best tactic is probably to pass him and find somewhere to stop further down the street or even carry on and turn at the next corner and then stop.

Alley – If the target turns into an alley or narrow road, following him into it is bound to attract his attention. You have the option of waiting to see if he comes back out the way he went in or of taking a parallel road in the hop of seeing him emerge at the other end. Stopping across the end of the alley will draw attention to you, especially if the alley is dark and the street where you are is brightly lit. With two or three cars you have more options. Even having a partner in a single car gives you the option of having him jump out and look down the alley to see what the target is up to.

U-Turns – If the target makes a U-turn, making the same move yourself will definitely draw the target's attention. The best you can hope to do in a single car is wait for the target to get out of sight before you turn and hope you catch up, or attempt a turn in a forecourt or side street that isn't as obvious as a U-turn. Again, having more than one car involved in the operation makes this easier to deal with.

Multiple Targets – If there are two or more targets in a car and one leaves the vehicle, do you follow the vehicle or the person? A single tail in a single car has to make this choice. If he's driving with a partner, the partner can leave the car and follow the pedestrian target. Multiple cars have more choices.

Tailing at Night

Driving after dark makes it harder for the target to see who is behind them, but car headlights are visible over long distances so they make it easy to spot that there is a car behind. Darkness also makes it more difficult to see who you are tailing. One suggestion I've seen is that you should mark the target car in some way – either by using a piece of reflective tape or a reflective sticker or by breaking or making a hole in a rear taillight.

Burt Rudd refers to 'blackout lights' that are shielded so that they cast light down onto the road but don't project a beam forward that can be seen by the car you are following. These are illegal for road use and don't work in smoke for fog, but you might find a use for them in a story. As far as I can tell, these are similar to the systems used in Britain during the Second World War – see www.aj-wilkinson.co.uk/blackout.html

GPS Tracking

GPS – global positioning system – uses satellites to pinpoint the position of a device anywhere on the planet, though its accuracy varies according to location and terrain. GPS or satellite navigation systems can be used by investigators in a number of ways. A simple example is to look at the last location programmed into the GPS in an individual's car – Does it reveal the location of the person they are having an affair with? More than one suspicious spouse has used this method.

You can also buy a device to attach to a target's vehicle that will either record or transmit the vehicle's location – for as long as the battery lasts or until it is discovered or damaged. Real-time transmission can use either code division multiple access (CDMA) wireless technology or the GSM (Global System for Mobile communications) network used by older (2G) cell phones. The devices are about the size of a pack of playing cards.

Another option a private detective might employ is to duct-tape a GPS-enabled phone to some part of a vehicle where it won't be discovered or damaged – inside a plastic bumper is ideal. If a location app is installed, the location of the device can then be tracked online – these apps are often sold so that parents can keep an eye on their children.

Tracking an individual by GPS without their consent is illegal in some states in the USA and in some other countries. In 2012, the U.S. Supreme Court ruled that law enforcement agencies needed a warrant to place a tracking device on a suspect's vehicle. This does not apply to private detectives.

Electronic Surveillance

There are three main areas to mention here – *tapping* telephones to listen to a conversation, *bugging* to obtain audio or video recordings, and *hacking* into someone's personal computer or other device. The portrayal of these three in television and film has tended to ignore what is possible in real-life in favour of what works for the story or what looks good on screen.

Technology in this area is changing all the time and I am not going to pretend that I understand any of it. I will mention a few things here, but if you want to use this sort of technology in a story, I recommend that you do your research – even if you're planning to make stuff up, you should be aware of how far you are going beyond the realms of the possible. There is a great deal of information available from both reputable sources and more 'underground' ones and the internet has made gaining access to interesting details much easier. You can also obtain all kinds of devices from retailers including Amazon and Radio Shack. Another source of gadgets is a store such as www.detective-store.com

Telephone Tapping

Telephone tapping or wiretapping is the monitoring of telephone conversations by a third party, usually by covert means. Originally tapping was conducted on physical telegraph wires to listen in on messages being sent, then it was applied to telephone conversations transmitted along the same copper wires, and it has now been extended to include cellular and internet-based calls. Approved wiretaps by official agencies are referred to as 'lawful interception' and in most countries has to be authorised by a court, with illegal wiretap evidence being inadmissible in court.

Official wiretaps on modern digital exchanges can be instigated remotely and it is virtually impossible to detect whether a line is tapped. Various technologies are available for unofficial wiretaps and most require physical access to the telephone or the line. Calls from cordless telephones can be picked up by some scanners. Where access to an individual's phone is possible, software can be installed that will allow their calls to be monitored – see www.retinax.com for example. Where access to a device isn't possible, cell phone calls can be monitored using a 'StingRay' device that tricks nearby cell phones into thinking it is a cell tower. It can also extract data from a phone. Cell phone manufacturers and software suppliers continue to develop ways to protect their users' calls and data. Criminals have increasingly used encrypted messaging services to avoid having their communications intercepted and to avoid leaving a 'trail' showing where they have made calls from and who they have contacted.

If you are thinking of using that old favourite the 'burner' cell phone in a story, it is worth looking online to see how 'untraceable' these really are.

Audio Surveillance by Remote Microphone

One device that you've probably seen in the movies or on television shows is the parabolic microphone, which uses a dish-like reflector to collect and focus sound waves and enable the user the pick up distant sounds. An example of this is the Bionic Ear and Booster Set which is on sale in a wide variety of places and can pick up sounds up to 300 feet away.

Another gadget that has been used in stories is the 'laser microphone' that shines a laser beam onto a distant object to detect sound vibrations via an interferometer. The beam is usually shone through a window onto an object such as a painting, detecting vibrations that are then converted back into an audio signal. Sometimes the beam is focussed on the window itself. One example is the Spectra Laser M see
http://lasermicrophone.com/spectra-laser-m/

There are many different microphones for recording sound under all kinds of different circumstances – including ones that can be fired from a sort of slingshot and stick to a distant wall or object and broadcast sound back to a receiver.

One of the main problems with bugging a subject's home or office is gaining access to it to plane the bug. TV shows make it look easy, but in real life we're talking about trespass or breaking and entering which may involve overcoming electronic alarm systems or sophisticated 'social engineering' to talk your way in. Either way, any evidence gathered using the bug would be inadmissible in court.

An interesting thriller that centres on audio surveillance is *The Conversation* (1974) starring Gene Hackman. The technology is outdated, but the action and the themes are still relevant.

Bugging

A 'bug' is typically a miniature radio transmitter with a microphone used for covert surveillance. Existing devices including cell phones, car tracking systems, and 'smart speakers' can also be used for bugging.

In placing a bug, it is important to keep it away from any sound sources that could impact the quality of sound being picked up and transmitted – avoid placing bugs near refrigerators and air conditioners. We've all seen television shows where people who suspect their homes have been bugged play loud music or stand by a running tap so that their voices will not be picked up clearly by the listening device.

Use of listening devices is governed by legislation which protects the privacy of individuals and also by laws designed to assist law enforcement and other agencies in preventing and investigating crime and terrorism.

A specific type of bug is a 'wire' that is hidden under a person's clothes to pick up the conversation the person has with a target individual. These devices are also referred to as body transmitters and you can find a number on sale online. Typically, in real life and in the movies, the transmissions from a wire are monitored by a back-up team at fairly close range so that they can react immediately to whatever they hear. The receiver is fairly compact, about the size of a briefcase and weighing only a few pounds.

Some people find wearing a wire uncomfortable because its discovery would put them at great risk. The associated anxiety makes it more difficult for them to convincingly carry out any interaction required with the subject of the surveillance operation. There are other devices that can be used to record or transmit conversations that do not have to be worn by an individual and they can be hidden in a briefcase, packet of cigarettes, baseball cap, a pair of glasses, or a cell phone.

In using wires or similar transmitters, it is usually the case that the recording of the conversation is only a back-up and serves as *part* of the evidence – the testimony of the person who was actually present and can provide context for the recording is the more important part.

Advances in technology and battery capacity mean that video recording and transmission can be used much more widely. Button-sized cameras can be hidden on clothing and in various other places to capture stills and moving images.

Computer Hacking

Official monitoring of internet usage by suspected criminals has been carried out since at least 1995. Illegal monitoring, now typically conducted via a Wi-Fi connection, has probably been going on for as long as individuals have had internet access. Techniques used to 'hack into' someone's computer – and methods used to protect computers from attack – are evolving all of the time and I am not going to attempt to cover them here as they will be out of date by the time you read this. Turning computer hacking into an original and dramatic sequence in a story is also quite tricky, which is the reason why movies about hacking have been relatively rare since the likes of *Sneakers* (1992) and *Hackers* (1995).

If your hero is going up against the computer system in a modern organisation, you're likely to have a lot of detailed research to do to create something plausible – especially if it involves an attack on national infrastructure systems. But if you just want your lone private detective to illegally obtain something from a person's private computer you can probably get away with having the owner of the target computer make one of the security errors that we all advised against making, such as using the same password or PIN for everything or using the default password that came with our modem.

If technology is not your thing, it can be much more fun to have your character engage in 'social engineering'. The weakest point in any computer system tends to be the people who use it and there are various ways 'social engineers' use to get people to give up things like passwords.

Counter-Surveillance

Counter-surveillance can be broken down into three broad types of countermeasure – electronic, software, and human. Electronic counter-surveillance involves activities such as 'sweeping' for bugs. Relatively low-cost devices can be bought online that pick up the radio transmissions given out by hidden transmitters, though these have limitations and do not detect all types of bugging device.

Software counter-surveillance includes programs that protect a computer from unauthorised external access and prevent data being altered by things like ransomware. Software can also encrypt stored data and anything that is transmitted from the computer. Use of software such as Tor can also protect an internet user's privacy.

Human counter-surveillance methods include the techniques that individuals use to lose someone who is shadowing them and physical methods of concealing one's identity.

Some private detective agencies specialise in counter-surveillance services, sometimes in combination with background checks or personal security (bodyguards) or cybersecurity. Search online for 'counter-surveillance services' to see what sort of things are offered by these agencies.

Physical searches for bugs are performed by people with knowledge of the best sorts of places to plant electronic listening devices. How well such devices are hidden depends on the length of time the person planting them had in the location. If he was able to dismantle internal features of a room or pieces of furniture, the bug might be almost impossible to spot.

Telephone taps can also be located by people who know how to tap a phone – they will examine the telephones and all internal sockets and wiring, and then continue outside the premises, going as far as a pole and a junction box. Wiretaps by official agencies are more likely to be made in the telephone exchange and so there will be no physical evidence of tapping.

If one bug is located, or several, it is safest to assume that others may still be present and that others may be planted in future.

18 | Missing Person Investigation

There are a number of different categories of missing persons. *Recently* missing people include runaways, child abductions, and kidnappings. *Long-term* missing persons include lost relatives and heirs, adult runaways, and people who have deliberately changed their identity. Another category is the person who was scheduled to attend court – who has often been released on bail – and failed to appear. Some people are 'misplaced' rather than missing – they are not deliberately hiding and may not know that anyone is looking for them. Old friends, school or college classmates, or estranged family members may even *want* to be found.

Adopted children may seek their birth parents or a person who gave up a child for adoption may seek the child. Sometimes such searches are initiated because a parent may wish to inform their biological child of the risk of an inherited medical condition or because parent or child may be seeking a matching organ or bone marrow donor. Other persons being sought might include siblings, heirs, witnesses, victims, stockholders, debtors, con men, and people who have 'skipped' in order to avoid financial or other obligations.

It should also be remembered that the person who initiates a search may actually be the villain – a stalker or jealous ex-lover, for example.

False Reports
Sometimes an individual will report a relative, friend, or acquaintance as being missing or abducted in order to cover up the fact that they have murdered this person. Investigators must bear this in mind and look out for any signs that the individual may be lying about what happened.

Long-Term Missing
Locating an adult who has been missing for a considerable length of time – say six months or more – requires a different approach to someone who has just gone missing. The long-term missing are more likely to have been listed in various forms of public and private records which can be searched. Documentary investigation will often be the first stage in the search because there are various databases that can be searched by computer. Some of these sources are freely accessible, some – such as those used by private investigators – require a subscription to be paid and may only be available to licensed investigators, and some are available only to official law enforcement agencies. If you have ever used an online genealogical resource such as Ancestry.com, you'll have some idea of how this kind of search can be conducted.

This kind of documentary investigation isn't particularly dramatic when presented in a story or film – despite the fact that in real-life finding a lost relative can be quite exciting. I'm not going to cover this here but there are several useful guides that list all manner of resources that can be used in searches, including *Missing Persons* by Fay Faron; Steven Kerry Brown's *The Complete Idiot's Guide to Private Investigating*; *Practical Handbook for Professional Investigators* by Rory J. McMahon, and Michael Bazzell's *Open Source Intelligence Techniques: Resources for Searching and Analyzing Online Information*.

It is worth noting that if an investigator finds *no* records on a subject, this may in itself be significant as it suggests that the individual either lied about who they are or are deliberately hiding.

Another form on long-term missing person investigation is the *cold case* which may involve a runaway or abductee who disappeared some time ago and whose case is not being actively pursued by the police. Private investigators may be asked to look into such cases and will have to examine what work was carried out by the police during their active investigation phase as well as conduct new inquiries of his own.

Recently Missing

People who have recently gone missing fall into three broad categories – *benign and involuntary*, *runaways*, and *abducted*. I will explore each of these in a little more detail below – the information presented here refers primarily to missing children as procedures for dealing with missing children are better developed and more likely to be implemented than those for adults – and also the time factor for locating a missing child is much more significant.

Benign Voluntary & Involuntary Missing Person Incidents

In some cases, the missing person has not been abducted or run away and the reason for their absence is not related to any form of crime. People who become lost or stranded and are unable to find their way home or to contact anyone for help fall into this category, as do those who are injured and unable to each help – including those taken to hospital for treatment who are not carrying any form of identification.

Where children are concerned, the causes may include missing a ride or travelling in a vehicle that has a flat tyre or some other mechanical failure; losing track of time; misunderstanding or disagreement over the time a child is meant to return or where they are allowed to go; flat cell phone battery; being talked into doing something by a friend; attending a party, or deliberately hiding in order to 'teach a lesson' to their parents or to avoid having to carry out some activity or chore.

With these types of incident, there is no probable or reasonable cause to suspect that the missing child has been abducted or run away.

Runaways

Runaway children tend to fall into the 11 to 17-year-old age range and they leave home for a reason which seems valid to them. There may be domestic violence or the child may have suffered neglect or physical, emotional, and/or sexual abuse. It is important that the home situation is assessed by experts – it may not be in the child's interest to locate them and return them to the family home. Statistics in the USA suggest that less than 25% of runaways are the victims of physical or sexual assault at home. Some parents who report that their child is a runaway have actually thrown their child out of the family home and then suffered remorse or guilt or some other feeling that has caused them to report their child missing.

Although we are treating runaways and abducted children separately here, a child who runs away from home becomes vulnerable and may then be abducted.

Sprague describes a five-phase cycle in the life of a runaway or teenager who is thrown out of the family home:

Phase 1 – Stress Building. There may be emotional, physical or sexual abuse; neglect; domestic violence; alcohol or substance abuse in the home; problems with school attendance, grades, or peer pressure.

Phase 2 – Runaway or Thrown Out. The child decides that they have had enough and runs away or a domestic argument results in them being thrown out of the house or barred from re-entry.

Phase 3 – Survival. The child relies on other relatives or friends to survive. May enter an unhealthy relationship in order to have needs met. Or may engage in crime or prostitution in order to have the money to live.

Phase 4 – Crisis. The child is located and returned home but there is no assessment of the family circumstances or risks posed to the child.

Phase 5 – Honeymoon. Parents nurture the child who is led to believe that all will be well. But after a short or long period of calm, the stress begins again returning the child to Phase 1.

Investigating a Runaway

Runaway teenagers are not seen as high-risk victims in the same way that abducted children are. Police tend not to treat such cases with the same degree of urgency. If it is the first time that a child has gone missing, the police will treat the incident with more resources than they will if it is the third or fourth time the child has run away.

When a child has run away on multiple occasions, parents may feel uncomfortable about 'bothering' the police again – or they may have other reasons for not drawing attention to themselves – and may approach a private investigator instead.

A private investigator has no legal right to pick up a runaway child and return them against their will to the family home. An investigator who acts in this way risks being accused of abduction or having the child make a false claim of physical or sexual abuse against them. There is also a possibility that the child will be staying with people who will attack the investigator in order to 'protect' the child.

In his book, Steven Kerry Brown advises private investigators that a missing child should always be reported to the police, even if the disappearance will not be investigated by police officers. If a child is registered as missing, their name will be flagged if they are picked up by the police for any reason. Reporting the incident also serves to show that the parents are concerned about it – questions might be asked later if they didn't report it and something serious happens to the child. When the child is located, the police can handle the pickup and return to the family home, avoiding the risk of complaints about abduction or inappropriate touching. The child will also, hopefully, be interviewed before being returned home to make sure that their home life is safe.

A private investigator may need to make a judgment call if it is suspected that the child may be involved in illegal activity – in such circumstances, involving the police may not be in the best interests of the child or the family. Eleven to seventeen-year-olds may be involved in drugs, alcohol, prostitution, or gang-related activity and involving the police may result in them gaining a criminal record that could blight the rest of their lives. The child might also end up in juvenile detention which can result in other life-changing encounters.

An investigator may need to warn the parents that the child may make false accusations of abuse by the parents.

As far as the investigation itself goes, the detective will need to interview the parents to try and understand why the child has run away. And he will have to convince them to trust him and tell the whole truth – especially if there has been conflict within the family. During this interview, the investigator will also have to assess the family situation and gauge whether it is safe to return the child to it – the parents may be his clients, but he also has a duty of care when it comes to the child. Part of the case may involve investigating the parents as well as trying to locate the runaway.

The detective will need to ask the parents if the child has ever run away before. If so, where did they go? Did they hide out at a friend's house or with a boyfriend/girlfriend? Are they still seeing that person? The parents may already have checked with friends and exes, but that doesn't mean that they discovered all that there was to know – the detective will need to speak to these people himself. He will need as complete a list of the runaways friends and school/college acquaintances as possible. It may also be worth checking whether the teenager had a crush on any of their teachers or if there was a particular teacher the child felt able to confide in. Social media contacts – both locally-based ones and friends in other parts of the country – should also be tracked down if possible. The investigator should also ask the parents for a recent photograph of the runaway; a description of the clothes they were wearing and of any that they have taken with them; any identifying marks such as scars or tattoos, and whether the child has a cell phone or bank card. He should also ask about any bicycle, motorcycle, or car that the runaway may have access to. If the bank card or cell phone subscription is in a parents' name, they may be able to gain access to the transactions online and these may give clues about the location it has been used or the people who have been called. If the parents do not have caller ID on their home landline, it is a good idea to get it activated in case the child decides to call home from a public telephone or 'burner' cell phone. Parents may feel tempted to cancel a child's bank card to 'teach them a lesson' or try to force them to return home, but this risks forcing them into criminal activity to obtain food or money.

In the case of a runaway, the investigation will almost certainly rely on interviewing people connected to the child. As well as close friends and school acquaintances, the detective should speak to the parents of these children – they may have overheard something or made some observations about the runaway and who they had been associating with. Another source is the runaway's siblings – especially if these are older and have moved away from home – they may offer insight into the family situation and the runaway's state of mind.

Grandparents are another source of information and provide another place where a runaway may go to hide.

In a relatively close-knit community, talking to neighbours can result in the sharing of gossip about the family of the runaway or details of any recent movements around the house. If the runaway got a ride from someone when they left, a neighbour may have seen this. Bear in mind that the car would probably have stopped some distance from the house and waited for the runaway. In the section on abductions below, I have included other questions that an investigator can ask neighbours.

If the family has relocated in the recent past, speaking to former neighbours and friends in that neighbourhood may yield results. The runaway may have been unhappy about the move and decided to return to the old location.

And if the child's parents are separated, the ex-spouse is an obvious person to speak to. The child may have contacted them or even gone to stay with them. The ex-spouse will be suspicious of anyone asking questions – especially if the child has made allegations (perhaps false) about what has been happening in the family home and they may lie to protect their child.

Child Abductions
Children may be abducted by family members, by individuals known to the family, or by complete strangers.

Family Abductions
Family child abduction includes taking or keeping a child in violation of a custody order usually involving some form of *concealment* – hiding the child in order to prevent return to, contact with, or visitation from the legitimate custodian; *flight* – transporting or intending to transport the child to prevent their recovery, perhaps even taking them to another country; and *intent to deprive indefinitely* – i.e. preventing the legitimate custodian of the child having contact with the child for an indefinite period. Children under the aged eleven and under are more likely to be abducted than children aged twelve to seventeen. The abductor will usually act alone. It is rare for the child to be physically harmed and the abductee is typically found and returned to their rightful guardian.

Motivations for Family Abduction
The reasons behind the abduction of a child by a parent or other relative can be complex and involve a high level of emotion. Typical motives include:

Revenge – the abductor wishes to 'punish' the legitimate guardian by taking away something that is important to them.

Reconciliation – the abductor seeks to force a reconciliation with their ex-partner.

Protecting the Child – from actual or perceived physical, sexual or emotional harm by the legitimate guardian or their new partner.

Fear of Losing Visitation Rights – the abductee may fear being prevented from seeing their child, perhaps due to a change of location or marriage of the legitimate guardian. Or they may suspect that the legitimate guardian is trying to 'turn the child against me.'

Religious or Other Beliefs – the abductor fears that the child will be raised according to beliefs that he or she finds unacceptable. They may want to have greater control over how the child is raised.

Fear of Being Forgotten or Replaced – the abductor may be concerned that the child will regard them as unimportant or unnecessary, especially if the legitimate guardian has a partner who can fulfil the role of the missing parent.

Projection – the abductee may confuse their own frustration and unhappiness toward the legitimate guardian with the feelings of the child and assume that the child would be better off with them.

Before a parent or other family member decides to abduct a child, there will usually be some event that triggers the decision. Stresses may build within the family situation to the point where definite action is seen as necessary.

During the abduction, the child often has to assume adult responsibilities and may have to provide emotional support to the parent-abductor. Parent and child go into hiding and contact with the outside world may be forbidden. Where contact with others cannot be avoided, the child may be forced to lie and will often have to use a new name. They may be home-schooled or receive no education. They will have no contact with children their own age. The child may be the victim of unintentional emotional or psychological abuse – but has been convinced that there is no one else they can turn to other than the parent-abductor. Physical or sexual abuse by the abductor-parent is rare.

Even where overt abuse does not occur, the child may suffer a traumatic experience as the abductor-parent typically lies about his or her reasons for taking the child away from their other parent. The child may be told that the other parent is dead – that they died in a car accident or committed suicide. Or the story may be that the other parent is dangerous or mentally unstable that they were plotting to hurt the child or wanted to keep the child from seeing the abductor-parent and that the legitimate guardian was abusive, a drug addict or a drunk, a prostitute, or some kind of criminal. Or the child may be told that the other parent never loved or wanted them and walked out, gave them away, or sold the child to the abductor-parent. Sometimes the other parent is simply never mentioned and there is a pretence that they do not exist.

Locating the abductor and the child is carried out in a similar way to the investigation into a runaway. The abductor will probably avoid locations that an investigator may immediately link to him, but in going into hiding the abductor is likely to choose a place where he feels safe – and that is likely to be a location with which he is familiar.

In family abduction situations, there is a high risk of violence – towards the legitimate guardian and their new partner, towards an investigator, and towards the child. The parent-abductor may be convinced that they are doing the right thing and 'protecting' their child. Or they may reach a point where killing the child seems the only option – either to protect the child from harm or because the abductor decides that 'if I can't have them no one can.'

After an abduction of this kind, things don't simply return to normal after the child is returned to their legitimate guardian – especially if they have been separated for a considerable period of time. Even assuming the family home is a safe place for the child, the trauma of the abduction may cause them long-term or short-term emotional and psychological issues which may require professional help. Where the abduction involved any form of abuse, the situation will be even more acute.

Non-Family Abductions

A non-family abductor *takes* a child by physical force or threat of physical harm or *detains* a child in isolation without lawful authority or parental consent. Also included are situations where a child under fifteen or who is mentally incompetent voluntarily accompanies a non-family perpetrator who conceals the child's whereabouts, demands a ransom, or intends to keep the child permanently.

Where the abductor is a family *acquaintance* or friend of the victim, the abductee is typically female and aged twelve to fifteen years. The motive for the abduction is usually sexual and the victim is usually released alive. The abductor is typically male, aged between thirteen and thirty, and is usually a friend, long-term acquaintance, or perhaps a boyfriend or ex-boyfriend. The abductor does not have an accomplice. The victim is taken from a street, park or wooded area, their home, or a vehicle to the abductor's vehicle or home. Abduction takes place between noon and midnight. The victim will be held and sexually assaulted for a period of between three and twenty-four hours. The police are often but not always contacted when the subject goes missing – sometimes the victim seeks to protect their abductor. The abductor may have carried out the assault in revenge for being spurned by the victim, to try and force a reconciliation, or because the victim's parents had tried to break up the relationship.

Where the abductor is a *stranger*, the abductee is likely to be female and aged between six and fifteen years old. The motive is sexual and/or murder and there is a high probability that the victim will be killed. In such cases, the police are almost always contacted, usually within two to four hours. Abductors are often white, male and aged between twenty and forty. They typically have no accomplice, completing the abduction alone. A typical suspect lives alone or with parents and has a previous history of sexual assault, attempted rape, or rape and may have committed other crimes against children. Many have had previous contact with the police, perhaps in the weeks before the attack. The abduction is opportunistic and is a sudden attack and subdue, usually completed without use of a weapon. The abduction occurs between noon and midnight and usually takes place on a street, in a park, or some other public area. Bindings are often used, possibly in a fetishistic manner. The body is then concealed – usually disposed of within 24 hours, and it is usually discovered by a passer-by. Perpetrators sometimes return to the disposal site or they may leave town.

In both cases, the victim is held for no more than three hours and they are transported less than fifty miles from the point of abduction.

Motivations for Abduction
Although sexual assault and/or murder are common motivations for abducting children, there are a number of reasons for them being taken:

- *Ransom* – to obtain money from the parents or authorities.
- *Profit* – to obtain money by selling the child to a third party.
- *Maternal* – infants are often abducted by women who want to raise the child as their own.
- *Sex Trafficking* – the child is to be used for prostitution.
- *Revenge* – where a parent is involved in gang-related or other criminal activity, for example, the child may be taken to 'punish' the parent.
- *Hostage* – to facilitate a criminal's escape.
- *Accidental* – if a car is stolen and the thief is unaware that a child is inside, for example.

Included in this category of abduction are paedophiles and sex traffickers who begin relationships with children online, usually posing as someone close to the child's age, and 'grooming' them, perhaps encouraging them to post explicit photographs of themselves online and then using blackmail to manipulate them. Children may be encouraged into meeting a stranger because they believe they are in a romantic relationship or that they can 'buy back' the 'incriminating' images.

While many abductions involve a surprise 'attack and subdue' approach, some abductors seek to lure their victims away with them. Methods used include seeking a child's assistance by asking for help finding a lost pet or for directions; telling the child that their parents sent the abductor to collect them – often backed up by them knowing the child's name; telling the child that their parent has been in an accident and they want the child to go to the hospital to see them; bribery with chocolate, ice cream, or money;

offering an opportunity to play video games; pretending to be a police officer or security guard, or flattering the child by praising their sports abilities or physical beauty. The type of approach attempted will vary according to the age of the child.

The Time Factor
Statistics in the USA suggest that 74% of children who are abducted by strangers are abused and/or murdered within three hours of being taken – and those taken by an acquaintance are sexually assaulted within a similar timeframe. If parents and neighbours conduct their own search for the missing child, it may be two hours before the abduction is reported to police. Each passing minute means that the child may be moved further from home and the risk of being victimised increases. The passage of time also increases the possibility that important clues may be lost.

Investigating a Non-Family Child Abduction
Bearing in mind the short time-frame, investigators responding to a report of an abduction have to achieve a great deal in a very brief period, including:

– interview the child's parents – including establishing if the child has any health issues such as diabetes or asthma which might put them in increased danger, or any mental health issues such as depression, self-harm, or suicidal thoughts. Issues such as drug or alcohol use or gang-related activity must also be explored, along with the possibility of them being the victim of an online sexual predator
– obtain a recent photograph and physical description of the child including the clothes they were wearing
– interview any witnesses
– classify the missing child as a runaway, family abduction, or stranger abduction
– alert other law enforcement officers – in the USA this means activating an AMBER (American Missing Broadcast Emergency Response) alert
– locate the child's last-known location
– determine the abduction location, which must then be treated as a crime scene

The reaction of the parents to a child abduction may be classed as *introverted* in that they feel helpless and depend on law enforcement officers to take control of the situation, or *extroverted* where the parents want to try and do something or perhaps grow angry and seek to blame others for their child's abduction. The police will usually assign a family liaison officer to support the family.

The investigation will include searching the neighbourhood, including vacant buildings, abandoned vehicles, sewers, ponds, rivers, and lakes. A request for civilian volunteer searchers may be sent out and these people will then need to be properly briefed and organised. An incident command centre will be set up close by, but avoiding any location that might be related to the abduction so as to avoid contaminating or destroying evidence. It will also be necessary to manage communications with the media and the public.

Interviewing Neighbours
The sorts of questions to ask neighbours – including any children in the neighbourhood – include:

- Did you see anything? Hear anything?
- Did you see anyone or any vehicles near the abductee's home or the abduction site?
- What sort of activities are usually going on at that time of day?
- Have you seen anything unusual or suspicious recently?
- Have there been any delivery trucks in the area today?
- What vehicles do you normally see around here?
- What people do you usually see? Have you seen anyone strangers around recently?
- Who is normally arriving or leaving the location at this time of day?
- Has anyone said anything about unusual activities – perhaps neighbours or local children have mentioned something?
- Can they suggest anyone the investigator should talk to?
- Have they any other information or thoughts about the incident?
- Are there any abandoned buildings or vehicles locally? Are there any other hiding places that children might use?

Investigators should also request to search the residence, grounds, garage, or shed.

Much of the information in this chapter was taken from Donald F. Sprague's book *Investigating Missing Children Cases: A Guide for First Responders and Investigators*. Additional information can be found on the website of the National Centre for Missing and Exploited Children (www.ncmec.org) in the USA or the National Crime Agency (www.nationalcrimeagency.gov.uk) in the UK.

19 | Murder Investigation

In this chapter I'm going to try and outline the stages of a generic homicide investigation. It is based on US and UK procedures, but hopefully the sequence will give you an idea of the kind of things that are likely to occur in most jurisdictions. This refers primarily to official law enforcement investigations – because they deal with virtually all real-life homicide cases – but I have included some references to where private investigators might be involved.

A homicide investigation begins with a murder – or at least a strong suspicion that a murder has occurred – though it may be that investigators are not able to locate the body.

The Murder Scene

When a body is discovered, 'ownership' of the scene is divided between two agencies – the crime scene 'belongs' to law enforcement investigators and the body 'belongs' to the coroner or medical examiner's office. There is the potential for some conflict with this arrangement – law enforcers will be concerned about the coroner's staff destroying or contaminating physical evidence at the scene and the coroner's staff will be concerned that the police will move or contaminate evidence on the body.

Until the coroner's/medical examiner's staff arrive on the scene, no one is permitted to touch, move, or remove the body or any items on the body. Photographs will be taken by the ME's staff and the police of the scene before anyone touches anything. The temperature of the body and the temperature of the location will also be recorded.

It may be determined that the body was not actually killed in the place where it was discovered – this means that law enforcement officers must seek another location where the incident actually occurred and this will be a separate crime scene.

The coroner/medical examiner has responsibility for determining the cause and manner of the victim's death. The detective investigating the case will liaise with the coroner's office and share any information which may help determine the cause and manner of death.

Not that not all death scenes are necessarily *crime* scenes – some, such as the location of an accident, are just *incident* scenes.

Death in the Emergency Room

In traditional whodunits, the dead body is little more than a prop that provides a puzzle for the detective to investigate. Real-life victims don't tend to die in such neat circumstances and you may want to reflect this in your story.

In some cases, the victim will be mortally wounded but still alive. Paramedics will be called and they will perform the usual checks of airway, breathing, and circulation and deal with any wounds. The victim will then be taken by ambulance to the Emergency Room. On route or in the ER, the victim may go into cardiac arrest and attempts will be made to resuscitate the patient. These may begin in the ambulance and continue in the ER and may continue for 20 to 40 minutes or in some cases longer. If this proves unsuccessful, the attending physician will pronounce the victim dead and announce the time of death that is to be recorded.

If a victim's clothes are removed while they are in hospital, these should be treated as evidence and handled accordingly.

There are certain types of case which ER staff *must* report to the authorities – these may vary according to jurisdiction but will typically include assault, child abuse, serious burn injuries, rape (the ER will use a standard 'rape kit' to collect evidence), shootings and stabbings including those reported as 'accidental', and any case where a person is dead on arrival. See also *Coroners & Medical Examiners* below.

Pronouncing a Death & Death Certification

Who can pronounce a person dead? This depends on the circumstances in which the death occurs or the place in which the body is found – and there are some variations according to jurisdiction. If death occurs in a hospice or at home, death may be pronounced by a family physician, registered nurse, or paramedic. The body will normally go directly to a funeral home with no need for further medical or legal intervention. In a nursing home death may be pronounced by a physician or registered nurse and the coroner may be asked to rule on the cause of death which may or may not require an autopsy – often the cause and manner of death can be presumed from the circumstances and a death certificate issued, allowing the body to be taken to a funeral home without further intervention. In a hospital, the physician will pronounce the death and the cause of death with be determined by a coroner. If a death occurs in an ambulance, treatment will usually continue until the vehicle reaches a hospital where medical staff will take over and pronounce the death.

Where a body is discovered or the death was unattended, death will be pronounced by a 'professional person' attending the scene – a police officer, paramedic, nurse, or physician. A coroner will determine the cause of death. A death certificate must be filed before a body can be released for a funeral. If a coroner's inquiry is necessary (see below) the death certificate may be withheld or the cause of death and/or manner of death may be entered on the certificate as 'pending' and be updated later.

Coroners & Medical Examiners

In the United Kingdom (excluding Scotland, which operates a different system) a *coroner* must hold a legal qualification (a solicitor or barrister) and is an independent judicial office holder. They are appointed and paid by the local authority whose area they serve and the laws and policies relating to their work are laid down by the Ministry of Justice.

Most deaths are not investigated by a coroner – if the deceased was under medical care or had seen a doctor in the two weeks preceding their death, a doctor can issue a death certificate. The coroner will conduct an *inquiry* if the deceased had not been under medical supervision or seen a doctor; if the cause of death cannot be established; where death seems to be the result of industrial disease or poisoning; where the cause appears unnatural or the result of violence, neglect, abortion, or other suspicious circumstances; when the death occurs during surgery or while under anaesthetic, or if death occurs while a person was in lawful custody.

An *inquiry* will be made by an officer appointed by the coroner – a deputy or assistant coroner or a police officer. The coroner may also request that an autopsy be performed. In many cases, a death certificate will be issued following the conclusion of the inquiry, but an *inquest* must be held if the death is violent or unnatural, if the cause of death cannot be established, or death occurred while the person was in lawful custody.

An *inquest* is a court of law and, depending on the type of death, may be conducted with or without a jury of between seven and eleven people. Witnesses can be summoned and questioned under oath and the normal rules of evidence are followed, but they are less stringent in terms of admitting hearsay.

It is the role of the coroner and/or the coroner's court to confirm the identity of the deceased and establish the cause and manner of their death. It is not within the jurisdiction of the coroner to seek or determine who was responsible for the death – that would be a matter for a criminal court to decide. The main verdicts available to a coroner are:

- Death by natural causes
- Death by misadventure
- Accidental death
- Lawful killing
- Suicide
- Unlawful killing
- Occupational disease
- Drug dependence
- 'Open' verdict – where it is believed that the circumstances of the death are suspicious but where none of the above verdicts can be reached based on the information available

Since 2004, the coroner may also make a 'narrative verdict' instead of one of the above. In all cases, the verdict is based on the 'balance of probabilities.'

In cases of homicide and some suicides, the coroner's inquest is opened and adjourned until criminal investigations and court proceedings are completed.

The system in the United States is similar to that of the UK, but there are variations across the different states or counties. Some jurisdictions have a *coroner,* some have a *medical examiner,* and some have both. In some areas, the coroner is an elected public official who may have no medical or legal training. He may appoint a deputy and/or a forensic pathologist to investigate deaths. In some jurisdictions, a medical examiner must be a forensic pathologist but in others, they may be a physician but not a pathologist. And in some places, the medical examiner needs no formal qualifications.

Local laws determine which deaths a coroner must investigate, but the categories are usually broadly similar to those in the British system above.

What Happens to the Body?

The sequence of events for an unexpected death following trauma and for an unattended unexpected death without trauma (e.g. a heart attack, suicide, or drowning) are very similar.

- The body is discovered.
- Death is pronounced.
- The coroner's office is notified and an investigator is sent to the scene.
- The body is taken to a morgue or funeral home.

- Where possible, the body is formally identified by a family member or close friend.
- Blood may be taken from the body to test for the presence of alcohol or drugs.
- An autopsy is performed if required. If not, cause and manner of death may be determined by the coroner or physician.
- The death certificate is complete, stating the cause and manner of death.
- All information obtained – autopsy report, photographs, toxicology test results, and the pathologist and/or coroner's opinion are turned over to the authorities to become part of the *corpus delicti* ('body of evidence') – the police investigator's report will also be added to this as appropriate.
- The body is turned over to the family and becomes their 'property' and the responsibility of the next of kin. In criminal cases, the body may not be released as the defence counsel may wish to have the body re-examined.

With suspected homicides, the hands of the deceased may be encased in special bags to preserve any evidence on the skin or under the fingernails. The whole body is then placed in a body bag – with anything that collects in the body bag also being retained as potential evidence after the body is taken from the bag at the morgue.

The Homicide Investigation

The *first officer(s) on the scene* must determine whether the victim is alive or dead and take appropriate action - e.g. calling for an ambulance. If paramedics are already on the scene, the officer should record any changes they have made to the scene such as moving the victim. If the victim appears to be near death, an attempt should be made to obtain a dying declaration. If a victim is taken away in an ambulance, an officer should ride with them in case it becomes necessary to take a dying declaration. A dying declaration or a statement from an injured victim can be obtained as long as it does not interfere with lifesaving measures by medical personnel. A dying declaration is legally admissible if the victim believes that they are going to die and they have no hope of recovery and can be used if they do die. The victim giving the statement must be deemed competent and rational. The declaration must refer to the manner and circumstances in which their life-threatening condition was caused and the identity of the person responsible. Ideally, the statement should be recorded or written down and then signed by the victim.

If the attacker is still present at the scene, they should be detained; if they are escaping or have escaped, an alert must be communicated so that they can be sought by other patrols. If a suspect is detained at or near the scene, they must be kept away from the scene so that they cannot contaminate or destroy evidence. Care has to be taken to ensure that the suspect has been made aware of his or her Miranda rights – investigators should never *assume* that uniformed officers at the scene have already done this.

Investigators or the homicide division such be notified of the incident.

Safeguarding the crime scene then becomes a priority - the officer must try and determine the full extent of the crime scene, all entrances and exits, and create a barrier to entry using police tape or some other means. An officer must remain at the scene until investigators arrive. Anyone who enters the scene, including paramedics or a priest, should do so via a single entry point and along a single narrow path that avoids disturbing evidence.

Any witnesses or suspects should be detained and their names and contact details recorded. Persons should be removed from the crime scene to avoid destruction or contamination of evidence. Witnesses should be kept separate from each other as far as possible to avoid them comparing stories and influencing each other. The person who first reported the crime or discovery of the body may need to be eliminated as a suspect or treated as a suspect, so recording their exact words is vitally important.

Once investigators arrive and take charge of the scene, the first officer(s) should stand by and assist them as required.

In the UK, the investigation is led by a Senior Investigating Officer (SIO) who works with a deputy and an incident room manager who co-ordinates all information and communications relating to the investigation. In the past, homicides were investigated by the Metropolitan Police, but in modern times each force now has its own homicide detectives who use procedures based on those devised by 'the Met.' The work of the SIO is supported by the HOLMES 2 (Home Office Large Major Enquiry System version 2) information technology system which co-ordinates data and allows it to be shared with all UK police forces.

Crime Scene Photographs

The scene of the crime will be examined by specially trained crime scene investigators, made famous in several *CSI* television series – the British equivalent is a scenes of crime officer (SOCO), forensic scene investigator (FSI), or crime scene examiner (CSE), though this person may be a specially trained and experienced civilian employee rather than a police officer and the role differs somewhat to that of the American CSI. The first stage will normally be to take photographs of the scene exactly as it was when it was discovered. Photographs will also be taken that indicate what lighting was available at the scene and what the weather was at the time. All photographs are taken at the highest possible resolution. Images are never deleted from the camera or memory card, even if blurred, as they received sequential numbering and time-stamps. Missing images are a red flag for defense attorneys who may suspect that evidence has been destroyed or lost. Details of the photographic equipment used, lenses etc. are recorded for inclusion with the images as part of the evidence package.

The first images taken are taken from a distance to establish the layout of the whole scene. These are taken from all four compass points. Images will also be taken of all routes in and out of the scene and any pathways through it. Then more detailed close-up photographs are taken and then similar photographs in the same sequence are taken with evidence markers, flags, rulers or other identifiers in place. In a building, the walls, floor and ceiling will also be photographed.

If a photographer returns to a scene at a later date, pictures of the seals or tape securing doorways will be taken to show their condition before the photographer enters.

The victim will be photographed as part of the crime scene photographs and then subjected to a separate detailed photographic record. Ideally, a clear facial image should be taken so that the individual can be identified, but this may not be possible until the body is turned over by medical examiners later. Photographs of any injuries and of the victim's eyes are also taken if possible. When the body is removed, the area under it will also be photographed. Video footage is now also taken of crime scenes – usually with the audio turned off so as not to include any off-guard comments by investigators which might be seized on by attorneys later. Crime scene sketches may also be used.

Photographs of the body will also be taken after the body has been taken to the pathology lab for autopsy. The body will also be photographed in detail after it has been undressed.

Search of the Crime Scene
A record will be made of the temperature and weather conditions at the scene as these may affect physical evidence or the condition of the body. Detailed investigation of the scene doesn't normally begin until photographs have been taken and the body has been removed by the coroner/medical examiner's staff. The search aims to find anything that will help identify the murderer. People examining the scene will wear sterile suits – sometimes called 'bunny suits' – and overshoes to ensure that they do not contaminate the scene with new fibres or other deposits.

If the crime scene is outside in the open, paths may be taped off and new routes marked out for police use so that evidence on the original path is not obliterated. Vegetation may be stripped down to ground level, bagged and taken away for closer examination. Fingertip searches of the ground, paths, and roads are conducted by teams of police officers.

The sorts of evidence investigators will attempt to locate include:

- Fingerprints, footprints, tyre tracks, and any other physical marks left by a person, weapon or tool
- Trace evidence (hairs, fibres, ashes, gunshot residue)
- DNA (from blood, semen, saliva or skin fragments)
- Other fluids or substances including chemicals, vomit, faeces, and sweat
- Objects such as drugs and paraphernalia, inhalants, or alcohol
- Blood spatter

Investigation into the life and background of the victim was covered in the 'Victimology' section of the chapter on serial killers.

Questions to Ask of the Scene
Things that the investigator needs to consider include:
- Are the scene, witness statements, and physical evidence consistent with a homicide?
- Was evidence normally expected at such a scene missing?
- By what means was the death caused?
- Was a weapon used? If so, is it present at the scene? Are the wounds consistent with this weapon? Are there any spent casings or bullet holes in or around the scene?
- Was the victim also armed?
- Based on the appearance of the scene, does it appear that any attempt has been made to mislead the police?
- Are witness statements consistent with what the physical evidence seems to show?
- Is the timing of the incident as suggested by witnesses confirmed by physical evidence such as the wetness of bloodstains or the condition of the body in terms of rigor mortis and lividity?
- Was the victim killed where the body was found or was it transported to that location? How might it have been moved?

- Are there other possible explanations for the crime scene evidence beyond the 'obvious' one?

Reconstructing the Crime

The senior investigating officer will try and piece together the sequence of events based on what he or she observes at the crime scene.

The Association of Crime Scene Reconstruction (www.acsr.org) defines it being to "...gain explicit knowledge of the series of events that surround the commission of a crime using deductive and inductive reasoning, physical evidence, scientific methods, and their interrelationships." We might describe it as trying to discover what happened.

In their introduction to crime scene reconstruction, Bevel & Gardner write that the crime itself is an *incident*. The incident is made up of a number of specific *events* and these events are in turn made up of smaller *event segments*. Data collected during the investigation can be used to try and determine these components of the incident:

- Collect data and, using all evidence, establish likely events.
- Establish from the data specific snapshots or event segments of the crime.
- Consider these event segments in relation to one another in order to establish related event segments.
- Order or sequence the event segments for each identified event.
- Consider all possible sequences and, where contradictory sequences exist, audit the evidence to determine which is the more probable.
- Determine the final order or sequence of the events themselves.

This process was discussed in the chapter on serial killers in terms of understanding the murderer's behaviour at the scene.

Informing the Family

The family should be notified as soon as possible after the identity of the victim has been established – this is usually done by the homicide detective leading the investigation. The media should never be informed of the identity before the next of kin have been informed. Where the next of kin cannot be located immediately, people are asked not to tell them anything until the police have had an opportunity to notify them formally. If family members reside in another area, local police will be contacted to deliver the notification.

The notification is kept simple: I have some bad news for you. Your husband is dead. The detective will also express his condolences to the family. Any questions the family asks will be answered tactfully and in a way which does not compromise the investigation. They will almost certainly want to know what happened, when and where it occurred, and how it happened.

Some relatives may refuse to believe what has happened and it may be necessary to provide some evidence to confirm the identification of the victim.

After the surviving family have dealt with the initial shock, they will be asked to answer some questions that will help with the initial stages of the investigation. They will also be asked to nominate a family member to formally identify the deceased. The family should also be informed that an autopsy will be required to establish the cause of death. A family liaison officer will often remain with the family and the detective will leave his contact details.

Canvassing the Neighbourhood

Uniformed police officers often conduct door-to-door inquiries to determine whether local residents saw or heard anything at the time of the murderer. They ask similar questions to those given in the chapter on missing person investigation. Detectives may conduct follow-up interviews with anyone who seems to have important information. The police also seek out locations that have security cameras and obtain the footage from them.

A week after the incident, the police may return to the area and stop and question people – pedestrians and motorists – to see if they were at the location the previous week and to ask if they may have seen or heard anything. The police also request dashboard camera footage from drivers.

At a later date, if the investigation needs a boost, the police may stage a reconstruction of events using an actor to play the victim dressed in clothes identical to those worn on the day – by doing this, investigators hope to jog the memories of witnesses who have not yet come forward. These reconstructions may also be broadcast on local television stations and/or made available online.

There are separate procedures for investigating police-related shootings and for so-called 'suicide by cop.'

Private Detectives and Homicide Investigations

In real life it is rare for a private detective to be the first person to investigate a homicide – where a death is known to be a homicide it is the responsibility of an official law enforcement agency to investigate. But private detectives may be asked to investigate if a client feels that the reported and certified manner and cause of death are inconsistent with the evidence or if new evidence has been uncovered. In such cases, the private investigator effectively reinvestigates the initial official investigation and conducts new inquiries of his own.

Private detectives may also investigate 'cold cases' that are no longer under active investigation by the police.

Types of Murder

Corvasce & Paglino identify more than a dozen different types of murder and their book *Murder One: A Writer's Guide to Homicide* has a chapter on each: business and financial; narcotics; gang murders; organized crime; contract killings; family murders; stranger and familiar stranger; crime of passion; thrill-lust and sexual murders; mass murders; serial killing; vehicular homicide, and 'bizarre' murders including rituals, voodoo, cannibalism, and delusions.

20 | Car Chases

I will begin by stating the obvious: A *car chase* is a scene or sequence of scenes in which a vehicle is pursued by another vehicle or multiple vehicles. The chase may or may not involve a police vehicle.

'Start Your Engines!' – Historical Development
The first car chase in a film is believed to occur in the 1903 five-minute silent short *Runaway Match*, also released as *Marriage by Motor* and *Elopement à la Mode*. The film was directed by Alf Collins and can be viewed on *YouTube*.

The car chase against which all others are judged is the ten-minute chase on the streets of San Francisco in *Bullitt* with Steve McQueen at the wheel of a 1968 Ford Mustang GT. Also cited in most people's top ten is the chase in *The French Connection* (1971) in which hero Popeye Doyle (Gene Hackman) chases after an elevated train in Brooklyn. Both films were produced by Philip d'Antoni and featured stunt driver Bill Hickman who was also worked on the chase scene in another d'Antoni film, *The Seven-Ups* (1973).

Vanishing Point (1971) is a road movie that both Quentin Tarantino (*Death Proof*, 2007) and Edgar Wright (*Baby Driver*, 2017) acknowledge as an inspiration. There were a number of more feel-good road movies in the late 1970s and early 1980s. *Smokey and the Bandit* (1977) stars Burt Reynolds as Bo 'Bandit' Darville as a bootlegger trying to transport 400 cases of beer from Texarkana to Atlanta while being pursued by the 'Smokey' – Sheriff Buford T. Justice. It was the second most successful film of the year after *Star Wars*. Sam Peckinpah's *Convoy* (1978) starring Kris Kristofferson, and based on a country and western song by C.W. McCall, was in a similar vein. And *The Cannonball Run* (1981) starred Burt Reynolds and a host of stars in an illegal cross-country race based on an actual race – the Cannonball Baker Sea-to-Shining-Sea Memorial Trophy Dash – held four times in the 1970s. Another take on the Cannonball dash was *Carquake!* (1976) starring David Carradine and there is also *The Gumball Rally* (1976). Australia brought us the Mad Max / Road Warrior movies and also *Midnite Spares* (1983). Escaping from a robbery is a good excuse for a car chase – both the 1969 and 2003 versions of *The Italian Job* are worth seeing and there is also an official Hindi remake called *Players* (2012) which I haven't seen, but the trailer makes it look like it should be fun. *The Burglars* (1971) is another movie using the getaway plot. Richard Rush, director of *Freebie and the Bean* (1974) describes his movie as having "four major chase scenes and over one hundred car crashes", making it sound like one for our list.

From 1979 to 1985, the TV series *The Dukes of Hazzard* brought car chases and jumps into people's living rooms on a weekly basis, running for a total of 147 episodes. It was created by Gy Waldron and Jerry Rushing based on Waldron's 1975 movie *Moonrunners* which was inspired by the experiences of ex-moonshiner Rushing. In the USA the series preceded *Dallas* on a Friday evening and in the UK the series became Saturday evening primetime viewing on BBC1.

Highlighting standout car chases in novels is more difficult because people tend not to remember a book for its car chase scene. Or two quote comedian Eddie Izzard (from *Unrepeatable*) "There are no car chases in books, are there?" Car chases, he says, are just people driving fast, looking in the mirror to see who is following, and then a crash. "Just doesn't fucking work, does it?" He's exaggerating, of course, but he does have a point. Car chases are about movement and that's harder to pull off in prose.

I have tried to recall examples from my own reading and I've looked around for recommendations online so have a few titles that you might want to have a look at. Ian Rankin's *Tooth and Nail* (1992) and Meg Gardiner's *The Memory Collector* (2009) are mentioned in a couple of online articles I've seen. Many films with car chases are based on novels – but that doesn't necessarily mean that the car chase was in the book. Robert Ludlum's Bourne series and Ian Fleming's James Bond novels – especially *Moonraker* – feature chases, but not on the scale of those in the films. The 2011 Ryan Gosling movie *Drive* is based on a 2005 novel of the same name by James Sallis who wrote a sequel *Driven* (2012). The 1974 film *Dirty Mary, Crazy Larry* starring Peter Fonda was based on a novel called *The Chase* (also published as *Pursuit*) by Richard Unekis.

If you're a novelist looking for examples of car chases, it is probably worth looking at the screenplays for movies that feature car chases – many are available online for free. The format is very different from a novel, but the structure and pacing of the sequence should still be instructional. You will probably find that the scene as described in the screenplay is very different from what finally appeared on screen – especially if the screenplay you read is an early draft. Another possibility is to look at the 'novelization' of a movie that wasn't based on a book – it might be interesting to see how the adapter has 'written up' the screenplay in novel form. *The Driver* (1978) was novelized by Clyde B. Phillips. There was even *The Dukes of Hazzard: Gone Racin'* by Eric Alter published in 1983. Dean Koontz's 1993 thriller *Mr. Murder* is a story about a family on the run. *The Getaway Man* (2003) by Andrew Vachss as the title suggests is a story about a getaway driver. Lee Goldberg's novella *McGrave* (2012) has been described as an action movie in book form. There's also David Morrell's *The Protector* (2003)

How to Write a Car Chase

I wrote a chapter on chase thrillers in *Suspense Thriller,* using films such as *The Fugitive* (1993) as examples and concentrating on a hero being hunted and running away on foot. Much of what I wrote there in terms of planning a chase also applies to the car chase. I will use the same headings here. In *Suspense Thriller* I also included a template for a story like *The Fugitive* which is basically one long chase.

1. Who is Being Chased?

In theory, the hero could be the one doing the chasing, but it is much easier for the audience to identify with an underdog who is being pursued by overwhelming odds – and this also gives the writer more scope for creating jeopardy and suspense. In a car chase, another question you have to answer is 'What is the hero driving?' American muscle cars and top of the line European saloons with big engines, or Japanese street racers are the obvious choices because they look cool. Gone are the days when movies featured battered old vehicles that were cheap to buy. But as well as thinking about what would look good – on the screen or in the reader's mind's eye – you need to think of the needs of the story. Is it reasonable that your hero will have the keys for a top of the line automobile? Is his character such that he would know how to drive one like a stuntman?

Putting your hero in a low-powered, ordinary family vehicle might be more believable and also increase the odds against him when the villains are in pursuit in top-of-the-line SUVs.

Something else to keep at the front of your mind for the hero and anyone else driving in the chase is to make sure that they are *in character* during the chase. These people should drive in the style of their character and not in the generic style of a stunt driver.

2. Who is Chasing the Hero?

You want to make it look as though the hero is facing overwhelming odds and almost bound to get caught. You can either make this obvious from the start or have things start off well for the hero and then add more pursuers – or more dangerous ones – to increase the odds against him as the chase progresses. You can also have the bad guys planning an ambush ahead of the hero so that it looks as if he's driving into trouble. And a helicopter overhead. And just around the corner, there's a flock of sheep or a herd of bicycling nuns that are really going to slow him down.

It used to be that having the hero pursued by three or four police cruisers was enough to establish 'overwhelming odds' but this has been used too often and audiences are used to the fact that police drivers don't seem to be able to drive a car around a corner without crashing into a building, a ditch, or the side of another police car. Numbers alone aren't enough to demonstrate a superior force so you will need to come up with something in addition to this – perhaps related to the ruthlessness of the drivers or the fact that the pursuers' vehicles are very obviously superior to what the fleeing hero is driving.

3. What is at Stake?

What terrible thing will happen if the hero doesn't manage to get away from his pursuers? Or what happens if his pursuers prevent him from reaching the destination he is desperate to reach? Build in suspense from the beginning by making it clear what is at stake. The hero must get to X or must escape from Y because if they don't something terrible will happen. *Getting to* or *escaping from* is the objective of a chase scene or sequence of scenes. Make sure that the stakes are something can audience can quickly understand and sympathise with.

If possible, add time pressure. And how much time does he have left to achieve his objective – is the clock ticking down? A clear deadline and an easy way of denoting the passage of time means that every delay you introduce into the chase adds to the suspense.

Then try and find some way of *increasing* the stakes or of increasing the pressure on the hero in some other way. Increase the distance the hero has to cover by forcing a change of route. Or add an extra objective for the hero to achieve along the way – taking a detour or having to backtrack to rescue an injured associate, for example. You can also take away the hero's options and reduce his available resources – these are things I discussed in *Suspense Thriller* as ways of increasing suspense. If the pursuers are armed, have the hero lose his gun. If he's driving a muscle car, have it damaged so that it can't achieve full speed – or have it stuck in reverse so he has to drive backwards. Or make the external terrain or situation such that he can't drive in top gear.

Put the hero in situations where he has to demonstrate his *ingenuity* to escape overwhelming odds, rather than rely on brute horsepower. Yes, you want to show that he's a better driver than the guys following him – unless he's not – but you also want to make the audience *believe* that the hero *might not* get away. Putting the hero at some kind of disadvantage increases the suspense and the audience also loves to see the underdog triumph.

If there is not something vital at stake – something that is important within the story as a whole – a car chase becomes a bit of a hollow exercise. Car chases are fun in their own right, but you don't want to get to the end of one and have the audience wonder what the point of it was. If the chase doesn't advance the story and reveal something about the characters – criteria against which every scene in a story should be judged – then it serves no purpose and shouldn't be there. In the old days, writers were brought in to 'spice up' a screenplay by adding 'tits and car chases' but – happily – people expect more from their stories these days.

What is at stake may be a 'MacGuffin' – something that has no intrinsic value as an object but which has significance within the context of a story and serves as a tangible representation of what the heroes and the bad guys are trying to achieve. Microfilm with secret plans or blueprints on is the clichéd example. I covered MacGuffins in *Suspense Thriller* – they were a plotting tool often used by Alfred Hitchcock.

4. Why is the Chase Taking Place?

There aren't really any rules when it comes to writing. But rule number one when it comes to writing a chase scene – or an action scene of any kind – would be: Make the scene be about something other than the chase. The chase is a by-product of what's really happening in the scene – a means to an end. You need to justify, within the context of the story, why a chase is taking place. It can't simply be there because your story needs a bit of action at that point. Well, yes, it can, but you need to disguise that by making the audience believe that its presence is justified for other reasons. The basic justification is simple enough – the hero needs to escape from somewhere and the pursuers want to catch him. Or the hero needs to reach some destination and the bad guys want to prevent him from getting there. Adding time pressure – the hero must get to his destination by a certain time or deliver a certain object to a certain place at a certain time or whatever – and you justify the need for the hero to be travelling at the fastest speed possible. Everything else is just dressing.

5. Where is the Chase Taking Place?

Geography and location are important in a chase sequence. A chase in a rural location will be very different from an urban one and crowded streets will allow a different sort of action to miles of empty blacktop. A chase has to take place somewhere. And it has to seem that the hero is travelling from one location to another place, not just driving round and round a movie backlot. Especially if you're writing a novel.

Changes in the location – or changes to it – can have an impact on the progress of the drivers. Think about ways to reduce the width of the road. Or send the vehicles off-road and onto some surface that is harder to drive on – grass, loose rocks, dusty earth, wet mud, sand, or anything else you can think of. Put your cars in places that cars don't normally go – *The Blues Brothers* demolished a shopping mall to good effect.

If your hero is trying to escape, a good question to ask yourself is 'What's the worst possible location that I can make him drive through?' How does this location disadvantage the hero and perhaps give the bad guys an edge? Again, if you can, make this specific to the character of the hero – if the hero is afraid of being over water, what's the best place to set your chase? Heights? Fire? Enclosed spaces? Open spaces? You need to establish his discomfort earlier in the story, obviously, but it can be an effective way of increasing the pressure on the hero.

In both novel and screenplay, you should be thinking in terms of trying to create specific images in the mind of the reader. Try to come up with something that the reader can visualise in their mind's eye – and make it original and specific so that the image sticks with them, rather than causing them to conjure up generic movie chase images. What's the most inappropriate place to put a car? What's the most unusual thing you could have a car crash into and demolish? What things would you not normally mix with a car chase? What is the least likely thing that characters might do during a car chase? If your first thought was fellatio, then shame on you.

6. Route Planning

Which way did he go? If your hero is travelling from one real-life location to another, you could use *Google Maps* and Street View to plan the whole route – or maybe even a GPS navigation system. You can also create variations on the route by avoiding certain roads or places. And you can look up points of interest and landmarks along the way. Or maybe old-fashioned printed maps are your thing. If you're writing something set in a particular period in the past, old maps may be your only option. Do you *have* to do this? Of course not. But you should give some thought to plotting your chase in a way that gives the feeling of geographical movement.

Be aware that if you get a route wrong or have your hero take a turn that doesn't exist or travel the wrong way along a one-way street, someone will spot your 'goof' and comment on it. Things aren't quite as strict in a novel where you have more poetic licence, but IMDb movie reviews are full of comments about incorrect geography. It matters to some people. It is up to you whether you want to run that gauntlet. In a novel, I usually make up a location that is loosely based on a real place as this helps me keep the geography straight in my head while giving me the freedom to 'cheat' with the layout of the land.

Time of day and the location of the sun is worth considering if your hero is travelling in a particular direction – especially if you want to have someone blinded by the sun. Or not. Same with the moon – if the hero looks out to his left and notices a full moon, make sure his left is towards the correct compass point.

Changes in terrain can help give the sense that the chase is moving from somewhere to somewhere – up into the mountains or downhill into the valley can affect the speed at which vehicles travel. As can a switch from wide urban streets to narrow country roads. Or vice versa. You can have your people getting closer to the sea or further inland. Anything that gives a sense of geographical movement.

You might also pick up some useful tips from the 'DVD extras' for movies – many have a 'making of' that shows how action sequences were put together, including storyboards and/or 'pre-viz' images. Many of these are also on *YouTube*.

7. Sequencing Events

A chase scene (or sequence) needs to be treated like a mini-story in its own right. It should have a beginning, middle, and an end and it needs rising tension or suspense and rising action – it should build to a climax which will serve as a turning point in the plot of the story, setting up whatever comes next.

To create *rising action* we need to start with small 'stunts' and build gradually to bigger and then biggest, saving the best for the climax of the scene/sequence. What other sorts of action can we use in our car chase?

Changing Vehicles – They used to do this will stagecoaches and horses in the Westerns – one character climbs out of one vehicle and across into another while the vehicles are still moving. The character can even be involved in a gunfight or a fistfight while doing this.

Near Misses – In most car chases either a truck pulls out of a side street or a homeless guy wheels a shopping cart full of trash out into the road – and the hero has to swerve to miss it. Sometimes a pursuing police vehicle runs into the thing the hero swerved to miss – showing that the hero is a much better driver than his pursuers. The homeless guy is never harmed. Sometimes two or three cars narrowly miss an obstacle before a final car slams into it. Audiences are thrilled by near-misses, but they like collisions more.

Jumps – Getting a car to leave the ground and fly through the air at a height that allows it to pass over another vehicle requires ramps at a certain height and a driver with expert skills – and when the car comes down and hits the ground the suspension will probably be destroyed. But in the movies cars make jumps all the time – they're part of the magic show. The trick these days is coming up on a new twist on the gag and this is often a matter of coming up with something original for the car to jump over. Or through. Going *under* something so that the roof is sheared off a car turning it into a convertible has been done so often that it is a bit of a cliché – but if you can put an original spin on the idea, go for it.

Collisions – You could write a car chase packed full of near-misses and never have your cars hit with anything – but why would you want to? If one of your cars doesn't demolish a fruit stand, have you really written a proper car chase? Or a wall of cardboard boxes, beloved of the lower budget TV car chase creator? Or a stack bales of straw? Okay, all of those are clichés, but you have to come up with shots that are fresh takes on these old ideas.

Ramming Other Vehicles – either those involved in the chase or those of other road users. Nobody suffers whiplash injuries in the movies so you can do this as often and as hard as you like.

Don't forget that car chases can also have a more sinister feel to them – remember Steven Spielberg's 1971 Plymouth Valiant versus Peterbilt truck movie starring Dennis Weaver? The fact that it was called *Duel* gives some idea of the way the action unfolds.

Add new and unexpected obstacles – sometimes bizarre or amusing is the way to go.

And don't forget to include brief pauses and moments of silence – 'I think we lost them...' – before having the pursuers reappear and closer than ever.

8. What Happened Before the Chase?

How did the chase begin? What was the catalyst? If your story opens with a chase scene, you won't need to show this necessarily, but you will need to imply it somehow. If your chase occurs two-thirds of the way through the story, there is plenty of time to set things up. But what we're really thinking about here is the stuff I mentioned under *stakes* above – What is the justification for having a chase occur at this point in the story? What events led up to this action sequence? The chase occurs as a *consequence* of something that happened earlier.

If you're going to have your hero leap into a high-powered vehicle and set off a break-neck speed it will look like a 'cheat' or *deus ex machina* – or a whim of the director – unless you have set-up or planted the possibility of this happening earlier in the story.

9. Weapons?

Ian Healy writes that weapons are more likely to be used in a car chase than they are in a chase on foot. This can include weapons mounted on the vehicle or pistols and machine guns fired by passengers. The people in one vehicle or both vehicles (or multiple vehicles) could be armed. He also notes that the vehicle itself can be used as a weapon.

There are a couple of things to bear in mind here, especially if you are writing a novel. Firstly, if you are riding as a passenger in a moving vehicle it is much harder to hit another moving vehicle than it appears in the movies. And targeting the tyre of a pursuing or escaping vehicle is even more difficult. Secondly, the cars shown in movies appear to be armoured and bullet-proof. Machine-gun bullets pierce the bodywork but never seem to penetrate into the vehicle. Law enforcement vehicles might have doors reinforced with Kevlar, but most normal vehicles don't. If you're writing a screenplay you can make use of the accepted conventions, but if you're writing a novel you probably need to be aware of what sort of damage different sorts of guns and ammunition can cause to a vehicle over different distances.

Again, weaponry and its use is an area where those in the know take pleasure in pointing out your mistakes – and probably more so than geography. Ian Fleming ended up recruiting one of his critics as an advisor.

10. Breathless Prose

Action scenes are fast-paced and that means you need to write them in a way that the reader – of your novel or screenplay – gets a real sense of rapid movement. You want your reader to *feel* what it is like to be travelling in a speeding car. You can gain first-hand experience of driving at speed if you think that will help – but I don't advise doing it in your own car on public roads. Book yourself an adventure day or 'experience' as a passenger at a local race track or similar location. Or go off-roading with an expert if that is more appropriate for your story. You'll learn things you never see in movies or video games – just make sure you wear brown trousers and take along a change of underwear.

If you are writing a screenplay, look at the scripts for fairly recent adventure movies to see how they lay out the action on the page.

A question to ask yourself – whether writing a novel or a screenplay – is 'Whose viewpoint are we seeing?' Are you sticking solely with the hero – first-person or restricted third-person viewpoint in a novel – or do you want to switch between the viewpoints of pursuer and pursued? Restricting yourself to the hero's p.o.v. limits what you can show to the reader. One of the tricks of suspense is to show the reader or viewer a danger that the hero isn't yet aware of – the helicopter closing in on their position or the roadblock that has been set up a few miles ahead.

Try and engage other senses rather than just relying on sight – especially in a novel. Changes in the texture of the surface the cars are moving on will affect the sound and the feel of the car – and the car will move differently on west asphalt versus dry, smooth surfaces versus broken or dusty ones. Pebbles may rattle underneath the car. Metal may scrape against concrete barriers or other metal vehicles. Plastic trim on a car crunches in a different way to metal bodywork. As impacts damage a car and its suspension, the sounds of the car and the way it moves will be affected. Try and evoke smells too – burning rubber, hot oil, hot metal, and exhaust fumes. Does the interior of the car have a new car smell? Leather? Or old vinyl and cigarettes? Is the back seat full of old fast food wrappers? Is the driver chewing gum? Or tobacco? Are they driving past wet earth or newly-mown grass? The sea? A garbage dump?

Writing Action
Don't describe anything other than the action and keep the description short. People who are moving and thinking quickly don't have time for long speeches – keep the dialogue short and punchy. Use verbs like 'streaked' and 'slammed' in a novel (present tense 'streaks' and 'slams' in a screenplay).

Use analogy to give the reader a chance to compare what the character experiences with something they have personally experienced. You have *simile* and *metaphor* to play with here. With simile, you tell the reader what something is *like* – or similar to: 'The car hit the ground and it was like being kicked in the ass by a mule.' Obviously, everyone has been kicked by a mule so can draw on this experience. With metaphor you say that one thing actually is another: 'The impact as he hit the ground was a kick in the ass from a mule.' Generally speaking, metaphor is more direct and better suited for action, but use what feels best as you write. Keep your comparisons in character – have your character refer to things that someone like him would be likely to think of.

11. Injuries Sustained
Other than gunshot wounds, people seem to emerge from movie chases relatively unscathed. And no one ever suffers neck injuries despite the fact that their car has been rear-ended at least once, collided with multiple stationary and moving obstacles, left the ground and flown through the air, and rolled and hit the ground on its roof. The drivers are just lucky, I guess.

The cars also survive pretty well. In those seventies car chase movies, you used to see a car leap and hit the ground nose first, bending the front wings like bananas and then they'd cut to a shot where the front of the car isn't creased. They used multiple cars and the audience was hip to the fact, but no one really minded. Today movie cars are like armoured tanks and hardly suffer a dent as they collide with concrete walls or land on their roofs. And the drivers can still open the doors and get out. Modern automobiles are obviously much better built.

It is up to you whether you want to accept these movie conventions in your story. In a novel, I'd probably want to lean more towards reality, unless it was a pure action-adventure.

12. Collateral Damage
I've mentioned this already under *sequencing events* but it bears repeating – Audiences like to see stuff trashed. It appeals to the anarchist or trickster in us. A little chaos is good for the soul. And if you can destroy something

impressive or unusual, that's even better. Often little thought is given to the consequences of an action sequence beyond what it means for the hero and the villain. You might get a long shot taking in the full extent of the chaos caused, and then we cut to something else.

Again, you have to decide to what extent your characters are going to be held accountable for the damage they have caused. And whether you are going to show the impact of the destruction on anyone other than the main characters. No one ever gives a thought to the innocent driver who gets t-boned at a junction – probably because we know he's a stunt driver. But what if he wasn't? Or what if hero or villain had to make their way back along the route they'd just taken, dodging the debris along the way?

It might be interesting to have a hero who is neither pursuer nor pursued who finds himself unexpectedly caught in the middle of a huge chase and has to avoid danger and thread his way through the wreckage. Maybe this has already been done.

13. What is the Purpose of the Scene?

I've said this a couple of times already, but it is important. The chase scene or sequence must serve a plot function – it must contain one or more turning points that affect the hero and/or villain's progress towards their story goal. And it must serve to set-up something that comes later.

14. How Does the Chase End?

A chase ends when the person being pursued either gets away or is captured or trapped, surrenders, or is killed. Whichever it is, the scene or sequence will have a climax and resolution, even if this hooks into the next action scene in the story.

If the person being chased gets away, we have to see *how* they get away. They must *do* something to earn their escape. It isn't enough to just have them disappearing at speed into the distance. Coincidence and/or luck shouldn't decide the outcome of the chase. We should see the hero doing something brave, foolhardy or ingenious – or all three combined. He should make a decision and commit to an action that allows him to get away. The more unexpected and dramatic the better. You can use any sort of 'cheat' that you can think of – and then go back and 'plant' something earlier in the story that prepares for the action and makes it not be a cheat. And you can also plant a red herring so that the audience *thinks* they know how the hero is going to get out of the situation and then you can pull the rug from under them.

You can end a chase with a 'twist' of some kind – something unexpected that spins the story in a new direction. The hero may reach the place or person he was racing to reach – and then discover that this person or place doesn't represent what he thought it/they did. He may be let down or betrayed. Or he may have raced straight into a trap. Or the hero may turn out not to be the person we thought he was – unless the twist is a double-bluff...

15. What Happens After the Chase?

Where do we go from here? Think in terms of consequences. What does the aftermath of the chase look like? How will characters react to it? There is often a moment of calm after intense action – and often it is a character-based moment where people express their emotions. Even if the emotion is only relief at having survived. The other thing to think about in terms of consequences is what your hero will do next and what your bad guys will do next – both in the short-term and the longer term. How does the outcome of your chase set-up the next confrontation in the story – assuming that the chase isn't the climactic action of the story?

'Just Follow the Sirens!' – Watching the Experts

Here's something cool – your homework tonight is to go on *YouTube* or *Vimeo* and search for 'car chase' and spend a couple of hours watching the best sequences that you can find. Look for the ones mentioned in this chapter or do a *Google* search for 'top ten car chases' and pick out some films that you are familiar with and some that you've never heard of. Also, try and find sequences that were shot *before* CGI was commonly used car chases – this may just be my personal prejudice, but even the best CGI scenes seem to look a little too computer-gamey and lack the crunch and grit of real-world physics. And then over the next few days, watch a few car chase movies in full – the *Fast and the Furious* series – especially the earlier ones; the 1978 film *The Driver* starring Ryan O'Neal and Bruce Dern; *The Bourne Supremacy* (2004); *The Blues Brothers* (1980); *Taxi* (1998) – the original French version by Luc Besson is better than the remake; *Ronin* (1998); *Jack Reacher* (2012); *Drive* (2011), and *Two-Lane Blacktop* (1971).

The best way to learn how to structure and write a chase sequence is to watch some good ones – watch them out of context as clips on *YouTube* and watch them in context by watching the whole movie.

Music & Movement

Many chase scenes – including *Bullitt*, *The French Connection*, and the 2011 movie *Drive* – rely on the sound of screeching tyres and vehicle impacts, but others make full use of soundtrack music or songs. And director William Friedkin said that he used music during the editing of the car chase in *The French Connection*, cutting the film to the rhythm of Santana's cover version of *Black Magic Woman*, even though the song was not used on the soundtrack. Edgar Wright, writer and director of the 2017 movie *Baby Driver*, says that he wrote the script for the six-minute opening sequence of the film to the song *Bellbottoms* by the John Spencer Blues Explosion which features on the soundtrack. The *Billboard* website published 'The Best 10 Music Moments in Famous Car Chase Scenes' including Juno Reactor's 'Mona Lisa Overdrive' used in *The Matrix Reloaded*, and the chase in *Bonnie & Clyde* being accompanied Wacky Races-style by Earl Scruggs 'Foggy Mountain Breakdown.'

We can all follow Edgar Wright's example and pick a song to inspire our chase scene. If you write while listening to something fast-paced and with a strong rhythm, you will probably find it influences the way that you write. Or if you have movie scores in your music collection, seek out the tracks that were written for chase sequences. The genre of the music doesn't really matter – anything from classical to pop is fine – just pick something that has the right tempo for a chase. Rock songs with a driving beat are an obvious choice – perhaps too obvious. Have a listen to 'The William Tell Overture' by Rossini – there's a great version by Hans Zimmer on the soundtrack for the 2013 movie *The Lone Ranger*. Or for a more old-fashioned sound try 'The Devils' Galop' ('galop' being a dance, though some versions of the music on *YouTube* and elsewhere use the spelling 'gallop') composed by Charles Williams, it was used by the BBC for the radio serial *Dick Barton - Special Agent*. Whatever you end up listening to, try and think of it in terms of the beginning, middle, and end of your chase sequence.

Jourdan Aldredge in an article aimed at filmmakers says "Move the camera around. Arguably, the best car chases are the ones that get creative and make the most use of diverse camera shots from many different places and angles." Look at the types of shots that have been used in classic car chases and "... make your plan to include shots you are certain will work and add a few that you might not be so sure about, as you haven't actually seen them pulled off before. As long as your main coverage is solid and controlled, you can free yourself to experiment." Aldredge also says "Don't focus on the cars. Focus on the action." He uses the analogy of a Chuck Norris kick – we don't focus on the boot, our attention is on what it comes into contact with and what happens to it.

More Homework?

Seeing really is better than reading when it comes to car chases, so I've found a few more things that you may want to watch. Ross Peacock has an interesting video essay called 'The Art of the Car Chase' on his *Rossatron* channel on *YouTube*:
https://www.youtube.com/watch?v=H8V4hXppLgE

And there is another great video essay 'Baby Driver: What Makes a Good Car Chase?' by Nelson Carvajal on the *Fandor* website:
https://www.fandor.com/posts/baby-driver-what-makes-a-good-car-chase

I also like the video 'Why Do Action Scenes Suck?' on the *Corridor Crew* channel on *YouTube* – it isn't about car chases specifically, but many of the points raised are relevant.
https://www.youtube.com/watch?time_continue=4&v=H_19rSdEWao

As I discover new content I will post links at
www.paultomlinson.org/crime

Bibliography

1 | Hardboiled Detective
Baker, Robert A. & Michael T. Nietzel – *Private Eyes: One Hundred and One Knights - A Survey of American Detective Fiction 1922-1984*. Bowling Green State University Popular Press, 1985
Campbell, Donna M. – 'Naturalism in American Literature.' *Literary Movements*. Washington State University, 2017 https://public.wsu.edu/~campbelld/amlit/natural.htm
Chastain, Thomas – 'The Case for the Private Eye,' in: Lucy Freeman, Lucy (ed.) – *The Murder Mystique: Crime Writers on Their Art*. Ungar, 1982
Duggan, Eddie – 'Writing in the Darkness: The World of Cornell Woolrich.' *Crimetime* 2.6, 1999
Frey, James N. – *How to Write a Damned Good Mystery*. St. Martin's Press, 2004
Gardner, Erle Stanley – 'The Case of the Early Beginning,' in: Howard Haycraft (ed.) – *The Art of the Mystery Story: A Collection of Critical Essays*. Simon & Schuster, 1946
Geherin, David – *The American Private Eye: The Image in Fiction*. Frederick Ungar Publishing Co., 1985.
Gregory, Sinda – *Private Investigations: The Novels of Dashiell Hammett*. Southern Illinois University Press, 1985
Grella, George – 'The Hardboiled Detective Novel,' in: Robin W. Winks (ed.), *Detective Fiction: A Collection of Critical Essays*. Prentice Hall, 1980
Grossman, Julie – *Rethinking the Femme Fatale in Film Noir: Ready for Her Close-up*. Palgrave Macmillan,
Heilbrun, Carolyn G. – 'The New Female Detective,' *Yale Journal of Law & Feminism*, 14(2), 2002
Keating, H.R.F. – 'Transatlantic Cousins and Others,' in: *Writing Crime Fiction* (2nd ed.). A & C Black, 1994.
Macdonald, Ross – 'The Writer as Detective Hero,' in: Francis M. Nevins (ed.) – *The Mystery Writer's Art*. Bowling Green State University Popular Press, 1970
MacDonald, Ross – *On Crime Writing: The Writer as Detective Hero - Writing the Galton Case*. Capra Press, 1973
Nevins, Francis M. (ed.) – *The Mystery Writer's Art*. Bowling Green State University Popular Press, 1970
Norville, Barbara – *Writing the Modern Mystery*. Writer's Digest, 1992
Ousby, Ian – *The Crime and Mystery Book: A Reader's Companion*. Thames and Hudson, 1997
Perelman, S.J. – 'Somewhere a Roscoe...' *The New Yorker*, 15 October 1938
Pronzini, Bill & Jack Adrian (eds.) – *Hardboiled: An Anthology of American Crime Stories*. Oxford University Press, 1955.
Ruehlmann, William – *Saint with a Gun: The Unlawful American Private Eye*. New York University Press, 1974
Todorov, Tzvetan – 'The Typology of Detective Fiction,' in: *The Poetics of Prose*, Blackwell, 1977.

2 | Gangsters
Bell, Daniel – 'Crime as an American Way of Life,' in: *Antioch Review* vol.13, no.2, Summer 1953
Burnett, W.R. – 'Introduction' in: *Little Caesar* by W.R. Burnett. The Dial Press, 1958
Cawelti, John G. – *Mystery, Violence, and Popular Culture*. University of Wisconsin Popular Press, 2004
Gardaphé, Fred L. – *From Wiseguys to Wise Men: The Gangster and Italian American Masculinities*. Routledge, 2006
Gomar, Carmen Guirait – 'The Transgressive Discourse of Rowland Brown's Cinema (1931-1933): A Brief career in Pre-Code Hollywood,' in: *La Revista de Comunicación de la SEECI* (Sociedad Española de Estudios de Comunicación Iberoamericana) Ano XX (40), Julio 2016
McArthur, Colin – *Underworld USA*. Viking Press, 1972
Mate, Ken and Pat McGilligan – Interview with W.R. Burnett in: *Film Comment*, Jan-Feb 1983. Reprinted in *Backstory 1: Interviews with Screenwriters of Hollywood's Golden Age*. University of California Press, 1986
Mitchell, Edward – 'Apes and Essences: Some Sources of Significance in the American Gangster Film,' in: *Film Genre Reader IV*, edited by Barry Keith Grant. University of Texas Press, 2012

Peña, Manuel – *American Mythologies*. Ashgate Publishing, 2012
Seldes, Gilbert – 'Foreword' in: *Little Caesar* by W.R. Burnett. The Dial Press, 1958
Warshow, Robert – 'The Gangster as Tragic Hero,' in: The Oxford Book of Essays (ed. John Gross). Oxford University Press, 1998. Originally published in *Partisan Review* #2, February 1948
Yogerst, Chris – *From the Headlines to Hollywood: The Birth and Boom of Warner Bros*. Rowman & Littlefield, 2016

4 | Police Procedurals

American Psychological Association – 'Eyewitness Accuracy in Police Lineups,' *American Psychological Association,* April 2014
https://www.apa.org/action/resources/research-in-action/eyewitness
Dove, George N. – *The Police Procedural*. Bowling Green University Popular Press, 1982
Gilbert, Michael – 'The British Police Procedural,' in: *Whodunit?* ed. By H.R.F. Keating.
Keating, H.R.F. – *Writing Crime Fiction*. A & C Black, 1994
Keating, H.R.F. – *Whodunit?: A Guide to Crime, Suspense and Spy Fiction*. Windward (W.H. Smith & Son Ltd), 1982
Lofland, Lee – *Police Procedure and Investigation: A Guide for Writers*. Writer's Digest, 2007
MacKay, Jenny – *Forensic Art*. Gale, Cengage Learning, 2009
Markman, Art – 'The Value of Proper Police Lineup Procedures,' *Psychology Today*, 2016.
https://www.psychologytoday.com/gb/blog/ulterior-motives/201610/the-value-proper-police-lineup-procedures
Miller, Aaron – '11 Things You Didn't Know About Cop Cars' – www.thrillist.com
O'Byrne, Michael – *The Crime Writer's Guide to Police Practice and Procedure*. Robert Hale, 2015
Russ, John C. – *Forensic Uses of Digital Imaging*. CRC Press, 2001
Shannon, Dell – 'Writing the Police-Routine Novel,' in: *The Writer's Handbook*, 1972.
Wade, Stephen & Stuart Gibbon – *The Crime Writer's Casebook: A Reference Guide to Police Investigation Past and Present*. Straightforward Publishing, 2017
Waugh, Hillary – 'The American Police Procedural,' in: *Whodunit?* ed. By H.R.F. Keating.
Wilkinson, Caroline M. – 'A Review of Forensic Art,' *Research and Reports in Forensic Medical Science*, Vol. 5, 16 September 2015

5 | Forensic Investigation

Genge, N.E. – *The Forensic Casebook: The Science of Crime Scene Investigation*. Ebury Press, 2004
Knight, Bernard & Pekka Sankko – *Knight's Forensic Pathology* (4th ed.), CRC Press, 2016
Leadbeatter, Stephen – 'Forensic Pathologist,' in: *The Oxford Companion to Crime & Mystery Writing*. Oxford University Press, 1999
Lyle, D.P. – *Forensics for Dummies* (2nd ed.). For Dummies/Wiley, 2016
Lyle, D.P. – *Forensics: A Guide for Writers*. Writer's Digest, 2008
Madea, Burkhard (ed.) – Handbook of Forensic Medicine, John Wiley & Sons, 2014
McDermid, Val – *Forensics: The Anatomy of Crime*. Wellcome Collection, 2015
Payne-James, Jason et al. (eds.) – *Simpson's Forensic Medicine* (13th ed.). CRC Press, 2011

6 | Forensic Psychology & Serial Killer Profiling

Bloom, Richard – *Foundations of Psychological Profiling: Terrorism, Espionage, and Deception*. CRC Press, 2013
Bronswick, Amy L. – *Using Sexually Related Crime Scene Characteristics to Profile Male Serial Killers: A Question of Motivation*. (2001, Unpublished dissertation) Alliant International University, Fresno, CA. [Quoted in Hickey]
Brussel, James – *Casebook of a Crime Psychiatrist*. Bernard Geis Associates, 1968.
Canter, David – *Criminal Shadows: Inside the Mind of the Serial Killer*. Harper Collins, 1994
Canter, David – 'Profiling as Poison,' *Inter Alia*, 2(1), 10–11, 1998. [quoted in Petherick]
Canter, David – *Mapping murder: The Secrets of Geographical Profiling*. Virgin Books, 2003.
Canter, David V. & Laurence J. Alison, Emily Alison and Natalia Wentink – 'The Organized/Disorganized Typology of Serial Murder: Myth or Model?' *Psychology, Public Policy, and Law*, 10 (3), 2004.
Canter, David & Donna Youngs – *Investigative Psychology: Offender Profiling and the Analysis of Criminal Action*. Wiley, 2009
Canter, David – *Forensic Psychology: A Very Short Introduction*. Oxford University Press, 2010
Canter, David – *Forensic Psychology for Dummies*. John Wiley & Sons, 2012
Douglas, John E. & Mark Olshaker – *Mindhunter: Inside the FBI's Elite Serial Crime Unit*. Scribner, 1995
Douglas, J.E., Ressler, R.K., Burgess, A.W., & Hartman, C.R. 'Criminal Profiling from Crime Scene Analysis'. *Behavioral Sciences and the Law*, 4(4), 1986
Federal Bureau of Investigation – *Serial Murder: Multi-Disciplinary Perspectives for Investigators*. Behavioural Analysis Unit, 2008

Ferguson, Claire – 'Investigative Relevance,' in: Petherick, Wayne – *Profiling and Serial Crime: Theoretical and Practical Issues* (3rd ed.). Elsevier, 2014
Field, John – *Caring to Death: A Discursive Analysis of Nurses Who Murder Patients*. PhD Thesis, University of Adelaide, 2007
Godwin, Grover Maurice – *Hunting Serial Predators: A Multivariate Classification Approach to Profiling Violent Behavior*. CRC Press, 2000
Hickey, Eric W. – *Serial Murderers and Their Victims* (5th ed). Wadsworth, Cengage Learning, 2010
Homant, Robert J. and Daniel B. Kennedy – 'Understanding Serial Sexual Murder: A Biopsychosocial Approach,' in: *Profiling and Serial Crime* (ed. Wayne Petherick), 2014
Petherick, Wayne – *Profiling Serial Crime: Theoretical and Practical Issues* (3rd ed). Anderson Publishing/Elsevier, 2014
Ramsland, Katherine – *The Psychology of Death Investigations: Behavioral Analysis for Psychological Autopsy and Criminal Profiling*. CRC Press, 2018
Ramsland, Katherine – 'James Brussel: The "Sherlock Holmes of the Couch".' *The Forensic Examiner*. (Spring 2009) www.theforensicexaminer.com/archive/spring09/22/
Rossmo, D. K. – 'Geographic profiling,' in: J.L. Jackson & D. Bekerian (eds.) – *Offender Profiling: Theory, Research and Practice*. John Wiley and Sons, 1997.
Taylor, Sandie – *Forensic Psychology: The Basics*. Routledge, 2015
Turvey, Brent E. – *Forensic Victimology: Examining Violent Crime Victims in Investigative and Legal Contexts* (2nd ed). Academic Press, 2014
Webb, David – 'Criminal Profiling Part 2 - Profiling: The FBI Legacy.' www.all-about-forensic-psychology.com/offender-profiling.html

7 | Undercover Cops
Motto, Carmine J. & Dale L. June – *Undercover* (2nd ed). CRC Press, 2000
Terrace, Vincent – The Television Crime Fighters Factbook. McFarland, 2003

8 | The Heist
Tout, T.F. – *A Medieval Burglary: A Lecture*. Manchester University Press, 1916

10 | Confidence Tricks
Abagnale, Frank W. & Stan Redding – *Catch Me If You Can*. Grosset & Dunlap, 1980
Braucher, Jean & Barak Orbach – 'Scamming: The Misunderstood Confidence Man,' *Yale Journal of Law and the Humanities*, Vol.27, Iss.2, 2015
Bellin, Andy – *Poker Nation: A High-Stakes, Low-Life Adventure into the Heart of a Gambling Country*. Harper Collins, 2002
Bergman, Johannes Dietrich Bergmann – 'The Original Confidence Man,' *American Quarterly* #21, Fall 1969.
Christie, Richard & Florence L. Geis – *Studies in Machiavellianism*, Academic Press, 1970.
Conwell, Chic – *The Professional Thief, by a Professional Thief*, annotated by Edwin H. Sutherland
Crosby, William C. – *Confessions of a Confidence Man: A Handbook for Suckers*, the life of William C. Crosby as told to Edward H. Smith (pg. 35)
Faron, Fay – *Rip-Off: A Writer's Guide to Crimes of Deception*. Writer's Digest Books, 1998
Hines, David T. – *The Life, Adventures and Opinions of Dr. David Theo. Hines of South Carolina*. Bradley & Clark, 1840
Jones, Daniel N. & Delroy L. Paulhus – 'Machiavellianism,' in: *Individual Differences in Social Behaviour*, ed. M.R. Leary & R.H. Hoyle. Guilford, 2009
Konnikova, Maria – *The Confidence Game: The Psychology of the Con and Why We Fall For It Every Time*. Canongate, 2016
Kuhlmann, Susan – *Knave, Fool, and Genius: The Confidence Man as He Appears in Nineteenth-Century American Fiction*. University of North Carolina Press, 1973
Maurer, David – *The Big Con: The Story of the Confidence Man*. Anchor Books, 1999
Mott, Graham M. – *Scams, Swindles & Rip-Offs*. Golden Shadows Press, 1994
Nash, Jay Robert – *Hustlers & Con Men*. M Evans & Co., 1976
Paulhus, Delroy L. & Kevin M. Williams – 'The Dark Triad of Personality: Narcissism, Machiavellianism, and Psychopathy.' *Journal of Research in Personality* 36 (2002)
Poe, Edgar Allan – 'Diddling Considered as One of the Exact Sciences.' *Saturday Courier*, 14 October 1843
Rayner, Richard – *Drake's Fortune: The Fabulous True Story of the World's Greatest Confidence Artist*. Doubleday, 2002
Sifakis, Carl – *Frauds, Deceptions, and Swindles*. Facts On File, 2001
Swierczynski, Duane – *The Complete Idiot's Guide to Frauds, Scams, and Cons*. Alpha, 2003
Whitlock, Chuck – *Chuck Whitlock's Scam School*. John Wiley & Sons, 1997

11 | Prison Thrillers
Crowther, Bruce – *Captured on Film: The Prison Movie*. Batsford, 1989.

Roffman, Peter & Beverly Simpson – 'Prison Films,' in: *The Political Companion to American Film*, ed. Gary Crowdus. Lakeview Press, 1994.
Tobias, Ronald B. – *Twenty Master Plots and How to Build Them*. Writer's Digest Books, 1993

12 | Noir Romance
Crowdus, Gary (ed.) – *The Political Companion to American Film*. Lakeview Press, 1994
Damico, James – 'Film Noir: A Modest Proposal,' in: *Film Noir Reader*
Derry, Charles – *The Suspense Thriller: Films in the Shadow of Alfred Hitchcock*. McFarland & Co. Inc., 1988
Grossman, Julie – *Rethinking the Femme Fatale in Film Noir: Ready for Her Close-Up*. Palgrave Macmillan, 2009
Horsley Lee – *The Noir Thriller*. Palgrave, 2001
Mellen, Joan – 'Film Noir,' in: *The Political Companion to American Film* edited by Gary Crowdus. Lakeview Press, 1994
Mulvey, Laura – 'Visual Pleasure and Narrative Cinema,' in: *Screen* 16(3), Autumn 1975
Place, Janey – 'Women in Film Noir,' in: *Women in Film Noir*, edited by E. Ann Kaplan. British Film Institute, 1988
Snyder, Scott – 'Personality Disorder and the Film Noir Femme Fatale,' in: *Journal of Criminal Justice and Popular Culture* 8(3), 2001
Wager, Jans B. – *Dames in the Driver's Seat: Rereading Film Noir*. University of Texas Press, 2005
Zinsser, David – 'James M. Cain, The Art of Fiction No. 69,' in: *The Paris Review* #73, Spring-Summer 1978

13 | Vigilantes & Enforcers
Cawelti John G. – *Adventure, Mystery, and Romance: Formula Stories as Art and Popular Culture*. University of Chicago Press, 1976
Kittredge, William & Steven M. Krauzer – *The Great American Detective*. Signet, 1978
Mengel, Bradley – *Serial Vigilantes of Paperback Fiction: An Encyclopedia from Able Team to Z-Comm*. McFarland, 2009
Polti, Georges – *The Thirty-Six Dramatic Situations*. James Knapp Reeve, 1924. (Originally published as *Les Trente-Six Situations Dramatiques*, 1895)
Tobias, Ronald B. – *Twenty Master Plots and How to Build Them*. Writer's Digest Books, 1993
Young, William Henry – *A Study of Action-Adventure Fiction: The Executioner and Mack Bolan*. Edwin Mellen Press, 1996

14 | The Buddy Movie
Ebert, Roger – 'Rush Hour.' *RogerEbert.com*
https://www.rogerebert.com/reviews/rush-hour-1998
Ellen, Barbara – 'Facials, Manicures, Emotional Outbursts... Is Metrosexual Man More of a Woman Than You?' *The Observer*, 29th April 2007.
https://www.theguardian.com/world/2007/apr/29/gender.features
Martin, Katherine Connor – 'The Rise of the Portmanbro,' *Oxford Dictionaries* blog, 9th October 2013.
http://blog.oxforddictionaries.com/2013/10/the-rise-of-the-portmanbro/
Mosse, George L. – *The Image of Man: The Creation of Modern Masculinity*. Oxford University Press, 1996
Simpson, Mark – 'Meet the Metrosexual.' *Salon.com*, 22nd July 2002.
https://www.salon.com/test/2002/07/22/metrosexual/

15 | Informants
Derry, Paul – *Inside a Police Informant's Mind*. CRC Press, 2016
Fitzgerald, Dennis G. – *Informants and Undercover Investigations: A Practical Guide to Law, Policy, and Procedure*. CRC Press, 2007
McMahon, Rory J. – *Practical Handbook for Professional Investigators* (3rd ed). CRC Press, 2014
Mono, Carmine J. & Dale L. June (eds.) – *Undercover* (2nd ed). CRC Press, 2000

16 | Interviewing Witnesses & Interrogating Suspects
Black, Inge Sebyan & Charles L. Yeschke – *The Art of Investigative Interviewing* (3rd ed.). Butterworth-Heinemann, 2014
Boyle, Michael & Jean-Claude Vullierme – *A Brief Introduction to Investigative Interviewing: A Practitioner's Guide*. Council of Europe, 2018
Bull, Ray & Tim Valentine & Tom Williamson (eds.) – *Handbook of Psychology of Investigative Interviewing: Current Developments and Future Directions*. Wiley-Blackwell, 2009
Gudjonsson, Gisli H. – *The Psychology of Interrogations and Confessions: A Handbook*. John Wiley & Sons, 2003
McGrath, Michael – in: Brent E. Turvey (ed.) – *Forensic Victimology: Examining Violent Crime Victims in Investigative and Legal Contexts*. Academic Press, 2014

Ministry of Justice (UK) – *Achieving Best Evidence in Criminal Proceedings: Guidance on interviewing Victims and Witnesses, and Guidance on Using Special Measures*. March 2011

Newman, A.W. & J.W. Thompson, Jr. – 'The Rise and Fall of Forensic Hypnosis in Criminal Investigation,' *Journal of American Academy of Psychiatry and Law* 29(1), 2001

Schollum, Mary – 'Bringing PEACE to the United States: A Framework for Investigative Interviewing,' in: *The Police Chief,* November 2017

St-Yves, Michel & Nadine Deslauriers-Varin – 'The Psychology of Suspects' Decision-Making During Interrogation,' in: Bull, Valentine & Williamson (eds.) – *Handbook of Psychology of Investigative Interviewing: Current Developments and Future Directions*. Wiley-Blackwell, 2009

Turvey, Brent E. (ed.) – *Forensic Victimology: Examining Violent Crime Victims in Investigative and Legal Contexts*. Academic Press, 2014

Wallace, Harvey – *Victimology: Legal, Psychological, and Social Perspectives*. Allyn and Bacon, 1998

Walters, Stan B. – *Principles of Kinesic Interview and Interrogation* (2nd ed.). CRC Press, 2002

Zulawski, David E. & Douglas E. Wicklander – *Practical Aspects of Interview and Interrogation* (2nd ed.). CRC Press, 2002

17 | Surveillance & Stake-Outs

Brown, Steven Kerry – *The Complete Idiot's Guide to Private Investigating* (3rd ed.). Alpha, 2013

Coleman, Roy & Michael McCahill – *Surveillance & Crime*. SAGE Publications, 2011

Jenkins, Peter – *Advanced Surveillance: The Complete Manual of Surveillance Training*. Intel Publications, 2003

Jenkins, Peter – *Covert Imagery - Photography & Video: The Investigators and Enforcement Officers Guide to Covert Digital Photography*. Intel Publications, 2015

Jenkins, Peter – *Surveillance Tradecraft: The Professional's Guide to Surveillance Training*. Intel Publications, 2010

Petersen, J.K. – *Understanding Surveillance Technologies: Spy Devices, Privacy, History & Applications* (3rd ed.). CRC Press, 2012

Plomin, Joe – *Hidden Cameras: Everything You Need to Know About Covert Recording, Undercover Cameras and Secret Filming*. Jessica Kingsley Publishers, 2016

Rapp, Burt – *Shadowing and Surveillance: A Complete Handbook*. Loompanics Unlimited, 1986

18 | Missing Person Investigation

Bazzell, Michael – *Open Source Intelligence Techniques: Resources for Searching and Analyzing Online Information*. Independently published, 2018

Brown, Steven Kerry – *The Complete Idiot's Guide to Private Investigating* (3rd ed.). Alpha Books, 2013

Faron, Fay – *Missing Persons: A Writer's Guide to Finding the Lost, the Abducted and the Escape*. Writer's Digest Books, 1997

McMahon, Rory J. – *Practical Handbook for Professional Investigators* (3rd ed.). CRC Press, 2014

Sprague, Donald F. – *Investigating Missing Children Cases: A Guide for First Responders and Investigators*. CRC Press, 2013

19 | Murder Investigation

Beer, Dean A. – *Practical Handbook for Professional Investigators*. CRC Press, 2014

Bevel, Tom & Ross M. Gardner – *Bloodstain Pattern Analysis with an Introduction to Crime Scene Reconstruction*. CRC Press, 2002

Bintliff, Russell – *Police Procedure: A Writer's Guide to the Police and How they Work*. Writer's Digest Books, 1993

Cole, D.J. – *A Writer's Guide to Police Organization and Crime Investigation and Detection*. Robert Hale, 1996

Corvasce, Mauro V. & Joseph R. Paglino – *Murder One: A Writer's Guide to Homicide*. Writer's Digest Books, 1997

Geberth, Vernon J. – *Practical Homicide Investigation: Checklist and Field Guide* (2nd ed.), 2014

Wilson, Keith D. – *Cause of Death: A Writer's Guide to Death, Murder & Forensic Medicine*. Writer's Digest Books, 1992

Wilson, Keith & David Page – *Code Blue: A Writer's Guide to Hospitals, including the ER, OR, and ICU*. Writer's Digest Books, 2000

20 | Car Chases

Aldredge, Jourdan – '6 Tips for Filming a Thrilling Car Chase Scene'. *PremiumBeat.com*, 17th January 2017
https://www.premiumbeat.com/blog/how-to-film-car-chase-scene/

Bibliography

Blauvelt, Christian – 'The Best 10 Music Moments in Famous Car Chase Scenes', *Billboard.com*, 15th June 2017
https://www.billboard.com/articles/news/movies/7832928/music-car-chase-scenes-best

Gardiner, Meg – 'Writing Chase Scenes.' *MegGardiner.Wordpress.com*, 4th December 2012
https://meggardiner.wordpress.com/2012/12/04/writing-chase-scenes/

Healy, Ian Thomas – '10 Types of Action Scenes: The Chase', *WriteBetterAction.IanHealy.com*, 10th January 2011
http://writebetteraction.ianthealy.com/2011/01/10/10-types-of-action-scenes-the-chase/

Healy, Ian Thomas – *Action! Writing Better Action Using Cinematic Techniques*. Local Hero Press, 2011

MacAvoy, Jordan – 'How All the Best Car Chase Scenes are Filmed.' *InterestingEngineering.com*, 30th December 2017.
https://interestingengineering.com/how-all-the-best-car-chase-scenes-are-filmed

Runaway Match (1903) – [film]
https://www.youtube.com/watch?v=CteD9ROdtKs

Thomas, Lou – 'Edgar Wright: What Makes the Perfect Car Chase?' *British Film Institute* website.
https://www.bfi.org.uk/news-opinion/news-bfi/interviews/edgar-wright-baby-driver-car-chases

VaRaces: The Car Chase Community (www.varaces.com) Has an A-Z of movies on 'The Chases' page – but doesn't appear to have been updated since 2015

INDEX

48 HRS (1982), 251, 335, 336, 337, 338, 339, 340, 341, 342, 343, 344, 345, 346
6 Bridges to Cross (1955), 219
87th Precinct, 88, 135
A Fool There Was (1915), 306
Abagnale Jr., Frank W., 265-266, 270, 278, 424
Abbot, Anthony, 140
ABC Murders (1936), 162
abduction, motivations, 398, 400
abductions, 43, 160, 173, 188, 190, 191, 192, 193, 196, 345, 394, 395, 396, 398, 400, 401, See also missing person investigation
About the Murder of a Startled Lady (1935), 140
absence of evidence, 17
Absolute Power (1996), 247
Accomplices to the Crime: The Arkansas Prison Scandal, 292
Accountant, The (2016), 148
ACPO, 111
action-adventure, 149, 231, 232, 333, 418
Acute Stress Disorder, 380
Adam Dalgliesh, 84
Adamson, Chuck, 220
Addie Pray, 266
Adrian, Jack, 20, 26, 27, 39, 422
Adventure, Mystery and Romance, 20, 65
Adventures of Jimmie Dale, The, 246
Affleck, Ben, 148
African Queen, The (1951), 336
After Dark, My Sweet (1955), 317
After Dark, My Sweet (1990), 304
Agamemnon, 305
Airport (1968), 118
Alcatraz — The Whole Shocking Story (1980), 290
Alcatraz Federal Penitentiary, 290
Aldredge, Jourdan, 420
Aldrich, Robert, 291
Alger, Horatio, 71
Alienist, The (1994), 142
All On a Summer's Day (1981), 88
Allain, Marcel, 242
allies, characters, 32, 34, 272, 296, 298
ally, character, 66
Alter, Eric, 412
Altman, Robert, 62
Amateur Cracksman, the, 242
amateur detective, 7, 10, 17, 89, 102, 117
Amateur on the run thriller, 7
Amazing Spider-Man, 332
AMBER, 401
ambition, theme, 70
Ambler, Eric, 220
Amelia Sachs, 191
American Academy of Forensic Sciences, 148
American Board of Forensic Odontologists, 145
American Board of Professional Psychology, 163
American dream, 69
American Dream, 56, 70, 71, 72, 217, 308

American Film Institute, 246
American Literary Naturalism: A Divided Stream, 26
American Missing Broadcast Emergency Response, 401
American Naturalism, 11
American Psycho (1991), 162
American Society of Questioned Document Examiners, 148
Ames, Aldrich, 378
Amnesty International, 101
analogy, 167, 418, 420
Anatomy of a Corpse, 141
Anderson, Edward, 62
Anderson, Jamie, 79
Anderson, Maxwell, 62
Anderson, Paul Thomas, 219
Anderson, Sherwood, 10, 27
Anderson, Sir Robert, 159
Angel of Darkness, The (1997), 143
Angel of Vengeance, 324
Angels with Dirty Faces (1938), 62
angry white men, 337
Annie Laurie Starr, 77
anti-hero, 64, 100, 243
Any Means Necessary, 199
Aoyama, Gosho, 243
appearance, character, 40
Apprentice, The (2002), 142
Arbuckle, Roscoe 'Fatty', 63
Armes, Jay J., 12
Armored Car Robbery (1950), 219
Arquette, Patricia, 304
Arrest of Arsène Lupin, The (1905), 242
Arsène Lupin, 242, 243
Arsène Lupin (1932), 242
Arsène Lupin (2004), 242
arson, 149
Arson Plus, 12
Art of Investigative Interviewing, The (2014), 366
Art of the Car Chase, The, 421
Ashbury, Herbert, 56
Asphalt Jungle, The (1950), 61, 219
assassination, 118
Asser, Jonathan, 292
Association of Certified Fraud Examiners, 262
Association of Chief Police Officers, 111
Association of Crime Scene Reconstruction, 408
assumed identity, 198
Astor, Mary, 305, 306
At Bertram's Hotel (1965), 212
A-Team, The (1983), 333
Atlanta Child Killer, 162
Atlanta Child Murders, The, 161
attacking behaviour, serial killers, 175
Attenborough, Richard, 58
attorneys, 10, 11, 14, 16, 18, 33, 34, 35, 44, 45, 101, 102, 113, 141, 150, 246, 262, 310, 343, 364, 366, 374, 375, 407
Audacious Crimes of Colonel Blood, The: The Spy Who Stole the Crown Jewels and Became the King's Secret Agent (2015), 212
Aykroyd, Dan, 87
Baby Driver (2017), 411, 420
Baby Driver: What Makes a Good Car Chase?, 421
Baby Face Nelson (1957), 78
Bacall, Lauren, 62, 305, 308
Bacon, Francis, 325
Bacon, Kevin, 324

badge scammers, 276
badger game, 277
Badlands (1973), 80
Bailey, Frankie Y., 20
Bailey, H.C., 140
bait-and-switch, 277
Baker, Stanley, 88, 212
Baldacci, David, 243, 247
Bale, Christian, 162
ballistics, 87, 140, 146, 378
Baltimore City Police Department Academy Report Writing Manual, 116
Bank Crime Statistics, 210
Bank Job, The (2008), 220, 221, 236
Bank of Australia, robbery, 212
Bank of Pennsylvania, robbery, 212
bank robbers, 8, 78, 198, 208
Bara, Theda, 306
Barker, Kate 'Ma', 78
Barker-Karpis Gang, 78
Barrow, Blanche, 80
Barrow, Clyde, 77, 79, 80
Barrymore, Drew, 77
Barrymore, John, 242
Barrymore, Lionel, 242
Basic Instinct (1992), 304
Bass, Jefferson, 141
Bass, Ronald, 243
Bass, William M., 141
BATF, 348
Batman, 320, 321
Batman (1939), 325
Battered Woman Syndrome, 380
Battle of Alcatraz, 290
Baumeister, 186
Bava, Mario, 243
Bazzell, Michael, 394
BBC, 57, 141, 143, 212, 219, 231, 242, 291, 420
Be Your Own Detective (1998), 16
Beatty, Warren, 62, 80
Beckett, Simon, 142
Beckham, David, 337
Bedtime Story (1964), 266
Behavioral Analysis Unit, 161, 165
Behavioral Research and Instruction Unit, 161
Behavioral Science Unit, 160, 161
Behavioural Evidence Analysis, 167, 171, 172
Bell, David, 71
Ben-Hur: A Tale of the Christ (1880), 324
Berg, Karl, 159
Bergman, Johannes Dietrich, 264
Bernie Rhodenbarr, 247
Bertillon, Alphonse, 114
Besson, Luc, 420
Best 10 Music Moments in Famous Car Chase Scenes, Billboard, 420
betrayal, 32, 38, 69, 78, 105, 202, 206, 208, 209, 217, 224, 229, 235, 236, 298, 301, 313, 314, 315, 316, 318, 331, 355, 419
betrayer, 22, 214, 215, 235, 236, 238, 239, 273, 305, 349, 359
Bevel, 409
Beverly Hills Cop, 93, 338
Beyond the Body Farm, 141
Bezzerides, A.I., 62
Big Caper, The (1955), 219
big con, 277
Big Con, The: The Story of the Confidence Man, 261, 280
Big House, The (1930), 289

big score, the, 210, 255
Big Sleep, The, 24, 42, 308
Biggs, Ronnie, 212
Bill Brockton, 141
Bind Torture Kill Strangler, 162
Biography of a Corpse, 141
biometrics, 146, 147
Birdman of Alcatraz, The (1962), 290-291
Birmingham, 57
Black & Yeschke, 366, 375, 376
Black Box (1999), 292
Black Hand, The (1906), 58
Black Lives Matter, 101
Black Maria, 111
Black Mask magazine, 10, 12, 13, 26
Black Mass (2015), 363
Black Mass: The True Story of an Unholy Alliance Between the FBI and the Irish Mob, 363
Black Samurai, The (1976), 332
black widow, 165, 305
Black, Lisa, 142
Blackboard Jungle, 88
Blacklist, The, 363
blackmail, 16, 359
Blackmailers Don't Shoot, 13
Blade Runner (1982), 304
Blaisdell, Anne, 87
Blake, Robert, 336
Blaming the Victim (1971), 380
Bleak House, 11
Blochman, Lawrence G., 140
block hustle, 276
Block, Lawrence, 247
blood splatter, 147, 172
blood stains, 17
Blood, Captain Thomas, 211
blood, drinking, 162
blood, evidence, 17, 146, 408
Bloody Murder, 56
Bloom, 158, 162
Blue Cross, The (1910), 242
Blue Dahlia, The, 303
Blue Velvet (1986), 304
Blues Brothers, The (1980), 336, 414, 420
Blye, Irwin, 12
Blyth, Ann, 305
Bob le Flambeur (1956), 219
Body Farm, the, 141
Body Farm, The - TV series, 144
Body Heat (1981), 304, 317
body language, 44, 141, 368, 369, 377
Body of Proof, 144
bodyguard, 19, 246, 335, 348
Boetticher, Budd, 308
Bogart, Humphrey, 62, 77, 308, 346
Boiler Room, 279
Boland, John, 219
Bomer, Matt, 267
Bond, Dr. Thomas, 159
Bone Collector, The (1997) 141, 190, 191, 192, 194
Bones, TV series, 142, 143
Bonnie and Clyde (1967), 62, 77, 80, 210
Bonnie Parker Story, The (1958), 78, 80
Book of Swindles, The: Selections from a Late Ming Collection, 263
Boone, Daniel, 39
bootlegging, 11, 69, 77, 411
Borde, Raymonde, 303, 304
Border Incident (1949), 87
Boston Strangler, 160, 162, 163

Index 429

Boston Strangler,The, 163
bounty hunting, 15, 18
Bourne Supremacy, The (2004), 420
Brando, Marlon, 266
Brannon, W.T., 265
Bratva, 57
Brave One, The (2007), 320, 324
Breaking In, 252
Breaking Point, The (1961), 219
Breen, Joseph, 63
Breton, Auguste Le, 219
bribery, 101
Brief Introduction to Investigative Interviewing, A, 364
Brighton Rock (1938), 58
Brigid O'Shaughnessy, 23, 25, 31, 305, 306
Brink's, 219
Brink's Job, The (1978), 219
British Psychological Society, 163
bro, 337
bromance, 337
bromantic comedy, 337
Bronson, Charles, 77, 320
Bronswick, Amy L., 174
Brooklyn, 411
Brooklyn Bridge, sale of, 265
Brooks, Pierce, 161
Brosnan, Pierce, 243
brotherhood, 217
Brown, Joe David, 266
Brown, Rowland, 58
Brown, Steven Kerry, 16, 366, 375, 385, 394, 396, 422, 426
Brown, Tom, 264
Brubaker (1980), 292
Bruce Wayne, 320
Brudos, Jerry, 171
Brussel, James, 159, 160, 423, 424
brutality, police, 100
Brute Force (1947), 290
BSU, 160, 161
BTK [Bind Torture Kill] Strangler, 162
Bug in the Martini Olive and Other True Cases from the Files of Hal Lipset, Private Eye, 16
bugging, **390, 392**, 393, *See* surveillance
Bulger, James J. 'Whitey', 363
Bullies, Bastards and Bitches, 307
Bullitt (1968), 212, 220, 411, 420
bunco, 261, 262
Bundy, 186
Bunyan, Paul, 39
Bureau of Alcohol, Tobacco, Firearms and Explosives, 147, 199
Bureau of Alcohol, Tobacco, Firearms, and Explosives, 348
burglar as detective, 250
Burglar in the Closet, 247
Burglars Can't be Choosers (1977), 247
Burglars, The (1971), 411
burglary, 79, 96, 176, 210, 219, 220, 242, 243, 244, 245, 248, 250, 251, 252, 253, 255, 256, 258, 259
Burnett, W.R., 56, 59, 60, 61, 62, 69, 77, 219, 422, 423
Burns, Robert Elliott, 290
Burton, Amanda, 143
Buster (1988), 212
Busting (1974), 336
Butch Cassidy and the Sundance Kid (1969), 80, 336
Butcher, The, 331, 332
Byrne, Richard, 249

Cabinet of Dr. Caligari, The, 304
Caeser, Gene, 12
Cage, Nicholas, 325
Caged (1950), 290
Cagney and Lacey, 335
Cagney, James, 58, 59, 61, 62, 63, 65, 68, 71
Cain, James M., 306
Caine, Michael, 212, 220, 266, 324, 331
Call Mr. Fortune (1920), 140
calling card, 173, 244, 251, 252
Cambridge Companion to Crime Fiction, 27
Campbell, Donna M., 25
Campbell, Ramsey, 162
cannibalism, 162, 176, 410
Cannonball Run, The (1981), 411
Canon's Yeoman's Tale, the, 263
Canter, David, 162, 163, 165, 167, 170, 177, 179, 180, 423
Canterbury Tales, The, 263
canvassing the neighbourhood, 409
capers, 8, 210, 219, 273, 302, 333
Capone, Al, 57, 58, 59, 60, 61, 71
card sharp, 264
Cardinelli, Sam, 59, 61
Carer archetype, 93, 149, 151, 322, 338
Carmilla (1871), 306
Carnegie, Andrew, 71
Carnegie, Dale, 268
Carquake! (1976), 411
Carr, Caleb, 142
Carradine, David, 290, 411
Carrey, Jim, 265
Carter, Asa Earl, 324
Carter, Forrest, 324
Carvajal, Nelson, 421
Carved in Bone (2006), 141
Casablanca, 308, 346
case files, 116, 171
caseload, 45
Caspar Gutman, 30, 31, 317
Cassidy, Butch, 213
Castellammarese War, 56
cat and mouse plot structure, 234, 243, 250, 251, 329
cat burglars, 8, 216, 242, 243, 246
Catch Me If You Can, 265, 266, 270, 278, 424
Caught on Camera, 114
Cawelti, John G., 20, 24, 32, 39, 65, 66, 70, 71, 74, 75, 331, 332, 333, 422, 425
CCTV, 19, 114, 115, 122, 125, 126, 183
Céline and Julie Go Boating, 336
Céline et Julie vont en bateau (1974), 336
chain of custody, evidence, 18
Chaloner, William, 264
Chandler, Raymond, 10, 11, 13, 20, 24, 25, 26, 27, 28, 33, 34
Chandlerisms, 11, 28
Chappell, Holly, 264
Character Creation (2018), 36, 64, 93, 269, 338, 339, 366
character development, 8, 96, 133, 339, 340
Characters, 8
Charlie Chan, 83
Charlie Resnick, 88
Charrière, Henri, 291
Charteris, Leslie, 246
chase, 7
Chase, James Hadley, 10
Chastain, Thomas, 42
Chaucer, Geoffrey, 263, 268
Chaumeton, Etienne, 303, 304

Chemistry of Death, The (2006), 142
Chen, David, 71
Chesterton, G.K., 242
chiaroscuro, 304
Chibnall, Chris, 212
Chicago, 11, 56, 57, 58, 59, 60, 61, 68, 72, 78, 425
Chief Inspector's Statement, The (1951), 87
child abductions, 398
child custody investigations, 15
Chinatown (1974), 304
Chiodo, Dan, 199
chivalric code, 23, **24**, 35
chivalry. *See* chivalric code
Choirboys, The (1975), 88
Christie, Agatha, 7, 10, 162, 212, 424
Christie, Richard, 269
CIA, 378
Circe, 305
citizen's arrest, private detectives, 18
City Bank of New York, robbery, 212
City on Fire (1987), 203
Clarice Starling, 189, 191
Clarke, Alan, 291
Clarke, Mae, 68
classic murder mysteries, 10
classical murder mystery, 28, 31, 33, 41, 85
Clean Break (1955), 219
Clement, Dick, 220
Cleopatra (1917), 306
clichés, 22, 41, 90, 96, 108, 122, 150, 288, 290, 295, 296, 379, 384, 416
clues, 17, 20, 42, 43, 86, 92, 106, 123, 124, 129, 132, 133, 136, 140, 153, 162, 164, 170, 178, 179, 180, 182-185, 188, 191, 193, 195, 196, 299, 343, 357, 370, 397, 401
Clues for Dr. Coffee (1964), 140
Clytemnestra, 305
Code of Practice on Police use of Firearms and Less Lethal Weapons, 111
code, the criminal, 216
Cody Jarrett, 63, 68
cold case, 395
Cold Case, TV series, 143
cold cases, 14, 34, 85, 123, 139, 143, 181, 354, 410
Cold Moon, The (2006), 141
College of Policing, UK, 98, 111, 115, 365, 366
Collins, Phil, 212
Collins, Wilkie, 84
Colonel Blood (1934), 211
Color of Money, The, 277
commitment, 36, 46, 89, 123, 192, 225, 253, 254, 255, 257, 281, 286, 287, 307
communications, police, 112
Complete Idiot's Guide to Private Investigating (2013), 16, 394, 426
computer forensics, 147
computer hacking, 147, **392**
Con Man: A Master Swindler's Own Story, 265
confessions, 373
Confessions of a Confidence Man (1920), 280
Confessions of a Master Jewel Thief (2004), 249
confidant, 32
Confidence (2003), 267, 285, 286, 288
Confidence Game, The (2016), 267, 269, 281
confidence man, 261, 264
confidence tricks, 210, 222, 246, 250, 261, 262, 266, 267,

269, 271, 272, 274, 277, 279, 280, 284, 285, 286, 287
confidence tricksters, 8, 262, 263, 264, 266, 267, 269, 279, 283
Confidence-Man, The: His Masquerade (1857), 264
Confidential Human Source Program, FBI, 350
confidential informant, 350, 352
confidentiality, 115
Connery, Sean, 212, 243
conscience, motivation, 353
conspiracy, 13, 22, 29-34, 41-43, 47, 49-54, 98, 105, 149, 150, 151, 156, 157, 215, 221, 222, 224, 236, 237, 238, 243, 247, 250, 274, 293, 297-299, 301, 302, 320, 344, 345
contamination of evidence, 406
Conti, Michael E., 111
Continental Op, 12
Contract on Cherry Street, 383
Convoy (1978), 411
Cook, Jr., Elisha, 30
Cool Hand Luke (1967), 291, 292
Cooper, James Fenimore, 40
Cop Hater (1956), 88, 135
Copperfield, David, 277
Cormack, Bartlett, 58
Corman, Roger, 77
Cornwell, Patricia, 141, 152
coroner, 141, 143, 403, 404, 405, 406, 408
corpus delicti, 406
Corridor Crew, 421
corruption, 20, 22, 24, 28, 30, 32, 34, 35, 36, 37, 39, 100, 101, 105, 200, 278, 293, 308, 325, 333
corruption, police, 100
Corvasce, 410, 426
Cosmic View of the Private Eye, A, 25
Coster-Waldau, Nikolaj, 250
Council of Europe, 364
Count of Monte Cristo, The, 324
Counter Terrorism Command, 199
counterfeiting, 264
counter-surveillance, 16, **393**
country house, 20, 84
couple on the run, 420
court appearances, 19, 118
covert policing, 199
Cox, Gary, 23
cozy mysteries, 7, 20, 29
Craig Kennedy, 140
Crais, Robert, 21
Crane, Stephen, 28
Crawford, Broderick, 203
Creasey, John, 87, 88, 89
Crichton, Robert, 265, 266
Crime as an American Way of Life, 71
Crime Classification Manual: A Standard System for Investigating and Classifying Violent Crimes (1992), 116, 161, 168
crime scene, 403
Crime Scene Investigation, 163, 423
crime scene photographs, 407
criminal enterprises, 149, 351
Criminal Interrogation & Confessions, 365
Criminal Investigation: A Practical Handbook (1906), 159
Criminal Investigative Analysis, 161, 167, 169
Criminal Minds, 161
criminal profile, 167
criminal profiling, 158, 159, 163, 172

Criminal Psychology: A Manual for Judges, Practitioners, and Students (1911), 159
criminologists, 94
Criss Cross, 303
Crockett, Davy, 39
crook-versus-cop, 210
crook-versus-crook, 210
Crosby, Bing, 336
Crossing Jordan, 144
Crowe, Cameron, 200
Cruel Gun Story (1964), 220
Cruise, Tom, 213
Cruising (1980), 203
Crusader, character archetype, 35, 36, 37, 38, 39, 40, 93, 322, 338
CSI, 17, 144, 163, 407
CSI effect, 143
CSI: Crime Scene Investigation, 143
CSI: Cyber, 143
CSI: Miami, 143
CSI: NY, 143
Cummins, Peggy, 77
cunning, 179, 269, 270, 304
Curtis, Tony, 219, 265, 266, 336
Cutter, John, 332
Cutting Edge: Confessions of an Undercover Cop, 199
cyber forensics, 147
cynicism, 36, 97, 203, 367
d'Antoni, Philip, 411
Dahmer, 186
Daji, 306
Dalton Gang, 77
Daly, Carroll John, 12, 26
Dalziel and Pascoe, 84, 335
Damico, James, 303, **425**
Damon, Matt, 363
Danger: Diabolik (1962), 243
Daniel, Frank, 8
Danny Ocean, 213
Darabont, Frank, 292
Daring Daylight Burglary, A (1903), 242
Dark Passage, 308
darkest hour, 51, 128, 189, 196, 197, 203, 229, 301, 315, 345
Darwin, Charles, 158
Dassin, Jules, 220
Data Protection Act (1988), 115, 117
Davis, Bette, 305
Davis, Volney, 79
Day of the Jackal, The, 118
De Niro, Robert, 79, 220, 231, 234, 278, 338, 341, 342
DEA, 348, 352
Deadly is the Female, 77
deadshrinker, 142
Deaf Man, The, 135
death certificate, 404, 406
Death in the President's Lodging, 84
Death of Jack Hamilton, The, 79
Death Proof (2007), 411
Death Sentence (1975), 324
Death Warrant (1990), 203, 293
Death Wish (1974), 320, 324, 325, 333
death, pronouncing, 404
Death's Acre: Inside the Legendary Forensic Lab, the Body Farm, Where the Dead Do Tell Tales (2004), 141
Deaver, Jeffery, 141, 190
Deborah Knott, 40
debt collection, 16
debugging. *See* counter-surveillance
DeBurger, James, 162
deception, 323, **376**, 377, 423, 424

Decoy Man: The Extraordinary Adventures of an Undercover Cop (1973), 199
deductive and inductive reasoning, 167
Deep Cover (1992), 202, 203, 205-209
Deerslayer, 13
defamation, 19
Defiant Ones, The (1958), 336, 338
deification of victims, 188, 189
Déjà Dead (1997), 142
Delany, Dana, 144
Delilah, 306
Demara Jr., Ferdinand Waldo, 265
Demara, Ferdinand Waldo, 266
democracy, 327
Dempsey, John S., 15
Denton, William, 29
Departed, The (2006), 203, 363
Department of Justice, 113
depositions, 19
Depp, Johnny, 363
Depression-Era Outlaws, List of (*Wikipedia*), 77
Derby, 57
Dern, Bruce, 420
Derry, Charles, 303
Derry, Paul, 353, 354, 356, 357, 358, 425
DeSalvo, 186
Desperate Housewives, 137
Desperately Seeking Susan (1985), 336
destroyer, archetype, 308
Destroyer, The, 331
Detective (1997), 118
Detective Story (1951), 87
Detective Story Magazine, 140
determinism, 26
deus ex machina, 85, 417
DeVito, Danny, 220
Devol, George, 264
Dexter, Colin, 84
Diabolik, 243
Diagnosis: Homicide (1950), 140
dialogue, 13, 22, 26, 27, 60, 121, 177, 219, 220, 231, 245, 247, 251, 255, 341, 364, 418
DiCaprio, Leonardo, 265, 266
Dick Barton - Special Agent, 420
Dickens, Charles, 11, 265
diddler, 264, 267
Diddler, The (1868), 264
Diddling Considered as One of the Exact Sciences, 264
Diesel, Vin, 205, 279
Dietz, Park Elliot, 381
Digital Forensic Art Techniques: A Professional's Guide to Corel Painter (2018), 114
digital forensics, 147
digital imaging, 115, 423
Dillinger (1973), 78, 79
Dillinger, John, 62, 78, 79
Dinneen, Joseph F., 219
Dirty Harry (1971), 320, 325
Dirty Mary, Crazy Larry (1974), 80, 412
Dirty Rotten Scoundrels (1988), 266
Dirty Secrets Club, The (2008), 142
disaster movies, 118
disguise, 124, 130, 198, 238, 242, 265, 388, 414
disorganized killer, 168
divorce investigations, 15
DNA, evidence, 17, 87, 109, 117, 144, 170, 175, 181, 193, 378, 408
Doc Savage, 331

documentary evidence, 17, 50, 364
Dodge, David, 243, 247
Dog Pound (2010), 291
Doherty, Paul, 212
Don Corleone, 31
Don Vito Corleone, 331
Donnie Brasco (1997), 201, 203, 205
Donnie Brasco: My Undercover Life in the Mafia (1988), 201
Doorway to Hell, The (1930), 58
Dortmunder, 219
double agent, informant, 355
Double Eagle, The, 250
Double Indemnity (1944), 303, 305, 306, 307, 312, 314
Douglas, John, 66, 160, 161, 164, 423, 426
Douglas, Kirk, 87
Dove, George N., 83, 84, 85, 89, 92, 94, 95, 98, 100, 102, 106, 119, 349, 359, 379, 423
Doyle, Arthur Conan, 11, 140
Dracula (1897), 306
Dracula (1931), 58
Dragnet, 87
Dramas of Paris, The, 242
Drames de Paris, Les (1857), 242
Dreiser, Theodore, 10, 28
Drew, Bernard A., 40
Drive (2011), 412, 420
Driven (2012), 412
Driver, The (1978), 412, 420
Drug Enforcement Administration, 112, 348, 363
Du Rififi Chez les Hommes, 219
Duchovny, David, 137
due process, 361
Duel (1971), 416
Dukes of Hazzard, The, 411
Dukes of Hazzard: Gone Racin', 412
Dumas, Alexandre, 324
Dunaway, Faye, 62, 80, 243
Dupin, C. Auguste, 11, 140
Duris, Romain, 242
dying declaration, 406
Eastwood, Clint, 247, 320
Easy Rawlins, 13
Ebert, Roger, 333, 338, 425
Edwards, Blake, 243
Edwards, Buster, 212
effeminacy, 337
Egan, Lesley, 87, 134
Egger, Steve, 162
Eichenwald, Kurt, 363
Eiffel Tower, sale of, 265
Ekman, Paul, 377
electronic surveillance, 16, **390**
Elise, Kimberly, 221
Ellen, Barbara, 337
Ellis, Brett Easton, 162
Ellroy, James, 13
Elopement à la Mode. See Runaway Match (1903)
Elvis Cole, 21
embezzlement, 148
Emergency Room, 403
emotion versus logic, **283**
endangered species, 149
Engel, Lyle Kenyon, 332
English country house, 7
Enkidu, 335
entrapment, 52, 117, 289, 361
Entrapment (1999), 243, 251
environmental crime, 149
envy/jealousy, motivation, 354
Epic of Gilgamesh, The, 335
Equalizer, The (1985), 333
Ericson, John, 79
Escobedo v. Illinois in 1964, 118
espionage, 42, 198, *See also* spies

Ethan Hunt, 213
ethics of policing, 98
Euripides, 324
evaluating witnesses, 379
Evanovich, Janet, 15
Evans, Rob, 199
Eve Duncan, 142
evidence, **16**, 18
Executioner, The, 325
existentialism, 22, 23, 24
Experiment, The (2010), 292
expert thriller, 83, 139, 148
Expert, The, 141, 143
exploitation thriller, 324
explosions, 59, 149, 231
exposure to risk, 185
exposure to risk, victims, 185, 187
Exterminator, The (1980), 332
extortion, 101
Eyewitness Evidence: A Guide for Law Enforcement (1999), 113
eyewitnesses, 113, 114, 115, 380, 423
Face Finder, The, 141
Face of Deception, The (1998), 142
Face That Must Die, The, 162
facial composites, 113
facial recognition, 147
Fairbanks Jr., Douglas, 66
Fairy Queen, The, 25
faith healers, 272
Fallis, Greg, 16
false allegations of crime, 381
false arrest, 18
False Burton Combs, The, 12
false confessions, 374
false witnesses, 380
Fandor, 421
Fantômas, 242
Fantômas (1911), 242
Fantômas (1964), 242
Fantômas contre Scotland Yard (1967, *Fantômas Against Scotland Yard*), 242
Fantômas se Déchaîne (1965, *Fantômas Unleashed*), 242
Farewell My Lovely, 28
Faron, Fay, 16, 269, 275, 394, 424, 426
Fast and the Furious series, 420
Fast and the Furious, The (2001), 203, 205, 206, 207, 208, 209, 221, 420
Fast Times at Ridgemont High (1981), 200
Father Brown, 242
fears, character, 37
Federal Aviation Administration Aircraft Registry, 112
Federal Bureau of Investigation, 199, 362, 363, 365, 423
Federal Communications Commission, 262
Federal Trade Commission, 262
Felix Ungar, 336
femme fatale, 22, 30, 31, **32**, 43, 48, 49, 50, 54, 55, 67, 77, 128, 214, 230, 290, 303, 304, 305, 306, 307, 308, 309, 310, 311, 312, 313, 314, 315, 316, 317, 318
Ferguson, Claire, 179
Ferrer, Miguel, 109, 137
fibres, evidence, 17, 123, 145, 163, 175, 181, 193, 408
Field, Charles Frederick, 11
Fields, W.C., 266
Fierro, Marcella Farinelli, 141
Fifth and Sixth Amendments to the US Constitution, 117
Fight for Right, The (1913), 289

Index

film noir, 8, 11, 87, 303, 304, 305, 307, 308, 309
find the lady, 276
Finder, Marilyn Greene, 12
Findley, Ferguson, 203
Finger Points, The (1931), 61
fingerprints, 17, 117, 146, 147, 153, 163, 170, 181, 193, 244, 378, 408
Fiorentino, Linda, 304
firearms, 18, **20**, 354
First Blood, 109
First Great Train Robbery, The (2011), 212
First World War, 7, 12, 57, 65
Fischer, Robert J., 15
Fitzgerald, 350, 354, 360
Fitzgerald, F. Scott, 66
Five Little Pigs (1942), 139
Flambeau, 242
Fleischer, Richard, 219
Fleming, Ian, 412, 417
Flight Characteristic and Stain Patterns of Human Blood (1971), 147
Florida, 62
Floyd, Charles 'Pretty Boy', 79
Fonda, Peter, 412
footprints, 17, 408
Ford Mustang GT, 411
Ford, Harrison, 147, 381
forensic accountancy, 148
forensic anthropology, 141, 142, 143, 145
forensic art, 114, 115, 147, 423
Forensic Art and Illustration (2000), 114
forensic ballistics, 146
forensic biology, 144
forensic chemistry, 145
forensic dentistry, 141
forensic entomology, 146
forensic investigator, 142
forensic linguistics, 148
forensic odontology, 145
forensic pathology, 405
forensic psychiatry, 142
forensic psychology, 109, 144, 148, 158, 162, 193
forensic sculpture, 142, 147
forensic taphonomy, 146
Forensic Thriller, 139
forensic toxicology, 144
Forensics: The Anatomy of Crime (2014), 139, 140
forgery, 148
Forsyth, Bill, 221
Forsyth, Frederick, 118
Fortune and Men's Eyes (1971), 291
Foster, Jodie, 220, 320, 324
Four Quarters Plus Midpoint, 43
Fourth Amendment to the U.S. Constitution, 19
Fox, James Alan, 162
Fox, Vivica A., 221
frame-ups, 101
Francesca Wilson, 40
Frank McCloud, 62
Frank, Nino, 303
Franklin, Benjamin, 71
fraud, **148**, 262, 278, 279
fraud investigation, 15, 148, 165, 261, 262, 272, 277, 279, 356, 359
Frechette, Evelyn 'Billie', 78
Freebie and the Bean (1974), 336, 411
Freeman, Morgan, 292
Freeman, R. Austin, 140
French Connection, The (1971), 383, 411, 420
Freud, Sigmund, 63, 163, 378
Frey, Charles Weiser, 203
Fried Green Tomatoes (1991), 336
Friedkin, William, 203, 219, 420

Friends of Eddie Coyle, The (1973), 220
Front Page Detective: William J. Burns and the Detective Profession, 1880-1930, 12
Fry, Stephen, 324
Fugitive, The (1993), 147, 289, 294, 412
funeral scams, 277
G Men (1935), 61
Gaboriau, Emile, 84, 87, 111
Gacy, 186
Gaddis, Thomas E., 290
Gallimard, 11, 219
gallows humour, 71, 97, 152
gamblers, 272
Game of Thrones, 250
Gang: A Study of 1,313 Gangs in Chicago, 59
Gangs of New York (2002), 56
Gangs of New York: An Informal History of the Underworld, The (1927), 56
Gangster as Tragic Hero, The, 69
gangster's mother, 68
gangsterism, 11, 20, 59, 67
Garcia, Eric, 266
Gardiner, Meg, 142, 412, 426
Gardner, 409
Gardner, Ava, 305
Gardner, Erle Stanley, 13, 16, 43
Garfield, Brian, 324
Garland, Judy, 58
Garner, Jennifer, 325
GDPR, 115
Geis, Florence L., 269
General Data Protection Regulations, 18, 115
genre conventions, 8, 11, 20, 84, 89, 149, 213, 243
Genre Writer series, 4, 7, 8, 94
gentleman burglar, 242, 245
Gentleman Thief, The (2001), 242
Gentleman Thief: The Recollections of a Cat Burglar (1995), 249
geographical profiling, serial killers, 172, 423
George Gideon, 87
Gerasimov, Mikhail, 140
German Expressionism, 304
Gerritsen, Tess, 142
Get Carter (1971), 331
Getaway Man, The (2003), 412
Ghost: My Thirty Years as an FBI Undercover Agent (2018), 199
Gideon of Scotland Yard, 88, 89
Gideon's Day (1955), 88, 89, 103, 135
Gilbert and Sullivan, 12
Gilbert, Michael, 12, 60, 86, 89, 95, 423
Gilda (1946), 305, 306
Gilgamesh, 335
gimmick, 59, 122
Giordano, Mario, 292
Gish, Lillian, 58
Giussani, Angela, 243
Giussani, Luciana, 243
Gladiator (2000), 324
Glass Key, The, 26
Go Down Together: The True, Untold Story of Bonnie and Clyde, The
God Bless America (2011), 324
Godard, Jean Luc, 219
Godfather, The, 31, 56, 72, **74**, 75, 76, 331
Goffman, Erving, 368
Goldberg, Lee, 412
Goldberg, Whoopi, 247
Goldblum, Jeff, 205

golden age murder mystery, 10
golden fleece, the, 211, 223
Goldman, William, 247
Goldthwait, Bobcat, 324
Gondorf, Charley, 265, 266
Gondorf, Fred, 265, 266
good cop/bad cop routine, 379
Good Detective, The, 16
Good Samaritan, 272
Good Thief, The (2002), 219
GoodFellas (1990), 65, 72
Google Maps, 415
Goring, Marius, 143
Gorky Park, 141
Gosling, Ryan, 412
Gothic, 13, 140, 306
Gould, Elliott, 336
GPS, 183, 184, 390, 415
Grafton, Sue, 13, 40
Grant, Cary, 243
Grapes of Wrath, The, 79
Gray Seal, The, 246
Great Armored Car Swindle, The, 219
Great Crown Jewels Robbery of 1303, The (2005), 212
Great Depression, 13, 20, 39, 57, 65, 68, 279, 289, 305
Great Detective, 12, 84, 86, 95, 99
Great Detective Stories, Allan Pinkerton, 12
Great Escape, The, 289
Great Gatsby, The, 66
Great Impostor, The (1959), 265, 270
Great Impostor, The (1961), 266
Great Train Robbery, The (1903), 210, 212, 213
Great Train Robbery, The (1941), 213
Great Train Robbery, The (1975), 212
Greek mythology, 305, 306
Green, Robson, 142
Greenberg, Ruth, 16
Greene, Graham, 58, 242
Greene, Marilyn, 12
Greenmask! (1964), 87
Greenstreet, Sidney, 30
Grella, George, 13
Griffith, D.W., 58
grifters and grifting, 261, 270
Grifters, The (1990), 266
grindhouse, 324
Grodin, Charles, 338
Groff, Jonathan, 161
Gross, Hans, 159, 423
Grossman, Julie, 307
Gruenfeld, Lee, 249
Guide to the Identification of Human Skeletal Material (1939), 145
Guinn, Jeff, 80
Gulino, Paul, 9
Gumball Rally, The (1976), 411
Gumshoe: Reflections in a Private Eye, 12
Gun Crazy (1950), 77
Guncrazy (1992), 77
gunsel, 30
Guttapercha Gang, 57
Hackers (1995), 393
Hackman, Gene, 220, 392, 411
Hail, Hail, the Gang's All Here!, 103
Hailey, Arthur, 118
Halpenny, Bruce Barrymore, 212
Hamilton, Ian, 148
Hammett, Dashiell, 7, 10, 12, 13, 23, 25, 26, 27, 30, 304, 422
Hamlet, 323, 324

handkerchief switch, 276
handler, 204, 349, 350, 351, 352, 353, 354, 355, 356, 357, 358, 359, 360, 361, 362, 378
handler, of an informant, 355, 356
Hanks, Tom, 87, 266
Hanrahan, David C., 212
Hard Eight (1996), 219
Hardboiled Dames: Stories Featuring Women Detectives, Reporters, Adventurers, and Criminals from the Pulp Fiction Magazine of the 1930s, 40
Hardboiled Detective Plot Template, 44
hardboiled dick, 10
Hardboiled: An Anthology of American Crime Stories, 20
Hardy, Tom, 58
Harlow, Jean, 68
Harris, Thomas, 161, 162, 188, 190, 192
Harrison, Harry, 249
Harry Brown (2009), 324
Harvey, John, 88
Hathaway, Anne, 266
Havers, Nigel, 242
Hawkeye, 13
Hayden, Sterling, 219
Hays Code, 63
Hays, Will H., 63
Hayworth, Rita, 292, 305, 306
Hazelwood, Roy, 381
He Walked by Night (1948), 87
Headhunters (2011), 250
Healy, Ian, 417, 427
Heat (1995), 210, 220, 221, 231, 232, 233, 234, 235, 251
Heat, The (2013), 336
Heath, William L., 219
Hecht, Ben, 58, 61
Heilbrun, Carolyn G., 40
heirs. *See* missing person investigation
Heist (2001), 220, 221
heists, 94, 118, 120, 136, 210, 211, 213, 214, 215, 216, 217, 218, 219, 220, 221, 222, 223, 224, 225, 226, 227, 228, 229, 231, 232, 233, 234, 235, 236, 237, 238, 240, 243, 244, 245, 250, 257, 293, 302, 333
Hell is a City (1954), 88
Hemingway, Ernest, 10, 27, 305
henchman, 30, 43, 49, 50, 54, 215, 220, 260, 271, 292, 295, 339, 341, 343, 344, 345, 346
henchmen, 22, 29, 48, 91, 229, 240, 338, 339, 340, 342, 343, 344, 345, 346
Hennessy, Jill, 144
Henry: Portrait of a Serial Killer, 162
Herbert, John, 291
Hercule Poirot, 7, 10, 83, 139, 162
Hickey, 27, 161, 162, 165, 168, 174, 181, 186, 423, 424
Hickman, Bill, 411
hierarchy, police force, 65, 98, 103, 104, 108, 150, 205, 291
Higgins, George V., 220
High Sierra (1941), 60, 62, 77
High Window, The, 24, 34
Hill Street Blues, 88, 335
Hill, Reginald, 84
Hines, David Thoedosius, 264
Hitchcock, Alfred, 7, 243, 414, 425
Hitman's Bodyguard, The, 335
Hoffman, Dustin, 267, 292
Hohimer, Frank, 220
Hollywood Genres, 22, 61
HOLMES 2, 407
Holmes, Ronald, 162
Holt, Patricia, 16

Homant, 164, 424
Home Invaders, The: Confessions of a Cat Burglar, 220
Home Office, UK government, 19, 111, 141, 143, 365, 407
Homeland Security, 112
homicide investigation, **406**
Homicide: Life on the Street, 88
Homme Criminel: Atlas, L', 158
homophobia, 31
homosexuality, 30, 31, 67, 185, 186, 226, 292
honey pot, 52
Honor System, The (1917), 289
Hoover, J. Edgar, 62, 78
Hope, Bob, 266, 336
Hornung, E.W., 242
Horsley, Lee, 56, 64, 66, 307, 425
hostages, 400
Hot Rock, The (1970), 219
Hotel (1965), 118
House of Games (1987), 266
House on 92nd Street, The (1945), 203
Houston, John, 12
Houts, Marshall, 143
How to be an Existentialist, 23
How to Win Friends and Influence People, 268
How to Write Killer Fiction, 29
Howard, Clark, 290
Howdunit Series, 110
Huckleberry Finn, 40
Human Rights Act (1998), 115
Human Skeleton in Forensic Medicine, The (1962), 146
Hunebelle, Andre, 242
Hunt, William R., 12
Hunter, Evan, 88
Hunting Humans (1986), 162
Hurt, John, 296
hustle, 261, 272, 276
Hustle, The (2019), 266
Hustle, TV series, 267
Hustler, The, 277
hustling, 276
Huston, John, 62, 219
Hutchinson, Robert, 212
Hutton, Timothy, 267
Hyams, Joe, 292
Hyams, Peter, 336
hypnosis, 378, 379
I Am a Fugitive from a Chain Gang (1932), 290
I Am a Fugitive from a Georgia Chain Gang!, 290
I Died a Thousand Times (1955), 77
I Have Lived in the Monster (1998), 161
I Love You Phillip Morris (2009), 265
I Love You Phillip Morris: A True Story of Life, Love, and Prison Breaks, 265
I Spit on Your Grave (1978), 324
I Was a Karpis-Barker Gang Moll, 79
I, Spy: How to Be Your Own Private Investigator (2016), 16
I, the Jury, 33
ICE, 348
Iconography, 8, 22, 69, 151, 216, 244, 274, 320
idealism, 97
Identifying the Culprit: Assessing Eyewitness Identification (2014), 380
Identikit, 113
identity, 202
identity parades, 113
Ides of March, The (1898), 242

Immigration and Customs Enforcement, 112, 348
impasse, 51
impossible mission, 213
imposters, 243, 261, 265, 266, 270, 278
improvisation, 204, 207, 211, 214, 248, 270, 295, 300, 330, 357
in medias res, 232
In the Heat of the Night, 338
Incredible Detective: The Biography of William J. Burns, 12
Independent Office for Police Conduct, 101, 102
individuation, 175, 193
inductive and deductive reasoning, 167
industrial pollution, 149
Industrial Revolution, 57
industrialization, 57
Infernal Affairs (2002), 203
informant, 97, **358**
Informant!, The (2009), 363
Informant, The: A True Story (2000), 363
informants, 348
informants, ethical issues, 361
Information Commissioner's Office, 115
informers, See informants
ingenuity, 52, 270, 361, 413
injustice, 13, 36, 37, 292, 320, 333
Innes, Michael, 84
inquest, 126, 312, 404, 405
inquiry agent, 10, 12
inside man, 212, 270, 278
Inside Man (2006), 215, 218, 220
insider, confidence man, 270
Inspector Bucket, 11
Inspector Clouseau, 243
Inspector Morse, 84, 335
Inspector West Takes Charge (1942), 88
insurance, 15, 16, 52, 106, 148, 165, 184, 209, 243, 245, 251, 261, 262, 272, 306, 310, 311, 312, 313, 314, 315, 366
insurance investigations, 15, 262, 279
Integrated Ballistics Identification System, 117
internal affairs, 102
Internal Revenue Service, 348, 363
International Association of Bloodstain Pattern Analysis, 147
International Association of Identification, 146
interrogation, 364
interviewing, 7, 9, 16, 44, 46, 51, 96, 109, 114, 232, 364, 365, 370, 379, 381, 397, 425
interviewing neighbours, **401**
interviewing witnesses & victims, **379**
Intolerance (1916), 289
Introduction to Private Security (2011), 15
Introduction to Security (2012), 15
inverted mystery story, 7
investigating a runaway, 396
Investigating Missing Children Cases: A Guide for First Responders and Investigators, 402
investigative interviewing, 364
Investigative Interviewing: A Guide to Interviewing, 365
Investigative Interviewing: The Interviewer's Rule Book, 365

Investigative Psychology, 167, 170, 423
IOPC, 101, 102
Ireland, Colin, 164
irony, 22, 26, 28, 71, 75, 86, 97, 209, 230, 231, 292, 316, 317, 319, 325, 330
IRS, 279, 348
Isabella Stewart Gardner Museum, robbery, 250
Italian Job, The (1969), 220, 411
Ivor Maddox, 87
Izzard, Eddie, 412
Jack Reacher (2012), 420
Jack the Ripper, 159, 323
Jack's Return Home (1969), 331
jailhouse informants, 351, 354
James 'Slippery Jim' diGriz, 249
James Bond, 31, 91, 149, 198, 242, 246, 332, 333, 354, 412
James, Jesse, 11
James, P.D., 40, 84
Jason and the Argonauts, 211, 305
Jason, Stuart, 332
Jay J. Armes, Investigator, 12
Jazz Singer, The (1927), 63
jealousy/envy, motivation, 354
Jefferson, Jon, 141
Jekyll and Hyde, 162
jeopardy, 7
Jeremy Diddler, 264
jewel thief, 79, 242, 243
Jezebel, 306
Jimmie Dale, 246
Jimmie Dale Alias the Gray Seal (1917), 246
Joel Cairo, 30, 31
Johansen, Iris, 142
Johnny Rocco, 62
Jones & Partners, 269, 270
Jones, William 'Canada Bill', 264
Jordan, Neil, 219
Joubert, John, 161, 163
Judges' Rules, 95, 117
Juliette, or Vice Amply Rewarded (1801), 306
Julius Caesar, 69
June, Dale L., 200
Jung, Doug, 267
justice, 13, 14, 21, 22, 24, 33, 34, 35, 37, 49, 50, 52, 56, 97, 99, 100, 107, 119, 122, 129, 139, 151, 170, 191, 202, 209, 231, 262, 274, 285, 302, 316, 319, 320, 321, 322, 325, 326, 327, 328, 330, 332, 333, 342
Justice is Served (1994), 161
kaitō, 243
Kaitō Tantei Yamaneko (2006), 243
Kalifornia (1993), 80
Kaminaga, Manabu, 243
Kantor, MacKinlay, 77
Karpis, Alvin 'Creepy', 78
Karpis-Barker Gang, 79
Kasdan, Lawrence, 304
Kate Martinelli, 40
Kate Miskin, 40
Kathryn Dance, 141
Katō, Kazuhiko, 243
Kava, Alex, 164
Keating, H.R.F., 25, 44, 86, 88, 91, 95, 134, 422, 423
Keats, John, 306
Kelly, George 'Machine Gun', 77, 78
Kelly, Grace, 243
Kelly's Heroes (1970), 220
Kemper, 186
Kennedy, 164
Kennedy, George, 291
Kennedy, Mark, 199
Kenney, James, 264
Kesey, Ken, 291
Key Largo (1948), 62, 308

Keyes, Israel, 164
KGB, 331, 378
kickbacks, 272, 278, 358
kidnapping. See missing person investigation
Kierkegaard, Søren, 23
Kill Bill, 324, 328
Kill Quick or Die (1971), 332
Killer Inside Me, The (1952), 162
Killer Reads, 142
Killers Among Us (2001), 162
Killers, The (1946), 303, 305, 306
Killing Game, The, 142
Killing, The (1956), 219
Kilmer, Val, 290
Kinesic Interrogation - The FBI Method of interviewing, **365**, 377
King Arthur, 306
King Zhou of Shang, 306
King, Laurie R., 40
King, Rodney, 101
King, Stephen, 79, 137, 292
Kingsley, Ben, 220
Kingsley, Sidney, 87
Kinsey Millhone, 13, 40
Kipling, Rudyard, 306
Kittredge & Krauzer, 332
Klugman, Jack, 143
Knight Rider (1982), 333
Knight, Bernard, 141
knight, medieval / chivalrous, 23, 24, 25, 29, 40, 91, 141, 306, 309, 336
Knox, Ronald, 85
Konnikova, Maria, 267, 269, 280, 424
Koontz, Dean, 412
Kotto, Yaphet, 339
Kraft, 186
Kray Twins, Ronnie and Reggie, 58
Kray, Ronnie, 58, 67
Kriminal-Psychologie (1898), 159
Kristofferson, Kris, 411
Krogman, Wilton M., 145
Kubrick, Stanley, 219, 278
Kuhlmann, Susan, 263, 268
Kunsthalle Schirn, robbery, 250
Kurosawa, Akira, 87, 336
Kürten, Peter, 159
Kyd, Thomas, 324
L.A. Takedown (1989), 220, 231
La Frenais, Ian, 220
La Plante, Lynda, 221
laddism, 337
ladette, 337
Lady from Shanghai, The, 32, 303, 304
Lamm, 'Baron' Herman, 78
Lancaster, Burt, 250, 290
Lane, Priscilla, 62
Lang, Fritz, 159
LAPD, 87, 88
Lardner, Ring, 10, 27
Larsen E. Whipsnade, 266
Las Vegas, 218
Las Vegas, TV series, 144
Last Bandit, The (1949), 213
Last Seduction, The (1994), 304
Last Seen Wearing... (1952), 87
Latifah, Queen, 277
Latin lotto, 276
Lau, Andrew, 203
Laurel and Hardy, 335
Law & Order, 88
Law Enforcement Techniques, 109
Law, Guidance and Training Governing Police Pursuits: Current Position and Proposals for Change (2018), 112

Index 433

Law, John Phillip, 243
lawyer. *See* attorney
Lazlo Kreizler, 143
Le Fanu, Sheridan, 141, 306
League of Gentlemen, The (1960), 211, 219, 222, 224
Leatherstocking, 13
Leblanc, Maurice, 242, 243
Lecoq, 84, 87, 111
Lee, Spike, 220
Legal Thriller, 7, 83, 105, 118
Legend (2015), 58
Legion of Decency, 63
Lehr, Dick, 363
Lemmon, Jack, 336
Lemon Drop Kid, The (1951), 266
Lethal Weapon, 335, 340, 341, 343, 344, 345, 346
Levenson, Thomas, 264
Leverage, TV series, 267
Levin, Jack, 162
Lew Archer, 13
Lewis, Jerry, 335
Lewis, M.G., 306
Lewis, Paul, 199
Lewis, Ted, 331
Leyton, Elliot, 162
licensing, private detectives, 14, 18, 19
lie detectors, 378
Life, Adventures and Opinions of Dr. David Theo. Hines of South Carolina, 264
Light of Day, The (1962), 220
Lights of New York (1928), 58, 63
Lilith, 306
Lincoln Rhyme, 141, 192
Lincoln, Abraham, 11
line-ups, 113
lingo, 274
Linington, Elizabeth, 87, 98, 134
linking crimes, 181
Lippmann, Walter, 306
Lipscomb, W.P., 211
Little Caesar, 56, 59, 60, 61, 65, 66, 67, 69, 70, 72, 217, 422, 423
Liverpool, 57
location. *See* settings
Lock Up (1989), 292, 293
Lock, Stock and Two Smoking Barrels (1998), 337
Loggia, Robert, 246
Lombroso, Cesare, 158
London, 11, 40, 58, 101, 143, 159, 199, 219, 220, 324, 331
lone operator, private detective, 14
Lone Ranger, The (1933), 325
Lone Ranger, The (2013), 420
Lone Wolf, The, 246
Lone Wolf, The (1914), 246
Lonely Hearts (1989), 88
Lonely Magdalen (1940), 87
long con, 262, 274, 275, 277, 285, 286
Long Goodbye, The, 25, 33, 34
Long Haul, 62
Longest Yard, The (1974), 291
Los Angeles, 21, 143, 267, 338
Lost Highway (1997), 304
lost relatives. *See* missing person investigation
Lucas, Henry Lee, 162
Ludlum, Robert, 412
Luis Mendoza, 87
Lupin III, 243
Lupino, Ida, 77
Lustig, Victor, 265, 268
M (film), 159
Ma Barker's Killer Brood (1960), 79
Maas, Peter, 105
Macbeth, 60, 69, 77
Macdonald, Ross, 13
MacDonell, Herbert L., 147

MacGuffin, 215, 220, 229, 236, 237, 239, 240, 241, 244, 274, 320, 340, 341, 342, 343, 414
Machiavelli, 60
Machiavelli, Niccolò, 269
Machiavellianism, 269, 270, 424
Machine-Gun Kelly (1958), 77
Mach-IV test, 269
Mack Bolan, 325, 331, 333, 334, 425
Mad Bomber, 160
Mad Max, 411
Mafia, 56, 57, 74, 201, 331, 333, 334, 359
Magic Kaito (1987), 243
Magnum Force (1973), 320
Maigret, 83, 84
Mak, Alan, 203
Maltese Falcon, The, 12, 23, 25, 30, 31, 32, 33, 42, 54, 244, 245, 303, 304, 305, 306, 317, 342
Maltese Falcon, The (1929), 12
Mamet, David, 220, 266
Man Who Broke 1,000 Chains, The (1987), 290
Manchester, 57, 424
Manhunt, 7
Mann, Michael, 220, 231, 234
Mantegna, Joe, 161
Manual of Guidance on Police Use of Firearms, 111
Marais, Jean, 242
Marble, Scott, 213
Mark Inside, The: A Perfect Swindle, a Cunning Revenge, and a Small History of the Big Con (2012), 265
Maron, Margaret, 40
Marriage by Motor. See Runaway Match (1903)
Marric, J.J., 87, 89, 103
Martin, Dean, 335
Martin, Steve, 266
Martin, Troy Kennedy, 220
Marvin, Lee, 219
masculinity, 105, 166, 336, 337
Mason, Bill, 249
Mass Murder: America's Growing Menace (1985), 162
Matchstick Men (2003), 266
Mate, Ken, 60
materialism, 69
Matrix Reloaded, The, 420
Matthau, Walter, 336
Mature, Victor, 219
Maurer, David, 261, 277, 280, 424
Mayo, Archie, 58
McBain, Ed, 88, 90, 96, 103, 118, 135, 137
McCall, C.W., 411
McCauley, Neil, 220
McCrery, Nigel, 143
McCutcheon, Wallace, 58
McDermid, Val, 139, 140, 141, 143, 423
McGilligan, Pat, 60
McGowan, Michael R., 199
McGrave (2012), 412
McMahon, Rory J., 16, 394, 425, 426
McMurtry, Larry, 79
McNaughton, John, 162
McQueen, Steve, 212, 243, 291, 411
McVicker, Steve, 265
mean streets, 11, 20, 24, 203
mean streets milieu. *See* urban milieu
Means, Motive and Opportunity, 119
Medea, 305
media and the police, 115
medical examiner, 120, 124, 140, 141, 142, 143, 144, 152, 154, 403, 405, 408
medical records, 18, 115, 145

Medical Thriller, 7, 149
Meet the Tiger (1928), 246
Meierhofer, David, 160
Mellen, Joan, 304, 305, 308, 425
Melville, Herman, 40, 264
Melville, Jean-Pierre, 219
Memory Collector, The (2009), 412
Mengel, Bradley, 332, 425
mentor archetype, 96, 189, 190, 273, 317, 318
Mermaids Singing, The (1995), 142
Metalious, Grace, 137
Metamorphoses of Leatherstocking, The, 13
metaphor, 418
Metesky, George, 160
Metropolitan Police, London, 11, 101, 159, 198, 199, 407
metrosexual, 337
Meynell, Laurence, 219
Miami Vice, 335
Michael Lanyard, 246
Midnight Cowboy (1969), 336
Midnight Express, 294, 295, 296, 297, 298, 300
Midnight Run (1988), 335, 338, 339, 340, 341, 342, 343, 344, 345, 346, 347
Midnite Spares (1983), 411
Mike Hammer, 13, 33, 331
Mildred Pierce (1945), 305
Miles Archer, 33
Milestone, Lewis, 58
Miller, William, 264
Mindhunter, TV series, 161
Mindhunter: Inside the FBI's Elite Serial Crime Unit (1995), 160, 164
Miranda, 117, 406
Mischief (1993), 118, 122, 135, 136
misogynism, 31
Miss Marple, 10, 212
missing children, 395
missing person investigation, 16, 394, 426
mission plot, 333
Mission: Impossible, 213
Mitchum, Robert, 58, 220
mob rule, 326
Mob, The (1951), 203
Modesty Blaise, 246
modus operandi, 167, 169, 174, 178, 181, 182, 192, 252, 330
Mohini, 306
Molly Maguires, The (1970), 11
money laundering, 148
Monk, The (1796), 306
Monkey Punch, 243
Monroe, Marilyn, 143, 219
Monuments Men, The (2014), 250
mood, 8, 82, 169
Moonraker, 412
Moonrunners (1975), 411
moral code, 22, 23, 35, 36, 46, 49, 50, 52, 97, 99, 203
moral values, 8, 22, 23, 24, 25, 33, 34, 35, 37, 38, 39, 62, 63, 64, 66, 68, 69, 73, 91, 94, 97, 203, 209, 214, 218, 269, 299, 301, 325, 326, 331, 340, 342, 344, 345
Morell, Jessica, 307
Morgan le Fay, 306
Morrell, David, 109, 412
Mosely, Walter, 13
Mosse, 336
Motion Picture Association of America, 63
Motion Picture Production Code, 63, 77
motivations for abduction, 398, 400
motives, serial killers, 165

Motorcycle Roadcraft: The Police Rider's Handbook, 112
Mottershaw, Frank S., 242
Motto, Carmine J., 200
MPAA, 63
Mr. Murder (1993), 412
Ms .45 (1981), 324
mugshots, 114
Mullany, Patrick, 160
Muller, Marcia, 40
multiple cases, 14
Multiple Storyline Plot, 134, 135
Mulvey, Laura, 308
Mumbai, 57
Muni, Paul, 61, 65, 290
Murder and the Mean streets: The Hardboiled Detective Novel, 13
Murder in Retrospect, 139
Murder One: A Writer's Guide to Homicide, 410
murder scene, 403
Murder, My Sweet, 303
murderer, 29, 30, 31, 33, 41, 42, 46, 49, 53, 54, 55, 85, 86, 88, 95, 100, 102, 107, 119, 122, 123, 126, 127, 129, 130, 131, 132, 140, 151, 156, 157, 159, 161, 162, 163, 168, 179, 181, 185, 304, 339, 408, 409
Murders in the Rue Morgue, The, 140
Murphy game, 277
Murphy, Eddie, 277, 339, 341, 343
Murphy, Warren, 331
Murray, Edna 'Rabbit', 79
Murray, Jack, 79
Murray, Natalie, 114
Murton, Tom, 292
Muscular Christianity, 336
Musketeers of Pig Alley (1912), 58
MWA Mystery Writer's Handbook, 110
My Life with Bonnie and Clyde, 80
Mysterious Thief Detective Yamaneko, 243
Mystery (2017), 7, 10, 17, 119, 167
Mystery Writers of America, 110
Mystery, Violence and Popular Culture, 70
naïveté, 65, 271, 272
Naked City, The (1948), 87
Nasty Women, 266
National Association of Bunco Investigators, 262
National Ballistics Intelligence Service, 117
National Centre for Missing and Exploited Children, 402
National Crime Agency, 108, 348, 402
National Crime Information Center, 116
National Incident Category List, 116
National Incident-Based Reporting System, 210
National Instant Criminal Background Check System, 116
National Insurance Crime Bureau, 262
National Integrated Ballistics Information Network, 147
National Law Enforcement Data Programme, 116
National Law Enforcement Telecommunications System, 112
National Policing Curriculum, UK, 111
National Policing Improvement Agency, 116

National Public Order Intelligence Unit, 199
National Standard for Incident Recording, 116
Natty Bumppo, 13, 40
Natural Born Killers (1994), 80
Naturalism, 11, 25, 26, 28, 422
Natwarlal, 265
NBC television, 363
NCIC, 116
Nebraska Boy Snatcher, 161
necrophilia, 162
needs, character, 37
Neel, Janet, 40
Nelson, George 'Baby Face', 78
neo-noir, 62, 304, 307, 310
Nesbø, Jo, 250
Never Give a Sucker an Even Break (1941), 266
New Centurions, The (1971), 88
New York, 21, 56, 57, 58, 88, 100, 103, 140, 159, 199, 203, 212, 265, 290, 292, 383, 422
New York City Police Department, 103, 199
New Yorker, The, 26, 60, 422
Newman, Paul, 265
Newton and the Counterfeiter, 264
Newton, Isaac, 264
Nicholas, Tom, 71
Nicholson, Jack, 363
Nick Carter, 12
NICS, 116
Night Stalker, the, 188
Nina Fischman, 40
Niven, David, 243, 266
NLETS, 112
No Man's Land (1987), 203
Noguchi, Thomas, 143
noir romance, 5, 8, 11, 32, 62, 303, 310, 317, 425
Nolan, Frederick, 12
Nolte, Nick, 339, 341, 342, 343
Nora Mulcahaney, 91
Norfleet, J. Frank, 265
Norris, Chuck, 421
North Side Gang, 57
North-Western Police Agency, 11
Norville, Barbara, 22, 422
Notebooks of Raymond Chandler, The, 28
Nottingham, 57, 88, 199
NSIR, 116
NYPD, 88, 199
NYPD Blue, 88
O'Banion, Dean, 57
O'Brien, Edmund, 63
O'Brien, Pat, 62
O'Connell, Jack, 292
O'Connor, 'Terrible' Tommy, 58
O'Donnell, Lillian, 91
O'Donnell, Peter, 246
O'Neal, Ryan, 243, 251, 266, 420
O'Neal, Tatum, 266
O'Neill, Egan, 87
O'Neill, Gerard, 363
Oates, Joyce Carol, 325
Oates, Warren, 78, 243, 251
objective, 14, 23, 38, 44, 53, 98, 171, 253, 281, 282, 326, 338, 339, 344, 345, 365, 369, 371, 373, 376, 379, 413
Ocean's 8 (2018), 221
Ocean's Eleven (2001), 210, 213, 219, 221
Odd Couple, The (1968), 336
odontology, 141
Odyssey, The, 305
Oedipal complex, 63
Officer's Guide to Police Pistolcraft: The New Paradigm of Police Firearms Training, The (2009), 111
Olden, Marc, 332
Olshaker, Mark, 161
omertà, 217
On Revenge (1625), 325
One Flew Over the Cuckoo's Nest (1975), 291
One Thousand and One Nights, 211
Open Source Intelligence Techniques: Resources for Searching and Analyzing Online Information, 394
opposition, 48, 62, 67, 228, 252, 253, 273, 285, 286, 327
ordinary mortal, hero, 90
organised crime, 57, 65, 149, 198, 199, 331, 332, 333, 348, 363
Organized Crime Control Act of 1970, 348
organized killer, 168
Osborn, Albert S., 148
Oscar Madison, 336
Ossana, Diana, 79
Ottolengui, Rodrigues, 141
Oursler, Fulton, 140
Ousby, Ian, 10, 422
Out of the Past, 303
Outlaw Josey Wales, The (1976), 324
outsider, 22, 35, 59, 91, 95, 98, 134, 203, 207, 273, 284, 285, 297
Overkill: Mass Murder and Serial Killing Exposed (1994), 162
Owen, Clive, 218
Oxford Companion to Crime & Mystery Writing, 20, 87
Oxford English Dictionary, 337
Pacino, Al, 74, 203, 205, 220, 231, 234
Packard, Frank L., 246
Paglia, Camille, 307
Paglino, 410, 426
Palance, Jack, 77
panhandling, 275
Paper Moon (1973), 266
Papillon (1973), 291
paraphilia profiling, 174
paraphilic footprint, 173
Pardoner's prologue, 263
Paretsky, Sara, 13, 40
Paris, 141, 242, 425
Parker, Bonnie, 77, 78, 79, 80
Parker, George C., 265
Parker, Robert B., 13, 25
Parkes, Henry Bamford, 13
Parshall, Sandra, 142
passing, assumed identity, 201
pathologist, 139, 140, 141, 143, 144, 151, 405, 406
Patience, Gilbert & Sullivan, 12
Patinkin, Mandy, 161
Patterson, John, 25
Paul Drake, 16
pay-off, the, 277
PEACE model of interviewing, 365, 373, 376
Peacock, Ross, 421
Peaky Blinders, 57
Pearce, Donn, 291
Peary, George, 58
Peckinpah, Sam, 411
Peel, Robert, 198
Peña, Manuel, 71
Pendleton, Don, 325, 331, 333
Penn, Arthur, 80
Pennycross Murders, The, 87
People's Magazine, 246
Peppermint (2018), 325
Perelman, S.J., 60
Perfect Evil, A (2000), 164
perjury, 101
Perry Mason, 13, 16
personal data, legal aspects, 18
personal life, detective's, 78
Persons in Hiding (1939), 62, 78
Petherick, 170, 171, 175, 423, 424
Petrified Forest, The (1936), 62
Peuchet, Jacques, 324
Peyton Place (1956), 137
Pezzullo, Ralph, 199
phantom thief, 243
Phantom Thief Yamaneko, The (2016), 243
Phantom, The, 331
Philip Marlowe, 13, 24, 25, 27, 33, 34, 39, 83, 91
Philips, John Neal, 80
Phillips, Clyde B., 412
Phoenix of Crime, The, 141
Photofit, 113
photographs, crime scene, 17, 159, 167, 178, 183, 184, 406, 407, 408
physical evidence, 17
PI. *See* private investigator
PI Magazine, 19
Picciarelli, Patrick W., 199
Picton, Bernard, 141
Piesman, Marissa, 40
pigeon drop, 276
Pink Panther, The (1953), 243
Pinkerton Detective Agency, 11, 12
Pinkerton, Allan, 11, 12, 264
Pinkett, Jada, 221
Pinkie Brown, 58
pirates, 211
Pistone, Joseph D., 201
Pitfall, 303
Place, Janey, 308, 309
plausibility, importance of, 85
Playback, 28
Players (2012), 411
Plot Basics (2017), 9, 85, 263
plot conventions, 8
plot structure, 8
Plummer, Bonnie C., 20
PNC, 116
PND, 116
poaching, 149
Poe, Edgar Allan, 11, 17, 140, 264, 267, 424
Poe's Deadly Daughters blog, 142
Point Break (1991), 203, 205, 206, 207, 208, 209, 221
Poisoned Pen, The (1911), 140
poisoning, 404
Polanski, Roman, 304
police, 33
Police and Criminal Evidence Act 1984, 111, 117, 118
police brutality, 100
police cars, 111, 358
police corruption, 100
police detective, 83, 84, 87, 93, 94, 98, 99, 100, 106, 107, 109, 117, 118, 119, 135, 142, 163, 245, 251, 338, 384, 384
police headquarters, setting, 22
Police National Computer, 116
Police National Database, 116
Police Pistolcraft: The Reality-Based New Paradigm of Police Firearms Training (2007), 111
police procedural, 149, 349
Police Procedural, The, 83, 89, 94
police sketch artist, 113
Police Story, TV series, 88
political investigations, 16
Political thriller, 7
Pollaky, Ignatious 'Paddington', 11
Polti, Georges, 323, 328, 425
polygraphs, 376, 378
Ponzi schemes, 265, 279
Ponzi, Charles, 264, 265
Popeye Doyle, 383, 411
populism, 326, 327
Porter, Dennis, 23, 24, 27, 28, 39
possessions, 17, 244
Postman Always Rings Twice, The (1946), 303, 305, 306, 308, 312, 314, 316, 317
Postmortem (1990), 141
Post-Traumatic Stress Disorder, 380
Practical Handbook for Private Investigators (2013), 16
Practical Handbook for Professional Investigators, 394, 425, 426
prejudice within police, 100
prejudice, racial, 31
Prepon, Laura, 142
Presentation of Self in Everyday Life, The, 368
Pretty Boy Floyd (1960), 79
Pretty Boy Floyd (1995), 79
Prince, The (1513), 269
prison rape, 290, 291, 296
private detective, 7, 10, 11, 12, 14, 15, 16, 17, 18, 19, 20, 22, 25, 33, 34, 35, 41, 42, 43, 44, 45, 50, 52, 83, 97, 203, 245, 246, 322, 338, 339, 341, 364, 366, 368, 375, 379, 383, 384, 385, 388, 390, 393, 410
private detective's office, setting, 21
private detectives and homicide investigations, 410
private eye, 10, 12, 21, 22, 29, 33, 34, 35, 38, 39, 40, 41, 42, 66, 83, 84, 85, 86, 91, 92, 95, 96, 98, 99, 102, 106, 107, 119, 127, 133, 149, 152, 191, 203, 232, 245, 303, 317, 338, 348, 349, 383
Private Eye's Guide to Collecting a Bad Debt, A, 16
private investigator, 10, 11, 13, 14, 18, 19, 21, 45, 386, 396, 410
private security, 15
Private Security Industry Act 2001, 19
privateers, 211
Proate, Ernest Marsh, 140
probable cause, 362
process serving, 16
Procter, Maurice, 87-88
Production Code. *See* Motion Picture Production Code
Professor Moriarty, 31
profiling victims, 181
Profiling Violent Crimes (1990), 162
Prohibition, 13, 20, 57, 68, 69
projection, 377
pronouncing a death, 404
Pronzini, Bill, 20, 26, 27, 39, 422
Prosecution Team Manual of Guidance For the Preparation, Processing and Submission of Prosecution Files, 116
Protected Persons Service, UK, 348
Protector, The (2003), 412
Proudhon, Pierre-Joseph, 249
Provost, Gary, 12
psychiatrists, 94, 158, 160
Psycho, 163
psychological autopsy, 142, 158, 181
psychological profiling, 144
Psychological thriller, 7
psychopaths, 163, 269, 376
PTSD, 226, 321
Public Enemies (1996), 79

Index

Public Enemies (2009), 79
Public Enemy No. 1, 78
Public Enemy, The (1931), 59, 61, 65, 66, 68, 72
Pudlicott, Richard of, 212
punisher, 35, 38
Punisher, The, 332
punishment, 100, 186, 196, 200, 209, 252, 268, 289, 291, 292, 297, 301, 319, 327, 328, 355, 372
Purloined Letter, The, 17
Pursuit. See The Chase
Puzo, Mario, 56, 74
pyramid schemes, 279
Queen of the Mob (1940), 78
Queen, William, 199
Queen's evidence, 348
Quincy, M.E., 143
Race Williams, 12
Racket, The (1928), 58
Rader, Dennis, 164
Radex model, 177
Raffles, 242, 243, 246, 333
Raffles (1939), 243
Raft, George, 58, 66
rag, the, 277
Ragged Dick, or Street Life in New York with the Boot Blacks (1867), 71
Raising the Wind (1803), 264
Ramirez, Richard, 188
Ramsland, 163, 169, 178, 180, 182, 183, 185, 424
Rankin, Ian, 412
ransom, 400
rape, 63, 176, 290, 292, 296, 324, 325, 328, 373, 378, 381, 400, 404
rape and revenge, 324
Rape Trauma Syndrome, 380
Rape: A Love Story (2003), 325
Rapp, Burt, 349, 383, 387, 388, 426
Rappe, Virginia, 63
Rascal and the Road, The (1961), 265
rationalisation, 319, 377
RCMP, 357
Rea, Christopher, 263
Reading, Amy, 265
Real McCoy, The, 252
realism, 7, 11, 23, 28, 29, 85, 91, 97, 136, 152, 295
Realism, 28, 85
Rebel Outlaw, The: Josey Wales (1972), 324
rebellion, 217
Rebels, 64
reconstructing the crime, **408**
recording conversations, legal aspects, 18
recording telephone conversations, legal aspects, 20
Red Dragon (1981), 162, 188, 190, 191, 192, 194
Red Harvest (1928), 12, 27
Red Thumb Mark, The (1907), 140
Redding, Stan, 266
redeemer, archetype, 308
Redford, Robert, 292
Reeve, Arthur B., 140
Reggie Fortune, 140
rehabilitation, 327
Reichs, Kathy, 142, 143
Reid Model, 376
Reid Technique™, 365
relationships, character, 29, 31, 32, 38, 40, 41, 49, 50, 81, 96, 104, 108, 114, 120, 125, 126, 127, 128, 133, 137, 152, 154, 163, 175, 181, 184, 185, 195, 200, 205, 207, 208, 226, 233, 237, 244, 251, 254, 257, 259, 269, 270, 298, 300, 301, 317, 336, 338, 340, 357, 358, 360, 400

reluctance to accept challenge, 46
Remember That Face!, 203
Remo Williams, 331
Remo Williams: The Adventure Begins (1985), 331
Remo: Unarmed and Dangerous, 331
Rendell, Ruth, 84, 89
repossession, 16
Reservoir Dogs (1992), 203, 221
Ressler, Robert, 160, 161, 423
Rethinking the Femme Fatale in Film Noir, 307
Return of A. J. Raffles, The (1975), 242
revenge, 265, 319, 323, **325**, 327, 353, 398, 400
Reynolds, Bruce, 212
Reynolds, Burt, 411
Ribacoff, Daniel, 16
Richard of Pudlicott, 212
Rico Bandello, 60, 61, 65, 69, 71
Rififi, 210, 217, 219, 220, 221, 222, 224, 226, 227, 230
Right to Counsel, 117
right to remain silent, 117
Riot in Cell Block 11 (1954), 290
rising action, 191, 415, 416
Rita Hayworth and Shawshank Redemption, 292
ritualistic behaviour, 174
rivalry between departments & agencies, 107
Rizzoli & Isles, 142
Road to Business Success: An Address to Young Men, The, 71
Road Warrior, 411
Roadcraft: The Police Driver's Handbook, 112
Roaring Twenties, The (1939), 20, 62
robbery, 58, 78, 79, 80, 81, 96, 165, 176, 208, 209, 210, 211, 212, 215, 219, 220, 221, 223, 225, 228, 230, 231, 232, 234, 238, 240, 241, 249, 250, 290, 411
Robbery (1967), 212
Robbins, Tim, 292
Robin Hood, 79, 99, 205, 217, 246, 252, 333
Robinson, 186
Robinson, Edward G., 58, 59, 60, 61, 62, 65
Rocambole, 242
Rochefoucauld, Francois, Duc de La, 272
Roffman and Simpson, 289, 291, 292
Roffman, Peter, 289
rogue tradesmen, 16
rogues' gallery, 114
Rohypnol, 378
Rolling Thunder (1977), 324
romantic co-protagonist, 67, 95, 150, 214, 246, 273
Romantic poetry, 306
romanticism, 29
Ronin (1998), 220
Rookie, The, 338
Room in the Dragon Volant, The, 141
roper, conman, 272
Rosener, George, 58
Rossatron, 421
Rossellini, Isabella, 304
Rossmo, 175, 424
Rubin, Martin, 13
Rucker, Allan, 11
Rules of Evidence, 117
Rumanian Box scam, 265
Runaway Match (1903), 411, 427
runaway teenagers. See missing person investigation

runaways, 189, 344, 394, 395, 397
Running Scared (1986), 336
Running with Bonnie and Clyde: The Ten Fast Years of Ralph Fults (1996), 80
Runyon, Damon, 266
Rush Hour, 338
Rushing, Jerry, 411
Rusk, Bruce, 263
Russell, Mike, 199
Russell, Steven Jay, 265
Russo, Rene, 243
Ryan, Robert, 58
Ryan, William, 380
S&M, 203
Sade, Marquis de, 306
Sadist, Der (1932), 159
Sadist, The (1938), 159
Safecracking: Tales and Techniques of the Master Criminals (1991), 249
Saint, The, 246, 333
Sallis, James, 412
Salome, 306
Sam Spade, 7, 12, 22, 23, 25, 30, 31, 33, 83, 342
San Francisco, 20, 142, 335, 411
Sandburg, Carl, 10
Sapir, Richard, 331
Saturday Evening Post, The, 77
Saturday Review, The, 25
scam artists, 264
Scarface (1932), 58, 59, 61, 64, 65, 66, 68, 72
Scarlet Street, 303
Scarpetta, Kay, 141
Schatz, Thomas, 22, 23, 61, 62, 64, 65, 67, 69, 77
Schifrin, Lalo, 246
Schrader, Paul, 324
Scientific Working Group on Bloodstain Pattern Analysis, 147
scopolamine, 378
Score, The, 252
Scorsese, Martin, 56, 203, 363
Scotland Yard, 87, 89, 109, 140, 242
Scott, Peter, 249
Scott, Ridley, 266, 304
Screenwriting: The Sequence Approach, 9
Scum (1979), 291
Se7en, 338
search and seizure, unreasonable, 19
search of the crime scene, 408
searching a crime scene, 17
searching, legal aspects, 18
Second World War. See World War II
Secrets of a Private Eye, 12
Security Industry Authority, 19
Seldes, Gilbert, 60
self-dramatisation, 268
self-interest, motivation, 353
selflessness, 36
self-protection, motivation, 355
self-worth, 217
Sellers, Peter, 243
Seneca, 304
Senior Investigating Officer, 407
Senter, A.E., 264
serial killers, 7, 142, 144, 158, 160, 161, 163, 164, 165, 166, 169, 173, 174, 176, 181, 185, 188, 189, 400, 409
Serial Murder (1988), 162
Serial Murder: An Elusive Phenomenon (1990), 162
Serial Vigilantes of Paperback Fiction, 332
Série Noire, 11
serienmörder, 161

serology, 144
Serpico, 105
Serpico, Frank, 105
Set It Off (1996), 221
settings, 8, 20, 68, 89, 151, 216, 244, 274, 321
Seven Suspects, 84
Seven-Ups, The (1973), 411
sex trafficking, 400
Sex, Art and American Culture: New Essays (1992), 307
sexual assault, 166, 170, 176, 177, 395, 400
Sexual Homicide: Patterns and Motives (1988), 161
Sexy Beast (2001), 220, 221
Seybold, John, 220
Shachtman, Tom, 161
shadow or dark side, character, 38
Shadow, The, 331
Shadowing and Surveillance: A Complete Guidebook, 383
shadowing, mobile surveillance, 386
Shakespeare, William, 324
Shannon, Dell, 87, 90, 96, 97, 98, 110, 134, 423
Sharon McCone, 40
Shaw, Joseph T., 12, 26, 27
Shawshank Redemption, The (1994), 292, 293, 294, 296, 299
Sheffield, 57
Sheppard, Sam, 147
Sherlock Holmes, 11, 21, 25, 31, 35, 44, 83, 91, 93, 140, 160, 162, 192, 242, 323, 333, 424
Sherwood, Robert E., 62
Shield, The, 88
shill, 272, 275
Shirley, John, 332
short con, 251, 273, 275, 285
short-changing, 276
Shulman, Morton, 143
Sideways (2004), 336
signature behaviours, serial killers, 164, 167, 173, 174, 191, 192
Silence of the Lambs (1988), 161, 162, 190, 191, 192, 194
Silent Witness, 143
simile, 28, 418
Simon & Simon, 335
Simon Templar, 246
Simple Art of Murder, The, 10, 24, 27
Simpson, Beverly, 289
Simpson, Mark, 337
Sinatra, Frank, 58
Single Case Plot, 119
Six Against the Rock (1987), 290
Sixth Amendment of the US Constitution, 117
Skylight Caper, the, 250
Sleeping Doll, The (2007), 141
Sloggers, 57
small con, 275
Smart Money (1931), 59
Smart Set magazine, 12
Smith, Edward H., 280
Smith, Martin Cruz, 141
Smith, Terence Lore, 243
Smokey and the Bandit (1977), 411
snake oil, 272
Snatch (2000), 337
Sneakers (1992), 393
Snyder, Ruth, 306
social milieu, 8, 20, 22
sociologists, 94
sociopathy, 217
Soderbergh, Steven, 363
sodium pentothal, 378
Some Like It Hot (1959), 336
Somewhere a Roscoe..., 60
Somewhere in This City, 88
Son of Sam, 161

South Pacific Trail (1952), 213
Southside Strangler, 141
Souvestre, Pierre, 242
Spader, James, 363
Spanish Prisoner, The (1997), 266
Spanish Tragedy, The (c.1587), 324
speakeasies, 57, 68, 71
Specialist, The (1994), 332
Spencer, Timothy Wilson, 141
Spenser, Robert B. Parker, 13, 25
Spicy Detective magazine, 60
Spider, The, 331
Spielberg, Steven, 265, 266, 416
spies & espionage, 7
Spillane, Mickey, 13, 60, 331, 332
Sprague, Donald F., 402
spree killings, 188
Srivastava, Mithilesh Kumar, 265
St. Valentine's Day Massacre, 57, 60
Stainless Steel Rat Saves the World, The, 249
Stakeout (1987), 336
stake-outs, 384
stakes, 33, 80, 81, 127, 129, 193, 196, 205, 206, 207, 208, 227, 230, 233, 235, 238, 239, 240, 254, 255, 285, 295, 343, 344, 345, 346, 413, 416
Stalking Trauma Syndrome, 380
Stallone, Sylvester, 109, 292, 332
Stanford Prison Experiment, 292
Stanwyck, Barbara, 305, 306
Star Wars (1977), 411
Starred Up (2013), 292
Stars My Destination, The (1956), 324
Stars' Tennis Balls, The (2000), 324
Starsky and Hutch, 335, 336
Startling Detective Adventures, 79
state's evidence, 66, 348, 353
statements, 16, 86, 95, 122, 123, 129, 148, 167, 178, 182, 184, 308, 364, 372, 408
Statue of Liberty, sale of, 265
Stealing the Past, 250
Steinbeck, John, 79
Stephanie Plum, 15
Sternberg, Josef von, 58
Steve Carella, 88, 135, 136
stick-ups, 78, 210
Sting, The (1973), 265, 266, 276, 278, 282, 283, 285, 286, 287, 319
Stoker, Bram, 306
stolen property, 16, 116, 362
Stone, Sharon, 304
Stray Dog (1949), 87, 336, 338
Street Gang (1983), 324
Street Hawk (1985), 333
Street with No Name, The (1948), 87, 203
Streets of San Francisco, The, 335
Stroud, Robert, 290
style, 7, 8, 10, 11, 12, 13, 22, **26**, 27, 28, 60, 78, 87, 93, 97, 143, 151, 183, 242, 244, 246, 264, 269, 303, 304, 308, 333, 366, 367, 368, 413, 420
St-Yves and Deslauriers-Varin, 374
sub-genres, 7, 8, 9, 83, 84, 87, 89, 109, 139, 198
subpoena, 19
sub-rosa justice, 100
Sûreté, 198
Surgeon, The (2001), 142

surveillance, 199, 383
surveillance using vehicles, 388
surveillance, legal aspects, 384
suspects, 18, 20, 29, 46, 49, 51, 52, 53, 54, 79, 86, 96, 99, 101, 105, 106, 107, 109, 111, 114, 115, 117, 118, 119, 120, 122, 124, 127, 129, 130, 131, 132, 155, 157, 158, 162, 164, 169, 182, 200, 202, 205, 252, 311, 313, 315, 317, 320, 325, 326, 333, 344, 364, 365, 372, 373, 374, 379, 387, 406
suspense, 7, 81, 84, 85, 87, 89, 102, 119, 127, 131, 133, 137, 156, 191, 213, 221, 224, 226, 229, 235, 237, 238, 239, 243, 247, 248, 256, 274, 279, 288, 296, 311, 313, 412, 413, 414, 415, 417
Suspense Thriller (2018), 7, 83, 105, 118, 149, 198, 236, 237, 243, 289, 293, 320, 333, 338, 364, 412, 413, 414, 425
Sutherland, Donald, 292
SWAT, 106
Swayze, Patrick, 205
Sweeney, The, 335
sweetheart, 272, 278
sweetheart scams, 272, 274, 278
Swierczynski, Dwayne, 270, 424
symbolism, 8, 186, 188, 297
Symons, Julian, 56
T.H.E. Cat, 246
taboo, 26
Tail-End Charlie, 88
tailing, mobile surveillance, 386
Taj Mahal, sale of, 265
Takeover (2008), 142
tangible evidence, 16
tapping telephones, 390
Tarantino, Quentin, 62, 203, 220, 324, 328, 411
Tatum, Channing, 79
Taxi (1998), 420
Taxi Driver, 324
Taylor, Karen T., 114
Taylor, William Desmond, 63
Techno-thriller, 7
telephone tapping, 391
Telling Lies: Clues to Deceit in the Marketplace, Politics, and Marriage (2009), 377
Temperance Brennan, 142, 143
Terrail, Pierre Alexis Ponson du, 242
terrorism, 163, 199
testimony, evidence, 16
Teten, Howard, 160
Tevis, Walter, 277
That Darkness (2016), 142
That Sinking Feeling (1979), 221
theft, 101, 249
thefts, 15, 245, 247, 248, 249, 250, 251
Thelma & Louise (1991), 80, 336
themes, 8, 22, 25, 69, 97, 151, 201, 216, 245, 279, 307
Thew, Harvey, 61
They Drive By Night (1940), 62
They Live By Night (1948), 62
They Stole $25,000,000 - And Got Away with It, 219
Thief, 259
thief & the crime boss plot, 257
Thief (1981), 220
Thief of Hearts (1984), 251
Thief Who Came to Dinner, The (1973), 243, 247, 251, 255, 256

Thief-Taker General, 198
Thieves Like Us (1974), 62
Thinker, character archetype, 35, 37, 40, 93, 149, 214, 322, 338
Thirty-Six Dramatic Situations, 323
This Gun for Hire (1942), 61
Thomas Crown Affair, The (1968), 243, 251
Thomas Hewitt Edward Cat, 246
Thompson, Jim, 162, 219, 266, 270, 317
Thompson, Josiah, 12
Thompson, William H., 261, 264
Thorndyke, Dr. John, 140
Thrasher, Frederic M., 59
Three Acts, 43
three-act structure, 8
three-card monte, 264, 272, 274, 276
Three-Gun Terry, 12
Thrillers (1999), 13
Thunderbolt and Lightfoot (1974), 336
Thurman, Uma, 324
Tiger! Tiger!, 324
Tillmann, John, 250
To Catch a Thief (1925), 243, 247
To Have and Have Not, 308
Tom Powers, 61, 65
tone, 8, 26, 71, 97, 152, 219, 245, 279
Tony 'Scarface' Camonte, 61
Tony Hill, 141, 143
Tooth and Nail (1992), 412
Topkapi, 210, 219, 220
Tormes, Lazarillo de, 264
Torture Doctor, 162
Touch of Evil (1958), 304
toxicology. See forensic toxicology
tragic flaw, 66
Train, The (1964), 250
training and experience, police, 110
Treat, Lawrence, 87, 89, 110, 119
Triads, 57
Tricksters, 64, 262
True Detective Mysteries, 290
True Romance (1993), 62, 80
Trumbo, Dalton, 77
trust, 32, 34, 44, 49, 70, 94, 107, 110, 155, 194, 198, 200, 201, 202, 205, 206, 216, 217, 239, 253, 259, 261, 268, 271, 277, 279, 281, 282, 283, 284, 296, 315, 317, 340, 344, 345, 346, 349, 350, 355, 356, 357, 358, 360, 369, 370, 371, 379, 397
trust, informants, 356
truth serum, 378
Turner, Kathleen, 304, 307
Turner, Lana, 305, 306, 308
Turvey, Brent, 171, 172, 181, 182, 183, 184, 187, 381, 424, 425, 426
Twain, Mark, 27, 40, 264
Twin Peaks, 109, 137
Twining, James, 250
Twists, Slugs and Roscoes: A Glossary of Hardboiled Slang, 29
Two-Lane Blacktop (1971), 420
tyre tracks, 408
U.S. Constitution, 11, 19, 57, 354
U.S. Marshals Service, 348
UCLA, 8
Under and Alone: The True Story of the Undercover Agent Who Infiltrated America's Most Violent Outlaw Motorcycle Gang (2005), 199

Undercover (2000), 200
Undercover Cop: How I Brought Down the Real-Life Sopranos (2013), 199
Undercover Policing Inquiry, 199
Undercover Research Project, 199
Undercover: The True Story of Britain's Secret Police (2013), 199
underworld, 30, 33, 35, 57, 235, 321, 348, 349
Underworld (1906), 61
Underworld (1927), 58
Unekis, Richard, 412
University of Tennessee Anthropological Research Facility, 141
urban environment, 11, 56, 57, 67
urban milieu, 20
urbanisation, 57
Urschel, Charles F., 77
US Constitution, 117
Using Sexually Related Crime Scene Characteristics to Profile Male Serial Killers, 174
USMS, 348
V as in Victim (1945), 87, 89, 119, 121, 122
V.I. Warshawski, 13, 40
Vachss, Andrew, 412
Valentin Follows a Curious Trail, 242
Valentine, Anthony, 242
Valley of Fear (1915), The, 11
vamp, 305, 306
Vampire of Düsseldorf, 159
Vampire, The (1897), 306
Vampire, The (1913), 306
Van Damme, Jean-Claude, 203
Van Dine, S.S., 85
Vance, Louis Joseph, 246
Vanishing Point (1971), 411
Vaughn, Robert, 267
Velvet Light Trap, The, 58
Vengeance: A Love Story (2017), 325
verdicts, coroner's, 405
Vernon, John, 143
ViCAP, 161
victim profiling, **181**
victim selection, 188
victimology, 9, 158, 167, 172, 178, **181**, 182, 188, 196, 380
victims, 9, 29, 30, 32, 33, 34, 37, 41, 42, 46, 47, 48, 50, 51, 52, 54, 55, 65, 80, 87, 96, 99, 101, 102, 106, 115, 119, 120, 121, 122, 123, 125, 126, 127, 128, 129, 130, 132, 135, 137, 139, 142, 145, 146, 147, 151, 152, 153, 154, 155, 157, 158, 159, 160, 164, 166, 167, 168, 169, 170, 171, 172, 173, 174, 175, 176, 177, 178, 179, 180, 181, 182, 183, 184, 185, 186, 187, 188, 189, 190, 191, 192, 193, 194, 195, 196, 200, 206, 210, 215, 218, 240, 245, 246, 252, 261, 262, 263, 265, 267-282, 285, 286, 289, 296, 298, 303, 304, 305, 308, 309, 317, 319, 320, 321, 322, 323, 324, 326, 327, 328, 329, 330, 331, 355, 367, 370, 380, 381, 382, 399, 400, 401, 403, 404, 406, 407, 408, 409, 410
victim's exposure to risk, 185
victims of violent crime, 380
Vidocq, Eugène François, 11, 198
Vietnam, 324, 331, 332, 337, 344
viewpoint, first-person, 26, 29, 43, 86, 247, 251, 417

Index

viewpoint, third-person, 29, 43, 417
Vigilante (1983), 324
Vikings, 211
vilification of victims, 188, 189
villain, **30**
violence, 13, 21, 22, 25, 26, 28, 30, 34, 35, 39, 56, 64, 65, 66, 70, 72, 75, 97, 105, 155, 165, 166, 175, 177, 183, 201, 210, 226, 231, 242, 259, 261, 267, 268, 270, 275, 290, 291, 295, 298, 299, 319, 321, 322, 326, 328, 330, 356, 364, 395, 396, 399, 404, 422
violent crime, victims, 380
Violent Criminal Apprehension Program, 161
Violent Saturday (1955), 219
Violent Streets, 220
violin case, 58
Visha Kanya, 306
vulnerability, 36, 185, 188, 261, 280, 340, 344
Wacky Races, The, 420
Wade, Henry, 87, 423
Wainwright, John, 88
Wainwright's Beat, 88
Waking the Dead, 143
Walcutt, Charles Child, 26
Waldron, Gy, 411
Walker, Gerald, 203
Walking and Talking (1996), 336
Wall Street, 279
Wall Street crash, 57
Wallace, Harvey, 380
Wallace, Lew, 324
Wambaugh, Joseph, 84, 88
War Against the Mafia (1969), 331, 333

Ward, Rachel, 304
Warne, Kate, 11
Warner Bros., 58, 60, 61, 290, 423
Warner Bros. Gangster Movies, 58
Warrior archetype, 24, 35, 40, 64, 66, 68, 93, 214, 322, 338
Warshow, Robert, 69, 70, 423
Washington, Denzel, 220, 333
Water Rat of Wanchai, The (2011), 148
Waterfront (1951), 203
Watson, character type, 29, 43, 83, 86, 140, 192, 242
Waugh, Hillary, 83, 84, 85, 87, 89, 95, 97, 348, 423
Way to Wealth, The, 71
weaknesses, character, 37
weapons, 17, 20, 108, 111, 146, 178, 223, 261, 309, 320, 417
Weaver, Dennis, 416
Weil, Joseph 'Yellow Kid', 265
Weir, Peter, 381
Weiss, Hymie, 57, 61
Welden, Paula Jean, 87
Welles, Orson, 304
Westlake, Donald E., 219, 266
Wexford, 84
What is Property? Or, an Inquiry into the Principle of Right and of Government (1840), 249
Wheat, Carolyn, 29
Where Death Delights, 143
whistle-blower, 363
White Collar, TV series, 267
White Heat (1949), 62, 68
White, Lionel, 219
Whitechapel Murders, 159
white-collar crime, 198, 348

Whited, Charles, 199
Who Killed Atlanta's Children? (2000), 161
whodunit, 7, 10, 11, 29, 43, 53, 83, 84, 85, 86, 95, 96, 97, 102, 106, 117, 119, 122, 124, 126, 130, 131, 143, 151, 152, 180, 252, 348, 403
Whoever Fights Monsters (1992), 161
Why Do Action Scenes Suck?, 421
Widows (2018), 221
Wild Bunch, 11, 77, 213
wild justice, 325
Wild West, 71
Wild, Jonathan, 198
Wilde, Oscar, 306
wildlife crime, 149
Wilkinson, Caroline M., 114
Will Graham, 191
Willis, Bruce, 324
Wilmer Cook, 30
Wilson, Charlie, 212
Wilson, Rebel, 266
Winstone, Ray, 220, 291
Winters, Shelley, 77, 79
Wire in the Blood, 142, 143
wire, the, 277
Wire, The, 88
Wired magazine, 378
Without a Trace, 143
Witness (1985), 381
Witness Security Program (or Federal Witness Protection Program), 348
witnesses, 9, 16, 29, 51, 52, 53, 54, 89, 96, 99, 106, 109, 113, 114, 120, 121, 123, 124, 130, 153, 158, 173, 182, 187, 188, 189, 190, 232, 240, 314, 348, 349, 358, 361, 364, 365, 372, 378, 379, 380, 381, 394, 401, 406, 408, 410
Wojeck, 143
Wolf of Wall Street, The, 279
Woman in Gold (2015), 250
Woman in the Window, The, 303
Woodley, Richard, 201
Woods, Edward, 66
Wordsworth, William, 26
World War II, 7, 87, 88, 159, 250, 290, 305, 390
Wright, Edgar, 411, 420
Writer's Digest Books, 110, 424, 425, 426
Writer's Digest magazine, 26
WritersDigest.com, 139
writing action, 418
Writing Crime Fiction, 25, 88, 422, 423
Writing the Modern Mystery, 22, 422
Wunza movies, 338
Yakuza, 57
Yates, Peter, 212, 220
Yellow Kid Weil: The Autobiography of America's Master Swindler, 265
You Can't Cheat an Honest Man (1939), 266
You Only Live Once (1937), 62
Young Dillinger (1965), 79
Young Scarface, 58
Zeta-Jones, Catherine, 243
Zhang Yingyu, 263
Zorro (1919), 325

ALSO BY PAUL TOMLINSON

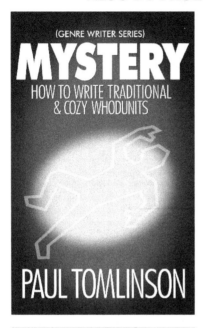

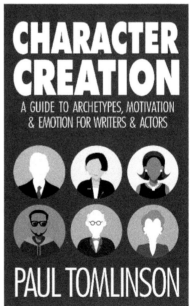

www.paultomlinson.org

Printed in the USA
CPSIA information can be obtained
at www.ICGtesting.com
LVHW071620090524
779705LV00023B/231